SECOND EDITION

LEARNING
AND
BEHAVIOR

Biological, Psychological,
and
Sociocultural Perspectives

LEWIS M. BARKER
Baylor University

Prentice Hall, Upper Saddle River, New Jersey 07458

Library of Congress Cataloging-in-Publication Data

Barker, Lewis M. (date)
  Learning and behavior : biological, psychological, and
sociocultural perspectives / Lewis M. Barker. — 2nd ed.
    p.   cm.
  Includes bibliographical references and indexes.
  ISBN 0-13-256975-2
  1. Learning, Psychology of.   2. Psychobiology.
BF318.B37   1997
153.1'5—dc20
                                    96-23094
                                      CIP

Editor-in-Chief: Peter Janzow
Assistant Editor: Nicole Signoretti
Director of Production and Manufacturing: Barbara Kittle
Production Liaison: Fran Russello
Project Manager: Linda B. Pawelchak
Manufacturing Manager: Nick Sklitsis
Prepress and Manufacturing Buyer: Tricia Kenny
Cover Art Director: Jayne Conte
Cover Design: Bruce Kenselaar
Electronic Art Creation: Asterisk Group
Copy Editing: JaNoel Lowe
Proofreading: Nancy Menges

*This book was set in 10/12 New Aster by Americomp, Inc.
and was printed and bound by RR Donnelley & Sons, Inc.
The cover was printed by Phoenix Color Corp.*

 © 1997, 1994 by Prentice-Hall, Inc.
Simon & Schuster/A Viacom Company
Upper Saddle River, New Jersey 07458

Printed in the United States of America
10 9 8 7 6 5 4 3 2

ISBN 0-13-256975-2

Prentice-Hall International (UK) Limited, *London*
Prentice-Hall of Australia Pty. Limited, *Sydney*
Prentice-Hall Canada Inc., *Toronto*
Prentice-Hall Hispanoamericana, S.A., *Mexico*
Prentice-Hall of India Private Limited, *New Delhi*
Prentice-Hall of Japan, Inc., *Tokyo*
Simon & Schuster Asia Pte. Ltd., *Singapore*
Editora Prentice-Hall do Brasil, Ltda., *Rio de Janeiro*

To my parents, Ronald and Sydona,
who shaped my views of love and life

BRIEF CONTENTS

DETAILED CONTENTS

CHAPTER 4   **COMPLEXITIES OF CONDITIONING   148**

CHAPTER 6   REINFORCEMENT AND PUNISHMENT   285

**CHAPTER 7   INTEGRATION OF LEARNING, PHYSIOLOGY,
AND BEHAVIOR   339**

CHAPTER 10   **LANGUAGE, INTELLIGENCE, AND CULTURE   478**

PREFACE

Learning and Behavior: Biological, Psychological, and Sociocultural Perspectives has been written as a primary text for a college-level course in learning. This book will be of interest to students and instructors who recognize the broad, pervasive role that learning and behavior theory play in our human lives. The subtitle reflects a range of interests that extends beyond typical treatments of animal learning.

This revision is designed to be as thought provoking, user friendly, and relevant to student interests as the first edition. Students want to know about themselves and the lives of others. A persistent theme in this text is that laboratory experiments using nonhuman animals can help us account for the behavioral complexity we encounter in our everyday lives. I offer students a deterministic, behavioral/biological perspective to counterbalance the softer explanations they may encounter in other courses in their psychology major.

Learning is too important to be relegated to some esoteric subfield called *animal learning*, one that the majority of psychologists and students make jokes about. Humans are animals too. Among our more interesting human behaviors is language. Language allows us a unique human culture, and written language has made civilization possible. Chapter 10 discusses how humans learn to use spoken and written language, what this has to do with thinking and intelligence, and why we are the only civilized animals that have evolved.

Offended by *Far Side* cartoons in a scholarly book? Dislike boxed topics? Of the opinion that footnotes have no place in modern textbooks? This one has a sprinkling of all three, and I have included them because they allow me the illusion of keeping my informal classroom voice. My major professor pointed out years ago that there's no sense talking if no one's listening. A few digressions and other surprises should reinforce page turning in the same way that some humor will make a 50-minute class seem a little shorter.

Nicole Signoretti, assistant psychology editor at Prentice Hall, and the following reviewers: David K. Hogberg, Albion College; Etan Markus, University of Connecticut; and Michael J. Renner, West Chester University shaped the manuscript. My good friends and colleagues Mike Best, John Flynn, and Chuck Weaver provided critical, personal mirrors for many of my ideas. My parents and extended family, my wife Beverly, and daughters Kristen, Melinda, Kira, and Jane are at one and the same time my sources of energy and the reasons I enjoy living. You will meet some of them in this book.

Early in an academic career, students are faced with many choices. This text is merely one path to explore. I hope that you find your formal education both enjoyable and profitable. Paraphrasing a Hindu expression, "if the journey is not what you expected, don't be surprised."

Lewis M. Barker

CHAPTER 1

ISSUES IN LEARNING AND BEHAVIOR

1

The horses were already moving. He took the first one that broke and rolled his loop and forefooted the colt and it hit the ground with a tremendous thump. The other horses flared and bunched and looked back wildly. Before the colt could struggle up John Grady had squatted on its neck and pulled its head up and to one side and was holding the horse by the muzzle with the long bony head pressed against his chest and the hot sweet breath of it flooding up from the dark wells of its nostrils over his face and neck like news from another world. They did not smell like horses. They smelled like what they were, wild animals. He held the horse's face against his chest and he could feel along his inner thighs the blood pumping through the arteries and he could smell the fear and he cupped his hand over the horse's eyes and stroked them and he did not stop talking to the horse at all, speaking in a low steady voice and telling it all that he intended to do and cupping the animal's eyes and stroking the terror out.
McCarthy, *All the Pretty Horses* (1992, pp. 103–104)

INTRODUCTION

This is a book about how humans and other animals learn and behave. In Cormac McCarthy's description of a young cowboy "breaking," or domesticating, a wild mustang, John Grady is behaving the way a human does, and, not surprisingly, the horse is behaving like a young colt. Both species behave in a manner that reflects their past learning, and both are learning new things through their experience with each other.

The colt is snorting and fearful and struggles to escape. (The other horses bunch in a herd and look on wildly.)

John Grady uses a tool (a coiled rope) to trip the colt, his five senses to perceive the colt's emotionality, his body to pin the colt, his hands both to cover the colt's eyes and "to stroke the terror out," and words to soothe the horse's soul.

Both are *learning* how to interact with each other—learning, among other things, what to expect from each other in the future.

What Is Learning?

For present purposes **learning**[1] is defined as *a more or less permanent change in behavior resulting from personal experiences with an environment.* Learning could be defined in other ways. For example, learning could be defined as an alteration in the way the brain works, or as a change in the way someone thinks. But over the years psychologists have settled on a definition tied to a change in *behavior*. Why? One reason is that behavior is more easily observed. We can typically see and readily measure changes in behavior.

By contrast, even though we assume that learning experiences produce changes in brain chemistry, the science of the neurochemistry of learning and memory is in its infancy. At present only the most basic neurochemical correlates of simple reflex learning in snails have been identified. Then why not define learning as "changed thinking"? Certainly thinking results from learning. But thinking is different from learning. What is normally called "thinking" depends on what a person says.

> *"What are you thinking?"*
> *"I'm thinking about what I learned on my date last night."*

Since we know that babies and birds and horses can learn, but we can't get a verbal self-report about what they are *thinking*, it is best to begin our study by defining learning in terms of *changes in observable behavior*.

Finally, much of what we learn in life, as we will see throughout the text, may only marginally involve thinking. Phobias, for example, are learned without "thinking." It is likely that John Grady didn't consciously think about the early childhood experiences that led to his ability to expertly train the wild horse. It is also likely that the horse learned to respond to its new rider without giving it much thought.

What Is Behavior?

Behavior is what you do, the ways you act, how you respond to your environment. Much of your behavior has been learned, but behavior change by itself is not "learning." Your behavior is affected by other factors as well as by learning. Drugs can change behavior, but typically the alteration is temporary

---

[1] Boldfaced terms appear as key terms at the end of each chapter and in a glossary appended to the text.

and behavior returns to normal. By contrast, learning is relatively permanent. A child's fatigue, as every parent knows, can drastically alter his or her behavior. A night's rest restores behavior to normal. By contrast, once a child has learned the alphabet, under most circumstances it doesn't go away.

Genes determine patterns of behavior in ways scientists are only now beginning to understand. A toddler does not *learn* to walk or to babble, and it is likely that horses do not learn to hang around in herds. Rather, these behaviors appear during the course of development, and each is an indication of the *genetic endowment* that an animal inherits at conception.

A summary statement: Your genetic endowment provides inherited tendencies. But in the course of a lifetime *what* is learned and *how* something is learned determine an individual's unique behavior. (Notice that all arguments thus far are applicable to animals in general, not just to humans.)

Genes and Environment.   Few readers would disagree with the observation that most of their behavior results from their personal interactions with a distinctive **environment**. Without any personal knowledge of each other, both you and I can deduce that we have learned a great deal in classroom settings. Classrooms provide a language-rich environment. You are reading this written text. Without extensive educational experiences, humans cannot understand written language.

Another way of saying this is that there appears to be nothing in the human **genotype** (the sum of your genetic endowment) that has specifically prepared you to read and to write. To speak, yes. Almost all humans speak even when raised in widely varying and less than optimal environments. But as every school child knows, learning to read and write requires much more effort than talking. Most humans talk: Only a highly organized environment, however, affords humans the experiences necessary to read and to write.

Culture as Environment.   Certain behaviors are important to society within a culture. Being able to work with horses was an essential part of the Texas ranching culture into which John Grady was born. Likewise, both male and female students in Western urban cultures learn how to solve math word problems and to think logically, as well as to read and write. *Learn* is the operative word. Human infants cannot read, write, or do math, nor do they engage in rational processes. If you lived in any of a number of third world countries, or if you weren't a good student in our culture, you would be unable to read this text. Your very capacity to reason and to think would be altered. Western culture provides environments that support reading or writing and restricts individuals who have not learned these skills to a lessened role in society.

The Realm of Behavior

Other assumptions about your behavior follow. Each of you has learned to like certain foods, songs, books, people—and to dislike others. Had you been raised in a different culture, that is, a different environment, presumably you would prefer other foods, songs, books, and people. For example, your choice of a best friend is likely to be a person presently sharing your local, immediate environment. Think of those you know who recently got engaged or married. More than likely they met at school, or at work, or at a dance, or in an apartment complex. Had one or the other been in a different location, they likely would have become involved with someone else. Environment determines opportunity. Environment shapes behavior.

Most people in our culture have learned to drive an automobile and to operate a TV, a VCR, a microwave oven, and other electronic appliances. The same cannot be said for people in other cultures. Even within a culture, learning experiences can vary from generation to generation. My grandfather never learned to operate a VCR. Likewise, I haven't a clue how to shoe a horse or to make and throw a lariat.

Depending on your unique *learning history*, you already know how to dance and to ice skate, and many of you are able to play soccer, the guitar, or the piano. You have *learned* to shop, to cook, to sing, and to sew, as well as to be coy and to control your temper—or not! Your thinking when expressed as language is *behavior*. Returning to an earlier distinction: Thinking reflects what you have learned, but you have learned many things without conscious thought. We are not always aware of how and when we are learning.

Here are some more examples: Some of us learn to be sick; others learn to perceive less pain. Many of us have learned how to "get our own way" in the immediate environment. Another way of saying this, as we see in Chapter 5, is that we have learned how to attain *reinforcers* and how to avoid *punishing* situations. Can more important lessons be learned than these? Arguably not, since these activities define the successful negotiation of our environments, of our happiness, and of our well-being.

Unconscious Processes.   Especially in our human interactions, we are not always aware of *when* we have learned something, or exactly *what* we have learned. For example, the playground bully says, "I taught him a lesson he will never forget." The nature of the lesson is illusive. What is learned from physical punishment, or when we argue, or when you persuade someone to do it your way? Quite often, verbalizing what it is that has been learned is difficult. For example, it is unlikely that John Grady could say exactly what it is he does that allows him to be so effective with wild horses.

Likewise, can you think of behaviors you have learned and now perform that do not involve conscious thought? Swimming, dancing, skiing, and playing a musical instrument after a period of inactivity reflect behaviors previously learned and not forgotten. I know an accordion player, for example, whose left-hand fingers still know "where to go" on the black buttons after 45 years of only sporadic playing. On this instrument he cannot see his fingers but still is able to guide their uncannily accurate placement. Furthermore, he has forgotten all the names of the notes and chords he is able to play. He is not aware of how his body "remembers" what to do.

Procedural Memory.   That our previously learned experiences often result in unconscious processes is what is meant by **procedural memory**. Like the accordion player and the black buttons, you likely have forgotten the details that were important when you were initially learning to spell, or to write your name, or to add a column of numbers. If you regularly drive a particular route—for me it is I-35, from Waco to either Dallas or Austin—you have shared with me the disconcerting experience of "waking up" and realizing that you have been driving unconsciously for many miles. There is other evidence that prior learning stored as *implicit memories* can unconsciously influence the learning of new materials. For example, research subjects who are shown certain target pictures (in a session in which hundreds of similar pictures are viewed) will, a week later during retesting, correctly identify the target pictures even though they have no conscious recollection of having previously seen them. Their memory was *primed* by the first viewing of the target stimuli.

Pointing out unconscious processes in learning is important for the following three reasons:

1. Newborn humans and other animals learn many things despite their lower level of consciousness relative to adult humans. Another way of saying this is that adult human awareness does not seem to be necessary for learning to take place.
2. Emotions, perceptions, and skilled behavior can be easily conditioned in humans independent of language and the rational processes that language affords. Procedural memory allows us to function capably without awareness.
3. A corollary of point 2 is that "book learning" accounts for only a small (but important) portion of all the things humans learn in a lifetime. We learn and remember the bulk of our behavior in a manner similar to how other animals accomplish these things.

Learning and Behavior: Biological, Psychological, and Sociocultural Perspectives

Your human ability to learn widely varying tasks during a lifetime complements other behavioral tendencies you inherited at conception. Likewise, it is clear that your behavior is highly dependent on the specific environment of the culture into which you were born. The research of psychologists and other behavioral scientists enhances our understanding of the interplay of these innate and learned behaviors. Let us first look at the more biological end of the spectrum.

Psychobiology is an interdisciplinary science concerned with questions of genetics, physiology, and psychology. Here the focus is on analyses of learning and behavior—an integration of observations and experiments in psychology, ethology, physiology, and genetics.

Psychobiologists recognize that learning and memory processes—indeed, all phenomena of the human and animal mind—are the end result of the interplay of genetically unique organisms behaving within their environments. To understand how animals learn, you must understand both the nature of the animal and the immediate environment with which it interacts.

That sounds good, but you may be asking, "What does it mean to 'understand' the nature of an animal?" The answer, unfortunately, is not simple. To fully understand an animal (such as yourself), you would need to know its evolutionary history, biology, psychology, and sociology. How does its brain work? How do its endocrine glands influence behavior? What does it eat? These "body" aspects in turn are related to questions of survival. What is its life cycle? In the niche it occupies, how does the animal's brain/behavior solve problems of reproduction and care of offspring? And, using the term *consciousness* in the human sense, to what extent is the animal *conscious* of itself and of its surroundings? Some scientists believe that we are now in a position to develop a model of an animal's "behavioral system" (Timberlake, 1994).

When the animal in question is human, the environment includes other people living in societies. **Culture** consists of learned ways of behaving, thinking, and feeling:

> A people's culture consists of all the ideas, objects, and ways of doing things created by the group. Culture includes arts, beliefs, customs, inventions, language, technology, and traditions. *World Book Encyclopedia* (1991)

We could then ask, "What is the role of learning in art and in the formation of beliefs, customs, and traditions?" What is the role of learning in the thinking that produces inventions and technology and in the language used to describe John Grady's exploits?

To summarize, the *how*, *what*, and *why* of animal learning and behavior can be analyzed from biological, psychological, and sociocultural perspectives. This undertaking becomes especially ambitious given that you and I are among the "animals" whose behavior we are trying to understand.

Learning and Behavior Contrasted

As we have just seen, *behavior* is a term that encompasses both learned (acquired) and innate (instinctive) components. Were you to make a list of behaviors acquired in your lifetime, more than likely you would consider only a few of them to be either "innate" or "instinctive." In comparison with simpler animals, such as spiders and newts, human behavior is especially variable. Evidence the multitude of cultural variations among humans. For this very reason the science of psychology focuses on a systematic analysis of individual differences (i.e., what *you* have learned and how *you* have learned over the course of your lifetime). Particular experiences have shaped you to be "you," and yet other experiences produced the young cowboy named John Grady.

Learning Theory.   Would it be fair to say that unless one knows *your* unique history—that is, all that you have experienced since conception—one really doesn't know *you*? **Learning theory** is an attempt to account for how your behavior has been shaped by your immediate environment—the people, places, relationships, and events you have experienced. What stimuli impinged on you, and what effect did they have? What were the outcomes of your unique encounters with your unique environment? It is likely that certain events had greater impact than others, including, as we will see in later chapters, stimuli that reward and punish and stimuli that afford predictability and control over the environment. John Grady's unique environment provided him the skills necessary to in turn shape a unique environment in which horses learned new responses.

Language is another example of behavior. Most readers of this text first heard the unique sounds of the English language—an environment that influenced but did not totally determine their language behavior. Obviously, this same language environment does not produce language behavior among pet dogs and cats and other nonhuman animals. Your unique human genetic makeup allowed you to be receptive to and to learn from a language environment. So *what* you learned in part has been determined by your human genotype. A tentative first conclusion: Learning theory by itself cannot account for any given acquired behavior, such as language. (The role of learning in language acquisition is further pursued in Chapter 10.)

Behavior Theory.   By contrast, **behavior theory** encompasses the interplay of genes and environment (Halliday & Slater, 1983; Plomin, 1990).[2] As noted earlier, your total genetic endowment—that which you received from biological parents at conception—defines your *genotype*. The combination of these innate tendencies *plus* the learned personal behaviors acquired in your lifetime determines your unique physical and psychological nature—your **phenotype**.

Do not confuse genotypes and phenotypes. Your genotype is the theoretical you, the potential "you" at the moment of conception. Your phenotype is the *real* you resulting from the special environment your genotype encountered. Another way of saying this? Phenotypes are genotypes expressed in environment.

Phenotypes are unique. You think and behave differently from your family, friends, and unknown others (a) because of your basic nature and (b) be-

---

[2] "Behavior theory" should not be confused with "behaviorism" as defined by John B. Watson, B.F. Skinner, and others (see Chapter 5). As we will see, behaviorism embodies an extreme environmental determinism that, for the most part, ignores genetic differences in behavior.

cause you have had unique experiences. By definition each of us has a one-of-a-kind genotype, and each of us has been raised in a unique environment.

Nature and Nurture. Learning is the "nurture" in the "nature-nurture argument." Learning is the "environment" in questions relating to the role of environment in gene expression. Take as an example the feeding behavior of titmice (various species of birds) native to England. Some individual birds of the species have been observed to remove the paper caps and to eat the cream from the top of bottles of home-delivered milk (Fisher & Hinde, 1949). Neither this nor any other species has evolved in an **ecological niche** (i.e., an immediate environment) that contained bottles of milk as a food source. Such feeding behavior, therefore, is not instinctive ("instincts" are discussed in the next chapter). These birds, however, have inherited eyes for seeing, a manipulative beak, an underlying physiology that regulates hunger, thirst, and so on. This basic equipment supports feeding in a variety of environments. Therefore, we can safely conclude that in their lifetime, birds *learn* to eat cow's milk from bottles.[3]

Notice the parallel of this feeding bird to our earlier discussion of reading and writing language. Reading, writing, and removing bottle caps are not instinctive behaviors. Nevertheless, we use visual, auditory, and motor systems that are inherited and that serve other functions to get the job done.

Behavior Theory Is All-Encompassing. Modern *behavior theory* is more global than *learning theory*. Reflect, for a moment, on why this is so. A "theory of behavior"—a theory ostensibly aimed at understanding why humans behave as they do—would encompass all of personality theory (normal and abnormal), motivation theory, learning theory, ethology, behavioral genetics, anthropology, neurophysiology, sociology, literature and the fine arts, and other relevant enterprises. Why? Because each of these ways of studying human behavior adds to our understanding of human complexity.

Learning theories help us to understand why humans behave as they do. In and of themselves, however, learning theories do not provide complete accounts of behavior. Box 1.1 discusses an example of a measure of complex human behavior—IQ—that requires both genetic and learning theories to account for our observations.

A Rationale for Studying Learning

Why study learning? If behavior theory is more all-encompassing than learning theory, why do psychologists emphasize learning? One answer has already been given. Behavioral scientists at present do not know enough to interrelate

[3] In a behavioral analysis of this situation (Chapter 5), the cream is the reinforcer for the bottle-top pecking response. The process of reinforcement makes it more likely that the bird will return to the next milk bottle.

BOX 1.1   ANALYSIS OF COMPLEX HUMAN BEHAVIOR: THE CASE OF IQ

Not all complex human behaviors are learned. Schizophrenia, alcoholism, manic depression, and intelligence have genetic determinants (Plomin, 1990). Take intelligence. One human measure of "intelligent behavior" is quantified by tests yielding an "intelligence quotient," or IQ. Behavioral scientists have gathered convincing evidence that both genes and environment are important determinants of IQ scores. An implication of this analysis is that learning and environment provide incomplete accounts of intelligent behavior. (A provocative book detailing some of the sociological implications of native differences in IQ is *The Bell Curve* by Richard Herrnstein and Charles Murray.)

How do we know that IQ has both genetic and learned components? The method is deceptively simple. **Monozygotic** (one-egg) twins, also known as MZ twins, have identical genotypes. Such twins separated at birth encounter different environments and, hence, different learning experiences throughout their respective lifetimes. Nevertheless, their IQ scores remain remarkably close together in comparison with **dyzygotic** (two-egg) twins sharing a common environment. (Recall that dyzygotic twins have two different genotypes at conception.)

Scientists have reached the conclusion that genetics, rather than environment, better accounts for much of the observed variance (i.e., differences) of IQ scores of MZ twins raised apart (Bouchard, Lykken, McGue, Segal, & Tellegen, 1990). Learning theory alone (or other sociological accounts) *cannot* account for individual differences in the intelligence test scores of monozygotic twins. In these and other studies, however, specific environmental interventions *do* affect intelligence scores in the short term. Project Head Start and other educational experiences, for example, allow children to initially score higher on IQ tests.

Interestingly enough, the Bouchard et al. (1990) study found that genetics better accounts for observed differences among *adult* as well as younger MZ twins. Specifically, IQ scores of adult MZ twins showed less variance than did those of child MZ twins. What is surprising about this finding is that the cumulative effect of environmental differences over the years would lead to the opposite prediction—that MZ twins would have grown apart under the influence of lifelong different environments. Perhaps this long-term stability can be attributed to similarities in personality that are also genetically determined. Each twin pair may be actively selecting similar environments that in turn influence their behavior (Bouchard, 1994).

Can we conclude from this study that genes rather than learning experiences account for *intelligent behavior* as measured by standard IQ tests? Not really. A simple thought experiment will suffice. Prior to age 2 (i.e., before verbal development is completed), maroon monozygotic twin *A* on a deserted island containing food and water but with no other socializing influences.

Box 1.1

Hence, no language, and no books. At age 50, retrieve twin *A* and compare her IQ scores with those of her middle-class, college-educated identical twin sister *B* living in San Francisco. You can predict the outcome. In this instance, environments determine the measured differences in intelligence. The unsocialized twin would be untestable.

The point is that no such animal as "pure learning," or "pure genetics," exists. Phenotypic behavior contains both elements, inextricably intertwined. MZ twin IQ scores that differ emphasize the role of environment, including culture; similar MZ twin IQ scores reflect both genes and environment. These two component elements of behavior will be analyzed throughout this text.

all of personality theory, all of behavioral genetics, all of neurochemistry, all of sociology, and so on. As we approach the 21st century, therefore, behavior theory remains woefully incomplete. And so we openly acknowledge what we don't know and concentrate on what we do know. After nearly 100 years of laboratory study, we know a great deal about the realm of learning and about applications of learning theory to the study of behavior. *Learning*, then, is our focus, even though an all-encompassing behavior theory remains one of psychology's goals.

Interim Summary

1. Learning is defined as a permanent change in behavior resulting from experiences with the environment.
2. Behavior is what you do, the ways you act, how you respond to your environment.
3. Inherited tendencies can be attributed to an organism's genes; learning determines unique behavioral tendencies.
4. The processes of learning and memory can both be mediated without awareness, that is, as unconscious processes.
5. Animal learning and behavior can be analyzed from biological, psychological, and sociocultural perspectives.
6. Individual organisms have a genotype (sum total of genes) and a phenotype (genotypes expressed in environment).
7. Intelligence, learning, and other psychological processes can be analyzed from a nature/nurture perspective.
8. Learning theory, a subset of a broader theory of behavior, is the focus of this text.

UNDERLYING ISSUES IN LEARNING AND BEHAVIOR THEORY

The foregoing discussion of human intelligence raises an issue that I frequently encounter in teaching a learning course. Students soon realize that the evidence underlying learning theory comes primarily from laboratory experiments using animals. Questions—and challenges—arise. Reading entertaining horse stories is one thing. But why study rats, pigeons, and dogs to find out how humans learn? Don't the facts that I can speak and that I can reason—and that animals can't—make animal learning experiments both irrelevant and meaningless to an understanding of humans?

Animal Learning Contrasted with Human Cognition and Memory

Let us identify five issues raised by these important questions:

1. Humans and other animals compared. First, how are humans the same as and how do they differ from other animals? *Which* other animals? What do we know of the genetic structure of different animals? Of their brains compared with ours? Of their behavior patterns compared to ours? Of how they are socialized compared to us? Answers to these questions are not simple. "Comparison" questions are entertained primarily in Chapter 2 and again in Chapters 9 and 10.

2. Individual differences. Do all *humans* learn in a like manner? For example, is it reasonable to assume that human neonates (newborns) and severely mentally retarded adults learn as other humans do or as nonverbal animals do? Likewise, do "smart" humans learn differently from the guy sitting next to you? Have you shared a classroom with the "learning disabled"? If so, did they learn differently from you? Do your friends who are more mechanically (or musically or mathematically) inclined learn these skills differently from the way you do?

These questions are variations on the theme of *individual differences* in learning, questions that will be entertained throughout the text. In general, the focus of learning in the 1990s is *not* on accounting for individual differences. The reason for this is that, exceptions notwithstanding, *basic* learning processes appear to be applicable to all vertebrates, which would include all humans, regardless of age, gender, and ethnicity. *Complex* learning processes, as well as species-specific differences in learning, are exceptions to these general rules.

3. Animal intelligence. What evidence should we accept to support or refute claims of so-called animal intelligence? Do we know whether animals are capable of thinking or whether they are able to reason? (You might want to try out these questions by analyzing your pet dog, cat, or goldfish.) As we see in Chapter 9, a number of chimpanzees have been taught American Sign Language (ASL) and other ways to communicate with humans. Now that they have language, do they use it? For example, we might ask whether chimpanzees with admittedly primitive language skills learn other tasks differently from chimps lacking these communication skills. One conclusion we will reach is that humans are *not* the only animals capable of both conceptual learning and thinking, broadly defined.

4. Problems of extrapolation. Another issue raised by experiments in this book is the problem of the **extrapolation**—that is, of applying experimental results from the laboratory to real life. How relevant can "artificial" findings be to everyday living? Can results from one experiment (let's say an analysis of how one learns to play the guitar) be applied to another experiment (i.e., learning how to tie shoes, or to program a computer, or to break a horse)?

Do you remember another type of extrapolation encountered earlier? How do we compare learning in one species of animal, let us say rats learning a maze, with another, pigeons guiding a rocket's trajectory?[4] Is a monkey learning the concept of "odd and even" (Chapter 9) similar to a child learning to discriminate and label round and oval objects (Chapter 5)?

There are no easy answers here; arguments for and against extrapolation of experimental findings will appear throughout the text. The student should realize that in successfully answering these questions, the stakes are high. If behavioral scientists are successful, then the goal of discovering *general principles* (as has been the case in chemistry and physics) *of learning and behavior* may be achieved and a science of behavioral analysis realized. The alternative is not too exciting—the mere cataloging of what each species is or is not capable of learning, with no general principles. Some may find such catalogs interesting, but I do not. Here we will search for general principles.

5. Scientific and nonscientific views of humans. Can the human mind and human behavior be understood by scientific methods? Three hundred fifty years ago Rene Descartes divided the psychological world of humans and animals into two realms: one—reflexes and instinct—that is shared and the other—voluntary behavior—that is restricted to humans. In this Cartesian view, animals are reflexive machines that behave instinctively, in contrast to humans who can act voluntarily and are purposive. Lost in Descartes' dichotomous argument is the fact that he thought humans could be studied scientifically.

Many people living within our "scientific" Western culture continue to hold prescientific views about human nature. Is it possible that ignorance

---

[4] Yes, during World War II, B. F. Skinner trained pigeons to function as inertial guidance systems to steer rockets! (See Skinner, 1960.)

about the human mind preserves its mystery? Many share with Descartes the belief in the division of humans from other animals. Some contemporary religious leaders, for example, continue to assert human preeminence over (as well as distinctiveness from) the animal world. Fully 80% of Americans espouse a belief in the "special creation" of humans as distinct from other animals.

Students' questions reflect our culture's understanding of what it means to be "human." The ideas developed by Charles Darwin and other scientists that focus on biological and psychological continuities of humans with other animals are not universally taught in U.S. public schools. In my view, this situation is untenable for students and scientists alike. As long as humans are considered to be mysteriously different from other life forms, a science of human behavior is not possible.

Some of you may think that humans cannot and/or should not be studied scientifically. Note in the following quotation how the intrigue of mystery promises understanding and comfort:

> *The heart is a mystery—not a puzzle that can't be solved, but a mystery in the religious sense: unfathomable, beyond manipulation . . . everything associated with the heart—relationship, emotion, passion—can only be grasped and appreciated with the tools of religion and poetry.*
>
> Moore, *Soul Mates* (1994, p. xii)

To the extent that you agree that humans cannot be studied scientifically, the present study of animal learning and behavior may seem to be an esoteric exercise in trivial research findings, an exercise unrelated to the human condition. I sincerely hope this is not the case. Science alone does not have all the answers about humans and their place in the universe, but scientifically formulated questions and experimental methodologies can further a tentative understanding. Box 1.2 highlights three individuals who in challenging us to think differently about ourselves helped bring about a scientific conception of human experience.

This text accepts the challenge of trying to analyze and understand the human mind from within a scientific framework. You may be surprised to find that behavioral scientists now have answers to questions about humans and other animals that Descartes didn't know enough to ask. The challenge to view humans from a scientific perspective begins here and continues through each of the following chapters.

Psychology of Human Learning and Cognition Compared

Thinking, memorizing, reasoning, reading, knowing. These terms are part of the vocabulary and psychological constructs of *cognitive psychology* and the study

Box 1.2   Three Intellectual Giants

What *is* a scientific understanding of human experience? Ask 10 people and get 10 answers. Most would agree that such a view would encompass mainstream findings and theory in chemistry and physics, including the big bang origin of the matter in the universe. Focusing more on the existence of life and that which constitutes *human nature*, here I offer my three candidates for "most influential thinkers," namely, Charles Darwin, Ivan Pavlov, and Sigmund Freud.

We will meet Darwin (in Chapter 2) and Pavlov (Chapters 3 and 4) in more detail. Sigmund Freud's ideas are not critically examined in this book, but his influence is ever present. What are the similarities and differences of these three individuals? All are DWEMs (dead, white, European males). All were born in 19th-century Europe, and all had biological interests. While none

were psychologists per se, each profoundly influenced modern conceptions of the human mind and behavior. Darwin addressed our phyletic and behavioral continuities with other animals. Pavlov showed us that we shared with other animals both common reflexes and common processes of conditioning those reflexes. Freud pointed out to us that although we are not always conscious of what we have learned during our lifetime, our adult mind is continuous with and is in part determined by childhood experiences. Hence, all were materialists who espoused various forms of biological determinism.

All three individuals addressed mental as well as physical aspects of human experience. All three addressed the uniqueness of human culture. Retrospectively, each can be characterized as having had a biopsychosociocultural perspective.

of **cognition.** Historically, "learning psychologists" have been concerned with laboratory experiments on animals. By contrast, cognitive psychologists tend to view learning as the acquisition of, and retrieval of information from, human memory. Cognition is interpreted from within an "information-processing" model of psychology.

Concepts of learning and memory are obviously related. Can you think of an instance of learning that does not presuppose a memory system or vice versa? Can you think of a concept of memory as other than the repository of that which has been learned? Seldom, however, do the terms *learning* and *memory* seem to interact in the minds of psychologists! Separate research journals report experiments on "animal learning" and on "human memory." Different courses using distinctive textbooks on "learning" or "cognition" (or "memory") are offered in our colleges and universities by psychologists with vastly different understandings of these two terms.

"Learning" or "Thinking"?   For the sake of argument and putting the questions of evolution and psychological continuity among animals aside for the moment, let us accept the assumption that humans are sufficiently different from animals that separate rules, or principles, may guide their learning. Let's listen to one of many students over the years who doubts that animal learning experiments mirror her own learning experiences in the classroom:

> *I sit here, listening to you, trying to make sense, thinking, comparing, contrasting, trying to understand. Then I go to the library and read, read, read . . . trying to learn the material in the textbook. Some of it I memorize.*
>   *My dog cannot do what I do; it does not learn in the same way. What good does it do to study animal learning experiments if animals don't think as I do?*

These are excellent observations, and you may likewise be entertaining similar reservations. But consider the following: This student's comments imply (a) that she fully understands the realms of human learning and cognition and (b) that she intuitively knows that human learning is distinct from animal learning and cognition.[5] Unfortunately, *behavioral scientists* do not presently know enough to arrive at these same conclusions. Since we don't have all the answers, isn't it preferable to adopt the behavioral scientists' strategy of (a) looking at the evidence, (b) noting that the evidence is incomplete, and (c) coming to some tentative conclusion that may change as more data are gathered? The hard part for both scientists and students alike is to be content with less than perfect answers to such complex questions. We must learn to be patient and accept the fact that more is unknown than known about human and animal minds.

Animals Have Minds?   Some evidence that bears on the "animal mind" may surprise you. For example, humans and nonhuman animals alike engage in "timing" behaviors; likewise, both make similar *choices* when presented with similar alternatives. Nonhuman animals and humans reason and learn some tasks in a similar manner. Nonhuman animals not only make choices but also think and otherwise behave in quite complex ways reflecting sophisticated psychological properties. Many species, not just humans, learn concepts. Humans and animals engage in communication. And, not unlike humans, a number of animal species pass on knowledge from generation to generation.

Let us suspend judgment for the present, then, regarding the inviolable uniqueness of humans, and return later to a serious treatment of these questions. My hope is that you, like the other student who raised these questions, will have a better idea of just how complex the questions are, even if the answers are less than satisfying. For now, consider the following questions: What evidence would convince you that animals can tell time? That animals can

---

[5] Note that the issue of psychological continuities among species can be legitimately raised even if one does *not* espouse a belief in "special creation."

think? That animals can make decisions? That animals can behave in a voluntary fashion?

The study of animal learning and behavior can help us better understand how humans learn and how they think. Likewise, many of the techniques used by cognitive psychologists to study human memory involve problem solving, list learning, and procedural memory, to name but a few methods. Interpreting the results of these human experiments makes use of *associative models* (Chapter 3) that are based on the study of laboratory animals. The point is that both animal learning and human cognitive approaches are complementary. Learning and memory theory for both animals and humans *are* increasingly interdependent.

Application of Theories of Learning. The psychology of learning also has an applied dimension. We had better understand how to educate our children, why some might have eating disorders and others a chemical dependency, and how each of us can learn to be sick and learn to be well. To the extent that your roommate or a close friend (or you) has problems with relationships, can we better understand such problems by studying that person's learning history—the rewards and punishments that have shaped the maladaptive behavior? By applying learning theory to our skilled performances, to our use of language, to our emotional and rational behaviors—both dysfunctional and normal—we attain insight and the power to change behavior. Let us look as some of these applications.

Relationship of Learning to Clinical Psychology

Many undergraduate majors studying psychology in U.S. colleges and universities have professional aspirations. Their goal is to go to graduate school and then through course work, practicums, and internships to become licensed—as clinical psychologists, as social workers, as professional counselors, or in other applied occupations. More often than not these career-oriented students do not see the relevance of courses in animal learning (or, for that matter, courses in perception, physiology, or cognitive or quantitative psychology!). Rather, most students view the "applied" courses (personality, abnormal, social, developmental, testing) as the relevant preprofessional curriculum.

Allow me to offer a different perspective. The study of animal learning is *critically* important to the practice of clinical psychology. The bulk of patients seeking therapy have emotional- and cognitive-based "lifestyle disorders." Most were *not* born that way. Many are presently dysfunctional because of a myriad of *aversive learning experiences*. As we will see in examples throughout this text, aversive conditioning is rapid, powerful, and long lasting under a variety of circumstances in differing environments. Our understanding of phobic and panic disorders, post-traumatic stress disorders (PTSD), reactive depression, eating disorders, educational problems, sexual disorders, marital disorders, and psychophysiological disorders, to name but a few, depends on theories of *learned* behavior.

Likewise, therapeutic regimens for these and other disorders are largely laboratory based. By that I mean that associative models used in behavioral and cognitive-behavioral therapy are predicated on, and documented by, laboratory research with animals. In summary, students with aspirations in clinical psychology are well served by learning the empirical research basis for their chosen discipline.

Relationship of Learning to Socialization and Parenting Skills

A psychology major attracts many students because they seek a better understanding of themselves, of friends, and of family members. Who am I? Why do I think, feel, and act as I do? To return to an earlier theme, a multifaceted behavior theory—including genetics, learning, sociology, and so on—addresses such questions. In many respects, each course in a psychology curriculum addresses one or more aspects of a broad "theory" (or "theories") of behavior.

Integral to a comprehensive theory of behavior are learning and the analysis of learned behavior that such theory affords. Beginning with your genetic endowment, you subsequently have learned to be who and what you presently are. Your present level of socialization reflects the total of your environmental experiences to date. Significant others have guided you (or not); reinforced and punished you (or not); and arranged formal learning opportunities in schools, camps, churches (or not).

Many of you will become parents during your lifetime and will be faced with making decisions about how you will rear your children. What do you want from them and for them, and how will you arrange their environment to maximize attaining your mutual goals?

This text exposes you to outcomes of experiments that reflect the results of environmental manipulations on animals, including humans. No guarantees, but your children might profit from your study of behavioral analysis in this text. At a minimum you will likely be more analytical about your parenting role.

Relationship of Learning to Culture

Ethnic and cultural differences fit a nature/nurture framework. Ethnicity denotes "ancestry, culture, language, nationality . . . religion, or a combination of these things" (*World Book Encyclopedia*, 1991). Ancestry is nature; the remaining factors are nurture—environmentally determined. In the course of your lifetime, not only have you learned to speak the language peculiar to your culture, but also you have learned about religious practices, about cultural foods and clothes styles, about dating practices and other habits of interacting, and . . . just about everything else you can think of. This could be a long book.

Interim Summary

1. Historically, research interests in animal learning differed from those in human cognition and memory.
2. Comparative psychologists study both learning processes and the behaviors of humans and other animals.
3. Individual differences can best be accounted for by unique learning experiences in unique environments.
4. *Extrapolation* refers to the application to humans of the results of studying learning processes in nonhuman animals.
5. While recognizing the complexity of humans, it is assumed that the human mind and human behavior can be understood by scientific methods.
6. Learning theories apply to clinical psychology, the socialization process, parenting skills, and to the very foundations of culture.

THE QUEST FOR A SCIENCE OF LEARNING

The study of learning is a formal science. As is the case in other areas in psychology, the methods used to study learning seem to be radically different from, say, those of chemistry, biology, or physics. In this section we briefly look at the methods of inquiry into psychological processes and then focus on particulars in the science of learning. Here you learn about operational definitions, the problem of reification, the learning-performance distinction, levels of analysis, and reductionism.

History of Science

Science is one of the more complex (and curious) activities in which humans engage. Those of us who enjoy Western culture take for granted the various methods by which science is accomplished, the knowledge attained, and the technology made possible by these findings. Some in our culture, however, ignore, devalue, and even reject scientific thinking. Various kinds of artistic and religious experience, for example, provide a type of knowledge that is independent of scientific criteria. An underlying premise of this text is that a scientific perspective aids our understanding of human behavior.

Those who study the history of science and scientific thinking find precursors of "modern" science in Greek philosophers who lived several thousand years ago. These mathematicians, astronomers, logicians, and inventors—to name but a few of the behavioral activities of *natural philosophers*—formulated problems and discovered a variety of philosophical tools, including mathematics and logic. The activity of these ancient philosophers found fruition in modern Western European scientific thinking that dates from the 1600s. Our present focus is on the behavioral sciences, arguably only about 150 years old. Behavioral studies on laboratory animals have only a 100-year history.

Generations of students have found the activities of psychologists working with animals in laboratories to be a curious enterprise, indeed. As mentioned earlier, "What are you trying to prove?" and "What can we learn about humans from the study of rats?" are legitimate questions.

The Science of Learning.   A behavioral scientist's activities in the laboratory can be divided into two parts. First, a decision is made as to *what* will be studied, followed by the questions of *how* the investigation will continue. In the same way that our understanding of any phenomenon depends on the perspective from which we view it, the results of learning experiments are directly influenced by the way in which the experiment is performed, that is, the method used. For this reason it is important at the outset to understand some of the underlying theory and methods used to investigate learning and behavior—in real life and in the laboratory.

Learning as a Hypothetical Construct

Earlier, *learning* was defined as *a relatively enduring change in behavior resulting from particular kinds of experiences*. Unfortunately, it is presently impossible to directly observe the learning process. We simply cannot crawl into the minds of the people (or, for that matter, the minds of much simpler animals) and actually see or feel or hear learning. The process is unobservable.

How is it possible to have a science of learning if learning is unobservable? Terms like *learning* are not unusual in psychology; consider, for example, *memory, motivation, fear,* and *intelligence*. These words describing processes of the mind are generally referred to as **hypothetical constructs.** *Intelligence,* for example, is assumed to exist but cannot be observed directly. (It is not even clear what it means to suggest that "it" *could* be observed directly, other than to assert that "it" is composed of neurochemical changes or of patterns of neural activity).

Hypothetical is perhaps a poor term because it implies that processes such as learning and intelligence are nonexistent or even imaginary. Nothing could be further from the truth. As every school child knows, memory and intelligence are routinely measured as *performance on paper and pencil tests*.

Operational Definitions

As we saw in Box 1.1, behavioral scientists define intelligence as performance on an IQ (or other kind of) test. To define intelligence as a score on a test is an operational definition. An **operational definition** means that the construct at hand is defined according to the operations that measure it. For example, performance on a final exam operationally defines what you have *learned* in the course.

Typically, arguments to the effect that IQ tests do not measure "real" intelligence or that final exams do not measure what was *really* learned in a class are disagreements about operational definitions. Yes, other performance measures can be used to measure "intelligence" and to measure what was learned in a class. But intelligence and learning do not exist independent of some measure of performance. Arguments to the contrary run the risk of **reification.** *To reify* means to assert the existence of something without having independent evidence that "it" exists. It doesn't help, for example, that everyone has a general idea of what intelligence is and that what intelligence is is something different from a score on a test. Likewise, to assert that you know more than what a test samples is at one and the same time true and begging the question. Tests are performance measures, and good tests are designed to allow you to express what you have learned. The futility of asserting that "intelligence cannot be measured" and that "there is no way to measure what I have learned" should be apparent.

Learning-Performance Distinction

Note that behavioral scientists measure "performance" and infer learning, intelligence, memory, and so on from these observations. As noted before, learning and memory formations are "invisible" processes. We infer such processes based on the changes in performance that *can* be measured. The difference between what is measured and what is inferred is known as the **learning-performance distinction.**

"Hard Science" and Psychology

The psychology of learning is characterized here as a science—that is, as a systematic, objective, analytical enterprise. Not everyone agrees that psychology is a science. Biologists, chemists, and physicists, for example, often object to the subject matter of psychology. How can one study learning (or motivation or memory), they ask, when these processes are unobservable?[6] After all, the primary goal of a science is to observe and analyze objectively the various phenomena of nature. Are not physical phenomena, such as the chemical reactions of basic biological processes, more objectively measured? Would it perhaps be better to be looking for the biochemical determinants of the learning process and not merely analyzing the behaving animal?

---

[6] All sciences deal with "constructs" such as gravity, acceleration, and so forth. For example, "acceleration" has no empirical referent. It can be computed as time divided by velocity. IQ can be computed as mental age divided by chronological age × 100.

Obviously, behavioral scientists think not. But let us analyze the hard science argument more carefully. What *are* the consequences of reducing the learning process to concrete physical and/or chemical entities? The argument is called *reductionism*.

Reductionism

As you well know, the world is described by several kinds of language. Artists and musicians and priests certainly see the world in different terms than engineers and politicians. Within the world of science there also exist *levels of analysis*.

While their activities vary widely, at best a communality of purpose and spirit exists among scientists. Some scientists investigate phenomena at a **molar level.** An example of a molar-level study is to analyze the behavior of a whole, intact organism. Others attempt to understand some aspect of behavior by determining which parts of the brain (anatomy) or which chemicals (biochemistry) are involved when a particular behavior occurs. They are pursuing a more **molecular level** of analysis. The tendency to explain a phenomenon by reference to a more molecular level of analysis, such as biochemistry, is called **reductionism.**

Chicken Example.   Let us use as an example a scientist wanting to understand the sand-eating behavior of a newly hatched chicken. Young chicks do in fact ingest sand. As far as is known, there are no more nutritive advantages for sand-eating chickens than there are for sand-eating kids.

Over a period of time, sand eating drops off. At that time, when given a choice between seed and sand, chicks eat only seeds. It appears that young chicks learn to develop a discrimination between grains of sand and similarly shaped seeds. Indeed, through clever, painstaking research, just such a learning analysis has been accomplished (Hogan, 1977).

Now it is certain that biochemical changes are occurring in the brain of the chick as it learns the sand-seed discrimination. Moreover, as researchers tell us *which* biochemicals change, *when* they change, and *how* they change, our understanding of the sand-seed discrimination will be enhanced. Recognize that a complete knowledge of these biochemical changes does not in and of itself constitute anything approaching a complete explanation of the sand-seed behavioral discrimination. It is, after all, the *behavior* of the creature that we are attempting to account for. How does the animal interact with the environment? Are there social factors involved in learning the discrimination, and so on?

A biochemical analysis might clarify a subtle difference in behavior, furthering the understanding of the behavior in question. However, in no way does the biochemical analysis constitute a *better* explanation of the phenomenon by comparison with the molar analysis of learning as Hogan (1977) described. Together, the molar and molecular analyses provide a better understanding than either alone.

Summary Statement Concerning Reductionism.   Molar analyses of a behavior are appropriate and necessary for a complete understanding of behavior. Reductionism alone constitutes neither a better explanation nor a better science.

Scientific Content and Method Compared

Science can be roughly divided into two components: *methodology* (how and what is done in an experiment) and *content* (what is found out). Students typically hate methodological considerations. ("I don't care who did what, when, or how! All I want to know is *what was found out!*") Unfortunately, content cannot be separated neatly from methodology. Indeed, as argued before, more often than not, methodology *determines* content.

An Example: Sleep Research.   The job of the behavioral scientist can be simply divided into two parts: first, deciding on *what* is to be studied and then deciding on *how* to study it. Consider, for example, sleep research. I imagine a sleep study in which the methodology is limited to watching a person's behavior overnight. The researcher records activity, tosses and turns, perhaps a verbal report of a dream upon awakening, and so forth. This method would give us a veridical (truthful, accurate) but limited understanding and perspective of one of the more fascinating aspects of our lives.

Various scientific methodologies (and some nonscientific approaches, such as Jungian dream analysis) have added other dimensions to our understandings of sleep and dreams during this century. For example, a psychoanalytic perspective might focus on the latent and manifest sexual content of someone's dreams and relate such findings to id-ego interactions during that person's waking hours. Alternatively, recording electrodes might be attached to the scalp during sleep, and sleep stages monitored (i.e., an electrophysiological measure). A comparative psychologist might compare the sleep patterns of vertebrates—of prey animals and of predators—and note the longer, deeper sleep enjoyed by the latter. Such patterns relate to questions of evolutionary adaptation. Finally, we could note the changes in serotonin levels during dreams and other sleep stages and develop hypotheses concerning the physiological restorative function of sleep (i.e., the biochemical method).

Note that each experimental methodology allows us only partial insight into the nature of sleep. Each method provides a different perspective or content. Likewise, each of the different methodologies used to investigate "learning" provides multiple perspectives of this process.

When learning methodologies successfully mimic "real-life" learning situations, laboratory studies become interesting in their own right. It is certainly true that individual investigators develop and become expert in a particular methodology, often because of "real-life" interests and applications.

Interim Summary

1. Scientific analyses and laboratory study yield knowledge about human behavior that complements our artistic and religious experiences.

2. Learning, memory, motivation, anger, and intelligence—processes of the mind assumed to exist but not directly observable—are called *hypothetical constructs.*

3. "Performance on a multiple choice test" is an *operational definition* of learning, that is, a definition based on how the presumptive process is being measured.

4. Performance is observed and measured, and from changes in performance, learning may or may not be inferred. The difference between the observed performance and the inferred (and invisible) process of learning is known as the *learning-performance distinction.*

5. The error of *reification* is to assert the existence of a psychological process in the absence of any performance measures.

6. Learning can be studied at different levels of analysis, from *molecular* to *molar*. Explanation of behavior by reference to a more molecular level (such as changes in brain biochemistry) is known as *reductionism.*

7. Explanations of behavior in physiological or chemical terms are neither better nor more scientific that molar observations.

8. The science of learning consists of both *method* (how an investigation was conducted) and *content* (what was found out).

PSYCHOLOGICAL EXPERIMENTS IN LABORATORIES

No one would mistake John Grady for a psychologist training an animal in a laboratory learning experiment. But there are similarities. John Grady arranged a unique environment for his wild mustang. The horse learned new responses as a result of this experience. Here we look at ways in which laboratory experiments resemble real-life scenarios. You may be surprised to find that what John Grady did and how the horse responded can be profitably analyzed from a formal learning perspective. Let us look, then, at psychological experiments in the laboratory.

Most of the experiments you come across in this text are designed to investigate cause-and-effect relationships. Certain precise experiences or manipulations are imposed on experimental subjects. Then the effects of these treatments are assessed in tests specifically designed to measure one or more aspects of the changed behavior. Laboratory studies in the behavioral sciences—in areas of learning and memory in particular—have common features. Indeed, experiments on rats and college students (and horses) more often than not use a similar scientific method.

The Black Box Approach

Students almost invariably ask why dogs, or rats, or pigeons are studied in the laboratory if the researcher is interested in human learning and memory processes. One answer is that each of these species can be considered an interchangeable "black box" in which stimuli go in one end and responses come out the other end (see Figure 1.1). For some researchers, what might be inside the black box is often of less interest than whether there are similarities in differing species' responses to stimuli going in the box. One assumption underlying this black box approach is that the behavioral processes under study are the same (or are similar) from species to species. For example, all animals respond in similar ways to confinement, food, pain, stroking, and so forth. John Grady's horse responded to stroking and "gentling" by becoming calm. Humans, rats in laboratories, and most land-dwelling vertebrates respond in a similar manner.

Yet other researchers justify the study of a particular species of animal, such as kangaroo rats, or Japanese quail, or honey bees because they are interested in the peculiarities of that particular species' behavior. *Homo sapiens*, after all, is only one of thousands of species whose behavior we do not understand! Certainly John Grady had a special interest in horses. A researcher I first met as a graduate student had a "thing" about snakes and continues to study their behavior to this day. The point is that there are legitimate reasons to study the behavior of all animals. Let us set up a laboratory learning experiment that deals with the distinctive behavior of humans. The results are applicable to other animals.

Stimulus → [ ] → Response

FIGURE 1.1   The Black Box Approach to Behavior

In the *black box* model of behavior, stimuli impinge on an animal, and the animal responds. The S-R relationships can be investigated regardless of what happens—either physiologically or psychologically—inside the animal. Behaviorists attempt to build a science of behavior using this approach.

The Effects of Study on Language Learning.   Consider, for example, an experiment using college students as subjects. The students are allowed to study Spanish language vocabulary for several minutes. Sometime later they are asked to recall these words in a test of vocabulary retention. Referring again to the black box in Figure 1.1, note that the *words* may be considered to be the **stimulus variables** (i.e., the experimental manipulation imposed on the subjects). The degree of retention—the number of words recalled or percentage of the list retained—is the **response variable.** This response or behavioral measure—specifically, the number of words recalled—is the evidence that learning has occurred in a subject (cf. operational definition of learning). For students already familiar with scientific methodology, *stimulus and response variables* are also known as *independent and dependent variables* (see later discussion).

Stimulus, Response, and Intervening Variables

In this example, you can see the sequence of events typical of all psychological experiments. Response variables are systematically related to preceding stimulus variables, rendering the process of "learning" into an observable event. The stimulus variable imposed on the experimental subjects is the *cause*, and the *effect* is reflected in the response measure selected by the experimenter. Learning in laboratory animals, then, is operationally defined as a change in behavior that can be related to a specific manipulation of the environment.

When a behavioral scientist is able to make a reliable, lawlike statement relating measured responses to preceding stimulus conditions, learning assumes the status of an "intervening variable." The behavioral scientist identifies the psychological process occurring inside the black box as the **intervening variable.** Intervening variables presumably mediate the cause-and-effect relationship between the experience and the behavior.

Freud's ideas of id and ego should not be conceptualized as intervening variables. For these "soft" constructs to be considered intervening variables, the manipulation of specific stimulus variables would have to be shown to be systematically related to changes in response measures used to define ego and id. Such research has not been accomplished. By contrast, learning does change systematically with the manipulation of stimulus variables and for this reason is considered to be an intervening variable (MacCorquodale & Meehl, 1948).

Independent and Dependent Variables

In all learning experiments—indeed in all psychological experiments—the goal is to identify the cause-and-effect relationship under investigation. The treatment or manipulation of stimulus variables imposed by the experimenter on the experimental subject is referred to as the **independent variable.**[7]

---

[7] Readers already familiar with the scientific method may want to skim this section.

In the previous example, the list of Spanish words is the independent variable.

In all experiments the experimental manipulation is called the *treatment,* and the group of subjects that receive the experimental manipulation—the *independent variable*—is known as the **treatment group.** Typically these subjects are compared to other group(s) of subjects given a *control* treatment. **Control groups,** therefore, are exposed to all conditions in the experiment that the treatment group experiences but *not* to the independent variable.

The response used to assess the treatment effects of the independent variable is known as the **dependent variable.** The measure of retention of Spanish words, then, constitutes the dependent variable in the previous example. The dependent variable is so named because the response outcome *depends on* the treatment.

What Constitutes an Experiment?

Experimental treatments are compared to control groups to determine whether an effect is real. You may wonder what the control group was in the foregoing "experiment" that measured the recall of foreign words. There was none. The example given was not truly an experiment!

Hypotheses.   An experiment involves **hypothesis** testing. For example, one might have a **working hypothesis** that more Spanish words will be recalled if a person studies more (which was implied but not specified in the example). Note that a working hypothesis is a simple statement of what you expect to happen if you run an experiment. Let us turn this example into a real experiment:

First, identify 30 students enrolled in a first-year Spanish course. Each student is given the same list of 20 Spanish words to study. Next, divide the 30 students into 3 groups with 10 students in each group (i.e., $n = 10$/group).

> **Group 1:** Studies for 60 seconds (enough to read the list one time). Then students are allowed to read a novel of their choosing for 59 minutes. Note that from the beginning of the treatment to the end, 60 minutes elapse.
>
> **Group 2:** Studies the Spanish words for 15 minutes and then students read a novel of their choice for 45 minutes.
>
> **Group 3:** Studies the Spanish words for 60 minutes.

Twenty-four hours later the students are given the English equivalents of the 20 words and are asked to make the Spanish translations. The mean number of correct responses is computed for each group. The results are displayed in Figure 1.2. Can you identify the treatment group(s) and the control group(s)? By interpreting the graph, can you verbalize the results before read-

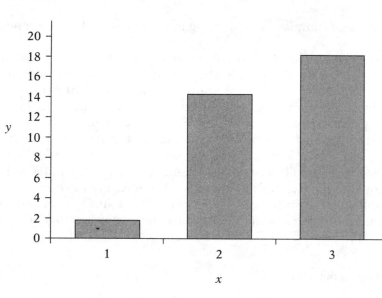

FIGURE 1.2   Bar Graph Depicting Results
of Spanish Vocabulary Experiment

Responses are plotted along the *y* axis as a function of conditions 1, 2, and
3, plotted along the *x* axis. Note the general form: *Any* response can be
plotted as a function of *any* stimulus condition. See text for description of
the conditions identified as 1, 2, and 3.

---

ing further? Another way to ask this question is: Can you label the *x* axis, the *y*
axis, and the *functional relationship* that is depicted?

Experimental Design

Note in this experiment that the independent variable—the amount of time
each group is allowed to study—is displayed along the *x* axis as a *category*.
Each category (1, 2, or 3) represents a treatment condition selected by the experimenter. This experiment is an example of a **between-groups design** in
that each group is assigned a different **parameter** (i.e., 1, 15, or 60 minutes) of
the independent variable. The idea is to test the hypothesis that a systematic,
or **functional relationship** exists between the independent variable and the
dependent variable. The working hypothesis is that amount of study (1 minute,
15 minutes, or 60 minutes) influences the number of Spanish words recalled in
a later test.

By contrast, a **within-groups design** compares a pretreatment measure
of the dependent variable with a post-treatment measure *in the same subjects*.
For example, the investigator might give the 20 Spanish words to all three

groups before allowing them to study. Their performance would constitute a pretest (or a *baseline*) from which to measure the effects of the treatment. After studying the Spanish words for 1, 15, or 60 minutes, they would then take a post-test. The post-test performance of each group would be compared with its respective pretest performance—hence, a *within-groups* design.

Look at Figure 1.2 once again. What parameter of the independent variable was manipulated?[8] Note that the dependent variable plotted on the *y* axis is the number of Spanish words recalled during the test. The mean values plotted are 1.8, 14.3, and 18.2 words, respectively, for Groups 1, 2, and 3.

Statistical Analysis.   These experimental results could be subjected to a statistical analysis to see whether the **null hypothesis** could be rejected. The null hypothesis in this experiment is that the three groups do not differ from each other. That is, that the results observed in Figure 1.2 would have occurred even if study time had been equated for the three groups. Yet another way to state this counterintuitive argument (i.e., the null hypothesis) is that the amount of time spent studying had nothing to do with the number of successful Spanish translations.

A statistical procedure called an *ANOVA* (analysis of variance) of these data would compare both the means and the variance (differences in the distributions of recalled words) of the three groups. The size of the mean differences in Figure 1.2 is sufficiently large that the results of the ANOVA would likely allow us to reject the null hypothesis. A statistically significant difference among the groups would allow us to conclude that the "amount of time studying the Spanish words" was *causally related* to the recall performance of these words. We can now accept the working hypothesis. From the performance of these students, we can infer that "study" (practice? familiarity? trials?) is related to the learning process.

John Grady's treatment of the wild mustang can be likened to a laboratory experiment. Confining, stroking, covering the animal's eyes, and whispering into its ear are stimulus variables. It is likely that such response variables as heart and respiration rate, pupilary dilation, adrenal gland secretions, and so on would have systematically changed as a function of the continued treatment. The "experimental" design was within-groups: The horse's wild behavior in the presence of a human became more gentle as a result of the treatment. Any of a number of behavioral response measures—such as rearing, whinnying, biting, pawing, or running—could have been quantified and compared with pretreatment measures. On the basis of these results, one could have concluded that there was a functional relationship between the treatment variables and the response outcome.

---

[8] The parameter of *time*—the amount of time students were allowed to study the Spanish words—was manipulated.

Interim Summary

1. Molar behavior can be studied scientifically.
2. Learning is an inference made from observations of an animal's performance.
3. A simple analysis of behavior employs a *black box* model in which incoming stimulus variables can be systematically related to response variables.
4. Researchers manipulate treatment conditions, or independent variables, and measure dependent variables (usually some form of behavioral response).
5. Treatment groups are compared to control groups in an experiment. The conditions of the control group are made as identical as possible to the treatment group except that the independent variable is not manipulated in the control group.
6. In a *between-groups* design, each group is assigned a level, or *parameter,* of an independent variable, and results are compared to a control group. In a *within-groups* design, the effects of the independent variable are compared with a pretest measure.
7. The basic design of a learning experiment:
   a. State working hypotheses about what is expected to happen.
   b. Operationally define terms.
   c. Set up treatment and control conditions for comparison.
   d. Measure performance.
   e. Test null hypothesis using statistics.
8. One outcome of a successful experiment is the identification of a *functional relationship* in which a response measure is related to stimulus conditions.

LEARNING AND BEHAVIOR: A PREVIEW

The remainder of this chapter provides a survey of issues raised in the rest of this text.

Evolution and Behavior

Where did I come from? What nature of creature am I? In Chapter 2, the role of learning in behavior theory is examined within the context of Darwin's theory of evolution. Extensions of evolutionary theory—ethology, comparative and evolutionary psychology, behavioral genetics, and sociobiology—shed light on life's mysteries. Some questions to guide your reading:

- In what ways are humans alike and in what ways are they unlike other animals? What is instinct? Do humans have instincts? Do *you* behave instinctively?
- Has our "mental life" evolved?
- We return to questions of extrapolation. What is the theoretical basis for research using animal models of human behavior? Can relatively simple associative models profitably be used to analyze the complex organization of human brains?
- What is ethology? How do bees and birds learn to navigate over long distances? How do psychologists' experiments differ in theory and method from those of ethologists?
- What are the strengths and weaknesses of a stimulus-response approach to the study of behavior?

Theoretical Approaches to Learning

Two dominant "connectionist" theories of learning—classical conditioning and instrumental learning—are introduced in Chapters 3 and 5, respectively. Together these approaches constitute the "meat," or basic science, of animal learning. Among the questions considered:

- Why are two theories necessary?
- What is associative learning?
- What is nonassociative learning?
- Why is it important that learning is "lawlike"? Are there "laws of learning"?
- Can animal models *really* account for skilled human performance—playing the piano, for example?

Complex Conditioning

Classical conditioning studies over the past century have surpassed Ivan Pavlov's classic demonstration that dogs will salivate to the sound of a bell. Indeed, demonstrations of the conditioning of human behavior are now commonplace.

By comparison with Pavlov's experiments, contemporary conditioning studies more often involve complex stimulus arrangements (Chapter 4). Such complexity mirrors behavior in the real world. These experiments often give us several kinds of information—how stimuli in complexes become associated, how the brain perceives stimuli (thereby affecting their association), and how contextual conditioning occurs in the "real world." Consider these questions:

- Why are some things easier to learn than others? For example, why do so many students have math phobia but not music phobia?

- How do children learn when and where it is acceptable to use profanity and when and where such language is inappropriate?
- Why do people have different fears?
- Why does conditioning sometimes fail?
- Can simple associative conceptions of learning really account for complex conditioning?

Carrots and Sticks

Psychobiology, the science of mind-body interactions, is exemplified by questions of how and why reinforcement (carrots) and punishment (sticks) control behavior. The role of motivation in learning is pursued in Chapters 5 and 6, where the following questions are addressed:

- What is hedonism? Are humans as hedonistic as other animals?
- Why is it that the most memorable things in life are most often associated with pleasure and pain?
- Are rewards and punishments universal? If so, why do humans differ so much in their likes and dislikes?
- Which controls behavior better, reward or punishment?
- What is known about reward circuits in the brain?

Physiology and Behavior

Still skeptical that the study of rats, pigeons, and other guinea pigs can tell you anything about your own behavior? Chapter 7 is designed to make a believer of you. The application of basic principles of conditioning and learning to human physiology and health is in its infancy but is nevertheless exciting. Consider the following:

- What is the role of learning in psychosomatic, or mind-body, disorders?
- Can your immune system be conditioned? If so, can you learn to be sick and learn to be healthy?
- Is your asthma a conditioned emotional response?
- Is becoming angry or falling in love a conditioned response?
- Does drug effectiveness depend more on pharmacology or psychology? To what extent do the reinforcing properties of alcohol and cocaine control behavior?
- How does learning affect your eating patterns? Can learning principles be applied to *understand* abnormal eating and drinking behaviors? To *change* unusual eating and drinking behaviors?
- What is the role of learning in psychotherapy?

Choice Behavior

Behavioral scientists approach their study of human behavior from a philosophical position known as **determinism.** Determinists assert that behavior is caused by both genetics (biological determinism) and environmental influences (environmental determinism). Whether or not you consider yourself a "free agent," animals and humans behave as though they make choices. To what extent are our choices truly voluntary?

Chapter 8 presents an analysis of research into the determinants of choice behavior. Among other interesting issues is the extent to which this animal research informs "economic theory" governing human behavior.

- Are humans and other animals free to make choices, or, as B.F. Skinner has argued, are our alleged choices shaped and determined by the environment?
- Are you an unwitting component of a market economy? Do advertisers know more about you than you do?
- Given a choice between going to a movie or studying, what would you do? You would likely answer, "that depends." Behavioral scientists make some other surprising predictions.
- What laws or rules govern choice behavior?

Conceptual Learning and Thinking

We come full circle in Chapter 9, again raising such cognitive issues as insight, concept formation, and thinking. Three questions guide our examination of cognitive issues:

- What higher-order processes do animals (pigeons, monkeys, chimpanzees) exhibit?
- To what extent can such cognitive processes in humans and animals be understood as extensions of basic associative theory?
- What psychological properties (if any) are unique to humans?

Language and Culture

The all-important topic of language is treated in Chapter 10. Language makes civilization possible and seemingly erects an insurmountable boundary between humans and other animals. Important questions to be considered follow:

- Are humans the only species capable of understanding and producing language?
- Is language learned, or is it a biological inevitability, like upright walking?

• What factors determine which children become good readers with large vocabularies?

• What is the relationship of written language to science and technology?

So much for questions you will come across throughout this text. Let us get on with it and focus our discussion. Do humans and other animals share common psychological properties? We join the argument in Chapter 2.

CHAPTER SUMMARY

1. *Learning* is defined as a relatively permanent change in observable behavior that results from experience.

2. Behavior theory includes both genetic and environmental components (i.e., behavior theory can be thought of as the nature/nurture analysis of behavior).

3. Behavior is (a) what you do, (b) how you act, and (c) the way you respond to your environment. The viewpoint of this text is that differences among humans result from each individual's personal experience with a unique environment.

4. A psychobiological approach to learning and behavior recognizes that both genes and environment affect the learning process and observable behavior. That is, behavior is best understood as the result of genetically predisposed organisms interacting with the environment in which they live their lives.

5. A psychobiosociocultural (phew!) approach to human learning and behavior is characterized by the interdisciplinary study of biology (especially evolution, behavioral genetics, ethology, physiology), of psychology (how individuals learn), and of the interactions of individuals in society and culture.

6. *Learning* is a hypothetical construct. Like other psychological constructs, such as *intelligence, memory,* and *personality,* learning is inferred from observations of behavior. The learning process can be distinguished, then, from the performance of behavior.

7. Learning can be analyzed and explained at several different levels of analysis. Explaining learning by reference to biochemical changes in the brain is called *reductionism.*

8. Theories of learning attempt to account for behavior by noting the effects of immediate, local environments. Environments include both the field and laboratory where animals are studied. Human environments include homes, classrooms, and rock concerts.

9. Issues in learning include questions regarding the universality of "laws of learning," the extrapolation of the results of animal experiments to humans, humans as objects of scientific study, individual differences in learning, the role of volition and choice in learning, and the influence of human language and cognition on conditioning and learning.

10. Learning theory derived from studying animals can be applied to an understanding of health issues such as obesity and chemical dependency, to psychopathology, to parenting skills and child development, to the learning of skilled behavior (i.e., playing a musical instrument), to the learning of emotional behavior, to the socialization process, and to the learning of concepts and language.

11. Although other kinds of experience and knowledge—art, music, interpersonal relationships—inform the human condition, human behavior and human experience can also be understood from a scientific perspective.

12. Learning can be studied scientifically, both in humans and in laboratory animals.

13. The study of learning is critical to the scientific analysis of human behavior.

DISCUSSION QUESTIONS

1. My mother says that there are some things we will never know about people and other things we shouldn't even try to find out. I love my mother and respect her opinions. But as a scientist, I respectfully disagree with her and think that an experimental analysis of human behavior is both desirable and possible. Do you think that human beings can and should be studied scientifically? How do you feel about being "an object of study"?[9]

2. You will likely find your future in your present. That is, your local, immediate environments of home/apartment, school/work will in part determine your present and future friends, your career, and so on. In a nutshell, that is all that is meant by the phrase *environment shapes behavior.* I give my children much freedom, but I encourage them to "stay in school" rather than to "go to work." What likely reasons other than completing their education contribute to my concern for where they spend their time?

3. Do you agree with the assertion that "book learning" accounts for only a small (but important) portion of all the things we learn in our lifetimes? If you disagree, are you prepared to explain to millions of illiterate humans how little they have learned in their lifetimes?

4. An accomplished pianist was asked how she came to play the piano so well. She replied that she chose her parents well. Have you contemplated your genetic endowment? Your early environmental experiences? Or do you think you are a free agent who can choose to make your own way in life irrespective of your specific nature and nurture? We will return to these questions in later chapters.

5. *But what is the correct answer?* I share the exasperation of students who ask questions that aren't yet answerable. (And as a psychology professor, I am well aware that there are more of those kinds of questions than any other!) However, consider the risks of *not* being able to live with tentative conclusions . . . the inability to live with indecision? How do you respond to someone who always has the "right" answer to your every question? Something of an anomaly, isn't it? Society considers *people who have all the answers* to be less educated than people who say *"I'm not sure . . . possibly this is the answer, based on this evidence."* In responding to the following questions, assume that the physiological mechanisms underlying learning are now

[9] Discussion starters may be found in the next section.

known: (a) Would a behavioral analysis of learning any longer be necessary? (b) Can you make the case that a black box approach might still yield valuable information?

6. Sigmund Freud reified the ideas of id, ego, unconscious, and so forth. What does the reification of "the unconscious" mean? Do IQ tests measure "intelligence"? Why or why not?

7. The opposite of *reductionism* is *emergence*. Can you think of an example in which a neuroscientist uses emergence (rather than reductionism) to "explain," for example, the biochemical called *beta-endorphin*?

DISCUSSION STARTERS

1. *Should people be studied scientifically?* A student once made the interesting observation that there would always be mystery in the human condition because science was slow and inefficient. Since the human brain is one of the universe's most complex creations, she argued, it will not be figured out in this lifetime regardless of how much study is devoted to it. Maybe never, given the logic that humans would have an even more complex brain to understand our present level of complexity. So we needn't worry so much about demystifying humans. I'll buy that.

2. *Given that environment shapes behavior, why am I concerned that my children stay in school?* My daughters will more likely meet interesting, challenging people in a university environment than in the workplace. In addition, a college environment is an excellent one for learning how to set short- and long-term goals and then to meet them. Obviously, their father's value system is embodied in a college environment.

3. *How much does "book learning" account for?* The movers and shakers in our Western culture—that includes you—spend 20–30% of their lives in highly structured educational environ-

ments. We become the doctors, lawyers, educators, government/business/military leaders who control the wealth and direction of our culture. Book learning is important.

4. *Have you considered your personal "nature-nurture" questions?* "The unexamined life is not worth living," asserted Socrates. The quest for self-understanding is a lifelong one. Reexamination of one's life is necessary throughout a lifetime for two reasons: the accumulation of new experiences and the unfolding of time-locked genetic predispositions. Ever found yourself embarrassed when you noticed that you were acting as your mother or father would have in some situation? Or, because of a book you read, that you now hold different views than you did before?

5. *Dissatisfied with uncertainty?* This is a tough one. Religion's great appeal is the assertion of absolutes. Science's great solution to the uncertainty of the world is to match it with conditional answers. Is learning to think in a probabilistic manner a worthwhile goal for the college graduate?

6. *What is meant by the reification of the id? Id* and *ego* are two of the many names Freud used to label his under-

standing of psychological (behavioral?) characteristics of the human personality. (Note that the term *personality* is also a psychological construct.) Once accepted as a label—used in reference to certain unconscious, usually biological, always selfish, motivations—the id became a real entity rather than just a label. It becomes easy to talk about "it." "It" was reified.

7. *Reductionism and emergence?* A neuroscientist studying beta-endorphin would be interested in the behavioral, or real-world, significance of the neurochemical. She might note, for example, that certain neurons in the brain of an individual reporting pain were secreting this neurochemical. Something having to do with the experience of pain and/or its absence *emerges* from the secretion of this chemical. Note that a better understanding of both pain and beta-endorphin accompanies the inquiry into their relationship.

Key Terms

Behavior The way in which an animal acts or responds within the environment.

Behavior Theory An analysis of the way in which animals act or respond with environments as encompassing the interplay of genes and environment.

Behaviorism An extreme form of environmental determinism. Behaviorists ignore genetic influences and attempt to account for individual differences in behavior in terms of the effects of reinforcement and punishment.

Between-Groups Design The design of an experiment in which the effect of manipulating an independent variable (i.e., the treatment group) is compared to a control group not having the independent variable. (Cf. *Within-Groups Design.*)

Cognition The acts of perceiving, thinking, knowing, and remembering.

Control Group A comparison group for a treatment group. In an experiment, a group of subjects exposed to all conditions that the treatment group experiences but *not* to the independent variable.

Culture The arts, beliefs, customs, inventions, language, technology, and traditions of a group of people.

Dependent Variable In an experiment, the treatment effect of an independent variable is assessed by measuring changes in the dependent variable. In the behavioral sciences, most dependent variables are changes in behavior. Example: A drug (independent variable) *caused* increased activity (dependent variable).

Determinism The philosophical position that behavior is caused by the joint actions of genes (i.e., biological determinism) and environmental influences (i.e., environmental determinism).

Dyzygotic Developed from two zygotes; fraternal, or two-egg, twins. Dyzygotic twins have different genotypes.

Ecological Niche The place of an animal or plant in nature; the interrelatedness of plants and animals with their local environments.

Environment The sum of conditions and influences affecting the growth and development of living things, including air, water, soil, other plants and animals, and so on.

Extrapolation The real-world application of experimental results found in field and laboratory experimentation (typically conducted with animals) to the human condition.

Functional Relationship An orderly relationship existing between stimulus and response. Example: Higher drug doses cause higher levels of activity.

Gene Composed of deoxyribonucleic acid (cf. *DNA*); a part of a chromosome that, during the reproductive process, influences the inheritance and development of characteristics in the offspring.

Genotype The total of an organism's genetic information.

Hypothesis A hunch, idea, or theory that is formally tested in an experiment.

Hypothetical Construct The psychological terms used to label alleged processes of the mind, such as personality, learning, memory, motivation, perception, and intelligence. (Cf. *Intervening Variable.*)

Independent Variable In an experiment, the variable that is manipulated to see how it affects the dependent variable. The *independent variable* is seen as the cause, and the dependent variable is the effect. Example: A drug (independent variable) *caused* increased activity (dependent variable).

Intervening Variable Processes of the mind, such as learning, memory, and motivation that are inferred from observations of behavior. When "learning," for example, is operationally defined and investigated, it is conceptualized as an *intervening variable* that bridges the gap between measurable

stimulus and *response variables.* (Cf. *Hypothetical Construct.*)

Learning A relatively permanent change in observable behavior that results from experience within the environment.

Learning-Performance Distinction The difference between what is measured (performance) and what is inferred from the measurement (learning). Example: Changes in lever pressing are measured; learning is inferred.

Learning Theory The proposition that a limited number of general principles of learning can account for much of the observed variability in animal behavior.

Molar Level In research, investigations of the behavior of whole, intact organisms. (Cf. *Molecular Level.*)

Molecular Level In research, investigations of behavior by determining which parts of the brain (anatomy) or which biochemicals are involved concomitant with the behavior. (Cf. *Molar Level.*)

Monozygotic Developed from a single zygote; identical, or one-egg, twins. Monozygotic twins have identical genotypes.

Null Hypothesis In an experiment comparing a *treatment* condition with a *control* group, the hypothesis that *no* differences exist between the groups. Rejecting the null hypothesis (using a statistical analysis) leads to the conclusion that the two groups in fact differ and that the treatment effect caused this difference.

Operational Definition A definition of a term or concept that refers to the operations that measure the presumptive process. Example: Intelligence is that which IQ tests measure.

Parameters   The various levels that an independent variable can assume. Example: Low, medium, and high dosages are the *parameters* of a drug treatment.

Phenotype   A genotype expressed in an environment; defining an organism by its appearance, and not by its genetic constitution or hereditary potential.

Procedural Memory   Memory for skills; a hypothesized memory store for conditioned responses.

Psychobiology   An interdisciplinary approach to questions of physiology, learning, and behavior that draws on and attempts to integrate observations and experiments in, among other sciences, psychology, ethology, physiology, and genetics.

Reductionism   Explaining a phenomenon by reference to a more molecular analysis (i.e., a biochemical level). Reductionism is the primary means of scientific explanation.

Reification   Asserting the existence of a presumptive process independent of evidence for that process. Example: Intelligence is *there*, awaiting its measurement.

Response Variable   The measured response in a behavioral experiment. (In chemistry, the response variable is typically called a *reaction*.) In the behavioral sciences, the response variable is a measure of behavioral change.

Stimulus Variables   The experimental manipulation imposed on a subject in an experiment; also called the *independent variable*. Stimulus variables impinge upon animals, causing responses.

Treatment Group   In an experiment, the group of subjects that receives the *independent variable*.

Within-Groups Design   The design of an experiment in which a pretreatment measure of the dependent variable is compared with a post-treatment measure *in the same subjects*. (Cf. *Between-Groups Design*.)

Working Hypothesis   A simple statement of what is expected to happen in an experiment. Example: A low dose of drug *X* will have less effect on activity than a high dose.

CHAPTER 2

EVOLUTION AND THE STUDY OF BEHAVIOR

Each of us is a tiny being, permitted to ride on the outermost skin of one of the smaller planets for a few dozen trips around the local star. The great internal engine of plate tectonics is indifferent to life, as are the small changes in the Earth's orbit and tilt, the variation in the brightness of the Sun, and the impact with the Earth of small worlds on rogue orbits. These processes have no notion of what has been going on over billions of years on our planet's surface. They do not care.

. . . Of course the individual organisms see nothing of the overall pattern—
continents, climate, evolution. They barely set forth on the world stage and are
promptly snuffed out—yesterday a drop of semen, as the Roman Emperor Mar-
cus Aurelius wrote, tomorrow a handful of ashes. If the earth were as old as a per-
son, a typical organism would be born, live, and die in a sliver of a second. We are
fleeting, transitional creatures, snowflakes fallen on the hearth fire. That we un-
derstand even a little of our origins is one of the great triumphs of human insight
and courage.
             Sagan and Druyan, *Shadows of Forgotten Ancestors*, (1992, p. 30ff)

INTRODUCTION

To understand our behavior, we must entertain a longer perspective than the
course of events in a lifetime. Another way to say this is that the determinants
of each human's behavior begin before conception. How can this be so, you
ask? Is human behavior predestined? Where did this counterintuitive notion of
prebirth influences on behavior come from?

A mere century and a third ago, the publication of Charles Darwin's monumental theory allowed humans a new way to think about their behavior. At
present, neoevolutionary theory is crucial to an understanding of the broad
brush strokes of behavior and to learning and memory processes in particular.
At an intuitive level, the logic and rationale for incorporating evolutionary theory into a textbook on learning may not be apparent. Consider, however, that
learning and behavior are the activities of all living creatures, and, further, that
evolution is the major scientific theory that addresses the meaning of life.

Evolutionary theory provides an account of the origin of life forms as
well as a rationale for and understanding of basic processes of biological and
behavioral motivation—in other words, where we came from and why we live
the way we do. Let us begin by considering learning and behavior in two broad
categories of life, plants and animals.

EVOLUTION

Plants

"Live and learn" is a common figure of speech. Living and learning are not synonymous, however. Not all life forms learn. Few would disagree with the statement that plants do not learn, remember, or, for that matter, even behave
much! What plants "do" is respond in curious and highly interesting ways to
certain physical features in their immediate environment. The manner in
which plants do this superficially resembles reflexive behavior in animals (see
Chapter 3). For example, the tendency for some plants to open leaves in sun-

light and to orient roots "down" and stems "up" are forms of tropistic behavior, or tropisms.

Tropisms are movement adjustments that simple organisms make in response to changes in the environment. Since most plants are sessile (attached, relatively unmoving), they are capable of making only minor, usually local, movements. Compared to animals, plants sense their environment poorly and move very little. Lacking sensory and motor neurons, synapses, and a central nervous system, plant behavior is not characterized by learning and memory processes.

Animals

Now contrast the behavior of plants just described with the behavior of animals. The animal kingdom is "full of life." Animals move (cf. *animation*). Because they move, animals come across much more variation in their environment than plants do. Among other "things" they encounter are other animals. Behavior of increasing complexity and variability is required to cope with the constantly changing environment movement produces. To test this theory, compare the amount of "environment" you would experience sitting for 5 minutes with that you would encounter walking around (or driving) for 5 minutes.

The Role of Learning in Animal Behavior

The behavior of animals is characterized by their ability to profit from what they meet in their environment. That is, animals can learn. They form memories. The range of responses in animals is considerably beyond that of the "blind" tropisms of plants: Animals are able to adjust their reactions on the basis of the outcomes of previous actions. Another way to say this is that animals are able to learn that certain features of the environment are more often than not associated with other features of the environment.

For example, bears can remember that buzzing gold and black insects with stingers also predict the nearby presence of honey. Humans and other land-dwelling vertebrates learn about and form memories of the environments they inhabit. For example, I have a memory of this particular stretch of muddy river. Last year I learned that this river floods over there when it rains; now I remember that it can be crossed where it narrows, by the large cottonwood tree.

What I have learned from experiences with this river will help me survive. That is, my ability to learn and to remember is **adaptive**. Such learning is neither frivolous nor random—rather, it tracks the environment. Learning very often promotes survival and enhances future opportunities to reproduce. Indeed, the argument has been made by many that in comparison with other animals, intelligence—that includes the ability to learn and to remember—is the most adaptive characteristic of human beings.

To summarize, unlike sessile organisms, moving animals can and do make complex behavioral adjustments based on prior learning experiences. Very often such learning promotes the animal's survival.

Complex Animals and Learning: A Preview

Some animals behave more simply than others. Animals with simpler nervous systems exhibit less complex behavior. Simple nervous systems are less amenable to change as a result of learning experiences. For example, the common housefly feeds reflexively (read "automatically") when taste cells on the fly's legs are stimulated, causing its proboscis (trunklike mouth) to lower (Dethier, 1978). Chickens, however, must learn how to eat. They initially peck at both grain and sand indiscriminately. Grain but not sand satisfies their hunger, and the chicks eventually learn to peck the grain and not to peck the sand (Hogan, 1977).

Should one surmise, therefore, that the housefly is born "knowing" what to eat? This is not a simple question. Humans cannot experience what a housefly "knows," since human brains do not allow the same qualities of mental life as that afforded by housefly brains. For present purposes let us simply say that feeding behavior in the housefly is reflexive and that the role of learning in behavioral expression varies considerably among species.

What is clear is that learning and memory formation play an increasingly important role in the behavior of complex animals as opposed to the tropisms and reflexes of plants and simpler animals. Why is the behavior of animals so variable? How did it come to be this way? Our focus here is on animals, and we might ask why some animals survive perfectly well by reflex while others must learn life's lessons. Further, we might challenge the notion that learning is adaptive. Always adaptive? If so, why is "maladaptive behavior" so often the result—especially among humans? In Chapter 7 we consider maladaptive behavior in some detail.

Let us begin by more carefully examining the idea of adaptation. The term **adaptation** refers to two related propositions. First, adaptation is an alteration in an animal's structure or function that promotes survival. Second, adaptations give the animal a reproductive advantage. Asking questions about adaptation across generations brings us to the theory of evolution.

Darwin's Theory of Evolution

We turn to Charles Darwin's theory of evolution for the purpose of addressing behavioral processes of motivation and adaptation. To help direct your reading of this section on evolution, let us first consider the following questions:

• How are humans and animals related?
• What is "instinctive" behavior in animals?

- Do humans have instincts?
- What laws govern how and why each species behaves, learns, and remembers?
- Do humans follow the same laws of learning and behavior as other animals?

Let us begin with a brief history of evolution related to behavior theory.

Charles Darwin (see Figure 2.2) proposed a theory of organic **evolution** in his 1859 book, *On the Origin of Species by Means of Natural Selection*. Social and scientific controversy regarding his theory has characterized the ensuing years. The biological and social sciences have incorporated Darwin's basic ideas of adaptation and **continuity of species**—that all life forms are related—into their respective accounts of life. At the same time, many highly educated individuals—and a majority of the lay public—have either rejected Darwin's theory or "revised" critical details to better accommodate their cultural/religious views. Indeed, a 1991 Gallup poll revealed that about half of all Americans think that God created the universe and humans within the past 10,000 years. An additional 40% believe that God directed evolution to specifically create humans.

Evolutionary Theory and Culture. Many people are uncomfortable with the position taken by Darwin and modern evolutionists that humans have a biological nature that is physically related to other animals. And, of course, for even more individuals, the very suggestion that psychological continuities might exist between humans and animals is considered preposterous.

Why is evolutionary theory so controversial? Sigmund Freud, writing in *Civilization and Its Discontents*, suggests that scientific thinking is the culprit:

> *Humanity has in course of time had to endure from the hands of science two great outrages upon its naive selflove. The first was when it realized that our earth was not the center of the universe, but only a speck in a world system of a magnitude hardly conceivable. . . . The second was when biological research robbed man of his particular privilege of having been specially created, and relegated him to a descent from the animal world.*

The importance of evolutionary theory for modern psychology should not be understated. Contemporary theories of both learning and behavior—the focus of this text—are predicated on evolutionary considerations. As we have noted, all organisms have a biological nature that allows them to learn in a predictable fashion. Psychologists work from the assumption that the human mind and human behavior can be understood best by examining evidence from both nature (biology) and nurture (the study of environment and behavior).

Part of the problem of acceptance of Darwin's "theory" may be that it encompasses a number of distinct component theories (Mayr, 1991). Each component theory is discussed in turn here.

FIGURE 2.2

Charles Darwin (1809–1882) is one of the most influential and controversial individuals in our species' intellectual history. His concept of the origin and meaning of life provides *the* unifying theoretical framework for the biological and behavioral sciences. (Photo courtesy of National Portrait Gallery, London)

Neoevolutionary Theory.   Modern evolutionary theory (cf. neoevolutionary theory) is a synthesis of Darwin's theory with the more recent science of **genetics**. Four ideas that define current evolutionary theory (theories?) and that relate to learning and behavior theory are covered here: *heredity, variability, reproduction,* and *natural selection*.

Heredity

The most obvious feature of life forms is physical—how plants and animals appear. Early taxonomies (groupings or arrangements) were primarily based on the physical features of plants and animals. At its most basic, the term **heredity** refers to the fact that chickens reproduce chickens and humans, humans— that there is a transmission of like structure, of physical form, through sexual reproduction. Offspring resemble parents.

The basic unit of the process of heredity is the gene, and readers are referred to any of a number of modern biology books to fathom the complexities of gene functioning. The idea of how genes might evolve is also beyond the scope of this text (see Lewontin, 1983). For present purposes, human genes are the mechanism for making the next generation of humans, chicken genes for chickens.

Related concepts of genotype, phenotype, and heritability will help us better understand the term *heredity*. As defined in Chapter 1, a **genotype** is the basic combination of genes that defines a species. The notion of genotype is often confused with that of **phenotype**. A phenotype is the genotype as expressed in the environment. Your genotype is the potential "you" at conception; the physical you, at conception through the present, is an example of a phenotype.

Phenotypes having the same genotype (as in "identical" twins) vary because they live in different environments. For present purposes, we can consider that phenotypes learn and form memories following interactions with environments. "Learning" can be considered a phenotypic characteristic.

Heritability.   One approach to questions of "instinctive" versus "learned" behavior is to try to divide a given behavior into component parts. **Heritability** is a mathematical concept that attempts to partition biological, behavioral, or psychological phenotypic characters into genetic or environmental components. On the assumption that genes and environment (a) are uncorrelated and (b) can be added, observed differences between individuals varying on a phenotypical character (for example, differences in learning rate) can be expressed as

$$Vt = Vg + Ve + Vm$$

where V is a measure of the observed variance or differences (for example, difference in learning rate among individuals), t = total differences, g = genetic differences, e = differences due to environment, and m = measurement error.

Heritability may vary between 0 and 1 (0.0 to 1.0); behavioral characteristics with measured values approaching 1.0 are defined as highly heritable; mostly environmental determinants of a behavioral character would have heritability nearer to zero. Returning to the question of whether human intelligence is learned or inherited (research on this question was discussed in Chapter 1), heritability values of 0.70 have been reported for measures of intelligence (Bouchard et al., 1990) and 0.50 for personality (Bouchard, 1994). As mentioned in Chapter 1, significant heritability values for schizophrenia, alcoholism, and manic depression have been reported (Plomin, 1990).

Given the foregoing observation that the phenotype and, more specifically, phenotypical behavior are influenced during interactions with the environment, is it also possible for the environment to influence the genotype? The answer is yes . . . and no. An understanding of "how yes" and "how no" will clarify the complex relationships of genotype, phenotype, heredity, and behavior.

Lamarckian Evolution.   Before Darwin, the noted French naturalist Jean Baptiste Lamarck (1744–1849) proposed a different theory now known as **Lamarckian evolution**. Lamarck believed that the environment caused changes in the genotype. That is, he thought (a) that slight changes experienced during an animal's lifetime gradually modified an animal and (b) that the next generation profited from the transmission of these acquired characteristics.

One ramification of this view is that children would benefit from the musical, or mathematical, or bowling abilities of their parents who patiently perfected these skills during their lifetime. What a great idea! Unfortunately (or fortunately, for the children of murderers, car thieves, and other criminals), evidence supporting the theory of Lamarckian evolution is lacking. Rather, the next generation's genotypes are relatively well protected from environmental influence. Specifically, the genes in sperm and eggs are not affected by the minute biochemical changes in the brain that are known to underlie memory and other experiences acquired during a lifetime. Therefore, the only environment that can influence one's genes (genes that produce the next generation's genotypes) during the course of one's lifetime consists of certain chromosome-damaging drugs, high levels of ionizing radiation, and other known mutagens responsible for genetic mutations.

Human Inheritance

Does your schoolwork come as easily for you as it does for your roommate? For your brothers and sisters? Obviously, not all humans are equal in their ability to learn and to memorize. Why are there individual differences?

Evolutionary theory and genetics become personal when you consider your own human identity. As an individual, you have both a unique and a shared inheritance. You are unique because of the one-of-a-kind **DNA** contributed by your mother and by your father. DNA is deoxyribonucleic acid, a complex protein structure containing all genetic instructions. Your behavior in part is determined by the DNA you received from each parent.

Genetic History Extends Beyond Parents. Each of your parents likewise was created by a unique combination of approximately 20,000 genes on each of their parent's 23 chromosomes. And so on. The *and so on*s become intriguing! Your *shared inheritance* refers to the process of genetic transmission—a process that has been ongoing in *Homo sapiens* for 100,000 or more years. (See Box 2.1.)

Prehistoric Minds. *Homo sapiens'* brain 100,000 years ago was probably not radically different from yours and mine (Stringer & Andrews, 1988). Is it presumptuous to speculate that our male and female predecessors enjoyed similar levels of sensory experiences and aspects of consciousness as we do at present?

Little is known about the presence of language beyond about 10,000 years ago or about other aspects of the mental life of men and women in prehistoric times.[1] Cranial endocasts (rubber castings taken from the inside of

BOX 2.1   WHAT IS A "RELATIVE"?

You are genetically unique, but you also share with all other humans common genetic material. Each of us had the same parents sometime in the past (i.e., a common ancestor). Regardless of racial origin, each of us shares common parents—a great, great, great . . . great grandmother and grandfather.

An example: A popular account recently asserted that more than 500,000 individuals in the United States are related to British royalty. By itself this figure is meaningless; the number of relatives a person has is determined by the genetic distance one is from a common ancestor. The figure 500,000 includes all of those individuals who were one-tenth cousins or closer in relationship. Obviously, if we counted every person

who was a cousin one-twentieth removed, the number of "royal" relatives would increase.

Many European-derived Americans take great pride in having had ancestors in the Revolutionary War (approximately 10 generations). Some are "Mayflower stock" (approximately 15 generations). Other individuals delight in tracing their ancestry over 1,000 years, roughly 50 generations, or more. (I now know three people who claim to be a distant relative of Charlemagne!) These lineages do not even begin to convey the immense period of time your direct human ancestors have been walking the earth—approximately 5 to 10 thousand generations of consorting *Homo sapiens*.

[1] For an intriguing commentary on language development and hemispheric specialization in prototypical hominids, see Corbalis (1989).

skulls, which allow estimates of brain size and shape) suggest few differences during the past 100,000 years, however. With the possible exception of the elaboration of language (allowing higher levels of cognition?), our ancestors probably lived, learned, laughed, and loved much as we currently do.

Beyond 200,000 years ago? Evolutionary theory is based on the assumption of continuity among species as well as relatedness within species. That is to say, humans have common ancestors with all life forms. Understandably, we are most interested in humans, and microbiological findings continue to elaborate on our origins. Estimates of human lineage have been made using mitochondrial DNA (mDNA) techniques. Though these models are tentative (Hedges, Kuman, Tamura, & Stoneking, 1991), researchers postulate a common origin of African women, a "mother of Africa," designated "Eve," who lived approximately 200,000 years ago (Vigilant, Stoneking, Harpending, Hawkes, & Wilson, 1991). Humans' closest living relative? The chimpanzee, with whom we share a common ancestor, living approximately 7 million years ago. How apelike are humans? Quite. See Box 2.2 for some comparisons.

BOX 2.2   CHIMPANZEES: SO CLOSE AND YET SO FAR AWAY

DNA, deoxyribonucleic acid, makes up the complex molecules from which each gene is constructed. Fifteen years ago scientists Charles Sibley and John Ahlquist took chimpanzee DNA and human DNA, separated the double helix of each into two strands and allowed one strand from each species to recombine. Then they measured the resulting match of the DNA of one species to the other. Their technique resulted in a 98% match of the DNA of humans and chimpanzees, and a 97% match of human DNA with mountain gorilla DNA. Humans diverged from chimpanzees about 7 million years ago, they estimated, and from gorillas about 10 million years ago.

More recent estimates? Humans are closer genetically to the pygmy chimpanzee, *Pan paniscus*, than to the common chimp, *Pan troglodyte*. The two chimps share 99.3% of their DNA, and we share 98.4% of our DNA with *Pan paniscus* (Sibley, Comstock, & Ahlquist, 1990). We are closer kin to chimpanzees than chimps are to gorillas, than mice are to rats. According to Washburn and Moore (1974, pp. 11–13), "Man and chimpanzee proved to be as (genetically) close as sheep and goat, two species that had always been regarded as very close. Man and chimpanzee are more closely related than horse and donkey, cape buffalo and water buffalo, cat and lion, or dog and fox."

The chimpanzee has a brain size of only 450 cubic centimeters (cc) compared with humans' large, 1350 cc brain. Nevertheless, it is a trifle discomforting to realize that human civilization depends on less than 2% of our "essence."

Human Nature

Let us shift our focus from individual differences among humans to similarities. Given our genetic relationships with other primates, the observation that all humans are related should come as no surprise. This shared inheritance is the physical basis for "human nature"—the tendency for humans to behave like humans and less like other species of animals.

"Human nature," which has produced human culture, has three components: our collective **phylogenetic history** (history of life on earth), our collective **ontogenetic histories** (an individual's ontogeny is defined as the total of life experiences from conception to death), and our **written history** (cumulative oral and written experiences of ontogenetic histories; cf. Sagan's, 1977, "extra-genetic history").

Of course, it follows that there is also "tiger nature," "pigeon nature," "bee nature," and so forth. Each member of a species shares common genetic material and common inherited behavior patterns. Indeed, common genetic material and common behavior patterns define the term *species* (see Figure 2.3a).

Do aspects of human behavior also resemble the behavior of other species of animals? Some, obviously, more than others. We behave more like other primates than chickens because we share more genetic material with primates (see Figure 2.3b). Likewise, in many particulars we behave more like rats, dogs, and cats than like chickens or trout. Humans, rats, dogs, cats, and monkeys are mammals and as such share certain common, yet important, psychobiological characteristics.

Summary of Heredity.   To summarize, *heredity* refers to the transmission of physical structure from one generation to the next. A new genotype is formed at conception. The proportion of a phenotypic character, such as learning, that can be attributed to the genotype can be estimated by mathematically measuring the character's heritability. Each individual's genotype is determined at conception; the phenotype, but not the genotype, changes during a lifetime. Changes in the phenotype, such as learned behavior, do not change the genotype, and therefore such changes cannot be inherited by the next generation.

Evidence from paleontology, comparative anatomy, and DNA matching techniques reveals that humans share common genetic ancestry with each other, and with other living animals. "Human nature" differs from that of other animals because humans have unique phylogenetic, ontogenetic, and written histories.

Let us return again to individual differences. We dress differently; we prefer certain kinds of music (and foods, and people) over others. Another aspect of Darwin's theory allows insight into these differences.

Variability

The second major idea defining evolutionary theory is **variability**. When genetic material is transmitted through sexual reproduction from a parent gen-

FIGURE 2.3 Phylogenetic Relationships

(a) In addition to fish and amphibians, the other three classes of vertebrates are mammals, birds, and reptiles. Most learning theory is aimed at discovering associative processes common to all vertebrates. (From Wallace, 1979)

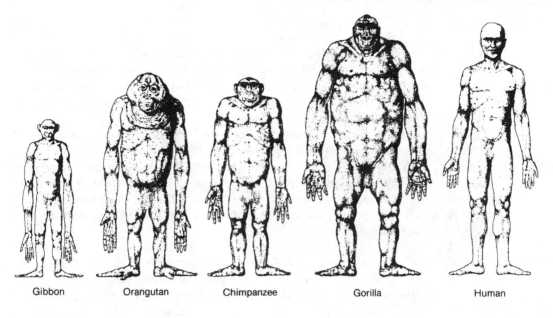

| Gibbon | Orangutan | Chimpanzee | Gorilla | Human |

FIGURE 2.3 *Continued*

(b) The extant primates with all hair removed, showing proportions
of adult apes, drawn to the same scale. (From Strickberger, 1990)

eration to offspring, differences in structure are introduced. Unless you have
an identical twin, you are an individual genetically different from all others.
We need not concern ourselves here with the mechanisms of variability; the
science of genetics points to both mutation and events during cell meiosis as
contributing factors. *Mutation* is a permanent, random chemical change in the
DNA molecule. *Meiosis* refers to the fact that during fertilization, each human
male and female contributes 23 chromosomes to produce offspring with 46
chromosomes.

Many have observed that "variety" makes life interesting. According to
Darwin, variety makes life possible. The slight differences introduced from
generation to generation determine the course of evolution. Variability in
part determines which individual organisms survive and which do not.
Why? Because some of the differences are advantageous to living and others
are not.

The significance of the concept of variability in Darwin's theory, therefore, is that some genotypes in interaction with environment (i.e., phenotypes)
are more viable than others.

Reproduction

Oftentimes in discussing Darwin's theory, **reproduction** is minimized. But heredity and variability are genetic mechanisms that can be expressed only as the result of a sexual act. In politics and the world of business, power lies with those who control the money. In biology, the name of the game is "who produces (reproduces) the next generation?"

Indeed, the reproductive urge appears to be central to the adult life of most animal species. We do not find it surprising that humans spend billions of dollars annually for perfumes and other odorants, the apparent purpose of which is to enhance opportunities for, and otherwise maximize, encounters that may lead to sexual reproduction (Stoddart, 1990). Nor does anyone find it surprising when a student passes on a study session for the opportunity to spend time with a potential mate.

Most psychologists view sex as a primary reinforcer and incentive (see Chapter 6 for a fuller discussion). Freud and Jung asserted that sexual energy and an innate "life force," respectively, motivated humans. What do you think? Is most (all?) of your motivation derived from the more primal motivations of sexual pleasure, that is, of your "selfish gene" (cf. Dawkins, 1976)? Before even considering the ideas of reward and the process of reinforcement, would you suspect that the opportunity to engage in sexual behavior would be high on a list of satisfying events?

Natural Selection

Both heredity and variability can be accounted for by the science of genetics. Even in the absence of a theory of genetics, in Darwin's time animal breeders selectively bred dogs and horses for specified phenotypic characters—color, size, temperament. Changes introduced from generation to generation were accomplished by human-directed, or artificial, selection.

Darwin postulated that similar selection factors occurred from one generation to the next under natural rather than artificial circumstances. He called this **natural selection**. He and others noted that too many offspring are reproduced in the course of a breeding lifetime and that typically there are insufficient resources to accommodate the abundance of new lives. Therefore, competition ensues for limited resources. The prize of winning this competition for nature's resources is life and the opportunity to be around long enough to reproduce. The cost of losing is death or lessened opportunities to successfully produce the next generation.

Darwin's theory of natural selection is as prone to misinterpretation as it is insightful and controversial. Essentially, he proposed that each species is best understood as a unique solution to specific problems of survival. Some individuals are better able than others to overcome the environmental obstacles they face in day-to-day living. Such obstacles, or impediments to survival, are called **selective pressures**. Not only might some birds have better protective coloration (i.e., camouflage), to use a popular example, but also they may learn more quickly than others. That is, some individuals may be bigger, stronger, and faster, and some others may be slower but smarter. The environment blindly "selects" behavioral characters (such as rapid learning) in the same way it selects adaptively colored individuals.

Protective coloration, rapid learning, and other behavioral adaptations facilitate survival for "lucky" individuals (Gould, 1989). When environmental conditions change between generations (i.e., if and when selective pressures change), some individuals live and some die—the luck of the draw. Yet others among the varying offspring that do survive will have more of an advantage in reproducing their offspring—in which case, nature again selects the more advantageous characteristics to be reproduced.

Darwin's theory continues to be vital even as it is modified (see Box 2.3). Nevertheless, his conceptual framework has been remarkably successful in accounting for seemingly contradictory (and certainly puzzling) features of life on earth. The result of evolution is a world populated by unique living organisms. So disparate in appearance and behavior are these plants and animals that Darwin's allegation that all are related, indeed, are continuous forms of life, seems bizarre. The sexual nature of animals is self-evident. Heredity successfully accounts for similarity and continuity; variability accounts for dissimilarity and diversity. And, depending on the nature of the environmental pressures, natural selection accounts for the historical progression of certain living forms and the exclusion of others. Little evidence supports the view that present conditions differ substantially from times past when the fossil record was accumulating. There is no good reason to suspect that humans are other than another end product of these processes.

Relation of Evolutionary Psychology to Learning.   Current theories of learning take into account both general and highly specialized features of living organisms. The behavior of many animal species reflects their genetic similarity. We humans in fact appear to learn some behaviors in the same manner that rats and pigeons do—that is, some behavior seems to be governed by general processes. At the same time, dissimilarity and diversity among life forms are apparent, and **species-specific behaviors** reflect unique evolutionary strategies in meeting environmental obstacles. Taken together, the theoretical approaches of general processes and species-specific behaviors help us to understand learning, the most adaptive of all behavior processes (Halliday & Slater, 1983).

You may question why a behavioral scientist must be an evolutionist to analyze behavior experimentally. Is an evolutionary perspective essential if one merely wants to study and characterize the learning and memory processes of humans, or of dogs, or of any other particular species? This question focuses on particular research strategies taken by behavioral researchers both in the field (i.e., where animals normally live) and in the laboratory (where animals can be brought for study).

BOX 2.3   STEPHEN J. GOULD: CONTEMPORARY EVOLUTIONIST

Stephen J. Gould simplifies the complexities of Darwin's theory in a popular series of essays and books (*The Panda's Thumb, Ever Since Darwin, The Flamingo's Smile*, etc.). In *Wonderful Life: The Burgess Shale and the Nature of History* (1989), Gould challenges existing taxonomies such as those depicted in Figure 2.3. The fossil record of early life forms belies, he argues, the "tree of life" conception of diversification of species. Rather, the random destruction of early life forms by cataclysmic environmental insults (e.g., impacts with asteroids) largely determined which phyla survived and which were killed off. Such accidents in large measure caused the present similarities and differences of life forms. Blind luck, Gould argues, accounts for more of the variance than does Darwin's theory of natural selection in producing variety.

Gould's arguments challenge neither Darwin's theory of continuity of life forms nor the role of natural selection in speciation. Rather, his analysis reinforces Darwin's view that in providing obstacles to survive, nature is blind. All extant (living, as opposed to extinct) creatures could tell interesting tales of how they got here.

For a variety of reasons, most behavioral scientists are specialized and study the psychological processes of only a single species. And, in the area of learning, that species is typically *not Homo sapiens*.

Research Strategies of Behavioral Scientists.   Obviously, not all behavioral scientists agree on what constitutes the most appropriate research strategy. There are certainly those who would disagree with the position taken here that a comparative perspective based on evolutionary theory is critical in developing theories of learning and memory. For example, among experimental psychologists, behaviorists—taking their lead from B.F. Skinner (see Chapter 5)—have been highly successful in describing and analyzing animal behavior from a laboratory-based, black box, stimulus-response perspective. Because most contemporary behaviorists are also evolutionists, the disagreement in research approach is *not* about discontinuity of species or other aspects of evolutionary theory.

In the next two sections we examine the diverse research strategies taken by behavioral scientists who work from an evolutionary perspective. Some conduct field research (ethologists), some do laboratory research (comparative psychologists), and yet others do a combination of the two (various other specialty fields will be noted). Although these fields have distinct histories, their methods and theoretical orientations often overlap. In particular, the relationship of ethology to comparative psychology constitutes a long and controversial history. The interested reader is directed to Domjan (1987a, 1987b), Galef (1984), Gottlieb (1984), Hodos and Campbell (1969), and Jaynes (1969). For a treatment of the role of women in the development of theory in ethology and comparative psychology, see Furumoto and Scarborough (1987).

We begin with classic ethology.

Interim Summary

1. Plant behavior is best described by simple movement adjustments, called *tropisms*, to sun, gravity, and so on. Moving animals meet changing environments, and their nervous systems adjust reactions accordingly.

2. The processes of learning and remembering are adaptive.

3. Adaptations are alterations in a plant or animal that promote survival and yield a reproductive advantage.

4. Darwin's theory of evolution describes adaptation and the origin and continuity of species.

5. Neoevolutionary theory weds the modern science of genetics (heredity and variability) to reproduction and natural selection.

6. Natural selection can be distinguished from human-directed, or artificial, selection. Organisms that overcome impediments, called *selective pressures*, breed the next generation. Luck accounts for many survivors.

7. Lamarckian evolution is the discredited theory that experiences acquired during one's life can be transmitted to offspring.

8. A genotype is the combination of genes that defines a species. A genotype expressed in the environment is called a *phenotype*.

9. Heritability is an estimate of the genetic component of a particular behavior.

10. Humans have been in their present form for 100,000 to 200,000 years.

11. Chimpanzees are the nearest living form of primate to humans. Our common ancestor with chimpanzees lived about 7 million years ago.

12. Each human has a unique nature that can be attributed to his or her phylogenetic, ontogenetic, and written history.

13. Human nature differs from chicken nature because each has a different genotype. Each species engages in species-specific behaviors.

ETHOLOGY

Ethologists study the role of learning within the context of species-specific behaviors—how animals behave within their naturally occurring ecological niches. Ethologists cite examples of free-ranging behavior among these animals (as opposed to laboratory observation and manipulation of animal behavior). Behavior, they propose, is lawful and best understood as instinctive. Particular behaviors are considered to be evolutionary adaptations that implement survival strategies. Classical European ethologists, therefore, heartily disagreed with the laboratory approach to animal behavior taken by psychologists.

Consummatory Behaviors

Classical ethologists focused their studies on several species of birds and only occasionally on a mammal. Among birds' behavioral repertoires are behaviors indispensable for survival: feeding, courting, reproducing, caretaking of offspring, and so forth. Collectively, these behaviors in birds and other animals are called **consummatory behaviors**. The idea of consummatory behaviors is often confused with feeding or ingestional behavior. The manner in which ethologists use the term is in the broader sense of behaviors necessary for survival.

Behavior as Adaptation

How does one explain the remarkable diversity of animal behavior observed in nature? Ethologists suggest that we first ask what selective pressures are currently operative in the niche the animal occupies. Second, what selective pressures must have been present in the animal's evolutionary past? Then ethologists ask how a particular behavioral pattern has helped the animal overcome a specific problem presented by the environment.

Ethologists argue that an animal's behavior (no matter how remarkable and seemingly uninterpretable) can be best accounted for by knowing the function of that particular behavior—that is, how the behavior helps the animal adapt to its niche requirements. Indeed, ultimately, the behavior is the adaptation. Behavior, therefore, is purposive, and the ultimate purpose of behavior is to survive and to reproduce.

Ethological Methods

The first step in any scientific study is systematic observation. Through patience, training, and perseverance, ethologists have given us a more meaningful understanding and appreciation of the diversity and adaptiveness of animal behavior. The ethologists' most noteworthy successes can be attributed to their skilled observation of naturally occurring behaviors in selected animals.

The second step of the ethologist is to systematically isolate the independent variables (stimuli in the environment) that are presumed to be responsible for eliciting the behavior under observation. One example of the ethological approach is their analysis of the phenomenon of *imprinting*.

Imprinting.   Nobel prize winner Konrad Lorenz found that geese behave in a peculiar manner if they are exposed to abnormal environments during a few critical hours shortly after hatching. If during this time period goslings view a moving human (instead of a moving mother goose), for the remainder of their lives they tend to treat humans as geese. At maturity, they even court and attempt to mate with humans (see Box 2.4). Lorenz called this phenomenon **imprinting,** which is now considered to be a special type of rapid, long-lasting learning.

Instincts

Many ethologists and laypersons continue to use the term **instinct** to describe patterns of behavior common to a species. Another use of the term refers to the motivation underlying consummatory behaviors.

Instinct is both a useful and a slippery term. At its worst the term is tautologically circular. Why do squirrels bury nuts? Squirrels bury nuts because this behavior has "survival value." A "survival instinct" ensures a "fit" with the niche into which the animal was born. According to this argument, those squirrel-like creatures in the past who did not instinctively bury nuts (or successfully engage in other consummatory behaviors) died. How do we know this? Because (completing the circle) the ones that are alive bury nuts.

Likewise, chickens (are motivated to) scratch to secure food. The scratching behavior is adaptive—is instrumental for survival. More often than not, these kinds of behaviors appear in animals naturally, meaning without elaborate training.

BOX 2.4   CRITICAL PERIODS IN GEESE

With childlike curiosity, Konrad Lorenz played with hatchling geese and recorded his valuable observations. He and other European ethologists identified critical variables in the gosling's behavioral development, including the phenomenon of imprinting.

Imprinting occurs only during a few critical posthatching hours, known as the **critical period**. "Following" behavior is depicted in the photo. The object (i.e., Lorenz) must be seen moving by the birds during their critical period. The critical period for these birds is a few hours after hatching. Seeing Lorenz moving at 1 to 2 days of age, for example, would have no greater effect on the birds' subsequent behavior than any other kind of visual stimulus. Imprinting to moving objects is an example of a species-specific behavior. Only a few species of birds exhibit this particular behavior (Lorenz, 1935). Other species also display behaviors specific to their particular niche requirements.

Fixed Action Patterns

Modern ethologists have recast the idea of an instinct as a **fixed action pattern (FAP)**. To qualify as an FAP, a behavioral sequence must meet four specific criteria (Moltz, 1963). First, the behavior must be stereotyped—it occurs in the same way each time. Second, once begun, this behavioral sequence should be difficult to disrupt and should continue to completion. A third characteristic of FAPs is that once completed, there is a latent period. Before the FAP will occur again, some time must pass. Finally, an FAP must be innate, or unlearned. That is, the animal must perform the full integrated behavioral sequence of the FAP the first time it is elicited. An excellent example of an FAP is the analysis of egg-retrieving responses of the Graylag goose (Lorenz & Tinbergen, 1938; see Box 2.5).

Sign Stimuli.   A *fixed action pattern* is a programmed sequence of behaviors triggered by specifiable environmental stimuli, called **sign stimuli**. An underlying brain mechanism called an **innate releasing mechanism (IRM)** is hypothesized to be particularly receptive to these stimuli. The IRM is the "lock" to which the sign stimulus "key" has been perfectly tailored. Encountering a particular stimulus unlocks the neural mechanism, causing release of the FAP. (Compare this analysis of FAPs with the description of reflexive feeding in flies on p. 44.)

FAPs and Reflexes.   Except for the complexity of motor behavior exhibited by geese, in many particulars FAPs resemble behavioral reflexes. The idea of simple reflexes (physiological, behavioral, and conditioned) is discussed in the next chapter (see summary of reflexes, Table 3.1). The modification of more complex reflexlike systems, as seen in drug tolerance and in the immune system, is discussed in Chapter 7. Reflexes are modifiable in interaction with the environment while FAPs apparently are not. Nevertheless, we may consider FAPs to be reflexlike and the concept of FAPs a more sophisticated analysis of the slippery term *instinct*. Let us look at a few more examples of complex behavioral reflexes.

Animal Navigation

The incredible navigation patterns of a variety of animals also fall into the category of complex instinctive-like behaviors. Commenting on the fact that migrating salmon find home streams with great accuracy, presumably by smell, Konrad Lorenz termed their behavior "a wonderful example of landscape imprinting" (Long, 1991). It would be interesting to know whether Lorenz would also consider grouping innate navigation patterns with other consummatory behaviors. Certainly migrations to spawning grounds are preparatory to elaborate courting and mating practices seen in many species.

Box 2.5   "Smart" Birds or "Smart" Genes?

It is not uncommon for an egg to slip from under a brooding female Graylag goose and roll a few feet from the nest. Upon noticing this, the goose will get up and approach the egg. The initial sighting and approach reaction to the egg are called *appetitive behaviors*. Appetitive behavior is modifiable; it is followed by a fixed action pattern (FAP), which, by definition, is not.

The egg is the sign stimulus (or sign-releasing stimulus—see text). The FAP consists of the goose placing the upper surface of her bill against the far side of the egg and systematically scooping it into the nest. If all goes well, the egg will be retrieved and the goose will sit on it. If the egg rolls off to the side once the retrieval sequence begins, however, something interesting occurs. The bird often simply continues the sequence to completion. She inefficiently scoops the area where the egg should be, waddles back into her nest, and assumes her position on an imaginary egg.

The more frequently the egg rolls out, the less vigorous is the retrieval response. If the egg stays in the nest (where it belongs) for a long period of time, the goose may well wind up retrieving an imaginary one anyway! In other words, she may perform the FAP in a vacuum (Lorenz's term) without the relevant sign stimulus.

What is really strange is that a particularly vigorous retrieval response can be elicited by an oversize egg. An egg—in the form of a bowling ball—will be retrieved even if it is so big that the goose is unable to get her bill over it. Finally, fulfilling the requirements necessary to be classified as an FAP, a brooding goose will react in this fashion to a "wandering egg" the first time it comes across one.

Birds and bees as well as fish accurately move over long distances. Consider the 18 Laysan albatrosses taken from their Midway atoll in the Pacific and released from various locations around the world. Fourteen returned; one from Washington, 3,200 miles away, averaging 317 miles per day. Another came 4,120 miles from the Philippines in 32 days. Most researchers suspect that navigational abilities such as these are innate, having evolved along with their underlying sensory capabilities. Representative examples of sensory abilities not shared by humans include the following:

> Homing pigeons are able to sense slight, 4 mm changes in altitude and can see ultraviolet light. Honeybees can detect minor fluctuations in the earth's magnetic field as well as the most sensitive magnetometers. Sharks can recognize and respond to five billionths of a volt changes in electric fields. (Long, 1991)

Classical ethology has spawned a variety of research approaches, which include neuroethology and sociobiology. These modern disciplines—along with comparative psychology—emphasize the evolutionary determinants of behavior: How do brain mechanisms and behavior reflect past selective pressures? How do the brain and behavior of an animal function to enhance adaptive fitness? In the following section, we continue to examine this question by taking a brief look at these animal behavior disciplines. Our focus remains on laboratory-based research.

Interim Summary

1. Ethologists study the adaptiveness of an animal's species-specific behavior within its ecological niche. The ultimate purpose of behavior is to survive and to reproduce.

2. Consummatory behaviors such as eating and drinking, courting and mating, and taking care of offspring are among the survival behaviors studied by ethologists.

3. Konrad Lorenz found that a critical period existed in young animals during which a type of rapid, long-lasting learning—imprinting—occurs under certain conditions.

4. Fixed action patterns (FAPs) are instinctive behaviors that
   a. Are innate, or unlearned.
   b. Occur in the same way each time.
   c. Are difficult to disrupt (once started, they continue to completion).
   d. Are followed by a latent period during which the FAP cannot occur.

5. FAPs are released by sign stimuli that normally occur in the animal's ecological niche. Sign stimuli are detected by innate releasing mechanisms (IRMs) hypothesized to be in the animal's brain.

6. Navigational abilities in many animals appear to be innately organized, complex, reflexlike behaviors.

Comparative Psychology and Other Behavioral Approaches

Types of Behavioral Scientists

Who are "behavioral scientists"? Most are found in psychology departments in universities in the United States and Europe. They usually call themselves *psychologists, experimental psychologists,* or *comparative psychologists.* (Although some identify themselves as *biopsychologists, psychobiologists, neuroscientists,* or *behavioral neuroscientists.*) Many would say that their research area is animal learning and that they might teach a course in learning.

Researchers other than psychologists study animal behavior. For example, breeding animals and the systematic identification of one or more genetic components of learning characterize behavioral geneticists. Researchers trying to find the neurobiological basis of a learned behavior that has a strong biological component (i.e., a species-specific behavior such as birdsong or navigation) might identify their field as neuroethology. Sociobiology is the realm of yet other researchers who use evolutionary theory to account for the origins of social behavior of animals.

The foregoing profusion of labels is not exhaustive, nor are the research areas mentioned mutually exclusive. Researchers and students alike have every right to be confused! An up side of this situation is the difference in education of these diverse scientists. Studying animal behavior from slightly different evolutionary perspectives has produced a healthy, productive research climate during the past 100 years. An excellent history of Darwin's influence on approaches to the mind and behavior can be found in Boakes (1984).

Comparative Psychology

Comparative psychology is the study of the motivation and behavior of animals for the express purpose of identifying similarities and differences among them. Again, Charles Darwin played an important role. His publication of *The Expression of Emotions in Man and Animals* in 1872 helped determine the direction of what was to become comparative psychology.

From the beginning of written history, humans have lived with domesticated animals. Since then, probably most cat and dog owners have at one time or another wondered what pets thought about. The first comparative psychologists were no different. What, they wondered, was the nature of animal minds?[2] One obvious clue to an animal's mind was the fact that animals showed evidence of learning. They readily learned where and when food is pre-

---

[2] Domjan (1987b) has identified the earliest scientists who specifically contributed to the field of comparative psychology as Charles Darwin (*The Descent of Man,* 1871); George Romanes (*Animal Intelligence,* 1884); C. Lloyd Morgan (*An Introduction to Comparative Psychology,* 1894); and Margaret Washburn (*The Animal Mind: A Textbook of Comparative Psychology,* 1908).

sented, how to get around in their surroundings, how to respond to signals and cues, and so forth. Understandably, animal learning became the focus of a number of these early scientists, including, as we will see, E. L. Thorndike and C. Lloyd Morgan.

Compared with feral (wild) animals, the niche of domesticated animals contains human beings. Animals reared in environments containing humans learn different behaviors in comparison with nondomesticated animals. Feral animal niches, for example, better allow for the appearance of FAPs and other species-specific behaviors.

Role of Environment in Controlling Behavior. Studying domesticated animals raises other issues. How could a domesticated animal's environment be arranged to better control its behavior? Such focus differed from the strategy of noninterventive observations of feral animals by ethologists. Obviously, the manipulation and control of animal behavior are best accomplished in an artificial laboratory environment. It is no accident that early comparative psychologists worked with animals in zoos (Greenberg, 1987). Note, however, that Konrad Lorenz (Box 2.5) also gained control over his domesticated goslings' *following behavior.* How? By his presence in their environment during a critical period.

Individual Differences Versus Species-Typical Behavior. Comparative psychologists brought the question of following behavior into the laboratory. They showed that individual birds could be trained to behave differently, depending on which particular environment they encountered. That is, by manipulating the environment, a scientist could gain control of a bird's behavior. At the same time, researchers gained a better understanding of species-typical behavior. They analyzed the way that both the animals' natural niche and the laboratory niche controlled the genetic expression of the following behavior. (The issue of behavioral control is addressed in detail in Chapter 5.)

Historically, comparative psychologists have concentrated their research on just a few species of animals: rats, cats, dogs, pigeons, monkeys, and humans. (Note that all of these animals have been domesticated for hundreds of years in various cultures.) A criticism of comparative psychologists is that their selection of animals for comparison with one another does not make good sense from an evolutionary perspective (Hodos & Campbell, 1969). Why? Because, if comparative psychologists were attempting to discover the "evolution of learning," the phylogenetic relationships among these animals made little sense. Evolution is *not* described by a simple progression of bird to rat to monkey to human.

Certainly the Hodos & Campbell (1969) argument has merit. But what if the behavior of animals with larger brains becomes "more organized" and "more versatile . . . due to enhanced perceptual, cognitive, learning, social, and/or motor skills" (Gottlieb, 1984, p. 454). There is, Gottlieb argues, a logic and an implicit theory, both in the range of animals selected for study and in the evolutionary strategy employed by comparative psychologists. The selection of both species of research animal and type of behavior studied continues to divide ethologists and comparative psychologists (Domjan, 1987b). A further rationale for "rat research" is presented in the concluding section of this chapter.

How do comparative psychologists decide whether a behavior is species specific or general? More specifically, what rule or rules guide the extrapolation of results from nonhuman animals to humans and from animal to animal? Let us explore this issue.

Consciousness as a Species-Specific Behavior?   In what ways do behavioral scientists think about human uniqueness? Taking cues from classical ethologists, we might raise the question of *species-specific behaviors* of humans. For example, we might note that we humans have *minds* that allow conscious reflection on, among other things, the differences between ourselves and other animals. Our human *language* allows us to think, to compare other animals with ourselves, and to comment on the differences we see. Among the major apparent differences are human consciousness, language, and cognitive processes—differences, it can be argued, that permit us an awareness of these differences![3]

On the basis of these observations, we might entertain rightly or wrongly the proposition that human cognitive properties allow us to transcend the animal mind, thereby making us different from other animals. Framing the question one last time, do human language and human cognition make meaningless the simple models of associative conditioning that are explored in Chapters 3–6?

The issue of the role of consciousness in conditioning has been raised. We need a rule of thumb to help us decide when behavioral changes in humans are due to "simple" conditioning procedures and when they are due to human levels of consciousness. One such rule follows.

The Law of Parsimony.   There is no escaping human uniqueness, and this text would not be credible if the complexities of the human mind were forced into the simple conceptual box labeled "general process learning." With this reservation, a research strategy suggests itself. Let us resort to complex explanations only if simple explanations will not suffice. This excellent, well-exploited heuristic is called the **law of parsimony**. In the sciences, the law of parsimony is often used interchangeably with the term *Occam's Razor*.

What are *parsimonious* explanations of behavior? Simply, those that assert simple rather than complex processes. Consider this example: You observe a 5-year-old boy taking a few sips of water from a water fountain. Is he likely to be exerting free will? That is, after some reflection, is he consciously, voluntarily choosing to drink water? Or can his behavior be better understood as a

---

[3] See Ludvigson (1989) for a brief history of how psychologists have wrestled with human/animal issues of mind during this century. A more detailed treatment of comparative human and animal mind can be found in Boaks (1984). Not all theorists are in agreement that humans have self-reflective consciousness. See Chapter 10.

procedural memory[4] intimately tied to unconscious, homeostatically regulated, physiological mechanisms of meeting his fluid needs? To continue, does he consciously decide, after reflection, *how much* water he should drink to slake his thirst, or does he mindlessly take a few swallows and continue on his way?

Both views may be partially correct. Recognize, however, that the latter explanation—invoking procedural memory—is the more parsimonious. Why? Because all living animals regulate water. If his behavior resembles that of other vertebrates in this situation, we do *not* have to speculate about higher-order cognitive processes. The procedural memory hypothesis allows scientists to bring to their investigation a wealth of research findings gleaned from psychological and physiological studies of nonhuman animals. We return to this theme in Chapters 7 and 9.

Anthropomorphism, Zoomorphism, and Morgan's Canon

Historically within comparative psychology, the law of parsimony has been synonymous with **Morgan's Canon**. As Box 2.6 shows, Morgan's Canon is related to questions of **anthropomorphism,** the attribution of human characteristics to nonhumans. Modern investigators are concerned with keeping humans separate from "animals." This can be seen in the following passage that relates the applicability of animal models to the development of a theory of PTSD (post-traumatic stress disorder):

> [While animal models] can and do illuminate many of the most prominent and cardinal features of the disorder ... [they] may not illuminate every feature or symptom of these disorders (*at least in part because humans have cognitive capacities that are different from and often exceed those of even the highest non-human primates*). (Mineka, 1985, p. 200, italics added)

A Darwinian perspective emphasizes the continuity of life forms rather than a dichotomy of humans and other animals. You might expect, therefore, that comparative psychologists such as Morgan would advocate **zoomorphism,** the attribution of animal qualities to humans. Zoomorphism is consistent with the evolutionary continuity of animal behavior and with parsimony. Though Morgan played a historic role in developing comparative psychology and in identifying both anthropomorphic and zoomorphic positions (see Box 2.6), he was uncomfortable in acknowledging our animal nature.

Species-Specific Defense Reactions

Many contemporary studies of animal learning blend the foregoing distinctions between ethology and comparative psychology. Consider, for example, laboratory research into innately organized behavior in mammals, which has

---

[4] In the next chapter we see that procedural memories are what Pavlov called *conditioned reflexes*.

BOX 2.6 DECANONIZING MORGAN

Comparative psychology's origins are easily traced. Charles Darwin published *The Expression of Emotions in Man and Animals* in 1872. About one decade later, Conwyn Lloyd Morgan wrote *An Introduction to Comparative Psychology* (1894). It is in this book that Morgan canonized his rule governing the study of humans and animals. (Yes, Morgan himself called it *Morgan's Canon!*)

> In no case may we interpret an action as the outcome of the exercise of a higher psychical faculty if it can be interpreted as the outcome of the exercise of one which stands lower in the psychological scale.

For a century this statement has been widely interpreted as a plea for parsimony—to use the simplest explanation possible. It has also been interpreted as an admonishment for psychologists not to commit the sin of anthropomorphism—that is, of attributing human characteristics to animals. Other writings by Morgan, however, suggest that he was concerned less with parsimony and anthropomorphism than he was with salvation.

Morgan apparently wrestled with the conflicts inherent in his Anglican faith and his understanding of Darwin's theory of evolution. You may recall that divine purpose is lacking in the latter. Yet as late as 1928, writing the chapter "Mind in Evolution" in the edited book *Creation by Evolution* (Mason, 1928), Morgan was still attempting to resolve this conflict:

> Only in the light shed by the concept of evolution does the full richness of Divine Purpose . . . appeal to some . . . in whom a spiritual attitude toward God has itself been evolved.
>
> . . . The acceptance of evolution through many ascending grades, reaching its culmination in the highly-developed mind that plays so great and increasing a part in later evolutionary progress, is not incompatible with belief in God as manifested in all advance from lower to higher.

Morgan's Canon then and now functions to keep humans separated from animals. In Morgan's view of God's plan, animals have not ascended to the highest grade; hence, they are unable to exercise the higher psychical faculties of humans. Humans alone can achieve a highly developed, godlike mind.

It is understandable that Morgan the Christian was concerned with the dehumanizing implications of a zoomorphic position. It is more difficult to understand the posture that comparative psychology has assumed during this past century. The canon is clearly not parsimonious: It assumes a priori that humans have "higher psychical faculties." A more parsimonious position is to assume a priori that humans *are* animals and that all animals learn and think and behave in similar ways (Griffin, 1978). Indeed, psychologists following Morgan's Canon seem to have applied the law of parsimony in only one direction, that of not attributing psychological complexity to non-human animals. The argument should also be applied to analyses of human "psychical faculties"; don't assume cognitive complexity (as Morgan did) if you can explain things more simply.

some similarity to FAPs described in birds (Bolles, 1972). An experimental psychologist, Bolles noted that rats respond to aversive stimulation in predictable, characteristic ways. For example, when given painful electric shock, they jump and run; in the presence of moving stimuli, they initially freeze and then run. By contrast, pigeons flap their wings and fly when shocked rather than jumping and running.

Can animals learn new responses rather than merely default to innately organized behavior? Yes, but at a significant cost in time and energy. For example, rats required to press a bar to avoid electric shock took thousands of trials, and not all of them learned the task (D'Amato & Schiff, 1964). Running in response to pain takes no training. Bolles called these innately patterned responses **species-specific defense reactions (SSDRs)**. The order in which such defensive behaviors occur is invariant both for the particular environmental stimulus and for each species of animal.

Thought question: In the face of adversity, do humans exhibit innately organized SSDRs?

Comparative Psychologists and Ethologists Compared

The respective orientations of researchers in comparative psychology and in ethology continue to provide two windows into the minds and behavior of animals (Timberlake, 1993). Ethologists observe a particular species' behavior in the natural environment (i.e., in "nature"). For this reason ethologists study species-specific behavior. Comparative psychologists typically bring a number of different animals into laboratories to conduct behavioral experiments, often studying how different animals learn the same task. They ask questions about general process learning.

In no small measure, differing methodologies account for many of the conceptual differences between ethology and comparative psychology. Psychologists who study learning prefer the more tightly controlled, contrived, artificial setting of the laboratory. Many of the species-specific tendencies that might otherwise intrude into an investigation of "pure" association formation are neutralized in the laboratory. In turn, the laboratory environment allows the researcher to seek general processes across species and situations, including consummatory behaviors studied by ethologists (Domjan, 1983).

Cross-Disciplinary Behavioral Research.   A great deal of contemporary research in animal learning reflects an interest in understanding innately organized behavior as distinct from, but influenced by, local environments. From the preceding examples it should be obvious that most observed patterns of behavior are combinations of innately organized and newly learned responses. Dr. Nancy Dess is a contemporary researcher who integrates ethological, physiological, and behavioral approaches with traditional animal learning approaches (see Focus on Research 2.1). She and her colleagues use laboratory

FOCUS ON RESEARCH 2.1

Studying the "Emotional Flow"

Dr. Nancy Dess, Department of Psychology, Occidental College, Los Angeles, California

"Humans are animals. Though unique in some very important ways, we are, along with other mammals, caught up in a visceral, emotional flow of events. I am intrigued by the primitive underpinnings of mammalian behavior: hedonic and response production systems and their modification by simple learning processes. My research currently concerns ingestion, fear, and learning. Taken together, these processes occupy a substantial part of most mammals' waking life. Studying how they interact in the lab will help us understand the general organization of mammalian behavior and perhaps some particular problems of our species, such as emotional and eating disorders."

animal models to study the developmental changes in fear (Dess, 1991; Dess & Minor, 1996; Minor, Dess, Ben-David, & Chang, 1994).

Personality Differences Among Psychologists and Ethologists?

The question of why ethologists and comparative psychologists approach the study of animal learning differently is a complicated one (Timberlake, 1993). Let me share my simple theory. It is that many individual psychologists have personalities and temperaments that differ from more biologically oriented ethologists. Many psychologists by interest and training are ultimately more concerned with an understanding of the human mind and human behavior than are classical ethologists. For example, I personally consider humans to be the most interesting animals of all. Humans provide the reference points to which I compare the behavior of all other animals. Not all researchers interested in animal behavior share this anthropocentric (human-centered) view. It is no accident that the revival of interest in comparative animal cognition and consciousness, including humans, reflects current interests of comparative psychologists.

Discussion question: What does your professor consider to be the appropriate domain of animal behavior? Does it include humans?

Animal Models

Psychologists often use animal models in their quest to better understand the behavior of humans. Examples of animal models include the search for the determinants of alcoholism or the formation of learned food aversions (both discussed in Chapter 7). The largest use of animal models by psychologists is found throughout the remainder of this text—namely, the use of laboratory animals to test associative theory and other general process learning theories. The results from experiments using rats, dogs, pigeons, and monkeys used as models are deemed applicable to all animals, including humans.

One Final Contrast.   The primary interest of ethologists is an in-depth understanding of a particular (nonhuman) species' animal behavior. The application of animal research to better understand human behavior and/or to test general theories sets psychologists apart from classical ethologists. Table 2.1 summarizes the major differences between psychological and classical ethological approaches to the study of behavior.

Behavioral Genetics

Genetic components of psychological and behavioral functioning have been known (and studied) for many years, especially in the breeding of domesticated animals and, more recently, from human studies. Findings in the field of **behavioral genetics** are peripheral to the learning emphasis of this text; stu-

TABLE 2.1   Two Methods of Studying Behavior

Psychological Approaches	*Ethological Approaches*
1. Focus on individual differences within a species/across species	1. Focus on species-typical behavior across species
2. Interest in general processes among vertebrates	2. Interest in species-specific behaviors
3. Study domestic animals under laboratory conditions	3. Study feral animals within (natural) ecological niche
4. Interventive manipulation of behavior	4. Unobtrusive observations
5. Human manipulation and control of animal behavior	5. Observation of animal in niche; no interest in controlling behavior
6. Use of animal models; extrapolation to human behavior; tests of general theories	6. Animals do not "model" behavior; little/no interest in extrapolation to human condition or testing "general" models
7. Ultimate focus is human species and human behavior	7. Focus on nonhuman animal behavior

TABLE 2.2 Heritability Estimates for
Psychological Characteristics
of a Particular Breed of Dog

Trait	Heritability
Nervousness	0.58
Suspicion	0.10
Concentration	0.28
Willingness	0.22
Distraction	0.08
Dog distraction	0.27
Noise distraction	0.00
Sound shy	0.14
Hearing sensitivity	0.00
Body sensitivity	0.33

*Source: Data from Goddard and Beilharz (1983) as cited in
Mackenzie, Oltenacu, and Houpt (1986).*

dents interested in the heritability of behavior can find many recent books in
this field. An example of representative research can be found in Table 2.2,
which lists heritability estimates of a number of psychological traits important
for guide dogs for the blind (Goddard & Beilharz, 1983; see Mackenzie, Oltenacu, & Houpt, 1986, for a review of canine behavioral genetics).

As discussed in Chapter 1, many types of human mental disorders (schizophrenia, manic depression, etc.) and "normal" attributes of mind such as temperament and intelligence have been shown to have a heritable component (see
Loehlin, Willerman, & Horn, 1988, for a review). Our future understanding of
complex human behavior awaits the synthesis of behavioral genetics with theories of environmentally determined (i.e., learned) behavior (Plomin, 1990).

Sociobiology

Complex human and animal social interactions can be successfully analyzed from within an evolutionary perspective. The models and concepts
of **sociobiology** (Wilson, 1975) have generated both excitement and controversy.

Sociobiologists argue that the determinants of each human's behavior begin before conception. Sociobiological theory at present lacks a compelling
database for vertebrates (Wilson's work described insect behavior). This philosophy, however, and related research in behavioral ecology (Hinde, 1981)
continue to influence the thinking of behavioral scientists. How does behavior
interact with—that is, how does it affect and how is it affected by—the evolutionary process?

Proximate and Ultimate Causation.   Sociobiologists are responsible for a shift in thinking about the determinants of behavior from **proximate causes** (psychological and sociological) to **ultimate causes** (genetic, Darwinian). A satirical expression attributed to Samuel Butler (1835–1902) captures their philosophy in a quite disturbing way. Butler turned a common expression— "An egg is a chicken's way of making another chicken"—on its head. He quipped that "a chicken is an egg's way of making another egg." Sociobiologists prefer to focus on the egg—the genetic material—of an animal. From their perspective, the phenotypic forms—adult frogs, chickens, and humans—are viewed as elaborately evolved devices. These devices have one purpose only, the perpetuation of the species. Everything about the adult human form, including our social behavior, is an elaborate adaptation to self-replicate.

Consider the following observation of human behavior from a sociobiological perspective. First, the facts. A stepchild is far more likely to be abused (and even murdered) by a stepparent than is a child living with his or her birth parents (Gibbons, 1993). Sociobiologists argue that humans, like other animals, have evolved to protect the interests of their own genetic material over and above the genetic material of others. In this example, they reason, genetic influences provide the ultimate (or distal) causes of parent-stepchild behavior. By contrast, psychologists and sociologists argue for proximate (or proximal) causes of behavior. A proximate cause of stepchild abuse would be the increased emotional and financial hardships of put-together families. It does not seem unreasonable in this example to conclude that both proximal and distal causes are at work.

Some theorists (Barash, 1979, 1982; Dawkins, 1976; Dennett, 1995) have attempted to synthesize contemporary theories of human motivation and behavior with sociobiology. They have been criticized on grounds that each and every behavioral feature and motivation cannot and should not be considered as representing an evolutionary adaptation (Gould & Lewontin, 1979; Lewontin, 1977). Nevertheless, sociobiological thinking permeates many contemporary psychological theories. Dawkins's (1976) provocative book *The Selfish Gene* is highly recommended reading, as is Sagan and Druyan's (1992) *Shadows of Forgotten Ancestors*.

Why Birds Sing: A Neuroethological Analysis

Our current understanding of birdsong illustrates the interplay of traditional ethology with both brain and comparative learning perspectives. This interdisciplinary merger is called **neuroethology**. Neuroethologists study the underlying brain mechanisms mediating the behavior in question as well as how environment modifies instinctive behaviors (Nottebohm, 1991). Whereas classical ethologists focused on fixed patterns of behavior, neuroethologists study how "fixed" patterns can be altered by learning.

Role of the Neuroendocrine System.   When two particular areas of the brains of songbirds are damaged, the appearance of song is prevented. In normal male birds, the size of these brain areas is determined by testosterone; if castrated, the size of these brain areas diminishes, and the male bird no longer sings. In addition, testosterone injected into female birds induces the relevant brain areas to grow, and nonsinging females begin to sing (Nottebohm, 1980).

Each species of bird has its own song. Males hearing recorded birdsong during a critical period (20–60 days of age, depending on species) will, upon maturity several months later, begin to sing the dialect they heard during the critical period. If they hear nothing during this period, they do not develop song (Marler & Peters, 1988).

Role of Reward and Punishment in Song Production.   How effective is the male bird's song in getting females to copulate? The study of cowbird song reveals several interesting anomalies. Male birds raised in isolation (called *isolates*) develop slightly different songs, which prove to be more effective in both attracting and successfully copulating with females. Males reared together have "normal song," which is relatively less successful in attracting females. When the isolates sing their smooth song within earshot of these socially grouped males, however, the isolates are attacked and driven off, thereby reducing their opportunities to copulate with females (West & King, 1980). Here we can see the effects of a rewarding (successful copulation) and punishing environment shaping the cowbird-specific behavior.

Interim Summary

1. Comparative psychologists, behavioral geneticists, neuroethologists, and sociobiologists all study animal behavior from an evolutionary perspective.

2. Comparative psychologists work from a zoomorphic perspective in which common behavioral processes—including learning, thinking, and consciousness—are compared across species.

3. Innately patterned responses of animals in response to pain are called *species-specific defense reactions* (SSDRs).

4. The major differences between comparative psychology and classical ethology are summarized in Table 2.1. Comparative psychologists use animal models to study general properties of behavior.

5. Behavioral genetics is the study of the heritability of behavior—how genes interacting in environments produce such diverse phenomena as temperament in dogs, migration in birds and fish, and mental illness in humans.

6. Sociobiologists stress that behavior is determined in two ways: proximate causes (psychological and sociological) and ultimate causes (genetic, Darwinian).

7. Neuroethologists study brain mechanisms underlying the ways in which environment modifies survival behaviors.

QUEST FOR GENERAL PROCESSES AND A SCIENCE OF BEHAVIOR

Lever-pressing rats and key-pecking pigeons? At first blush, these laboratory scenarios appear to be unrelated to natural behavior. Indeed, that something quite fundamental and basic might be discovered about the learning process—independent of the animal's niche behaviors—is one reason they are used. In developing his now famous experimental chamber, called the Skinner box, B.F. Skinner (1959) did not want FAPs, SSDRs, or other rat-specific or pigeon-specific behavior to interfere with "pure" association formation. He wanted to make an objective analysis of how new responses might be learned in the laboratory.

Pure association formation has proven to be an elusive goal, however. Skinner's position that lever-pressing and key-pecking responses are arbitrary behaviors is incorrect. In recent years (as we see in Chapter 5), almost all animal responses have been shown to be heavily influenced by species-specific factors. Nevertheless, from laboratory studies we have learned a great deal about learning.

Assumptions Underlying General Process Learning Theory

A primary assumption of **general process learning theory** is that a set of laws exist that can adequately describe the learning process. Behavioral scientists who do learning experiments attempt to identify these laws as systematically and objectively as possible. Let us look at a few of their assumptions.

Behavioral Flexibility.   At the outset, most behavioral scientists acknowledge the importance of learning in the development of behavior. Biological influences on behavior are not ignored, but *learning is viewed as the primary source of identifiable behavioral variability*. Another way to state this is that instinctive behavior is important, but what is of most interest in both human and animal behavior comes about through both nonassociative and associative learning processes.

Lawfulness of Learning.   A further assumption of behavioral scientists is that behavior is neither capricious, accidental, nor random. Rather, it changes in predictable, adaptive ways. A simple example: You get mad and kick at a jammed door and break a toe. More than likely you will not repeat that behavior. Why? Because *most animals* change their behavior rather than continue to induce painful outcomes. Most animals respond to rewards and punishments in predictable ways.

Generality of Learning.   General process learning theory implies that many of the phenomena of learning are both *general across species* and *transituational*.

That is, *general processes* can be observed under comparable sets of conditions in a variety of species. The biological and behavioral continuities offered by Darwin's evolutionary theory provide the conceptual basis for assuming common psychological processes.[5] *Transituational* means that the same stimuli conform in a lawlike manner at different times, in different experiments, and in different laboratories.

Replicability.   Scientists assume that the various phenomena of learning are reproducible—that they can be demonstrated in other laboratories under similar sets of circumstances. Both replicability and predictability of outcome, therefore, illustrate what is meant by the "lawfulness" of learning.

Desirability of Laboratory Analysis.   Comparative psychologists assume that a laboratory is the best place to study learning and behavior for the following reasons:

1. Laboratories allow for more careful measurement of the learning process than do observations made in natural settings.
2. Manipulation of one or more independent variables in laboratory research allows for the use of control procedures.
3. Control procedures in turn allow the experimenter to deduce with confidence the *necessary* and *sufficient* conditions for learning. For example, is temporal contiguity *necessary* for learning to occur? If not, is it a *sufficient* condition? A logical analysis of these questions requires scientists to control the experimental environment in which learning occurs.
4. Laboratories allow for the control of various nonlearning effects, or **confounded variables**. In the absence of specific control procedures, many experiences (such as light-dark cycles, changes in diet and sleep, age of organism, to name a few confounded variables) contribute to changes in behavior that are easily mistaken for learning effects.

Is Comparative Psychology's Approach Justified?

Both ethological and laboratory methods are "best" in furthering our understanding of extremely complicated behavioral processes of adaptation and of learning. Both ethology and psychology have learned from the shortcomings of the other, and a modern synthesis incorporates method and theory from both approaches (Gould & Marler, 1987; Halliday & Slater, 1983). Ethologists

---

[5] Invertebrate neurons for all intent and purposes are like vertebrate neurons. Common processes such as habituation and sensitization are in part due to the functioning of individual neurons. Moreover, all vertebrates have similarities of nervous system functioning (forebrain, midbrain, hindbrain, cranial nerves, etc.), which underlay common processes of learning. Similarities and differences in nervous system structure are noted as animal learning experiments and are presented throughout the text.

recognize the role of learning in adaptation—as illustrated by the research highlighted in the box on Dr. Nancy Dess—and psychologists increasingly incorporate both ecological and phylogenetic considerations into their experiments and subsequent theory development. There is no reason to suspect that this merger will not continue in the future. There is also no good reason to think that the comparative approach is on the wrong track.

How Basic Is General Process Learning Theory?

Consider some tentative integrative statements: First, learning is a very basic, fundamental process that has been around for a long time—even by evolutionary time-scale standards. Nonassociative learning processes (discussed in the next chapter) are found in all extant vertebrates and most invertebrates. Simple sensitization and habituation processes, for example, modify an animal's responsiveness to stimuli. As we shall see, such changes in basic reflexes are mediated by relatively permanent changes in memory and qualify, therefore, as learning phenomena.

Certainly a science of behavior is being built along zoomorphic guidelines. General features of learning and behavior among vertebrates are emerging. But other problems remain. Let us look at a few.

Why White Rats?

Many psychologists continue to use white mice or rats or pigeons in laboratory studies of learning. We have seen that ethologists (and some psychologists) object to these laboratory experiments. Why do so many comparative psychologists continue to use so few species in learning experiments?

Two opinions regarding the use of white rats in psychology have emerged during the past 80 years; namely, rats are, and alternatively, are *not* worthy of study. On one hand, white rats remain the most commonly used laboratory animals (and experimental subjects) in learning research. From this observation it can be concluded that at least one large group of scientists continues to think their use is justified. Indeed, the majority of experiments cited in this text used white rats as subjects.

Most students, many ethologists, and some psychologists, however, decry the use of these "loathsome" creatures because they are convinced that no good will come from their study—except the dubious goal of better understanding the behavior of white rats. "The proper study of mankind is man" (and of womankind, woman?)—so the saying goes (and as modified). Indeed, a comparison of the mental mechanisms and capacities of white rats and humans is no contest. (The size of the rat's brain can be approximated by measuring from the top joint to the tip of your little finger.)

Are White Rats Degenerate? Arguments against using animals in psychological research take many forms. (Some animal rights activists would outlaw all animal research on the grounds of cruelty. At the risk of oversimplifying complex issues, the benefits accruing from the responsible use of animals in medical and neuroscience research would seem to outweigh the negatives.) White rats capture most of the general criticism. For example, citing the unusual breeding history of white lab rats, Lockard (1969) asserted that albino rats were deviant from creatures "naturally" evolved on this planet. Artificially selected for gentleness, Lockard asserts, white rats became "degenerate"—so degenerate they could not exist at present outside of environmentally controlled laboratories.

These are serious allegations, indeed. If it is improper to study white rats, 90 years of behavioral investigation and the time and talents of many researchers have been tragically wasted. And if white rat usage was a problem over 20 years ago, when Lockard proposed his argument, the situation has only worsened. Rats and mice dominate the laboratory animal world.

History of White Rats.   In part, scientists continue to use white rats for the simple reason that they have been successfully used in the past. A researcher named Small (1901) first used them in tests of mental processes. Successive generations of graduate students became researchers who also adopted rats as laboratory subjects.

White laboratory rats continue to be used because they are hardy, fecund, and relatively inexpensive. *Fecundity* refers to reproductive capability. White rats have large litters throughout their normal lifetime, allowing many researchers to breed their own research subjects. Large litters are quite a feat for a species alleged to be on the brink of self-destruction through degeneracy! Rats (and mice) are used because they are small, require minimal facilities and support personnel, and are resistant to infection. They are social (they are mammals!) and can be group housed at little risk to life and limb. A rat's life span (indeed that of all rodents) is relatively short compared with that of other mammals. They have, therefore, been exploited in neonatal studies, studies of aging, and other investigations involving life-span development.

Are White Rats "Normal"?   Back to the issue of degeneracy. A comparison of the behavior of albino rats with *Rattus norvegicus* (the wild stock from which it was derived) finds quantitative rather than qualitative differences. For example, comparisons of food neophobia (wariness of novel foods) (Mitchell, 1976), of taste preference behavior (Shumake, Thompson, & Caudill, 1971), of burrowing behavior in climatic extremes (Boice, 1977), and of learning (Boice, 1973; Eibl-Eibesfeldt, 1970) reveal no major differences among strains of rats, including albinos.

As a result of nine decades of experimentation, we know much about the brain and behavior of mice and rats. Yes, the rat's brain is grossly less complex than a human's. Yet it has proven to be sufficiently complex to keep several generations and many thousands of scientists busy. The study of sweet peas and *Drosophilia* (a fruit fly) have allowed geneticists a better understanding of the general mechanisms of genetics. In the same way, the white rat is revealing knowledge of both brain-behavior relationships and generalized mammalian learning and memory processes.

Would Brown Rats Be Any Better?   Psychologists who study learning assert that they are interested in "general processes." Given that white rats are not substantially different from brown rats,[6] one may inquire as to whether brown rats are sufficiently representative of "generalized mammals." That is, are rats "general" enough for the study of general process learning?

Although the argument is not an easy one to make, rats in fact are primitive, nonspecialized mammals. That is, if one were to select from extant mammals a species that is somewhat prototypic of all mammals, rats are not a bad choice. The opossum may be considered a better representative of the common ancestor of mammals, but for many of the reasons cited, rats are a much better laboratory subject.

Ethics of Animal Experimentation

The fact that most humans are not too fond of rats and mice raises questions of ethics. Two such questions will be touched on here; one regards the human food chain and the other concerns using animals in research. Because much has been written in the popular press regarding animal rights and because few minds will be changed regardless of the arguments presented here, I will be brief. Suffice it to say that some individuals and organizations would prohibit boiling live lobsters. Why? Because the reflexive twitching can be interpreted as being a painful experience for the lobster. As the next section discusses, the highly organized brains of more complex mammals would presumably support their perception of (humanlike?) pain and the generation of evasive responses to pain. Imprisoning and inflicting pain on vertebrates, then, are ethical issues. But objecting to the boiling and eating of a lobster, an invertebrate lacking a central nervous system, is a bit effete.

Animal rights activists would outlaw all animal research on grounds of cruelty. At the risk of oversimplifying complex issues, the benefits accruing from the responsible use of animals in medical and neuroscience research would seem to outweigh infrahuman rights. I for one am not interested in living in a prescience, or nonscience, culture. A cost-benefit analysis of this issue by a high school student is presented in Box 2.7.

Comparison of Representative Brains

Learning takes place in the brain. The size of my human brain can be approximated by placing my two closed fists together. The rat brain is no larger than the tip of my finger. How can these two brains be compared for their respective

---

[6] *Brown* is used here simply to denote the color of *Rattus norvegicus* as it occurs in its nonlaboratory ecological niche. A more accurate term is *agouti*, the mixture of brown, tan, white, and black hair found in deer, field mice, squirrels, and so forth.

BOX 2.7   ETHICAL ISSUES OF ANIMALS IN RESEARCH

Jan Hison, a senior at D. H. Conley High School (Pitt County, CA), captured first place at a National Health Occupations Students of America (HOSA) Research Persuasive Speaking Contest. Prior to researching the speech, Ms. Hinson was against the use of animals in research. Studying the issue changed her mind. Major points in her speech included these:

• Animal research has extended human life spans by 20 years.
• By law, research facilities provide animals with humane living conditions . . . that are less stressful than the struggle for survival in the wild.

• 90 –95% of animals suffer no pain in research.
• The majority of 20th-century medical advances have depended on animal research, as follows: cardiac catheterization; organ transplant techniques; discovery of insulin and DNA; treatments for tetanus, rheumatoid arthritis, whooping cough, and leprosy; and development of the heart-lung machine, Salk and Sabin vaccines.
• Animal research has resulted in millions of pets that are free of heart disease, leukemia, and kidney failure.
• Five million abandoned animals are destroyed at animal shelters each year— animals that could be productively used in medical research.

Source: INTERNET bulletin board, September 1992.

---

learning capabilities, you ask? More important, why assume that these brains learn anything in the same manner?

Vertebrate Plan.   Many researchers have studied the brains of representative species of vertebrates. Two comparison outcomes are noted here, beginning with observations by C. Judson Herrick. Common features of brain organization, which Herrick (1948) called the **vertebrate plan**, reflect the evolutionary relatedness and continuity of vertebrates. Humans have in common with other vertebrates a spinal cord containing similarly organized sensory and motor nerves, a medulla (brain stem), 12 cranial nerves and their attendant motor and sensory nuclei, a hypothalamus, and a thalamus.

Reptilian Brain.   Further brain organization common to all vertebrates can be seen in Figure 2.4. MacLean (1970, 1977) describes "reptilian" features of the human brain common to all vertebrates, which are overlain by "old mammalian" and "new mammalian" features. Higher cognitive processes of humans, MacLean argues, are among the functions of the cerebral hemispheres (new mammalian).

New mammalian

Reptilian

Old
mammalian

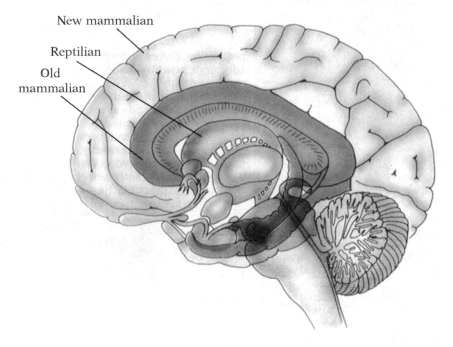

(a)

FIGURE 2.4   Common Brain Features Yield
Common Learning Processes

(a) The human brain as conceptualized by MacLean (1977) consists of a
primitive "reptilian" brain, overlaid successively by "old" and "new"
mammalian brains. Cerebral hemispheres are larger in the more recently
evolved forebrain of mammals, a process called *corticalization*.

Conclusions from Brain Comparisons

Rats, birds, monkeys, and humans certainly have old mammalian brain
structures, conform to a vertebrate plan, and possess other features of physiological organization, including common neurotransmitters and neuroendocrine systems. The rat's brain may be only as big as the tip of your finger,
but its organization is sufficiently complex to allow it to process information
and to readily learn from interactions in its environment. Indeed, as we see
in the next chapter, associative learning is easily investigated in a number of
invertebrates—animals that lack central nervous systems (Abramson, 1994).

In an earlier argument, zoomorphism was presented as an alternative to
Morgan's Canon that functions to isolate humans from other animals. Here we
have learned that humans have brains built on guidelines that are common
with other animals. The not-so-simple bilateral organization of vertebrates

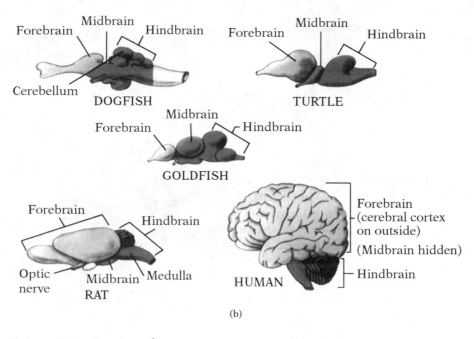

(b)

FIGURE 2.4 *Continued*

(b) Note the three major divisions of hindbrain, midbrain, and forebrain in representative vertebrate brains (not to scale). (After Kalat, 1984)

---

provides the underlying neuroanatomical basis for a common stimulus-response (S-R) psychology. These common brain features support the contention that processes of learning and behavior may be general to all animals.

Species-specific behaviors are often accounted for by reference to special brain structures. For example, it is possible that the visual tectum of some goslings (lacking in others) promoted better following behavior. Both similarities in behavior (general processes) and species differences in behavior can in part be accounted for by brain structure and other anatomical/physiological bases. Anatomical and physiological similarities among species lend some justification to the previously mentioned black box approach to the study of behavior. Results of research into basic behavioral and physiological processes in rats can be extrapolated with caution to other mammals and with somewhat more caution to all vertebrates.

What of humans? We learn like other animals, and we learn like no other animals.

We are fleeting, transitional creatures, snowflakes fallen of the hearth fire. That we understand even a little of our origins is one of the great triumphs of human insight and courage.

(Sagan & Druyan, 1992, p. 31)

Interim Summary

1. Comparative psychologists and other behavioral scientists recognize that all life forms are evolved from a common source and that speciation has produced the peculiarities of each class, order, and species.

2. Aware of species-specific behaviors, comparative psychologists conduct learning research on only a few species of animals and cautiously extrapolate results to other animals. Their goal is to investigate *general process learning theory*.

3. Comparative psychologists assume that learning accounts for most individual differences in behavior, that behavior is lawful, that learning is lawful and that these laws can be found, and that laboratories provide the best means of studying learning and behavioral change.

4. All vertebrates and many invertebrates have sufficiently developed brains to support most nonassociative and many associative learning processes.

5. Conclusion? The laboratory study of animal learning and behavior is well grounded in evolutionary theory, genetics, anatomy, and physiology.

CHAPTER SUMMARY

1. Concepts of learning and behavior in both the biological and behavioral sciences have been presented. Findings from diverse methodologies have been integrated.

2. The ability to learn new behaviors complement more innately organized behaviors. Hence, learning is adaptive.

3. Darwin's theory of evolution provides an understanding of continuity among species as well as the basis for such concepts as species-specific behaviors, instinct, motivation, and learning as adaptation.

4. Neoevolutionary theory incorporates the modern science of genetics (genes and heredity) along with the concept of speciation through natural selection.

5. Humans share many physical and behavioral characteristics (and much DNA) with other primates; *Homo sapiens* have lived for about 100,000 to 200,000 years.

6. Biologically oriented scientists seek the ultimate, or phylogenetic, determinants of behavior. These include an understanding of evolutionary processes, of how species are adapted to their environmental niches, of behavioral genetics, and of comparative brain structures.

7. Ethologists study species-specific, consummatory behaviors in the field. Lorenz described imprinting, a type of rapid, long-lasting learning, and fixed action patterns (FAPs) that are released by sign stimuli.

8. Behavioral scientists who study animal learning in laboratories are most concerned with an animal's ontogenetic history—the proximal events that describe how the environment influences behavior.

9. The zoomorphic perspective of comparative psychologists guides their search for common learning processes among all animals. They use animal models to study general properties of behavior.

10. Emphasis on species-specific differences (by ethologists) and on general, associative processes (by comparative psychologists) is presently being synthesized through interdisciplinary research. An example is laboratory research on species-specific defense reactions (SSDRs), innately patterned responses to pain.

11. The heritability of behavior, including personality characteristics and intelligence in humans, is studied by behavioral geneticists.

12. Sociobiologists differentiate between proximate causes (the effects of reinforcers and punishers) and ultimate causes (genes) of behavior. Neuroethologists and evolutionary psychologists stress that evolved brain mechanisms underlie such behaviors as birdsong, navigation,

courting rituals, male-female differences, and so on.

13. General psychological processes exist across species in part due to similarities of brain and other physiological measures. Because chimpanzees, for example, have so much DNA in common with humans, results from experiments with chimps are easily extrapolated to humans.

14. Rats and other laboratory animals are appropriate animal models for general behavioral studies. What different animals learn is highly variable; the process by which they learn has many features in common.

15. The study of learning processes and the development of behavioral theory are well grounded in evolutionary theory, genetics, anatomy, and physiology, and they are the proper domain of psychology and behavioral neuroscience.

DISCUSSION QUESTIONS

1. Are cats smarter than mice? If you answered yes, ask yourself why there are so many mice in the world.
2. Is sleep an FAP according to Moltz's four criteria? Is human coitus?
3. When I was about 13 years old I became fascinated with female breasts and since then have discovered that I was not alone. Why age 13, and why the near universal interest among males in female breasts?
4. The history of our species is a short, recent one. Our human brains are essentially mammalian, and they differ little from those of other primates. In particular, except for size, the human brain is remarkably similar to the chimpanzee brain. Assume that a goal

of neuroscience is the complete understanding of the human mind and behavior. What are the implications of the fact that our brains have been nonhuman a great deal longer than they have been human?

5. Given our nonhuman ancestry, perhaps we are too cautious in extrapolating findings from research animals to ourselves. Do you agree that our culture, in not adopting a zoomorphic perspective, underestimates animal intelligence and overestimates human intelligence? Can you think of examples that do not involve Lassie? (We return to questions of extrapolation in Chapter 7 and to the comparison of minds in humans and animals in Chapters 9 and 10.)

DISCUSSION STARTERS

1. *Are cats smarter than mice? If you answered yes, ask yourself why there are so many mice in the world.* The complexities of behavioral interactions among species—such as predator-prey relations—cannot be summarized in terms of which animal is "smarter." The larger problem is that of inferring *intelligence* from animal behavior on the assumption that humanlike intelligence is exhibited by animals other than humans. And to the extent that humanlike intelligence *is* exhibited by other animals, it is necessarily *adaptive*. An extended discussion of comparative thinking and complex learning can be found in Chapters 9–10.

2. *Is sleep an FAP according to Moltz's four criteria?* Yes. *Is human coitus?* Yes, in many respects, but not according to criterion 4.

    1. Stereotyped—occurs the same way each time.
    2. Continues to completion once begun—difficult to disrupt.
    3. Latent period—once completed, some time must pass before behavior appears again.
    4. Innate (unlearned; we return to this in Chapter 7).

3. *Why males' interest in female breasts at age 13?* Are the author's assertions correct that there is "near universal interest in female breasts"? Males entering puberty? Males only? Are breasts and buttocks sign releasers that trigger a human innate releasing mechanism? If breasts and buttocks *are* sign releasers, why have they evolved? Do advertisers understand the roles of conditioning and learning in viewer interest?

4. *What are the implications of the fact that our brains have been nonhuman far longer than they have been human?* As a culture we should not be quite so surprised when humans exhibit "animal" behavior. Corticalization has resulted in inhibitory processes that act to suppress behavior. The cortex merely overlays a larger, more primitively functioning brain, which continues to be involved in consummatory behaviors. The cortex allows for, but does not guarantee, civilized behavior. Where does civilized behavior come from?

5. *Is it possible that we underestimate animal intelligence and overestimate human intelligence? Can you think of examples that do not involve Lassie?* This question can be taken in at least two directions. First, note the enormous individual differences evident within our species; not all humans exhibit high levels of consciousness, intelligence, and so on. We continue to live in a culture that is alienated from nature and that thinks a lifetime is a long time. Better adapted than other animals? No, primates are at risk around the world. It is highly likely that the dinosaur era, for example, will have outlasted the *Homo sapiens* era by millions of years. A second direction to take this question is to note the successes (albeit without language, technology, and minimal cross-generation transfer of knowledge) of dumb animals.

KEY TERMS

Adaptation   Any characteristic that improves an organism's chances of transmitting its genes to the next generation.

Adaptive   Describing a characteristic or behavior that enhances survival.

Animal Model   The use of animals in research that bears on the human condition. Example: an animal model of alcohol addiction.

Anthropomorphism   The attribution of human characteristics to animals, deities, and others.

Behavioral Genetics   The study of the interaction of environment and patterns of inheritance in expressed behavior.

Comparative Psychology   The study of animal behavior, stressing both similarities and species-specific differences.

Confounded Variables   Variables that contribute to changes in behavior and can be mistaken for learning effects. These variables include light-dark cycles, changes in diet and sleep, age and sex of organism, and so on.

Consummatory Behaviors   (Ethology) Innate, genetically determined "survival" behaviors, including fixed action patterns, which determine species-specific patterns of feeding, courting, reproduction, social interactions, and so on.

Continuity of Species   (Darwin) The theory that all living organisms are evolutionary adaptations of earlier life forms and, therefore, are all genetically related.

Critical Period   (Ethology) A specific time period (usually early in an animal's development) when an animal is particularly sensitive to certain features in the environment. Exposure to such sign stimuli "releases" genetically determined behavioral responses. (Cf. *Imprinting; Sign Stimulus*.)

Distal Causes   (See *Ultimate Causes*.)

DNA   (deoxyribonucleic   acid)   A double-stranded, helix-shaped structure containing genetic material.

Evolution   Changes taking place in the genetic makeup of populations. Darwinian, or neo-Darwinian, evolution is a complex theory (comprised of many subtheories) proposed to account for the history of life on earth.

Fixed Action Pattern (FAP)   (Ethology) A fixed series of movements ordered in time and space and triggered by an environmental stimulus. FAPs are species-typical and, once initiated, proceed through sequence to completion.

General Process Learning Theory   The theory that animals have common parts of the brain (cf. *Vertebrate Plan*) that mediate common learning processes. General processes are contrasted with species-specific processes of learning and behavior.

Genetics   The study of patterns of heredity and variations in plants and animals.

Genotype   The genetic constitution of an individual organism.

Heredity   The genetic transmission of characteristics from one generation to the next.

Heritability   The fraction of the total phenotypic variance that is accounted for by genetic variation.

Imprinting   (Ethology) A genetically programmed aspect of behavior change involving the rapid development of a response to a specific stimulus at a particular stage of development. (Cf. *Critical Period; Innate Releasing Mechanism*.)

Innate Releasing Mechanism (IRM) (Ethology) A postulated neural mechanism that, when stimulated by a sign-releasing stimulus, triggers an innately organized motor program. (Cf. *Critical Period; Sign Stimulus.)*

Instinct Innately organized behavior.

Lamarckian Evolution The theory that genetic changes in populations (i.e., evolution) can occur through the inheritance of characters acquired during a lifetime.

Law of Parsimony The strategy of explaining phenomena in terms of simple mechanisms and/or processes, rather than by appealing to complex ones (also known as *Occam's Razor*).

Morgan's Canon Morgan's (1894) belief that we should not attribute complex psychological processes to animals if their behavior could be understood from the perspective of lower (simpler) psychological processes.

Natural Selection (Darwin) An aspect of the theory of evolution that stresses the reproductive advantage of certain offspring suited to their environment over others not suited. Darwin argued that environment (i.e., nature) selects those individuals who will reproduce the next generation depending upon their relative fitness. Animals not able to overcome these selection pressures drop out of the gene pool. (Cf. *Selective Pressure.)*

Neuroethology The study of the relationship between the nervous system and consummatory behaviors.

Ontogenetic History A history of an animal's entire development—from fertilization through death.

Phenotype The physical expression of features in an individual animal that results from the interaction of its genotype with the environment.

Phylogenetic History The entire evolutionary history of a specific taxonomic group of organisms. Collectively, the natural history of life on earth.

Proximate Causes (of behavior) Causes of behavior that focus on immediate, local (psychological and sociological) determinants as opposed to ultimate causes (genetic).

Reproduction The behavioral and physiological means by which animals produce offspring.

Selective Pressure Any feature of an environment that allows one phenotype to have reproductive advantage over another.

Sign Stimulus (Ethology) A specific environmental stimulus that triggers innately organized behaviors. (Cf. *FAP; IRM*.)

Sociobiology The study of the genetic determinants of social behavior.

Species-Specific Behaviors Innate perceptual and response patterns typical of a species.

Species-Specific Defense Reaction (SSDR) An innately organized hierarchy of defense behaviors elicited by signals indicating potential danger.

Tropism A differential growth movement in a plant away from or toward a directional stimulus.

Ultimate Causes (of behavior) Causes of behavior that focus upon evolutionary and genetic determinants rather than psychological and sociological explanations.

Variability (Darwin) An aspect of the theory of evolution that describes the role played by the wide range of genetic variation (i.e., variability) within a species. Genetic variance is the raw material upon which natural selection works. (Cf. *Natural Selection; Selective Pressure*.)

Vertebrate Plan   The observed similarities in brain structure among all vertebrates characterized by their common bilaterality, cranial nerves, thalamus, medulla, and other structures.

Written History   The transmission of cultural knowledge; a cumulative record of the ontogenetic histories of many individuals that provides the basis for civilization, which is an invention unique to *Homo sapiens*.

Zoomorphism   The attribution of animal qualities to humans.

CHAPTER 3

FROM REFLEXES TO SIMPLE CONDITIONING

[An insect] . . . can see, walk, run, smell, taste, fly, mate, eat, excrete, lay eggs, metamorphose. It has internal programs for accomplishing these functions—contained in a brain of mass, perhaps, only a milligram—and specialized, dedicated organs for carrying the programs out. But is that all? Is there anyone in charge, anyone inside, anyone controlling all these functions? . . . Or is the insect just the sum of its functions, and nothing else, with no executive authority, no director of the organs, no insect soul?

Sagan and Druyan, *Shadows of Forgotten Ancestors* (1992, p. 167)

REFLEXES

Animals are born with innate, unlearned response tendencies. These responses, called **reflexes**, occur involuntarily when elicited by specific stimuli in the environment. Reflexes are more complex than tropisms and often simpler than fixed action patterns (FAPs). We now turn to the reflex and to reflexive behavior for three reasons: (a) reflexes are of interest to ethologists, physiologists, and psychologists alike; (b) reflexes provide the basis for simple conditioning; and (c) both reflexes and *conditioned* reflexes are important in understanding the complexities of human behavior.

A number of diverse reflexes and reflexlike behaviors are listed in Table 3.1. The survival value of each is self-evident. A human infant, for example, will draw up arms and legs reflexively in response to a sudden, loud noise or a loss of equilibrium—a response known as the *Moro reflex*. Further disturbance will elicit crying. Noise, the eliciting stimulus, triggers the reflexive-like response, crying, that in turn triggers the infant's caregiver to action. Thus, re-

TABLE 3.1 Types of Reflexes

ELICITING STIMULUS (Stimuli originate in the environment; i.e., Darwin's "nature")	*REFLEX* (Reflexes are the DNA's programmed responses to stimuli)
1. "Motor" (touch) reflexes	
PATELLAR TAP --> KNEE JERK	
PRESSURE ON THE--> EYE BLINK SURFACE OF THE EYE	
2. Light and sound reflexes	
LOUD NOISE, LOSS OF EQUILIBRIUM ----------> MORO REFLEX	
DECREASE/INCREASE --------------------------------> DILATION/CONSTRICTION IN LIGHT INTENSITY OF THE PUPIL	
3. Temperature reflexes	
INCREASE IN BODY TEMPERATURE-------------> SWEATING	
LOCALIZED INTENSE HEAT (BURN) -------------> BLISTER	
MATCH BURN ON ARM ---------------------------------> ARM WITHDRAWAL	
SUDDEN DROP IN BODY TEMPERATURE -----> GOOSEBUMPS	
4. Feeding/Ingestional reflexes	
TASTE OF FOOD --> SALIVATION	
TASTE OF SOUR LEMON -----------------------------> SALIVATION	
FINGER, FOOD IN THROAT -------------------------> GAG REFLEX	
INGESTION OF TOXIN --------------------------------> NAUSEA, LOSS OF APPETITE, VOMITING	
SALT LOSS ---> ALDOSTERONE RELEASE	
5. Immune system reflexes	
CEDAR POLLEN ---> HISTAMINE RELEASE	
ANTIGENS --> T-LYMPHOCYTE RELEASE	

flexes in humans and insects are, without exception, adaptive. Most of the re-flexes listed in Table 3.1 are retained into adulthood.

Note that the stimulus in the simple stimulus-response (S-R) framework of the reflex can be directly tied to the environment—Darwin's "nature." Each response reflects the operation of an organism's inherited anatomy, physiology, and behavior as it meets with the environment. A newborn roots and then sucks in response to the stimulus of a warm nipple around its mouth. Pupils dilate in bright light. The environment is the *source* of reflexive behavior in that it places a *selective pressure* on evolving animals. Animals with adaptive reflexive tendencies were selected over those lacking them.

Sherringtonian Reflexes

Not all reflexes have the underlying anatomical simplicity of the patellar (knee-jerk) or the eye-blink reflex. These two well-known reflexes are characterized by identifiable *sensory neurons* synapsing on identifiable *motor neurons*. Typically, one or more *interneurons* separate the direct sensory and motor component. For the patellar and eye-blink reflex, the synapses occur in the spinal cord and medulla, respectively. Sensory-to-motor nerve activation completes what is known as a *reflex arc.*[1] The motor component of the reflex was identified by Sherrington (1906) as the "final common pathway." Hence, simple reflexes are often called **Sherringtonian reflexes**.

Look, however, at other reflexes listed in categories 3 through 5 in Table 3.1. Sweating and salivation are glandular responses, not skeletal muscle contractions, yet by convention both are considered reflexive. But what about blister formation to burns? Remember that in the patellar reflex, motor neurons compose the "final common pathway" causing the lower leg to jerk when the patella is tapped. What is the final common pathway that directs *histamine* release and extracellular fluids that are secreted around cells that have been injured? What of nausea and vomiting in response to toxins?

The Poison-Illness Reflex

Assuredly, these latter responses are more complex behaviorally and neurologically than the eye-blink and patellar reflexes. Consider sickness or nausea. Many environmental toxins and poisons are sensed by neurons in the *area postrema*. Also known as the *chemical trigger zone*, or *CTZ*, the area postrema lies in the posterior part of the brain, just underneath the cerebellum. Neurons from the CTZ project to a portion of the *solitary nucleus* (a group of neurons in the brain stem). Next to the solitary nucleus can be found neurons of the *vagus* nerve that project to the esophagus and stomach. Activating the motor portion of the vagus nerve can result in "gagging" and reverse peristalsis of the esophagus—vomiting. A poison-illness "reflex," then, is initiated by environmental toxins. The reflex continues: → CTZ → solitary nucleus → vagus nerve → nausea and vomiting.

Extending the Idea of Reflex

For present purposes let us simply observe that all reflexes are not Sherringtonian. The underlying physiology of poisoning, of immune system functioning, of temperature regulation, of fluid and electrolyte regulation, and so on, though more complex, can be thought of as reflexlike. Recall the opening de-

[1] Kalat (1994) provides an excellent, readable review of the physiology of reflexes, of sensory and motor nerves, and of the physiochemical events that take place at synapse.

scription of the reflexive life cycle behaviors of insects—walking, eating, smelling, and so forth. Such complex reflexes raise the possibility that at least some components of functionally similar human behaviors may also be reflexive. Walking, for example, doesn't seem to be learned. Nor do chewing and swallowing. But learning does seem to be involved in the selection of spinach over ice cream.

Unlearned responses serve to protect the newborn and adult organism alike against any number of environmental dangers. However, this arsenal of reflexes falls woefully short of the complex responses (e.g., running, shouting, climbing) and the chains of responses (stalking prey, escaping predators, fighting, eating and drinking, communicating) required for survival. These seemingly more "voluntary" responses are acquired through learning.

Hardwiring Versus Plasticity.   Reflexes are primarily studied by physiologists. The brain organization underlying reflexive behavior is fairly well understood. Indeed, innately organized sensory and motor nerves are often referred to as the brain's *hardwiring.* By contrast, modification of brain physiology (which is presumed to underlie learned behavior) is often referred to as the brain's *plasticity.* Our working assumption is that complex behavior is mediated by both hardwired and more plastic brain functioning.

What is the importance of plasticity? From plasticity we get individual differences.[2] Basically, incoming stimulus elements become associated with other stimulus elements, expanding the range of responsivity. Through a process of conditioning, reflexes then come under the control of the newly associated stimuli. However, let us begin our analysis of learning by first looking at nonassociative processes.

Interim Summary

1. Reflexes are unlearned responses to environmental stimuli. Reflexive behavior can be best understood as involuntary, adaptive responses that have evolved because they promote survival and enhance reproductive success.

2. Reflexes are composed of sensory components (elicited by the appropriate environmental stimulus) and motor nerve components that complete a reflex arc. The patellar and eye-blink reflexes are often called *Sherringtonian reflexes* because only a few interneurons precede the motor component, or *final common pathway.*

3. More complex reflexive-like tendencies involve more brain components. Immune system functioning and the physiology of ingestion are two examples.

4. Reflexes are considered to be hardwired, and learned behaviors presumably involve a modification of these inherited response tendencies.

[2] Note that there are also hardwired individual differences that can be attributed to genes.

NONASSOCIATIVE LEARNING

> *While riding with her father through a brief North Florida thunderstorm, 4-year-old Kristen fearfully watched bright flashes of lightning and heard the sharp cracks of thunder. Then, over the next 10–15 minutes, the storm began to dissipate.*
>
> *"Where's the thunder?" she asked.*
>
> *Distracted, dad pondered how to explain the physics of thunder and lightning to a 4-year-old.*
>
> *Far off in the distance where the storm had moved, another flash brightened the dark sky.*
>
> *Again Kristen asked, "Where'd the thunder go?"*
>
> *At this point dad realized that she had learned a thunder-lightning association. She could still see the flashes, but the low growl of thunder was too distant to be heard.*

Learning by association is what this book is about. But something called *nonassociative learning* also occurs. Before analyzing the association that Kristen learned, let us first see what happens when two common stimuli, thunder and lightning, impinge on our nervous systems. The stimulus events experienced by the 4-year-old can be depicted in a 2 × 2 table of possible outcomes (see Figure 3.1). The stimulus event of lightning (S_1) occurs or doesn't occur. The second stimulus event (S_2), thunder, also may or may not occur. The two stimuli may occur together, or neither may occur. The effect of only one stimulus acting on an organism is called a **single-stimulus effect.**

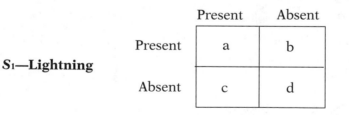

S₂—Thunder

	Present	Absent
Present	a	b
Absent	c	d

S₁—Lightning

FIGURE 3.1   An Association Matrix

The joint occurrence of S_1 and S_2 occupies the upper left cell, labeled a. Either stimulus may occur alone, for example, cell c, thunder alone, or cell b, lightning alone. Note that stimulus association occurs only in cell a; the effect of either stimulus by itself (cells b and c) is called a *nonassociative effect.* Cell d indicates the absence of both stimulus events. Cell d can be labeled *context* in that stimulus events always occur against a background of ambient conditions, or context. In the example given, wind and rain, the moving automobile, the radio, and voices compose some of the context against which thunder and lightning might be experienced.

Habituation

Direct your attention for a moment to an example of a *single-stimulus effect*. First consider "silent" lightning displays many miles away. The child might reflexively turn her head to see the lightning. In doing so, she orients (directs attention) to it. Over a period of time, faraway lightning would elicit less responsiveness from the child; she would orient less to each new occurrence. This reduced responsiveness of an organism to repeated stimulation is called **habituation**. Habituation is typically considered to be an example of **nonassociative learning** because it is a relatively permanent change in behavior resulting from a single stimulus.[3]

Habituation is a basic property of behaving organisms. Stimuli that by themselves are not too meaningful tend to be ignored. If you asked the 4-year-old, she might say she quit looking because it was boring. Habituation is the most basic form of learning, that is, learning *not* to respond to repetitious, meaningless stimuli. Other examples of habituation include not hearing the ticks of a clock, not feeling the clothes you are wearing, and not seeing the page numbers as you read this book—until your attention is directed to these stimuli.

Every waking minute we are exposed to thousands of stimuli (auditory, visual, cutaneous, chemical, etc.). Fortunately, we can't possibly attend to all of them. Only the most critical, meaningful stimuli that *demand* attention get it. The other stimuli *must* fade into the background stimulus conditions (cell d, Figure 3.1), or we would constantly be in sensory overload.

Habituation is the process that allows this fading to occur. In a sense, we are learning what *not* to respond to, what *not* to attend to . . . and this seems to be a perfectly reasonable use of the term *learning*. Single-stimulus events that are repeatedly encountered become relatively permanently "habituated." Such stimuli, for example, less readily form new associations. The reduced associability of familiar stimuli is a phenomenon called *latent inhibition*, discussed in the next chapter.

Habituation Is Not Receptor Adaption.   The process of habituation is often confused with the more peripheral processes of receptor adaptation and/or receptor fatigue. For example, rods and cones become less sensitive to light stimulation immediately after they are exposed to light. Following sound stimulation, hair cells in the cochlea of the ear likewise have refractory periods during which their responses are inhibited. In the absence of further stimulation, these sensory adaption processes typically recover within a few seconds to a few minutes. By contrast, habituated responses may remain so for days, weeks, and months.

Remember the distinction made earlier between learning and perfor-

---

[3] An alternative view, that habituation is an *associative* phenomenon, is presented in Chapter 4.

mance? We infer learning from performance, but not all changes in performance constitute learning. The present example of sensory adaption is an excellent example of performance changes (i.e., reduced sensitivity to sights and sounds) that do *not* constitute learning.

How "General" Is Habituation?   We have begun to entertain arguments to the effect that learning is a *general process*. A general process allows one to make meaningful behavioral comparisons across widely divergent species and in a variety of learning situations. Habituation is a general process. For example, if we were to compare the effects of rhythmically stroking the "arm" of a starfish and the arm of a human infant (i.e., an invertebrate and a vertebrate), the initial reflexive movements of the arms of both species diminish following repeated stimulation. In both instances we would say that the response is *habituated*. Because of highly dissimilar nervous systems, the mechanisms underlying these responses presumably differ (see Box 3.1).

Perhaps we should not be surprised at the similar outcomes of habituation experiments displayed in Box 3.1. Apparently, there are no exceptions to the generality of nonassociative processes throughout the animal kingdom. Razran (1971) cites the similarity of patterns of habituation in a variety of responses in planaria, worms, snails, goldfish, frogs, turtles, birds, and humans.

Sensitization

Repetitive stimulation does not invariably lead to reduced responsiveness. Had Kristen, for example, experienced lightning flashes right next to her, it is probable that a somewhat different outcome would have ensued. Intense visual, auditory, cutaneous, and chemical stimuli do not habituate readily. In fact, often one or more presentations of a powerful stimulus has the opposite effect. Rather than reduced responsiveness, animals tend to become yet more activated when the stimulus is presented again—a phenomenon called **sensitization**.

Nervous systems are constantly being attuned to the environment in which they interact. The stimulus effects of lightning and thunder are good examples of the nonassociative processes of sensitization and habituation. A sharp crack of thunder sensitizes 4-year-olds and adults alike. After one or more bone-jarring stimulus events, one's "nerves" are on edge; and other noises tend to elicit a greater-than-normal response. We await, we anticipate, the next crack of thunder. Such is the nature of sensitization. Not so the gentle rumbling of distant thunder. In fact, low-intensity, rhythmic stimulation (such as petting a cat) has a calming effect (on both the stroker and the strokee).

Sensitization can produce a relatively permanent change in a person's behavior. For several years after experiencing thunderstorms, the 4-year-old in question was aroused at their first approach. Her memory of close lightning strikes remains with her and has sensitized her to that particular class of auditory stimulus events. Likely this learning will last throughout her lifetime.

BOX 3.1   HABITUATION: A GENERAL BEHAVIORAL PHENOMENON

Most general process arguments you will encounter presuppose a common underlying neural mechanism. Habituation, however, is a behavioral phenomenon that apparently can be accomplished by many different types of nervous systems. Note in the figure the similarity of the time course of decreased responsiveness to repeated stimulation in spinal rats, normal rats, and adult humans (Lehner, 1941).

a. Withdrawal response decreased for tail-pinched rats after 13 trials in the first "habituation cycle." (These rats had transected spinal cords, thereby eliminating the brain's control over the habituation response.) Fifteen seconds

later, the same tail-pinch stimulus habituated in seven trials (second habituation cycle). By the sixth cycle, habituation was accomplished in two trials.

b. "Startle," or jerking, reflex to a loud sound habituates more slowly in intact rats, compared with the tail-pinch reflex in spinal rats. Again, the interval between blocks of rapidly repeated stimulations is 15 seconds. Note that half as many stimulations (approximately 15) are sufficient to habituate the response in the second cycle, compared with 30 stimulations in the first cycle.

c. Note the same pattern of habituation of the abdominal reflex of adult humans, again with 15 seconds between each block of response habituation.

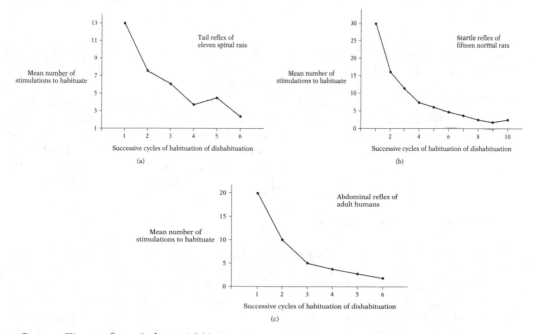

Source: Figures from Lehner, 1941.

Note that being sensitized to thunderstorms is adaptive. Perhaps this is the stuff phobias are made of. Are phobias adaptive? We address these questions in Chapter 7.

Habituation and Sensitization Compared

To reiterate, some responses to repetitive stimuli tend to habituate, and others tend to sensitize. Both processes occur in all species of animals (Peeke & Petrinoviche, 1984). As a general rule, responses to regularly occurring presentations of stimuli of low to moderate intensity tend to habituate (Thompson & Spencer, 1966). Moderate to high intensity stimuli tend to sensitize the organism. To give you some idea of the complications that can arise in assessing nonassociative effects, consider the following experiment by Davis (1974). He compared the effects of presenting a loud noise (110 decibels, dB) lasting only a fraction of a second to two groups of rats. The rats differed only in the level of background noise in their experimental chamber; either 60 dB (relatively quiet) or 80 dB (relatively loud), respectively. Davis measured the rats' startle response to aperiodic presentations of the loud, 110 dB noise. The startle response decreased over trials in the group with low background noise but increased in the group with the high background noise. That is, the same 110 dB stimulus had two opposing effects—habituation and sensitization, respectively!

Simple-Systems Research: Neural Mechanisms of Nonassociative Learning

Nonassociative learning (sensitization and habituation) has been studied in a California marine snail called *Aplysia*. The chemical events at synapse in sensory and motor neurons subserving a gill-withdrawal reflex have been described by Kandel and his associates (Carew, Hawkins, & Kandel, 1983; Kandel & Schwartz, 1982). This simple-systems approach to understanding the neural underpinnings of nonassociative learning is described in Box 3.2.

Analysis of Nonassociative Learning

These examples readily illustrate the importance of the concepts of habituation and sensitization for understanding important changes in response patterns. There is irony in the fact that all psychologists cannot agree on the importance of single-stimulus events. This is true even to the point that some theorists ignore nonassociative phenomena. Why is this so? How has learning come to be defined as "due to association" and single-stimulus effects relegated to other areas of psychology? Answers to these questions are not simple. Consider the following arguments.

Box 3.2 **Neural Mechanism**
of Nonassociative Learning

MECHANISM OF HABITUATION

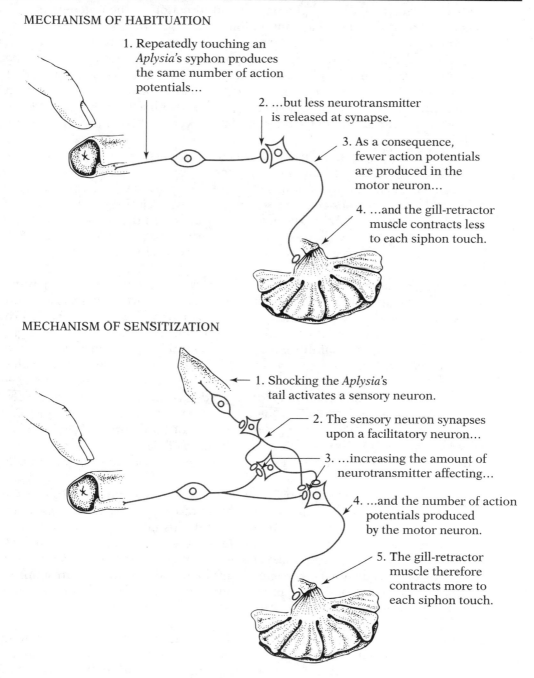

1. Repeatedly touching an *Aplysia*'s syphon produces the same number of action potentials...

2. ...but less neurotransmitter is released at synapse.

3. As a consequence, fewer action potentials are produced in the motor neuron...

4. ...and the gill-retractor muscle contracts less to each siphon touch.

MECHANISM OF SENSITIZATION

1. Shocking the *Aplysia*'s tail activates a sensory neuron.

2. The sensory neuron synapses upon a facilitatory neuron...

3. ...increasing the amount of neurotransmitter affecting...

4. ...and the number of action potentials produced by the motor neuron.

5. The gill-retractor muscle therefore contracts more to each siphon touch.

Source: Adapted from Pinel, 1993, p. 512.

Post Hoc Analyses of Nonassociative Effects.   Ideally, scientists would like to be able to predict in advance the nature and direction of the outcome of an experimental treatment. Take habituation. A scientist interested in investigating habituation would want to select a stimulus, present it to an animal a few times, and measure the reduced responsiveness. Unfortunately, our experimental psychologist may find that the response outcome is in the nonpredicted direction, that is to say, one of *enhanced* rather than diminished responsiveness. And to complicate the matter, another test subject, or the same test subject on another day, or one with different background conditions might give a different result.

   All too often in studying nonassociative processes one is restricted to post hoc analyses of the presumptive process. The experiment is done, results recorded, and *then* a hypothesis is formed. Not good science! This loss of predictability retards the scientist's search for lawlike relationships. It may be for this reason that not many psychologists specialize in the study of nonassociative learning. As a result, less is known about these processes than about the laws of association between two stimuli. A curious situation, indeed!

Example of Learned Helplessness.   Even general rules concerning the nature of stimuli that typically lead to habituation or to sensitization do not always hold. A case in point is the phenomenon known as **learned helplessness**. Learned helplessness is a condition initially described by Overmier and Seligman (1967). After a rather painful experience, a research animal no longer responds in an adaptive fashion. Experimentally, a dog or rat in an experimental chamber is administered one or two very intense electric shocks. One would expect the organism to be sensitized, to respond vigorously to even mild electric shock in the future. Yet in fact there is an overall *reduction* in responsiveness to subsequent electric shocks, characteristic of habituation. Why? Probably because the shocks were too intense! (The learned helplessness model may underlie some forms of human psychopathology, a topic we return to in Chapter 7.)

   So very low intensity shocks habituate; medium- to high-level shocks sensitize; and *very* high intensity shocks again produce a reduction in responsiveness that resembles habituation. Single-stimulus effects are difficult to conceptualize and difficult to investigate in the laboratory. To summarize, predicting whether certain independent variables will act to sensitize, to habituate, or to have some other effect is problematic. The animal's response depends critically on the species under study, the nature of the physical stimulus, and the animal's prior history with the stimulus in question.

Adaptiveness of Nonassociative Learning.   Single-stimulus effects, including sensitization and habituation, are important for their inherent survival value. Recall that FAPs are released by a single stimulus, called a *sign stimu-*

lus. One interpretation of the complex responses elicited by such a stimulus is that the infant goose's visual brain is preprogrammed to be sensitive to movement during a critical period of development. Neurons allowing the perception of movement are tuned to whatever moving stimulus is experienced. The goose's *following behavior* is tied to activation of these neurons. It is also the case that specific neurons in the brain are preprogrammed to be sensitive to other complex stimuli, including food and water. Drugs have their complex effects to the extent that they can stimulate naturally occurring receptor sites on neurons. As indicated in Table 3.1, our brains and behavior have evolved to be especially sensitive to nature's stimuli that affect our survival. Such processes presumably are part of the "operating equipment" present at birth.

Ethology and comparative psychology are not the only sciences that are concerned with the nonassociative effects of stimuli. Psychologists who study processes of *sensation* and *perception* are very much interested in single-stimulus effects in humans and other animals. The discipline of *psychophysics* has been successful in measuring response characteristics to a variety of stimuli. Other behavioral and biological scientists have traced physical stimuli through our sensory systems and throughout the central nervous system. *Physiological psychologists* and those in the neurosciences investigate the effects of complex stimuli such as foods, drugs, spoken words, and so on acting on the body.

To summarize the adaptive significance of sensitization and habituation, consider the following: Living organisms either "drowsy" or "wired" are at less than their optimal arousal level for coping with environmental demands. Sleepy? Predators are watching. Likewise, nervous twitches may give away the position of a prey animal. In large measure, a learned balance of habituation and sensitization is critical for optimal awareness.

Potentially important stimuli are better perceived against a background of habituated stimuli. Animals are more likely to respond adaptively under these conditions. Likewise, for a period of time following a "stronger" stimulus, the nervous system displays a greater than normal sensitivity.

Neural Basis of Sensitization and Habituation.   Studies of *long-term potentiation (LTP)* and *long-term depression (LTD)* are encouraging research into the neural substrates of nonassociative learning. In LTD, neurons are rapidly stimulated with a train of high-frequency electrical impulses for a brief period of time. Such treatment facilitates these neurons to discharge more easily when further stimulated—an effect that lasts for days and even weeks (Bliss & Lomo, 1973). Furthermore, stimulating several axons simultaneously produces more LTP than when only one neuron is stimulated. We will return to studies of long-term potentiation and long-term depression when the neural substrates of associative conditioning are considered.

Interim Summary

1. An association matrix summarizes the effects of two stimuli presented alone or in association.
2. *Nonassociative learning* is the concept that single stimuli acting alone can produce relatively permanent effects known as *habituation* and/or *sensitization*.
3. *Habituation* refers to a relatively permanent reduced responsiveness following repeated stimulation with low-intensity stimuli.
4. *Sensitization* is the term used to identify increased responsiveness for a time period following a relatively intense stimulus.
5. Stimuli can be characterized as lying along a dimension from simple (both physically and perceptually) to complex (both physically and perceptually).
6. Simple stimuli have less effect on animals (both associative and nonassociative) than do complex stimuli.
7. Nonassociative effects such as sensitization and habituation are behaviorally adaptive.
8. Relatively long-lasting changes in the sensitivity of individual neurons, called *long-term potentiation* (LTP), may underlie habituation and sensitization.

THE ASSOCIATION OF STIMULI

Saint Ildefonso used to scold me and punish me lots of times. He would sit me on the bare floor and make me eat with the cats of the monastery. These cats were such rascals that they took advantage of my penitence. They drove me mad stealing my choicest morsels. It did no good to chase them away. But I found a way of coping with the beasts in order to enjoy my meals when I was being punished. I put them all in a sack, and on a pitch black night took them out under an arch. First I would cough and then immediately whale the daylights out of the cats. They whined and shrieked like an infernal pipe organ. I would pause for awhile and repeat the operation—first a cough, and then a thrashing. I finally noticed that even without beating them, the beasts moaned and yelped like the very devil whenever I coughed. I then let them loose. Thereafter, whenever I had to eat off the floor, I would cast a look around. If an animal approached my food, all I had to do was to cough, and how that cat did scat!

Lope de Vega, *El Capellan de la Vergen (The Chaplain of the Virgin)* (1615); trans. by J. H. Arjona, as cited in Bousfield (1955)

Most present-day investigations of learning and of memory are *associative* in nature. Complex animals move freely throughout wide, ever-changing niches. Even though sign stimuli can have unusually large effects on behavior, complex animals (including humans) meet comparatively few such innate-releasing stimuli in their lifetime. Rather, we solve many of our problems by learning to associate and remember the important stimuli in our environments. We learn by the reinforcing and punishing consequences of our behavior, also an associative process. It is to associative theory we turn.

Modern learning theory is a form of *philosophical associationism*. The formal theory of associationism can be traced to the writings of 17th-century philosophers now known as the *British Empiricists:* John Locke, Thomas Hobbes, George Berkeley, and others. Obviously, simple ideas of association have been around for a long time, as the protagonist in Lope de Vega's play indicated by his cat-conditioning experiment. John Locke was more interested in how humans learned from their immediate environment. Our ideas, wrote Locke, result from the association of simple sensory events. These "raw sensations" became associated to produce complex associations:

> All the ideas we have of particular distinct sorts of substances, are nothing but several combinations of simple ideas. . . . It is by such combinations of simple ideas, and nothing else, that we [mentally] represent particular sorts of substances to ourselves. . . .
> Thus, the idea of the sun—what is it but an aggregate of those several simple ideas—bright, hot, roundish, having a constant regular motion (etc.)

> Locke, *An Essay Concerning Human Understanding* (1690)

Empiricism. The British associationists assumed that a primary source of knowledge about the world is based on *experience* with the world. Hence, knowledge is *empirical,* that is, guided by observation. Modern science uses empirical methods; laboratory study involves seeing, hearing, and otherwise observing, testing, and measuring. **Empiricism** is the main method (and philosophy) that distinguishes science from other ways humans can get knowledge about the world (cf. *intuitionism,* which has no real-world referents).

The British empiricists, also known as *associationists,* did not do experiments in laboratories. Nevertheless, many of their ideas about **associationism** (cf. *association theory*) have proven to be remarkably insightful. Modern scientists retain the basic approach of these philosophers: The most simple learning process is operationally defined as the association of two or more sensory experiences.

Four Tenets of Association Theory

From the British associationists and subsequent findings of researchers, modern **association theory** may be summarized as follows:

1. *Temporal contiguity.* The process of association formation is integrally dependent on **temporal contiguity**. That is, for stimulus events to be associated, they must occur close together in time (we explore how close is close enough later). You did not learn what "watch out!" means by experiencing a near miss with an 18-wheeler 30 minutes after someone yelled at you. Vertebrate nervous systems readily make associations when stimuli sensed by them occur closely together in time. That two stimuli must occur close together in time for them to be associated defines the **contiguity theory of association.**

2. *Intensity.* The **intensity** of two sensory experiences influences the process of association formation (more intense stimuli being more readily associable). Larger reinforcers (or punishers) influence the rate of learning more than smaller ones. In addition, for reasons not well understood (but TV advertisers know only too well), loud sounds and bright lights are associated more quickly.

3. *Frequency.* The **frequency** of occurrence of stimuli strengthens their association. Many of us have learned math facts or another language using flash cards. Mastery depends on time spent studying. The more frequently you go through the cards (i.e., the more trials), the better the material is associated: $9 \times 7 = ?$

4. *Similarity.* **Similarity** of experiences influences their associability. Some events seem to "belong" together, and, as a result, they are more easily associated. For example, assume that you visit a zoo. While there, you experience new animal smells and hear a new song played over the loudspeaker. Which association would be stronger two years later? Would the smell or the music most likely put you in mind of the zoo? We explore several hypotheses about similarity later in this chapter. Presumably, the role of similarity in association has something to do with hardwiring in the brain.

Association Theory: Example and Analysis

With these principles in mind and in the spirit of John Locke, let us return to the storm. Recall that Kristen wanted to know what happened to the thunder. She could still see the lightning in the distance, and her question indicated that she had learned to associate the two stimuli. At that point she had an "idea" that a storm is composed of rain, thunder, and lightning (in the same way that Locke's idea of sun was warm, red, and round). After being experienced together, the elements belong together. In the presence of only one element, the other is missed.

Learning About Causality. In this 4-year-old's perceptual world, however, **causality** was probably *not* inferred from her observations. Because of the nature of thunderstorms, thunder sometimes seems to precede and sometimes to follow lightning. It is likely that Kristen learned that thunder and lightning were highly correlated, but she had not yet learned that lightning *causes* thunder. That is, she most likely had *not* learned that lightning is the *antecedent condition,* or *cause,* of the thunder.[4] Having learned the thunder-lightning (or lightning-thunder) association, the absence of thunder was puzzling. Her still-not-quite-predictable world had become even less so.

Contiguity and Contingency

Given that knowledge provided by correlation is incomplete, how do animals learn about causality? Let us look in more detail at what is known as *contingency theory of association* and see what it adds to the associationist's theory of contiguity. Implicit in the comparison of these two theories is the notion that humans and other animals process incoming sensory information. The comparison of contiguity and contingency theories, therefore, can also be thought of as *information-processing* theories.

A **contingency theory of association** focuses on the *information* value of one stimulus preceding and thereby *signaling* a second stimulus (Rescorla, 1968). For simplicity, let us call the lightning stimulus S_1 and the thunder stimulus S_2. Contingency theory highlights an additional aspect of what an animal learns during an association, namely, the predictability of S_2 by S_1 due to the lightning $\rightarrow$ thunder *sequence.*

A *contingent* relationship exists between these two stimuli to the degree to which one predicts the other. For example, if the contingency between S_1 and S_2 is perfect, the probability of S_2 given the occurrence of S_1 equals 1. Every time there is an instance of thunder, lightning has preceded it. Symbolically (where p means probability),

$$p(S_2/S_1) = 1.0 \tag{3.1}$$

This equation reads "the probability of S_2 given S_1 is equal to 1.0." Recognize that this perfect relationship between thunder and lightning can be altered in several ways. For example, S_1 can be presented to the animal in the absence of S_2:

$$p\ (S_2/S_1) = 0.0 \tag{3.2}$$

or S_2 can be presented to the animal in the absence of S_1.

---

[4] Careful observation over a number of trials with a nearby storm *might* allow human observers to detect the fact that thunder is contingent on (invariably follows) lightning strikes. Unless one learns about (and remembers) the physics of lightning and thunder in a science class, however, one will *not* know that a lightning strike *causes* thunder by heating and expanding air molecules that "thunder" on contraction.

$$p \ (S_2/\text{no } S_1) = 1.0 \tag{3.3}$$

What if Kristen had heard thunder follow lightning on only half the occasions? There would not be a perfect contingency of $p(S_2/S_1) = 1.0$. The equation reflecting this "half" predictability is

$$p(S_2/S_1) = 0.5 \tag{3.4}$$

Would Kristen have learned the contingent relationship? If so, would she have learned as quickly? We analyze this question and related issues in contingency theory in the next chapter. The important thing to remember here is that predictable sequences of two stimuli add more information than two stimuli merely occurring together.

Two-Stage Theory of Association

From the foregoing example, it is clear that association formation has two distinct stages. In stage 1, two stimuli are perceived simply as being *correlated,* but one stimulus is not perceived as reliably preceding the other. The association occurs by *temporal contiguity*—two events happening at about the same time. After a number of trials (cf. *frequency* of association) in which one stimulus is perceived as always preceding the second stimulus, a more complex association is learned. The first stimulus is perceived as being the *cause* of the second.[5] The more complex second stage is association by *contingency*. Together, contiguity and contingency constitute the **two-stage theory of association.**

Association Theory and S-R Theory

Behavioral science began when philosophers crawled out of their armchairs and into their laboratories. The raw sensory experiences of John Locke became the psychologist's stimuli. Since Locke's "ideas" are difficult to measure, the behavioral scientist instead concentrates on relating the organism's response to an incoming stimulus—both of which are measurable. Coughing and pain are readily associated by cats. Association theory easily becomes translated into the stimulus-response (S-R) theory of the laboratory.

More often than not, S-R analyses do not refer to what is happening inside the organism, for example, the changes assumed to be taking place in the

---

[5] Is there a psych major alive who has not heard the old saw that "correlation does not imply causation"?

brain as learning occurs and as memories are formed. Recall that for this reason S-R psychology is also known as a *black box approach.*

U.S. Laboratories.   Darwin's influence on the development of comparative psychology at the end of the 1800s has already been noted. At Columbia University E. L. Thorndike moved the study of animal behavior into the laboratory. In 1898, Thorndike placed hungry cats in boxes and measured how many trials it took for them to learn to escape. He then formulated basic general principles of instrumental learning, so named because the animals' responses were "instrumental" in escaping the box. In 1913, psychologist John B. Watson (1879–1958) promoted an objective science of behavior at Johns Hopkins University. Working within an S-R framework, Watson studied the effects of conditioning responses of both laboratory animals and humans. In later chapters we look more carefully at the contributions of both researchers to general process learning theory.

Russian Reflexology.   During this same time period, Ivan Pavlov in Russia was independently arriving at a philosophical position similar to Watson's. Pavlov studied both reflexive and conditioned reflexive (learned) behavior. Both Pavlov and Watson encouraged their students to conceive of behavior as a "mirror of the mind." Learning would be objectively measured by observing behavior.

   Watson, Pavlov, and others were influenced by several generations of contemporary learning theorists. The result was that learning would be studied in the laboratory as an observable change in *behavior* rather than as a mental process. Modern learning theory follows the lead of these early behaviorists. Ultimately, however, the elusive constructs we call "learning" and "memory" will be understood from a variety of perspectives, including biological, psychological, and sociocultural.

   Ivan Pavlov, the great Russian physiologist, recognized the complexities of associative learning as he began to investigate "psychic secretions" in dogs. Let us turn next to his work.

Interim Summary

1. Seventeenth-century philosophers now known as the *British associationists* proposed that knowledge was derived through the association of sensory stimuli.
2. Four tenets, or rules, proposed by the British associationists that govern the formation of associations are (a) temporal contiguity, (b) frequency, (c) intensity, and (d) similarity (or belongingness) of stimuli.
3. A two-stage theory of association posits that events are first perceived as being correlated and second interpreted as being causally related.

"Pavlov . . . Pavlov . . . That name rings a bell."

FIGURE 3.2

Cartoon by R. L. Zamorano

Causal relationships are inferred from contingent sequencing of two stimuli.

4. By the beginning of the 20th century, the study of learning moved into the laboratory. Learning was an inference made from observing changes in behavior in response to arranged stimulus events.

Pavlov's Salivary Conditioning

Experiments that we now refer to as **Pavlovian conditioning** (also known as **classical conditioning**) were first reported at the turn of this century by a Russian physiologist, Ivan Pavlov.[6] His main work in this area, *Conditioned Reflexes*, was published in 1927.

Pavlov's research and that of his associates originally focused on the digestive process in dogs. In the course of his physiological studies, he described the **salivary reflex;** that is, he carefully measured the amount of salivation caused by precisely measured amounts of food placed on the dog's tongue. Not too interesting, perhaps, but these and other studies in digestion earned Pavlov a Nobel Prize in 1906.

Pavlov's other observations that we continue to study *are* more interesting. He noted that salivation occurred not only as a reflexive response to food being placed in the mouth. His dogs also salivated just prior to actual ingestion—almost as if the animal "anticipated" eating. Because salivation occurred without real-world food, Pavlov called it a **psychic secretion.** Pavlov the physiologist knew that without the appropriate eliciting stimulus, reflexes weren't supposed to work this way. Could he understand the dog's higher mental faculties by investigating the role of the dog's cerebral hemispheres as new associations to the salivary reflex were learned? Pavlov took a chance and devoted 30 years of his life to a thorough examination of this question (Pavlov, 1927/1960).

Association of Bell and Food.   On closer examination of the phenomenon, Pavlov found that the mere sight of food being prepared was sufficient to produce salivation in his dogs. Figure 3.3 shows a dog in a conditioning apparatus that Pavlov and his associates used to study association formation. The sight of food and the taste of food were always paired in time. Pavlov reasoned that the animal had learned to salivate to a broader range of stimuli because it had associated sight with taste.

Pavlov tested his hypothesis of association by pairing the sound of a bell[7] with the taste of food. He noted that the dog pricked up its ears and turned its head to the source of the bell's sound but did *not* salivate. This **orienting reflex** to the bell differed from the salivary reflex to the food. After a number of paired presentations with food, the bell's sound elicited salivation even before

---

[6] In 1902 an unpublished dissertation by E. B. Twitmyer, "A study of the Knee Jerk," was defended at the University of Pennsylvania. In his laboratory research, Twitmyer repeatedly sounded a bell a half second before hitting the patellar tendon of students, thereby causing the patellar, or knee-jerk, reflex. The sound alone came to elicit the reflex (Twitmyer, 1974). Pavlov, not Lope de Vega, not Twitmyer, is credited with the "discovery" of conditioning because of the 30 years he devoted to its study.

[7] In addition to an electronic bell, Pavlov used the sounds of a metronome and "bubbling water," tuning forks, various pictures, vibration, and so on in pairings with food. For ease of illustration, most examples given refer to a bell.

FIGURE 3.3   Inside Pavlov's Laboratory

Pavlov and his colleagues trained dogs to stand in a harnesslike apparatus during experimental sessions. During the experiment the dog would be isolated and could see and hear only the sights and sounds presented by the researchers. Food was placed on the animal's tongue and salivation was collected and measured by a mechanical apparatus not depicted in the photograph. The dogs were well cared for, and Pavlov's lab set high standards for animal experimentation.

---

food was tasted—a process Pavlov called *conditioning*. He immediately grasped the adaptive nature of this type of learning:

> It seems obvious that the whole activity of the organism should conform to definite laws. If the animal were not in exact correspondence with its environment, it would, sooner or later, cease to exist. To give a biological example: if, instead of being attracted to food, the animal were repelled by it, or if instead of running from fire the animal threw itself into the fire, then it would quickly perish. The animal must respond to changes in the environment in such a manner that its responsive activity is directed towards the preservation of its existence. (Pavlov, 1927/1960, pp. 7–8)

Questions of adaptation aside, on the face of it, Pavlov's description of conditioning sounds like an esoteric laboratory exercise. Present-day behavioral scientists are not especially interested in the digestive processes of dogs, nor, as we will see, in the lever-pressing or maze-running abilities of rats. But we continue to study behavior in experiments such as these. They inform the process by which basic learning occurs in all species in a variety of situations.

Application of Conditioning to Humans.   The general form of research in the remainder of this chapter begins with an inborn reflex. Through association, the original eliciting stimulus is replaced with a new, arbitrary stimulus. Are such simple conditioning processes determining factors in human behavioral repertoires? Certainly. Consider, for example, the many domestic creatures who inhabit kitchens. The rattling of a box of milk bones or the lid of the cookie jar is sufficient to cause both orienting responses and conditioned salivation. For most of us, the mere mention of a thick, juicy steak or chicken *fajitas* sizzling over a bed of hot charcoal often have the same effect. But not for vegetarians. Why is that? A perfume or distinctive voice may bring to mind a particular individual and cause your stomach to flip-flop. Why is that? Similarly, running toward an icy lake will raise goose bumps. The sight of a fast-approaching dust cloud (or fist) will produce an eye blink—over and above the reflex elicited by touching the cornea. The appearance of a green sheen on a slice of turkey elicits a disgust response in adults but not in very young children. Why is that?

Remember Sherringtonian reflexes? It turns out that they can be modified by experience. The environment can come to control reflexes in new ways. One result is that each individual has a unique conditioning history. Some have learned things that others have not.

Thought experiment: You now know how Pavlov brought the salivary reflex of a dog under the control of a neutral stimulus (i.e., the bell). Could you describe how it might be possible to condition a person to be disgusted at the sight of green meat? Or to sneeze when he or she merely *sees* a cat? Or to love to read? You will have the basic mechanics of conditioning by the end of this chapter. Chapter 7 investigates applications of learning to an understanding of physiology and behavior.

Elements of Pavlovian Conditioning

Simplicity in theory and method may not guarantee scientific success. We recognize the enduring nature of Pavlov's research a century after the fact in part, however, because of its simplicity. Only four basic components (two stimuli, one response, and time) are involved. Let us now consider **excitatory conditioning** as initially demonstrated by Pavlov (see Figure 3.4). More specifically, the following preparation is an example of **appetitive salivary conditioning** (or **appetitive conditioning**) in that Pavlov elaborated a conditioned salivary response to a food stimulus (cf. *appetite*).

Two of the four components you already know—the unlearned *stimulus* and the *response* that form the salivary reflex. Pavlov labeled these unlearned components the **unconditioned stimulus (US)** and the **unconditioned response (UR).** For Pavlov's dogs, the taste of *food* is the unconditioned stimulus that automatically elicits the reflexive response of *salivation*, the unconditioned response.

To this basic reflex is added a learned, or conditioned, component. A new stimulus such as a bell is thrown into the mix. Before training, the bell has no special effect on the animal's appetitive behavior. That is to say, the bell ini-

STIMULUS --> **RESPONSE**

1. **Before training**
   US (food) --> **UR** (reflexive salivation)
                        (elicits)
   CS (bell) --> **OR** (orienting response)
                  (no effect on salivation)

2. **Initial training:** First paired presentation of US and CS:
   CS (bell) + **US** (food) ----------------------------> **UR** (salivation)

3. **Final training:** After 5–9 paired presentations of CS with US:
   CS (bell) + **US** (food)---------------------------> **UR** (unconditioned salivation)
                                                                +
                                          ------> **CR** (conditioned salivation)

4. **Testing:** Present CS alone.
   CS (bell) -----------------------> **CR** (conditioned salivation)

FIGURE **3.4**   Pavlovian Conditioning Procedure

---

tially is a *neutral stimulus* with respect to the salivation response. After training, a new response is learned. The animal now salivates to the bell. When the bell comes to control salivation, it is called the **conditioned stimulus (CS).** The newly learned response—salivation to the bell—is called the **conditioned response (CR).** In summary, after repeated pairings of the CS (bell) with the US (taste of food), the bell is able to produce the learned, or conditioned, response of salivation.

Orienting Response.   As noted earlier, the bell doesn't initially cause salivation, but it does produce an *orienting reflex*. The dog makes head and ear adjustments in localizing the source of the sound. Recall that the four basic elements of conditioning are the CS, the US, the CR, and the time interval relating these two stimuli. The orienting reflex (OR) is not considered basic because (a) the OR rapidly changes with repeated trials; (b) during conditioning the experimenter's focus shifts to the conditioned response; and (c) changes in the OR are considered to be nonassociative (habituation), whereas Pavlovian conditioning is associative.

A Typical Pavlovian Conditioning Experiment

Let us conduct an idealized experiment along the lines that Pavlov reported. Our experiment can be characterized as appetitive *excitatory* conditioning (*in-*

hibitory conditioning is discussed later). Let us first set the CS, US, and time interval parameters. Recall from Chapter 1 that the specification of intensity, frequency, and duration of stimuli are *parameters* of the stimulus. As we shall see, conditioning outcomes are critically dependent on stimulus parameters.

Conditioning Parameters.   As experimenters, we set the parameters. Let the CS be a 500 hertz (Hz) frequency tone sounded at 70 dB loudness for 10 seconds (think of a 10-second-long doorbell). Let the US be 5 grams of meat powder dropped onto the animal's tongue (about ¼ teaspoon). The **CS–US interval** will be 30 seconds. By convention, the CS–US interval is measured from stimulus onset to stimulus onset—in the present example, from the first sound of the tone to the first taste of the meat.

Next, let us set the **intertrial interval** at 3 minutes, where a **trial** consists of a CS–US pairing, and the *intertrial interval* the amount of time between pairings. We will condition the dog for a total of 20 trials but will measure every fifth trial to see how much conditioning has taken place.

To summarize our hypothetical experiment, the stimulus parameters are

CS = 10.0 sec, 500 Hz tone at 70 dB
US = 5.0 gm meat powder
CS–US interval = 30.0 seconds
Intertrial interval = 3.0 minutes
Trials: *n* (number) = 20

Recognize that if we changed any of these stimulus parameters entering the dog's brain, the conditioning outcome would be different. Another way to say this is that within an S-R paradigm, the R is dependent on the S.

Measuring Conditioning.   How do we know if and when conditioning is completed? The researcher can measure changes in salivation only if he or she has some idea how much dogs salivate in the first place. Since an animal salivates when food is placed on its tongue, Pavlov was able to measure both *un*conditioned salivation (i.e., salivation to the food alone) as well as conditioned salivation when the tone was sounded (see Figure 3.4).

The first measure of salivation in the presence of the tone, prior to conditioning, is called a **baseline** measure of salivation. The baseline measure answers the question of how much saliva flows normally. That is, from where does the animal start? We may even want to present the 500 Hz tone and measure salivation before conditioning, just to assure ourselves that dogs don't salivate to this sound. After five trials, we want to test for conditioning. To do this, we measure salivation to the tone in the absence of the food. A test trial, presenting the tone (CS) without the food (US), is called **experimental extinction.** In this and many other conditioning procedures, tests of learning are "measured in extinction."

In our experiment, let us measure the total amount of saliva during the

10-second tone CS and, say, for 20 seconds following (total = 30 seconds). Also, let's measure salivation to the tone alone before the first trial (i.e., before conditioning) to establish a baseline of salivation and again on every fifth trial thereafter.

Conditioning Results.   The results of our hypothetical experiment are shown in Figure 3.5. Note that in this graph *only* the conditioned responses to the tone in extinction (i.e., in the absence of food) are plotted.

How Can We Conclude That Conditioning Has Occurred?

In Figure 3.5 how do we know that the change in salivation on test trials reflect conditioning? Might not salivation have occurred even if food was regularly presented but not the tone? Or if the tone *had* been sounded repeatedly and no food presented? Perhaps sounding a tone for 30 seconds every 3 minutes might drive the dog nuts, thereby increasing salivation!

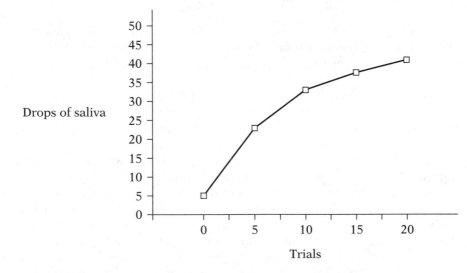

FIGURE 3.5   The Growth of Association

Typical plot of an acquisition function. Only the CS is presented on trials 0, 5, 10, 15, and 20. On all other trials, the tone and food are paired, and salivation to the food is not plotted.

Control Groups.   This is a conditioning experiment, and experiments need control groups. Pavlov's control group was a *within-subjects control*. During pretesting, the dog's baseline salivation was measured in the absence of either the CS or US. Note that this condition closely resembles cell d in the association matrix (Figure 3.1, p. 94). To conclude that conditioning is due to a tone-food association, however, additional control groups are needed. Recall that several nonassociative control groups are possible. A **habituation control group** receives only the CS, and a **sensitization control group** receives only the US (cells b and c, respectively, assuming that lightning can be considered a CS and thunder a US). The logic is to compare the effects of each stimulus alone to both together. Treatment effects due to the **association** of two stimuli can then be separated from single-stimulus effects.

Control groups in learning experiments are often referred to as *sham-treatment groups*. (Some researchers call the sensitization control group a *pseudoconditioning control*.) Rescorla (1967) has suggested the inclusion of a **random control group** in which both the CS and US are presented but never together in time. A random control group precludes association of the CS and US by not allowing them to be temporally contiguous.

Thought question: Why do experimenters almost always run groups of subjects rather than merely gathering data on a single animal?[8]

Experimental Extinction and Spontaneous Recovery

If, after conditioning, the CS continues to be presented without the US, the conditioned response diminishes. Because the CS is presented without the US, this procedure is also called **extinction** or **experimental extinction.** The plotted decline in the conditioned response is called an **extinction curve** or **extinction gradient** (see Figure 3.6). In the example we have been considering, salivation during *experimental extinction* is our measure of the strength of conditioning.

Theories of Extinction.   Why does extinction occur? Two possibilities are offered. First, the intentional "unpairing" of the CS and the US might be seen as breaking the learned association between them. An alternative approach, however, is to note the similarities between habituation and extinction. In both instances, responses diminish to repeatedly presented stimuli. It may be that one function of the US is to prevent habituation to the CS. When the US is removed (as is the case during extinction), the CS merely habituates. Recall that habituation is nonassociative. In the next chapter we further examine the interplay of associative and nonassociative factors under the topic of *latent inhibition*. Recall the acquisition function in Figure 3.5, and the argument that the

---

[8] By chance a given animal might not be representative of the population from which it is selected. Measuring the mean and variability of the behavior of a group of dogs, for example, would be a more reliable estimate of all dogs.

rate of conditioning is reflected by the slope of the line. We can also compare the slope of the extinction curve and measure the rate of extinction (see Figure 3.6). Indeed, the strength of conditioning typically is inferred from how long it takes the conditioned response to extinguish. Recall that the conditioned response is dependent on such conditioning variables as the nature of the CS and US and the number of previous conditioning trials. As a general rule, the conditioned response lasts longer, and the rate of extinction is slower, following many as opposed to a few conditioning trials.

Spontaneous Recovery. Suppose that the conditioned response has extinguished to the level depicted on the 14th extinction trial (solid line in Figure 3.6). Instead of conducting the next extinction trial in that session, we mercifully remove the dog from the conditioning laboratory and return it to its home cage. The next day we bring the dog back for the remaining extinction trials. We would measure a different outcome under these conditions (dashed

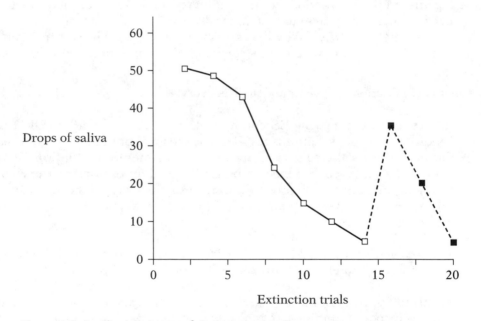

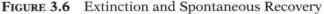

Extinction trials

FIGURE 3.6   Extinction and Spontaneous Recovery

A salivatory response to a CS has been previously conditioned. On extinction trials 1–14, the CS continues to be presented but food is no longer forthcoming. The drops of saliva decline over trials (open squares). If time is allowed to pass (i.e., the animal is returned to its home cage overnight) and experimental extinction trials resume the next day (dotted lines), the animal salivates more than would be expected, a phenomenon called *spontaneous recovery* (dark squares).

line). The level of extinction is not as great after the 24-hour interruption. As Figure 3.6 indicates, the conditioned salivary response on the 16th trial is stronger than it would have been without the 24-hour interruption.

Pavlov called this reappearance of conditioning following a delay in the extinction process **spontaneous recovery.** He argued that normal extinction is hastened by a process he called **internal inhibition.** He attributed internal inhibition to the dog's frustration at not receiving its expected food during the extinction trials. The frustration dissipates with the passage of time, allowing the true extinction rate to be seen.

Appetitive and Defense (Aversive) Conditioning

Pavlov used a sour solution instead of food as the unconditioned stimulus in some of his experiments. Dogs salivate unconditionally to sour tastes just as they do to tasty food. You might want to try dripping lemon juice on your tongue to test this. If you have a good imagination, just the thought of lemon juice on your tongue will produce salivation.[9]

In contrast to food-based appetitive conditioning, Pavlov used the term **defense conditioning** to describe experiments that used aversive unconditioned stimuli. In addition to sour solutions placed on the tongue, he used mild electric shock to condition a leg-withdrawal reflex. Conditioning experiments using aversive stimuli (as opposed to a food stimulus) are now referred to as **aversive conditioning.** A later section introduces three contemporary *aversive* conditioning procedures: eyelid conditioning, conditioned suppression (cf. *fear conditioning*), and taste aversion conditioning.

Conditioning and Perception

When an optometrist asks which of two lenses makes your visual world clearer, or when an audiologist asks you to press a button when you can no longer hear a sound, your responses communicate your personal sensory experiences. The study of how your responses are related to incoming physical stimuli is called *psychophysics*. In the same manner, measuring a dog's responses to systematically presented stimuli allows insight into its perceptual world. The results of Pavlovian conditioning experiments have provided important windows into the nature of the minds of dogs, nonverbal human infants, and other animals.

Because a dog initially salivates to food placed on the tongue but does not salivate to a ringing bell, we can infer that the dog can discriminate between tasting and hearing. When Pavlov's dogs began to salivate to the sight of the

---

[9] "Thinking" that produces reflexive responses sounds suspiciously like Pavlov's "psychic reflexes." Throughout this text we confront the fact that *thoughts* and *words* acquire conditioned stimulus properties. If, imagining a bite into a lemon, you do salivate, you are likely to be an excellent subject for hypnosis. Interesting, eh?

white lab coats worn by technicians, he concluded that the dog's visual world differed from its auditory world. Pavlov (1927/1960) called the portions of the dog's brain responsible for the different senses *analyzers*. In his late 19th-century understanding of brain functioning, the sound of the bell was perceived by the dog's "auditory analyzer," a picture by the "visual analyzer," touch by a "cutaneous analyzer," and so forth. Vision, audition, touch, taste, and smell, among other senses, define how animals discriminate their environment, and conditioning was viewed as a way to get one of these analyzers to signal another.

Likewise, Pavlov found that his dogs responded to similar stimuli in a similar manner. For example, a tone of 500 Hz heard by dogs (and humans) sounds more similar to a tone of 512 Hz than to one of 530 Hz. How do we know that? For humans this is an easy experiment. Because we have learned to use language to track the environment (words denoting concepts such as *greater than, more than, equal to,* and so on are learned early in life), we can simply ask humans, "Which two of these stimuli are more alike?" German psychophysicists did these experiments with humans more than 100 years ago.

Generalization.   But what about dogs and other animals? What do their psychophysical functions look like? Researchers this past century have measured the sensory functions of a variety of animals using Pavlovian methods. These animal psychophysicists have found that vertebrate nervous systems track the environment in a manner similar to the way humans do. One method used with dogs is given as an example. First condition a dog to respond to a 500-Hz tone and then measure salivation to various tones of differing frequencies. You would find that responses track the stimuli. That is, dogs respond most to the original CS (500 Hz), next most to closely related stimuli (for example, 490 and 510 Hz), and least to highly dissimilar stimuli (for example, 400 and 600 Hz). This tendency of animals to respond similarly to like stimuli is called **generalization.**

Generalization is a nonassociative process. The natural hardwired tendency of animals is to treat similar stimuli in a similar manner. This process is reflected in part by a brain organization honed by natural selection. There is survival value in recognizing that a snake is a snake no matter whether they all look or sound exactly alike. The importance of the concept of generalization is that we can account for responses to stimuli that have never been experienced firsthand. Learning one response to a particular situation generalizes to others. Our language reflects these properties, which are characteristic of all animal nervous systems. Following a particular experience (such as getting a traffic ticket in a school zone), we "learn" about similar situations never before encountered. I slow down not only in that particular school zone but also in all school zones. That is, my learned response generalizes to other school zones, hospital zones, and so forth. I exhibit highly adaptive behavior predicted from a limited but meaningful experience.

The nuances between stimuli can be trained. Musicians, artists, writers, and scientists cannot afford to generalize all musical notes, all colors and forms, all words and grammatical rules, and all laws and axioms. In the next chapter—under the topic of conditioned discrimination—we see how fine discriminations between stimuli can be learned.

Pavlov's Second Signal System

You look up and notice that your psych teacher is walking toward you. Too late to escape and worried about the exam you took from her a few days ago, you reluctantly make eye contact. She stops. You tense. "Congratulations," she says. "You made a high *B* on your last exam." "Yes!" you blurt out, your relief evident in every pore.

How can the words *congratulations* and *a high B* evoke elation? Pavlov extended his analysis of conditioning to learning human language. How do humans learn to attach meaning to words? The process is so basic that it is included here, early in the text. My intention is to alert students to the power and importance of Pavlov's ideas in accounting for important aspects of human behavior. As we see in later chapters, classical conditioning involves much more than how Russian dogs salivate!

Pavlov described how words can become conditioned stimuli that control conditioned responses. He called "words as CSs" the **second signal system** (Pavlov, 1927/1960). He reasoned that all words derive their meaning by *association* with signals from the environment. For example, seeing an apple is a signal, which, in his terminology, stimulates the animal's "visual analyzer." The visual representation of the apple is a signal of the real-world apple, one level of reality removed. Attaching the word *apple* to the visual signal of the apple is accomplished by the *second signal system*. The word *apple* is yet another level of reality removed from sensing the real-world apple.

The apple is real. "Seeing" the apple is the first signal of the real apple. Naming the apple *apple* is the second signal of the apple—hence, the *second signal system*.

Conditioning Language.   Pavlov further avowed that conditioning in the second signal system was not different from other kinds of conditioning. All the rules governing the formation of conditioned responses applied equally to language, he argued. More often than not, repetitions of word with object (i.e., trials) are necessary. Additionally, more intense stimuli lead to more rapid learning. The sequence of stimulus presentation is important.

A parent interacts with a child who is learning to talk. She presents to the child objects, relations, and actions and names them in close temporal contiguity—*apple* for apple and *hot* for a heated object. The word *good* is accompanied with a loving embrace. *Good* is the CS, and the loving embrace that follows it is the US. The sight and warmth of a flame are CSs. The words that signal these CSs—*hot, burn*—are paired with the pain of the flame. The flame and words describing it are thus conditioned. Later the child learns that more complicated behavior can be signaled by the word *congratulations*. That word, and many others, have been conditioned to control emotional responses. The Japanese word for *congratulations* does not control the emotional responses of English speakers.

Pavlov's observations are important for a number of reasons. As discussed further in Chapter 10, humans make only about 40 phonemic sounds. Cross-culturally, language patterns using these sounds vary widely. Languages as spoken sounds are meaningful only to the extent that particular sounds are associated with the environment through the process of Pavlovian conditioning. The nature of the word-object or word-activity associations determines the meaning of the word. *Algebra* has a different meaning to a mathematician than to a failing student. The word *algebra* produces different conditioned responses for the *A* and the *F* student. For a small child, no associations to the word *algebra* have formed, but most small children come to know the meaning of *good* and *no* early in their language environment.

Why do some students have a sinking feeling when they merely look at their algebra textbook or their psych professor? Ever cry after receiving bad news on the phone? These signals are controlling your emotional behavior. We return to the role of conditioning language in Chapter 10. There we see that another level of conditioning gives meaning to arbitrary visual signals—a process called *written language*. The written word is associated with the spoken sounds is associated with objects and actions in the environment through the process of conditioning. For the present, suffice it to say that words are arguably the most important CSs controlling human behavior.

Neural Basis of Association

Changes in the strength of connections between neurons parallel some associative conditioning phenomena. For example, neurons rapidly stimulated for a brief time show potentiation effects lasting for days and even weeks—a phenomenon called **long-term potentiation (LTP)** (Bliss & Lomo, 1973). Under some conditions, synaptic responses can be shown to express either LTP or similarly **long-term depression (LTD)** effects (Kombian & Malenka, 1994; Xie, Berger, & Barrionuevo, 1992). Furthermore, stimulating several axons simultaneously produces more LTP than stimulating only one neuron. This finding raises the possibility of long-lasting *associative* effects between neurons (Kelso, Ganong, & Brown, 1986).

LTP and LTD.   Are LTP and LTD likely mechanisms underlying associative learning in vertebrates? Perhaps, perhaps not. Extrapolating the measured effects of LTP or LTD on one or two "cooperating" neurons to the probable integration of hundreds of thousands of central nervous system (CNS) neurons in associative learning is a tremendous leap.

The question of neural substrates of behavior arises each time we look at different conditioning situations. Most contemporary conditioning preparations involve vertebrates, as we see in the next section, but a CNS isn't necessary for simple associative processes such as classical conditioning. Invertebrates, including *Aplysia* and insects, can be conditioned. Let us take a closer look at these experiments.

Invertebrate Conditioning Preparations

This chapter was introduced with descriptions of insect behavior: They see, walk, run, smell, taste, fly, mate, eat, lay eggs, and so on. The inference was that their primitive brains are programmed to do these things—by instinct, if you will—and that they live without either conscious awareness or an "executive in charge." The fact of the matter is that insects and other invertebrates can also benefit from their experiences. They can adaptively adjust their behavior; they can learn.

Associative processes are so general among animals that invertebrates are commonly used in learning experiments. You have already read about *Drosophilia*, a lowly invertebrate commonly used in studies of genetics (including behavioral genetics). The anatomy, physiology, and behavior of a close cousin, the common fly, have been investigated so thoroughly by Dethier (1978) and others that the functional significance of 280 of the animals 287 neurons is now known. Comparative psychologists who study learning in invertebrates recognize that simple animals account for 97% of all animal species. Lacking a CNS, they nonetheless learn in an associative manner (Abramson, 1994).

Conditioning Honeybees. The honeybee learns quickly, both in the field and in the laboratory (Batson, Hoban, & Bitterman, 1992; Bitterman, Menzel, Fietz, & Schäfer, 1983). A recent example of classical conditioning in the honeybee is provided by Buckabee and Abramson (1995). Brought into the laboratory, the bee's body is placed in a small metal tube with its head and antennae exposed (see Focus on Research 3.1). A sugar solution (US) is brought to the bee's mouth, and the reflexive response is proboscis extension. Bees do not extend their proboscis in response to smelling cinnamon oil, so this odor was used as a neutral CS. After 12 pairings of the cinnamon CS with the sugar water US, the smell of the cinnamon alone reliably produced proboscis extension.

Simple Animal Conditioning: Aplysia. Simple animals with simple nervous systems provide researchers with simple black boxes in which to poke around. In addition to bees, a tiny California marine snail, *Aplysia*, has been studied extensively (see Box 3.3). It is assuredly the case, however, that "conditioning" the few neurons found in *Aplysia* is different from the neuronal changes subserving associative conditioning in vertebrate brains. Why? By contrast with invertebrates, the brains of dogs, humans, and even pigeons are large and highly organized. Vertebrate brains allow a richness of sensitivity to environmental change, of perceptual knowledge of environment enhanced and medi-

FOCUS ON RESEARCH 3.1

Pavlovian Conditioning European Honeybees

Dolores Buckbee, Laboratory of Comparative Psychology and Behavioral Biology, Department of Psychology, Oklahoma State University, Stillwater

"The European honeybee (*Apis mellifera*) has proven to be an excellent invertebrate species that can be used to test traditional vertebrate learning paradigms. My research goal is to make certain that when we test any animal's learning capacities, we do so in a manner that is friendly to the physiology of the species. In Pavlovian conditioning, for example, we can't expect a honeybee to respond to the same unconditioned stimulus (meat powder) that elicited reflexive salivation in Pavlov's dogs! However, we do know that a honeybee will reflexively extend its proboscis when it is presented with a sugar-water US.

"Honeybees show remarkable abilities for associative learning. By pairing a neutral olfactory conditioned stimulus with a sugar-water US, we find extremely rapid acquisition of the conditioned proboscis extension response. This deceptively simple methodology, when performed with an eye to the physiological requirements of honeybees, is a sound basis for understanding the development of complex behavioral patterns. And since we are using a standard classical conditioning paradign, interspecies comparisons of learning abilities are possible."

ated by memory, and of plasticity of responsiveness unknown to and unknowable by *Aplysia*'s brain.

Where in the Vertebrate Brain Is Conditioning?

Several features of vertebrate brains were compared in Chapter 2. The purpose was to provide a neurological substrate for general processes of learning. Given the fact that so much of the brain is common among different vertebrates, learning can be compared readily from one species to another. Vertebrate brains have even more common processes at the cellular level.

As noted earlier, the brain/behavior questions arise each time we condition different animals. Dogs share with humans CNSs that have common fea-

Box 3.3   SIMPLE SYSTEMS APPROACH
TO ASSOCIATIVE LEARNING

In addition to sensitization and habituation, the gill-withdrawal reflex has been conditioned (Carew, Hawkins, & Kandel, 1983) by pairing a light touch (CS) of the siphon with electric shock to the tail (US). After several pairings, the CS elicits the CR of gill withdrawal. Shown is a discriminated Pavlovian conditioning preparation (also reported by Carew et al., 1983). In this preparation, lightly touching the mantle is the CS^- (not reinforced), whereas touching the siphon is the CS^+ reinforced. The changes in synaptic activity are indicated.

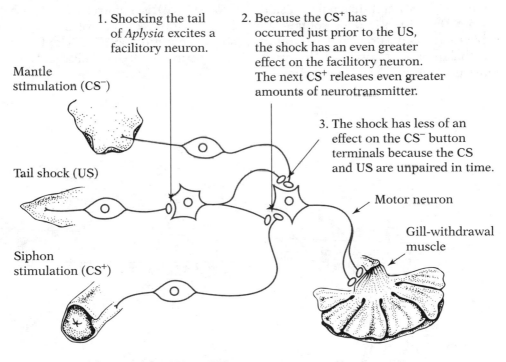

1. Shocking the tail of *Aplysia* excites a facilitory neuron.

2. Because the CS^+ has occurred just prior to the US, the shock has an even greater effect on the facilitory neuron. The next CS^+ releases even greater amounts of neurotransmitter.

3. The shock has less of an effect on the CS^- button terminals because the CS and US are unpaired in time.

Mantle stimulation (CS^-)

Tail shock (US)

Siphon stimulation (CS^+)

Motor neuron

Gill-withdrawal muscle

Source: Adapted from Pinel, 1993, p. 515.

tures. In Box 3.4, some of the parts of the brain that must be involved in conditioning responses to sights and sounds are indicated. Note that the schematic follows an S-R framework in tracing the auditory and taste stimulus in and the salivary response out. Other integral brain parts involved in food-based learning *not* indicated in Box 3.4 are the hypothalamus, limbic system, and hippocampus.

Box 3.4 Peeking Inside the Black Box:
Spotski's Brain

Salivary conditioning in dogs is initiated by nerve pathways in the brain. The salivary reflex begins with stimulation of the dog's taste nerves, primarily the *chorda tympani* (branch of Cranial Nerve VII), which synapses in the *solitary nucleus* in the medulla (brain stem). Interneurons from the solitary nucleus synapse in the adjacent *salivatory nucleus*, also in the medulla, completing a Sherrington-like reflex of salivation. For sights and sounds to activate the salivatory nucleus, both the thalamus and cortex of the brain must become involved. For sights, the *optic nerve, lateral geniculate nucleus* (LGN), *striate cortex,* and other areas subserving vision can come to elicit the reflex. For sounds, the *cochlear nucleus* (and other nuclei) in the *medulla, medial geniculate nucleus* (MGN) of the thalamus, and primary and secondary projection areas of *auditory cortex* are involved. For all conditioning, a midbrain structure called the *hippocampus* (not shown) is involved. The cerebellum is intimately involved in tone-shock conditioning. See Klopf (1988) for a neuronal model of classical conditioning of vertebrates.

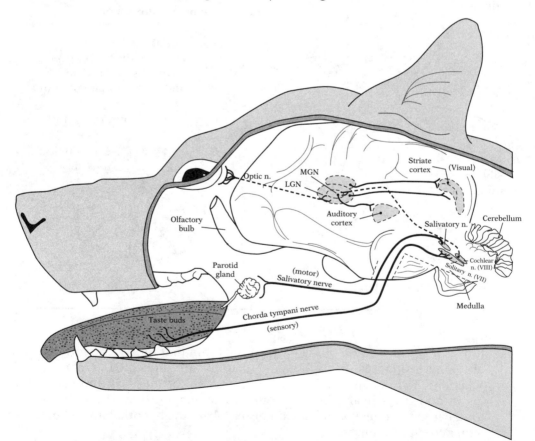

Interim Summary

1. Pavlovian *salivary conditioning* involves modification of the food-saliva reflex. Pavlov called food the *unconditioned stimulus* (US) and salivation to food the *unconditioned response* (UR).

2. Neutral stimuli that do not control the feeding reflex produce *orienting responses.*

3. By pairing neutral sights and sounds—Pavlov's conditioned stimuli (CSs)—with food for a number of trials, CSs alone produce the conditioned response (CR) of salivation.

4. The *CS–US interval* is measured from the onset of the CS to the onset of the US. The *intertrial interval* is the time between conditioning trials.

5. Associative conditioning is inferred after comparing conditioning results with one or more between-subjects control groups. Control groups include *habituation* controls, *sensitization* controls, and *random* controls.

6. The rate of conditioning and extinction is determined by the parameters of the CSs and USs.

7. In *extinction*, the CS is presented in the absence of the US. Following extinction, recovery of the conditioned response to a higher level is known as *spontaneous recovery.*

8. Using food as the US defines *appetitive conditioning;* using aversive stimulation defines defense, or *aversive conditioning.*

9. *Generalization* is the nonassociative process by which similar stimuli produce similar responses.

10. Pavlov's *second signal system* describes how words can become CSs that control emotional responses. The most important CSs controlling human behavior are words.

11. The associative process is mediated by brain mechanisms. Long-term potentiation (LTP) and long-term depression (LTD) are relatively long-lasting physiological changes in the functioning of neurons that possibly underlie conditioning.

12. Bees and *Aplysia*—two invertebrates lacking CNSs—can be conditioned. Cinnamon oil has been used as a CS to condition a proboscis extension (CR) in the honeybee. The proboscis reflex is elicited by sugar water (US).

13. Vertebrates have CNSs with many common features. It is likely that some similarly conditioned responses in different species use homologous parts of the brain.

Contemporary Conditioning Methods: An Introduction

Note again the variety of physiological reflexes outlined in Table 3.1. Though few laboratories now conduct appetitive conditioning experiments with dogs,

Pavlov-inspired experiments continue to be conducted and the results published. Different reflexes in other species of animals are conditioned. Data and theory development using contemporary methods far exceed those gathered from Pavlov's salivary reflex experiments. A brief introduction to a few of the more important methodologies follows.[10] All but one use aversive conditioning. The reader is advised to become familiar with the basic terminology and procedures used in each method. Methods and results from each procedure are used interchangeably to build and expand on a general theory of conditioning.

Fear Conditioning

Any of a number of intense environmental stimuli produce pain or fear-inducing responses in animals. For example, loud noises, electric shocks, and sudden loss of support disrupt normal homeostatic functioning in animals. Such stimuli induce changes in the *autonomic nervous system* that in turn activate us to action. When a normally neutral stimulus (such as a tone CS) is repeatedly paired with a disruptive stimulus (such as an electric shock US), conditioned fear to the tone results. An example of fear conditioning in humans is presented in Box 3.5.

One way to measure a **conditioned emotional response** in the laboratory is to sound a tone (CS) that has been paired with electric shock (US) while a rat is pressing a lever to obtain food (Estes & Skinner, 1941). The intensity of the shock is adjusted just high enough to cause the rat to momentarily stop the lever-pressing response. After a number of tone-shock pairings, the rat learns (is conditioned) to interrupt lever pressing when the tone is sounded. Because the lever-pressing response is disrupted in the presence of the tone, this method is called **conditioned suppression.** The conditioned suppression technique is one of the most popular methods used in the contemporary study of classical conditioning. A conditioned suppression experiment and the results of fear conditioning in the laboratory are presented in Figure 3.7.

Both positive and negative conditioned emotional responses are easily attached to words via Pavlov's second signal system. For example, a father's booming voice saying "No!" attaches fear to the word. When someone says "good job"—accompanied by a pat on the back—a state of well-being accompanies, and is conditioned by, those words.

Rabbit, Rat, and Human Eye-Blink Conditioning

A puff of air to a human, rabbit, or rat's eye elicits a reflexive blinking response. When a tone (CS) is presented immediately prior to the air puff (US),

---

[10] A method called *autoshaping* is discussed in Chapter 5. Autoshaping contains instrumental and species-specific tendencies as well as classical components.

Box 3.5 AN UNUSUAL EXAMPLE OF FEAR CONDITIONING

During the 1960s I was one of a number of paid U.S. Air Force volunteers who rode "impact sleds." In one phase of this research, airmen tested space suits that eventually were worn by Apollo astronauts. Would the suits tear on impact, or would critical helmet fittings fail during takeoffs, landings, EVAs (space walks), moon walks, and so on? Short on money, we volunteered to be strapped to a sled that was propelled along rails. Impacts were varied to simulate the various angles and *g* forces astronauts would experience in emergency situations. (Notice the bent nose and lips in this photo, taken with high speed film at the point of impact.)

A 40-second countdown preceded the sled acceleration and final impact. During these 40 seconds, a European-style emergency vehicle horn ("dee doo, dee doo") reverberated throughout the test site. This distinctive signal accompanied the anticipation and high autonomic nervous system arousal of being strapped to a sled soon to be slammed into a barrier. To this day, emergency vehicles in Paris and London cause heart palpitations and sphincter-control problems for at least one of these now aging airmen.

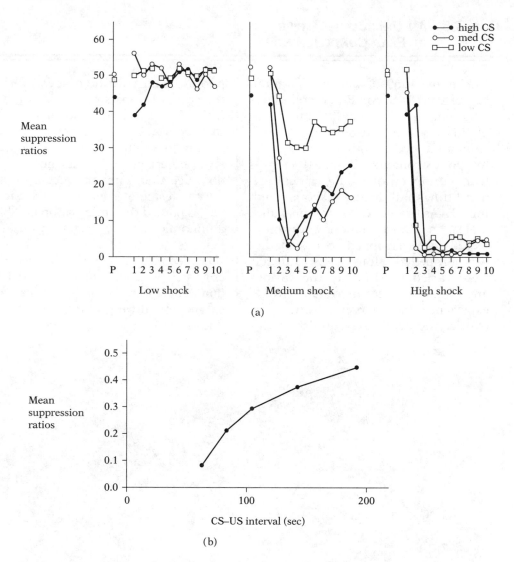

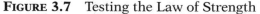

(a)

(b)

FIGURE 3.7   Testing the Law of Strength

Conditioned suppression tests of Pavlov's law of strength are reported by Annau and Kamin (1960). Upper panel: Note that increasing CS intensity (low, medium, and high) and US intensity (left, middle, and right panels, respectively) led to both faster acquisition and lower suppression ratios. (Lower suppression ratios equal better conditioning.) In the lower panel (redrawn from Kamin, 1965), suppression ratios are plotted as a function of the interval between a 1.5-second tone CS and a brief electric shock US. Data are means for acquisition days 2 through 5.

these animals can be conditioned to blink to the sound of the tone. A number of investigators have used this classical preparation for many years. The generality of associative theory has been addressed (Gormezano, Kehoe, & Marshall, 1983).

Two examples of the outcome of conditioning eye-blink responses in rabbits and humans can be found in Figure 3.8. Rabbit conditioning is shown in Figure 3.8a. The percentage of conditioned responses (out of 82 conditioning trials per day) is plotted for 8 acquisition days. Note the relative lack of conditioning in the early trials. There is a regular growth of response (as indicated by the percentage of conditioned responses on each day) throughout the 600 plus trial acquisition periods.

Figure 3.8b shows the outcomes of conditioning eye-blink responses of humans (Hartman & Grant, 1960). Students were paid to be attached to an apparatus not unlike the one used with rabbits. In different treatment groups, the tone CS was always followed by an air-puff US (Group 100%), and the results were compared with treatment groups that received extra CSs (i.e., Groups 75%, 50%, and 25%).[11] For present purposes, simply note the growth of the acquisition of the conditioned response over 40 CS–US trials.

Salivary and Eye-Blink Conditioning Compared. In comparing Figures 3.8a and 3.8b, note that the form of the acquisition curves are similar to those depicted for salivary conditioning in dogs (cf. Figure 3.5b). Both rabbits and humans (and rats; Schmajuk & Christiansen, 1990) require many more trials to condition an eye-blink response, however. Dogs required 5 to 9 trials for salivary conditioning, yet humans took 15 to 40 trials, and rabbits several hundred trials in eye-blink conditioning. What is going on? Why does eye-blink conditioning require more trials than salivary conditioning? And why do rabbits require hundreds more trials than humans? A literature review by Lennartz and Weinberger (1992) found that acquisition during conditioning could be characterized as being either fast or slow. Fast acquisition included the conditioned suppression procedure and conditioned changes in blood pressure, respiration, pupil size, and heart rate. Reflex systems that were conditioned slowly included eyelid, nictitating membrane, and flexion responses. Why this is the case is not known.

Neural Basis for Eyelid Conditioning. Many neuroscientists in this century assumed as did Pavlov that the cerebral hemispheres mediated learning. This is not the case. Several neuronal models for eyelid conditioning have been proposed (for reviews, see Lavond, Kim, & Thompson, 1993; Thompson, 1986; for representative research, see Sears & Steinmetz, 1991). Neurons in a discrete area of the cerebellum (called the *lateral interpositus nucleus*) have been found to underlie the tone–air puff conditioning of the rabbit's nictitating membrane (McCormick & Thompson, 1984). One implication of Richard F. Thompson's

---

[11] Extra CSs were presented but *not* followed by a US.

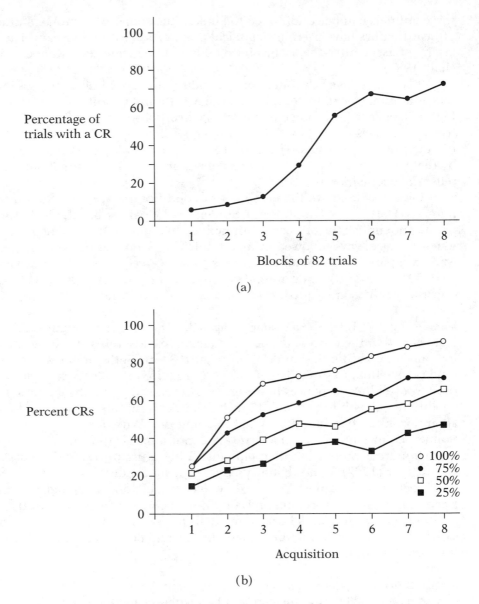

FIGURE 3.8 A Comparison of Human and Rabbit
Eyelid Conditioning

The increase in percentage of conditioned eye-blink responses in rabbits is
plotted as a function of training days. (See text.) Four groups of humans
received 40 pairings of a light (CS) followed by an air puff (US) to the
eye. Group 25% received 120 additional CSs without USs; Group 50%
received an additional 40 CSs; and Group 75% received an additional 14
CSs. Note that conditioning was degraded to the extent that the CS was
presented in the absence of the US.

research is that "Pavlovian conditioning" is not centrally represented. Rather, certain brain areas will underlie salivary conditioning, others taste aversion learning, and yet other areas eye-blink conditioning. Appetitive and defense conditioning, though behaviorally similar, may have quite different anatomical loci.

Taste Aversion Conditioning

Several thousand experiments on a variety of animals over the past 30 years have made **taste aversion conditioning** another popular method of studying Pavlovian conditioning (see Riley & Tuck, 1985, for a bibliography of these experiments). In animal experiments, rats are allowed to drink a novel flavored solution (the CS) and then are made sick by radiation or illness-inducing toxins (the US). Conditioned taste aversions to the novel flavor result. In comparison with control rats not made sick, the conditioned rats no longer prefer the target flavor (Garcia, Kimeldorf, & Koelling, 1955).

Humans have an intuitive grasp of this kind of conditioning because in our lifetimes, many of us become sick after eating or drinking. Often a particular flavor or food item is tagged as the culprit. A personal vignette: At the age of six I became sick after eating fresh pineapple. I disliked pineapple for many years afterward, and even today I remember the incident all too vividly. Humans can also have taste aversions conditioned through Pavlov's second signal system. A student related that her grandfather lived with her family, and she grew up listening to his complaints about one particular food item. It seems that he had nothing to eat except lamb for weeks at a time while stationed overseas during the Korean War. As a result, he was vociferous as to how repugnant lamb tasted. Years later, this student relates that she first encountered lamb at a formal meal. When the host announced that they were having a leg of lamb, she was overcome with cold sweats, a churning stomach, and nausea. She poked the food around as long as she could and then took a bite and gagged. The taste, she related, was fine; it was the idea of it—associatively conditioned through words describing the meal—that made her sick.

This application of learning to an understanding of both normal and abnormal appetites continues in Chapter 7. Eileen Bernstein (Focus on Research 3.2) applies taste aversion conditioning concepts to her research. She is attempting to understand eating disorders in children who are undergoing treatment for cancer.

One-Trial, Long-Delay Learning. Taste aversion learning by humans and animals takes place quickly—often in a single trial. Add to that the fact that conditioning occurs over a long delay between taste and illness. These two aspects of taste aversion learning made it difficult for John Garcia to convince journal editors that it was a classically conditioned response. Because tastes and illness can be associated over a long delay in a single trial, this conditioning methodology is a popular one. For example, taste aversion methodology is

FOCUS ON RESEARCH 3.2

Tumor Anorexia: Application of an Animal Model

Eileen Bernstein, Department of Psychology, University of Washington, Seattle

"My early work in the area of taste aversions and cancer indicated that food aversions arise not only as a consequence of chemotherapy treatment but also as a consequence of the disease itself. Using an animal model, our findings suggested that aversions that develop as a result of the association of tumor growth with consumption of specific foods were causally related to the depressions of food intake and body weight known as *tumor anorexia*. These observations led me to ask whether food aversion acquisition involves . . . classical conditioning. Thus, a taste previously paired with nausea could, upon reexposure, be capable of triggering an illness or nausea response. My current work explores the hypothesis that conditioned illness triggered by food stimuli plays a mediating role in the development of anorexia symptoms. Relevant publications are Bernstein and Borson (1986) and Meachum and Bernstein (1990)."

now used to condition immune system functioning (Ader, 1985; Husband, 1992), as we see in Chapter 7. The apparent simplicity of this preparation also makes it a favorite for those researchers attempting to find the neural basis of conditioned taste aversions (see Chambers, 1990).

Summary of Contemporary Conditioning Methods

Table 3.2 summarizes the contemporary conditioning methods discussed in this section. Each is compared with Pavlov's appetitive and defense salivary conditioning preparations.

Interim Summary

1. In *conditioned suppression*, tones or lights (CS) are paired with electric shock (the US). Conditioning is measured by the degree to which the tone or light CS suppresses lever-pressing responses (the CR) in rats.

TABLE 3.2 Comparison of Contemporary Conditioning Methodologies

Name of Procedure	*US*	*UR*	*CS*	*CR*
Pavlov's appetitive salivatory conditioning (dogs)	Food	Salivation	Bell, metronome, pictures, cutaneous stimuli	Salivation
Pavlov's defense (aversive) conditioning (dogs)	Sour flavor	Salivation	Bell, metronome, pictures, cutaneous stimuli	Salivation
Proboscis extension (bees and other insects)	Sweet flavor	Proboscis extension	Cinnamon odor	Proboscis extension
Rabbit eyelid conditioning (rabbits, humans)	Air puff to eye	Eye blink	Tone, lightflash	Eye blink
Conditioned suppression (*Conditioned fear*) (rats, pigeons)	Electric shock	Stops lever-pressing response	Tone, lightflash	Stop lever-pressing response
Conditioned taste aversion (rats, humans)	Toxin	Sickness, loss of appetite	Flavored fluid	Loss of appetite

2. When tones or lights (CSs) signal an aversive air puff to the eye (US), the procedure is known as *eye-blink conditioning*. Eye-blink conditioning is typically conducted on rabbits and humans. After conditioning, the CS can evoke a reflexive eye-blink CR.

3. Conditioned taste aversions are studied in rats, humans, and other animals. A flavor (the CS) is paired with toxin (the US), and conditioned responses take the form of learned aversions to flavors. One-trial, long-delay learning can be studied using the taste aversion conditioning methodology.

VARIABLES THAT AFFECT CONDITIONING

Pavlov was interested in discovering what events, or variables, control the conditioning process. Why did some of his dogs learn more quickly than others? Why were some CSs more effective in producing conditioned salivation than others? Why is it that conditioning tends to persist (last longer) following conditioning procedure A compared to procedure B?

Resistance to Extinction.   For example, Pavlov noted not only that his dogs would salivate more after 20 conditioning trials than 10 trials but also that the conditioned response lasted longer in extinction. That is, there is more **resistance to extinction** of the conditioned response after more trials have been accomplished compared to extinction after only a few trials. Resistance to extinction is one of the more important ways in which we can compare conditioning outcomes.

Five Rules of Conditioning

Let us begin by listing five rules that Pavlov and other experimenters have discovered that govern how associations are formed:

1. Number of trials rule.
2. CS intensity rule.
3. US intensity rule.
4. CS–US interval rule.
5. CS–US, or US–CS sequencing rule.

1. Number of trials rule. Pavlov was the first laboratory scientist to measure how conditioning systematically improves as more trials are conducted. In Figure 3.5 note that more salivation is evident on the 15th trial than on the 5th or the 10th trial. As a general rule, *the magnitude and persistence of the conditioned response are directly related to the number of conditioning trials.*

Intuitively obvious though it may be, why more than one trial is typically necessary for conditioning is a matter of speculation. Sometimes only one trial is necessary for conditioning to occur. The questions of how many trials and why more than one trial continue to be raised.

What else leads to *faster acquisition* and greater *resistance to extinction* of the conditioned response? In addition to the number of trials, Pavlov found three other interrelated factors of conditioning. Collectively, these next three rules are known as Pavlov's **law of strength** (where strength refers to the magnitude, or amount of, conditioning).

2. CS intensity rule. If a louder bell is used (i.e., a stronger, more intense CS), the dog conditions faster and the training lasts longer. This finding is not as intuitively obvious as the number of trials variable. Perhaps it is the case that Pavlov is better able to capture the dog's attention during conditioning by using a louder bell. For whatever reason, we know from this and other experiments that *attentional factors* are as important in conditioning as they are in other learning situations. For example, most of us must pay attention to what we are reading if we want to learn and remember the material. One theory is that the CS "signals" that the next few seconds (minutes?) are important, that is, that something important is about to happen. More intense signals also activate more of the nervous system that may in some way enhance the associative process.

3. US intensity rule. If more food is used in the conditioning situation (i.e., a more intense US is used), dogs condition more rapidly and the training lasts longer. From this and other experiments, we know that the magnitude of a food reward is an important variable in conditioning. A related variable is the quality of the reward. Tastier foods also lead to better conditioning than do nontasty foods.

Magnitude of *punishment* is also an important variable in *aversive* conditioning, as we see later. Stronger poisons condition greater food aversions, and higher intensities of shock produce more rapid acquisition and longer-lasting conditioned fear responses (see Figure 3.10).

4. CS–US interval rule. When the interval between the bell and the food is short (i.e., when the CS–US interval is only a second or two), dogs condition faster and the training persists longer over time than is the case if the bell and food were separated in time. That is, *contiguity* of stimuli in time, or temporal contiguity, is an important factor in conditioning. Likewise, the tone-to-shock interval in conditioned suppression (as is shown in Figure 3.7) is an important variable in learning fear responses. As predicted, the longer the interval between tone and shock, the less conditioning is likely to occur.

5. CS–US, or US–CS sequencing rule. The fifth rule of Pavlovian conditioning is that the *sequencing of stimuli determines the nature, or direction, of the response to be learned.* Let us do another thought experiment. Assume that you are a rat trapped in an experimental test chamber. Every time you hear a tone, you receive a brief electric shock within 5 seconds. More than likely, after 10 trials you would use the tone to prepare yourself for the shock—perhaps by adjusting your posture—to minimize the effects of the shock. (In fact, rats do just that.)

Now imagine a slightly different conditioning situation: You are first shocked, and then 5 seconds later you hear the brief tone. The tone no longer predicts the shock; rather, the shock predicts the tone. The tone is an "all-clear" signal; it predicts a safe period, the intertrial interval, during which no shocks will occur. *Question:* Would your responses to the tone differ in the two instances? Obviously, yes. Just as the tone acquires fear-inducing properties in the first situation, in the second situation, after 10 conditioning trials, you can begin to relax when you hear the tone. The tone predicts that the ordeal is over.

What have we learned from our thought experiment? That merely knowing the first four rules of conditioning described in the preceding section did not allow us to predict the experimental outcome. Note that the only thing that differs in the two situations is the *sequencing* of the stimuli. Even with full knowledge of the number of trials and by holding constant both tone and shock intensity and the time interval connecting the stimuli, two very different response outcomes were learned.

Law of Strength.   As noted earlier, the three rules of conditioning dealing with CS and US intensity and the interval of time relating them are collectively known as Pavlov's *law of strength*. Such rules governing conditioning outcomes are not really "laws" comparable to Henry's law or Boyles' law in chemistry. Rather, the law of strength is better understood as a series of three interrelated functional relationships that summarize the outcomes of three separate experiments. Pavlovian conditioning has three variables (i.e., CS, US, and CS-US interval). Holding any two constant and systematically manipulating the other one has a predictable outcome. Knowing this, experimenters can adjust stimulus parameters to better predict experimental results. Extended discussion of the law of strength can be found in Gray (1964) and in Razran (1971). Tests of the law of strength by Kamin (1965) using the conditioned suppression methodology are detailed in Figure 3.7.

Summary of Five Rules of Conditioning.   To summarize, five main factors determine the *rate* of acquisition of conditioning, the *magnitude* of the conditioned response, and the *persistence* of conditioning as measured by resistance to extinction. Rule 1 is that the number of conditioning trials determines how much conditioning occurs. Rules 2, 3, and 4 compose Pavlov's law of strength: Other factors held constant, the magnitude of a conditioned response varies as direct functions of CS and US intensity and as an indirect function of the CS–US interval. Rule 5 states that the order of the CS and US determines the nature, or direction, of the response to be learned.

Other dimensions of stimuli that play an important role in conditioning are *qualitative* parameters (whether the stimuli are sights, sounds, foods, etc.) and other *quantitative* parameters (including *how long* a stimulus lasts). More is said about these latter variables in the next chapter dealing with more complex conditioning situations.

Temporal Factors in Conditioning

Our preceding thought experiment did not begin to exhaust the many possible ways in which two stimuli can be related in time. Several of the more important of these *temporal relationships* between the CS and US are diagrammed in Figure 3.9. This type of diagram emphasizes the quantitative parameters of *onset, duration,* and *offset* of the stimuli, as well as their relationship to each other in time. Not depicted are other dimensions of stimuli that play an important role in conditioning: *quantitative* parameters such as stimulus inten-

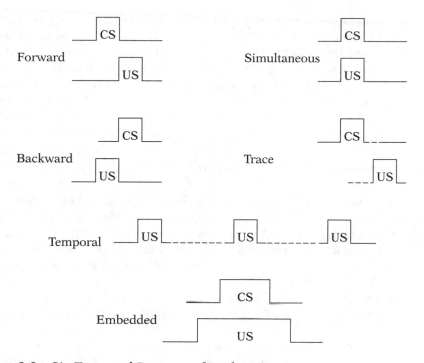

FIGURE 3.9   Six Temporal Patterns of Pavlovian Conditioning

In Pavlovian conditioning, stimulus events with measurable onsets, durations, and offsets are arranged in time. Note that in temporal conditioning, the US events are presented on a regular schedule without an explicit CS. The passage of time becomes the CS, and dogs reliably salivate prior to the presentation of the food stimulus.

sity (brighter, quieter, etc.) and *qualitative* dimensions (sights, sounds, tastes, etc.).

Forward and Trace Conditioning.   Let us begin by more formally defining the now familiar instances of Pavlovian conditioning that have already been introduced, namely, forward conditioning and trace conditioning. In **forward conditioning,** the CS onset precedes the US onset, and both stimuli overlap in time. Compare the stimulus arrangements of both types of conditioning in Figure 3.9. Note that **trace conditioning** is a special example of forward conditioning in that both the CS onset *and offset* precede the US onset. Both arrangements are typical of experiments described by Pavlov and others in this chapter.

Remember that Pavlov's law of strength describes how conditioning diminishes if the CS and US are separated in time. Hence, in trace conditioning there are limits as to how much gap can exist between the CS and US.[12] If the interval is too long, the two stimuli cannot be associated. For example, imagine being the dog that is conditioned with a (tone) CS-US (food). The tone sounds for 10 seconds, and the food is presented 30 seconds from the tone's onset (hence the CS-US interval is 30 seconds). After a number of trace-conditioning trials such as these, you would likely learn a conditioned salivary response. If, however, the CS–US interval were 2 hours rather than 30 seconds, you would most likely *not* be conditioned to salivate to the tone.

Simultaneous and Embedded Conditioning.   You would be mistaken if you were led to conclude from this example that conditioning results when stimuli are contiguous (close together in time) but does *not* result when stimuli are far removed in time. As Figure 3.9 illustrates, among the most contiguous of stimulus relationships is one called **simultaneous conditioning,** in which the CS and US have identical onsets, durations, and offsets. Simultaneous conditioning involves relatively brief conditioned stimuli (tones and lights lasting only a second) paired with short duration unconditioned stimuli (a tiny amount of food or a brief electric shock). Under these circumstances, very little conditioning occurs, even after many trials (Kamin, 1965; Pavlov, 1927/1960). Apparently, strict contiguity of stimuli is *not* a sufficient condition for association to occur.

Embedded conditioning is a variation of simultaneous conditioning in which the onset and offset of one of the stimulus elements occur sometime during the other element (Heth, 1976; see also Figure 3.9). Embedded conditioning situations often involve the pairing of longer duration stimuli. For example, in taste aversion conditioning, a flavor might be experienced for several minutes in the middle of an illness episode lasting several hours. The flavor (CS) can be said to be *embedded* in illness (US). Conditioned flavor aversions *do* occur in these situations (Barker, Suarez, & Grey, 1974).

The differentiation of embedded conditioning from simultaneous conditioning is important for another reason. Outside of the laboratory, timing arrangements encountered by animals are not as neat as they are made by laboratory researchers. Most stimuli encountered in natural contexts are of longer duration than 1.0 seconds, and the relationship of these stimuli with other stimuli often varies across trials, yet conditioning occurs despite the lack of precision in timing. The embedded conditioning category includes (but is not restricted to) conditioning situations using drugs, flavors and foods, toxins, recovery from illness, and other long-duration stimulus complexes.

---

[12] Historically, the term *trace* in *trace conditioning* refers to a memory trace theory. In this theory when the conditioned stimulus is presented, it is conceptualized as being entered into memory. At stimulus offset, it persists as a memory trace just long enough to be associated with the US when *it* is presented.

Backward Conditioning.   In **backward conditioning,** the US onset precedes the CS onset. The outcome of this temporal sequencing confused even Pavlov! Again, contiguity predicts that stimulus association should occur, and it does. The *direction* of conditioning, however, is less predictable. That is, many such stimulus arrangements produce what is called *inhibitory* conditioning, the *opposite* of excitatory conditioning, especially after many conditioning trials have been conducted.

Recall the discussion in the section on stimulus sequencing. In forward conditioning with dogs, the animal salivates to the tone CS. In backward conditioning the dog suppresses salivation to the tone. In conditioned suppression experiments with rats, tone-shock (forward) sequences condition fear responses while shock-tone (backward) sequences condition "safety" responses. We have much more to say about excitatory and inhibitory conditioning in the next chapter.

Temporal Conditioning.   **Temporal conditioning** is unusual in that other than the passage of time, the CS is unspecified. Pavlov noted that following regularly spaced placements of food on the dog's tongue, salivation eventually began to occur just prior to food delivery. Pavlov's observation is an important one. Time schedules are principal ways that civilized humans organize events and responses in their world, and the passage of time can and does act as a signal to control these responses. We often eat at 12 noon *because* it is 12 noon, whether we are hungry or not. Moreover, in laboratory experiments, the passage of time can be a confounding factor. That is, animals (like humans) may anticipate when certain treatments are likely to occur and adjust their responses accordingly. Another way to say this is that "time of day" and "time between treatments" provide the animal important contextual cues. That these cues affect their responses must be taken into account in the interpretation of treatment effects.

The real world is where we are headed. While introducing you to basic laboratory methods, this chapter should have raised some questions as well. In comparing John Grady's horse-training experience with laboratory studies, we raised the issue of ecological validity of laboratory studies. How relevant are laboratory studies? Another issue has to do with mapping the behavioral complexity found in the world to laboratory experiments. Can we design experiments that resemble learning experiences in the real world? One solution, as we see in the next chapter, is to make experiments more complicated. The experiments become more difficult to follow, but the outcomes are more satisfying. Let us move on.

Interim Summary

1. Time arrangements connecting stimuli determine their associability and the direction of the conditioned response.

2. *Forward* and (short) *trace* arrangements are the best for conditioning most stimuli.

3. *Simultaneous* and *embedded* timing relationships work for some intense, long-duration stimuli but typically *not* for brief stimuli.

4. The conditioned response following a few *backward* conditioning trials *may* reflect excitatory conditioning, but many more trials *usually* indicate inhibitory conditioning.

5. Finally, *temporal conditioning* results from regularly scheduled unconditioned stimuli; the passage of time can act as a conditioned stimulus.

CHAPTER SUMMARY

1. Reflexes are involuntary, adaptive responses. Most learned behaviors involve a modification of these inherited response tendencies.

2. Single stimuli acting alone can produce relatively permanent nonassociative learning effects known as *habituation* and *sensitization*.

3. *Habituation* refers to reduced responsiveness to a stimulus following repeated stimulation by that stimulus.

4. *Sensitization* refers to increased responsiveness for a time period following a relatively intense stimulus.

5. Stimulus events range from simple to complex. Associative and nonassociative effects vary as a function of stimulus complexity.

6. The two-stage theory of association describes how animals first learn that two events are correlated and second that one event appears to cause the other.

7. General process learning focuses on association formation that is common to all animals.

8. Reflexive behavior can be modified by simple conditioning procedures developed by Ivan Pavlov and others.

9. Pavlovian, or classical, conditioning involves modification of a reflex by pairing it with a neutral stimulus, which eventually comes to control the reflex.

10. Pavlovian salivary conditioning involves modification of the food-saliva reflex. Food, the unconditioned stimulus (US), causes reflexive salivation (the UR). A bell (conditioned stimulus, or CS) paired with food soon produces salivation, the conditioned response (CR).

11. Control groups for associative conditioning include habituation controls, sensitization controls, and random controls.

12. Pavlov's second signal system describes how the sounds making up words can act as CSs that signal objects and actions in the environment.

13. Simple systems approaches include measurement of individual neurons in the invertebrate *Aplysia* and classical conditioning in invertebrates such as the bee.

14. Conditioning methodologies in current use include simple systems, eyeblink, taste aversion, and fear conditioning.

15. Five rules that predict the effectiveness of conditioning are (a) the number of trials, (b) CS intensity, (c) US intensity, (d) CS-US interval, and (e) the order of presentation of the CS and US.

16. Learning is typically measured in extinction.

17. Forward conditioning and trace conditioning (CS before US) are more effective than backward (CS follows US) or simultaneous conditioning.

DISCUSSION QUESTIONS

1. Recently, I asked several hundred students about thunder and lightning and found that more than half did not remember the physics taught in elementary and secondary schools (see footnote 4). Most thought that thunder and lightning occurred simultaneously and that lightning only seemed to occur before thunder "because light travels faster than sound in air." Why do you think that more people remembered the physics of sound and light transmission in air rather than the physics of lightning heats air that causes thunder when the expanded air molecules collapse? Do one or more of the *British associationists'* four rules (i.e., contiguity, intensity, frequency, and similarity) help to explain this misattribution of causality? *Hint:* Which of these two rules of physics have you heard most often?

2. The Coolidge effect (Carlson, 1992) refers to the fact that males of some (most?) species of mammals and birds respond with more interest to new sexual partners than to familiar partners (i.e., ones they had copulated with in the immediately preceding time period). Is this an example of habituation to familiar partners? Can you identify in this example a learning-performance distinction?

3. Note that in Box 3.1, successive blocks of habituation and "rehabituation" eventually produce near zero respond-

ing. Imagine that you are the human subject depicted in the lower figure and that you no longer respond to the stimulation after the sixth block of trials in a given session. What do you think would happen if you were to be stimulated the next day or a week later? Is it likely that your "fully habituated" response would return? Is this similar to the phenomenon of *spontaneous recovery?*

4. Manual stimulation of the genitals typically produces sexual arousal. Erotic daydreams can also produce sexual arousal. Can you identify unconditioned and conditioned reflexes in these examples?

5. For years digitalis has been used pharmacologically to stimulate the heart's pumping action, thereby increasing cardiac output. A typical daily dosage maintains a fairly constant level of digitalis in blood serum. Often patients maintained on this drug suffer both nausea and appetite suppression (anorexia) that physicians and pharmacologists alike treat as side effects of the drug's action. Can you make the case that some of the appetite disturbances might be learned?

Now frame the foregoing in terms of the attribution of causality within *contingency* and *contiguity* frameworks. Is it obvious that contingency arguments *demand* discrete trials and that conditioning over a longer time period is likely the result of association by contiguity?

6. Flashing red or blue lights in rearview mirrors reliably elicit fear responses in most people in our culture. Identify conditioning situations that have produced other fear-eliciting stimuli in your life. How about your father's voice?

7. Are you sometimes anxious without knowing why? Is it possible that there are fear-eliciting stimuli of which you are not conscious? Of which you are not aware? Of which you cannot verbalize the contingencies?

8. Compared with the occasional ob-

server, sports fanatics enjoy athletic contests at a different level. In knowing the intricacies and nuances of the game, including the players and the win-loss records, fanatics can be characterized as more *discriminating* observers. Given the relationship between *generalization* and *discrimination*, how would you characterize the occasional observer? What experiences enhance the fanatic's *discrimination* abilities? Why is a 3–2 pitch "not just another pitch"?

9. Is it likely that a human suffering cortical damage in an automobile accident would no longer be able to be classically conditioned? Why or why not?

DISCUSSION STARTERS

1. *More people seem to remember that light travels faster than sound than that thunder is caused by air molecules collapsing. Why?* Probably because the first sound bite is heard more often than the second; that is, children memorize that light travels faster than sound through repeated exposure. The physics of a thunderstorm is more complicated, first involving lightning, then heated and expanding air, then collapsing air, and then thunder.

2. *The Coolidge effect describes males responding with more sexual interest to new partners than to familiar ones. Is this habituation? Is there a learning-performance distinction in this example?* The physiology of sexual arousal is clearly not as simple as food causes salivation. Male-female differences in sexual and other complexly organized behaviors have both heritable and con-

ditioned components (Barash, 1982). For example, during the course of a meal, humans become habituated (Rolls, Rolls, & Rowe, 1982), as reflected by both reduced intake and changes in palatability of particular foods. The reader should be able to come up with a learning-performance distinction in this example.

3. *Do fully habituated responses return in a way that is analogous to spontaneous recovery following extinction?* This is called an *empirical question*. The answer likely depends on the nature of the stimulus to which you are habituating. For example, most of us more or less permanently tune out the background hum of a fan, an air conditioner, or a refrigerator. We don't hear it the next day or a week later. A louder or more complex stimulus, such as the sounds at a busy intersection, may

never habituate fully. It may be instructive for you to come up with personal examples in both categories.

4. *Unconditioned and conditioned sexual arousal?* This should be intuitively obvious: Manual stimulation is a US; daydreams, erotic photos or voices, and so on are learned. These stimuli have been conditioned, and the arousal they produce can be characterized as a conditioned response (CR).

5. *Drug side effects and appetite disturbances are learned?* Researchers have shown that some anorexia experienced by patients undergoing chemotherapy can be attributed to conditioning (i.e., meals eaten in too close proximity to treatments). Elderly patients at risk of a stroke and maintained on warfarin to thin the blood, for example, are dosed with a rat poison that has been shown to be highly effective in conditioning taste aversions. Physicians are typically not aware of research that demonstrates the power and pervasiveness of taste aversion conditioning and are too prone to dismiss even life-threatening anorexia as being an inevitable side effect of drug therapy.

6. *Are you sometimes anxious without knowing why?* Gantt (1964) developed a concept called *schizokinesis* that is in essence a conditioning model for being anxious without knowing why. In schizokinesis, generalized anxiety is what is left after the specifics of aversive conditioning episodes have been forgotten. The specific CSs or even more insidiously, the *context* in which the CS was conditioned, are no longer accessible from memory. Years later the context alone may evoke the conditioned emotional response. For example, let us suppose that as a small child you were punished by being confined to your room. The room happened to be blue. Now, as an adult, blue rooms may be a CS for anxiety. Note that neither as a child nor as an adult are you aware that blue rooms were being aversively conditioned. All you are aware of is that you sometimes become anxious for no apparent reason.

7. *Why is a 3–2 pitch not just another pitch?* Ask a ball player.

8. *Can brain-damaged humans be classically conditioned?* Risking oversimplification, classical conditioning of some responses in cortically damaged humans is a likely outcome. Single-unit neurons can be conditioned, *Aplysia* can be conditioned, decerebrated cockroaches can be conditioned, unconscious rats can be conditioned, human fetuses can be conditioned, and so on.

KEY TERMS

Appetitive Conditioning (Pavlov) Food-based Pavlovian conditioning. (Cf. *Appetite.*)

Appetitive Salivary Conditioning (Pavlov) Pavlovian conditioning in which a conditioned salivary response to a food stimulus is measured.

Association Theory The relationship (connection, union) that results when two or more stimuli are paired together in time.

Associationism Basic learning defined as the association of two or more sensory experiences. (Cf. *Association Theory.*)

Aversive Conditioning Conditioning experiments using aversive unconditioned stimuli (as opposed to an appetitive food stimulus). Three contemporary *aversive* conditioning procedures are eye-blink conditioning, conditioned suppression, and taste aversion conditioning, employing aversive air puffs to the eye, electric shock, and toxins, respectively.

Backward Conditioning (Pavlov) A conditioning procedure in which the onset of the unconditioned stimulus precedes the onset of the conditioned stimulus. Both inhibitory conditioning (often) and excitatory conditioning (rarely) can result from backward pairings of US and CS. (Also referred to as a *negative contingency* between the CS and the US.)

Baseline The preexperimental, or normal, level of a measured response. The baseline often constitutes the control condition to which the effects of an experimental treatment are compared.

Causality The relationship of cause and effect. A goal of science is to investigate why events occur, on the assumption that nothing can happen without a cause.

Classical Conditioning See *Pavlovian Conditioning.*

Conditioned Emotional Response (CER) The outcome of an experimental treatment in which emotional responses are conditioned to neutral (non-emotion-inducing) stimuli. (Cf. *Conditioned Suppression.*)

Conditioned Response (CR) (Pavlov) A new response, learned to the CS, following pairings of a neutral stimulus (i.e., the CS) with an unconditioned stimulus. Salivation to the sound of a bell is an example.

Conditioned Stimulus (CS) (Pavlov) A stimulus that comes to control a reflexive response following pairings with an unconditioned stimulus. Example: A bell controls salivation after pairings with food.

Conditioned Suppression A laboratory technique used to measure aversive (fear) conditioning. A neutral stimulus is paired with electric shock while an animal is lever-pressing for food. Following tone-shock conditioning, the tone disrupts (suppresses) lever pressing, allowing the experimenter to easily quantify the amount of fear conditioning the animal has experienced.

Contiguity Theory of Association The theory that stimulus-stimulus associations occur when two stimuli are perceived close together in time.

Contingency Theory of Association The theory that stimulus-stimulus associations occur when one stimulus precedes and *signals* the occurrence of a second stimulus.

CS-US Interval A time interval measured from the onset of the conditioned stimulus to the onset of the unconditioned stimulus.

Defense Conditioning Pavlov's term for experiments that used aversive unconditioned stimuli, such as sour solutions placed on the tongue and electric shock to condition a leg-withdrawal reflex. Experiments using noxious USs are now referred to as *aversive conditioning.*

Embedded Conditioning A variation of simultaneous conditioning in which the onset and offset of either the CS or US occurs during the other element. Embedded conditioning situations often involve the pairing of long duration stimuli, such as flavors experienced during meals, and sensory events during drug effects.

Empiricism   The primary method (and philosophy) of observation and experimentation that distinguishes science from other ways humans obtain knowledge about the world. (Cf. "intuitionism," which has no real-world referents.)

Excitatory Conditioning   "Normal" forward conditioning in which a CS is paired with a US and the conditioned response resembles the unconditioned response.

Extinction   (Experimental Extinction) (Pavlov) A reduction of the CR in the presence of the CS. The conditioned response is said to *extinguish,* and the procedure is called *extinction,* or *experimental extinction.*

Extinction Curve (Extinction Gradient)   A plot of the magnitude of the conditioned response as a function of extinction trials. In a typical extinction curve, response magnitude diminishes to preconditioning levels.

Forward Conditioning   (Pavlov) CS onset precedes US onset. The most common form of excitatory conditioning. Example: A bell CS is followed immediately by a food US.

Frequency   (Association theory) The number of times two stimuli occur together.

Generalization   The tendency of animals to both perceive (*stimulus generalization*) and respond (*response generalization*) in a similar manner to stimuli that share common properties.

Habituation   The reduced responsiveness of an organism to repeated stimulation.

Habituation Control Group   A nonassociative control group that is presented the CS but not the US during conditioning.

Intensity   (Association Theory) The association of two stimuli influenced by their perceived intensity. More intense stimuli are more associable. (Cf. *Law of Strength.*)

Internal Inhibition   (Pavlov) A term Pavlov used to account for the loss of a conditioned response during an extinction procedure. Spontaneous recovery was interpreted by Pavlov as evidence for an active process of *internal* inhibition (i.e., within the dog) as opposed to the disruptive effects of an *external* inhibitor (i.e., a stimulus occurring external to the dog).

Intertrial Interval   The elapsed time between conditioning trials in a conditioning experiment.

Law of Strength   (Pavlov) Three interrelated factors that account for the *strength* (or magnitude) of a conditioned response: the intensity of the CS, the intensity of the US, and a close interstimulus interval between the CS and US.

Learned Helplessness   The outcome of an experimental treatment in which an animal is initially prevented from escaping intensely painful stimuli. Thereafter, when allowed the opportunity, the animal fails to respond in an adaptive fashion and does not attempt to escape pain.

Long-Term Depression (LTD)   Decreased responsiveness of certain neurons stimulated rapidly and repeatedly that may last for days and even weeks. LTD may mediate associative effects between neurons.

Long-Term Potentiation (LTP)   Increased responsiveness of certain neurons stimulated rapidly and repeatedly that may last for days and even weeks. LTP may mediate associative effects between neurons.

Nonassociative Learning   Relatively permanent changes in behavior that result from an animal experiencing a particular stimulus. Sensitization and habituation are two examples. (Cf. *Association Theory.*)

Orienting Reflex   (Pavlov) The response that occurs when a CS such as a tone is first sounded. A dog will prick up its ears and turn its head, locating the source of the sound.

Pavlovian Conditioning An experimental procedure in which a basic *reflex*, consisting of an *unconditioned stimulus* (*US*) and an *unconditioned response* (*UR*) is paired in time with a neutral stimulus (the *conditioned stimulus, CS*). After several pairings, the CS by itself can elicit components of the original reflex, called the *conditioned response* (*CR*). (Also called *conditioning* and *classical conditioning.*)

Psychic Secretion (Pavlov) Pavlov's term for salivation attributable to psychological factors—the dog's thoughts, memories, expectations, prior learning—rather than a physiological reflex.

Random Control Group A nonassociative control group in which the CS and US are both presented separately, never together, in time.

Reflexes Innate, involuntary responses an animal makes to specific stimuli in the environment. Example: Iris closure in response to sudden bright light.

Resistance-to-Extinction An indirect measure of the amount of conditioning that has occurred based on a comparison of the number of extinction trials necessary for a conditioned response to extinguish provides. As a general rule, greater *resistance-to-extinction* is found following many conditioning trials compared to a few conditioning trials.

Salivary Reflex An innate response (salivation) to food placed on a dog's tongue.

Second Signal System Pavlov's theory that words are arbitrary auditory (i.e., spoken) and visual (i.e., written) signals that are associated with real-world sensory impressions, such as "red sun" and "cold water." *Red sun* and *cold water* are the first signals of the real world. Words are symbols that represent these raw sensory experiences. Words are one level of abstraction removed from the world they represent. In Pavlov's view, words are the signal of signals, hence, the second signal system.

Sensitization   Increased responsiveness following presentation of a stimulus. Sensitization is an example of nonassociative learning.

Sensitization Control Group   A nonassociative control group (also referred to as a *pseudoconditioning* control) that is exposed only to the US during conditioning.

Sherringtonian Reflexes   Reflexes characterized by identifiable *sensory neurons* synapsing upon identifiable *interneurons* and *motor neurons.*

Similarity (Association Theory) Two stimuli that are perceived as being similar to each other are more associable. (Cf. *Preparedness.*)

Simultaneous Conditioning (Pavlov) The CS and US have identical onsets, durations, and offsets in simultaneous conditioning. Very little conditioning results in these trials.

Single-Stimulus Effect (Association Theory) Behavioral change due to the action of a single stimulus, as opposed to the association of two or more stimuli. (See *Habituation; Nonassociative Learning; Sensitization.*)

Spontaneous Recovery (Pavlov) The

reappearance of a higher level of conditioned response following a delay in the extinction process.

Taste Aversion Conditioning   A method of studying aversive Pavlovian conditioning. Rats drink a flavored solution (the CS) and then are given an illness-inducing toxin (the US). Conditioned taste aversions to the target flavor result from one or a few pairings.

Temporal Conditioning (Pavlov)   A variation of conditioning in which dogs are presented food at regular intervals. After many such trials, salivation is found to occur just prior to food administration. Pavlov interpreted these results by postulating that the interfood time interval had acquired conditioned stimulus properties and that the salivation was a conditioned response.

Temporal Contiguity   Two events perceived as being closely related in time.

Trace Conditioning (Pavlov) An example of forward conditioning in which both the CS onset *and* offset precede the US onset.

Trial   (Pavlov) A CS-US pairing.

Two-Stage Theory of Association   Stage 1: two stimuli are perceived as being temporally contiguous and correlated. Stage 2: S_2 is perceived as being contingent upon, and caused by, S_1.

Unconditioned Response (UR)   (Pavlov) The reflexive response to an unconditioned stimulus (the US). Salivation is the unconditioned response to food.

Unconditioned Stimulus (US)   (Pavlov) A stimulus that innately and involuntarily elicits a reflexive response (i.e., the UR). Example: Food is an unconditioned stimulus that elicits reflexive salivation.

CHAPTER 4

COMPLEXITIES OF CONDITIONING

148

Sometime in late March, after the Indian violets had come, we would be gathering [acorns] on the mountain and the wind, raw and mean, would change for just a second. It would touch your face as soft as a feather. It had an earth smell. You knew springtime was on the way. . . .

Then the yellow dandelions poked up everywhere along the lower hollow, and we picked them for greens—which are good when you mix them with fireweed greens, poke salat, and nettles. Nettles make the best greens, but have little tiny hairs on them that sting you all over when you're picking. . . .

Everything growing wild is a hundred times stronger than tame ones. We pulled the wild onions from the ground and just a handful would carry more flavor than a bushel of tame onions. . . . Bitterroot has big lavender-pink faces with yellow centers that hug the ground, while moonflowers are hidden deep in the hollow, long-stemmed and swaying like willows with pink-red fringes on top.

Carter, *The Education of Little Tree* (1976, p. 100)

INTRODUCTION

We have seen that simple conditioned responses may result when one CS enters into association with one US. It is in fact the case, however, that environments seldom present us with such solitary, "simple" stimulus events as seen in the laboratory. Nature, as a Cherokee Indian named Little Tree learned in his first few years of life, is complicated. Unlike laboratory experiments, knowing seasons and where to find plants and how they taste and whether they are poisonous is not an easy subject matter to master. Nature doesn't break stimuli down into discrete elements.

Does predictability disappear when *several* stimuli are placed in contiguous and/or contingent arrangements? When natural stimuli are used? When the duration of the CS and US is varied from fractions of a second to minutes and even hours? When a stimulus is one with which the animal is already familiar? We begin by asking a number of questions that are addressed in this chapter.

Question 1. Can laboratory learning experiments be designed to allow experimenters to investigate real-world problems?

Ecological Validity.   Experimenting on the learning abilities of caged animals raises a number of problems. This research appears to lack **ecological validity**. To be ecologically valid, an experiment should ask an animal to learn a task that it is likely to encounter in its ecological niche. Learning about foods, the location of predators, and how to use language are examples of ecologically valid tasks. In Chapter 2 we learned that questions of ecological validity were more a concern to ethologists than comparative psychologists. They attempted to understand animal behavior in natural environments and were critical of comparative psychologists working in labs. Too often, ethologists argue, the precision that laboratory researchers achieve by using carefully timed sequences of bells and whistles, flashing lights, tiny food rewards, and brief electric shocks limits the real-world applicability of experimental results. But this criticism places laboratory researchers in a catch-22 situation. How so? Scientific analysis of causal relations suffers as more variables are left uncontrolled. When animals are confronted with complex stimulus situations in laboratories (similar to what they might encounter in a natural environment), their responses become more multidimensional and less predictable. Nevertheless, *laboratory learning experiments that allow researchers to investigate real-world problems have been designed.*

Question 2. Prior learning affects present learning. Can this simple observation be investigated in the laboratory—again, using relatively simple associative conditioning methodologies?

How Does Learning Influence Learning?   To be ecologically valid, an experiment should also reflect the fact that most of what we learn in the real world is an accumulation of a lifetime's experiences. That is, each new instance of learned behavior is built on a background of other experiences. Most laboratory learning experiments, however, are conducted using young animals bred specifically for the short-term task they are required to perform. Such animals are described as naive—never before having experienced any of the conditions to which they will be exposed in the experiment.

Experimenters typically use naive laboratory animals. The reason is that when an animal has previously learned something, it biases the results of the next experiment. The animal's responses in the second experiment must be attributed to a combination (cf. *interaction*) of the present and previous treatment conditions.

The problem of how prior learning affects subsequent learning has practical implications. College algebra teachers, for example, are often heard decrying the methods by which their students were taught algebra while in high school. What students previously learned, they argue, often interferes with the students' performance in college classrooms. Furthermore, students bring to college different high school learning experiences. It is difficult to judge the effectiveness, for example, of two classroom methodologies, such as comparing an algebra lecture method with an interactive computerized tutorial. Some students may be better prepared through prior learning to do better under one or the other "new" method.

Obviously, what is called for is research that addresses how prior learning affects new learning. Many of the experiments described in this chapter provide answers to the knotty question concerning prior experience.

Question 3. Is it possible to mirror in the laboratory the complexity presented by "nature"—that is, to deconstruct nature into simple stimulus elements, accomplish associative experiments, analyze results, and then reconstruct and synthesize the complex behavior of animals (humans) going about their business of living in their niches?

Is Association Theory Too Simple?   A related issue is the *extrapolation* of results attained from laboratory research. Given the differing evolutionary histories of animals and the different niches they occupy, is it reasonable to think about learning as a *general* process shared by all species? One solution is to think of common features of all vertebrate niches, including the laboratory. For example, the environmental *context* in which experiments are conducted in laboratories can be understood as the laboratory animal's ecological niche. This niche, or context, includes home-cage housing, feeding schedules, laboratory light/dark cycles, experimental chambers, prior learning experiences, and interactions with human caretakers.

Human learning also occurs in contexts of classrooms, automobiles, televisions, and meals and in interactions with other humans—as well as surviving in Little Tree's natural setting. Some have argued that the ecological niche of humans living in cities is in many ways as artificial as that of a laboratory animal (see Richter, 1942). Research begun by Pavlov and continued by others addresses the complexity of human and animal behavior in laboratory environments. We shall see that *latent* and *conditioned inhibition, blocking, discrimination learning, overshadowing, higher-order conditioning,* and *potentiation* are among the many possible outcomes of these stimulus-response interactions in complex laboratory environments.

Question 4. Why are certain stimuli and certain responses in certain animals conditioned relatively easily, and why do others apparently fail to be conditioned? To what extent do these observations present a problem for learning theory?

Failures of Conditioning? An important section of this chapter addresses apparent failures of conditioning theory. Failures mean problems for general theories of learning. Why do animals learn some responses after a single experience and yet fail to learn others after many trials? Sound familiar? How is it possible that humans are able to remember a face over a period of many years even after a brief meeting while an acquaintance's name may escape them even as they interact? Why is it that we can conjure up a face by merely hearing the person's voice on the phone yet have a hard time making name-face associations?

Why is it important to raise these four questions? For one reason, if it turns out that laboratory analyses of behavior are merely esoteric exercises—games that researchers play to test meaningless theories—no matter how interesting the experiments may be, such research ultimately is worthless. Questions of ecological validity and behavioral complexity and species differences and failed experiments present very real problems for laboratory analyses of learning and behavior. The astute reader realizes that these questions likely would not be raised if there were no good answers to them! As we see, psychologists and other neuroscientists have been most clever in designing meaningful laboratory studies that accurately model complex human behavior.

LEARNING AND RELEARNING: EFFECTS OF PRIOR EXPERIENCE ON CONDITIONING NEW RESPONSES

Let us begin by looking at an example of complex human behavior (see Box 4.1). Throughout this chapter we return for further analysis to the taste aversion conditioning example in Box 4.1. It is likely that you already have several hypotheses for Tracy's, Candace's, and Carlos's behavior. (You may want to take a minute to jot down in the margins your best guesses for their differently learned responses.) Recognize that analyzing the complexities of their behavior is possible by applying results of laboratory animal experiments. Unless you already have a good background in learning theory, you will probably be surprised by the range and sophistication of arguments that can be brought to bear on their human behavior based on these laboratory animal experiments. By the end of the chapter, you will have a better idea why Candace, Tracy, and Carlos learned, remembered, and behaved as they did.

In this section we look in turn at the following phenomena related to complex conditioning: latent inhibition, sensory preconditioning, higher-order conditioning, overshadowing, potentiation, and blocking.

BOX 4.1   CONDITIONING FOOD AVERSIONS

Three years ago, Candace and Tracy, identical twins living in a rural part of Nebraska, came to Miami, Florida, to visit their cousin Carlos. All three had previously eaten pepperoni pizza and were hungry for it, so Carlos took them to his favorite restaurant, Momma Rollo's. Neither Candace nor Tracy had eaten at Momma Rollo's before this occasion.

In addition to the pepperoni pizza, Candace and Carlos each ordered a can of Dr. Spicey® while Tracy drank only water. Since Dr. Spicey® was unavailable in rural Nebraska, neither Candace nor Tracy had ever before experienced its distinctive taste. All ate three slices of the pepperoni pizza.

Hours later, the twins became sick, experiencing both nausea and vomiting. Carlos felt okay and a phone call home confirmed that the twins' mother was sick with the same symptoms. Because Carlos did not get sick but their mother was, Candace and Tracy reluctantly concluded that their meal at Momma Rollo's did *not* make them sick. They probably had a stomach virus they had brought from Nebraska.

After this incident the following changes in their behaviors were noted:

1. For several months after returning to Nebraska, neither Candace nor Tracy had any desire to eat pizza. Why?*

2. Carlos returned to Momma Rollo's three weeks later and ate pepperoni pizza. Why the difference between Carlos's and the twins' behavior?

3. (Assume that prior to their experience at Momma Rollo's the twins had identical taste preferences.) After several months elapsed, the twins once again began to eat pizza. Candace ordered a cheese topping only, and Tracy, a sausage pizza. Why did neither order pepperoni? What is your hypothesis as to why Candace ordered a cheese topping rather than sausage?

4. Two days after the illness incident (while still in Florida), Tracy drank a Dr. Spicey® at Tom's apartment and loved it. Candace still dislikes the taste of Dr. Spicey® three years later. Why the difference?

5. Candace dislikes Dr. Spicey® more than she dislikes pepperoni pizza. Why the difference?

6. Candace and Tracy visited Carlos a year after the illness episode. Candace says she will eat pizza but would rather not go back to Momma Rollo's; Tracy also says she will eat pizza and, furthermore, is indifferent about the choice of restaurant. Why do the twins respond to Momma Rollo's restaurant differently?

7. Candace says, "Just mentioning Dr. Spicey® or seeing the Dr. Spicey® can makes me ill." Why?

* You probably know the answer to this question already since taste aversion conditioning was discussed in Chapter 3. Other experiments presented in this chapter will help you answer the remaining questions.

Latent Inhibition

Pavlov was the first experimenter to observe that a *novel* CS more readily entered into association with an unconditioned stimulus than did a *familiar* CS. That is, he found that if a dog had previously heard a bell, whistle, or metronome of a particular timbre and intensity before the stimulus was used as a conditioned stimulus in pairings with food, the dog required more CS–US trials to acquire a conditioned response. Novel stimuli condition more easily than do familiar stimuli.

A systematic demonstration that familiar stimuli condition less readily than novel stimuli was made by Lubow, who called the phenomenon **latent inhibition** (Lubow, 1989; Lubow & Moore, 1959). Many demonstrations of latent inhibition, also known as the **CS preexposure effect,** now exist. Familiar stimuli have less *associative potential* than do novel stimuli in the same way that more intense CSs and USs have greater associative potential than do weaker CSs and USs. The latent inhibition effect is diagrammed in Figure 4.1.

Similar differences are also found to exist between novel and familiar unconditioned stimuli. That is, when an animal is exposed to a drug, or an electric shock, or a food reinforcement prior to using these stimuli in conditioning a novel CS, less association of the CS with the US occurs. This phenomenon is called the **US preexposure effect** (Randich & LoLordo, 1979).

Why Are Familiar Stimuli Less Easily Conditioned? Hypotheses abound as to why novel stimuli are more readily conditioned than familiar stimuli. The question

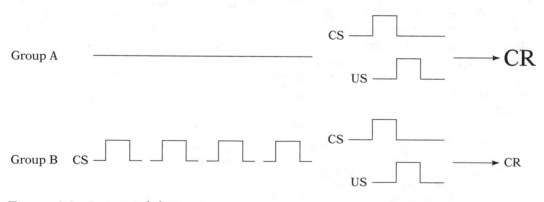

FIGURE 4.1 Latent Inhibition

If a conditioned stimulus (such as a tone) is presented several times before it is paired with an unconditioned stimulus (for example, food) in a conditioning situation (B), the conditioned response (salivation) is less than if the conditioned stimulus were novel (A). The same design (not shown) substituting the US as the preexposed stimulus would yield similar results following conditioning.

is an important one. With apologies to Pavlov, the adage "you can't teach an old dog new tricks" comes to mind. Probably the saying refers more to "being set in one's ways" than it does to the inability of an aging brain to learn new tasks. Prior experience *does* influence later learning, and the latent inhibition phenomenon may be the most elementary demonstration of this point.

Nonassociative Theories of Latent Inhibition.   Students often confuse *habituation* with *latent inhibition,* and for good reason. The two phenomena are similar. *Habituation* refers to response diminution following repeated presentations of a stimulus; *latent inhibition* refers to lowered associability when a familiar stimulus is used in conditioning. The orienting response is diminished in both cases; humans and animals so habituated appear to pay less attention to the familiar stimulus.

One theory proposed to account for the latent inhibition effect, then, is *nonassociative.* Stimuli that have become habituated and that capture less attention during conditioning are less associable than novel stimuli to which attention is directed. Novel stimuli are more surprising (Wagner, 1976). The habituation hypothesis has a particularly difficult time accounting for the *US preexposure effect.* By definition, USs are less susceptible to habituation and are more "attention getting" than are CSs. And yet preexposed USs (including even electric shock; Baker & Macintosh, 1977) do not work as well as novel USs in conditioning. Both CS and US preexposure effects seem to be better accounted for by associative theories.

Associative Theories of Latent Inhibition

A nonassociative theory involving reduced attention-capturing properties of familiar stimuli has been noted. In addition, two associative theories of latent inhibition have been proposed.

1. *Interference theory of latent inhibition.* In this theory, presenting the CS alone allows the CS to become associated with background contextual cues. The CS thereby effectively becomes part of the context. By merging into the context, the signal-to-noise ratio of the CS is diminished. The now familiar CS is less a signal and more a part of the background, thereby reducing its associative potential (Grahame, Barnet, Gunther, & Miller, 1994; Rudy, 1994; Wagner, 1976).

One prediction from this theory is that the more preexposure to the CS, the more associations would be made and the greater would be the latent inhibition effect. Just such a finding has been reported (Ayres et al., 1992). These researchers preexposed different groups of rats to the CS for varying time periods in conditioned suppression experiments and found predictably varying amounts of latent inhibition. Habituation of the context cues also increased the signal value of the CS. In summary, prior associations of the CS with other contextual cues are presumed to interfere with the formation of new associations.

2. *Learned irrelevance theory of latent inhibition.* A second associative theory also posits that associations are made when the CS is presented alone. The animal learns that the CS does not predict anything new; hence, an "association" is made between the CS and "nothing new." According to this theory, to an information-processing animal, the CS signals safety (Kalat, 1977; Kalat & Rozin, 1973), or becomes irrelevant (Baker & Macintosh, 1977; Best & Gemberling, 1977).

An implication of this theory of latent inhibition is that animals have expectations. For example, rats and other animals are hesitant the first time they taste a novel flavor. This **neophobia** (fear of the new) reflects a built-in expectation "to be wary of novel flavors." Given this biological predisposition to expect aversive consequences, when nothing bad happens, the rat associates the flavor with "nothing bad happening" and learns that the new flavor is safe (Kalat, 1977; Kalat & Rozin, 1973).

Comparing Theories of Latent Inhibition.   Closer to the truth would be a revised saying that "it is *more* difficult to teach an old dog new tricks." Older animals (don't forget humans) typically have been exposed to more environments, have encountered more stimuli, and have made more associations. You have both experienced more and learned more now compared to what you had experienced and learned 10 years ago.

Habituation has been characterized as being (a) nonassociative and (b) a "theory" that accounts for a large proportion of your environmentally determined behavior (i.e., "learning" that most of the stimuli you sense in your immediate environment can be ignored). The phenomenon of latent inhibition may be an even more likely explanation for what we learn (and don't learn) during the course of our lifetimes. Let us compare the theories of habituation and latent inhibition by way of an example.

Algebra, Algebra, and More Algebra.   The first day of class in a new school, you are awash in a sea of new faces, new desks, smells, and sounds. Alert and excited, you are processing your environment at an incredible rate. You make many orienting responses to rapidly changing stimuli. If you are a new student in a new country, the amount of new information may be overwhelming.

The college classroom context in which you find yourself is composed of a combination of new and old experiences. That is, classrooms have features in common with most institutional buildings. In this classroom, you may notice windows (if most other classrooms you sat in did not have them) or not notice windows (if most other classrooms you have experienced *did* have them). Padded seats noticed, or not. Amphitheatre noticed, or not. The signaling strength of any stimulus in this new classroom is related to its novelty as well as to its intensity.

This new algebra classroom signals other previously learned associations as well. For example, your algebra failures in the high school classroom share many features with the college classroom: *algebra* written on the blackboard and textbook, formulas, and other students who by their verbal and nonverbal behavior expressed the anxiety you now feel. The instructor writes on the board a "familiar" equation:

$$y = ax + b$$

You recognize the equation as one you have seen before but were unable to master in a previous class. Your heart sinks, as does your performance.

Skip to the end of the semester. You now realize that only with great difficulty were you able to understand this particular equation, $y = ax + b$. You recall that you had readily learned several new equations (i.e., novel ones that you had not previously seen). Why? Which of the following theories best accounts for your behavior?

Habituation Hypothesis. According to the habituation hypothesis, you would be less likely to learn new associations to familiar stimuli because familiar stimuli are attended to less than novel stimuli. (*I doubt it. Evidence to the contrary would be the sinking feeling you had when that equation was written on the board. No lack of orienting response there! Rather, the evidence presented here leads to the conclusion that the difficulty of forming new associations to the equation* y = ax + b *was not due to habituation to the stimulus.*)

Learned Irrelevance Hypothesis. According to the learned irrelevance hypothesis, you had more trouble learning $y = ax + b$ because the equation had been previously associated with other events and no longer predicted anything new when reencountered in the college classroom. (*Hardly! We've already determined that you associated the formula* y = ax + b *with anxiety and feelings of failure. Nothing irrelevant about this particular equation. In this example the learned irrelevance hypothesis does not apply.*)[1]

Associative Interference Hypothesis. The clue to understanding how prior associations with a stimulus can influence new associations with that stimulus is readily evident in this example. Stimuli in previous algebra classrooms shared common contextual features with the equation $y = ax + b$. Presumably, the equation, blackboards, textbooks, and anxiety became associated together (we see how later). The "new" classroom is a complex CS eliciting both anxiety and "feelings of failure." The new teacher's job, moreover, is somehow to explicate the latently inhibited $y = ax + b$ stimulus from the "math phobia stimulus con-

---

[1] You could make the case that for some individuals, $y = ax + b$ is both familiar and is "irrelevant" in the sense that the student verbalizes no interest in math (i.e., "math is irrelevant to what I want to do with my life"). The *learned irrelevance hypothesis* does not address this cognitive usage of the term *irrelevance*.

text" in which it occurs. Until that is done, new associations to the equation will be learned only with great difficulty. (More is said about the formation and treatment of phobias in Chapter 7.)

Summary of Latent Inhibition.   In summary, your difficulty in making new associations to the equation $y = ax + b$ can be attributed to two previous associations: (a) The equation "merged" into (became associated with other features of) the contextual background, in effect, becoming part of it and (b) the equation was conditioned through association with an aversive state of anxiety and other emotional stimuli relating to failed expectations. Although both associative and nonassociative theories have been proposed, simple associative models best account for our observations.[2] The study of latent inhibition has ecological validity in that the effect of prior learning is readily demonstrated and incorporated into an account of learning in the present. There is predictability even using old dogs.

Are you able to apply what you have learned about *latent inhibition?* Box 4.1 (Question 5) asks you to provide a hypothesis to account for the fact that Candace dislikes Dr. Spicey® more than she dislikes pepperoni pizza after a sickness experience. Reread the account of conditioning and see if you can relate *latent inhibition* to Candace's observed behavior. Again, for future reference, you might want to jot down your hypothesis in the margin.

Sensory Preconditioning

In the preceding example, the observant reader may have wondered how blackboards, the word *algebra*, formulas, textbooks, and faces can become associated together in a college classroom. All are stimuli, but where is the *unconditioned* stimulus (such as food, electric shock, illness-inducing toxin, etc.) that we have noted in all previous examples of conditioning? How can CSs become associated with each other in the absence of USs? Is a CS_1-CS_2 association possible?

An honest answer is that our theories of association are not adequate to answer this question. Recall that John Locke merely asserted that the sun was an associative complex of warm, round, and red stimulus characteristics. When this problem is brought into the laboratory, we typically measure CS-CS associations only indirectly. One method called **sensory preconditioning** is outlined in Figure 4.2.

Note that in Figure 4.2 prior to conditioning with an unconditioned stimulus (which is depicted in the middle panels for both Groups A and B), conditioned stimuli are presented together (Group A) or separately (Group B). CS_1 is then conditioned to a US in both groups, and CS_2 is tested in extinction in

---

[2] Hundreds of experiments have been conducted to investigate the similarities and differences of habituation, generalization, discrimination, and latent inhibition. See Hall (1991) for an introduction to this literature.

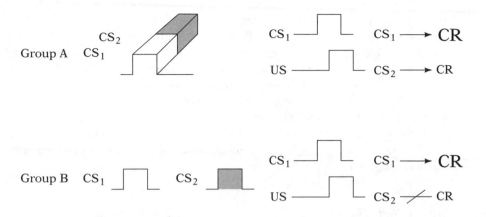

FIGURE 4.2 Sensory Preconditioning

Prior exposure to CS_1 and CS_2 *simultaneously presented together* (Group A, left panel) produces a CR to both CS_1 and CS_2 (right panel) after CS_1 alone is conditioned with a US (middle panel). Compare with Control Group B in which CS_1 and CS_2 are first presented but *separate from each other* (left panel). In this case, conditioning CS_1 does *not* produce a CR to CS_2 (right panel). Why is the CR larger to CS_1 than to CS_2 in Group A? Example:
Let

CS_1 = the equation, $y = ax + b$
CS_2 = the blackboard
US = a punishing stimulus (such as the teacher saying "wrong") or simply not understanding what is going on when other students apparently do.

Any combination of these US events produces the stress of failure associated with the stimulus complex of *equation, blackboard, school,* and so on.

---

both groups (right panel). CS_2 yields a conditioned response only in Group A, animals that had experienced CS_1 and CS_2 together in time.

Sensory Preconditioning and Background Context. The importance of *sensory preconditioning* lies in the fact that we can understand "background context" as a stimulus complex of associated elements—associated because these stimuli are experienced together. The reader is referred to Figure 3.1, cell d, on page 94. When we attempt to condition a CS with a CS, a CS with a US, or a US with a US, the contextual background, held together in associative fashion, is always present. The context in which conditioning occurs is also conditioned (Bouton & Swartzentruber, 1986).

Let us return to the algebra classroom. It is unlikely that a student can ever "start over" or follow an instructor's advice to "forget everything you have learned [meaning mislearned] up to now." Too many contextual stimuli with prior negative associations are always present. It is impossible to wipe the slate clean and start over. Relearning is, of course, possible. From what we have learned in Chapter 3, one form of remediation would be to extinguish aversive conditioned responses by presenting the stimuli ($y = ax + b$, the blackboard, etc.) without the negative USs. This procedure would begin to extinguish the emotional responses that were previously conditioned to these stimuli (Bouton & Bolles, 1979a, 1979b). Sounds like therapy, and we talk about that in Chapter 7.

Higher-Order Conditioning

In the preceding college classroom example, blackboards, formulas, textbooks, and the student's anxiety were identified as stimuli that had become associated together. "Anxiety" and "fear" are not neutral stimuli. But anxiety and fear make up math phobia. Given that algebra-related stimuli are initially neutral, by what process can students form fear associations to them?

In Chapter 3 we saw that when a tone is paired with an electric shock in rats (and, in Box 3.1, when a "dee-doo" sound is associated with a nasty sled ride), the auditory stimulus comes to produce a *conditioned emotion response* (CER). Another name for a CER is a *conditioned fear response*. In the college classroom, fear of failure is best understood as a conditioned response (CR). Here we show how a conditioned fear response can in turn be used to condition associations with new CSs.

The process of **higher-order conditioning** was initially described by Pavlov. The procedures differ, but the outcome of *higher-order conditioning* resembles *sensory preconditioning* in one respect. Both are associative conditioning processes in which there is no unconditioned stimulus.

Remember Pavlov's distinction between the stimuli he called CSs and those he labeled as USs? USs are "biologically meaningful" to the animal. They include food, water, and pain. In *higher-order conditioning* the end result is to take an arbitrary stimulus, such as a neutral sound, and show that it has acquired unconditioned stimulus properties.

A three-step process illustrating two levels of higher-order conditioning is presented in Figure 4.3. Pavlov (1927/1960) describes an experiment in which a dog is conditioned in Step 1 to salivate to the sound of a metronome (CS_1) in pairings with food (the US). Then "a black square [CS_2] is held in front of the dog for 10 seconds, and after an interval of 15 seconds the metronome is sounded during 30 seconds" (Pavlov, 1927, p. 34).

The procedure is repeated for 10 trials. On the 10th trial Pavlov reported that the dog salivated 5.5 drops to the black square, compared to a range of 9.5 to 13.5 drops of conditioned salivation to the sound of the metronome. Note that the black square had never been directly associated with food, yet a re-

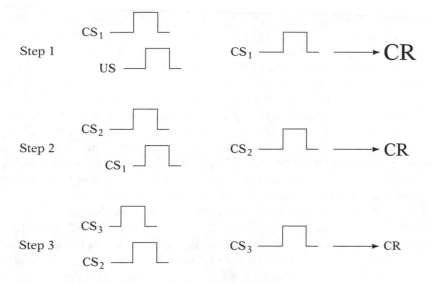

FIGURE 4.3 Higher-Order Conditioning

A stimulus associated with the US in Step 1 acquires US-like properties. Note that even in the absence of a US in Steps 2 and 3, conditioning nevertheless occurs due to these US-like properties.

sponse had been conditioned to it. Pavlov called this phenomenon **second-order conditioning** (Pavlov, 1927/1960, p. 34).

Interestingly enough, Pavlov reports that he was able to accomplish *third-order conditioning* (see Step 3, Figure 4.3) only when he conditioned his dogs with an electric shock US. That is, he could not use the food-based conditioned response to the black square to condition yet a third stimulus. (The conditioned response established by a food reward was not powerful enough.)

Pavlov (1927) then reported the results of experiments by Dr. Foursikov, another researcher in his laboratory. First, Foursikov elaborated a leg withdrawal conditioned response (CS = touching the hind paw, US = briefly shocking the front paw, CR = withdrawing the front paw when the hind paw is touched). He then presented the sound of bubbling water (CS_2) followed by touching the hind paw (CS_1). Second-order conditioning was noted. Finally, Foursikov presented a tone (CS_3), which he paired with the sound of bubbling water (CS_2). After a number of pairings, CS_3 (the tone), when sounded alone, produced the conditioned response of leg withdrawal (Step 3, Figure 4.3). Such "conditioning of the third order" and the more common second-order conditioning are collectively known as *higher-order conditioning*.

The significance of higher-order conditioning is twofold. First, the process allows conditioning in the absence of an unconditioned stimulus. Second, higher-order conditioning is another demonstration that prior conditioning experiences can continue to influence the present. Once "neutral" stimuli are conditioned, they in turn can be used to condition other responses.

Let us return to the language examples. Most humans inhabit language-rich environments. We know that language attains meaning through associative processes. Let us look at the possibilities presented by the higher-order conditioning of language. Referring back to Step 1 in Figure 4.3, let CS_1 be the word *no* and the "biologically meaningful" US be a stimulus complex represented by a parental figure. The parental figure's voice (intonation, intensity, etc.) or the parent's withdrawal of affection (or physical punishment or a "time-out", etc.) is a potentially aversive US that enters into association with the word *no*. In Step 1, then, the word *no* acquires punishing/fear-inducing properties not unlike that acquired by the tone in tone-shock conditioning.

CS_1, the word *no*, can now be used in association with other neutral stimuli in second-order conditioning during Phase 2.[3] More to the point, the conditioned emotional responses associated with the word *no* can now attach to other neutral stimuli. The word *algebra* was conditioned through the process of higher-order conditioning. *No, wrong,* and *incorrect* with attendant conditioned emotional responses became associated with the formulas and equations found in a book labeled *algebra*.

Test your understanding of this section. First read Box 4.2. See if you can incorporate (a) Pavlov's *second-signal system* conditioning, (b) the process of *higher-order conditioning*, and (c) *generalization* to show how failure experiences in an algebra classroom might contribute to problems in other school subjects.

Overshadowing

When an animal is conditioned, both the CS and the context (background stimulus conditions) become associated with the US. The CS competes successfully with the context to capture most of the associative potential of the US for reasons already discussed. The context is latently inhibited, and the CS intensity allows this signal to emerge from background stimulus conditions.

What would happen if two novel CSs were presented simultaneously? Would both become conditioned, or would only one be attended to, the other merging into the background? Pavlov and others have done these experiments. The basic design is shown in Figure 4.4. As the figure illustrates, the result of conditioning the two stimuli simultaneously is compared with the results of conditioning each stimulus separately. In the example given, CS_1 competes with and captures more of the associative potential of the US than does CS_2. When both are conditioned together and tested separately (Group A in Figure

---

[3] Among other stimuli that can be conditioned by the word *no* are other words such as *don't, wrong, incorrect, stop,* and *yuk.*

BOX 4.2 HOW SYMBOLS ACQUIRE MEANING

Is money an important part of your ecological niche? A fistful of $100 bills gets the attention of most of us. What about a ¥100 (Japanese yen) or £100 (English pounds)? Obviously, the value of any given currency is relative to the values of other currencies. If you have specific knowledge of exchange rates (that *associate* the value of one currency with the value of other currencies), you may already know whether $100 is more or less than £100 or ¥100.*

How does money attain "value"? Aside from international macroeconomic considerations that fine tune each currency's value, a $1 bill is a CS (a symbolic token) that has been associated with "biologically meaningful" events (USs) in one's niche. As a child you learned the value of money by its association with candy, toys, and clothes and later with food, beverages, perfume and other cosmetics, sex, music, shelter, tuition, automobiles, and other stimuli and activities that can be purchased in our culture.

As we see in Chapter 6, *secondary reinforcers* attain value through Pavlov's process of *higher-order conditioning*. Money is one of the most important *secondary reinforcers*. Language is the most important secondary reinforcer governing human behavior. Just talking about money makes me salivate. Can you identify any conditioning of the third order in your past? Using the concept of higher-order conditioning, can you describe why someone might "fall in love with a car"? Finally, can you explain why people feel differently about the following artificial symbols?

HIV+   BMW   ✝

* ¥100 = approximately 7¢; £100 = approximately $150.

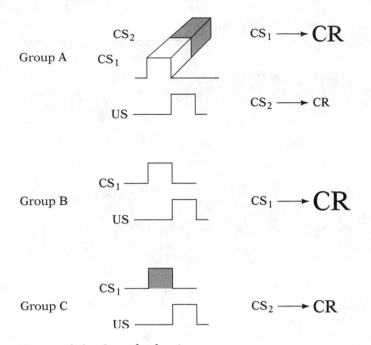

FIGURE 4.4 Overshadowing

In Group A, both CS_1 and CS_2 are conditioned; CS_1 overshadows CS_2 because the CR is larger to CS_1 than to CS_2. Note that when CS_1 and CS_2 are conditioned separately (Groups B and C, respectively), the CRs are greater to both stimuli than when they are conditioned concurrently. In Group A, only a fixed amount of US associative strength is shared with both CSs; hence, the CRs are less than when they are conditioned separately.

4.4), the CR to CS_1 is larger than the CR to CS_2. The procedure is called **overshadowing** (Pavlov, 1927/1960, p. 269ff). CS_1 is said to *overshadow* CS_2.

Salience. Because CS_1 is more easily conditioned than CS_2, CS_1 is said to be more *salient* than CS_2. The **salience** of a stimulus depends on many factors, including the quality and intensity of the stimulus, the context in which the animal experiences the stimulus, and the nature of the evolved nervous system of the animal.

When two or more CSs are presented simultaneously, which stimulus will overshadow and which will be overshadowed are best predicted by Pavlov's law of strength. The most intense stimulus captures most of the associative potential of the US. Between-species differences in perception of visual, auditory, taste, smell, and so on may play an important role in *which* stimuli overshadow and *which* get overshadowed. Pavlov (1927/1960), for example, reported that in salivary conditioning, dogs associated food (the US) better with auditory than with visual CSs (i.e., sounds rather than sights were more easily learned). Equating stimulus intensity across modalities is problematic. This makes it difficult to judge whether any given auditory stimulus is more intense than a given visual stimulus. We return to this question and the possibility of cross-modality differences in overshadowing later in this chapter.[4]

Potentiation

Overshadowing is a demonstration that not all stimuli are equally associable with a given US. If two flavor stimuli (for example, a pepperoni pizza and Dr. Spicey®) were tasted during the same meal, likely one would overshadow the other in association with an aversive event. But flavors have other unique properties not shared by other stimuli. For reasons that are not readily apparent, when a flavor stimulus is simultaneously presented to an animal with another stimulus (e.g., a sight, sound, or odor), *potentiation* rather than *overshadowing* is the outcome. **Potentiation** means that the sight, or sound, or odor is conditioned *better* in the presence of a taste than it would have been if conditioned alone (see Figure 4.5).

Experiments by Dr. Mark Bouton and his colleagues (Bouton, Dunlap, & Swartzentruber, 1987) and by Dr. Michael Best and his colleagues reveal the special power of flavors to potentiate the conditioning of background environments during training procedures (see Focus on Research 4.1).

Return with me to Momma Rollo's. Many flavors were experienced there, and some were conditioned aversively. Did any of the flavors *potentiate* the conditioning of other stimuli? *Hint:* Based on the phenomenon of potentiation, can you come up with a hypothesis explaining why Candace was more hesitant than Tracy to return to Momma Rollo's? (See Box 4.1, Question 6, page 153.)

Blocking

We have seen that stimulus intensity best predicts which stimulus will overshadow and which will be overshadowed when both are paired with a US. What would happen if CS_1 were familiar and CS_2 novel? Will CS_2 overshadow CS_1 or vice versa?

In an earlier section, we learned that the theory of latent inhibition addresses the question concerning why familiar stimuli are less conditionable

---

[4] Assume that the complex stimulus is a fruit salad composed of grapes, pineapple, banana chunks, nuts, marshmellows, and jello. If you were to get sick after eating the fruit salad, would you be likely to attribute more of the sickness to one of the elements—let's say the pineapple chunks—than to another component part? If so, why? This example pinpoints the problems of trying to equate stimulus intensity both within (i.e., flavor) and across modalities.

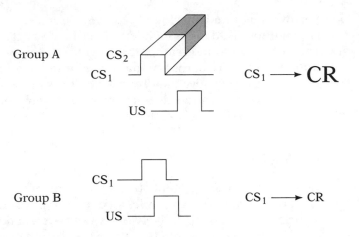

Group A CS_2
           CS_1 $CS_1 \longrightarrow$ CR

           US

Group B CS_1 $CS_1 \longrightarrow$ CR

           US

FIGURE 4.5   Potentiation

When either a simple stimulus CS_1 or a stimulus compound, such as the sights and sounds making up your friend's apartment, is conditioned simultaneously with a flavor stimulus (CS_2), conditioning to CS_1 is facilitated. (Compare the CR in Group B with that of Group A. *Note:* CS_2 *must* be a flavor.) Getting sick after eating in your friend's apartment is more likely to produce an *apartment aversion* than merely getting sick there without eating.

than novel stimuli. Familiar stimuli are apparently less associable in a subsequent pairing with a US because familiar stimuli have already become associated with other stimuli. Our prediction is, therefore, that a novel stimulus will overshadow a familiar stimulus when both are presented simultaneously.

Let us test this hypothesis by first conditioning an association to CS_1. Then pair CS_1 with a novel CS_2 in an overshadowing design, as shown in Figure 4.6. Kamin (1968), for example, used a conditioned suppression design in which he first conditioned rats to fear a tone (CS_1) using electric shock (US). Then Kamin simultaneously presented the tone with a novel light (CS_2) followed by electric shock. Remember that our prediction is that the novel light will capture most of the associative strength of the shock (US).

The results may surprise you. We predicted that a novel stimulus would overshadow the familiar stimulus. Kamin found, however, just the opposite. The surprising result is that prior conditioning to CS_1 *blocks* conditioning to CS_2. The procedure is a *blocking* design, and the counterintuitive phenomenon is called **blocking** (Kamin, 1968, 1969).

Why did the novel light fail to be conditioned? One hypothesis is that the novel light is a *redundant* stimulus, not useful in predicting the occurrence of electric shock. That is, the tone already predicts shock, and the rat may simply ignore the light when it occurs. Why is the CR to CS_1 larger in Group A (Figure

FOCUS ON RESEARCH 4.1

"I'll Never Go Back *There*...."

Dr. Michael R. Best, Department of Psychology, Southern Methodist University

"We have known for years that the sights, sounds, and smells of environments can be associated with illness produced by drugs and toxins. G. Andrew Mickley and I conducted some of the first experiments demonstrating this in Phillip Best's lab at the University of Virginia. Subsequently (and with considerable difficulty, I might add) we eventually published them (Best, Best, & Mickley, 1973).

"Since that time it has become clear to everyone working in animal learning that environmental contexts can be connected with sickness. Perhaps ironically, we now know that tastes can even enhance or *potentiate* the association of the environment with illness.

"Rats that drink a novel saccharin flavor in a distinctive environment and are then poisoned are less likely to consume familiar, nonaversive fluids (including water) in that conditioning environment—even though the rats never got sick after drinking them there (Best, Brown, & Sowell, 1984; Best & Meachum, 1986). It is therefore not surprising to find that you may be reluctant to eat at a restaurant if you become sick shortly thereafter. In these cases, it isn't just the food. It is also the location and other attendant stimuli to which you have been conditioned which motivate your decision.

"Although decisions about what you put in your mouth each day are possibly the most important you make, apparently you also keep track of *where* you eat and drink."

4.6) than it is in Group B? Because CS_1 captures *all* the associative potential of the US in Group A. In Group B, the associative potential of the US was split between the two CSs. A fuller discussion of what is meant by the *associative potential of the US* occurs later in this chapter.

Let us return to the algebra classroom. The college teacher says that she will use a different (new) method to help you learn a familiar (previously conditioned) mathematical equation. For the sake of the argument, let us assume that the previous CS (the equation in question) was aversively conditioned by association with anxiety-inducing stimuli ("wrong," "no," "incorrect," a grade

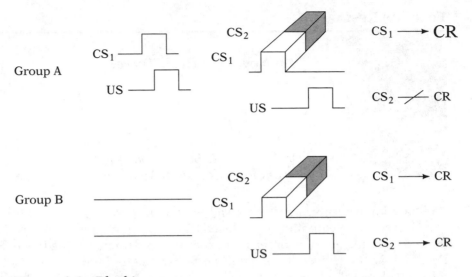

FIGURE 4.6 Blocking

Prior conditioning to CS_1 (Group A, left-hand panel) can block association to CS_2 (right-hand panel) after both CS_1 and CS_2 are conditioned in a compound (middle panel). Note that CRs to both CS_1 and CS_2 are learned in the absence of blocking (Group B) and, further, that neither stimulus overshadows the other during conditioning in Group B. CS_1 and CS_2 are equally salient in Group B.

of D, etc.). Given Kamin's findings about blocking, what is your prediction concerning the success of new conditioning? This is one more reason that it is difficult for an old dog to learn new tricks (see Figure 4.7).

Interim Summary

1. Familiar stimuli are less easily conditioned than novel stimuli. This phenomenon is known as *latent inhibition*.

2. Both associative and nonassociative theories help account for latent inhibition. These include habituation, interference, and learned irrelevance theories. Latent inhibition is best explained by an associative interference hypothesis.

3. *Sensory preconditioning* is a demonstration that two CSs can become associated with each other. Sensory preconditioning is measured indirectly. The transfer of associative effects from CS_1 to CS_2 is seen following conditioning of one of the CSs with a US.

THE FAR SIDE   By GARY LARSON

High above the hushed crowd, Rex tried to remain
focused. Still, he couldn't shake one nagging
thought: He was an old dog and this was a new trick.

FIGURE 4.7   Teaching an Old Dog New Tricks

4. *Higher-order conditioning* is a procedure in which the transfer of associative strength from CS_1 to CS_2 occurs *after* CS_1 has entered into association with a US. CS_1 acquires US-like properties and can then be used to condition CS_2.

5. *Overshadowing* sometimes results when two CSs simultaneously enter into association with a US. When one CS acquires more associative strength (i.e., conditions the better of the two), that CS is said to overshadow the other CS.

6. *Salience* refers to the characteristics of a stimulus that allow it to enter into association more or less easily relative to another. Among other factors, salience is due to the quality and intensity of the stimulus.

7. *Potentiation* describes a phenomenon in which the presence of a taste stimulus allows sights, sounds, and odors to acquire more associative strength in a pairing with a US.

8. If CS_1 has already entered into association with a US and CS_1 is then presented simultaneously with CS_2 followed by a US, CS_2 does not acquire associative strength (i.e., does not condition). CS_1 is said to have *blocked* conditioning to CS_2. *Blocking* may be complete or partial.

INHIBITORY CONDITIONING

Latent inhibition, sensory preconditioning, higher-order conditioning, potentiation, and blocking so far have revealed the extent to which prior learning experiences can affect the conditioning of new responses. *Conditioned inhibition* is the last and one of the most important of this set of phenomena. We see that many of Pavlov's experiments dealt with what he considered to be "inhibitory properties" of the nervous system. His experiments helped to illuminate mysterious processes that contribute to the inhibition of behavior. Following Pavlov's studies, Konorski (1948) and Rescorla (1969) have made the most important contributions to the study of conditioned inhibition. Let us begin by looking at the many ways in which the term *inhibition* has been used.

Excitatory and Inhibitory Conditioning Compared

You have already been exposed to numerous ways in which the terms *inhibitory* and *inhibition* have been used. At several places in Chapter 3, "inhibitory conditioning" was identified as the outcome of *backward conditioning* procedures. The result is that performance of the conditioned response is opposite in direction to the unconditioned response. For example, if tone-shock sequences predict conditioned fear, shock-tone sequences produce conditioned "safety." Tone → shock sequences define forward, excitatory conditioning. Shock → tone sequences define backward, inhibitory conditioning. Excitatory conditioning produces more salivation in Pavlov's dogs, and inhibitory conditioning produces less-than-normal salivation. Let us look more closely at an example of emotional conditioning.

Negative, or US-CS, Contingencies Procedure

Using the conditioned emotional response (CER) procedure, Heth (1976) conditioned rats using forward and backward pairings. One group was exposed to

60 US-CS (i.e., backward or shock → tone) pairings. A backward pairing sets up a **negative contingency** of CS and US. By measuring their rate of lever-pressing responses, Heth inferred first that the rats feared the tone and later that the tone had become a safety signal. (Remember that in forward conditioning, rats ostensibly fearing the tone suppress their lever-pressing responses during the tone; rats that treat the tone as a safety signal increase their rate of response following backward pairings.)

Given what we now have learned about conditioned inhibition, the reader should not be surprised at Heth's (1976) finding that *excitatory* (fear) conditioning to the tone preceded the appearance of *inhibitory* (safety) conditioning. You be the rat, trapped again in the scientist's box. If at the beginning of the experiment tones and shocks were introduced into your environment—no matter which came first—wouldn't you be fearful? Only later, after quite a few conditioning trials in which you were first shocked and then heard the tone, would you interpret the tone as a signal that no shock would be forthcoming for a given time period (i.e., a "safe period"). Heth found that even after 20 trials, the rats feared the tone. Inhibitory conditioning (accelerated responding in the presence of the tone) took 60 trials.

Is it obvious that the tone became a safety signal only in the context of fear? That merely presenting the tone without shock would not make the tone a safety signal?

Excitatory and inhibitory conditioning resulting from forward and backward conditioning procedures is diagrammed in Figure 4.8. CSs that result from one or the other procedure are renamed either **conditioned excitors** or **conditioned inhibitors.** The CS takes on the properties of the US, a process described earlier as higher-order conditioning. After conditioning, the CS alone can set up an excitatory or inhibitory state.

Inhibitory Conditioning of Flavors.   In a standard taste aversion conditioning experiment, rats first drink a flavored fluid and then are made sick by exposure to an illness-inducing agent, such as a drug or toxin. Flavor → illness contingencies make rats (and humans) no longer like the flavor in question. What if we reversed the contingency—made the animal sick and then allowed it to drink a novel flavor? The rat comes to prefer the flavor it tastes while presumably recovering from the illness—a phenomenon known as the *medicine effect* (Green & Garcia, 1971).

Is the flavor initially aversive, only later becoming preferred, as is the case in other measures of inhibitory conditioning? Yes. Rats tasting a coffee flavor find it aversive after two illness-flavor (i.e., backward conditioning) trials but show a preference for the flavor after eight such trials (Barker & Weaver, 1991).

Note that in both examples an initial excitatory conditioning component (fear of tone and avoidance of flavor, respectively) is followed by the development of conditioned inhibition (tone = safety signal and flavor is preferred, respectively).

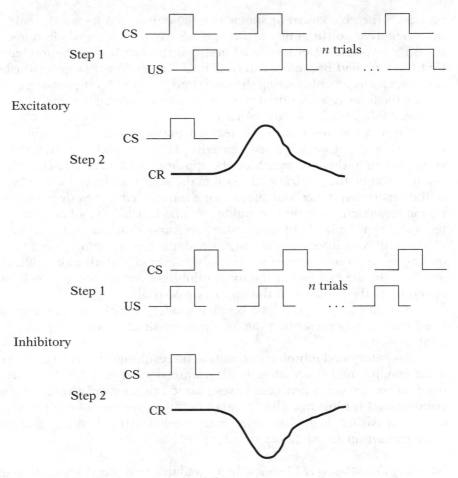

FIGURE 4.8 Excitatory and Inhibitory
Conditioning

A comparison of excitatory (forward) and inhibitory (backward)
conditioning. Note that the conditioned response following inhibitory
conditioning is opposite in direction to the conditioned (and
unconditioned) response following excitatory conditioning. In Step 2,
the CS has become either an *excitor* (top) or an *inhibitor* (bottom).

Pavlov's External and Internal Inhibition

Pavlov used the term *inhibition* in several contexts. First, he identified as **external inhibition** the temporary disruption in conditioned salivation that occurs when a dog's attention is distracted during conditioning. To understand what he meant, place yourself in the dog's position. You are hung up on a sling in a conditioning chamber in a controlled laboratory environment. The background context against which the tone CS and food US are delivered is stable (i.e., the background cues have become latently inhibited). During the preceding two days, you have been excitatory conditioned to salivate to the sound of the tone. On this, your fifth trial of the day, the 30-second tone has been sounding for about 5 seconds when Igor, Pavlov's clumsy assistant, blunders in, slamming the door behind him. Your salivation goes to zero as you orient ears and head to locate this distracting sound. Pavlov's notation in your training log is that the reduced salivation on trial 5 was attributed to external factors, that the door slam *externally inhibited* the salivation response. After waiting a minute or so, trials are resumed, and your conditioned salivary responses return to normal.

Pavlov, the physiologist, used the term **internal inhibition** to explain a number of phenomena.[5] One previously discussed is *spontaneous recovery* following extinction. Recall that spontaneous recovery is measured while a conditioned response is in the process of being extinguished. If the animal is rested during this process, a larger-than-expected conditioned response follows the rest period (see Figure 4.5). Pavlov thought that spontaneous recovery reflected active psychological properties. That is, extinction involved both the loss of the excitatory conditioned response (passive) as well as an active inhibitory process (that suppressed the excitatory process). This inhibitory process (Pavlov likened it to frustration at not getting food) would apparently diminish if the spacing between extinction trials was lengthened (presumably allowing the frustration to dissipate).

Conditioned Discrimination

Pavlov also thought that the inhibitory process was basic to discrimination training. In a classic experiment that demonstrated both generalization and **conditioned discrimination,** a black circle served as the conditioned stimulus (see Figure 4.9). A dog was trained to reliably salivate in the presence of the circle (CS_1). Then an ellipse (CS_2) was substituted. Initially, the dog salivated to the ellipse. We can infer that the dog perceived the ellipse and the circle as being similar—that the dog *generalized* its response from the circle to the ellipse.[6]

The circle (CS_1) continued to be paired with food. On alternate trials, the ellipse (CS_2) was shown to the dog, but it was never followed by food. By convention, CS with food is designated as a **CS⁺ trial.** CS without food trials are

---

[5] Pavlov's "internal inhibition" became Hull's (1943) "conditioned inhibition."
[6] Bush and Mosteller (1951) argue that each stimulus is composed of many elements and that similar stimuli have more of these elements in common than do dissimilar stimuli. Generalization, then, occurs most to a stimulus that has the most elements in common to the target stimulus.

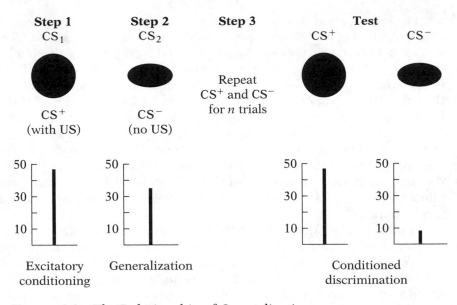

FIGURE 4.9   The Relationship of Generalization
                 to Conditioned Discrimination

In Step 1 a circle (the CS) is paired with food (the US) until a dog's
salivation reliably occurs (excitatory conditioning). In Step 2, an ellipse
rather than the circle is shown. The amount of salivation to the ellipse is
more than would be expected in an unconditioned animal (not shown) but
is less than to the circle CS. Salivation to the ellipse shows *generalization*
from the circle. After repeated trials of circle-food, ellipse-no food,
generalization disappears, and a conditioned discrimination of the circle
and the ellipse is the result. As we see in Chapter 5, the ellipse also
acquires inhibitory properties.

designated as **CS⁻ trials.** (These are simply read as *CS plus* and *CS minus* trials.) A conditioned discrimination is said to develop when the dog reliably salivates to the CS⁺ but not to the CS⁻ stimulus. Note that in the present experiment, the dog had to overcome an innate tendency to generalize from the
circle to the ellipse.

Why did Pavlov think that conditioning discriminations involved an inhibitory process? Where in the preceding example is there evidence of an active inhibitory process, akin to the "frustration" he saw in his dogs during extinction? Pavlov found evidence of an active process of inhibition as he
continued to train the dog, forcing it to make finer and finer discriminations
between the circle and an almost circular ellipse. When the dog could no
longer tell the difference between the CS⁺ and CS⁻, the discrimination broke
down. And so, apparently, did the dog. In Pavlov's words:

At the same time the whole behavior of the animal underwent an abrupt change. The hitherto quiet dog began to squeal in its stand, kept wriggling about, tore off with its teeth the apparatus for mechanical stimulation of the skin, and bit through the tubes connecting the animal's room with the observer, a behavior which never happened before . . . the animal now barked violently . . . in short, it displayed all the symptoms of acute neurosis [for several weeks]. (Pavlov, 1927/1960, p. 291)

Neurosis? From a discrimination training procedure? Apparently, the combination of excitatory and inhibitory processes put the dog into an extreme emotional state.

The outcome of this experiment aside for the moment, learning to discriminate is an adaptive process. After two meals at my favorite restaurant—a bad experience with catfish but a delightful flounder dinner—it is important that I discriminate (differentiate) between the two stimuli. One bad experience with catfish should not be overgeneralized to all fish. But all of us have been in this situation. The balance is precarious. In making fine discriminations, animals seem to incur a psychological cost. Let us look more closely at this interesting dynamic.

What Accounts for "Inhibition"?

> *Hurry, hurry, hurry. In another 10 minutes you'll be late for your appointment, and your destination is still many blocks away.*
> *Damn. The light turned red as you approach the next intersection.*
> *In our culture, a red light sets up an expectancy to respond in a certain way. Hit the brakes, and start an internal timer. Since you've come this way often, you know within a few seconds how long the cycle of green to yellow to red to green should take.*
> *The signal doesn't change. You impatiently wait. The horn behind you honks. Decision time. Is it broken? Should I go? Look for cops.*

Here, as in Pavlov's laboratory, the inhibitory context is also *the passage of time,* conditioned by our prior (excitatory conditioning) experiences. We have a conditioning history in which a red traffic light means "stop and wait." The long time delay can be interpreted as an *inhibitory stimulus,* which has signal value only in relation to prior excitatory conditioning at shorter intervals.

Conditioned inhibition on the surface appears to be no more than the mirror image of conditioned excitation (see Figure 4.8) in that the conditioned response changes direction when the CS-US relationship is reversed. Conditioned inhibition is more complex than conditioned excitation, however, because inhibition requires an *excitatory context* in which to be expressed (Rescorla, 1969, 1985). Excitation must both precede and set the stage for inhibition. A light not turning green is irritating only in the context that after a lengthy excitatory state, it usually does turn green. From this and other examples, we see that demonstrations of conditioned inhibition require that

1. The animal have a prior history of conditioned excitation.
2. The animal be in an excitatory state when the inhibitory CS is present.

Stuck at the traffic light that won't change. After inhibiting your response, you used the passage of time as a cue to respond by pressing the accelerator. In the presence of the red light, the time delay can be identified as a *conditioned inhibitor*. The red light is the excitor. The red light (excitor) controlled your "foot-on-the-brake" response. The combination of the excitor and time passing (inhibitor) produced the "go" response, opposite to the "stop" response to the red light alone.

Explaining Internal Inhibition.   Let us briefly review Pavlov's several demonstrations of internal inhibition to see whether these criteria were met. First the dog is conditioned in an excitatory manner (CS = tone followed by US = food). Now, during extinction, the tone is presented, setting up an excitatory state. Trial after trial, food is *not* forthcoming in the presence of the tone. The extended passage of time (with the tone and without food) becomes an inhibitory stimulus.

The conditioned discrimination procedure described here has in common with this example the element of extinction. After excitatory conditioning to CS⁺, CS⁻ occurs in extinction. The apparent buildup of inhibition takes place over a lengthy work session of alternating states of excitation and inhibition.

Let us look more closely at the inhibitory effect of the passage of time.

Inhibition of Delay Procedures

Boring. Absolutely boring. Is this prof ever going to say something interesting? This 50 minutes seems like 50 hours. If only I could lay my head down. I'm gonna break my neck jerking awake like this.

Pavlov was fascinated that inhibitory processes had the effect of inducing sleepiness in animals. One of his experiments—a procedure he called **inhibition of delay**—may help us to understand this process. First a dog is conditioned to salivate to a tactile CS (stroking its paw for 30 seconds). Figure 4.10 shows the results of measuring *when* during the 30 second CS the dog salivated. After many conditioning trials, salivation was *inhibited* during the first part of the interval. Note that in the figure most of the salivation occured *just before* delivery of food. Such timely salivation is highly adaptive in that it helps the animal begin the digestive process. The experiment also tells us that dogs, like humans, are sensitive to the passage of time.

How do we know that salivation is being *actively inhibited* during the initial 15-second period? Pavlov used two lines of evidence to argue his case. First he noted that many of his dogs became drowsy—some even fell asleep—during conditioning over long delays. Reduced attentiveness (drowsiness) is an ob-

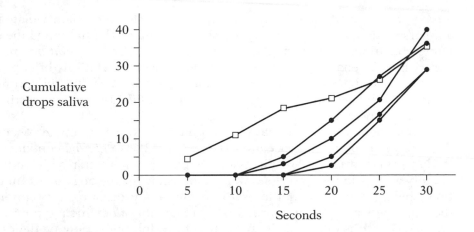

FIGURE 4.10   Inhibition of Delay

> A dog is conditioned to salivate to a 30-second tactile stimulus. Pavlov
> (1927/1960, p. 93) then measured salivation during the 30-second period
> on four occasions (circles). Note that the dog does not salivate an equal
> amount throughout the 30-second period; rather, salivation is inhibited
> during the first 15 seconds, a phenomenon Pavlov called *inhibition of
> delay*. On a fifth trial, Pavlov added a metronome's sound to the tactile
> stimulus and measured salivation (open squares). Note that the
> metronome had the effect of *disinhibiting* the inhibited salivation to the
> tactile stimulus, as evidenced by salivation throughout the entire 30-
> second period.

servable consequence of active inhibition. Second, Pavlov ran a test in which
he introduced another stimulus—the sound of a metronome—during the 30
second tactile stimulus. The metronome-plus-tactile stimulus (open squares)
released the process of inhibition, causing the dog to again salivate throughout
the 30-second interval (Figure 4.10). Pavlov called the process *inhibition of inhibition* (awkward) or **disinhibition** (better). The metronome is a *disinhibitor*.

Can you make the case that a boring lecture is one in which your mind is
in extinction and one in which there are no disinhibitors? What would you advise your professor to do to help students not sleep? Still stuck at the red light?
Perhaps your mind has wandered (become drowsy during the wait) and you
haven't noticed that the light has changed to green. A honking horn is a pretty
fair disinhibitor, isn't it?

Comparing Inhibition Procedures.   Remember Pavlov's phenomenon of *external*
inhibition? Igor slammed the door during an acquisition trial in which the
tone CS was providing an excitatory context. The door slam could be consid-

ered a *disexcitor* (Pavlov did not use the term). The door slam violated the animal's food expectancy, thereby acting as a stimulus that inhibited the excitatory conditioned response. Pavlov's *internal* and *external inhibition* are temporary phenomena; both dissipate with the passage of relatively brief periods of time. They are best understood, therefore, as nonassociative in nature. By contrast, both *latent inhibition* and *conditioned inhibition* are long-lasting associative phenomena.

Conditioned inhibitors have been produced from a variety of other conditioned discrimination procedures (Hearst, 1972). We can be confident that Pavlov was essentially correct in assuming that the interaction of powerful excitatory and inhibitory processes were responsible for the dogs' aberrant emotional behavior. In the conditioned discrimination procedure, not reinforcing the ellipse was an extinction procedure. Presumably *all* extinction procedures are stressful.[7] It is highly likely that conditioned inhibitors, among their other effects, produce measurable stress responses in the form of stress hormones (Dantzer, Arnone, & Mormede, 1980).

Table 4.1 summarizes the various uses of the term *inhibition*.

Induction Method of Producing Conditioned Inhibition

> *Presents. Presents. Presents. The expression on young Melinda's face reveals all too clearly her disappointment on opening her next present, the book* Black Beauty. *Her father is equally dismayed that he has apparently been unsuccessful in instilling good manners in her. How can she be so unappreciative of this beautiful book? (Not to mention her lack of courtesy in not hiding her displeasure.) After all, she likes horses. And she likes to read. Why the adverse reaction to the book?*

Indeed, why is it the case that normally well-behaved children—and adults—all too often look a gift horse in the mouth and find it lacking?

The answer may be found by applying the results of experiments on inhibition conditioned by the **induction method** (illustrated in Figure 4.11). Let us examine the animal model before returning to the example. An excitatory context is first created (see Phase 1, Figure 4.11) by normal excitatory conditioning. (As an example, let us use conditioning a fear response to a tone as measured in a conditioned suppression experiment.) In Phase 2, the tone—now a conditioned excitor—is presented in conjunction with a neutral stimulus, such as a light, and the rat is *not* shocked. Finally, the light is tested alone. The animal's response to the light is opposite to that of the tone. In the *induction method*, then, the light enters into association with (is induced by) the inhibitory process accompanying extinction of the excitatory tone.

---

[7] Ever been in a situation in which someone you cared for put you on extinction by withholding reinforcement (not talking with you on the phone, not returning your hello)? Can you identify the CSs during which extinction occurs? Now address the question, Is extinction stressful?

TABLE 4.1   Procedures Using the Term *Inhibition*

Name	Description of Phenomenon
Latent inhibition *(Lubow and others)*	Reduced associability of familiar stimuli relative to novel stimuli
External inhibition *(Pavlov)*	Temporary disruption of conditioned excitatory process due to presentation of extraneous stimulus during conditioning
Internal inhibition *(Pavlov)*	Process occurs during extinction of conditioned excitatory response; dissipates with time, as evidenced by spontaneous recovery
Conditioned inhibition *(Hull, Rescorla, & others)*	A state opposite to that of conditioned excitation; a process that produces a stimulus with conditioned inhibitory properties
Conditioned Discrimination *(Pavlov and others)*	Begins with conditioning an excitatory response (CS^+), followed by alternating trials with a CS^-, ends with responding to one but not the other stimulus
Inhibition of delay *(Pavlov)*	Reduced responding and drowsiness during the first part of a long CS presented in extinction

Notice the similarity of this "induction method" to simple extinction. An inhibitory process was implicated in extinction; spontaneous recovery occurred as inhibition dissipated.

Returning to the birthday party, did I mention that before opening *Black Beauty*, the first present that Melinda unwrapped was a small color TV for her bedroom? Let the TV be an excitor, setting up an excitatory state in the form of expectations in young Melinda. Let the book *Black Beauty* be a neutral stimulus that occurs during the excitatory state. Are the conditions right for the book to become a conditioned inhibitor? If so, what effect will the book have on Melinda's excitatory state?

What should you do, as a representative of the next generation of parents, to ensure that *your* child won't be a monster at her own party?[8]

---

[8] a. Not celebrate birthdays.
   b. Celebrate birthdays but not give gifts.
   c. Punish the child by taking back any gift the child is not thankful for.
*d. Arrange for your child to open the gifts in an ascending order of perceived value (i.e., save the best for last).

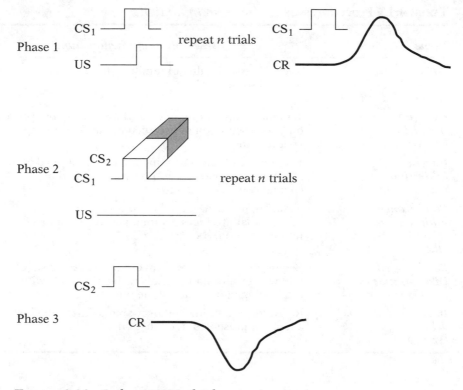

FIGURE 4.11 Induction Method

> After having been made excitatory in Phase 1, CS_1 is presented in compound with CS_2 in Phase 2. Notice that the compound is presented without the US during Phase 2. In Phase 3, CS_2 is demonstrated to have acquired inhibitory properties.

Indirect Methods of Measuring Conditioned Inhibition

Four methods that produce conditioned inhibition have been presented: *negative contingencies, induction, conditioned discrimination,* and *inhibition of delay*. These procedures are important because they demonstrate many of the subtleties and interactions of excitatory and inhibitory processes during conditioning. Equally important, these experiments show us how our mood swings can be modulated by conditioned stimuli in the environment.

Animals learn to increase or decrease response tendencies, depending on prior conditioning and on the context of the conditioning experiment in which they find themselves. Since Pavlov's experiments, two *indirect* methods of measuring conditioned inhibition, *summation* and *retardation,* have been devised. Why are they important? Because these methods provide demonstration experiments showing that inhibitors and excitors combine algebraically to modulate emotional behavior (Rescorla, 1971). Are the summation and retardation procedures necessary to demonstrate conditioned inhibition? No (Williams, Overmier, & LoLordo, 1992). As we have already seen, conditioned inhibitory properties can be demonstrated using any of a number of methodologies.

Inhibitory Processes in Using Language.   Let us look at how these processes work in reading this text and in listening to a lecture in the classroom. Both activities involve responding to words. Words and combinations of words in sentences were initially learned in an excitatory conditioning context. Understandable words—words with meaning—act as excitors. They keep your attention from wandering as you read. In a lecture, understandable words and sentences are interesting. Get it! By contrast, words and sentences that are not understood act as inhibitors. In the preceding sentence, if you do not understand how the word *inhibitors* was used, you did not understand the sentence. The frustration of not understanding the sentence is evidence of an inhibitory process. If too many of the sentences you read are not understandable, or if you do not understand the point of a lecture, your attention wanders. You become drowsy—further evidence of the inhibition that accrues under these conditions. In reading or in a lecture, we hope that the momentary excitatory processes outweigh the momentary inhibitory processes. An occasional disinhibitor, such as "Get it" does wonders in both lectures and in reading.

Let us look at an animal model.

Summation Test.   As the name implies, the **summation test** refers to a procedure in which CS_2 (a conditioned inhibitor) is presented with (added to) CS_1 (a conditioned excitor). The outcome is the sum of these two processes. Excitatory and inhibitory conditioning are initially accomplished separately (as indicated in Figure 4.12). A tone CS is conditioned by presenting the tone followed by shock (i.e., excitatory conditioning). This produces conditioned *suppression* of lever pressing. On another day a light CS is *preceded* by an electric shock US (i.e., a negative contingency procedure that produces inhibitory conditioning). Recall that in this example, inhibitory conditioning produces *enhanced* lever-press responding.

What would you predict would happen if, following this training, the *excitor* and *inhibitor* were presented simultaneously to the animal? The procedure and results are outlined in Figure 4.12.

Note first in Figure 4.12 that adding the light (CS_2) to the excitatory conditioned tone (CS_1) produces *less* suppression than would be expected to the tone alone. The CR to the combined stimuli indicates that the CR to each stimulus summated algebraically. In the conditioned suppression example, adding

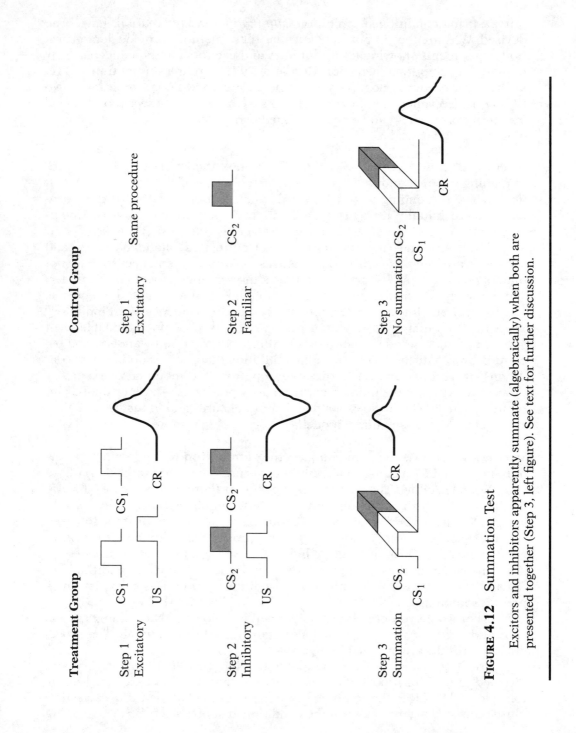

FIGURE 4.12 Summation Test

Excitors and inhibitors apparently summate (algebraically) when both are presented together (Step 3, left figure). See text for further discussion.

the light *diminishes* the ability of the excitor to suppress lever-press responses (Solomon, Brennan, & Moore, 1974).

The speed at which you drive a car in traffic is an illustration of the summation of excitatory and inhibitory elements. You approach a green traffic signal in a 35-mph zone. What stimulus elements contribute to your constantly adjusted speed? It is raining (inhibitor); the traffic is flowing smoothly (excitor); a police car is in the next lane (inhibitor); you are late for an appointment (excitor); you hear a siren (major inhibitor); the cop turns, and your rearview mirror is clear (major excitor). Your speed reflects the summation of these various elements.

Back in the laboratory, the experimenter must control for the possibility that *any* stimulus might interfere with an excitatory conditioned response, not just one that was conditioned in an inhibitory manner. (Remember the slamming door in Pavlov's external inhibition phenomenon and what it did to the dog's excitatory conditioned response?) A control group in which the light is made familiar prior to adding it to the tone is shown in Figure 4.12. Note that the control group sees the light the same number of times as the treatment group but that for the treatment group the light is a conditioned inhibitor. Merely presenting the light with the tone does not produce summation as it did with the treatment group. Can you figure out why, in the control group, the familiar light did *not* externally inhibit the tone in the same way that a slamming door inhibited the dog's conditioned salivatory response?[9]

The interaction of excitatory and inhibitory processes can be seen in driving a car, playing a basketball game, and reading the preceding paragraph. Eyes drowsy? Too many unexplained ideas (i.e., too many inhibitory, partially understood sentences)? Get up and walk around, and allow some of the inhibitory process accompanying a long session of processing difficult material to dissipate. It would be a good idea if your professors gave everyone 2 to 3 minutes in the middle of long lectures to accomplish the same end.

Retardation Test.   A final procedure that allows experimenters to indirectly measure conditioned inhibition is called the **retardation test**. Simply put, once a stimulus has been made a conditioned inhibitor, it is more difficult to turn that stimulus into an excitor. Let us return to the algebra classroom: In high school, you read too many words and too many formulas that you did not understand. Inhibitory processes built up to those CS^-s. These inhibitory processes will interfere with trying to learn similar material. To the laboratory.

Let us use as an example flavor preference and aversion conditioning, as outlined in Figure 4.13. First condition a preference to a flavor using a negative contingency (cf. the *medicine effect*). That is, in Step 1 (Figure 4.13) an illness experience (US) is always followed by a flavor CS, eventually making the flavor a conditioned inhibitor. In Step 2, the same flavor is now paired

---

[9] The key is that the light was made familiar (loss of orienting response) in the present example. Therefore, when presented along with the tone, the light presumably captured little of the animal's attention.

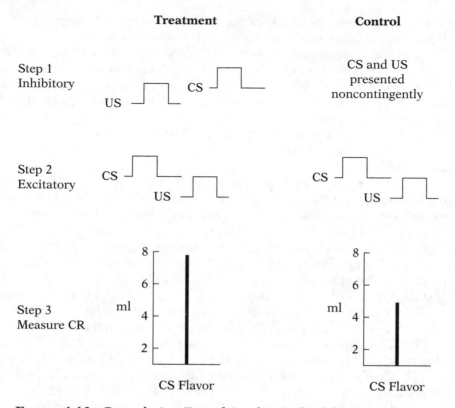

FIGURE 4.13   Retardation Test of Conditioned Inhibition

In the figure more aversion to the flavor is conditioned in the control group (5-ml intake) than the inhibitory treatment group (~8-ml intake). Why? Because following inhibitory training in Step 1, an inhibitory flavor is less easily conditioned when used as an excitor (Treatment Steps 2 and 3) relative to an equally familiar flavor (control). Hence, the inhibitory treatment "retarded" the excitatory aversive conditioning. *Note:* Greater excitatory conditioned taste aversion is reflected by *lower* intake values.

with illness in an excitatory framework. Can a conditioned inhibitor be made into a conditioned excitor? As we see in the next paragraph, only with difficulty.

The results of this retardation treatment are compared with those of a control group in Figure 4.13. The control group experiences both the flavor and the illness but not in a contingent (or contiguous) way. Then the flavor is made a conditioned excitor in Step 2, as in the retardation treatment (i.e., the flavor is made aversive by having the rat experience sickness *after* tasting the flavor). Note that in Figure 4.13, Step 3, after conditioning, the control group dislikes the flavor more (consumes fewer milliliters of the flavor in a test) than does the treatment group.

Conclusion: The treatment group was *retarded* in acquiring an aversion to a flavor that was previously conditioned in an inhibitory manner. A conditioned inhibitor can become a conditioned excitor, but more trials are required relative to a control group. You can learn new responses to algebra symbols and formulas to which inhibitory processes were attached in high school, but it will be more difficult. Likewise, if you decide on the first day that your prof is a nerd, his presence becomes a conditioned inhibitor. The prof's presence will likely retard the learning of new material.

Current Status of Conditioned Inhibition

The relationship of conditioned inhibition procedures and processes to second-order conditioning (Yin, Barnet, & Miller, 1994) and to extinction and spontaneous recovery (Fiori, Barnet, & Miller, 1994), to take but two examples, have been reported recently.

A summary of ways by which inhibitors are conditioned and the indirect tests for conditioned inhibition are presented in Table 4.2.

At the beginning of this chapter, a number of questions were posed concerning both the ecological validity and extrapolation of results of condition-

TABLE 4.2 Contemporary Methods of Producing and Measuring Conditioned Inhibition

Methods of Production	
Method	**Description**
Negative contingency	A backward conditioning procedure that produces a CR opposite in direction to the unconditioned response (i.e., if fear is the excitatory CR, safety is the inhibitory CR).
Induction procedure	A neutral stimulus is added to an excitatory CS in extinction; the neutral stimulus acquires inhibitory properties.

Indirect Methods of Testing	
Method	**Description**
Retardation procedure	An inhibitory conditioned stimulus is slower to acquire excitatory properties during excitatory conditioning.
Summation procedure	An inhibitory conditioned stimulus is placed in compound with a novel CS, thereby slowing excitatory conditioning to the novel CS.

ing experiments on animals in laboratories. Ultimately, you, the reader, must be the judge of these issues. From your reading so far, have *you* derived any insight into your personal behavior in:

> Classrooms (bored and sleepy, waiting for the bell, or hopeless in the face of algebra)?
>
> Your reaction to gifts?
>
> Automobiles (how fast you drive or how your attention wanders while you are waiting at red lights)?
>
> Your personal interactions with others?
>
> Your attitudes toward foods and restaurants?
>
> The effects the words of this text have on you (aroused or bored)?
>
> The effects spoken language has on you?

Given what you have learned so far, what do you think of general associative models of learning? Do learning experiments using laboratory animals tell you anything about yourself?

Interim Summary

1. Pavlov identified two types of inhibition that directly affected excitatory salivary conditioning. The first type, *external inhibition*, occurred when an extraneous stimulus such as a sudden noise disrupted conditioning of a salivary response. The second, *internal inhibition*, occurred during extinction, as evidenced by spontaneous recovery.

2. Other evidence of an inhibitory process occurs during a *conditioned discrimination* procedure. Excitatory conditioning (CS⁺) is alternated with inhibitory conditioning (CS⁻). The animal learns to respond to CS⁺ and not to respond to CS⁻. Under these conditions, emotional responses are evident in the presence of CS⁻.

3. During a long CS presented in extinction, Pavlov found drowsiness and reduced salivary response during the first part of the interval. He called this an *inhibition of delay* procedure.

4. *Conditioned inhibition* is readily conditioned using two contemporary procedures, namely a *negative contingency* and an *induction procedure*. Both result in a conditioned response opposite in effect to that of conditioned excitation. The CS acquires conditioned inhibitory properties and is called a *conditioned inhibitor*.

5. Two contemporary methods of measuring conditioned inhibition are the *retardation procedure* and the *summation procedure*. Using *retardation*, an inhibitory conditioned stimulus is demonstrated to acquire excitatory properties slowly during excitatory conditioning. In summation, an in-

hibitory conditioned stimulus is placed in compound with a novel CS, thereby slowing excitatory conditioning to the novel CS.

GENERAL PROCESS, PREPAREDNESS, AND OTHER LEARNING THEORIES

Two views of behavior were presented in Chapter 2. On the one hand, ethologists focus on phyletic relationships among animals, and species differences of animals living within distinctive ethological niches. They note that animals appear to behave in highly adaptive ways. Animals engage in those behaviors that promote survival. They engage in behaviors that produce the next generation. Birds and mammals take care of the resulting offspring.

On the other hand, comparative psychologists and other neuroscientists who study behavior focus more on behavioral *plasticity*. How do relatively large-brained vertebrates respond to changes in their immediate environment? How do they learn and remember from their interactions with the environment they encounter and, in the case of humans, the environment they create?

A suggestion was made in Chapter 2 that psychologists focus on plasticity in behavior (rather than on fixed action patterns, critical periods, and consummatory behaviors) because their ultimate goals are different from those of ethologists. Historically, psychologists' *primary* interests lie in understanding the mind of the creature with the most variable behavior of all, *Homo sapiens*. In addition to being used to study the behavior of a *particular* animal in the laboratory, laboratory animals become a convenient means to test theories and *to model human learning and memory processes* as well. Hence, the interest throughout this chapter is in applying the results of animal experiments to real-life human situations. Indeed, Chapter 7 in its entirety is devoted to further applications of animal learning experiments and theory to the human condition.

Reexamination of Issues. In this concluding section, we reexamine several issues raised earlier. Are there species differences in learning? Does each animal bring genetically coded behavior and innate reaction patterns to the laboratory? Is *general process learning theory* sufficient to account for most instances of animal learning? Why are certain stimuli and certain responses in certain animals conditioned relatively easily, but others are conditioned with great difficulty? What is the status of contemporary theories of learning?

Can Any Stimulus Become a Conditioned Stimulus?

Earlier we asked whether the laboratory is a valid ecological niche in which to study learning. One question raised about laboratory research has to do with the use of "artificial" stimuli in conditioning animals. Where can electric shock be found in nature? Or, for that matter, carefully timed bells, whistles, and metronomes? Given the divergent evolutionary histories of animals and the different niches they presently occupy, is it reasonable to think that *any* stimulus is arbitrarily interchangeable with another? If some animals rely primarily on taste and smell to negotiate their niche, for example, isn't it reasonable to expect that they would learn differently using these stimuli than, for example, a visual or an auditory stimulus? Can learning measured in laboratories using arbitrary stimuli and arbitrary responses (such as lever pressing) ever reflect real-life learning?

Pavlov's Assertion: "Yes."   After studying the issue for 30 years, Pavlov's conclusion follows:

> We must now take some account of the agencies which can be transformed into conditioned stimuli. This is not so easy a problem as appears at first sight. Of course to give a general answer is very simple; *any agent in nature which acts on any adequate receptor apparatus of an organism can be made into a conditioned stimulus for that organism.* This general statement, however, needs both amplification and restriction. (Pavlov, 1927/1960, p 38; italics added)

Among the "amplification and restriction" were pages and pages of experiments with dogs in which *particular* stimuli selected to be CSs conditioned either with ease or with difficulty. The law of strength held for a wide range of stimulus intensities, but if a stimulus was *too* intense, it could not be used effectively as a CS. Another troubling example is that of *temporal conditioning.* The mere passage of time (for which there is no apparent "receptor apparatus"!) can become an effective conditioned stimulus. In yet other experiments, Pavlov found that the *cessation* of a stimulus could become a conditioned stimulus. In his words,

> A metronome is sounded continuously in the experimental laboratory when the dog is brought in. The sound of the metronome is now cut out, and immediately an unconditioned stimulus, say food or a rejectable substance, is introduced. After several repetitions of this procedure it is found that the disappearance of the sound has become the stimulus to a new conditioned reflex. (Pavlov, 1927/1960, p. 39)

Growth of General Process Learning Theory

Laboratory researchers took Pavlov at his word and by the mid-1960s had developed a *general process learning* philosophy that made the following assumptions:

1. Choice of research animal is relatively arbitrary.
2. Choice of stimuli used in experiments is relatively arbitrary.

TABLE 4.3   General Process Learning: A Comparison
of Conditioning Parameters

Researcher (Subject)	CS (Duration)	US (Duration)	CS-US Interval	Number of Trials
Pavlov (1927) (dog)	Metronome (30 s)	Food (~10 s)	30 s	5–9
Watson and Rayner (1920) (human)	White rat (~5 s)	Loud clang (~2 s)	~2–3 s	7
Kamin (1965) (rat)	81-dB white noise (2.0 min)	0.85-mA shock (0.5 s)	3.0 min	6–8
Gormezano (1965) (rabbit)	800-hz tone, 72 dB (0.6 s)	Air puff (0.5 s)	0.5 s	~200

3. Choice of reflexes and types of responses by which to measure learning is relatively arbitrary.

From many different laboratories had come results with a variety of animals in different conditioning situations that seemed to support a *general process* approach to learning. A sampling of these experiments is presented in Table 4.3.

Note both the similarities and the differences in these experiments. For example, four different species (albeit all mammals) were used: dogs, a human infant, rats, and rabbits. Three sounds (a metronome, white noise, a pure tone) and one visual stimulus (the sight of a moving white rat) were used as CSs. Four different USs (three aversive, one appetitive) were used: electric shock, a loud clang, an air puff, and food. CSs were a half second to 2 minutes in duration; USs ranged from less than a second to a few seconds in duration. Interestingly enough, the number of trials to accomplish conditioning (with the exception of eye-blink conditioning) ranged from five to nine trials even in these highly diverse situations.

The basis of a *general process* position, then, is that conditioning outcomes are predictable in a variety of animals and in a variety of stimulus situations.

Challenge to General Process Learning Theory

Several new experiments have been published—one in 1955, others in the mid-1960s—that didn't seem to fit general process learning theory. Let us take a closer look at them.

Ionizing Radiation as an Unconditioned Stimulus. For many years following World War II, the U.S. government supported research into the biological effects of ionizing radiation. Among its other effects, ionizing radiation had been demonstrated to disrupt eating and drinking patterns. An important paper published in the journal *Science* suggested that some of the feeding changes had been conditioned (Garcia, Kimeldorf, & Koelling, 1955).

If so, the conditioning was unlike anything Pavlov had previously reported. Rats had been allowed to drink a 0.1% saccharin solution during a 6-hour low-level ionizing radiation exposure. Several days later these rats' preference for saccharin was tested; after the radiation exposure, the rats avoided the saccharin.

Over the next several weeks, the rats drank increasing amounts of the saccharin solution. John Garcia and colleagues' analysis was that the saccharin had functioned as a CS during the radiation exposure and that the radiation acted as a US. The aversion to saccharin was interpreted as a conditioned response. The CR (aversion to saccharin) extinguished over the next few weeks as inferred from the rats' increasing acceptance of the saccharin-flavored water.

Compared to the methods and results of experiments in Table 4.3, the Garcia et al. (1955) finding raised several problems for traditional learning theory:

1. The CS and the US each lasted 6 hours rather than a few seconds or minutes.
2. Conditioning was accomplished in one trial.
3. Stimulus *contiguity was apparently unnecessary:* Assuming that the rats tasted saccharin early in the 6-hour interval and that the response to radiation (radiation sickness?) occurred some time *after* the 6-hour interval, the taste-to-illness interval could be interpreted to be more than 6 hours in duration.

Such rapid, one-trial, long-delay learning was unprecedented. Was it unique? Was it outside the pale of general process theory? Many thought so. General process learning theorists frankly did not know what to do with John Garcia's experiments.

The "Bright, Noisy, Tasty Water" Experiment

After a number of rejections by the editors of journals of animal learning research, Garcia finally published the results of another controversial experiment (Garcia & Koelling, 1966) that provided further insight into his first paper. Garcia and Koelling's "bright, noisy, tasty water" experiment is now considered a classic.

Rats were placed in an experimental chamber and allowed to lick a tube

	Radiation	Electric shock
Bright, noisy water	No conditioning	Aversive conditioning
Tasty water	Aversive conditioning	No conditioning

FIGURE 4.14   The Bright, Noisy, Tasty Water Experiment

The results of Garcia and Koelling's (1966) "bright, noisy, tasty water" experiment are summarized in the 2 x 2 matrix of two CSs (bright, noisy water or tasty water) and two USs (radiation or electric shock). Notice that not all CSs were conditioned with all USs. Garcia's conceptual schema of two conditioning systems—telereceptors (eyes, ears) with cutaneous stimuli (skin pain), and gustatory stimuli (taste) with visceral stimuli (gut pain)—was proposed by Garcia, Hankins, and Rusiniak (1974).

containing water. By adding saccharin, the water could be made "tasty." Every time the animal licked the water tube, an electric circuit was completed to briefly flash a ("bright") light in the rat's environment. The same circuit also produced a brief click ("noisy"); hence, the water had bright, noisy, and tasty (as well as wet) conditioned stimulus properties.

Half the rats were trained to drink the bright, noisy, tasty water, following which they were exposed to ionizing radiation (the US). The other half were punished by being exposed to a brief electric shock after licking the fluid for a short time.

To test whether the audiovisual (noisy, bright) or the taste component of the water conditioned best with the electric shock or with the radiation US, the bright, noisy, tasty water was separated into component parts during extinction tests. Rats had the choice of drinking either bright, noisy water or tasty water. The results are shown in Figure 4.14.

In the bright, noisy, tasty water experiment, rats associated the audiovisual components of the compound stimulus with electric shock and the taste component with the radiation exposure. Garcia and Koelling (1966) interpreted these results to mean that not all stimuli were capable of entering into association; rather, there was **stimulus specificity in conditioning.** Taste and sickness were easily associated together, Garcia argued, because rats were evolutionarily prepared to associate flavors with the normal consequences of eating. Likewise, the sights and sounds of predators were more likely to be conditioned with pain rather than with gut sickness. This experiment, he argued,

FOCUS ON RESEARCH 4.2

Types of Learning

John Garcia, Professor Emeritus,
University of California at Los Angeles

"The entwined enigma of learning and the nature-nurture issue continues to amaze me. When any two events, such as signal-food and noise-shock, appear in close proximity, an association will be learned by various species. And when taste is followed by delayed nausea, animals will learn a taste aversion, be they snails, insects, fish, amphibians, reptiles, birds, humans, or other mammals. Genetic differences among species have surprisingly little effect on learning. In contrast, Americans all belong to the same species, exhibiting minor biological variation but major subcultural variation. When they are given 'intelligence tests,' which are memory tests composed of cultural bits, some psychologists think the scores reflect the genetic differences more than the subcultural differences among Americans. Other psychologists think the tests are unfair; many feel such tests are trivial. Why the disparity? I agree with Szent-Gyorgyi, a 1937 Nobel laureate in physiology. He said, 'The brain in not an organ of thinking, but an organ of survival like claws and fangs. It is made in such a way as to make us accept as truth that which is only advantage.'"

provided evidence for two quite different learning systems, a telereceptor-cutaneous system and a gustatory-visceral system (Garcia, Hankins, & Rusiniak, 1974).

Taste aversion conditioning has been investigated in many species of both vertebrates and invertebrates. Focus on Research 4.2 highlights Dr. John Garcia, a pioneer researcher in the field of conditioned taste aversions. Note that Garcia is also interested in using learning and behavioral theory to analyze cultural differences.

A number of methodological problems in Garcia and Koelling's (1966) experiment clouded interpretation of their results. However, a replication of the bright, noisy, tasty water experiment by Domjan and Wilson (1972) using a between-groups design both simplified the methods and clarified the theoretical issues. For this reason, their experiment rather than Garcia's will be the basis for further discussion. Domjan and Wilson used lithium chloride to induce sickness and conditioned a taste aversion. The taste cue failed to become associated with electric shock. Likewise, a "pulsed buzzer" was associated with electric shock but not with lithium. Not all cues are equally associable with all consequences.

Preparedness: An Evolutionary Learning Theory

Several other learning theorists (i.e., Rozin & Kalat, 1971; Seligman, 1970) agreed with Garcia's analysis. These theorists broadened the evolutionary argument. In developing a theory of **preparedness,** they argued that certain animals are (evolutionarily) *prepared* to readily make some associations and are *unprepared,* or even *contraprepared,* to make others.

> What an organism learns in the laboratory or in his natural habitat is the result not only of the contingencies which he faces and has faced in his past but also of the contingencies which his species faced before him—its evolutionary history and genetic outcome. (Rozin & Kalat, 1971)

Preparedness and Neophobia.   The rapid learning about flavors found in experiments by Garcia and others complements other species-specific behavioral tendencies in rats that together facilitate their success at securing food. Rats display neophobia (*fear of new*) when they confront unfamiliar flavors (tastes and smells) of foods and fluids.[10] Their innately organized feeding behavior prepares even hungry rats to approach new foods cautiously. Rats sniff, retreat, approach, sniff and nibble (taste), and retreat. On their next approach, they sniff, nibble, and ingest a small amount (the exact amount depending on hunger and the taste, smell, and temperature characteristics of the food). After minimal ingestion, again they retreat. On subsequent encounters they eat increasingly more (Domjan, 1977). One theory is that if rats experience no immediate ill-effects from what they ate, they shortly return to eat more.

Given this innate wariness, or "bait shyness," about new foods, complemented by the rats' ability to form flavor-illness associations in only one trial, it is easy to see why "rats as pests" are so difficult to poison (Rzoska, 1953). Let us look more closely at the "number of trials to learn" evidence for preparedness.

Preparedness and "Number of Trials."   Rozin and Kalat (1971) used the "number of trials to learn" metric to support evolutionary arguments. For example, learning taste aversions in one trial, they argued, constitutes evidence of preparedness in learning. The brains of animals that learn certain behaviors in one trial have been selected through the evolutionary process. Animals possessing brain structures that were able to learn rapidly about poisoned food

---

[10] Including, of course, rug rats. Neophobic tendencies in humans are so strong that children attribute draconian motivations to parents who attempt to introduce new foods. Indeed, more than one of my children, even at 10 years of age, have accused me of trying to poison them.

sources lived; those that didn't died. Why? Because more than one poisoning trial increases the likelihood of a fatal encounter with poison.

Unprepared and Contraprepared Learning.   Pavlov's dogs, the argument continues, took five to nine trials to learn that sights and sounds predicted food. The dogs were **unprepared,** or, at best, neutral regarding these stimuli; the intermediate number of trials necessary for conditioning to occur is evidence for their unpreparedness. Using similar reasoning, rabbits and humans are apparently **contraprepared** to learn about sights and sounds that predict air puffs to the cornea of the eye. Such conditioning is not ever likely to happen in *any* animal's ecological niche. That such conditioning can occur at all attests to the inherent plasticity of mammalian brains.

Birds Associate Color, Not Taste, with Poison?   Given the diversity of life forms and of the niches they occupy, what predictions can be made concerning cross-species comparisons? Unless animals occupy very similar niches, the preparedness argument goes, one should not expect them to associate stimuli in the same way. Birds, for example, conduct visual rather than olfactory searches for food. They make ingestional decisions more on what something *looks* like than how it tastes, and they should learn better about foods using visual rather than taste cues (i.e., the reverse of rats).

This hypothesis was tested by Wilcoxson, Dragoin, and Kral (1971). They allowed both laboratory rats and Japanese quail to drink blue (food coloring) or sour (slightly acidic) water and then poisoned the animals with a drug called *cyclophosphamide*. The entire procedure was accomplished in one trial. As in the bright, noisy, tasty water experiment, the compound CS was separated during extinction testing. The rats and quail were tested with a choice of drinking either blue or sour water. Rats, they reported, chose blue and declined the sour water. Quail rejected the blue-colored water but drank the sour water.

Again, these results constitute evidence for *stimulus specificity in conditioning*. The quail and rats were evolutionarily *prepared* to make these selective associations.

Preparedness Versus General Processes

The preceding experiments present problems for general process learning theory on several counts: First, one trial learning over *very* long delays is possible for taste paired with illness-inducing stimuli. Second, specific stimuli appear to enter into association, and others not, depending on species of animal. The preparedness challenge to general process theory is an important one because most humans consider themselves to be *truly* unique among species. If special rules of association formation are found to hold for some species, it must certainly be the case that learning accomplished by humans will be found to be the most different of all. Let us take a further look at these issues.

TABLE 4.4 Conditioning Failures?

Researcher	CS (Duration)	US (Quantity, Duration)	CS-US Interval	Number of Trials
Domjan and Wilson (1972)	Pulsed buzzer (35 s)	Lithium chloride (~20 ml/kg, ip)	35 s	3
	0.2% saccharin (35 s)	Electric shock (140V, 0.5 s)	35 s	3
Wilcoxson, Dragoin, and Kral (1971)	Blue water (30 min)	Cytoxan® (66 mg/kg)	30 min	1

Analysis of Conditioning Failures

Why did rats fail to associate the audiovisual stimulus with the radiation stimulus? Is the rat really unable to make flavor–electric shock associations in the bright, noisy, tasty water experiment? Why are quail apparently unable to form a sour taste–sickness association? Let us take a closer look at the conditioning failures noted in these two experiments. Conditioning parameters used in these experiments are summarized in Table 4.4.

Compare the procedures in Table 4.4 with those in Table 4.3. Note in Table 4.4 the main difference in these experiments compared with conditioning "failures." Only *one* conditioning trial (Wilcoxson et al., 1971) and *three* conditioning trials (Domjan & Wilson, 1972) were conducted (compared to a minimum of five trials in Table 4.3). Perhaps conditioning failed simply because not enough conditioning trials were conducted. Would we conclude that salivary conditioning was impossible if Pavlov had conducted a single bell–food trial?

Is it easier to condition a taste with illness in rats and a visual cue with illness in Japanese quail? Apparently so. Is it *possible* to condition a taste with illness in quail and visual cues with illness in rats? The answer for quail is *probably* "yes," and for rats, *definitely* "yes" (see Best's experiments, Focus on Research 4.1, p. 167). Species differences exist among birds. Hawks, for example, *require* taste cues to make visual associations. Hawks poisoned after eating black mice learned *not* to eat them only if the mice were also made bitter flavored; only after the black-bitter-poison association was made did they quit eating black mice and continue eating white mice (Brett, Hankins, & Garcia, 1976).[11]

---

[11] Why did the taste cue allow the hawk to begin to associate the visual cue with poison? (Why was Candace reluctant to return to Mamma Rollo's?) See Box 4.3.

Taste-Shock Associations.   Given the findings that visual cues *can* be associated with poisons, is there comparable evidence that *taste* can be associated with electric shock? Yes. An interesting experiment reported by Krane and Wagner (1975) indicated that an important variable in making taste-shock conditioning work was to delay the shock. Saccharin has a relatively long-lasting aftertaste. Krane and Wagner compared taste-shock conditioning at various intervals and found that associations formed only if the taste's duration did not extend past delivery of the electric shock.[12]

Analysis of *Preparedness* Conditioning

The earlier conditioning "failures" were accounted for by simply noting that stimulus-stimulus associations cannot be expected to form in one to three trials. Were associations found to be *impossible* after many trials, the *specificity in conditioning* position could be considered a more serious threat to a general process learning position. But, you may argue, taste aversions *do* form in one trial over long CS-US delays. Doesn't that observation by itself violate general process learning theory? Maybe, maybe not. Consider the following arguments:

1. Within a sensory modality, both intensity and duration effects are important factors in conditioning (see Pavlov's law of strength).
2. Although beginning with Pavlov, many have tried, but no one has yet solved the problem of equating stimulus intensities *across* modalities.
3. Regarding "tastes" and "poisons," general process learning theory predicts that both intensity and duration effects are important factors that predict ease of conditioning.
4. Most demonstrations of one-trial taste aversion conditioning over delays of several hours have used very intense taste stimuli, that is, strongly flavored solutions consumed for several minutes (Smith & Roll, 1969) or hours (Garcia et al., 1955), followed by long-lasting illnesses induced by radiation or lithium (Barker & Smith, 1974).

Preparedness or Stimulus Intensity Effects?   What would happen if taste aversion conditioning parameters were altered so that they more closely resembled *other* general process procedures? That is, would you still find one trial conditioning over a 30-minute delay if a *very brief* flavor (lasting only a few seconds) were paired with a tiny amount of toxin that produced only a mild illness?

---

[12] A student once suggested that if the electric shock were made intense enough, it presumably would take on some of the same characteristics of an "illness-inducing agent" (e.g., nausea). Why is this an important observation?

These brief, less potent stimulus presentations are more comparable to the conditioning parameters reported in Table 4.3. One-trial taste aversion conditioning has been found to be impossible under these conditions (Monroe & Barker, 1979). A mild conditioned aversion to the taste of saccharin *was* found after eight such trials. Monroe and Barker concluded that general process learning theory rather than preparedness theory better accounts for these results. Other theorists (Domjan, 1983; Logue, 1979) have come to similar conclusions.

General Process Learning Versus Preparedness: Tentative Conclusions

Animals bring not only specialized sensory and motor apparatus to the laboratory but also an associative apparatus that has a long and specialized evolutionary history. Each animal's nervous system apparently makes certain contingencies easier to learn than others in that, as Pavlov first noted, some stimuli are conditioned in a few trials, and others require many trials. This finding became yet more clear when Garcia-like experiments were conducted.

Role of Stimulus Salience in Conditioning. The number of trials it takes for a stimulus to become a CS defines the *salience* of that stimulus. Among other variables, the best predictor of salience is stimulus intensity. As a general rule, more intense stimuli are more salient in that they require fewer trials to be associated. That stimulus intensity is the best predictor of stimulus *salience* seems to be invariant across species.

Role of Stimulus Specificity in Conditioning. Evidence for stimulus *specificity* in conditioning across species is not as compelling as evidence for stimulus *intensity* in conditioning across species. For example, Pavlov noted that his dogs associated sounds better than visual stimuli with food during excitatory conditioning and sights better than sounds with food during inhibitory conditioning over a delay. But the general rule he formulated still holds, namely, that any stimulus can be made into a conditioned stimulus.

General Process Learning Can Incorporate Preparedness Observations. Most observations of how and what animals learn can be incorporated into general process learning theory (Domjan, 1983; Logue, 1979). Some researchers disagree (see Timberlake, 1994). General process learning theory was put to the test in accommodating the results of preparedness experiments. The end result is a synthesis, an evolutionarily based general process theory that accounts for many hundreds of behavioral observations in the field and in the laboratory. Humans are not rats or quail. And rats and quail learn some things differently (more or less rapidly) than humans. But evidence for a general process associative mechanism among vertebrates remains convincing.

Interim Summary

1. Most stimuli can be made into conditioned stimuli, but both stimulus intensity and stimulus quality affect the ease of stimulus associability.

2. A number of experiments have demonstrated that some stimulus-stimulus associations are easy and others are difficult. This has been interpreted to mean that there is a *stimulus specificity of association.*

3. *Preparedness* theory argues that some animals are evolutionarily predisposed to learn those tasks that promote survival more quickly than tasks that are unrelated to survival.

4. Animals are said to be *prepared, unprepared,* or *contraprepared* to learn certain tasks if it takes few trials, an intermediate number of trials, or many trials, respectively.

5. Rapid learning about the consequences of ingestion is aided by innately organized feeding behavior. *Neophobia* toward new foods and reduced neophobia with continued exposure to these foods are adaptive in that poisoning is minimized.

6. Flavors are easily associated with illness-inducing toxins and less easily associated with electric shock. With optimal stimulus parameters, flavors and toxin effects can become associated in one trial over a delay of several hours, said by Garcia and others to be evidence of prepared associability.

7. Garcia and others also suggested that visual and auditory stimuli were easily associated with pain but were contraprepared to be associated with illness.

8. Stimuli in "prepared" experiments often vary in modality, intensity, duration, and number of conditioning trials compared to stimuli in "contraprepared" experiments.

9. Matching shock intensity with illness intensity, intensity and duration of taste stimuli with audiovisual stimuli, and number of conditioning trials has not been accomplished, making comparisons across these experiments most difficult. Appealing to evolutionary arguments to account for different conditioning outcomes is confounded by these procedural differences.

10. *General process learning* complements prepared learning. The former remains the best account of observed plasticity in animal behavior, including complex human behavior.

Comparing assumptions of preparedness and general process approaches to learning brings us to the concluding section of this chapter. Let us now take our first look at formal theories of learning.

THEORIES OF ASSOCIATION FORMATION

To this point Pavlovian conditioning has been labeled, described, and defined but not explained. That is, a *theory of conditioning* has not been presented. For good reason. No matter how simplistic (and, by way of hindsight, intuitively obvious) Pavlovian conditioning may seem to be, contemporary theories of conditioning remain incomplete. That is to say, existing theories are neither exhaustive nor mutually exclusive. Nor is there agreement about whether the theory should be at the level of either brain functioning or observable behavior.

In the remainder of this chapter, several theories of learning are presented. Some you are familiar with, and others are presented to extend your thinking about what form brain-based and behavioral theories of conditioning might take. We start by reconsidering contiguity theory. Pavlov's law of strength described how associative conditioning could be degraded by separating the CS and US in time. Implicit in this formulation is the "theory" that association formation depends on perceived *contiguity* of stimuli; hence, we *should* expect that trace conditioning produces poorer conditioning due to less association of stimulus elements.

Dominance-Contiguity Theory

In addition to maintaining his own program of animal research, Gregory Razran read and translated Russian experiments for 30 years following Pavlov's death. His book *Mind in Evolution* (1971) presents an evolutionary schema in which animals learn at different conceptual levels depending on their brain development. In this respect his book anticipates a number of the major themes of this one.

Razran (1957, 1971) shifted the theoretical focus of Pavlovian conditioning from that of association between *stimuli* to association of *responses* to those stimuli. According to Razran's dominance-contiguity theory, afferent neural activity (i.e., sensory nerves signaling events in the environment to the brain) underlies each conditioning experiment. The CS and US produce the "R_o" (his abbreviation for the orienting *r*esponse to the CS) and the UR, respectively. The association is made between the R_o and the UR via unspecified *neural activation* (Razran, 1971).

According to Razran, *contiguity is necessary but not sufficient for conditioning.* In each conditioning situation, the neural events must occur close in time, and for conditioning to occur, two conditions typically are met: R_o slightly precedes the UR, and the UR *dominates* R_o. By "dominate," Razran refers to both the quantity and quality of the unmeasured neural activity that underlies the UR. Razran's theory helps account for numerous demonstrations of simultaneous and excitatory backward conditioning that cannot be accounted for by contingency theory. The learning literature is sprinkled with reports of excitatory backward conditioning since Pavlov's research in 1927 (see Spetch, Wilkie, & Pinel, 1981, for a review). For example, rats can be made sick prior to tasting a flavor, yet they learn aversions to the flavor (Barker & Weaver, 1991). Excitatory backward conditioning can occur in Razran's model by postulating that the second stimulus in the sequence (whether a CS or US) is merely the "dominating stimulus" of the pair. For example, if a weak US were used as the first stimulus and paired with a strong CS as the second stimulus, excitatory associative conditioning could result.

Criticism of Dominance-Contiguity Theory.   Razran uses unmeasured nervous activity to speculate about the outcomes of various behavioral manipulations. As such, like Pavlov's role of "visual and auditory analyzers," the "theory" makes predictions based on unobservable brain events. The circumstances of many (most?) experiments do not allow researchers to specify in a meaningful way either the magnitudes nor the onsets, durations, and offsets of neural responses to stimuli. In addition, Razran's theory is post hoc; only in the most general way can predictions about conditioning outcomes be made before the fact. Tests of dominance-contiguity theory then are difficult.

US-US and Bidirectional Conditioning

Two other theories are not inconsistent with Razran's focus on the brain's response to intense USs. Rather than the role reversal of CS and US proposed by Razran, both of these theoretical positions posit that two USs may enter into association, that is, *US-US conditioning*. For example, Solomon (1977) interprets the rapid, one-trial acquisition of flavor aversions as being the result of a flavor *US* (rather than a flavor CS) entering into association with a toxin (illness-producing) US. US-US conditioning would also predict that two flavor USs would rapidly associate with each other. An unusual *within-compound association* experiment by Rescorla and Cunningham (1978) showed this to be the case. First they made a compound solution composed of salt mixed with quinine that only a rat would love (but they don't). Then they conditioned an aversion to the salt/quinine solution by having the rats drink it and then a toxin US. Finally, they extinguished the quinine solution by repeatedly presenting it to the rats and not poisoning them. A control group did not have the quinine aversion extinguished. Relative to this control group, these researchers found that the aversion to salt was also extinguished. A likely interpretation is that the two flavors—both with US properties—became associated with each other while in the compound.

In addition, Gormezano and Tait (1976) cite Russian literature and some of their own research to develop a theory of *bidirectional conditioning*. They propose that conditioned responses develop concurrently both to the first and to the second stimulus presented the animal during conditioning. That is, *all stimulus pairings* produce both forward and, to a lesser degree, backward associations. They point out that researchers never measure the backward associations that may have formed to the US, but only the conditioned responses that have formed to the CS.

Little empirical evidence exists to support a theory of bidirectional conditioning. Three recent studies using very different methodologies conditioned animals over long intervals. Each finding suggested that both excitatory and inhibitory properties can be simultaneously conditioned in fear conditioning studies in rats (Anastasia & LoLordo, 1994), in fixed-interval appetitive schedules with pigeons (Palya, 1993), and in backward taste aversion conditioning with rats (Barker & Weaver, 1991). However, none of these studies specifically discussed bidirectional conditioning.

Pavlov never mentioned what the dog's ears did when, after bell-food conditioning, he merely fed it without ringing the bell. Why would this observation be relevant to a theory of bidirectional conditioning?

Contingency Theory

In Pavlov's traditional experiments there was always a perfect positive contingency between the CS and the US. That is, during acquisition, the US was always presented with the CS and was never presented in the absence of the CS.

Negative Contingencies. What happens in "backward" conditioning experiments? Interestingly, contingency theory predicts that if the US reliably *precedes* the CS, when the CS occurs it predicts a time period following during which no US will occur. These *negative contingencies* are as informative to the animal as positive contingencies. If, for example, a shock US reliably is *followed* by a tone CS, the tone predicts a safe period (i.e., one in which no shock will occur).

Note that learning does occur when negative contingencies are employed; however, *what* is learned differs from pairing the same stimuli in a positive contingency. In the present example, tone followed by shock (a positive contingency) produces excitatory conditioning; shock followed by tone (a negative contingency) produces inhibitory conditioning. As described earlier, the tone predicts a safe period in which no shock occurs.

But the story is even more complicated than this. During the first few conditioning trials of a negative shock-tone contingency, the animal learns a fear response (excitatory conditioning) to the tone. Only after many more trials does the animal learn that the tone is signaling a safe period (Heth, 1976). Note that contingency theory accounts for association formation in both forward and trace conditioning experiments. Likewise, contingency theory predicts the absence of conditioning in a "simultaneous" or "embedded" design (see Figure 3.9). In both stimulus arrangements the conditioned stimulus (S_1) does not precede, and therefore does not predict, the unconditioned stimulus (S_2).

Contiguity and Contingency Theories Compared

Both **contingency** and **contiguity theories of association** formation are necessary to account for the conditioning examples we have considered to this point. Contingency theory can better account for the fact that a very slight delay between the CS onset and the US onset (delay and trace procedures) produces much better conditioning than if the stimulus onsets are simultaneous. In both delay and trace procedures, a relatively neutral stimulus *predicts* a biologically more meaningful stimulus. Contingency theory also predicts that conditioning is *not* the inevitable outcome of the pairing of two stimuli, as follows: (a) if enough USs are presented in the absence of the CS, for example, the ones that *are* paired with the CS do not form associations as readily and (b) simultaneous and backward procedures, both lacking US predictability by the CS, typically produce less excitatory conditioning.

Neither theory predicts some conditioning outcomes particularly well. For example, as pointed out by Papini and Bitterman (1990), overshadowing and blocking procedures impair the conditioning of one stimulus even though that stimulus remains positively correlated (and contiguous) with the US. In addition, neither theory accounts for many instances of one-trial conditioning especially well. Consider, for example, the many reports of one-trial, long-delay taste aversion conditioning in humans (Bernstein, 1978) and rats (Smith & Roll, 1967). In these examples stimulus contiguity is violated when tasting a flavor and getting ill are separated by several hours. Second, an animal cannot learn much about "the contingent relationships of two stimuli" after only one trial! Yet learning occurs in these situations.

Taste aversion learning is especially problematic for contingency theory. Elkins (1973), for example, was able to condition rats to avoid a saccharin solution in one drinking trial that led to illness, even though these rats had many hours of previous experience with the saccharin solution over many days. The contingency probability could be computed in this experiment to be less than

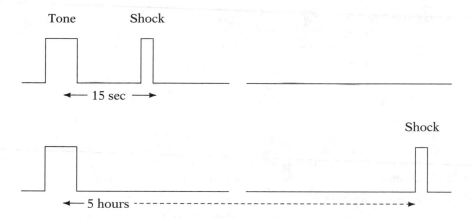

Tone   Shock

← 15 sec →

Shock

← 5 hours - →

FIGURE 4.15   Contiguity Is Necessary
                 for Contingency

The top group receives 20 trials consisting of a 5-second duration tone
followed 15 seconds later by a 1-second electric shock. The bottom group
experiences the same stimuli. The shock, however, is presented not 15
seconds but 5 hours later. Note that over 20 trials both groups enjoy the
same contingency:

$$p(S_2/S_1) = 1.0$$

Conditioning is a highly likely outcome for contiguous stimuli (top) and
highly unlikely for contingent but noncontiguous stimuli (bottom).

1% (i.e., $p[S_2/S_1] = 0.01$), yet an aversion was conditioned to saccharin that
proved to be highly resistant to extinction.

Necessity of Contiguity.   In the preceding chapter we learned that association by
contiguity necessarily preceded association by contingency (cf. *the two-stage
theory of association*). Are there instances of association by contingency in the
absence of contiguity? Consider the following thought experiment using a conditioned suppression methodology: What would you predict to be the outcome
of presenting a 5-second duration tone to a rat in an experimental chamber
and *5 hours later* delivering a 1-second electric shock? Even if this pairing were
to continue for 20 days, where $p(S_2/S_1) = 1.0$, an association of tone with shock
would be unlikely (see Figure 4.15).

  Conclusion? Every example of conditioning by "contingency" is confounded by the contiguity of the stimuli involved. If two stimuli in a contingent
relationship are too far removed in time from each other, no association will

TABLE 4.5   A Comparison of Contiguity and Contingency
Theories

Contiguity

Arguments for

1. Two stimuli presented closer together are better associated than two stimuli presented further apart.
2. Simultaneous and embedded stimuli (either with fuzzy stimulus onsets or when both CS and US may last for minutes to hours) can be associated together.
3. Backward excitatory conditioning can result from negative contingencies.

Arguments against

1. Contiguous stimuli may be less associable when the contingent relationship is degraded.
2. Direction of stimulus sequencing should not affect conditioning. It often does, resulting in either excitatory or inhibitory conditioning.
3. Contiguity cannot account for blocking or overshadowing.

Contingency

Arguments for

1. Positive contingencies produce excitatory conditioning, and negative contingencies often produce inhibitory conditioning.

Arguments against

1. Contingent stimuli must be close together to be associated.
2. All demonstrations of simultaneous, embedded, and backward excitatory conditioning constitute arguments against contingency theory.
3. Contingency cannot account for blocking or overshadowing.

occur. Vertebrate nervous systems were designed through natural selection to operate this way.

Summary of Contiguity and Contingency Theory.   Two theories of association formation can be conceptualized as information-processing models. Contiguity theory merely states that when two stimuli are presented together in time, they are likely to be perceived by the animal as belonging together. Contingency theory stresses that animals process the sequencing of two stimuli, such that the first stimulus predicts the occurrence of the second stimulus. A comparison of arguments supporting and refuting each position is found in Table 4.5.

Two important theoretical formulations that attempt to account for basic phenomena of conditioning are presented next: the theoretical position of Robert Rescorla and his colleagues (Rescorla, 1967; Rescorla & Wagner, 1972) and the *comparator hypothesis* of Ralph Miller and colleagues (Miller & Matzel, 1988).

Rescorla-Wagner Model

The *information-processing* approaches described earlier allow us to make valuable generalizations and predictions about the basic nature of association formation. Another approach is to attempt to model how humans and animals actually learn.

Learning English-Spanish Associations.   Consider, for example, using flip cards to memorize English-language equivalents of Spanish words. This task can be conceptualized as learning by association. The word *amarillo* is associated with *yellow* (*yellow* was associated with the sensation of seeing yellow earlier in the English speaker's life). Two items connected by association in this manner are called *paired associates*. One question that can be asked concerns the growth of association. Can we measure the association of *amarillo* with *yellow* as the student uses the flip cards, in which each encounter with the *amarillo— yellow* card constitutes one trial? Let us assume that it takes 10 trials to learn the association. Would you predict that most of the learning occurred in the first few trials, the middle trials, the last few trials, or in equal amounts on each trial?

The **Rescorla-Wagner model** addresses this and many other questions regarding the growth of associations between CSs and USs (Rescorla & Wagner, 1972; Wagner & Rescorla, 1972). Before seeing their solution, let us first look at three graphs of the question that has been posed.

Modeling the Growth of Association.   Three alternative models of the growth of association with each conditioning trial are presented in Figure 4.16. In the two upper panels, the association of the CS and the US increases either at a faster rate (Figure 4.16a) or at a constant rate (Figure 4.16b) with each successive pairing of CS and US. That is, if you had predicted that most of the flip-card learning had occurred in the last of the 10 trials, the graph on the left depicts this model. If you predicted that associations are learned in equal amounts on each trial, the middle graph depicts this model.

Both of these models have *intuitive* appeal (which means that they feel right—the models jive with what it feels like when you are memorizing a list of words). These intuitively appealing notions about the growth of association do not accord with the facts, however. Figure 4.16c better models the real world. Compare the idealized learning curve in Figure 4.16c with the acquisition function of salivation (Figure 3.5) and of fear conditioning using the conditioned suppression methodology depicted in Figure 3.7 (note especially the middle and right-hand panels; data of Annau & Kamin, 1961). In both graphs depicting real data *most of the associative learning occurs during the first few pair-*

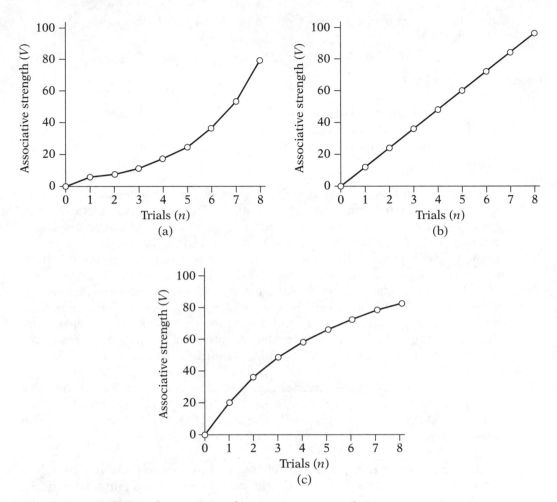

FIGURE 4.16   Three Alternatives of Associative Growth

Three alternative models of the growth of association are compared. In Figure 4.16a, each successive trial contributes a greater amount of associability and in Figure 4.16b an equal amount of association. Note that for the upper two panels there are no upper limits to the degree of association between stimuli. In the lower panel (Figure 4.16c) each successive trial contributes less, resulting in the negatively accelerated learning curve typical of most (but not all) conditioning experiments.

ings. In the last few trials very little is added to the strength of the association. Mathematical equations of both the growth of association and the shape of extinction functions have been proposed by two psychologists, Allan Wagner and Robert Rescorla. The Rescorla-Wagner model states that

$$\Delta V_n = \mathring{a}\beta(\lambda - V_n) \tag{4.1}$$

The left side of the equation defines how a conditioning trial changes the strength of association: Δ refers to "the change in," V_n refers to the amount of learned association that exists at the beginning of Trial n. The equation reads as follows: The growth of association (learning change in each trial) is determined by (equals) CS and US parameters ($\mathring{a}$ and β, respectively) times a quantity

$$\lambda - V_n \tag{4.2}$$

where λ (lambda) represents the maximum amount of conditioning possible in this experiment and V_n represents how much conditioning has already occurred.

Equation 4.2 is actually quite simple even for those of us not mathematically inclined. It states:

> The amount of association that occurs on any trial is determined by the maximum learning (association) possible (λ) minus how much has already been learned (V_n), taking into consideration the nature of the CSs and US ($\mathring{a}$ and β, respectively) that are being associated.

Referring to the curve depicted in Figure 4.16c, let us work through the equation with an example. Note that ΔV_1 (the change on Trial 1) is greater than ΔV_2 (the change on Trial 2) and that ΔV_3 (the change on Trial 3) is less than ΔV_2. Assume that the salience of the CS = 0.2. Further assume that the total amount of possible conditioning (lambda) = 100. We now can determine the amount of learning that will take place on the first trial:

$$\Delta V_0 = (0.2)(100 - V_{sum}) \tag{4.3}$$

(This is the first trial. Assume no previous conditioning. Therefore, $V_{sum} = 0$.) Let us do the math.

$$\begin{aligned} \Delta V_1 &= (0.2)(100 - 0) \\ &= (0.2)(100) \\ &= 20 \end{aligned} \tag{4.4}$$

After the first trial, then, $\Delta V_1 = 20$. Since V_{sum} is equal to the total amount of conditioning to this point, V_{sum} is also equal to 20.

For Trial 2, we plug the V_{sum} value into equation (4.1) as follows:

$$\Delta V_2 = (0.2)(100 - V_{sum}) \tag{4.5}$$
$$\Delta V_2 = (0.2)(100 - 20)$$
$$= (0.2)(80)$$
$$= 16$$

After two conditioning trials, $V_{sum} = \Delta V_0\,(0) + \Delta V_1\,(20) + \Delta V_2\,(16) = 36$. Continuing, then, for Trial 3,

$$\Delta V_3 = (0.2)(100 - 36) \tag{4.6}$$
$$\Delta V_2 = (0.2)(64)$$
$$= 12.8$$

V_{sum} now $= (0) + (20) + (16) + (12.8)\ldots$ and so on (see Figure 4.16c).

Notice that the most "units of association" accrued in the first trial, fewer in the second trial, even fewer in the third trial, and so on. This *learning curve* approaches the asymptotic limit of 100 that was arbitrarily set at the start of this example. Comparing the values determined in Equation (4.4) with those in Equations (4.5) and (4.6), you can see that 20 units of association were gained on the first trial, 16 on the second, and 12.8 on the third. More units of association, therefore, were learned in earlier trials than in later trials.

We can now predict that more flip-card learning of paired associates (English and Spanish words) takes place on earlier trials than on later trials.

Salience in the Rescorla-Wagner Equation.   Does the Rescorla-Wagner model allow researchers to predict how many trials will be necessary to effect conditioning? No. Only the form of the acquisition function is predicted; the *rate* of acquisition is determined by å and β, values representing the salience of the CS and US, respectively. Salience is a descriptive rather than an explanatory term. The salience of a stimulus refers to its relative associability. Take as an example the following statement in which the term is used: "The flavor stimulus was more *salient* than the tone stimulus." The only way to interpret the statement is to assume that an experiment was conducted, and the flavor stimulus conditioned either more quickly (in fewer trials) or to a higher level than did the tone stimulus. Hence, the flavor was more salient than the tone *under these conditions, in this experiment.*

The concept of salience—indeed, the Rescorla-Wagner model—should sound familiar to the reader. A number of the five rules of conditioning discussed earlier in this chapter are conceptualized mathematically in the Rescorla-Wagner model. For example, the growth of association over conditioning trials is implicit in Rule 1 (p. 134). In addition, Pavlov's law of strength (Rules 2 and 3) states that more intense CSs and USs enter into association more readily and lead to better conditioning. CS and US intensity, then, are two parameters of *salience* that Rescorla and Wagner plugged into their equation.

What about Rule 3 (relating to the role of the CS-US interval in conditioning)? Rule 3 is not specifically addressed in the model. Increasing the CS-

FOCUS ON RESEARCH 4.3

Simple Animals but Complex Processing

Robert Rescorla, Department of Psychology,
University of Pennsylvania, Philadelphia

"My research interests focus on elementary learning processes, particularly associative learning. Much of my earlier work concerned how animals learn relations among events in the environment, as exemplified by Pavlovian conditioning. More recently, I have been concerned with the organism's learning of relations between its own behavior and the consequences of that behavior, as exemplified in instrumental learning (see Rescorla, 1990a, 1990b).

"In both cases, the goal of the analysis is to understand the way in which organisms represent the richness of the environment. The striking thing is that even relatively simple animals seem to have an amazingly complex representation of the world. The trick for the scientist is to expose how the organism develops that representation using only simple associative mechanisms."

US interval, however, would slow the growth of associative strength in a predictable manner. Rule 5 (concerning the direction of the conditioned response when S_1-S_2 sequencing is reversed) can be accommodated in that this model predicts the growth of inhibitory potential as well as excitatory potential.

Limits of the Rescorla-Wagner Model. The Rescorla-Wagner model predicts what should happen in *extinction, latent inhibition, blocking, overshadowing,* and some aspects of *conditioned inhibition* designs. Indeed, associative learning theory since Pavlov has in large measure been defined by the research and theory of Robert Rescorla and his colleagues (see Focus on Research 4.3). The intricacies of predictions made by this theory when CSs are combined sequentially and in compound are beyond the scope of this text. The model's heuristic value has no contemporary parallel in animal learning: Since its publication, many hundreds of research reports have been published to test its various assumptions. The interested reader is directed to Williams, Overmier, and LoLordo (1992) for a review of the model's failure to predict conditioned inhibition phenomena, and to Bouton (1991, 1993), who addresses the shortcomings of the model regarding extinction, spontaneous recovery, and the myriad effects that can occur during conditioning through simple manipulations of time and context.

Summary of the Rescorla-Wagner Model.   The Rescorla-Wagner model is a relatively straightforward prediction about the growth of association between a conditioned stimulus and an unconditioned stimulus presented together in a forward sequence. The model asserts that an asymptotic level (a limit) of associative strength is approached with each conditioning trial. Further, the model of the growth of the association best resembles that depicted in Figure 4.16c in that more associative strength accrues on earlier rather than later conditioning trials. Certain parameters of the CS and US, as well as the number of trials, influence the rate of growth of the associative function. CS and US parameters that lead to more rapid growth of association are described as being more *salient* stimuli. The model intuitively predicts that stimulus intensity and many trials produce conditioning.

Comparator Hypothesis

In a typical conditioning situation, the experimenter specifies one stimulus as the CS and tests the association of that CS with a given US. In theory, all other stimuli that compose the context for the CS are also present and are also being conditioned by the US. Miller and his colleagues have proposed that the animal *compares* what happens to it in the presence of the CS with what happens to it the rest of the time it is in the experimental situation, that is, the comparator hypothesis (Balsom & Tomie, 1985; Miller & Matzel, 1988; Miller & Schachtman, 1985a, 1985b). The *comparator hypothesis* makes the following three assumptions about the nature of associations that are made during conditioning trials:

1. Associations between the target CS and the US are learned.
2. Associations between the target CS and the context CSs within which the target is embedded are learned (cf. *sensory preconditioning*).
3. Associations between the US and various CSs composing the context of the experimental situation are learned.

As we saw earlier when, during excitatory conditioning, the target CS is *always* accompanied by a US, more conditioning accrues to the CS. The comparison of the events during the CS (i.e., with the US always present) stand out more than when the US is sometimes present with CS and always present with context. The comparator hypothesis simply states that when an animal is conditioned to respond to a specific CS, that stimulus takes more of the associative strength of the US than do other CSs embedded in the context. The CS is always being compared with other potential CSs that compose the context of a conditioning experiment. A CR can be measured only when the CS acquires more of the associative strength than the context.

The comparator hypothesis accurately predicts the results of experiments in which contextual cues are altered following conditioning (Balsam & Tomie, 1985; for a critical review of these experiments, see Bouton, 1993). For example, if, after conditioning, the contextual cues are first *extinguished* before measuring the conditioned response to the target CS, a greater response to the target CS is seen (Miller & Schachtman, 1985a). This means that the contextual cues took some of the associative strength during conditioning to the target CS. In summary, the comparator hypothesis accurately describes a number of performance parameters affecting both the acquisition and extinction of conditioned responses.

Interim Summary

1. *Contiguity* and *contingency* theories of conditioning can be compared and contrasted. *Contiguity* refers to association of two stimuli occurring close together in time. *Contingency* refers to the probability that a given US is preceded by a CS, a value that varies between zero and 1.0. The sequence of two stimuli is stressed in contiguity theory: A first stimulus predicts (or not) the occurrence of a second stimulus.

2. Temporal contiguity is a necessary but not sufficient condition for association to occur. Some conditioning procedures (such as conditioned suppression) are amenable to a contingency analysis, but contingency of stimuli is neither necessary nor sufficient for the associative conditioning process. Contingency accounts of conditioning are *always* confounded by contiguity of stimuli.

3. In addition to information-processing models of *contiguity* and *contingency*, theories of association formation include Razran's dominance-contiguity theory, bidirectional conditioning theory, the Rescorla-Wagner model, and the comparator theory.

4. Razran's dominance-contiguity theory stresses that the association that forms during conditioning takes place in the brain and is largely determined by the interaction of neural responses to the stimuli. For conditioning to occur, the neural response to the second of the two incoming stimuli must (in some unspecified way) dominate the neural response to the first stimulus.

5. The Rescorla-Wagner model mathematically describes the growth of associative potential with each successive conditioning trial. The formula, $\Delta V_n = \mathring{a}\beta(\lambda - V_n)$, includes a role for CS ($\mathring{a}$) and US (β) *salience* (relative conditionability), the limit of conditioning (lambda), and the number of conditioning trials (n) in the growth of associative potential (V).

6. The *comparator hypothesis* posits that animals in conditioning situations compare what is happening to them in the presence of the CS with what is happening to them in the absence of the CS. Conditioning is said to occur when the US is reliably predicted by the CS, and, by comparison, when the US is *not* reliably predicted by other contextual cues.

CHAPTER SUMMARY

1. By being sensitive to the *ecological validity* of an experiment, conditioning procedures accomplished in laboratories can account for increasingly complex behavior. The experiments in this chapter elaborate on Pavlov's simple associative model.

2. Among the procedures that have been developed to measure the effects of prior experience on subsequent learning are latent inhibition, sensory preconditioning, higher-order conditioning, overshadowing, potentiation, blocking, and inhibitory conditioning.

3. Compared to novel stimuli, conditioned responses to familiar stimuli take longer to develop, a phenomenon called *latent inhibition*. Both CSs (cf. *CS preexposure effect*) and USs (cf. *US preexposure effect*) can be latently inhibited.

4. Two CSs can become associated together without the benefit of an unconditioned stimulus, a phenomenon known as *sensory preconditioning*. If one of the two CSs is then made a conditioned excitor, the other when tested also shows conditioned excitor properties.

5. When CS_1 is paired with a US, it becomes an excitor. Pairing CS_2 with the CS_1 makes CS_2 an excitor also. This phenomenon, called *higher-order conditioning*, is the basis for secondary reinforcement.

6. When two CSs are simultaneously conditioned, one is typically conditioned better than the other. One CS is therefore said to *overshadow* the other CS. The *overshadowing* stimulus also is said to be the more *salient* of the two CSs.

7. If taste is added to an exteroceptive CS (i.e., an audiovisual CS) in a conditioning situation, the exteroceptive CS conditions better than it would by itself. Taste is said to *potentiate* the conditioning of nontaste cues.

8. CS_1 is first conditioned as excitor. It is then put in a compound with CS_2 and both are conditioned with a US. Under these conditions, CS_2 does *not* become an excitor. CS_1 is said to have *blocked* CS_2 by this *blocking* procedure.

9. In addition to *latent* inhibition, Pavlov identified *internal* inhibition, *external* inhibition, and *conditioned* inhibition, inhibition of delay, and conditioned discrimination procedures. In all examples of inhibition, or inhibitory conditioning, the CR is opposite in direction to the excitatory CR.

10. Conditioned inhibitors can be produced by four methods: (a) by *negative, or US–CS, contingencies;* (b) in a *conditioned discrimination procedure* in which a CS⁻ becomes an inhibitor in contrast with CS⁺ excitor; (c) by the *induction method* in which a neutral CS becomes an inhibitor after having been simultaneously paired with an excitor in extinction; and (d) through an *inhibition of delay* procedure in which the early portion of a long duration CS becomes inhibitory.

11. Two *indirect* methods of measuring conditioned inhibition are the *summation test* and the *retardation test*. Inhibitors and excitors algebraically *summate* when added together in extinction. When inhibitors are put into an excitatory conditioning context, the acquisition of excitation is slowed (*retarded*).

12. Any stimulus can be made into a conditioned stimulus, but the species of animal and stimulus intensity and quality affect the associability with a US.

13. A number of experiments demonstrate that some stimulus-stimulus associations are easily learned and others are difficult (i.e., that there is *stimulus specificity of association*).

14. *Preparedness* theory argues that some animals are evolutionarily predisposed to make some associations and to learn some tasks more easily than others. If many trials are required for learning, the animal is said to be *contraprepared;* for an intermediate number of trials, the animal is *unprepared*.

15. Rapid learning about the consequences of ingestion is aided by innately organized feeding behavior. *Neophobia* toward new foods and reduced neophobia with continued exposure to them minimizes poisonings.

16. Flavors are easily associated with illness-inducing toxins and less easily associated with electric shock. With optimal stimulus parameters, flavors and toxin-effects can become associated in one trial over a delay of several hours.

17. Matching shock intensity with illness intensity and intensity and duration of taste stimuli with audiovisual stimuli has been difficult to accomplish.

18. Preparedness arguments are confounded by procedural differences among experiments, including failure to equate stimulus intensity and number of conditioning trials.

19. *General process learning* remains the best theory to account for observed plasticity in animal behavior, including complex human behavior.

20. Temporal contiguity is a necessary but not sufficient condition for association to occur: Stimulus contingency is neither necessary nor sufficient for conditioning.

21. Theories of association formation include Razran's dominance-contiguity theory, bidirectional conditioning theory, the Rescorla-Wagner model, and the comparator theory.

DISCUSSION QUESTIONS

1. Eating foods in pizza parlors, studying algebra equations in college classrooms, and monitoring emotional expressions while opening gifts at birthday parties are among the many examples of human behavior analyzed from the perspective of animal laboratory-based learning theory. How do these examples bear on questions of *ecological validity*?

2. Why is it so important to investigate the effect that prior learning experiences have on new learning?

3. What do you suppose Dr. Spicey® tastes like? Do you remember the learning concept introduced in Chapter 4 that might help you account for the fact that you know what a fictitious drink tastes like?

4. An early reader of this text thought that I had overstated the power of taste aversion conditioning. Specifically, he said that he shared with me an aversion to pineapple but "didn't get sick at the thought of it." Furthermore, he "doubted that the sight of the can of Dr. Spicey® [Box 4.1] would make a person ill." What do you think? Is the thought of an aversive learning experience sufficient to produce a conditioned response?

5. The twins became sick after eating pizza, but they also had found out that they probably had a stomach virus. Shouldn't this (cognitive) knowledge override the conditioning of their food aversion?

6. Don't you just love it that U.S. idiom embodies animal learning theory as well as human behavior? Based on what you have learned in this chapter, what evidence can you use to dispute the saying that "you can't teach an old dog new tricks" while at the same time acknowledging the wisdom of the saying? How about "practice makes perfect"? Also, in what way are professors who are *so boring they put me to sleep* like Pavlov's dogs (see the section on *inhibition of delay*)? If I belabor this issue, I risk making you *sick to your stomach*—but one individual has already suggested that this isn't possible! Come up with some other examples of idiom that reflect learning principles and send them to me. I'll acknowledge you by name if your example is included.

7. Some people can't study with the TV on or in the presence of other distracting sounds; others can't study in a room that is too quiet. Pavlov and his successors were interested in individual differences such as these, and you can read about them in a book entitled *Pavlov's Typology* by J.A.B. Gray (1964). Can you use Pavlov's concept of *external inhibition* to account for the psychological dimension of noise where *noise* is defined as *unwanted sound?*

8. Unable to release my foot from the accelerator, I recently wrecked my car. A wild dog in a rural environment was attempting to get in the passenger-side door, and I was attempting to get my family and myself out of danger. My superexcitatory state seemed to prevent me (a) from taking my foot off the gas and (b) placing it on the brake. I crashed into another car. Can you help explain to my insurance company what went wrong in terms of excitatory and inhibitory processes controlling my erratic driving behavior?

9. Chapter 10 deals in part with language behavior. Given what you know about the concept of preparedness, can you guess which of the following aspects of language behavior is (are) *prepared* and which is (are) *unprepared?* Babbling? Speaking? Reading? Writing? Spelling? Which should take the most trials to learn?

10. This chapter was introduced with a passage from *The Education of Little Tree*. A bit of the cultural knowledge of Cherokee Indians in this century illustrates how much can be learned merely from noting the associations between stimuli. Is language necessary to acquire this knowledge? Is language necessary to transmit this knowledge to the next generation?

DISCUSSION STARTERS

1. *How do eating pizza, studying algebra, and analyzing the sequence of opening birthday gifts bear on questions of ecological validity?* Two ideas are stressed: (a) Laboratory models are applicable and highly predictive of comparable human behavior and (b) there is not a good alternative to "an experimental analysis of behavior." General process learning theory is the best (only?) encompassing behavioral theory applicable to humans and other animals.

2. *Why is it so important to investigate the effect that prior learning experiences have on new learning?* Because we're only *naive* for (possibly) a few hours, days, weeks, after which we remain "experienced" for the rest of our lives.

3. *What do you suppose Dr. Spicey tastes like?* Dr. Pepper® by way of generalization from Pavlov's second signal system?

4. *Is the thought of an aversive learning experience sufficient to produce a conditioned response?* I have personally "retched" at the thought of a bad experience and often cry at the theatre or while reading a good book. It may be understandable even without learning theory that some people might faint while viewing a surgery. In the course of two decades of teaching, however, I've had two students faint in class listening to a description of implanting an electrode in a rat's brain. One of my daughters described an accident at school in which a student climbing a rope in a P. E. class fell and suffered a compound fracture of the wrist. In an emotional description of the bone protruding through the skin, she retched. The thought of an aversive learning experience, mediated by language, was sufficient to produce a profound conditioned response.

5. *Shouldn't cognitive knowledge (i.e., rational thought processes) override the conditioning of a food aversion that is caused by a virus?* Recall in the previous chapter the student whose grandfather had been forced to eat lamb daily during the war, had hated it, and had never allowed lamb in their home. When as an adult the student was told at a dinner party that a "leg of lamb" was being served, she suffered cold sweats, a churning stomach, and nausea. She "knew better" because she had never even tasted lamb and in fact did not find the taste offensive. Yet she had associatively conditioned an aversion to lamb merely through words describing the meal. In this instance, cognitive thought processes could not overcome conditioning. On the contrary, the cognitive thought processes were themselves the *result* of conditioning.

6. *External inhibition accounts for the psychological dimension of noise?* In Pavlov's experiments, a banging door distracted the excitatory process of Spotski, disrupting saliva flow. A noise while studying, or while carrying on a conversation, or while listening to music has similar distracting properties.

7. *Excitatory and inhibitory processes controlling erratic driving behavior?* The autonomic nervous system (ANS) modulates the actions of the central nervous system. In the example, an adrenalin rush apparently blocked the conditioned responses normally involved in operating a vehicle.

8. *Which aspects of language behavior are unprepared?* Readin', 'ritin', and 'rithmatic.

9. *Is language necessary to acquire and transmit cultural knowledge of the kind described by Little Tree?* Tough question. Nonhuman animals do it without language. *Homo sapiens* likely did it for thousands of years with minimal language. Language certainly would afford a selective advantage.

KEY TERMS

Blocking   The failure of conditioning to CS_1 in a CS_1-CS_2 compound when CS_2 has been previously conditioned. One hypothesis is that CS_2 is blocked because it is a *redundant stimulus,* i.e., not useful in predicting the occurrence of the US.

Comparator Hypothesis   The proposal that during conditioning an animal compares what happens in the presence of the CS with what happens in its absence (Miller).

Conditioned Discrimination   A procedure used to train an animal to respond differently to two stimuli. One stimulus (CS^+) is reliably paired with an unconditioned stimulus, and, on alternating trials, another stimulus (CS^-) is *not* paired with the US. The animal learns to respond to CS^+ and not to respond to CS^-, thereby demonstrating that it can *discriminate* one from the other. (Cf. *Generalization,* in which an animal responds in a *similar* manner to different stimuli.)

Conditioned Excitor   A descriptive term for the CS after it has been conditioned in a forward, or excitatory, manner. The CS acquires excitatory properties; for example, the excitor can be used as a US in higher-order conditioning.

Conditioned Inhibition   The usual result of "backward" procedures (Cf.

Negative Contingencies) that is the opposite of conditioned excitation. For example, if *fear* is the conditioned (excitatory) response, *safety,* or *elation,* is the conditioned inhibitory response.

Conditioned Inhibitor   A descriptive term for the CS after it has been conditioned in a backward, or inhibitory, manner. The CS acquires inhibitory properties; for example, the inhibitor can retard the conditioning of another stimulus.

Contiguity Theory of Association   The theory that stimulus-stimulus associations occur because the animal perceives the two stimuli close together (Cf. *Contiguous*) in time.

Contingency Theory of Association   The theory that stimulus-stimulus associations occur because the animal perceives the relationship, or pattern, or sequence, of one stimulus preceding and *signaling* the occurrence of a second stimulus.

Contraprepared   The opposite of a prepared, or easily conditioned, response. When associations between two stimuli, or a stimulus and a response, require many trials to learn, an animal is said to be *contraprepared* for association.

CS^+ and CS^- Trials   A method used to produce conditioned discrimination. One CS is paired with food (a *CS^+ trial*) and another CS is presented without food (a *CS⁻ trial*). CS⁺ trials yield excitatory conditioning, and CS⁻ trials produce inhibitory conditioning.

CS Preexposure Effect A reduction in conditioning due to familiarity of the conditioned stimulus. The reduced associability of familiar stimuli is also known as *latent inhibition*.

Disinhibition (Pavlov) The process by which an extraneous stimulus disrupts the ongoing effects of an inhibitory stimulus, typically allowing a release of excitation. The stimulus involved is called a *disinhibiting stimulus*. An example is the effect of a loud noise on a drowsy state.

Ecological Validity In animal experiments, requiring an animal to learn a task that is likely to be encountered in the real world, for example, learning about foods. Learning to maintain balance on a hind paw while inebriated is of questionable ecological validity.

External Inhibition (Pavlov) The process of temporarily disrupting the ongoing process of conditioned excitation by introducing an extraneous stimulus. The extraneous stimulus acts as a distractor, a temporary inhibitory stimulus.

Higher-Order Conditioning (Pavlov) The process by which an arbitrary (conditioned) stimulus (CS_1) acquires unconditioned stimulus properties. CS_1 is first paired with a US. Following conditioning, CS_1 is then paired with another arbitrary stimulus (CS_2). CS_2 acquires US properties through the higher-order conditioning process.

Induction Method A procedure used to condition an inhibitory response. An excitatory stimulus (such as a tone) is paired with shock. When another stimulus (such as a light) is paired with the tone and the stimulus pair is not shocked, the tone induces the light to become an inhibitory, or safe, stimulus.

Inhibition of Delay (Pavlov) The production of an inhibitory process by the passage of time. Responding is suppressed, or inhibited, during the first part of regularly spaced intervals. An extraneous stimulus can disinhibit this inhibition of delay.

Internal Inhibition (Pavlov) A process alleged to account for spontaneous recovery (following inhibition produced by extinction); proposed by Pavlov as a counterpart to external inhibition.

Latent Inhibition The condition that preexposed, or familiar, conditioned stimuli require more trials to become associated with a given US than do novel conditioned stimuli. A preexposed CS is said to be *latently inhibited*. Reduced associability of familiar stimuli is also known as the *CS–preexposure effect*.

Negative Contingency A US-CS, or backward, pairing. By contrast, a forward pairing sets up a positive contingency. Negative contingencies often result in the formation of conditioned inhibition.

Neophobia A behavioral tendency to approach new objects cautiously (literally, *fear of the new*). When applied to rats and humans responding to unfamiliar foods, their innate feeding tendencies are to cautiously approach and sniff before tasting, to be generally finicky, and (for a few human children) to suspect that someone is trying to poison them.

Overshadowing One CS acquiring more associative strength than another when two CSs are conditioned simultaneously. The CS that conditions best is said to overshadow the other CS.

Potentiation   The finding that a CS conditions better when it is simultaneously paired with a flavor stimulus. The flavor stimulus is said to *potentiate* the conditioning of the CS with which it is paired.

Preparedness   The argument that animals are (evolutionarily) prepared to readily make associations between certain stimuli and between some stimuli and certain responses because such rapid learning enhances fitness.

Rescorla-Wagner Model   The growth of association during conditioning (a) by quantifying the effects of using stimuli of different novelty and salience, (b) by predicting and quantifying the greater growth of associative potential in early training trials, and (c) by predicting and quantifying the effects of extinction and blocking procedures modeled by Rescorla and Wagner.

Retardation Test   A procedure that allows indirect measurement of conditioned inhibition. A stimulus is first made a conditioned inhibitor and is then conditioned as an exciter. The acquisition of conditioned excitation is retarded, relative to a neutral stimulus, when a conditioned inhibitor is used.

Salience   A descriptive (not explanatory) term that refers to the relative associability of a stimulus. More *salient* stimuli are more easily conditioned.

Second-Order Conditioning   (Pavlov) The first step, and the lowest level, of higher-order conditioning. After CS_1 has been paired with a US, CS_1 is then paired with CS_2, called *conditioning of the second order*. CS_2 acquires US properties through the process called *higher-order conditioning*.

Sensory Preconditioning   A method used to measure CS-CS associations. In the first step, two conditioned stimuli (CS_1 and CS_2) are repeatedly paired. CS_1 is then conditioned to a US, after which CS_2 is tested as if it had been conditioned. In sensory preconditioning, CS_2 shows (indirect) evidence of conditioning through its prior association with CS_1.

Stimulus Specificity in Conditioning   Genetically determined (prepared) brain structures that allow rapid learning of certain (specific) stimuli and make the learning of other associations more difficult. An example is Garcia's telereceptor-cutaneous and gustatory-visceral conditioning systems. (Cf. *Preparedness*.)

Summation Test   A procedure that allows indirect measurement of conditioned inhibition. Following conditioning of CS_2 (a conditioned inhibitor) and CS_1 (a conditioned excitor) and when presented together in extinction, CS_1 and CS_2 will algebraically combine, or summate to lessen both the excitatory and inhibitory responses.

Unprepared   The theory that although some learning is *prepared* (i.e., learned in one or only a few trials) and other learning is *contraprepared* to be associated (i.e., many, many trials to learn), other stimuli and responses are *unprepared* (i.e., are relatively neutral in their associability [requiring an intermediate number of trials]).

US Preexposure Effect   A reduction in conditioning due to familiarity of the unconditioned stimulus. (Cf. *CS Preexposure Effect*.)

CHAPTER 5

INSTRUMENTAL LEARNING

Granpa told me that frogs can feel the ground shake when you walk. He showed me how the Cherokee walks, not heel down, but toe down, slipping the moccasins on the ground. Then I could come right up and set down beside a frog.

There is a way to run up a mountain. . . . Granpa showed me the way Cherokees do it. You don't run straight up, you run along the side and angle up as you go. But you don't hardly run on the ground; this is because you place your feet on the high side of brush and tree trunks and roots, which gives you good footing, so you'll never slip.

Granpa taught me how to hand fish. . . . This is when you lay down on the creek bank and ease your hands into the water and feel for the fish holes. When you find one, you bring your hands in easy and slow, until you feel the fish. If you are patient, you can rub your hands along the sides of the fish and he will lie in the water while you rub him. Then you take one hold behind his head, the other on his tail, and lift him out of the water. It takes some time to learn.

Carter, *The Education of Little Tree* (1976, pp. 58, 73, 94)

INTRODUCTION

Until now the lens we have used to study learning has focused somewhat narrowly. In Chapters 3 and 4 we examined basic ways in which animals make associations between stimuli—namely, through the process of Pavlovian conditioning. In Pavlovian conditioning, environmental stimuli impinge on animals. In turn, animals respond in reflexive ways. Ultimately, through a process called *conditioning*, modified reflexes may result from these reflexive interactions with the environment.

In describing Pavlovian conditioning as "the modification of basic reflexes," we relegate animals to automatons—highly interesting but nevertheless robotlike creatures programmed to sense and to respond in certain ways. We are not robots, but a great deal of evidence suggests that, indeed, we are programmed to sense and to respond in identifiable patterns. Our reflexes and other innately disposed behavior patterns have evolved in ways that guarantee matches with environments we are likely to encounter during our lifetimes. That is, our reflexes are adaptive, and their modification, no matter how mechanical the process may be, also tends to increase our fitness with the environment.

Is All Behavior Reflexive? Animals are *not* just reflexive machines, however. In many instances we have seen the conditioning of emotional behavior as well as the conditioning of reflexes. Interesting robots, indeed! Animals engage in a variety of behaviors that seem to be initiated from within (i.e, from the internal environment, including the brain) rather than from without (the external environment). Humans and other complex animals seem to exhibit volition and will; they seem to engage in spontaneous voluntary behavior as well as involuntary reflexive behavior.[1]

People behave in highly idiosyncratic ways. Genetic arguments aside for the moment, the very existence of individual differences has been interpreted here as the result of particular learning experiences. In Little Tree's culture, certain patterns of movement and skilled behavior have direct survival value. In Western urban cultures we drive automobiles, operate VCRs and computers, play soccer and guitars, talk on the phone, and read books. People in all cultures learn to like particular foods, songs, dances, books, people—and to dislike others. Some of us excel, some are average, and others never quite get the hang of these learned behaviors. We can account for the many observed differences in human behavior by analyzing the *learning histories* of individuals.

In this chapter we begin to expand the study of learning by considering changes in such *nonreflexive* behaviors. How do animals learn as they move

---

[1] Questions regarding "voluntary" and "involuntary" behavior are asked throughout this chapter and again in Chapter 9. For present purposes, based on common language usage, accept the distinction as meaningful.

and act on the environments they occupy? That is, how do we learn when we *do* something, as opposed to having something done to us? Such behavior that acts on the environment has been called *instrumental* behavior, as in "Carl's driving skills were *instrumental* in getting him to Miami safely" and "Wyomia's assertive behavior is *instrumental* in getting her teacher's attention." The learning of instrumental behavior allows us to construct "new" behavioral units rather than being restricted to modifying reflexive behavior.

In this chapter we also entertain the possibility that what humans and animals learn can be controlled. John B. Watson, the founder of the behaviorist movement in psychology, thought that he could raise any child to become whatever he wanted him or her to be. Behaviorists believe that the personalities of all individuals are the end result of environments acting on them.

Have we no choice in the matter? Let us begin to analyze these issues.

Instrumental and Thorndikean Conditioning

Acquiring and modifying "voluntary" or nonreflexive behavior has historically been called **instrumental learning** or **instrumental conditioning.** E. L. Thorndike (1898) was among the first of behavioral scientists to describe how laboratory animals learn to make instrumental responses. Hence, another name for instrumental learning is **Thorndikean conditioning** (or *Thorndikean learning*).[2]

A question raised throughout this chapter and the next is the extent to which classical conditioning and instrumental conditioning result from different processes. As a first consideration, however, note that reflexive and instrumental behaviors more often than not work together. Thus, a woman caught walking in a dust storm blinks as the swirling cloud approaches her face (a reflexive response), turns her head, pulls her hat brim lower, and wraps a scarf about her face (all **instrumental responses**) to avoid the full brunt of the blast. Her eye-blink response is acquired through Pavlovian conditioning (taking advantage of a reflex) while the instrumental responses of bowing her head and making other shielding gestures are learned through instrumental conditioning (by escaping the punishment of blowing dust).

Shooting Free Throws and Kicking Soccer Balls.   Other examples. We learn to aim a basketball shot toward a hoop by taking advantage of sensory-motor reflexes as well as by making skeletal-muscle adjustments. The eye involuntarily accommodates (the lens becomes thinner) while viewing the moving ball as it approaches the hoop. We shift weight, make minor adjustments in body posture via skeletal muscle flexion and extension, and perhaps change our timing for the next shot. Some of these adjustments are under conscious control; others are not. If the next shot is successful, the previous posture (composed of both

---

[2] In conventional usage, *instrumental conditioning* is often contrasted with *classical conditioning*, and, likewise, comparisons are made between *Pavlovian* and *Thorndikean* conditioning.

reflexive and voluntary components) is reproduced on succeeding shots. As we will see, instrumental conditioning of new behaviors, such as making a successful hook shot or kicking a soccer ball with accuracy, are strengthened or weakened, depending on whether the ball goes where it is supposed to go. These skills take many thousands of trials to develop (see Figure 5.1).

STIMULUS CONTINGENCIES AND RESPONSE CONTINGENCIES

Instrumental conditioning differs from classical conditioning in other ways. One distinction described earlier, that of contrasting "reflexes" with "voluntary behavior," is not as simple as it seems. Not everyone agrees on what constitutes "voluntary behavior." A distinction between classical and instrumental conditioning that *can* be agreed on has to do with the requirement of a **response contingency** in instrumental conditioning.

Tail Wagging and Saliva Flow.   Recall that during Pavlovian salivary conditioning, an experimenter arranges stimulus elements to be presented to the dog. Spotski is given food on a certain schedule in relation to a ringing bell. Spotski does not have to make any particular response to attain the food. Another way to say this is that a stimulus-stimulus (i.e., CS-US) contingency is in effect in Pavlovian conditioning. Salivation is measured as the reflexive response to the US and as the conditioned reflex to the CS.

Dogs invariably make other responses, however, during Pavlovian conditioning. For example, they look around, they wag their tails, and they pant when they are about to be fed. Are these other responses also reflexive? Are they voluntary or involuntary.

What if the experimenter arranged conditions such that Spotski was *required* to wag his tail or otherwise to "beg" for his food? That is, rather than merely pairing a ringing bell with food (a stimulus-stimulus contingency), the experimenter required tail wagging before giving food to the dog (a response-stimulus contingency). An experimenter requiring a tail wag has set up an instrumental contingency between tail wagging and food. Would tail wagging increase under these circumstances? Would salivation also increase?

S-S Versus R-S Conditioning.   A shorthand designation for a Pavlovian (bell-food) contingency is stimulus-stimulus conditioning, or **S-S conditioning.** A Thorndikean contingency requiring a response before presenting food (such as tail wag → food) is called response-stimulus conditioning, or **R-S conditioning.** The most straightforward distinction that can be made, then, between Pavlovian and Thorndikean conditioning is the S-S versus R-S contingency.

Why is this distinction important? What does it matter if an experimenter requires a dog to wag its tail for food (R-S contingency) rather than merely

FIGURE 5.1   Learning Skilled Behavior

Learning to play soccer requires hours of practice. Reinforcement theory plays a role in our understanding of how skilled performance is acquired and maintained. First, recognize that movement is intrinsically reinforcing. It feels good as a child to get out and run around. Second, humans and other animals learn some skilled behavior through imitation; they watch a ball being kicked, for example, and then they model the behavior they see (Bandura, 1962). Reinforcement theory helps account for the way in which players acquire and maintain these skilled motor behaviors. Reinforcers include the praise of others (peers, parents, coaches), self-satisfaction for good play, meeting goals, and learning not to make mistakes (i.e, learning via negative reinforcement—to be covered in the next chapter).

pair the food with the sound of a bell (S-S contingency)? The example may appear trivial, but let us consider the *range of behaviors* that may be conditioned using either S-S or R-S contingencies. Instead of having the dog wag its tail, let's require it to climb stairs, or to sit quietly "on command," or to "point" a bird while hunting, or to race other dogs around a track, or to sniff out explosives hidden in airport luggage. Do such accomplishments seem on the surface to be more complicated, more impressive, than being conditioned to salivate to the sound of a bell? Why? What is the difference?

Knowing what you now know, could you train a dog to accomplish these instrumental behaviors? Recognize that we are also talking about the incredible realm of learned behaviors that you and I entertain.

Range of Possible Responses.   One answer to the question of differences between S-S and R-S conditioning is that *what* animals can learn by S-S contingencies is limited to the range of reflexive responses the animal can make. That is, only inborn response tendencies can be conditioned. By contrast, animals make a wide range of responses using their skeletal muscles to physically move within their niche. Risking oversimplification, to successfully operate in their environment requires the integration of both sensory and motor aspects of the animal's brain and body. Relative to reflexive responding, animal behavior becomes both more complicated and more interesting as it operates on a much wider environment. Think you could learn to catch a fish by hand? What if your life depended on it?

Smelling someone's perfume may elicit an orienting response (i.e., elicited behavior) but getting up the nerve to *act* on it (i.e., voluntary behavior) is another matter. That is getting ahead of the story, however, because not everyone agrees that these two types of response tendencies are as separable as they have been drawn here. Let us begin by looking at a classic experiment.

Thorndike's Experiments

In his famous "puzzle box" studies, Thorndike (1898) constructed an experimental chamber with a latching door that could be opened by animals trapped inside (see Box 5.1). Placed in the box for the first time, hungry cats "moved." Their movement included scratching, climbing, and bumping against the walls in a frenzied reaction both to the confinement and to the sight and smell of food available just outside the box. Eventually, by chance movement, the animal might bump against or claw at a simple latching mechanism. The door would release, allowing the cat to escape from the box.

Some time later the cat was returned to the puzzle box for second and third trials. Thorndike found that it took the cat less time to successfully locate and operate the latch. Eventually, after many more trials, on being put in the box, the cat performed the specific behavior required to unlatch the door with-

BOX 5.1   THORNDIKE'S PUZZLE BOXES

Edward L. Thorndike (1874–1949) confined cats, dogs, and chickens in a variety of boxes to study their associative processes. Some boxes were easier to escape from than others. Pictured is Box K in which a lever had to be de-

pressed and a rope pulled to unlock the door. Another (Box Z) required that a cat make a response selected by Thorndike—such as scratching its belly—that cued Thorndike to open the door and allow the cat to escape to its food. Thorndike found that the arbitrarily selected scratching response "degraded" over a period of time to the point that the cat merely made swiping motions at its underside rather than effectively scratching itself. Later in this chapter you will see that Marion and Keller Breland, who trained circus animals to perform crowd-pleasing instrumental tasks, provided theoretical insight into the nature of these "response degradations."

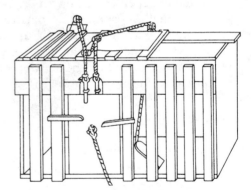

out hesitation. Thorndike's measure of learning, then, was "time to escape from the puzzle box as a function of trials" (see Box 5.1). He also observed dogs and chickens operating in different box environments. Thorndike then formulated basic general principles of instrumental learning, so named because the animals' responses were "instrumental" in escaping the box.

Thorndike's Law of Effect

Thorndike (1911, 1932) postulated an elementary principle governing *all* behavior, namely, the *law of effect*. The **law of effect** simply states that a *response that is followed by a pleasant consequence will tend to be repeated and a response followed by an unpleasant consequence will tend to decrease in frequency*. He called such pleasant and unpleasant consequences **satisfiers** and **annoyers,** respectively. Instrumental movements (responses) that led to the hungry cat's escape through an open door and to food (both pleasant consequences) tended, in Thorndike's terms, to be "stamped in." "Stamping in" can be likened to "writing" on John Locke's (1690) *tabula rasa* (blank slate); both are metaphors for hypothesized changes in the brain when learning occurs. Unsuccessful movements by the cat (i.e., those that did not allow escape, thereby maintaining both hunger and the annoying confinement) tended to drop out. The end result of the law of effect? Successful responses increase, and unsuccessful responses decrease; animals learn to be more efficient and more effective in operating on the environment.

Hedonism. Another way to describe the law of effect is to note that all organisms are born with hedonistic tendencies. Seeking pleasure and avoiding pain are both adaptive and "normal" for us. Note that Thorndike neither discovered nor invented the law of effect; rather, he recognized the importance of this commonly known general rule governing behavior.[3]

In a discipline for which exceptions to the rule *are* the rule, **hedonism** is best understood as a psychobiological law. Most animals most of the time engage in behaviors that produce pleasure and discontinue behaviors that produce pain. Among the best understood incentives for hedonistic tendencies are the taste and olfactory components of palatable foods. Following Thorndike's use of the puzzle box, many thousands of laboratory animals have been conditioned and have learned instrumental responses based on food rewards. (The aversive control of behavior in laboratory animals—typically through the use of annoyers such as electric shock—is discussed in Chapter 6.)

The Psychobiological Law of Effect

Combine Thorndike's original conception of the law of effect with that of hedonism as an evolutionary behavioral tendency. Add the results of nearly 100 years of laboratory animal experimentation. The resulting psychobio-

---

[3] My grandmother (and hers) understood and applied basic *carrot and stick* psychology without the benefit of exposure to Thorndike's theory. Carrots (dangled in front) and sticks (applied to the rear) were traditionally used as incentives to motivate donkeys to move in accordance with their human owners' wishes.

logical law of effect occupies a unique position in contemporary learning theory.

General Process Learning Theory.   The law of effect is a deceptively simple concept. Asserting that satisfiers increase and that annoyers decrease the probability of occurrence of *all* preceding behaviors, in *all* animals, however, covers a lot of ground! The law of effect complements classical conditioning in providing support for *general process learning theory*.

Both hedonism and the law of effect are firmly grounded in biology. Each can be accounted for as evolutionary adaptations. Risking a tautology, most pleasurable activities in life promote fitness, survival, and reproduction. Food, shelter, and mating (Thorndike's satisfiers) are all pleasurable and adaptive, but the opposite is true of annoyers in the form of hunger, pain, and adverse climate. For most animals in their ecological niches, therefore, the very behaviors they engage in are instrumental in producing food; securing shelter and mates; and avoiding predators, toxins, and reproductive extinction. In summary, the law of effect embodies adaptive responses to selective pressures.

Dennett (1975) beautifully describes both the adaptive nature of hedonism and the law of effect. He argues that the law of effect is an inevitable outcome of natural selection. Box 5.2 presents his theory of human cognitive behavior based on these innate response tendencies.

Determinism and the Law of Effect

How well does the law of effect account for human learning and behavior? Again, the reader must ultimately be the judge. Most of us are vaguely aware that environment at a minimum influences our behavior even if we might disagree that it *determines* our behavior. Indeed, differences in philosophy and in learning theories hinge on this very distinction.

A position of *hard determinism* asserts that all human behavior can be accounted for by combining **biological determinism** with **environmental determinism.** A *biological determinist* asserts that genes expressed in a given environment severely restrict alternative response outcomes. Hardwired reflexive behavior, FAPs, instincts, and so on are examples of biologically determined behavior. Such behaviors are typically seen as being more or less "involuntary."

An *environmental determinist* asserts that choice is delimited by reinforcement and punishment contingencies (i.e., the law of effect). In Thorndike's terms, such learned behavior is (involuntarily) "stamped in" by satisfiers. A *hard determinist* position, then, proposes that humans and other animals do not have "free choice." John B. Watson and B.F. Skinner are famous advocates of a hard determinist position (see following sections).

Box 5.2   THINKING GOOD THOUGHTS AND MAKING GOOD CHOICES

Why do reinforcers reinforce? Why does the presentation of food to a hungry animal (or water to a thirsty animal) allow responses that preceded these reinforcers to be so readily learned and repeated on future occasions? Dennett (1975) in an article entitled "Why the Law of Effect Will Not Go Away" argues that the role of reinforcement is to "select" behaviors and responses much the same way that the environment in Darwin's theory of natural selection "chooses" which organisms are to live and which will die. (A similar position has been advanced by Shettleworth, 1975.)

According to Dennett, those animals in past times who were *not* sensitive to "positive reinforcers" or "punishers" (i.e., those aspects of the environment that promote survival) would have gone extinct. Therefore, all extant animals were selected to obey the law of effect. The analogy of learning and natural selection has also been put forth by Dawkins (1995). He argues that pain is the analogue of death;

learning to avoid pain is learning to survive.

Dennett further argues that "good ideas" are also selected by the same general mechanism. In response to a complicated stimulus environment (i.e., one in which simple reflexive responses are not elicited), all humans *generate* hypotheses, or ideas. The generation of such hypotheses is accomplished by brain structures that have also been selected through evolution; some genotypes underlying some brain structures are better than others at generating likely hypotheses. Intelligent humans *select* those ideas that provide the most optimal consequences (in the same way reinforcement selects appropriate responses). Therefore, according to Dennett, a Darwinian *natural selection* of intelligent behavior, mediated by the law of effect, ensues.

In light of Dennett's arguments, under what conditions is behavior "maladaptive"? Does the law of effect provide an ethic of "right" and "wrong"?

By contrast, a philosophy of *soft determinism* asserts that both genes and environments influence but do not determine human behavior. Genes and environment limit response alternatives but do not prohibit choice (i.e., voluntary behavior) from among these alternatives. To test your understanding of the distinction between hard and soft determinism, review Dennett's position in Box 5.2. Is Dennett a hard or soft determinist?[4]

---

[4] Hard.

John B. Watson's Behaviorism

> Give me a dozen healthy infants, well-formed, and my own specified world to bring them up in and I'll guarantee to take anyone at random and train him to become any type of specialist I might select—doctor, lawyer, artist, merchant-chief, and yes, even beggar-man and thief, regardless of his talents, penchants, tendencies, abilities, vocations, and race of his ancestors. (Watson, 1924, p. 30)

One of the first psychologists to espouse a position of hard environmental determinism was also one of the more amazing characters in the history of psychology (see Box 5.3). John B. Watson's belief that human behavior is directly, inevitably determined by the environment is evident in his famous statement that opens this section. This clarion call announced a philosophy he called **behaviorism.**

The term *behaviorism* is unfortunate: Characterizing Watson's position as *environmentalism* is better. Why? Because genetic predispositions are ignored in Watson's theory, and, as we saw in Chapter 1, a general theory of behavior must include both innate and environmental components.

While we may be generous and forgive Watson's trumpeting of environment over biology (due, presumably, to a relative paucity of evidence for behavioral genetics in 1920), the fact is that he offered little experimental evidence to support even his environmental claims. He never trained a lawyer, physician, or thief. As we see in more detail in Chapter 7, Watson's laboratory investigations bearing on the preceding quoted assertion consisted of only a few published papers. One was a classic that dealt with conditioning a fear response in a child (Watson & Rayner, 1920). Nevertheless, Watson's influence was profound. Behaviorism dominated academic psychology for the next 40 years and influenced both U.S. educators and popular culture (Buckley, 1989). Among those Watson influenced was a young experimental psychologist just embarking on a 50-year research career. Burrhus Frederic Skinner (1904–1990) and his many students *were* successful in accomplishing laboratory research on which a formal experimental analysis of learned behavior could be built.

Interim Summary

1. Behavior has both reflexive and nonreflexive (voluntary and involuntary) components.
2. Nonreflexive behavior can be modified by a process called *instrumental conditioning* or *instrumental learning*. Also known as *Thorndikean conditioning*, instrumental conditioning complements *classical conditioning* (the modification of reflexive behavior).
3. Researchers who condition animals by Pavlovian, or *S-S* procedures, arrange *stimulus contingencies:* A CS is followed by a US. Researchers conditioning animals by Thorndikean, or *R-S*, procedures, arrange

BOX 5.3   JOHN B. WATSON AND THE HISTORY OF BEHAVIORISM

John B. Watson during his student days at Furman University, circa 1899.

In his 1989 book *Mechanical Man: John Broadus Watson and the Beginnings of Behaviorism*, Kerry W. Buckley asserts that Watson's *behaviorism* played a major role in the modernization of American society. At the turn of the century, Watson left the South Carolina farm where he had been reared in poverty. After taking his doctorate at the University of Chicago, he moved to Johns Hopkins University, where, within a few short years, he founded the behaviorist movement and became one of America's most influential psychologists.

At the pinnacle of his academic career, Watson and his graduate student, Rosalie Rayner, published the infamous "Little Albert" experiment in which an 11-month-old child was classically conditioned to fear a white rat. Their point? Not unlike other animals, Watson argued, humans are buffeted by instinct on the one hand and an all-controlling environment on the other. We are programmed throughout our childhoods. According to Watson, human minds, consciousness, and will are illusions.

Watson's academic successes came crashing down in 1920 following a scandalous divorce (his extramarital escapades made the front pages of the *New York Times*). Forced to resign his academic position at the age of 42, Watson married Rayner and headed for a more lucrative job with the J. Walter Thompson advertising agency. There Watson promoted his behaviorist philosophy to a far wider audience than would have been the case had he remained a university professor. Together John and Rosalie wrote popular magazine articles, published books, and gave radio interviews, on, among other topics, their bizarre philosophy of child rearing. Fathers should be remote and inaccessible, they asserted. And even mothers should severely limit the amount of affection they give their children.

Buckley points out that the behaviorist philosophy fit well with the emerging urban culture of the "roaring '20s." A *New York Times* review of Watson's *Behaviorism*, published in 1924, called it "perhaps the most important book ever written."

response contingencies: A response is followed by a positive reinforcer or a punishing stimulus.

4. E. L. Thorndike proposed that behavior is modifiable by the *law of effect:* Responses followed by *satisfiers* will be repeated and responses followed by *annoyers* will not be.

5. The psychobiological law of effect asserts that the hedonistic experience of pleasure and of pain avoidance (a) constitutes an evolutionary selective pressure and (b) selects, or reinforces, behavior.

6. Instrumental learning based on the law of effect addresses how *all* animals learn in *all* circumstances and is therefore a *general process learning theory.*

7. John B. Watson's philosophy of *behaviorism* espouses a hard environmental *determinism* in which the expression of behavior is controlled by reinforcers and punishers.

OPERANT CONDITIONING

As a graduate student, B.F. Skinner objected to the way animal learning experiments were conducted in the laboratory. By the 1930s rats in mazes were "in" and Thorndike's puzzle boxes were "out." Rats were placed in runways and given food rewards for their successful negotiation of right and left turns (see Figure 5.2). How many trials did it take before the rat made no errors (such as turning right when it was supposed to turn left)? How many seconds did the rat take to get from the start box to the goal box on the first trial and on the last trial?

By his own account Skinner decided to automate the runway procedure (see Figure 5.2). First he attached a feeder to the runway; the weight of the moving rat was *instrumental* in tilting the runway, mechanically activating the feeder. Skinner eventually did away with the runway altogether. He next simplified the apparatus so that the rat merely pushed open a door to get food:

> The behavior of the rat in pushing open the door . . . was obviously learned, but its status as part of the final performance was not clear. It seemed wise to add an initial conditioned response connected with ingestion in a quite arbitrary way. I chose the first device that came to hand—a horizontal bar or lever placed where it could be conveniently depressed by the rat to close a switch that operated a [feeder]. (Skinner, 1959, p, 366)

The Experimental Environment

With the invention of what became known as a **Skinner box**, Skinner's research strategy for many years focused on analyzing how food rewards influ-

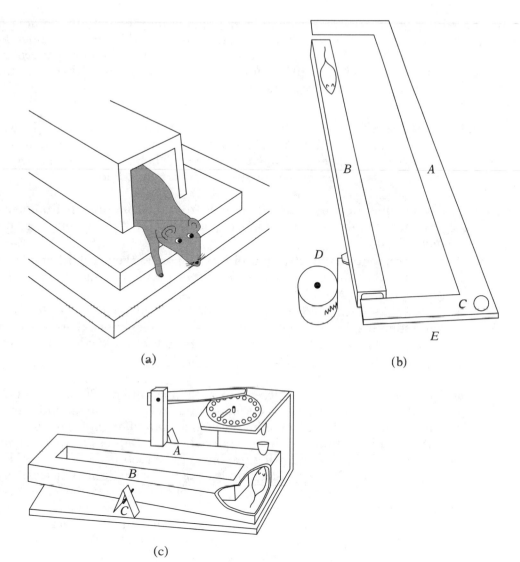

(a)

(b)

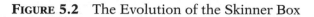

(c)

FIGURE 5.2   The Evolution of the Skinner Box

B.F. Skinner describes the evolution of the Skinner box in a tongue-in-cheek article decrying formal scientific method (Skinner, 1959). He points out two instrumental factors in his career: first, the role of serendipity (finding something you aren't looking for and pursuing it). Second, he claims that being personally lazy (which he wasn't) led him to design the Skinner box to automate the collection of data rather than continue the labor-intensive use of runways (a), of circular runways (b), and of a circular runway with an automated feeding device (c).

enced key pecking by pigeons and lever pressing by rats and other animals. The primary dependent variables that can be measured in this experimental environment are (a) rate of lever pressing, (b) control of response patterning under different conditions of reinforcement, and (c) "choice" behavior (in boxes with more than one response key).

Skinner's Research Strategy.   Skinner was aware of the criticism of ethologists regarding the study of animal behavior in laboratories. He was also sensitive to the ethologists' concept of innately organized behavior (Skinner, 1966). How did he justify his use of the conditioning box methodology?

1. Skinner intentionally removed animals from their natural environments to better identify and isolate independent variables controlling the animals' responses.
2. Skinner intentionally selected arbitrary responses (key pecking and lever pressing) that were presumably *not* akin to FAPs or other biologically prepared responses (Skinner, 1963).
3. Skinner designed a convenient, economical, and reliable way to automate stimulus delivery and to measure animal responses, thereby ensuring a standardized methodology that investigators could adopt in laboratories around the world. They did.

The Skinner Box.   Let us take a closer look at Skinner and his Skinner box (see Figure 5.3). The small chamber consists of four walls, a ceiling, and a grid floor. From one wall a lever (sometimes called a *manipulandum*) protrudes. A rat or other small mammal is trained to press the lever. Depressing the lever activates an electrical switch, allowing responses to be recorded. In another version of the chamber, the manipulandum is a backlit panel or lighted key. Positioned on the wall at an optimal height for a pigeon to peck, the key is also connected to a microswitch allowing the pigeon's responses to be electrically recorded. Food or water can be delivered into a small container attached to the wall for the rats. For pigeons, a "grain hopper" from which food can be pecked is made available for a few seconds.

The chamber may also be fitted with a speaker over which background masking noise (or any other auditory stimulus) can be introduced and with lights for both illumination and signaling purposes. Finally, aversive control of behavior can be investigated by applying electric current to the grid floor.

The Study of Operant Conditioning

How did Skinner begin the experimental analysis of behavior? Starting in the 1930s and continuing for 50 years, he and his many students systematically studied **operant conditioning** in these experimental chambers.

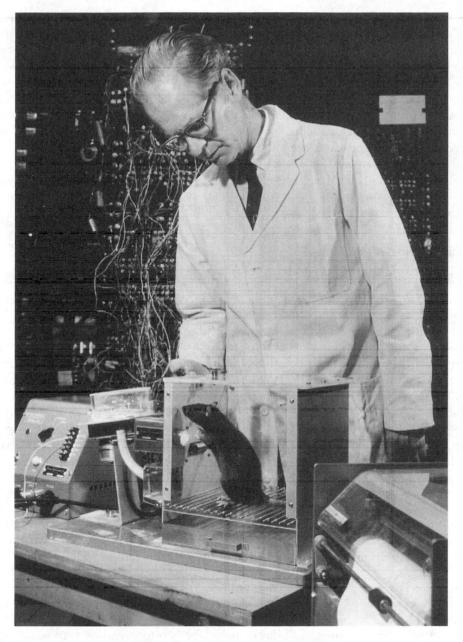

FIGURE 5.3   Burrhus Frederic Skinner, 1904–1990

Operant Responses.   First, Skinner defined the terms he would use to analyze behavior. He defined an **operant** as any response that "operated" on the environment (cf. *instrumental response*). Because a lever-pressing response is an easily repeated operant, Skinner's **free operant** method can be contrasted with the **discrete trial** methods characteristic of other types of behavioral analysis. Examples of discrete trials are Pavlovian conditioning, escaping from a puzzle box, and negotiating a maze. Each has a discrete beginning, duration, and end—a sequence called a *trial*. By contrast, in operant conditioning, one lever-pressing response is *not* called a trial. Rather, learning is measured during periods, or sessions, of lever pressing typically lasting 30 to 60 minutes.

Operant conditioning is best understood as a variant of instrumental learning. The methodology is unique, and its specialized terminology standardizes the experimental analysis of behavior.

Operant Methodology in Action

The power of the law of effect can be seen in operant conditioning. Naive rats can be trained readily to lever press and pigeons trained to peck at a lighted disc on the wall of a Skinner box. A hungry rat when placed in the chamber will explore the new environment for several minutes by sniffing, rearing on its hind legs, and touching objects with its front paws. The rat's exploratory behavior appears to be both voluntary and purposive rather than reflexive. For this reason, the rat's behavior is said to be *emitted* rather than *elicited*. We explored examples of **elicited behavior,** such as reflexive salivation, in earlier chapters; food placed on the dog's tongue involuntarily *elicited* a salivation response. By contrast, instrumental responses—including arbitrary operants such as pressing a lever—are examples of what Skinner called **emitted behavior.**

Operant Levels.   Every emitted behavior has an **operant level,** or *baseline,* of occurrence. For example, the likelihood that the rat will sniff floors and walls on first entering the box is high and will deftly depress the lever in the box is low. Operant conditioning, then, involves selecting a low-level operant and, through reinforcement, making the target response more probable.

Magazine Training.   During the rat's initial exploration, the experimenter initiates the first phase of training, called **magazine training.** Approaches to the food cup (cf. *magazine,* where military provisions are kept) are *reinforced* when the rat finds food in the cup. That is, behavior is reinforced by providing food immediately following the desired response. The food is called a **positive reinforcer** (cf. Thorndike's *satisfiers*).

Secondary Reinforcers.   What has the rat learned up to now? *Where* the food is located. An electrical feeder is activated by the experimenter, delivering more food to the cup. (The feeder noise may initially produce a startle response that quickly disappears.) After a few trials the sound of the electrically activated feeder becomes a *conditioned stimulus* signaling food. Furthermore, after the feeder sound has been paired several times with food delivery, the feeder sound becomes a **secondary reinforcer** via the process of higher-order conditioning (discussed in Chapter 4). The sound of the feeder stands for food, and animals will work merely to hear the sound. We return later to the secondary reinforcing effects of the feeder in another context. For now you might consider what secondary reinforcers control your behavior.

What has the rat or pigeon learned up to now? *Where* the food is located and *when* food becomes available (signaled by the feeder's sound).

Shaping Behavior.   After the animal is fully trained, the experimenter will reinforce only the **target response** or *target behavior.* In this instance, the target response is depressing the lever or key with sufficient force to close an electrical contact. Shortly after magazine training, however, the rat initially is reinforced for merely approaching the lever, conveniently located next to the food cup (or the key, illuminated, next to the feeder and conveniently placed head high on the wall for easy pecking). This intermediate procedure is necessary because the rat has yet to learn the target behavior. For example, should the animal retreat to the rear of the cage and then turn its head back in the direction of the lever or make any movement toward the lever, the orientation behavior is reinforced by delivery of positive reinforcement. Next only the intermediate behavior of approaching and touching the lever is reinforced. This method of training responses that are approximately like the target behavior is called **shaping by successive approximation.** Eventually, only the target response (i.e., lever pressing) will earn the food reward.

Positive Reinforcement.   The process by which selected operants are altered by the application of positive reinforcers is called **positive reinforcement.** The process of positive reinforcement is similar to Pavlov's conditioning.

What has the rat or pigeon learned? *Where* the food is located, *when* food is delivered to the food cup, and, most important, the response contingency—*which* operant response is associated with the positive reinforcer, food.

Thought question: Can you verbalize the difference between the concept of reinforcement and a reinforcer?

Measuring Operant Responses

We saw earlier that Skinner quickly discovered that programming reinforcements and measuring animal responses are difficult and tedious to accomplish without automatic equipment (Skinner, 1959). Let us look more closely at how operant behavior is measured.

Cumulative Records.   At present, computer control equipment is used to connect the animal with its programmed environment. A popular and relatively simple way to visualize behavioral effects of reinforcement is to use an instrument called a *cumulative recorder,* a device that generates a **cumulative record.** The operation of a cumulative recorder is quite simple, as is the reading of the record (see Figure 5.4).

The Home Environment as a Skinner Box

Can human behavior be shaped? In his earliest writings, Skinner asserted that human behavior could be systematically changed by the judicious application of reinforcement and punishment. For example, his famous utopian novel *Walden Two* (Skinner, 1948) created a carefully controlled community. Adult "planners" and "programmers" shaped appropriate behaviors in both children and adults by carefully reinforcing only certain behaviors. Likewise, the programmers modified unwanted behaviors either by extinction or punishment or by rewarding alternative behaviors.

Are there similarities in the methods by which humans, rats, and pigeons acquire new patterns of responding in Skinner boxes and home environments? Let us look at a few examples.

A Game of "Hot and Cold"

A favorite game played by children (and some adults) resembles experimenters with their rats. The task of the person that is selected to be "it" is to determine a *target behavior*—to find a particular object that has been hidden or to guess a secret word. The experimenters *shape* the behavior (moving around in the environment or guessing categories of words) by saying "you're hot" (for getting close) or "you're cold" for unwanted responses. For example, if a marble has been hidden in a vase on a shelf, movements toward that side of the room would be reinforced with the words "you're getting hot." Likewise, adults lead small children to Easter eggs by *successive approximation.* The words "hot" and "cold" can be construed as *secondary* reinforcers and punishers. (Recall that words acquire meaning in Pavlov's second signal system through the process of higher-order conditioning.)

Thought Question: Depending on the child's age and other circumstances, might one get better performance if M&Ms® candy was used in place of the words "you're hot"? Why or why not?

Training Rats and Children.   More often than not we underestimate the power of operant conditioning and the lessons that can be learned by its study. Prospective parents might profit by first training laboratory animals under the supervision of a behaviorist. Two things would very quickly become evident: first, the power of reinforcement and the law of effect and, second, how easy it is to mess up an animal's (and a child's) behavior. Let us look at two examples.

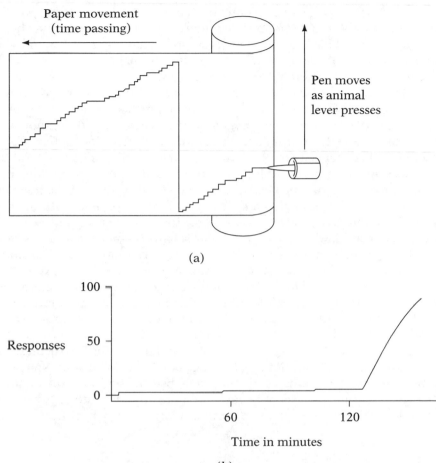

Paper movement
(time passing)

Pen moves
as animal
lever presses

(a)

Responses

100

50

0

60   120

Time in minutes

(b)

FIGURE 5.4   Measuring Operant Responses

Operant responses distributed in time are easily visualized on a
cumulative recorder. A motor turns the drum of the instrument, pulling the
paper through at a constant speed. A pen resting on the paper writes on
the passing paper (a). When the animal makes a lever-pressing or key-
pecking response, a ratchet moves the pen sideways. In (a), then, the
passage of time is indicated by the direction of the moving paper and
responses by sideways pen movements. In (b), only a few responses have
been made in the first 2 hours, as indicated by the flat line indicating the
passage of time. You can see several sideways excursions of the pen during
the first 2 hours and the rapid increase in lever pressing after 2 hours
(after Skinner, 1938).

A behavioral expert can efficiently train animals to bar press responses in less than an hour. Without appropriate attention to detail, novices may be ineffective in shaping skilled rat behavior even after many hours of training; and some may never get the hang of it. Even a skilled animal trainer can sometimes end up with behavior different from what was envisioned. For example, a graduate student once asked me to look at a rat that had been shaped to depress a lever for food reinforcement. The rat was lying on its back, under the lever, and pulling on the lever as if it were doing chin-ups. When I asked him how in the world he had managed to train such a complicated behavior pattern, he confessed that he had stepped out of the room for a few hours and left the rat to its own devices. Apparently, the rat had been reinforced several times while in that position; extensive retraining was necessary to get the rat up off the floor.

Another example that all of us have seen involves parents with their "out of control" children in grocery stores. Behavioral experts recognize that it is the parent, not child, who has lost *behavioral control*. When used in this formal sense, the term **behavioral control** refers to the reinforcement and punishment contingencies in operation at the time a behavior is being exhibited. In this usage, *behavioral control* is not equivalent to "parents disciplining their children." For example, the same parent whose commonsense approach precludes "bribing a child to do something" will inadvertently perpetuate an undesirable behavior by buying candy for the child after the 10th annoying "pleeeezzz." Achieving behavioral control in child rearing is expedited by a knowledge of operant conditioning. Playing "hot and cold" works. Nonsystematic observations of grandma's *carrot and stick* psychology, however, do little to further the scientific analysis of behavior pursued by Thorndike, Watson, and Skinner. Let us return to the more formal analyses of behavior afforded by Skinner.

Interim Summary

1. B.F. Skinner's research strategy was to pick an arbitrary response (that he called an *operant*) and to analyze how reinforcement modified and controlled that response.

2. Skinner and his students measured the operant responses of lever pressing and key pecking in an experimental chamber called a *Skinner box*.

3. The sequence of training operant responses is (a) to measure the baseline, or *operant level*, prior to reinforcement; (b) to initiate *magazine training* in which the sound of a feeder becomes associated with the *positive reinforcer* of food; (c) to *shape* responses similar to the *target response* by the method of *successive approximation;* and (d) to finally reinforce only the target response.

4. The process of training a specific response using a reinforcer is called *positive reinforcement*.

5. Skinner boxes are now computer programmed to present stimuli to the animal and to measure the animal's operant responses. Lever-pressing responses can be displayed on cumulative records.

6. Operant conditioning can be accomplished outside the Skinner box. Conditioning the desired target behavior requires both attention to detail and specific training skills.

SCHEDULES OF REINFORCEMENT

Recall that Skinner opted to analyze behavior using both rate and patterning of lever-pressing responses as his dependent variables. Among his many findings are that peculiar, highly distinctive patterns of lever pressing result when animals are subjected to different **schedules of reinforcement** (see Reynolds, 1968). Obviously, behavioral scientists are interested in how reinforcement produces patterns of behavior beyond the lever-pressing response. Before applying reinforcement theory to complex human behavior, let us examine the effects of scheduling reinforcement in the Skinner box.

Continuous Reinforcement

Continuous reinforcement (CRF) is important in the acquisition of many operant responses. CRF indicates that each emitted response produces a positive reinforcement. Simply stated, animals appear to learn an "if-then" contingency: *if* I turn left in the maze or *if* I peck the key, *then* a food pellet (or drink of water) magically appears.

The acquisition of this new pattern of lever-pressing behavior proceeds in a predictable manner. During acquisition, CRF schedules characteristically produce *positively accelerated* patterns of response. This same pattern was seen in classical conditioning. A positively accelerated slope merely means that as time passes, increasingly more responses are made and less time is taken between responses. After training, bar pressing proceeds at a rate dictated by how rapidly the animal eats (or drinks) the positive reinforcer.

By contrast, if, early in training, each response is not reinforced, more time is required to achieve steady lever-pressing responses. Many types of partial, or intermittent, reinforcement schedules have been studied. A few examples follow.

Partial, or Intermittent, Reinforcement

In contrast to continuous reinforcement, **partial reinforcement,** or **intermittent reinforcement,** schedules have three main characteristics: (a) they result in *slower acquisition* of stable responding; (b) partial reinforcement schedules produce *more responses* in a session of fixed duration (presumably because reinforcement occurs aperiodically, slowing down the ingestive process); and (c) partial reinforcement produces greater *resistance-to-extinction* when reinforcement is no longer forthcoming (see later discussion). Let us take in turn four schedules of reinforcement that have been most intensely studied: fixed ratio (FR), variable ratio (VR), fixed interval (FI), and variable interval (VI).

Fixed Ratio Schedules

In a **fixed ratio (FR) schedule,** reinforcement is contingent on the completion of a fixed number of operants, such as lever-pressing responses. For example, if every 10th response is reinforced, the schedule is designated FR-10. The animal can bar press quickly or slowly in making the 10 responses. In a given session, more positive reinforcers can be earned if the animal presses the lever faster.

The Postreinforcement Pause on FR Schedules.   When the ratio of unreinforced to reinforced responses is relatively small (such as when every fifth response is reinforced, i.e., an FR-5), the responding reflects how quickly the animal eats (or drinks) the positive reinforcer. As the ratio becomes larger (e.g., FR-180, every 180th response produces a positive reinforcer), the response that produces food is typically followed by a long pause, called the **postreinforcement pause.** The duration of the pause before responding resumes is directly related to the size of the ratio.[5]

Variable Ratio Schedules

As is the case with *fixed ratio* schedules of reinforcement, the **variable ratio (VR) schedule** requires a specified number of responses before the reinforcer is delivered. A rat responding on a VR-10, for example, is reinforced, on the average, for every 10th response. But the number of responses required for a particular positive reinforcer varies during the work session. Computer programs determine that the rat is reinforced after 1 or 2 responses (or after 15 or 20 responses). On a VR-10 the average during a work session is 10 responses.

The *postreinforcement pauses* seen for animals working on fixed ratio schedules of reinforcement are longer than those seen when variable ratio schedules are in effect (see Figure 5.5). Why? Put yourself in the rat's place.

---

[5] Postreinforcement pauses are seen in everyday life in a variety of situations and bear little resemblance to lever pressing and the presence or absence of food. For example, extended periods of study and daily class attendance are usual responses immediately prior to an exam. What pattern of behavior is typically found in the class period following an exam? Another example: We seldom hear from politicians until just before election time. Why then? What is the "availability of reinforcement" in both examples?

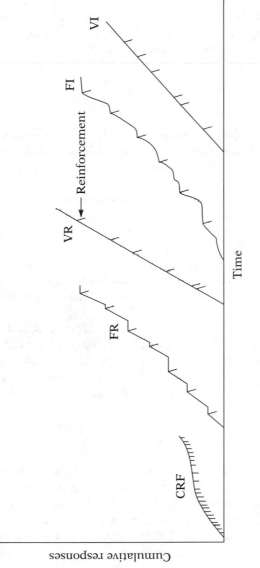

FIGURE 5.5 Cumulative Records of Common Schedules of Reinforcement

Cumulative records of continuous reinforcement (CRF), fixed interval (FI), fixed ratio (FR), variable ratio (VR), and variable interval (VI) schedules of reinforcement. The steepness (slope) of each line reflects the *rate* of response. Notice that while the VR produces a higher rate of response than the VI, both schedules produce straighter lines than CRF, FR, and FI schedules, indicating more stable, evenly spaced responding. When the reinforcing frequency of VI and VR schedules are equated, the rate of responding on the VR schedule might be 2 to 4 times higher than on the VI schedule. The reasons are that (a) "pausing" decreases the frequency of reinforcement on the VR more than it does on the VI and (b) animals are apparently sensitive to the relationship of their work (rate of responding) to their pay (rate of reinforcement). "Work for pay" is discussed further in Chapter 8.

Can you first come up with a *cognitive hypothesis* involving "expectancies"? Again, this time as a hungry rat, can you come up with a *behavioral hypothesis* of maximizing your responses to get the most reinforcers per unit time?[6]

Lacking the postreinforcement pause, VR schedules generally produce high, steady rates of operant responding (cf. Figure 5.5). Can you think of an example of human behavior that resembles rats working on a VR schedule of reinforcement? If you owned a gambling casino in Las Vegas and you could program the slot machines that your customers would play, what payoff schedules (reinforcement schedules) would *you* use to maximize your profits? CRF? FR-50? VR-50?

Fixed Interval Schedules

An animal on a **fixed interval (FI) schedule** is reinforced for its first response following a specified *time interval*. Another way to say this is that *interval* schedules of reinforcement make the positive reinforcer available after a programmed amount of time passes. Time-based interval schedules are contrasted with fixed or variable *ratio* schedules in which reinforcement is dependent on *amount* and *rate* of work, irrespective of time.

For example, in a fixed interval 60-second schedule of reinforcement (abbreviated *FI-60*), the first response after 60 seconds has elapsed is reinforced. (The interval is measured from the time of delivery of the preceding reinforced response.) Note that even though a time contingency has been added, the delivery of the food reinforcement is still *response* contingent. The animal must respond to get the food.

You be the hungry pigeon. Would you rather earn food for the first response you make after 10 seconds (FI-10) or for the first response you make after 45 seconds (FI-45)? After experiencing these two payoff schedules for several sessions, would you respond the same way on each? That is, can you predict what your postreinforcement pause would look like on these two FI schedules? Think about it. After receiving a food pellet, what are your chances of getting another one any time soon? Better on the FI-10. On the other schedule, 45 seconds must elapse before food is available again.

Scalloping.   Because *fixed interval schedules* of many seconds in duration preclude back-to-back reinforcers, these schedules typically produce cumulative curves showing a zero or near zero response rate immediately following reinforcement. As the end of the fixed interval approaches, a gradual increase in rate occurs. This distinctive pattern, called *scalloping*, appears on the cumulative record (see Figure 5.5). These scallops are seen only following extensive training on longer VI schedules. Can you visualize the shape of the respective scallops on FI-30 and FI-120 schedules of reinforcement?

---

[6] On a VR schedule, the very next response might be reinforced. Pausing delays what may be immediate gratification.

Do we see scallops in human behavior? For example, do employees work harder on payday than on other days? Why or why not? Under what conditions might they? A remarkable example of the patterning of responses leading to the self-administration of morphine on an FI schedule is described in Box 5.4.

Variable Interval Schedules

Rather than being fixed, in a **variable interval (VI) schedule** the interval of time between positive reinforcer availability varies from a few to many seconds. Compare an FI-45 with a VI-45. A computer-generated VI-45-second schedule might deliver response-contingent reinforcement after 1 second or after 100 seconds. In a given work session, the interreinforcement interval *averages* 45 seconds.

What is the effect of scheduling reinforcement availability so that it *averages* 45 seconds rather than being *exactly* 45 seconds? Again, the postreinforcement pause is eliminated. Both variable interval (VI) and variable ratio

---

BOX 5.4   SELF-ADMINISTERING ADDICTIVE DRUGS

While visiting a friend in his hospital room where he was recovering from surgery, I had the opportunity to observe him self-administering morphine to control pain. An automated pump dispensed the morphine through an indwelling intravenous catheter. His physician had determined both the amount of morphine available and the interval of time between dosages. My friend could administer the morphine to himself by pressing a button exactly at the end of each 2-hour interval (i.e., delivery of the drug was response-contingent on a FI-2.0 hour schedule of reinforcement).

By watching his wristwatch, this patient learned to accurately time the 2-hour interval. After a number of such trials, his response pattern emerged clearly and predictably. As the 2-hour period wound down, his button-pressing responses increased in frequency. During the final 30 seconds (as best he could estimate by his wristwatch), he made responses every few seconds until morphine was delivered. A clear scalloping pattern had emerged.

Was this response pattern inevitable? Other studies investigating the use of morphine to control pain (Melzac, 1990) report individual differences in drug-seeking (cf. *sensation-seeking*) behavior. Not all individuals crave the pleasurable effects of morphine; rather, their behavior (including verbal reports) indicates that they fear its addictive properties. Although they experience pain, these individuals do not self-administer the drug as described here even when placed on the same schedule of reinforcement.

(VR) schedules (see Figure 5.5) generate short postreinforcement pauses, while both long fixed ratio (FR) and long fixed interval (FI) schedules produce long postreinforcement pauses. Why? Because in both "variable" schedules reinforcement is possible with the very next response following the last reinforced response.

Stable Responding.   Indeed, the passage of time rather than the number of responses determines the availability of reinforcement. As a result, VI schedules produce highly stable, moment-to-moment operant responses throughout a given work session. Lever-pressing responses are evenly distributed in time. VRs and FRs produce the highest rates of response; the variable interval (VI) schedule produces the most evenly spaced, or stable, rate of responses. Another way to describe the effects of VI schedules is to note that they produce the least variation in interresponse intervals.

VI and VR Schedules of Reinforcement in Everyday Life

Assume that positive reinforcers can be identified in our daily lives and that reinforcement maintains patterns of behavior. We have already noted two examples of the outcomes of scheduling reinforcement on human behavior—how people continue to play slot machines with little payoff (VR schedules) and (at least in one individual) how the periodic availability of morphine determined a distinctive pattern of responses. Let us look at one or two other examples.

For most people, courteous behavior is typically ignored and only occasionally reinforced. Drivers who reduce their speed to allow other cars to merge into traffic or who allow left-hand turns in front of them only rarely get a smile or wave acknowledging (reinforcing) their behavior.[7]

Maintaining Behavior over Long Periods.   More typically, all forms of courteous behavior are "in extinction"; that is, they are not being reinforced. (Have you recently been reinforced for saying "please"?) "Courteous behavior" is maintained on an aperiodic schedule of reinforcement. In your opinion is response-contingent reinforcement (public acknowledgment of courteous behavior) more time dependent (i.e., on a VI schedule) or more rate dependent (i.e., on a VR schedule)? As another example, consider a third-grade school teacher's lesson plan. She contracts to make two to three response-contingent positive comments per week to each student during classroom activities. How would you characterize this schedule of reinforcement? In your estimation, would this plan have the desired effect?

Surprising Reinforcers.   Especially in the absence of continuous reinforcement, responding can be maintained at high levels on partial reinforcement sched-

---

[7] Yes, it is likely that courteous drivers also incur fewer "fender benders" and that their driving behavior is maintained as much by negative reinforcement (discussed in Chapter 6) as by positive reinforcement.

ules. Why is this so? One aspect characteristic of variable schedules of rein-forcement that may increase their power to reinforce and thereby maintain be-havior is that each aperiodic reinforcement is unexpected, that is, is surprising (Kamin, 1969; Rescorla & Wagner, 1972; Terry & Wagner, 1975). Unexpected events capture attention. The response that produces an unexpected positive reinforcement stands out more than the rest. ("What did I do to deserve *this?!*") The occasional reinforcement therefore selects a particular instance from ongoing behavior and makes it noteworthy. ("A little reinforcement can go a long way!")

As students progress from elementary to secondary schools to college, parents and teachers alike pay less daily attention to both courteous behavior and scholastic performance. Tests and course grades at fixed intervals serve as opportunities for reinforcement, yet these opportunities are only loosely at-tached to complex behaviors such as reading, writing, comprehending, and memorizing that characterize academic performance. Only rarely does one hear "good answer!" in the college classroom.

Humans set goals and standards. Meeting goals demands a great deal of our time and attention, and achieving them periodically is an important rein-forcing event. Shooting 9 of 10 free throws is reinforcing, as is getting all As and Bs in a semester. Likewise, earning college degrees, receiving promotions, and buying BMWs and new homes are important experiences, but they occur only a few times in one's life. What experiences are reinforcing and therefore have incentive value day to day? Securing, preparing, and eating good foods; drinking safe water; breathing clean air; living in safe homes and apartments; staying disease free; meeting sexual needs; and attaining other human con-summatory behaviors continue throughout a lifetime.

Extinction and the Partial Reinforcement Effect (PRE)

Back in the Skinner box. We saw earlier that continuous reinforcement (CRF) produces the fastest acquisition of stable responding. For this reason, when training animals (including humans) on *any* schedule of reinforcement, the ex-perimenter typically begins with CRF. After lever pressing occurs reliably, the animal is shifted to the target schedule. Now assume that the response re-quirements of the target schedule are high (such as FR-100 or VR-50) or that the interval between reinforcements is long (such as FI-60 or VI-30). To allow the animal to accomplish these difficult schedules, the experimenter typically "weans" it from continuous reinforcement to (low) ratio schedules. For exam-ple, an FR-2 or FR-3 gradually introduces the partial reinforcement contin-gencies to the animal; going from CRF to FR-100 would likely be unsuccessful because of the phenomenon of experimental extinction.

Pavlovian and Thorndikean Extinction Compared. The concept of experimental extinction was introduced in Chapter 3. Remember what happened to the con-ditioned salivary response of Pavlov's dog Spotski when the bell kept ringing but food was not forthcoming? The conditioned response of salivation extinguished, and extinction set the state for inhibitory conditioning.

A similar process is evident in operant conditioning. Instrumental responses (operants) that are being maintained by reinforcement undergo *extinction* when they are no longer reinforced with food. Extinguished responses never return completely to baseline (i.e., to preconditioning operant levels), but within a given session, lever pressing stops.

Resistance to Extinction.   It should be obvious, then, if the target schedule is a difficult one to achieve, why an experimenter must "wean" animals from CRF. Animals with a CRF history will soon stop responding (i.e., will extinguish when reinforcement is not forthcoming). Animals maintained on CRF show little resistance to extinction. By contrast, animals with a history of responding for long periods of time in the absence of reinforcement (i.e., FR-100, VR-50, FI-60, VI-45) are highly resistant to extinction.

Remember from our study of Pavlovian conditioning that resistance to extinction is an important measure of the success of conditioning. Typically, resistance to conditioning increases with (a) more conditioning trials, (b) more optimal conditioning parameters, and (c) more "prepared" responses (see p. 273ff in this chapter and p. 193ff in Chapter 4).

Here, however, we have something of a conundrum. Partial reinforcement by definition results in *fewer* reinforced responses. How can partial reinforcement result in better conditioning (as measured by resistance to extinction) than continuous reinforcement?

The Partial Reinforcement Effect (PRE).   The tendency for animals maintained on partial reinforcement schedules to be highly resistant to extinction is called the **partial reinforcement effect (PRE).** The PRE addresses both intuitive and counterintuitive observations about learned behavior. We might start by asking whether what the rat learned during acquisition is being reflected in extinction. For example, during training, the animal experiences partial reinforcement while lever pressing, and many of its responses are not reinforced. It may be that if the animal is now put on an extinction schedule, it cannot tell the difference. Many responses were not being reinforced then, and many responses are not being reinforced now. Therefore, it continues to respond longer than an animal trained and maintained on continuous reinforcement.

Again, the best insight into the phenomenon is to ask you, the reader, to be the rat. For example, describe your behavior the last time you put a quarter into a telephone or a vending machine and came up blank. Zero. Quarter gone. No call. No reinforcement. Extinction.

Frustration Theory.   Amsel (1958) points out that following a history of continuous reinforcement, one consequence of extinction is a state of negative emotions such as frustration.[8] Amsel's **frustration theory** also includes the cognitive component alluded to in the preceding example. This is, one can be frustrated only if one has *expectations* concerning what the consequences of responding *should* be. By this analysis, past candy bars vended, successful telephone connections, and food pellets delivered on a continuous basis set up predictable expectations of what should happen "the next time." Now imagine living in Italy where local phone systems are unpredictable at best. In using public phones over the years, Italians have lost many coins. That is, their telephoning operants have never been consistently reinforced. Sometimes they connect with the first coin; other times they must try several times (and lose coins) before connecting.

In which phone system would you be more likely to continue feeding your coins—the Italian system, in which patrons have a history of nonreinforcement, or a phone system that reliably reinforces most responses? In which system would nonreinforcement be more frustrating? Given this understanding, can you explain why Italians are surprised when Americans become angry at telephones?

Let us return to your Las Vegas casino. There you can control the payoff schedules in your slot machines. Now that you know how to maximize resistance to extinction, how might you go about minimizing the frustration of nonreinforcement in your customers? Can you conceptualize a trade-off between customer frustration and customer satisfaction? What are the optimal conditions guaranteeing that you, the owner, maximize profits?

To summarize, different expectations are set up when animals are trained on partial reinforcement and continuous reinforcement. If trained on partial reinforcement, the animal may not even become aware of the difference when it is put into an extinction period. By contrast, the animal trained on continuous reinforcement immediately becomes aware of its absence of reinforcement and will stop responding. Frustration results from thwarted expectations.

Work and Efficiency

Continuous reinforcement and FR and VR schedules of reinforcement allow animals to adjust their work output to determine the amount of food they can receive in a given session. Generally speaking, the harder the animal works (the more lever presses the animal makes per unit time), the more food is forthcoming. A fair analogy is the factory worker who does piece work in which the more units produced (for example, dresses in a clothing factory), the more money the worker earns. Within a work session, however, local rate of responding is unimportant. For example, workers may be considered less effi-

---

[8] Recall that Pavlov thought that the same process occurred during extinction of a salivary conditioned response.

cient for working slowly on completing a dress, but nonetheless they receive full pay for completed items.

How can local rates of responding be controlled? With what you have learned, could you manipulate reinforcement schedules of the workers in your factory to generate more precise timing of their responses? Let us look at another example of behavioral technology.

DRH and DRL Schedules of Reinforcement

Two schedules of reinforcement have been designed to reinforce *local rates of responding*. A **differential *r*einforcement of *h*igh rate (DRH)** of responding schedule reinforces bursts of lever pressing. A computer program monitors local rates of lever pressing and defines the response contingencies. A burst, for example, may be defined as five or more lever presses by a rat (or 10 or more pecks by a pigeon on a lighted key) in a 2-second time period. Only when the target level of responding is reached is a food reinforcer made available.

Instead of speed, what if the desired target behavior is very slow, accurately timed responding? A researcher might use a **differential *r*einforcement of *l*ow rate (DRL)** schedule of reinforcement. For example, an animal on a DRL-15-second schedule must minimally wait 15 seconds before a response will produce reinforcement. Each response made before 15 seconds has elapsed resets a clock, and the animal must wait an additional 15 seconds before reinforcement is again available.

I have trained several *Rhesus macaque* monkeys on DRL-15 schedules. After several weeks, they become incredibly efficient. In one representative session, monkey #079 produced interresponse latencies (time between responses) of 15:04 seconds followed by 15:08, 15:02, 15:04; 14:97 (nonreinforced), 15:14, 15:07, 15:04, and so on, with no further misses during a 4-minute session.

Of what practical use are schedules of reinforcement that by their operation produce fine control over local rates of response? Absolutely none that I can think of.[9]

Analysis of Schedules of Reinforcement

Why have we spent so much time on schedules of reinforcement? Why should we care how a pigeon or rat responds when reinforcement is scheduled contingent upon time and rate of lever pressing? Consider the following arguments. First, these laboratory investigations have produced a body of findings that has considerable application to the human condition. Humans in fact re-

---

[9] Actually, many. For example, *all* behavior requiring rhythm and pacing—*all* skilled movement requiring precise local control over rate of response, including the artist's brush strokes, playing a piano, and reading and writing. Observe two people having a conversation, and note the subtle cues controlling speaking and listening. Can you reconstruct the likely reinforcement history of individuals who lack conversational skills—who have not learned when to inhibit responding?

spond as predicted by these studies—not all humans, and not all of the time. For a wide variety of human behaviors, however, reinforcement—especially partial reinforcement—determines patterns of responding—be it morphine administration, gambling behavior, piano playing, using machinery, or being courteous to one another.

Perhaps a more important point is one that both Skinner and Watson were preoccupied with, namely, the prediction and control of human behavior. These studies of laboratory animals demonstrate the power of reinforcement and, as we see in the next chapter, of punishment to manipulate and control behavior. There are only so many things one can do with a lever, so we should not be surprised that the focus of Skinner's research has been on *rate and patterning of responding* on the lever. While one might criticize the narrowing of behavior demanded by the Skinner box, at the same time one must recognize the power of prediction and elegance of behavioral control afforded by this simple methodology. We turn in the next section to the issue of behavioral control.

Interim Summary

1. *Schedules of reinforcement* describe the manner in which reinforcement delivery is patterned, or scheduled, following operant responses.
2. The delivery of reinforcement for each response is called *continuous reinforcement (CRF)*. If each response is not reinforced, the animal is said to be on a *partial*, or *intermittent, reinforcement schedule.*
3. Schedules delivering reinforcement based on the *number of responses* an animal makes are called *ratio schedules*, including fixed ratio (FR) and variable ratio (VR) schedules.
4. Schedules delivering reinforcement based on *time* between reinforcement are called *interval schedules*. These include fixed interval (FI) and variable interval (VI) schedules.
5. An animal's behavior on different schedules of reinforcement can be compared with respect to acquisition: patterning of responses, including bursts (DRH), pauses (DRL), stability, and resistance to extinction.
6. In general, longer FI and FR schedules produce postreinforcement pauses; FI schedules produce scalloping patterns; VI schedules produce stable responding; and ratio schedules produce faster responding.
7. CRF extinguishes quickly, and partial reinforcement schedules are resistant to extinction. One measure of the partial reinforcement effect (**PRE**) is resistance to extinction.
8. Differential reinforcement of high (DRH) and low (DRL) schedules of reinforcement control bursts of responding or patience in responding, respectively.
9. Behavior in the real world is under the control of schedules of reinforcement.

ISSUES OF BEHAVIORAL CONTROL

Let's go to the supermarket. The whining is nonstop as you stand in line waiting to be checked out. You join other uncomfortable shoppers watching the battle of wills. Every time mom says, "No, you can't have it," little Joey's hand in the candy counter clutches his choice more tightly. He turns up the volume: "Why not?" he whines. "I want this one. Pleeeease . . . ? You said if I was good. . . ."

After several more iterations, mom's "no, and that's final!" is followed by loud crying. Mom counters, "If you'll be a good boy and not cry, you can have it, but this is the last time." Joey nods contritely, quits crying, and tears open the wrapper. Both mother and son (and everyone within earshot) appear content.

Let us begin our analysis of this behavioral encounter by answering the following questions:

1. In this scenario,
   a. Is mom controlling Joey's behavior?
   b. Is Joey controlling mom's behavior?
   c. Are both (a) and (b) correct?
   d. Is neither person in control of the other?
   e. Are both out of control?

Who's in Charge Here?   Answers (d) and (e) are both appealing. As a figure-of-speech answer, (e) seems to be self-evident but is incorrect when we analyze the problem as a behaviorist would.

The problem is one of semantics. A behaviorist analyzes behavior in terms of *control* issues, thereby using the word *control* somewhat differently than the lay public does. For a behaviorist, *all* behavior is controlled, or determined, by environment. Therefore, mom is controlling Joey, and Joey is controlling mom. Answer (c) covers all the possibilities.

In what way is mom controlling Joey and Joey controlling mom? Can you identify the reinforcement contingencies at work in this example? At a minimum is it possible that Joey's persistence in responding is being maintained by some sort of partial reinforcement schedule?

The Concept of Behavioral Control

The manner in which the environment comes to control human and animal behavior is a continuing theme in B.F. Skinner's writings.[10] His behaviorist

---

[10] *Behavior of Organisms* (1938), *Walden Two* (1948), *Verbal Behavior* (1957), and *Beyond Freedom and Dignity* (1971).

philosophy, like John B. Watson's, is an extreme form of *environmental determinism*. The method of behaviorism is to identify and analyze the way in which environmental stimuli exert control over an animal's behavior. The success of the method is measured (a) by the manipulation and control over ongoing behavior via reinforcement and (b) given a knowledge of past reinforcement history, to predict which behavior will occur next.

A formal definition of *stimulus control* is discussed later. For present purposes, an organism's behavior is said to be under control at that point in training when an experimenter can make highly accurate, reliable predictions that a particular response will occur in a particular situation. Before analyzing mom and Joey, let us again detour by the Skinner box.

Controlling Operant Behavior

Why does a pigeon peck a lighted key or a rat press a lever? The obvious answer is to obtain food. And with a few exceptions, this commonsense analysis is essentially correct.[11] Stimulus cues of hunger motivate an animal to move instrumentally, seeking food within its ecological niche. Prior learning in the Skinner box now allows specific responses to operate on the environment, that is, to be instrumental in securing food.

Stimulus Context in Skinner Boxes

Placing trained, hungry animals in a Skinner box, therefore, provides the occasion for specific operants to occur. The sights, sounds, and smells of the box are environmental stimuli (i.e., the context) that *control* the specific response of bar pressing. Change the stimulus context, for example, by moving the lever to a different wall, or change background noise in the box. Even subtle changes will disrupt the operant response. In this example we see that *environmental context* is a major controlling factor in whether or not an operant response will occur.

The importance of context in the control and prediction of behavior is currently being investigated using a number of methodologies (see Balsom & Tomie, 1985; Bouton, 1984, 1991; Miller & Schachtman, 1985a, 1985b). An oversimplified way of appreciating the relevance of these experiments is to think about being the new kid in a new school. Or imagine that you first learned to drive one particular car over a 1-year period of time. Then you are asked to drive a different car that has all the same operating features (steering wheel, brake and gas pedals, shifter, etc.), but the positions of these manipulanda and the sights, sounds, and smells differ (i.e., the context differs). Your

---

[11] But see the phenomenon of *autoshaping*, p. 269.

driving ability (operant responses) would suffer because of these contextual differences.

Getting Control of Responses

An easy way to demonstrate how a stimulus in the animal's environment can come to control operant responding is to arrange for a specific stimulus to be present when a response-food contingency is in effect. For example, the rat or bird can be trained to bar press or key peck when the house lights are on and not to make these operant responses when the house lights are off. How? By having a response-food contingency in effect only when the house lights are on. When the house lights are turned off, the lever is electrically disconnected from the feeder mechanism. With the lights off, the operants are no longer instrumental in securing food. The response-food contingency has been broken.

After several sessions of lights on/responses produce food and lights off/responses do *not* produce food, the animal soon learns to respond in the presence of the lights and not to respond in darkness. (The opposite can also be trained, when responses in the dark are reinforced but not those made in the light.)

Discriminative and Negative-Discriminative Stimuli. Skinner called a stimulus (such as a house light) that signals that response-food contingencies were in effect a **discriminative stimulus (S^d,** pronounced "essdee"). Therefore, *discriminative stimuli* (S^ds) set occasions in which trained operant responses become highly probable; S^ds control high rates of operant responding because the responses are reinforced. Conversely, a stimulus that signals that response-food contingencies are *not* in effect is called a **negative discriminative stimulus (S^Δ,** pronounced "essdelta"). There being no payoff when the S^Δ is in effect, the responses drop out.

Stimulus Control. We are now able to formally define the stimulus control of behavior. When trained animals reliably make operant responses in the presence of S^ds and do *not* respond in the presence of S^Δs, the animal is said to be under **stimulus control.** In a Skinner box environment, an S^d (such as a 500-Hz tone) sets the occasion for a high rate of response, and an S^Δ (no tone, or perhaps a tone of a different frequency) sets the occasion for a low rate of response. Responses in the presence of the S^d are reinforced, but not in the S^Δ condition. An animal reliably lever pressing in the presence of one stimulus but not another is said to be "under stimulus control."

My dog Sadie will crawl up on the couch in the presence of my children but not when I'm in the room. She begs for food from them but not from me. My presence is an S^Δ for her crawling on furniture and begging at the table. Note that Sadie is under stimulus control in the presence of both me and my children: She has been differentially reinforced and responds predictably, depending on the stimulus context.

Losing Stimulus Control

Note that an S^d-S^Δ discrimination is not unlike Pavlov's CS^+-CS^- conditioned discrimination procedure (see Figure 4.11, p. 173). The difference is that S^ds control *operant* responding and CS^+s control *reflexive* responding. Recall that Pavlov trained dogs to salivate in the presence of a circle and *not* to salivate to an ellipse; that is, he required that the dog discriminate a circle from an ellipse. When the ellipse had become too circular (beyond the dog's capacity of visual resolution), the dog began to salivate to both stimuli indiscriminately. In Skinner's terms, Pavlov had "lost stimulus control" over the animal. Likewise, after successfully training an S^d-S^Δ discrimination, if, for whatever reason, operant responses are no longer reliably controlled by the S^d and S^Δ, the trainer (or parent) is said to have lost stimulus control.

Red and Green Traffic Lights

As an example, if you reliably stop your automobile at a red light and go on green, Skinner would say that you are under stimulus control. The red and green traffic lights are S^ds that control the operant responses of *foot pressure on the brake* and *foot pressure on the accelerator*, respectively. The same red and green traffic lights are S^Δs for *foot pressure* off *the accelerator* and *foot pressure* off *the brake*, respectively (that is, *not* to press the accelerator or brake, respectively).

The stimulus control properties of red and green lights on driving an automobile are relatively simple. Can you identify the control characteristics of the *yellow* caution light? See Box 5.5 for some help.

Generalization and Stimulus Control

Traffic lights in Mexico control the behavior of Americans who drive there. The reds and greens are often of different hues, and the positions of the signals may vary (i.e., reversed so that a green "go" light is on top of a standard and the red "stop" light is below). The result is that the lights control our behavior less effectively, but, nevertheless, our responses to these light signals generalize.

We take for granted that learning in one situation applies to others. In Chapter 3 the concept of *generalization* was introduced to account for such transfer of learning effects. Recall that Pavlov had trained a dog to salivate to a tone of 1500 Hz and then found that it would also respond to tones of 1490 and 1510 Hz. Presumably, the tones sounded similar to the dog.

BOX 5.5   BEHAVIORAL ANALYSIS OF FREE WILL

As we see in Chapter 9, Tolman (1932) believed that both a formal psychology of learning and a relatively complete understanding of human behavior would result from the laboratory study of the behavior of a rat at a choice point in a maze. That is, if we could predict 100% of the time when a rat would turn left or right (or, presumably, around) at any point in time, our scientific understanding of behavior would be complete.

The merits of Tolman's arguments aside for the moment, let us attempt to analyze our "choices" when confronted with the appearance of a yellow caution traffic light. Are both operant and reflexive responses under stimulus control? Can we shed light on the enigma of "voluntary" behavior when the light turns yellow?

Operating an automobile can be described as a complex sequence of operant responses. The accelerator, brake, clutch, turn signals, and steering wheel are among the manipulanda necessary for successfully operating the vehicle. Stimuli controlling the operants in driving include visually detected movements of other cars, the speedometer, and traffic control signs and signals.

Recall how bewildering driving was on the first few occasions! The op-

erants of steering, braking, and controlling the clutch and accelerator—all at the same time—had to be coordinated with a flux of signals from the environment. Some of us even had dear old dad in the immediate environment.

And now you encounter a dreaded *yellow* light. How fast am I going? How long until I arrive at the intersection? To brake or not to brake—*that* is the question. The S^ds controlling the braking operant include speed of travel, distance to intersection, performance of brakes, road surface conditions (wet or dry), presence of police, past accidents, driving record, duration of the yellow light, presence of parents in car, alcohol (or other drugs) affecting performance, and so forth.

It is easy to overlook the Pavlovian conditioned reflexive responses that occur when the light turns yellow (not to be confused with the ANS arousal of seeing flashing blue and red lights in your rearview mirror). The dilation of your pupils is one indication of heightened activity in the reticular activating system (RAS) and increased sympathetic nervous system activity.

Do you begin braking or increase your rate of speed? If it makes you feel any better, you can continue to believe that you have a choice in the matter.

Another example follows: My voice command for Sadie to "Stay!" does not generalize well when my children use this word. First, their high-frequency voices do not sound like my voice. Second, because they have repeatedly used the word *stay* without appropriately reinforcing (or punishing) Sadie, their

"Stay" has been conditioned to mean something entirely different from my "Stay!"

Stimulus Generalization Gradient.   Not surprising, experiments using operant conditioning methodology have demonstrated similar findings. In a classic study (Guttman & Kalish, 1956), pigeons were reinforced with food on a VI schedule when they pecked at a key backlit with, for example, a yellow light (the yellow light's wavelength was 580 nanometers, or nm).[12] After training, the wavelength of light was changed on successive test trials, and the number of responses to a variety of wavelengths around the original wavelength were measured. (During the test trials only the responses to one wavelength were re-inforced; the VI schedule kept the pigeons responding during extinction as the S^d was changed to other wavelengths).

As you might expect, more responses were made to the most similar wavelengths and the least responses to the most different (most easily dis-criminated) wavelengths. This orderly pattern of responses is called a **stimu-lus generalization gradient** (see Figure 5.6).

The Guttman and Kalish (1956) experiment addresses previously raised questions concerning the *ecological validity* of laboratory investigations. Let us look at the real-world applicability of these findings.

Invariant Stimuli?   One criticism of laboratory research concerns the nature of stimuli used in experiments. Seldom is a "pure" stimulus repeatedly presented and consistently reinforced in the real world. In the present case, the "visual stimulus" that sets the occasion for response-contingent food availability was an invariant 580-nm "yellow" in a laboratory setting. In nonlaboratory niches, one could argue, a predator sees form and movement as well as color in locat-ing prey. The color may change as the prey moves. Movement also guarantees different patterns on the predator's retina from moment to moment. Does the learning that occurs under these stimulus conditions resemble learning using static stimuli in the laboratory?

The Guttman and Kalish (1956) findings demonstrate that a stimulus does not have to be perfectly reproduced on each occasion to control respond-ing. Presumably, views of shapes and movements that differ from those ini-tially reinforced also come to control responses. Generalization across varying stimuli produces meaningful, predictable, patterns of responses. I can recog-nize the difference in each of my children's voices, yet I recognize the words they speak as having the same signal value. An Episcopal service generalizes to a Methodist service. A meal in England is similar to one in Texas. We don't have to relearn each new environment as long as it is somewhere on our gen-eralization gradient.

---

[12] Recognize that the "yellow" experienced by humans is likely to be perceived differently by pigeon brains.

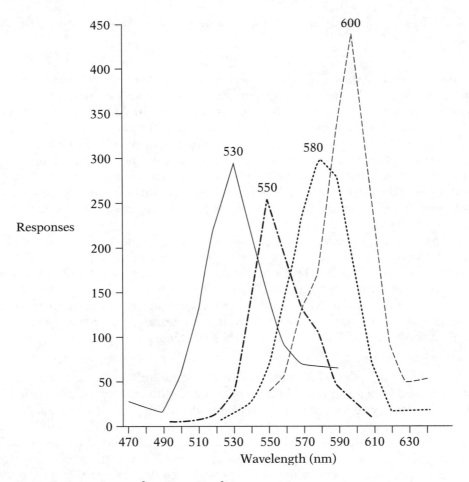

FIGURE 5.6   Generalization Gradients

Pigeons were food reinforced to peck at backlit discs illuminated with wavelengths of either 530, 550, 580, or 600 nanometers (to humans these wavelengths appear green, greenish yellow, yellowish orange, and red, respectively). Each bird was then put on extinction. Pecking responses to the wavelength it was trained with and immediately neighboring wavelengths were measured. Each pigeon's pecking responses distributed around the peak of the original training wavelength. The pattern of responses is called a *generalization gradient* (after Guttman & Kalish, 1956).

Stimulus Control of Reinforced and Nonreinforced Responses

Let us analyze a small child learning her multiplication tables in terms of stimulus control: Discriminative stimuli (S^ds, the multiplication problems) control responses (answers) that are reinforced (correct) or not (incorrect). This real-world example points out a methodological difference compared with Guttman and Kalish's (1954) training procedure. In most examples of learned behavior (especially of skilled performance), the subject learns which responses are reinforced and at the same time which are *not* reinforced: "$4 \times 4 = 16$" (correct); "$4 \times 4 = 15$" (incorrect). Shooting the basketball "this way" is reinforced; shooting the ball "that way" is not reinforced.

By way of contrast, Guttman and Kalish's (1956) pigeons did *not* initially learn that nonyellow stimuli were S^Δs. That is, during training, the birds only saw one stimulus, the 580-nm S^d that was always reinforced. What would happen if the pigeon initially learns that one stimulus is associated with reinforcement and that another is not? That is, what is the effect of initially learning S^d-S^Δ discriminations on subsequent patterns of generalization? In the real world, does it matter if a child also learns that "$4 \times 4 \neq 17$," or is it enough that she merely learns that "$4 \times 4 = 16$"?

Role of Nonreinforced Responses.   Recall that Pavlov's dog learned to salivate to a circle (CS^+) and not to salivate to an ellipse (CS^-). In investigating the role of S^Δ in S^d-S^Δ discriminations, the question that Hanson (1959) asked his pigeons was related both to Guttman and Kalish's (1956) and to Pavlov's findings. Specifically, what differences result when a correct response is trained in the presence of one stimulus (the S^d) versus training the correct responses in the context of both reinforced and nonreinforced stimuli (i.e., an S^d-S^Δ discrimination)?

In a design similar to that used by Guttman and Kalish (1956), Hanson (1959) used the following three treatment conditions to answer questions about the role of the S^Δ during training:

Group 1: S^d = 550 nm ; S^Δ = 590 nm (S^d-S^Δ difference = 40 nm)
Group 2: S^d = 550 nm ; S^Δ = 555 nm (S^d-S^Δ difference = 5 nm)
Group 3: S^d = 550 nm ; no S^Δ; (S^d-S^Δ difference = ∞)

Note that all three groups of pigeons were trained with the same reinforced stimulus, a light of 550 nm. They differed by having a very similar S^Δ condition (i.e., 555 nm), a dissimilar S^Δ condition (i.e., 590 nm), or no S^Δ during training.

Stimulus Generalization of Operant Responses.   After training, all pigeons were tested for stimulus generalization. Pigeons in Group 3 produced a familiar generalization gradient around 550 nm (See Figure 5.7) quite similar to that

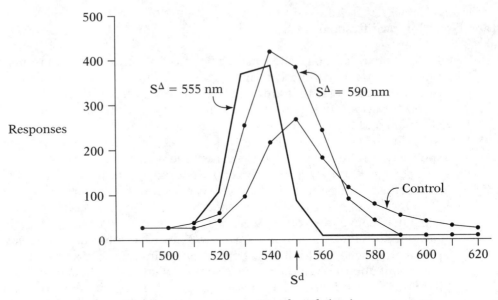

FIGURE 5.7   The Peak-Shift Phenomenon

> Three groups of pigeons were food reinforced to peck at a backlit key
> (wavelength = 550 nanometers), the S^d condition. One of the three groups
> was also trained with an S^Δ = 555 nm, another with S^Δ = 590 nm, and the
> third group with no S^Δ (a control condition). The generalization gradients
> for all three groups responding to S^d = 550 nm, in extinction, are plotted.
> Note that the gradients for both groups trained with S^Δ are shifted to the
> left of the peak wavelength of 550 nm.

found by Guttman and Kalish (1954; cf. Figure 5.6). Note that the peak of responding is precisely at 550 nm, the reinforced wavelength.

Of interest in Figure 5.7, however, are the generalization gradients of the
pigeons in which S^d-S^Δ discriminations had been trained. Even though pigeons
in all three groups were reinforced for responding to an S^d of the same wavelength, all three generalization gradients were found to differ.

Peak Shift.   First, note that the generalization gradients of both groups trained
with S^d-S^Δ discriminations are *shifted to the left*. The peaks of their generalization gradients are to the left of the 550-nm wavelength. A question immediately arises: Why should pigeons make more responses to wavelengths of light
for which their responses had never been reinforced? And, perhaps more important, why should the peak of responding be shifted *further* when, during
training, the S^Δ is closer to the S^d? Note that the peak of responding by Group
2 is shifted further than the peak of responding of Group 1. This phenomenon

is called **peak shift**. The peak of responding to the S^d is shifted *away* from the S^Δ experienced during training. Peak shift provides a clue to the role of the S^Δ in S^d-S^Δ discrimination learning.

A second difference that arises during S^d-S^Δ discrimination training is that the generalization gradients are *narrower* than the S^d-only group (see Figure 5.7). Third, when the S^Δ = 555 nm (only 5 nm different from S^d = 550 nm), the generalization gradient is narrower than when S^Δ = 590 nm (40 nm different from S^d = 550 nm).

To summarize, after S^d-S^Δ discrimination training (a) the shift in peak response is greater and (b) the generalization gradient is narrower if the S^Δ was more similar to the S^d.

S^d-S^Δ Training Sharpens Discriminations. What is the importance of these findings? First, the presence of a nonreinforced stimulus, the S^Δ, appears to *sharpen* the discrimination of the reinforced stimulus. Furthermore, the closer the stimulus characteristics of the reinforced are to the nonreinforced stimulus, the more *discriminable* are the two stimuli. It is as if the bird is forced to pay more attention to the *exact* attributes of a stimulus that provide information about reinforcement: 4×4 is not 15, and 3×4 is not 16; only the exact stimulus, 4×4 is reinforced by the exact response, 16. Likewise, when playing the piano, a G7 major chord *is* different from a G7 chord. Only by repeatedly comparing two stimuli having highly similar attributes can one distinguish, for example, that one red wine is slightly better than another.

Second, something rather than nothing is learned when a stimulus is *not* reinforced in the training context of a related stimulus that *is* reinforced. In Hanson's (1959) research, the presence of a nonreinforced wavelength during training changed the bird's response tendencies to all other wavelengths. Another way to say this is that what the bird learned in the presence of the nonreinforced stimulus was measurable, but only indirectly. The effect could be assessed only in the presence of other stimuli.

The Inhibitory Nature of S^Δ Training. The necessity of measuring the effects of nonreinforced stimuli indirectly by the peak shift phenomenon is reminiscent of Pavlovian conditioned inhibition. Remember that *conditioned inhibition* was also measured indirectly via summation and retardation tests, and then only in the presence of a conditioned excitor (for a review, see Chapter 4, p. 178). In the present situation, the S^d can be construed as an excitor and the S^Δ as an inhibitor. The peak response to the excitatory S^d is shifted, indirectly reflecting the role of S^Δ. Can the responses to S^Δ also generalize in the same way that responses to S^d generalize? Yes, *inhibitory* generalization gradients have been reported by Honig, Boneau, Burstein, and Pennypacker (1963).

Controlling Human Verbal Behavior

You may or may not be impressed with the behaviorist's analysis of your behavior at the choice point of a yellow traffic signal. More than likely you conceptualize human behavior as being far more complicated than a mere succession of operants controlled by discriminative stimuli. What role, for example, do language and thought play in controlling behavior? As we see in Chapter 10, our use of language (and the thought processes that language allows) *does* make human behavior different from animal behavior. But, as Skinner and others have pointed out, language usage can also be analyzed from a behavioral perspective (Skinner, 1957).

Back to the supermarket. We left mom and Joey exchanging words at the checkout counter. At that time, mom was characterized as being in control of Joey's behavior, and Joey of mom's. Can we bring the behaviorist concept of stimulus control to each person's behavior, including verbal behavior?

Discriminated Operants.   The bright candy wrappers in the checkout lane are CSs that have been associated with the appetitive chocolate USs they contain. In addition to these learned associations, Joey's past reinforcement history includes a sequence of operant behaviors that have been positively reinforced. "Reaching for candy" is a **discriminated operant** that reflects the stimulus control the candy has over Joey's behavior. That is, on previous occasions in this part of the Skinner box, these particular operants (reaching, grabbing, removing wrapper) have produced response-contingent reinforcement.

Mutual Control in Human Interactions.   Mom and her words are part of this stimulus complex. On past occasions her words were S^ds controlling Joey's behavior. How so? "No, you can't have it" was part of the stimulus complex in the presence of which Joey's operant behavior was ultimately reinforced by the candy. The word *no* in this stimulus context is an S^d for Joey to turn up the volume of his cry and to hold onto the candy even more tightly. Why? Because that response in this context produced reinforcement in the past.

In turn, Joey's vocalizations (and the caustic looks of other shoppers) are the S^ds for mom to respond verbally: "If you'll be a good boy and not cry, you can have the candy, but this is the last time." Joey stops crying, which reinforces mom's verbal behavior, just as it did the last time. (As we see in the next chapter, stopping an aversive event is an example of *negative reinforcement*.) Table 5.1 summarizes both the S^ds and the discriminated operant responses characterizing this human interaction.

Recognize the controlling role of context in this example. The presence of a second parent (as part of the context) would likely have precluded Joey's exchange with his mother.

Occasion Setting

Many laboratory experiments have investigated the features of a context that in turn control S^d-S^Δ discrimination learning (Holland, 1986). If a stimulus, such as a light or a room, comes to control discriminated responding, that

TABLE 5.1   Who's in Control?

Joey

S^ds *Controlling Behavior*	*Discriminated Operants*
Supermarket stimuli	Reach for candy.
Sight of candy	(a) Approach candy; (b) reach for candy; (c) "Mom, I want this piece" (verbal behavior).
"No, you can't have it."	Louder vocalizations.
"Okay, but this is the last time."	Tears off wrapper and eats candy.

Mom

Sight of Joey moving toward candy	"No candy" (verbal behavior).
Joey says "Please."	"No, you can't have it."
Louder vocalizations; others stare.	"O.K., but this is the last time."
Joey eats candy.	Mom resumes shopping.

stimulus is called an *occasion setter*. To the extent that Mom's and Joey's behaviors were under the control of the supermarket, this example mirrors **occasion-setting** experiments in which one stimulus sets the occasion for another stimulus to be reinforced or not. Ross and Holland (1981), for example, trained rats to use a light to give meaning to a tone. The presence of the light meant that a tone sounded a few seconds later would be an S^d (i.e., that the tone would in turn be followed by reinforcement). If unsignaled by the light, the tone would be an S^Δ. The tone set the occasion for discriminated learning in the same way that the supermarket context set the occasion for mom's and Joey's verbal behaviors.

Several points from the preceding example are worth emphasizing:

1. Words can and do function as *discriminative stimuli*. Words in some contexts mean different things than the same words in other contexts.
2. Speaking words (using language) can be understood as an *operant* behavior that, like any other operant, can result in reinforcement or punishment. Reinforcing and punishing an individual's words increases and decreases, respectively, the probability that they will be used in the future.
3. In all human interactions, the operant responses of one individual have stimulus properties that set the occasion for operant responses of the

other person. From this example it is easy to see how Joey's behavior is controlling mom's, and vice versa.[13]

4. Behavior always occurs in a context, and the context can become an occasion setter. Among humans, occasion setters can control when to argue and when to make love.

Complex Behavior as Chained Operants

Another point to be made concerning Table 5.1 is that seemingly complex human interactions can be analyzed into simpler behavioral sequences that are "chained" together. In these **stimulus-response chains,** each response has stimulus features that control the next response. Thus, Joey's verbal response "please" is the stimulus for mom's "no, you can't have it."

The concept of **chained operants** also allows us to analyze Joey's behavior in terms of discriminative stimuli, operant responses, and reinforcement: He sees candy at distance (S^d); approaches candy (operant); sees candy up close (S^d); reaches for candy (operant); sensory input as fingers touch candy (S^d); picks up candy (operant); candy in hand is stimulus (S^d) for "Mom, I want this piece" (verbal operant). Joey puts the candy in his mouth and bites off a piece (operants). The taste of candy (positive reinforcer) reinforces all preceding operants.

Thought question: Can you describe student-teacher interactions in the classroom in terms of stimulus-response chains? What are the discriminative stimuli controlling the behavior of student and teacher? *Hint:* Identify the operant responses of both students and teachers. Note the stimulus characteristics of students' operants that control the teacher and vice versa. For starters, you may want to analyze eye contact, pauses in lecture, students yawning, responses to hands raised, and so forth.

Behavioral Analysis of "Volition" and "Will"

Earlier mom and Joey's interaction was described as a "battle of wills." John B. Watson and B.F. Skinner objected to the use of words such as *volition* and *will* to describe presumed intrapsychic events. Watson denied the premise of human consciousness, and Skinner merely ignored it. Both thought that analyses of observed behavior were more productive, that explaining behavior was best accomplished by reference to past reinforcement histories rather than to hypothetical personality characteristics.

What do you, the reader, think? Which terminology lends itself best to a scientific analysis of human behavior? What, if anything, is added to an un-

---

[13] If you routinely argue with someone, both of you know which buttons to hit to keep it going. Also, the codependency relationship of human couples is an example from clinical psychology that profits from this analysis (see Chapter 7).

INSTRUMENTAL LEARNING   **265**

derstanding of Joey's behavior by describing him as a "brat" or as a "strong-willed individual"? In this instance, might not the label be inappropriate, given that Joey's mother is controlling his behavior?

Sequence of Learning Complex Chains

Complex sequences of operant behavior are learned with difficulty. Remember learning to swim, to ride a bike, or to painstakingly print the alphabet? Pianists take many years to learn hand and finger movements and months of intense practice for recitals. In all these examples, operants must be performed in sequence. What do we know about how these sequences are learned?

Rules for Learning Chains

Each operant can be performed only if the preceding operant has been successfully accomplished. Whether it be driving a car, writing your name, tying your shoe, or whistling a tune, all complex chains require the successful completion of individual operants.

In working with children, parents, teachers, and coaches should be sensitive to differences in sensory-motor development (don't ask fingers to do what they are not capable of doing). Parents should simplify the shoe-tying task, for example, as follows:

1. Separate each component response and have the child practice each operant separately.
2. Practice each operant in the reverse order of the shoe-lacing sequence. For example, initially tie the bow, and require the child only to tighten it.
3. Reinforce each operant (such as making the bow) separately.

Errors in Mazes.   Why the *reverse* order? An analysis of the errors of rats learning mazes indicates that they make fewer errors at the end of the chains than at the beginning (Hull, 1932). That is, the last response (for example, a *left turn* before entering the goal box) that produces reinforcement is learned first, then the next-to-last response, the third-from-last response, and so on. For this reason, after practice with all operants involved in lacing shoes, the child should be helped up to the last step, then allowed to accomplish it with minimal guidance. After several trials, allow the child to work alone on the last two steps. These two operants will be chained together by the terminal reinforcement (as well as by the verbal reinforcement—secondary reinforcement—of the caretaker at each step).

Interim Summary

1. Behavior control is a concept that certain stimuli in the environment (called *discriminative stimuli* or S^ds) become associated with reinforced

responses; other stimuli (called non*discriminative stimuli* or $S^\Delta s$) are not associated with reinforced responses.

2. The animal is said to be under *stimulus control* if, after S^d-S^Δ training, the response reliably occurs to the S^d but not to the S^Δ. The discriminative stimulus is said to *control* the response.

3. Laboratory demonstrations of stimulus control have recently focused on the way in which the context of the experiment controls responding.

4. One stimulus can also control the response to another similar stimulus. The response is said to have *generalized* to the second stimulus. The second stimulus is within the *generalization gradient* of the first simulus.

5. S^d-S^Δ training sharpens discrimination of the S^d. The presence of the S^Δ causes the response (which normally peaks to the S^d) to shift in a direction opposite the S^Δ (i.e., the *peak shift* phenomenon).

6. Introducing the S^Δ condition (in S^d-S^Δ discrimination training) produces results similar to the CS^- in the CS^+-CS^- discrimination. Both the CS^- and the S^Δ acquire inhibitory properties.

7. Human interactions, including verbal behavior, can be analyzed from the perspective of reinforced operant responding under stimulus control.

8. Contextual stimuli can come to control the occasions during which a stimulus can be a CS^+ or a CS^- (alternatively, an S^d or an S^Δ). These stimuli are called *occasion setters* and the event, *occasion setting*.

9. Learning complex behaviors can be analyzed as the acquisition of simple operant responses being chained together.

INSTINCTIVE BEHAVIOR AND OPERANT CONDITIONING

To this point we have contrasted Skinner's analysis of how reinforcement can modify emitted behavior with Pavlov's conditioning of innate reflexes. Both are examples of learning. But, as conceptualized in Chapter 2 and as implied by the name of this book, *behavior* is more than learning. Behavioral analysis involves the interplay of species-specific behavior and learned responses.

Recall that Skinner assumed that lever pressing by rats and key pecking by pigeons were relatively arbitrary "operants." That is, the responses were neutral with respect to the ingestive behaviors involved in eating the positive reinforcement. Why did Skinner think that the distinction between "arbitrary responses" and "innate feeding responses" was important? Simply because the range of possible behaviors that can be "arbitrarily" conditioned is greater than innately organized responses. Humans in fact write poetry and play the piano as well as basketball. None of these behaviors evolved in response to selective pressures, and none are as important as the *consummatory behaviors* discussed in Chapter 2. A fortunate few can make a living reading and writing and playing games and musical instruments, but eating, drinking, courting, mating, and taking care of offspring are more important. These latter behaviors are essential in maintaining individual life as well as ensuring the continuity of species.

Is Key Pecking Arbitrary?   Skinner and others have recognized that a great deal of behavior exhibited by humans and other animals does not appear to be innately organized or otherwise reflexive. To investigate how "arbitrary behavior" was learned, therefore, required an arbitrary "operant" that was not innately organized. Lever pressing and key pecking seemed to fit the bill. Surely the positioning of neck muscles and the postures of pigeons pecking at backlit keys are unrelated to eating food and drinking water.

But look closely at the photos in Figure 5.8. A pigeon is reinforced with food (top photos) or with water (bottom photos) for pecking at a backlit key. The difference is obvious. Water-reinforced pecking responses produce open-mouthed drinking postures (bottom), and food-reinforced pecking responses

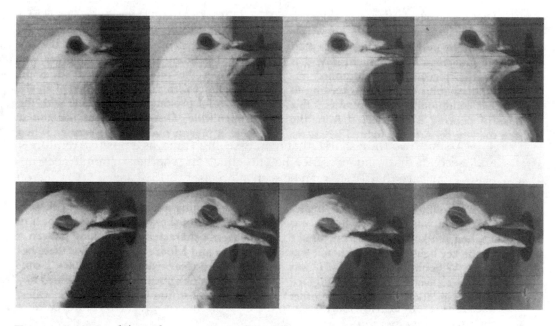

FIGURE 5.8   Birds' Beaks: Eating and Drinking Positions

Pigeons peck keys differently, depending on whether they are food (bottom panels) or water (top panels) reinforced. Apparently, open beaks are for picking up grain and closed beaks for drinking. The response topography is not as arbitrary as Skinner thought operant responding should be (photos courtesy of Dr. Herbert Jenkins).

model those made by pigeons eating grain (Jenkins & Moore, 1973). At least in this instance, the operant is not as arbitrary as Skinner had hoped.

Preparedness and Instrumental Behavior

Should we be surprised that an analysis of operant responses reveals a certain degree of "innate" organization? Certainly not. Skinner's assertion that instrumental responses are "emitted" does not change the fact that animals have evolved to behave in specific ways. Their innately organized behavior patterns match the niches they have occupied over many years (Skinner, 1966).

Evidence for innately organized behavior was presented earlier: In Chapter 2 we examined various examples of *species-specific behaviors* and in Chapter 4 we studied the concepts of *preparedness* and *stimulus specificity* in the conditioning of responses. What else can we find out about the interactions of instinctive behavior and operantly conditioned responses? We begin with an example of complex human courtship behavior.

Human Courtship Patterns.   Have you ever found yourself wandering back to a place where you had a chance encounter with a "hot" guy or gal? Imagine that one day you are driving around and see this magnificent person whose smile seems to be just for you. Over the next few days you begin to go out of your way to attempt to locate your goal—let's call this person Tracey. For the sake of argument, let us consider this complex behavior of "I'm attracted to you and want to see you/please notice me" a form of innately organized human courtship behavior.

Assume two things: first, that merely seeing Tracey is a positive reinforcer and, second, that your presence has no effect on whether or not Tracey appears. You learn that Tracey can be seen at precisely 8:15 A.M. and 5:30 P.M. You continue to check at other times even though you are seldom reinforced. As a matter of fact, you shower, change your clothes, and brush your hair before driving by at various times during the day and night. To your embarrassment, you find yourself parking nearby on the off chance. . . .

Further assume that Tracey finds out about you, considers you a pest (who *is* this strange person always smiling at me?), and without your knowledge begins to punish your behavior. Noticing your ever-present car, Tracey uses a different entrance and exit to the apartment complex. No reinforcement for this strange person.

Aware that you no longer see Tracey with the same frequency, you nevertheless continue your pattern of behavior. Unaware that your behavior keeps you from seeing Tracey as often as you might, you nonetheless manage to encounter your "satisfier" at least some of the time.

How can we account for this pattern of behavior? What maintains your persistence? Recognizing that much of our sexual behavior defies rational analysis, should we suspect that some innate patterns of human courtship behavior are involved? Is it possible that associative reinforcement theory may also help explain what is going on?

Let us begin our analysis by observing a pigeon in a (marginally) similar situation.

Autoshaping and Automaintenance

Place a pigeon in a Skinner box and on the average of once a minute light the bird's pecking key for 8 seconds. After 8 seconds, turn off the light and raise the grain hopper to allow the hungry pigeon to eat for several seconds. Simple enough. All the bird has to do is walk over to the grain hopper when it notices the light is on, wait for the food reinforcer to appear a few seconds later, and then eat. This procedure resembles classical conditioning: The light is the CS and the food is the US, and no response contingency is required. (Compare: Tracey's apartment is the CS; the sight of Tracey is the US; and no response on your part is required to make Tracey appear.)

Of the 36 birds trained in this manner by Brown and Jenkins (1968), *all* of them began to peck at the lighted key, even though pecking had nothing to do either with the light coming on or the food becoming available. Note that these researchers did not use the method of successive approximation to shape the naive birds' key-pecking behavior. Rather, they set automatic timers for the lights to come on and food to be delivered, and then walked away. Hence, the Brown and Jenkins training procedure came to be known as **autoshaping** (also called **sign tracking**).

Analysis of Autoshaping.   On the surface, autoshaping appears to be procedurally more like classical conditioning than instrumental conditioning. However, the initial key-pecking response is problematic. Food elicits reflexive salivation. Why does the light induce pecking behavior? The size of the backlit key is presumably too large to elicit generalized feeding responses (see Hogan, 1973). Since the bird doesn't confuse the large spot of light with food, most researchers concur that a simple light-food Pavlovian association is learned quite quickly. Because food and the light appear together in time, the pigeon begins to peck the light "as if" it were food.

Thought question: Would you predict that Tracey's apartment complex becomes "hot" by its association with Tracey? Is our hero "courting" the apartment complex as well as "courting" the person?

Automaintenance.   Why does the pigeon continue pecking the key? Probably because the unnecessary pecking is being reinforced both by the food (primary reinforcer) and by the light (a secondary reinforcer established by higher-order conditioning). First, and most important, for the pecking response to continue, the availability of food must be positively correlated with the light being on. That is, pigeons will *not* peck at lighted keys if food is predicted less than 50% of the time that the light is on (Gamzu & Williams, 1971, 1973). Moreover, if grain availability continues to be associated with the light, pigeons maintain their (unnecessary) key-pecking responses indefinitely. Gamzu and Schwartz (1973) called this phenomenon **automaintenance.**

What else is known about the phenomena of autoshaping and automaintenance? Perhaps the most striking finding is that pigeons seem to be relatively insensitive to the consequences of their key-pecking responses. This is quite ironic. Reinforcement theory demands that animals be exquisitely sensitive to the consequences of their responses, and, indeed, the subtle patternings of key pecking and bar pressing in response to the various schedules of reinforcement described earlier attest to such sensitivity. But if the experimenter changes the reinforcement rules for pigeons on automaintenance schedules, another surprising finding emerges.

"Maladaptive" Key-Pecking Responses?   Suppose that key pecking *delays* reinforcement. That is, arrange the contingency so that key pecks to the lighted key turn the light off and are *not* reinforced with food. (Note in this arrangement that both the *primary* and *secondary reinforcers* have been removed. In the human example, your presence drives off Tracey.) If the bird makes *no* key-peck responses while the light is on, food *is* forthcoming. Therefore, it pays the bird not to key peck because key pecking is punished by not getting the expected food reinforcement.

After several hundred such trials of not pecking → food, pecking → no food, birds continued to peck the lighted key about one-third of the time (Williams & Williams, 1969). This procedure, called *negative automaintenance,* produces birds that miss being fed due to their persistent pecking.

The nonreinforced key-pecking behavior seen on negative automaintenance schedules is troublesome. Such behavior seems to be both maladaptive (expending energy without payoff) and contrary to the law of effect (engaging in behavior that delays reinforcement).

But is it?

Significance of Autoshaping and Automaintenance

What is the theoretical significance of autoshaping and automaintenance phenomena? These experimental results require us to analyze behavior within both innate and "arbitrary" categories and see how each is affected by positive reinforcers. We begin with a question: Why do pigeons continue to expend energy to key peck in these situations? If we can answer this question, we may gain some insight into the human courtship pattern described earlier.

Pigeons Know How to Peck.   First, the pigeons. Pigeons know how to peck at backlit keys without special training, and, as Figure 5.8 indicates, their pecking responses reflect innately organized behavior patterns for eating and drinking. Innately organized feeding responses of birds are not restricted to pecking. Mature hens, for example, visually search for food, peck at a variety of nonfood objects, make clucking noises to their chicks, and pick up and drop pieces of food near their chicks (Wickler, 1973).

Even though laboratory researchers are interested only in "operant key-pecking responses," pigeons have no alternative but to bring their species-specific behaviors into laboratory settings. Cocking the head and visually orienting to a lighted key that predicts food are also reinforced—along with the key-peck response. We can safely conclude that autoshaping and automaintenance procedures result in the partial reinforcement of a variety of innately organized feeding responses (see Timberlake & Grant, 1975).

Reinforcement of Innate Feeding Responses.   Pecking responses of hungry pigeons are neither arbitrary nor trivial. Success in finding and ingesting food helps define their adaptive fitness. Recall that during automaintenance, when more than half of pigeon key-pecking responses went unreinforced, the pigeons would stop pecking the lighted key. Thus, these pigeons *were* adaptively responding to reinforcement contingencies. Earlier it was noted that during a negative automaintenance procedure (Williams & Williams, 1969) about one-third of the pigeons' key-pecking responses were "wasted." The focus on unreinforced responses clouds the fact that *two-thirds* of all key pecks were (partially) reinforced with food.

Furthermore, "wasted" or "inefficient" pecking at a lighted key has parallels with other niche behaviors that are *not* considered maladaptive. Birds peck for other reasons than to secure food. While most pecking responses *do* result in food ingestion, other pecking responses—at nonfood objects and dropping food near offspring are two examples—do not result in food ingestion. It may be that when all pecking responses are considered within the bird's niche, producing food two-thirds of the time may be *very* efficient.

Pigeon's Light Becomes Secondary Reinforcer.   In the Skinner box, visual orientation and non–food-pecking responses are components of these innately organized feeding patterns that are *also* reinforced by food. Because of the light/food association, the light becomes a secondary reinforcer. Both the appearance of the light and the partial reinforcement with food appear to maintain these component behaviors (orientation and pecking) indefinitely.

Conclusion? The behavior of a pigeon on an automaintenance schedule in a Skinner box is neither maladaptive nor contrary to the law of effect. Indeed, predictions derived from associative reinforcement theory complement innate feeding behavior analyses. Together these theories provide an adequate account of the observed pecking behavior.

Automaintenance of Human Courtship Patterns.   The outcome of feeding strategies may determine life or death. Likewise, courting patterns of sexually mature humans that bear on reproductive success are neither arbitrary nor triv-

ial. To the extent that we were successful in analyzing the pigeon's feeding behavior, can we identify innate behavior patterns, reinforced responses, and
their interactions in our example of human courtship behavior?

Needless to say, human courting behavior appears to be far more complicated than the manner in which pigeons secure food. But common elements
can be identified. Both feeding and courting require a visual search. (Where is
the positive reinforcer located?) Both require locomotor responses (approach
behaviors) and other instrumental responses (preening?) necessary to secure
the reinforcer.

Driving by Tracey's apartment can be likened to the pigeon's orienting responses to the light. Both the apartment complex and the light have something
to do with reinforcement (i.e., both have been previously associated with reinforcement). Pecking is a component behavior of an innately organized feeding
response. *Grooming* and "notice-me" behaviors are components of innately organized human courting responses. While on automaintenance, pecks at a
lighted key are not instrumental in producing food. Likewise, grooming and
"notice-me" behaviors are not instrumental in producing Tracey. In both cases,
however, these innately organized behaviors are being maintained by partial
reinforcement (i.e., both responses are associated with food and Tracey's appearance, respectively).

Under certain conditions, both pecking responses and "notice-me" behaviors may be punished. Food reinforcement can be made contingent on not
pecking, and Tracey can disappear contingent on your persistent responses.
Both pigeon and human responses will continue, however, as long as some reinforcement is ultimately forthcoming (i.e., persistence pays).

Thought question: Does pigeon behavior on an automaintenance schedule successfully model the example of human courtship behavior? Why or why
not?

Let us look at other ways in which reinforcement theory can modify innate predispositions to respond and vice versa.

Misbehavior of Organisms

Marion and Keller Breland were students of B.F. Skinner. They applied behavioral methodologies developed in laboratory research with pigeons and rats to
other animals. Specifically, they trained chickens, pigs, raccoons, and other animals to perform cute circus acts for sideshows.

If you have trained animals to do tricks, you already know how difficult it
is to achieve a consistent and reliable performance. In 1960 the Brelands wrote
The Misbehavior of Organisms, a book describing their animal training difficulties.[14] Their book is important because it calls for nothing less than a modification of the law of effect.

---

[14] The title is a parody of Skinner's *Behavior of Organisms* (1938).

Among their other trained animal acts, pigs and raccoons were reinforced for response chains that ended with depositing a coin in a bank. For example, a raccoon would work to earn a coin and would then pick it up and drop it into the bank. Depositing the coin was the operant response that resulted in food reinforcement.

Failure of the Law of Effect?   The law of effect predicts that reinforced operant behavior such as dropping a coin would be learned efficiently. After a sufficient number of trials, the hungry animal should rapidly and effectively perform the operant and eat the food reinforcer. Many of the Breland's trained animals did something else, however. Instead of depositing the coin, they played with it, delaying reinforcement.

Listen to the Brelands describe a raccoon required to drop *two* coins in the bank to secure reinforcement: "Not only [would] he not let go of the coins, but he spent seconds, even minutes, rubbing them together . . . and dipping them into the [bank]. . . . The rubbing behavior became worse as time went on, in spite of non-reinforcement" (Breland & Breland, 1961).

Likewise, pigs would repeatedly push coins along the floor with their snouts (cf. "rooting behavior") rather than deposit them in the bank as they had been trained to do. Observations of the pigs' rooting behavior corroborated that of raccoons' "washing" behavior in two ways; namely, both patterns of behavior delayed reinforcement, and both patterns of behavior became worse with repeated trials.

Do you recognize parallels in the behavior patterns of these pigs and raccoons with previously encountered pigeons on automaintenance schedules?

Instinctive Drift.   How did the Brelands explain such instances of "misbehavior"? First, they reasoned that in their respective niches, raccoons routinely wash their food before eating, and pigs routinely root with their snouts. These innate patterns of feeding appear to intrude on newly learned, highly arbitrary operants maintained by food reinforcement. The Brelands' term **instinctive drift** captures two of the most important aspects of the misbehavior they observed, namely, that arbitrarily established responses erode (drift) in the face of more innately organized behavior (instinct).

Comparing Instinctive Drift and Preparedness.   In Chapter 4 we saw that rats have an innate tendency to be wary of novel foods, a phenomenon called *neophobia*. A rat's phobic response to new foods appears to *complement* its rapid (evolutionarily prepared) learning of flavor-toxin associations. By contrast, the Brelands' formulation of *instinctive drift* suggests that rather than working together, innate feeding patterns can also *conflict with* the learning of new associations. To the extent that instinctive drift works against prepared learning, it would seem to be an example of *contraprepared* learning. Let us look more closely at details of the Brelands' experiments.

What Controls Instinctive Drift?

What would happen if, instead of using small coins, food reinforcement were made contingent on the operant response of rolling a large, heavy bowling ball into the bank? Or if reinforcement were contingent on the operant response of pushing a wheelbarrow through a door in the bank? Would you expect to see *instinctive drift* in these circumstances? Or is it likely that *instinctive drift* is restricted to instances in which components of the animal's normal feeding niche are incorporated into the "arbitrary" operant?

The question being asked is whether the raccoon and pig are treating the coin as a *substitute* for food in the same way pigeons pecked the light "as if" it were food. Consider that the coin, or token, is a conditioned stimulus associated with the unconditioned stimulus of food (see Wolfe, 1934, for an account of chimps hoarding tokens that had been associated with food reinforcement). Note that these coins are also similar in size to the foods eaten by raccoons and pigs. After many trials, feeding responses may have become associated with the sight of the coin, and responses to the coins may have generalized from their responses to foods (Timberlake, Wahl, & King, 1982). Such a theory of **stimulus substitution** was proposed initially by Pavlov (1927/1960).

Associations can be made between a wheelbarrow and food, but can bowling balls and wheelbarrows also be *substitutes* for food? To the extent that these objects fall outside the stimulus generalization gradient of "food objects," substitution is highly unlikely. If they *were* on the generalization gradient, we would expect to see raccoons attempting to "wash" bowling balls, and pigs "root" at wheelbarrows.

(You would likely attach positive feelings to Tracey's apartment complex by association but, being off the generalization gradient, would not "court" it. On the other hand, you *might* wash her car.)

Reconciling "Misbehavior" and the Law of Effect

Among other researchers, Shettleworth (1975) has studied the behavioral complexities of hungry animals. She has found that reinforcement worked to increase responding of some innately organized behaviors of the golden hamster (digging, rearing, pawing a wall). She found, however, that reinforcement minimally affected other behaviors, such as face washing, body scratching, and scent marking.[15] Are these truly failures of reinforcement? Her analysis emphasized the fact that reinforced or not, the first three behaviors increased

---

[15] It is difficult to make the argument that a response cannot be reinforced. A more powerful reinforcer, such as electrical stimulation of the brain (ESB; next chapter), may be effective in increasing the frequency of face washing, body scratching, and scent marking. What *can* be concluded from these findings is that a given reinforcer works better for some responses than others.

during food deprivation. Hungry animals dig, rear, and paw as they search for food; they do not expend energy face washing, scent marking, or scratching. All six behaviors increased when reinforced. The behaviors that are innately instrumental in securing food increased the most, the others minimally.

Do the findings from automaintenance studies from Shettleworth (1975) and the Brelands' account of misbehavior support the Brelands' conclusion that instinctive behavior is more powerful than acquired, or reinforced, behavior? I don't think so. A more parsimonious explanation is that primary and secondary reinforcement helped to maintain the behaviors that the Brelands attributed to instinct. In automaintenance, innate response tendencies and reinforcement principles interact in intricate ways to cloud even a "simple" key-pecking response. General process learning theory aids our understanding of these animals' interesting innate feeding tendencies.

Interim Summary

1. Contrary to B.F. Skinner's assertion that a pigeon's key peck is an "arbitrary" response, several lines of evidence reveal pecking to be a niche-specific feeding behavior.
2. *Autoshaping* and *automaintenance* describe pigeon-in-the-box methodologies that apparently produce nonreinforced responding.
3. In autoshaping, aperiodic presentation of a lighted key followed by food (a Pavlovian stimulus-stimulus contingency) produces unnecessary pecking at the lighted key. If food is paired with the light on at least half of the occasions that the key is lit, key-pecking responses will be maintained indefinitely (automaintenance).
4. Key pecking in the absence of a food reinforcement contingency occurs because (a) species-specific key pecking is emitted for reasons other than feeding, (b) the global feeding response involves orientation and approach behaviors (such as to the lighted key) as well as pecking behaviors, (c) the lighted key has become a secondary reinforcer (due to pairings with food) that reinforces both approach and pecking, and (d) responding is maintained by partial reinforcement with food (primary reinforcer).
5. The Brelands trained circus acts and reported what they believed to be *misbehavior of organisms* due to the failure of the law of effect.
6. Because the Brelands' pigs and raccoons delayed the food-reinforced terminal response of "dropping coins," and instead "washed" and "rooted" them, the animals' behavior was said to be caused by *instinctive drift*.
7. Analysis of the "misbehaving" animals revealed that they were under the behavioral control of the coins for two reasons: (a) The coins were on the food's reinforcer's generalization gradient and (b) the coins had also be-

come secondary reinforcers that maintained the washing and rooting behavior.

8. Shettleworth's findings that a given reinforcer affects some responses more than others is similar to Garcia's stimulus specificity in conditioning. In both instances, our understanding of each experimental outcome is enhanced by a knowledge of each animal's innately predisposed eating and drinking behavior.

9. Human courting behavior and pigeon-feeding behavior were both analyzed from the perspective of how reinforced behavior interacts with innate response tendencies.

Preview: Reinforcement and Punishment

Throughout these first five chapters, two themes have recurred. Associative theory provides a powerful account of learned behavior. Second, learned associations interact with and modify innately organized behavior. Pavlovian and Thorndikean conditioning represents our modern conceptions of associative learning and requires "biologically meaningful" stimuli for learning to occur. That is, we have already noted that Pavlov's *unconditioned stimuli* and Skinner's *reinforcers* are very often food and that "responses" produce "stimuli" that are available for association with food. Similar underlying processes of association are assumed to exist in both forms of learning.

In this and preceding chapters we have also noted more similarities than differences in these two versions of associative theory. For example, from both S-S and R-S perspectives, similar rules of acquisition, generalization, discrimination, and resistance to extinction govern learning. Both Pavlov and Thorndike also thought that associations were similar in outcome whether the "biologically meaningful" stimulus was appetitive/aversive or satisfying/annoying, respectively. Is this truly the case? Does it matter if we raise our children using punishment in place of reward? Are pleasure and pain equally effective in allowing us to modify our more innately organized behavior?

In the next chapter we look more closely at Pavlov's *USs*, Thorndike's *satisfiers* and *annoyers*, and Skinner's *positive* and *negative reinforcers* and *punishers*. One question we will try to answer is why, each in its own way, do pain and pleasure control so much of our behavior?

CHAPTER SUMMARY

1. In *instrumental learning* a response is learned or modified when it is followed by a positive reinforcer or a punishing stimulus. The association is made between the response and the reinforcer or punisher.

2. E. L. Thorndike's *law of effect* states that responses followed by *satisfiers* (Skinner's positive reinforcers) will increase in frequency, and responses followed by *annoyers* (Skinner's punishers) will decrease in frequency.

3. The *law of effect* "works" because animals are hedonistic. Reinforcement typically selects adaptive responses.

4. John B. Watson's and B.F. Skinner's *behaviorism* is best understood as a strict *environmental determinism*. In this philosophy, voluntary behavior is nonexistent because reinforced behavior is brought under stimulus control.

5. B.F. Skinner's *operant conditioning* method experimentally analyzes behavior in terms of how reinforcement contingencies control response tendencies. Operant behavior in the laboratory is analyzed in computer programmed Skinner boxes that present stimuli and measure the animal's responses.

6. B.F. Skinner's *emitted operants* reflect inborn response tendencies.

7. Control of responding is analyzed by measuring the effects of *schedules of reinforcement* on responding, including *continuous reinforcement* (*CRF*) and *partial*, or *intermittent, reinforcement*.

8. Partial reinforcement schedules include fixed ratio (FR), variable ratio (VR), fixed interval (FI), variable interval (VI), and differential reinforcement of high (DRH) and low (DRL) schedules of reinforcement.

9. Longer FI and FR schedules produce postreinforcement pauses, FI schedules produce scalloping patterns, VI schedules produce stable responding, ratio and DRH schedules produce faster responding, and the DRL schedule teaches withholding of responses (patience).

10. CRF extinguishes quickly, and, by comparison, partial reinforcement sched-

ules are resistant to extinction. The partial reinforcement effect (PRE) points out the roles of *frustration* and *surprise* in the maintenance of behavior.

11. *Behavior control* is a theory that identifiable features in the environment control behavior. An animal is said to be under *stimulus control* if a response reliably occurs in the presence of one but not another stimulus.

12. A *discriminative stimulus* (S^d) sets the occasion for reinforced responses; a *negative discriminative stimulus* (S^Δ) predicts nonreinforcement. S^d–S^Δ *discrimination training* sharpens discrimination of the S^d. The *peak shift* phenomenon is evidence that the S^Δ condition acquires an inhibitory influence on behavior.

13. Reinforcement theory and the analysis of stimulus control enhance our understanding of various aspects of human verbal behavior, of how complex behaviors are learned, and of how social interactions are maintained.

14. *Autoshaping* and *automaintenance* entail procedures that include both Pavlovian and Thorndikean conditioning components.

15. In automaintenance, pigeons peck lighted keys due to both inborn response tendencies (i.e., behaviors appropriate to their feeding niches) and because their key approach and key pecking are reinforced by a secondary reinforcer (the lighted key) and partial reinforcement with food, respectively.

16. Marion and Keller Breland reported instances of the *misbehavior of organisms* that they thought violated the law of effect. They proposed that the example of misbehavior was due to *instinctive drift*.

17. *Misbehavior* was analyzed in terms of both innate feeding niche behaviors and the secondary and primary reinforcing stimuli maintaining the behavior.

18. Innately organized feeding behavior was seen to interact in a predictable fashion with attempts to increase its frequency through reinforcement.

19. Human courting behavior was analyzed from the perspective of how reinforced behavior interacts with innate response tendencies.

DISCUSSION QUESTIONS

1. Skinner's distinction between elicited and emitted behavior is controversial. Remember his observation that when a hungry rat is placed in a Skinner box, it will explore the new environment for several minutes by sniffing, rearing on its hind legs, and touching objects with its front paws. A familiar environment does not elicit such behavior. Would a hungry rat behave differently from one just fed in such a situation? Why does such behavior occur in a novel environment? Is such behavior elicited or emitted (or both)? Is it reflexive? Is it adaptive?

2. Eating good foods, drinking safe water, breathing clean air, living in safe homes and apartments, staying disease free, meeting sexual needs, and attaining other human consummatory behaviors are reinforcing experiences, as are such experiences as earning college degrees, receiving promotions, and buying new homes and BMWs. Which are primary, and which secondary, reinforcers? Which of these experiences are most likely to reinforce you and maintain your behavior? Could you make a reinforcement hierarchy?

3. In an earlier discussion concerning the partial reinforcement effect (PRE),

you were asked about the relationship between customer frustration and customer satisfaction. How is the optimal fee for service that maximizes customer satisfaction and your profit determined? Given Amsel's *frustration theory*, can you make the case that "the customer is always right"?

4. Remember learning to ride a bike? Can you identify chained, component operants of this acquired skill? If anyone helped you to learn, did that person use successive approximation? Remember painstakingly printing the alphabet? Learning to play a musical instrument?

5. We trained the professor of our graduate learning class to write only at the very top of the blackboard, an uncomfortable position that he could reach only by stretching. He never knew what we were up to. We took advantage of his behavior of writing on the board while at the same time attempting to make eye contact with students. Before class we got together, made two little marks on each side of the blackboard about one-third down from the top, and reinforced the professor only when he wrote above but not below the imaginary line connecting our

marks. What is reinforcing to a professor? Eye contact. Expressions of interest in students' eyes. When he wrote below the line, we looked away. When he wrote above the line, we smiled, nodded sagely, and paid rapt attention. By successive approximation we inched him up, class by class. After several weeks he was on his tiptoes.

Get together with other students before class and . . .

6. My major professor was James C. Smith of Florida State University. Among the many valuable things I learned from him was his analysis of *behavioral control* in the classroom. It only seems, he argued, that teachers are in control of their students. *Good* teachers are as much *controlled by* their students as they are *in control* in the classroom. What do you think Smith means by his analysis? Taking your clue from what our class did to our learning prof described in Question 5, can you make the case that *good* teachers always respond to the reinforcement and punishment contingencies to which they are exposed?

7. Those of you who have been horseback riding know what happens at the end of your ride when you and your horse are on the way back to the stable. It takes off like a shot. Why?

8. Cigarettes kill more people than heroin or cocaine. Should we make cigarettes illegal or continue to let people "choose" to smoke? How much behavior control should society be allowed to exercise in the land of the free?

9. Reread the passages from *The Education of Little Tree* at the beginning of Chapters 4 and 5. Little Tree is learning adaptive survival skills in each reading. Can you characterize how they differ?

DISCUSSION STARTERS

1. *Skinner's distinction between elicited and emitted behavior?* The discussion of Skinner's distinctions of elicited and emitted behavior can take several tacks. It is not possible for a *black box* to emit behavior, for example. Behavioral analyses must incorporate biological principles to make sense. Hungry animals behave differently from sated animals in novel and familiar feeding environments. Novel environments are potential sources of food. Would it be incorrect to say that novel environments elicit food-seeking behaviors?

2. *Which are primary and which are secondary reinforcers?* The traditional distinction between primary and secondary reinforcers is that the former are biological in origin while the latter are learned through association. That humans as well as animals exhibit consummatory behaviors cannot be denied. Many cultures make a distinction between biological, psychological, and spiritual needs. For example, Maslow (1954) has conceptualized a "need hierarchy" for humans in which lower (biological) needs must be met before higher (psychological and sociocul-

tural) needs can be addressed. Indeed, a tension between our animal (biological) needs and our human (psychological, sociocultural) needs exists in much of Western culture. In the next chapter we look as Premack's (1962) discussion on how reinforcing opportunities differ from time to time among individuals.

3. *Why, to a businessperson, should "the customer always be right"?* Violating expectations typically results in frustration. Have you ever decided "never to return" to a restaurant or a dry cleaners because your expectations were violated? Conversely, if you have ever complained about your meal and the manager "comp'ed" it (i.e., gave you a complimentary meal), would you likely return?

4. *In learning to ride a bike, do you remember successively approximating this operant behavior?* Yes, balancing is separate from pedaling is separate from steering. You likely learned these component parts slowly and separately. Learning to ride a bike is analyzed from a *negative reinforcement* perspective in the next chapter. Lacking this concept, it is difficult to account for how we learned to ride. This example illustrates the necessity of employing psychological constructs in accounting for nuances of human behavior.

6. *Do good teachers respond to the reinforcement and punishment contingencies to which they are exposed?* Subtle cues and rules govern the way humans talk with each other. Lecturing is different from conversing because when you converse, you pause to allow the other person to say something. The pauses are reinforcing (unless they are long and awkward) in part because they are courteous. Good lecturers can introduce these pauses by watching facial expressions, stopping, and asking questions. Laughing and inquiring are also reinforcing. Can you make the case that your "best friends" are those that reinforce your verbal behavior?

7. *Analyzing the behavior of a horse returning to its stable?* It is likely that horses are reinforced as much by "not having to carry weight" (negative reinforcement) as they are by food and water in the stables (positive reinforcement). Instinctive drift is an unlikely explanation for horses that ignore a rider's instructions. The apparent loss of stimulus control by the rider can be accounted for by the reinforcing events on returning to the stables.

8. *How much behavior control should "society" be allowed to exercise?* As an introduction to behaviorism's contribution to political philosophy, Skinner's *Walden Two* is highly recommended reading. In this book Skinner suggests that freedom and choice are illusions. Behavior is controlled by parents, cults, and other organized religions, schools, peers, and so on. His main point is that children can and should be raised to be good citizens so that all their choices will be good ones. By controlling early environment, he would argue, children could be raised (conditioned) not to smoke—ever.

9. *How do the adaptive survival skills that Little Tree learns as described in Chapters 4 and 5 differ?* S-S learning in the Chapter 4 excerpt; R-S learning in Chapter 5.

KEY TERMS

Annoyers Aversive stimuli. Thorndike's *law of effect* proposed that when unpleasant stimuli, which he called *annoyers*, followed a response, the response would less likely be made thereafter. (Cf. *Punisher.*)

Automaintenance Maintenance of key-pecking behavior due to the contiguity between response and reinforcement. Pigeons that have a history of being fed in the presence of a lighted key will unnecessarily peck at the light even though their pecking response has no effect on when food is made available.

Autoshaping Occurrence of key-pecking responses in the absence of a reinforcement contingency. An untrained pigeon is placed in a Skinner box, and food is presented in the presence of a lighted key. Without specific training, the bird will begin to peck at the lighted key. See *Signtracking.*

Behavioral Control The past and present reinforcement and punishment contingencies that determine the expression of a behavior.

Behaviorism A philosophical position espousing an extreme environmental determinism. The assertion that human and animal behavior is directly and inevitably determined and controlled by the reinforcing and punishing contingencies of the local environment. (John B. Watson and B.F. Skinner are two famous proponents of behaviorism.)

Biological Determinism The philosophical position that behavior is caused by the immutable action of genes. (Cf. *Environmental Determinism.*)

Chained Operants A behavioral sequence analyzed in terms of a succession of discriminative stimuli that set the occasions for operant responses, eventually leading to reinforcement. (Cf. *Stimulus-Response Chains.*)

Continuous Reinforcement (CRF) Reinforcement of each emitted response.

Cumulative Record A visual record of responses and reinforcement patterns in time generated by an ink-writing instrument called a *cumulative recorder.*

Differential Reinforcement of High Rates (DRH) A schedule of reinforcement designed to reinforce bursts of lever pressing. (Example: The 10th response within a 5-second time period would be reinforced.)

Differential Reinforcement of Low Rates (DRL) A schedule of reinforcement designed to reinforce timed pauses between operant responses. (Example: The first response after 5 seconds of nonresponding is reinforced.)

Discrete Trial Testing an animal's response on a single trial, such as presenting a stimulus requiring a single response. (Cf. *Free Operant.*)

Discriminated Operant A particular operant response under stimulus control. Example: removing the wrapper [S^d] from a stick of gum [reinforcer].

Discriminative Stimulus A stimulus that signals that a particular response-reinforcement contingency is in effect, therefore setting occasions during which operant responses become highly probable.

Elicited Behavior Reflexive or otherwise innately organized behavior, sometimes characterized as *involuntary* behavior. (Cf. Skinner's distinction between *elicited* and *emitted* behavior.)

Emitted Behavior Instrumental responses, sometimes characterized as *voluntary* behavior, that are not readily tied to specific eliciting stimuli. (Cf. Skinner's distinction between *elicited* and *emitted* behavior.)

Environmental Determinism The philosophical position that behavior is caused (determined) by environmental influences. (Cf. *Behaviorism; Biological Determinism.*)

FI See *Fixed Interval Schedule.*

Fixed Interval Schedule (FI) A schedule of reinforcement in which an animal is reinforced for its first response following a specified *time interval* from the preceding reinforcer.

Fixed Ratio Schedule (FR) A schedule of reinforcement in which reinforcement is contingent on the completion of a fixed number of operant responses.

FR See *Fixed Ratio Schedule.*

Free Operant An easy, repeatable operant response, such as a lever press. (Cf. tasks requiring *discrete trials.*)

Frustration Theory Following a history of continuous reinforcement, the theory that an extinction procedure produces a state of negative emotions such as frustration (Amsel).

Hedonism A philosophical position to the effect that the sole motivation of humans and other animals is to seek pleasure and to avoid pain.

Instinctive Drift The theory that arbitrarily established responses erode (drift) in the face of more innately organized (instinctive) behavior (Breland).

Instrumental Conditioning See *Instrumental Learning.*

Instrumental Learning Acquiring and modifying so-called "voluntary," emitted, or otherwise nonreflexive behavior by the application of reinforcers or punishers (Thorndike). (Cf. *Pavlovian Conditioning; Operant Conditioning.*)

Instrumental Response Voluntary, nonreflexive responses that act on the environment in a meaningful, or instrumental, fashion.

Intermittent Reinforcement See *Partial Reinforcement.*

Law of Effect (Thorndike) An elementary principle postulated by Thorndike to govern *all* behavior, stating that a response that is followed by a pleasant consequence will tend to be repeated and a response followed by an unpleasant consequence will tend to decrease in frequency.

Magazine Training An initial stage of operant conditioning in which the sound of the food delivery mechanism becomes associated with food delivery.

Negative Discriminative Stimulus (S^Δ) A stimulus that signals that response-food contingencies are *not* in effect. Responding in the presence of this stimulus is not reinforced.

Occasion Setting A procedure in which stimulus or context signals that a following stimulus will be either a discriminative or a negative-discriminative stimulus.

Operant (or Operant Response) (Skinner) A designated response, such as a lever press, that effectively *operates* upon the environment (Cf. *Instrumental Response.*)

Operant Conditioning (Skinner) A variant of instrumental conditioning. (See *Instrumental Conditioning.*)

Operant Level (Skinner) An existing baseline rate of a response as measured prior to the administration of reinforcement and punishment contingencies. (Cf. *Baseline* or *Free-Operant Level.*)

Partial Reinforcement Any reinforcement situation other than continuous reinforcement. Also called *intermittent reinforcement.*

Partial Reinforcement Effect The tendency for animals maintained on partial reinforcement schedules to be highly resistant to extinction.

Peak Shift The observation that following S^+/S^- discrimination training of two wavelengths, the peak response of the generalization gradient to the target S^+ is shifted in a direction opposite to (away from) the S^- wavelength.

Positive Reinforcement The process by which the application of a reinforcer contingent on a desired response increases the frequency of that response.

Positive Reinforcer Any stimulus (such as food) delivered to an animal immediately following a designated response that leads to an increase in the frequency of that response. (Cf. Thorndike's *satisfiers.*)

Postreinforcement Pause A break in responding following delivery of a reinforcer. Longer pauses are seen for higher FR schedules than for lower FR schedules (i.e., for FR-100 vs. FR-10), and very *short* postreinforcement pauses are typically found using VI and VR schedules of reinforcement.

Reinforcement See *Positive Reinforcement* and *Negative Reinforcement.*

Resistance-to-Extinction The number of extinction trials necessary for a conditioned response to extinguish; an indirect measure of the amount of conditioning that has occurred. Greater *resistance-to-extinction* is found following many conditioning trials compared to a few conditioning trials in Pavlovian conditioning and following partial rather than continuous reinforcement in instrumental conditioning.

Response contingency In instrumental conditioning, making a reinforcer or punisher contingent on a specified response. No such requirement exists for Pavlovian conditioning.

R-S Conditioning In instrumental conditioning, the requirement of a response prior to presentation of a food stimulus. Hence, instrumental conditioning is sometimes referred to as response-stimulus, or *R-S conditioning.* (Cf. *S-S Conditioning.*)

Satisfiers Positive stimuli. Thorndike's law of effect proposed that when pleasant stimuli, which he called *satisfiers,* followed a response, the response would more likely be made thereafter. (Cf. *Reinforcer.*)

Schedules of Reinforcement Rules specified by the experimenter that govern the relationship of reinforcing events to an animal's responses. Example: In *continuous reinforcement* the rule is that each response is reinforced. Other schedules include fixed ratios, variable intervals, and so forth.

Secondary Reinforcers Neutral stimuli that acquire reinforcing properties via the process of higher-order conditioning; also called *conditioned reinforcers.* An example is money.

Shaping by Successive Approximation A training system that involves the selective reinforcement of responses that approximate the target behavior. Increasingly stringent response requirements are placed on the animal, until only the successful completion of the target response (i.e., a lever press) is reinforced.

Sign Tracking   See *Autoshaping.*

Skinner Box   An experimental environment consisting of a small box containing one or more (a) levers or response keys, (b) lights/speakers, and (c) feeding/watering devices used in animal learning experiments (named for B.F. Skinner).

S-S Conditioning   In Pavlovian conditioning, a stimulus is paired with another stimulus (such as food). Hence, Pavlovian conditioning is sometimes referred to as stimulus-stimulus or *S-S conditioning.* (Cf. *R-S* or *Instrumental Conditioning.*)

Stimulus Control   Trained humans and animals that reliably make a specified operant response in the presence of an S^d, but do not make that response in the presence of an S^Δ.

Stimulus Generalization Gradient Following training to a target stimulus, a pattern of responses to similar stimuli, in which more responses are made to the most similar, and the fewest responses are made to stimuli most different from the target.

Stimulus-Response Chains   The theory that in learning to perform a sequence of responses (such as left and right turns in a maze), each response may acquire stimulus properties that cue the next response. (Cf. *Chained Operants.*)

Stimulus Substitution   (Pavlov) The theory that in the course of conditioning, animals come to consider the conditioned stimulus to be a "substitute" for the unconditioned stimulus. (Example: chimpanzees that hoard tokens associated with prior food reinforcement.)

Successive Approximation   See *Shaping by Successive Approximation.*

Target Response   The instrumental or operant response that, when executed, is reinforced.

Thorndikean Conditioning   See *Instrumental Learning.*

Variable Interval Schedule (VI) A schedule of reinforcement in which an animal is reinforced for its first response following a *variable interval* of time from the preceding reinforcer. Example: An animal on a VI-60 is reinforced at varying time periods averaging 60 seconds from the preceding reinforcement.

Variable Ratio Schedule (VR) A schedule of reinforcement in which delivery of a reinforcer is contingent on the completion of a variable number of operant responses from the preceding reinforcement. Example: An animal responding on a VR-10 is reinforced for different numbers of responses, their average being 10.

VI   See *Variable Interval Schedule.*

VR   See *Variable Ratio Schedule.*

CHAPTER 6

REINFORCEMENT AND PUNISHMENT

"Beat me! Beat me!" said the masochist.
    "No!" said the sadist.

Anonymous

INTRODUCTION

In previous chapters we saw that learned changes in behavior result from either stimulus-stimulus associations (*Pavlovian conditioning*) or response-stimulus associations (*instrumental learning*). In both conditioning procedures, learning occurs when the consequences of a behavior are either *satisfying* (i.e., tasty food, a smile) or *annoying* (i.e., a painful electric shock, a disproving glance). The similarities of procedures in and results of both systems suggest that these processes are related. Underlying brain mechanisms appear to be common to both kinds of learning.

Before this, the question of *why* associations are formed in both Pavlovian and instrumental conditioning has been raised only informally. The present chapter entertains *theories* of reinforcement, punishment, avoidance behavior, and other questions of *motivation*. A goal of this chapter is to develop a theory that integrates reinforcement and punishment in both Pavlovian conditioning and instrumental learning—a mighty tall order.

Atheoretical Behaviorists

Why devote an entire chapter to motivational *theories* of reinforcement and punishment? B.F. Skinner, for example, espoused the well-known and highly influential *behaviorist* position that such theories were unnecessary for the development of a science of behavior (Skinner, 1950). Responding in part to Clark L. Hull's *drive theory* of behavior that postulated many intervening variables (Hull, 1943, 1952), Skinner countered that a quantified *description* of how reinforcement and punishment controlled behavior in carefully conducted experiments was sufficient to develop a science of behavior.

Espousing an atheoretical behaviorist position may have been defensible at the time. The lack of an overall organizing theory did not impede the conduct of literally thousands of experiments directed at discovering the determinants of behavior. The results of decades of research, however (100 years, going back to Pavlov's first experiments) now permit—and perhaps demand—attempts to formulate an encompassing theory. The alternative is to continue to merely describe isolated instances of learning and motivation.

As discussed in Chapter 1, a grand theory of behavior that would encompass and integrate diverse findings in behavioral genetics, neuroscience, psychology, sociology, and so on, has not yet been achieved. Although Hull (1943) outlined the problem more than 50 years ago, no one has been quite so ambitious since. After reviewing traditional theories of reinforcement and punishment, in this chapter we try to organize and integrate a number of contemporary theories that address different aspects of learning and motivation.

Learning and Motivation

Our understanding of how learning affects behavior seems to be intimately connected to our understanding of what *motivates* our behavior. Everyone knows the student who doesn't try, who isn't motivated, and hence, doesn't learn. In athletics and other skilled performances, we recognize that motivation separates the haves from the have-nots. Some individuals are "hungrier" than others. Some achieve more because they want it more.

During the course of this chapter, when we begin to focus on concepts of reward and punishment and on *incentives,* we enter the realm of motivated behavior. Questions as to *what* do we learn and *how* do we learn shift ever so subtly to *why* do we learn what we do and what are the conditions under which we learn best.

Maladaptive learned behavior—as illustrated by the chapter opening exchange of the sadist and the masochist—intrigues us all. What motivates these

individuals? Is their pleasure learned? How is it that pain can become pleasure, and inflicting pain can give some people so much pleasure? One way to
address these questions is to ask *why* some events bring us pleasure and others
are so annoying.

Reinforcers and Reinforcement

The process of *reinforcement* and the class of stimuli known as *reinforcers* are
of sufficient complexity and of such importance that both demand extensive
analysis. What is reinforcement? What determines whether a given stimulus is
a reinforcer? What do food, sex, water, some drugs, and electrical stimulation
of a part of the brain have in common? Why does association formation and
memory acquisition depend on the special properties of these diverse stimuli?

More interesting questions cannot be asked than those that concern the
wellsprings of human motivation and behavior. In courts of law and in personal relationships, we ask questions and puzzle over answers:

What motivated you to leave me for her?
Why did you try to kill yourself?
Do you still love me?

These questions go to the very heart of human nature. We now turn to
such questions of motivated behavior.

TRADITIONAL THEORIES OF REINFORCEMENT AND PUNISHMENT

A Review of Pavlov, Thorndike, and Skinner

For almost 100 years, learning theorists have struggled with the complexities
presented by the fact that humans and other animals not only are born with
but also in the course of their lifetimes acquire motivated behaviors. We have
studied three such systems to this point and here review the theories underlying them.

Pavlov's Biological Theory

Pavlov (1927/1960) focused on biologically meaningful stimuli in the environment that produce reflexes in animals. He observed that both humans and
dogs struggled against confinement and hypothesized that all animals have a
freedom reflex. He identified *appetitive* USs such as food and *aversive* (defensive) USs such as sour fluid placed on the tongue. Both of these stimuli produce reflexive salivation in dogs and humans. Pavlov also studied the aversive

motivating properties of electric shock that elicited leg-flexion reflexes. He found that the latter entered into association with neutral conditioned stimuli in the same manner as observed in appetitive conditioning. Pavlov's theory, then, is a biological statement:

1. Animals are motivated to survive.
2. Reflexes are physiological adaptations that promote survival.
3. Neutral stimuli paired with these innate reflexes alter the brain's connections so that conditioned reflexes may eventually occur to formerly neutral stimuli.
4. More often than not the conditioned reflexes are also adaptive in that they promote well-being and survival.

Thorndike's Psychological Theory

Thorndike (1898, 1932) provided an early theory of human motivation. Recall from Chapter 5 that he labeled stimuli in the environment based on their perceived effect. Some stimuli are *satisfiers*, others are *annoyers*, and yet others are *neutral*. Recall that his animal subjects were motivated to get out of *puzzle boxes* presumably because they found confinement (innately) *annoying*. Escape from confinement is (innately) *satisfying*. The satisfaction associated with escape, in Thorndike's way of looking at the world, had the effect of *stamping in* the immediately preceding instrumental escape responses. Therefore, innately satisfying and annoying events provide motivation for learning. The learned responses, as governed by the *law of effect*, were the inevitable results of associations with satisfiers and annoyers.

Pavlov and Thorndike Compared. Is it obvious that Thorndike's perspective is similar to that of Pavlov? For both, the satisfactions of appetite and freedom are in opposition to the annoyances of aversive events. For both, positive and negative events support parallel systems for learning new responses. Differences? Pavlov studied physiological reflexes and Thorndike, instrumental responses. Although the similarities may seem to outweigh the differences, consider that the organization of this textbook in part emphasizes their differences: Pavlov's methods and results (Chapters 3–4) are considered separately from those of Thorndike and Skinner (Chapter 5). This chapter and the next emphasize similarities rather than differences. Before examining these similarities, let us again review Skinner's contributions to a theory of motivated human behavior.

Skinner's Behavioral Theory

B.F. Skinner (1950) insisted that his positions on questions of reinforcement, learning, and motivated human behavior were *atheoretical*, a most interesting theoretical position to take! As a strict behaviorist (and following the lead of John B. Watson), Skinner proposed that questions relating to motivation were both unnecessary and undesirable. For example, in Skinner's view the very term *learning* exemplified a *hypothetical construct* (i.e., an inference from changes in an animal's performance). To say that an animal is *motivated* to learn and now has a *memory* for what it has *learned* does not, in Skinner's view, add anything to the observation that the animal's behavior changed as the result of experiences *a*, *b*, and *c*. (Note that all these italicized terms are *intervening variables*.) The description of the performance change based on the operations of the experiment (cf. *operational definitions*) constitutes a sufficient explanation for the behavioral change. For the strict behaviorist, the use of terms such as *motivation, incentive, learning,* and *memory* adds nothing. These terms allude to unobservable events, and each is an additional step removed from the reality of the observations of performance changes.

Skinner's Definitions of Reinforcement and Punishment.   B.F. Skinner's atheoretical position had the intended effect of making behavioral analysis more rigorous and scientific. As noted in Chapter 5, most behavioral scientists presently follow his lead in operationally defining reinforcers and punishers according to the effect each has on the preceding response. A *reinforcer* is therefore defined as any stimulus whose application following a response has the effect of increasing the probability of that response. Though awkward to state, this operational definition differentiates a reinforcing stimulus from Thorndike's requirement that the stimulus be pleasing. How so?

Are All Reinforcers Rewards?   With their respective concepts of *unconditioned stimuli* and *satisfiers,* both Pavlov and Thorndike clearly had in mind that such stimuli *innately* elicited pleasure. That is, pleasure-producing properties were inherent in the stimulus. B.F. Skinner, by way of contrast, makes no such requirement. If the effect of the stimulus is to increase the rate of emission of the preceding response, by definition the stimulus is a *reinforcer,* and the process is called *reinforcement.*[1] From Thorndike's perspective, all rewards (such as candy) are reinforcers; but for Skinner, a reinforcer need not be a reward.

The same distinctions hold for aversive stimuli. For Pavlov and Thorndike, such stimuli were *inherently* aversive. By contrast, Skinner also defined punishment operationally. If the effect of the stimulus is to decrease the rate of emission of the preceding response, by definition the stimulus is a **punisher,** and the process is called **punishment.**

Removing or Preventing Satisfiers and Annoyers.   Skinner pointed out that responses can also have the effect of removing a stimulus or preventing a stimulus from occurring. Obviously, withholding one of Thorndike's satisfiers is

---

[1] Yes, this is a circular definition. "Why is a given stimulus reinforcing? By increasing the rate of the preceding response, it acts as a reinforcer." In a later discussion we find a way out of this circularity by noting other defining properties shared by all reinforcers.

punishment. Parents more often punish teenagers by *preventing* them from driving a car or watching television than by spanking or applying some other aversive stimulus. Likewise, withholding one of Thorndike's annoyers can be a reinforcing event (it feels good when you stop hitting yourself in the head).

Later in this chapter we look at evidence for both the reinforcing and punishing effects, respectively, of withholding aversive stimuli and withholding rewarding stimuli. We merely note here that these concepts, too, are operationally defined. A descriptive summary of the way in which responses can be strengthened or weakened by the effects they have in producing or preventing either positive or negative environmental stimuli is presented in Figure 6.1.

Hull's Drive Theory of Behavior

Given that Figure 6.1 accurately summarizes behavioral definitions of reinforcement and punishment and noting that these definitions provide our *zeit-*

Effect of Stimulus on Preceding Response

	↑ Probability, or rate, of response	↓ Probability, or rate, of response
Response **produces** stimulus	Process is *Reinforcement* Stimulus is a *Reinforcer*	Process is *Punishment* Stimulus is a *Punisher*
Response **prevents** stimulus	Process is *Negative Reinforcement* Absence of stimulus is a *Negative Reinforcer*	Process is *Punishment* Absence of stimulus is a *Punisher*

FIGURE 6.1   Diagram of Reinforcement and Punishment

Summary of B.F. Skinner's operationally defined concepts of *reinforcement* and *punishment* and the operational labeling of *reinforcers* and *punishers*. See text for discussion.

geist, you might wonder what is to be gained by considering Hull's theoretical system. Contemporary learning theorists ignore Hull's system for the most part. Recall that Skinner's experimental analysis of behavior restricts observations and theory to that which can be measured—stimuli impinging on and responses emanating from the organism (see Figure 1.1). This black box approach has served us well. Why did Hull intentionally put madeup intervening variables inside the black box?

Hull's Neobehaviorism.   Dissatisfied with a limiting S-R behavioral approach, Hull proposed an alternative. Isn't it better, he asked, to characterize animal behavior as a complex of physiological *drives* and *need states* that could in part be met through learning experiences? Writing in *Principals of Behavior (1943),* Hull stated that learning is "driven" (motivated) by the necessity of meeting these physiological demands. Hull proposed a **drive theory** of behavior as an alternative to descriptive behaviorism (Hull, 1943, 1952).

S-O-R Theory.   Hull self-consciously described himself as a *neobehaviorist* to contrast his position with that of other behaviorists. Strict behaviorists, he thought, failed both in their lack of formal theoretical analysis and in their tendency to ignore crucial details of behavior. Hull developed *methodological objectivism* more sharply. He deviated from a pure S-R orientation by specifically including *intervening variables.* Hence, his position is characterized not as S-R but as **S-O-R theory** (*O* stands for such *organismic variables* as thirst and hunger). Given our knowledge of physiology (even in 1943!), he questioned the reason for continuing to treat the organism as a black box. Obviously, his reasoning is even more valid today.[2]

Drive Reduction Theory.   Following Pavlov's lead, Hull emphasized physiological variables critical for survival. Skinner did not. In *Behavior of Organisms* (Skinner, 1938), *behavior* became a description of operant responses. Taking his lead from John B. Watson, Skinner concentrated on the *environmental* control of behavior. In adopting a position of *environmental determinism,* Skinner minimized biological determinants of behavior (Skinner, 1957).

By contrast, Hull's behavioral theory intimately tied learning to physiology. Innately determined homeostatic mechanisms allowed organisms to survive. Food and water deprivation set up conditions of specific physiological **needs,** and these needs were translated into motivated behavior by specific

---

[2] Skinner acknowledged biology: "Where inherited behavior leaves off, the inherited modifiability of the process of learning takes over" (1953, p. 83). In one of his last articles, he wrote: "Behavior analysts leave what is inside the black box to those who have the instruments and methods needed to study it properly. There are two unavoidable gaps in any behavioral account: one between the stimulating action of the environment and the response of the organism, and one between consequences and the resulting change in behavior. Only brain science can fill those gaps. In doing so it completes the account; it does not give a different account of the same thing. Human behavior will eventually be explained (as it can only be explained) by the cooperative action of ethology, brain science, and behavior analysis." (Skinner, 1989, p. 18)

drive states. When these drives resulted in behavior that fulfilled the specific needs, restoring the organism's homeostatic balance, the drive was said to be *reduced*—hence, **drive reduction theory.** "Reducing" drives by eating and drinking has the effect of reinforcing behaviors that are instrumental in securing food and water.

Hull's System of Quantification.   Hull's (1952) system represents a monumental attempt to construct a theory of learning built on observations of behavior and assumptions about their causes. From these observations he derived corollaries, postulates, and theorems. His *drive reduction theory of learning,* stated in the form of a mathematical equation, follows:

$$_sE_R = {_s}H_R \times D \times V \times K - (IR + {_s}I_R) \tag{6.1}$$

Though imposing, in reality equation (6.1) is not difficult to understand. We are not going to elaborate all of the intervening variables Hull postulated, but we can begin by noting that the terms he specifies in the equation are merely being added, subtracted, or multiplied.

What is Hull attempting to model with this equation? The notation $_sE_R$ refers to *reaction potential,* a probability that the *performance* of a learned behavioral response (R) has the potential (E) to occur under certain stimulus conditions (S). In other words, Hull is attempting to write a learning equation that predicts the probability of a learned response in a given situation, such as how quickly a rat can learn a maze using food reinforcement.

What factors *are* important in how rapidly a rat learns to negotiate straight-alley and T-shaped runways? Among the variables included in Hull's equation are $_sH_R$ (*habit strength,* or how much has already been learned), D (*drive*), V (*stimulus intensity dynamism,* a variable akin to intensity effects in Pavlov's law of strength), K (*incentive motivation,* both innate and acquired), I_R (*reactive inhibition,* a variable that includes fatigue effects), and $_sI_R$ (*conditioned inhibition*). These variables are in turn operationally defined; for example, *drive* is defined in terms of hours of food or water deprivation. Other terms in Hull's equation are in turn defined by reference to such variables as Ng, Mg, and Tg—the nature, amount, and delay of reinforcement, respectively. The quality and amount of a reinforcer in part determines the degree of **incentive motivation** underlying behavior. Larger amounts or tastier food provide greater (primary, or innate) incentive for hungry animals.

Acquired Incentives.   Stimuli paired with innate incentives such as food and water become **acquired incentives.** Earlier, a player who performed better than another was described as being "hungrier." The allusion to a psychological hunger or an acquired incentive may better be described as competitiveness. Animals can be trained to acquire incentives as well. For example, a distinctively colored goal box or the muscle cues associated with a left-turn entry into the goal box can acquire reinforcing properties. Acquired incentives in

Hull's theory are *secondary reinforcers* in Skinner's system. Presumably both are acquired by the process of *higher-order conditioning* as described by Pavlov.

Hull's system models negatively accelerated learning curves similar to those predicted by the Rescorla-Wagner model (see p. 205). That is, the increment of $_sH_R$ (habit strength) that accrues with each reinforced trial is a fraction of the amount remaining to be learned. Hull's theory further predicts that the upper limit of learning tends to be at a maximum when need reduction (M_g) is greatest (i.e., when incentive motivation is highest) and when the delay between response and reinforcement (Tg) is shortest.

Finally, can you look at the equation and determine why Hull is described as a *drive reduction* theorist? Note that without *drive* (in the equation, let $D = 0$), there can be no reinforcement, and, hence, the right side of the equation when multiplied by zero goes to zero. Solving the equation, when $D = 0$, $_sE_R$ also is zero. No drive (no hunger), no learning.

Drive-Stimulus Reduction Theory

We have seen that Hull initially conceived of both reinforcement (and punishment) as being mediated through *drive reduction*. Because of a simple experiment reported by Sheffield and Roby (1950), Hull modified his position and endorsed a theory of **drive-stimulus reduction.**

Recall that if any of the terms in Hull's equation go to zero, no learning should occur. Sheffield and Roby (1950) demonstrated that satiated (nonhungry) rats could learn an instrumental response using non-nutritive saccharin as a reinforcer. In this experiment a hunger drive is not reduced; apparently, the stimulus properties of saccharin are a sufficient incentive for learning to occur. Hull reasoned that reducing the drive caused by this stimulus was reinforcing, hence, the (unfortunate) term, *drive-stimulus reduction*.

Is Stimulation or Satiation Reinforcing?   Once the implications of Sheffield and Roby's (1950) simple demonstration sank in, other examples of non–drive-reducing reinforcement appeared in the literature. The concept of reinforcement changed rapidly. For example, Sheffield and his colleagues next demonstrated that rather than reducing a drive, engaging in a behavior that presumably *increased* a drive (or at least increased the level of excitement) could also act as a reinforcer.

These experiments (Sheffield, Wulff, & Backer, 1951) first demonstrated that male rats learned to run quickly to a female in estrous to engage in copulatory behavior. Drive reduction theory predicts that achieving orgasm would *reduce* the sex drive. The resulting reinforcing effects of orgasm would enable the rat to effectively learn the preceding instrumental behaviors. In this experiment, however, the rats were separated *before* achieving orgasm. The male rats learned despite the lack of drive reduction, presumably because sexual excitement is itself reinforcing (Sheffield et al., 1951).

Analysis of Hull's Theory. Hull had a profound impact on both behavior analysis and learning and behavior theory. First he recognized the complexity of behavior. He insightfully differentiated *learning* variables from *performance* variables. He developed a *hypothetico-deductive model* of how data can be used to generate a formal theory of behavior. Despite drive theory's incompleteness, both drive reduction theory and the prominent role played by acquired incentives remain as his legacy. Although both premature and too ambitious, Hull's attempt to integrate biological and psychological variables into a general theory of behavior is commendable.

Equation (6.1) does *not* serve the function that Hull envisioned because it does not allow us to predict the course of learned behavior in other than the most general terms. Nevertheless, his overall approach to a theory of learning is better than Skinner's atheoretical position because contemporary investigations in behavioral neuroscience proceed from adaptive-evolutionary premises and use integrated physiological and behavioral methodologies. Modern neuroscience is more in tune with Hull's theory in that purely descriptive behaviorism is too limiting. In the next section we turn to physiological observations and behavioral data that have expanded the concept of reinforcement beyond the formulations of Pavlov, Thorndike, Skinner, and Hull.

Interim Summary

1. Pavlov hypothesized that biologically meaningful stimuli elicit survival-promoting reflexes. Examples include innate responses to food and withdrawal from aversive stimuli. New behaviors, also typically adaptive, can be learned by the association of these reflexes with neutral stimuli.

2. Thorndike proposed the law of effect, a simple statement that responses followed by a satisfying state tend to increase and responses followed by an aversive state (annoyers) tend to decrease in frequency.

3. Skinner defined *reinforcement* as the process of increasing the probability of response by applying a reinforcer. He further defined a *reinforcer* (in a circular manner) as any stimulus that increased the rate of the preceding response.

4. Hull's drive reduction theory of behavior is a formal model theory involving data gathered from behavioral observations. Corollaries, postulates, and theorems were derived from this theory. Hull attempted to predict performance in a learning task by specifying physiological and psychological variables within the black box (i.e., an S-O-R model rather than an S-R model). Physiological needs induced drives that when reduced (satisfied) reinforced behavior.

5. Drive-stimulus reduction theory attempted to account for observations that some effective reinforcers not only failed to reduce drive but also sometimes induced behavior. Drinking a saccharin-flavored solution

empty of calories is an example of a reinforcing event that does not reduce a hunger drive.

CONTEMPORARY THEORIES OF REINFORCEMENT

We should not be too surprised by the fact that saccharin and sexual foreplay
can act as reinforcers in both rats and humans. Many activities we engage in
are pleasurable in spite of the fact that our survival doesn't depend on them.
We ski, flirt, ride bicycles, take pleasure-inducing drugs, play (pianos, soccer,
and computer games), read, worship, swim, sweet-talk, watch TV, invest
money, spend hours cooking gourmet meals, high-five, listen to CDs, celebrate
holidays, tell jokes, sunbathe, talk on telephones and the net, soak in a tub,
brush hair, rub backs, and receive paychecks. What an impressive list! Let us
modify an earlier statement to propose that after primary needs are met, *most*
activities that humans engage in are pleasurable in spite of the fact that our
immediate survival doesn't depend on them.

Acquired Motivation.   At the end of this chapter you are asked to sort the preceding list of behaviors and events into three categories: those that are innately
reinforcing, those that are acquired through experience with the environment,
and those that include both components. Perhaps because Hull recognized the
importance of the concept of **acquired motivation,** he can be forgiven for requiring all motivation to be drive reducing in the first place. You will find that
all these activities normally give pleasure, but many do not involve drive reduction. A paycheck is a common example of a reinforcing, but not drive reducing, stimulus. In fact, the satisfaction of *social approval* may be among the
items at the top of the list of effective reinforcers for both children and adults
(Bandura & Walters, 1963). Is social approval drive reducing? We now turn to
Albert Bandura's social reinforcement theory; to understand it, we must first
look at his insightful analysis of the origins of much of human behavior.

Bandura's Theories of Imitation
and Social Reinforcement

A theory of imitation and social reinforcement has been proposed to account
for modeling behavior of children (Bandura, 1971). Bandura's theories contain
nonlearning accounts of human behavior (see Box 6.1). He argues that much
of human behavior is imitative and persists in the absence of overt reinforcers
as conceptualized by Thorndike and Skinner. Bandura proposes as an alternative **social reinforcement theory.** From an instrumental learning perspective,
social reinforcers can be understood as the application of a specific subset of
learned secondary reinforcers (including smiling, paying attention, and saying
"good").

BOX 6.1 IMITATION: INSTINCTIVE OR LEARNED?

I have enjoyed having a new baby girl in the house four times in my life. Few activities gave their mother and me more pleasure than our hours of intensely personal contact with each. You don't have to be a psychologist to wonder at the nature of developing consciousness and personality that unfolds before you.

Among the mysteries of human life are these first psychological contacts. What is it like to see and hear and cry without knowing what it is that you are seeing and hearing and crying about? As newborns, all of us were once in this position.

Then came the first contact. Her eyes begin to focus and follow the movement of other eyes and facial features. You stick out your tongue, and she sticks out hers. Wait a minute! What's going on here? How does she know how to do that? Following the way in which questions have been asked throughout this text, did she *learn* how to imitate sticking out her tongue or is this imitation instinctive? By comparison, a sweet-tasting, warm nipple elicits a sucking response, but sucking is understood in terms of the innate reflexive properties of cranial nerves.

If not a reflex, could sticking out the tongue be an example of an FAP elicited by the sign stimulus of seeing someone else's tongue being stuck out? The truth is that we don't have good answers to these questions. Meltzoff and Moore (1983) suggest that imitative ability is a more general property of the human nervous system, allowing a wider degree of imitative response (see photo). Because as adults we don't stick our tongues out everytime someone else does, this behavior doesn't resemble the FAPs of other animals. Indeed, other early behavioral predispositions of infants, including facial recognition and the ability to track another face with their eyes, disappear within the first 2–5 months of age (Johnson, 1992).

Art and music teachers, swimming and tennis coaches, and other educators have long recognized the ability of humans to learn by observing and imitating, called *observational learning* by Bandura (1971). The imitated response becomes an instrumental or operant response that can be manipulated by reinforcement or punishment. The model (parent, teacher, or coach) provides the reinforcement or punishment for the imitated response. Under these conditions, Bandura refers to them as *social reinforcers*. Bandura's social reinforcers are no different from Skinner's secondary reinforcers or Hull's acquired incentives. We return to further examples of social learning in the chapter on applications of learning.

Inside the Black Box: The Brain's Basis
for Reinforcement

Let us entertain the possibility that almost *all* behaviors that humans repeat-edly engage in are being maintained by a common process of reinforcement. Skinner's objections aside, pleasure certainly seems to be a common element in soaking in a warm tub and receiving some unexpected money for a birthday. What is the nature of this alleged *common reinforcer?* Could it be other than pleasure? We must look inside the black box for an answer.

Serendipity.   Over and above being a pleasant-sounding word, *serendipity* plays an important role in the conduct of science. Horace Walpole coined the word to describe a mythical faculty possessed by scientists that allowed them to make important discoveries—by accident. Others have noted that a successful discovery is often best attributed to being in the right place at the right time. Indeed, Skinner, in eschewing the role of theory in this research, asserted that serendipity (including equipment breakdowns!) best accounted for both the direction and the successes of his behavioral discoveries (Skinner, 1959). As it turns out, serendipity also played a crucial role in a classic experiment that opened a window in the black box. For the first time researchers glimpsed the brain's mechanisms of reinforcement (Olds & Milner, 1954).

Electrical Stimulation of the Brain (ESB).   Two psychologists, James Olds and Peter Milner, implanted electrodes deep into subcortical areas near the hypo-thalamus of rats. Assessing the effects of **electrical stimulation of the brain (ESB)** in a conscious, free-ranging rat, they passed minute amounts of electric current through an implanted electrode. The current stimulated neurons at the electrode tip. Serendipitously, Olds and Milner noted that some of the rats re-turned to the particular place in the open field apparatus where they had re-ceived the ESB on previous trials. The researchers had prepared minds (i.e., they were in the right place at the right time). They recognized that the ESB in these rats seemed to be acting as a reinforcer. They reasoned that the rats were learning an instrumental response as a result of the effects of the ESB (Olds & Milner, 1954).

To test their hypothesis, they programmed a Skinner box in a way that made ESB contingent on lever pressing. They reasoned that if ESB acted the same as food and water reinforcers in deprived rats, rats should press the lever to secure ESB (Olds, 1962). Their hypothesis proved correct. ESB passed through certain electrode placements near the hypothalamus acted as a rein-forcer. Rats would "self-stimulate" by pressing a lever that delivered electrical stimulation to select neurons in the brain (see Figure 6.2).

In the decades since Olds and Milners' original observations, neuro-science research has illuminated the brain mechanisms for reinforcement to a level that goes well beyond the scope of this book (see Pinel, 1993, for a read-

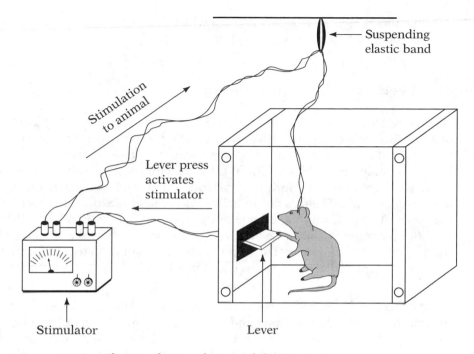

FIGURE 6.2   Electrical Stimulation of the Brain

Rats increase the rate of lever pressing when each lever press delivers electrical stimulation to a rewarding site in its brain.

able overview). A summary of some of the more important findings of this diverse research follows:

1. ESB has been demonstrated to have reinforcing properties for all species tested, including humans (Heath, 1963).

2. A factor common to many successful electrode placements (i.e., those that yield reinforcing effects) is that a structure called the *medial forebrain bundle (MFB)* is activated (Stein, 1969). (The MFB is a *limbic system pathway* that courses through portions of the hypothalamus.) More recent research has indicated that stimulation of the *mesotelencephalic dopamine system* plays a crucial role in ESB (Phillips & Fibiger, 1989). Brain structures other than the MFB and neurotransmitters other than dopamine have been implicated in the reinforcing effects of ESB (see Vaccarino, Schiff, & Glickman, 1989, for a review).

3. ESB can have motivational effects as well as reinforcing effects. Rats that are neither food, water, nor sex deprived can nevertheless be induced to eat or drink (Valenstein, Cox, & Kakolewski, 1969) or initiate sexual be-

haviors (Caggiula & Hoebel, 1966) when ESB is delivered in the presence of food, water, or a sexual partner, respectively.

Comparison of ESB with Traditional Reinforcers

How effective is ESB? How does ESB (from a positive electrode placement— one that "works") compare with a traditional reinforcer such as food? One way to answer this question is to arrange for rats to choose between one of two levers: pressing one produces ESB reinforcement; pressing the other produces food. Routtenberg and Lindy (1965) conducted such an experiment using daily 1-hour trials. The rats chose ESB reinforcement. Since the rats had only the 1 hour to eat during the course of this experiment, by choosing ESB they died of starvation within a few days. It can be concluded that ESB is an extremely effective reinforcer. The implication of this finding for an understanding of maladaptive behavior is discussed in a later section.

FI-10 Schedules Using ESB or Food Reinforcement.   Another demonstration of the relative effectiveness of food and ESB reinforcement can be found in an elegant experiment by Anderson, Ferland, and Williams (1992). Because this experiment provides both a review of material learned in the previous chapter and illustrates several new concepts as well, we look closely at its methods. Anderson et al. first trained rats on an FR-10 schedule for food reinforcement until stable responding ensued throughout a 90-second time period. Each FR-10 segment (signaled by S^d = light) alternated with 30 seconds of forced nonresponding by using a DRL-30" (S^D = tone). Recall that in this schedule each response resets a timer for an additional 30 seconds. The more responding during the DRL, the longer the delay in accessing food available on the FR-10 schedule. (The S^d signaling food availability on the FR-10 acted as a secondary reinforcer to maintain stimulus control on the DRL schedule.) The results following many sessions of responding on alternating FR-10, DRL-30" schedules of reinforcement can be seen in Figure 6.3a. A representative rat's rate of response on the FR-10 is high but is low on the DRL-30".

Anderson et al. (1992) then began alternating two kinds of reinforcement available on the FI segments; namely, food and ESB (electrical stimulation of the MFB). The same S^d controlled responding on both the food and ESB schedules; the DRL-30" segment effectively separated them. The way in which this rat responded on alternating FI segments with either food or ESB reinforcement allowed for a continuing comparison of their relative effectiveness. First, note in Figure 6.3a that the first ESB experience disrupted the pattern of (non)responding on the DRL. Electrical stimulation of the brain on the FI segment seemed to carry over into the following DRL segment; the rat no longer inhibited its responses. Remember that responding on the DRL resets the timer, delaying entry into the next food-reinforced segment. At this point we do

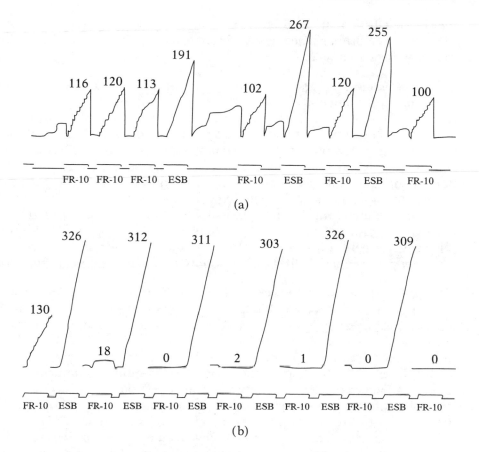

267   255
191
116 120 113   102   120   100

FR-10 FR-10 FR-10 ESB   FR-10   ESB   FR-10   ESB   FR-10

(a)

326   312   311   303   326   309
130
18   0   2   1   0   0

FR-10 ESB FR-10 ESB FR-10 ESB FR-10 ESB FR-10 ESB FR-10 ESB FR-10

(b)

FIGURE 6.3 Rats Prefer ESB to Food—Absolutely!

Rats are trained to bar press on multiple schedules of reinforcement, beginning with FR-10 for food, alternating with DRL-30 (not labeled) for the first three segments (top cumulative record). The DRL-30 was reinforced by reentry into the FR-10 segment. Then (fourth cycle from left) for the first time the rat's FR-10 was reinforced with ESB rather than food. Note how the rat responds at a higher rate and continues lever pressing through the DRL portion of the schedule, thereby resetting the timer, delaying reentry to the FR-10 portion of the schedule. Four sessions after the last session depicted, the hungry rat stops responding entirely for food while continuing to bar press at a high rate for ESB stimulation. Numbers in (b) reflect responses during each segment. Compared to ESB, food is apparently irrelevant to a hungry rat. This example is a very powerful demonstration of negative contrast.

not know whether the ESB has merely induced (excited) the bar pressing or whether the ESB has acted as a different kind of reinforcer and changed the pattern of responding during extinction.

Negative Contrast.   After several more iterations of FI, DRL, ESB, DRL, and so on, a new phenomenon emerges. By session 4—(Figure 6.3b)—the rat's bar pressing for food virtually stops. At the same time, by inhibiting responses on the DRL segment, the rat does *not* delay reentry into the FI segment for ESB reinforcement. And once in the FI segment maintained by ESB reinforcement, the rat rapidly bar presses for ESB. Having experienced both forms of reinforcement, apparently food reinforcement is now perceived as *less* reinforcing to the rat—a phenomenon called **negative contrast.** Negative contrast is an example of **behavioral contrast** in which reinforcement and punishment effects are determined in part by the context in which they are delivered (see Flaherty, 1982, 1991, for reviews).[3] In this study, we can use evidence of *negative contrast* to conclude that ESB is a more powerful reinforcer than food.

Choosing Between Two Reinforcers.   Although the results of the Anderson et al. (1992) and Routtenberg and Lindy (1965) studies attest to the power and efficacy of ESB as a reinforcer, they also raise questions concerning reinforcers and adaptiveness. Rats that died because they chose the pleasures of ESB reinforcement over food (Routtenberg & Lindy, 1965) might invite a sermon about the evils of hedonism or the perils of succumbing to immediate gratification. An alternative is to pose two serious questions about (a) the relationship of reinforcement to adaptive and maladaptive behavior and (b) the relative value of two reinforcing events at a given moment in time.

Most examples of the effects of reinforcement on behavior are adaptive, which is why the law of effect is so pervasive (see Box 5.2, p. 229, in which Dennett, 1975, outlines the argument that reinforcement selects behavior in an analogous manner to the role natural selection plays in evolutionary theory). Ironically, we take for granted that humans often behave maladaptively. It is an interesting commentary that we are truly surprised when other animals seem to behave so. The fact that humans are the only animals that exhibit masochistic and sadistic behavior does not rule out the possibility that nonhuman animals can exhibit maladaptive behavior. Let us look more closely at the relationship of the law of effect to maladaptive behavior.

Reinforcers and Maladaptive Behavior

The Routtenberg and Lindy (1965) finding that rats chose the pleasures of ESB reinforcement over life-giving food parallels an experiment on adrenalec-

---

[3] A human example of *behavioral contrast:* When you make *C*s on several tests throughout the semester and a *B* on the final exam, you are pleased. When you make *A*s throughout the semester and the same *B* on the final, you are disappointed.

tomized rats (Harriman, 1955). The adrenalectomized rats had a daily 1-hour choice between a salt solution and a sucrose solution. Because adrenalectomized rats do not secrete aldosterone, they excrete too much salt in their urine. Unless salt is replaced, these rats die within about 10 days. When given the opportunity to select the life-affording salt solution, some (but not all) adrenalectomized rats instead drink the sucrose solution and die of salt depletion (Harriman, 1955).

In the two experiments being compared, both the sucrose and ESB were more reinforcing than the salt solution and food, respectively. Why? Using Skinner's ideas, sucrose and ESB were more reinforcing because each stimulus better controlled the animals' responses in the two-choice situation. Also by definition, however, selecting sucrose and ESB appears to be *maladaptive* because each behavior resulted in death. How can we account for this apparent violation of the law of effect?

What Is Reinforcing for Normal Rats?   Normal rats prefer sucrose solutions to salt solutions, presumably because "sweet" predicts calories within the feeding niches in which rats evolved (Richter, 1942). Furthermore, in normal rats, a host of physiological mechanisms serve to conserve salt; destruction of the adrenal glands is certainly a rare, most likely lethal, event. Finally, except in laboratories, rats feed throughout the nighttime, not during 1 hour in the middle of the day.

Conclusion? It is normal for rats to select sucrose over salt. To expect otherwise in a 1-hour feeding period merely because a rat's adrenal glands have been removed is wishful thinking. Rats have been naturally selected to be sensitive to calories but not to survive removal of their adrenal glands. The fact that several rats *did* choose salt over sucrose is an example more of the remarkable redundancy of salt-conserving mechanisms than of *maladaptive* behavior on the part of those that selected sucrose.

Is ESB Like Food?   So much for salt and sucrose. Why was ESB selected over food in the Routtenberg and Lindy (1965) experiment? Again, the daily 1-hour feeding periods demand tremendous feeding plasticity on the part of the rat. The question is why a starving rat would select ESB (that presumably it has little experience with) over eating food (an innately predisposed behavior). One suggestion is that the sensations attendant with ESB are both highly pleasurable and in some sense "reminiscent" of the pleasures of eating palatable foods (Pfaffman, 1960). In this scenario, lacking the cognitive abilities of humans to talk about what the sensation of ESB *is like*, rats might simply confuse ESB sensations with eating sensations.

We have much to learn about brain mechanisms underlying reinforcement. The artificial stimulation of drugs, ESB, and perhaps the "normal" stimulation of other very powerful reinforcers and punishers (cf. post-traumatic stress disorders, p. 383) can apparently override the correspondence normally seen between adaptive behavior and the law of effect.

ESB in Humans

Watching rats respond to electrical stimulation of brain sites that supported lever pressing, Olds thought that they looked as if they were enjoying the ESB. Humans who have experienced ESB in similar areas of the brain report that the sensation is generally pleasurable, although one, unable to achieve orgasm no matter how often he pressed the button to stimulate himself, reported being frustrated (Heath, 1963). Such self-reports, coupled with the effect ESB has on animals in learning experiments, force the conclusion that the sensations produced by ESB can be thought of as highly pleasurable Thorndikean satisfiers.

Integrating Brain Mechanisms with Reinforcement Theory

What are the implications of the finding that vertebrate brains have "reinforcement" areas that, when stimulated, can either induce or reinforce behaviors? In the first place, recall that Hull's drive theory had to be modified to a drive-stimulus theory because of research showing that both non-nutritive saccharin and nonorgasmic sex had reinforcing properties. Both instances are arguably pleasurable. The reported effects of recreational drugs such as cocaine and marijuana can be added to the list. Activities are reinforcing because they involve activation of the MFB (see Milner, 1976, for discussion) and of the *mesotelencephalic dopamine system*. Given that activation of these areas both induces and reinforces behavior, the necessary and sufficient conditions for reinforcement seem to be the activation of these and other brain areas. At least for humans, if a stimulus, event, or activity is described as producing pleasure, it probably involves specific structures such as the MFB and the mesotelencephalic dopamine system and is highly likely to act as a reinforcer.

Another possibility. Perhaps ESB is more pleasurable than eating tasty food because ESB elicits more palatable feeding sensations than the real food alternative. For example, the ESB might produce a chocolate-chip cookie sensation compared to the bland rat chow alternative. In fact, many humans report a preference for the pleasures of a cocaine high over that of sexual orgasm. Our understanding of this phenomenon is that the cocaine molecule is a more or less perfect key to activate locks on the endorphin receptor mechanism. As was noted earlier, it is likely that ESB also works on these same receptor mechanisms (Phillips & Fibiger, 1989).

We return to these ideas in the next chapter when we look at the addictive properties of such potent reinforcers as alcohol, morphine, cocaine, and other drugs.

Premack's Theory of Reinforcement

David Premack (1962) deemphasized reinforcement through both drive reduction and drive-stimulus reduction. Instead he proposed that engaging in pleasurable activities (i.e., those that presumably stimulate the pleasure-producing brain areas) was the reinforcing event. Prior to Premack, a reinforcer was considered to be a stimulus event. Pavlov's unconditioned stimulus, Thorndike's satisfier, and Hull's need-satisfying food are examples. Premack set out to demonstrate that the reinforcing effects of food could not be separated from the behavior of eating the food. That is, both the eating behavior and the food occurred during the reinforcement event. For Premack, *eating* the food, rather than the food itself, was the reinforcing event. He then designed experiments to demonstrate that not all behavioral activities were equally reinforcing; rather, certain behaviors were more or less reinforcing at different times within an individual.

Drinking and Running Rats.   How did Premack demonstrate these ideas? In an early experiment, he deprived rats of water for 23 hours and then measured how much time they spent either drinking water or running in a running wheel (Premack, 1962). (Running in a running wheel is reinforcing to caged rats in the same way that most physical activities are reinforcing to humans confined in prison.) On another day he allowed rats unlimited access to water in their home cages to establish baseline drinking. He measured how much time they spent running or drinking in a 1-hour test session. Under these test conditions, rats predictably spent more time running than drinking during the test hour.

The Premack Principle.   Having established these baselines of behavioral activity, Premack then demonstrated that under certain conditions running would reinforce drinking behavior. How? By restricting running and allowing the rat to drink during the preceding 23 hours, running was made more probable during the next day's 1-hour test. Rats would even engage in overdrinking behavior (drink when not thirsty) if drinking was reinforced by the opportunity to run.

In a series of similar experiments, Premack and his students found that the more probable of two responses would always reinforce the less probable response, a relationship now known as the **Premack principle.** Note that this reinforcement relationship is *reversible*. Restrict drinking or eating (as is normally done in most animal learning experiments) and afterward eating and drinking will reinforce most other behaviors. Why? Because in a given testing session, *most other behaviors are less likely to occur* than eating (if the animal is hungry) or drinking (if the animal is thirsty).

Eating Candy or Playing Pinball.   In a clever experiment Premack (1965) demonstrated that more probable behaviors will reinforce less probable behaviors in children. First, the investigators measured two behavioral baselines for each child in the study. Given the choice of playing a pinball machine or of eating candy, which activity does each child prefer? Having established that some children preferred candy over pinball and vice versa, Premack then determined under what conditions candy would reinforce pinball playing (and under what conditions pinball playing would reinforce candy eating). Remember that the Premack principle predicts that playing pinball reinforces candy eating only for those children who preferred pinball to candy during the baseline measurement (and that eating candy reinforces pinball playing only for those children who preferred eating candy to playing pinball during the baseline measurement). These predictions held true (Premack, 1962). And, as you might expect, the less probable behavior would *not* reinforce the more probable behavior, even though both were pleasurable.

Biological Basis of the Premack Principle.   In an earlier section we saw that ESB can have motivational as well as reinforcing effects. That is, rats can be induced to eat, drink, and initiate sexual behaviors when certain neurons in their brain are stimulated. Those ESB-induced behaviors are called *stimulus-bound behaviors*. The electrode sites that produce stimulus-bound behavior can also be shown to reinforce instrumental responding (Gratton & Wise, 1988). This finding is similar to the Premack principle, namely that *engaging in certain behaviors can be reinforcing*.

Analysis of the Premack Principle.   At the time Premack was proposing his theory, reinforcers were things that behavior produced or avoided, and the process of reinforcement was the effect that such things had on the preceding responses. By extending the concept of reinforcement to the opportunity to engage in (pleasurable) behavior and by providing a method that demonstrated that reinforcement relationships were reversible as conditions changed, Premack shifted the focus of analysis away from things and back to behavior. The Premack principle remains just one of many ways to conceptualize reinforcement, however. Consider the following criticisms:

1. Reinforcers do not go away merely because one chooses to measure engaging in behavior. When rats engage in drinking behavior, they drink *water.* Likewise, children eat *candy.* Put bitter quinine in water and candy, and the behaviors involved in their consumption cease. The point is that the process of reinforcement in part is determined by properties of things, and the behavior being measured is determined by these properties.

2. Running in a running wheel, playing pinball, skiing, and riding bicycles are reinforcing events that presumably share with candy and water the activation of pleasurable brain sites. One does not need the Premack principle to account for the pleasure derived from engaging in certain behaviors.

3. That engaging in reinforcing behavior varies during the course of the day or, for that matter, in the course of a lifetime is not surprising. All traditional theories of reinforcement recognize that the reinforcing properties of food and water are conditional on hunger and thirst, respectively. To take another example, the opportunity for a 15-year-old to drive a car is a highly probable behavior and taking out the trash is not. New drivers will move mountains

of trash for a spin around the block. After driving for a year or so, however, the suggestion that "I'll let you drive around the block if you take out the trash for me" does not seem like such a good deal. Likewise, given the alternative of purchasing either a new car or a face-lift, the choice can be expected to vary as a function of a person's age, sex, and other factors.

Is Reinforcement Necessary for Learning?

Premack, then, joins other reinforcement theorists in stressing that the incentive value of reinforcers changes from hour to hour and throughout a lifetime. Not all theorists would be comfortable, though, with Premack's view that the opportunity to run in a running wheel or to play pinball was reinforcing. Why? Because there is no specifiable reinforcing "event" in these examples as there is in drinking behavior. Nor are traditionalists especially comfortable with an analysis suggesting that reinforcement is the (unobserved) stimulation of pleasure-producing areas in the brain. There is no escaping the circularity of arguing for the presence of a reinforcing event just because the behavior changed "as if" a reinforcing event occurred. Recall that Bandura believes that learning occurs by imitation of observed behavior, minimizing the traditional role of reinforcement in behavioral change. Here we again raise a question that has plagued theorists: Is reinforcement necessary for learning to occur?

How Do Rats Learn to Run Mazes?   The problem of accounting for behavioral change that looks like learning under conditions in which a specific reinforcer is absent has a long history. Classic experiments by Tolman and Honzik (1930a; 1930b) studied the role of reward in the manner that rats learned their way through a complex maze. Their maze had more than a dozen choice points prior to arrival in a goal box. On each trial, the number of errors (reversals in the runways and entries into blind alleys) was counted along the way to the goal box. Once there, one group of rats was rewarded with food in the goal box. In one study (Tolman & Honzik, 1930b), for the first 10 trials, two other groups were simply removed and put back in their home cages without being fed. The prediction of traditional reinforcement theorists is that the food reinforcement allows the first group to learn the maze more quickly than the other two. And, as Figure 6.4 illustrates, for the first 10 trials the number of errors decreased by over 60% for the food-reinforced group. Notice, however, that even in the absence of a food reward, the other two groups showed a more modest but still substantial 35% improvement in their error rate.

In addition to the obvious question concerning the role of food reinforcement in learning, several more basic questions are raised by the Tolman and Honzik (1930b) experiment. In order of behavioral complexity: Why do rats move in a maze? Why do rats find their way to the goal boxes in mazes? Why do rats reduce the number of wrong turns on their way to the goal box in a maze?

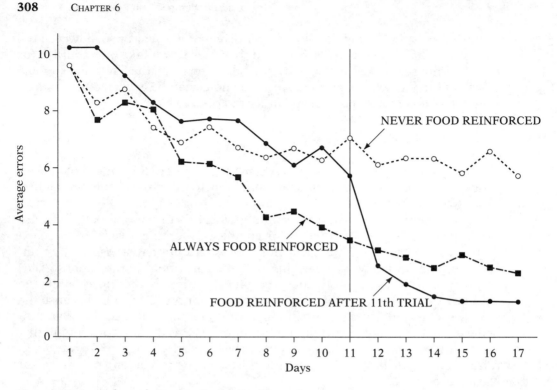

FIGURE 6.4   Tolman's Latent Learning Experiment

In Tolman and Honzik's latent learning experiment, the performance of rats labeled NEVER FOOD REINFORCED is compared with those labeled FOOD REINFORCED AFTER 11th TRIAL. Note the latter group's rapid improvement in performance relative to the group labeled ALWAYS FOOD REINFORCED, evidence for the phenomenon of *latent learning*. (Tolman & Honzik, 1930b)

Species-Specific Foraging Behavior.   We can make only educated guesses as to a rat's motivation. Here we note that food deprivation increases movement in rats and that increasing movement is adaptive because active rats are more likely than inactive rats to encounter food. So the fact that all rats in the Tolman and Honzik (1930b) experiment were food deprived provides them basic motivation to forage within a novel environment. The answer to the second question is not unrelated to the first; rats also have species-specific foraging tendencies that allow them to rapidly and efficiently "map" the environment they traverse (see Olton, Collison, & Werz, 1977; Olton & Samuelson, 1976; and discussion in Chapter 9, p. 443). These *cognitive maps* allow rats to become increasingly efficient at getting to the goal box. Once there, one of two events takes place: either the rats are fed (which is reinforcing) or they are removed from a place in which there is no food to a place where there is food (also reinforcing). The better performance of rats finding food in the goal box suggests that food is *more* reinforcing than merely being removed from the goal box and placed in a home cage in which the rat has a history of being fed.

Latent Learning

The second part of Tolman and Honzik's (1930b) experiment is not so easily explained, however. Note that in Figure 6.4 on the 11th trial, after traversing the maze, one group of rats that had never been food reinforced found food in the goal box. The effect of this single food-reinforced trial was dramatic; on the very next trial, these rats' performance equaled that of rats who had been food reinforced from the beginning. The remaining group of rats (that never experienced food reward in the goal box) continued to make the same number of errors as before. Tolman reasoned that the dramatic improvement in one trial reflected a change in *performance* rather than *learning;* that is, he assumed that all groups had learned the maze more or less equally after 10 trials. According to Tolman, more experience with the maze in the absence of food reinforcement was sufficient for learning to occur. Adding a food reward increased the animal's performance only. Tolman used the term **latent learning** to describe the learning that occurred in the absence of food reward.

Interpreting Latent Learning.   Tolman admitted to the possibility that some form of weak, nonfood reinforcement is responsible for the improved performance of all rats over the first 10 trials. How do we now interpret the relatively more rapid learning of the rats that were food reinforced beginning on trial 11? These rats experienced the following cumulative reinforcement: (1) learning where food *wasn't* while foraging on trials 1–10, (2) being taken out of a nonfood environment and placed in a home cage that had acquired secondary reinforcing properties, and (3) after trial 10, discovering food in the goal box. So it is incorrect to say that this group learned the maze in the absence of reinforcement.

So much for the latent learning of this group. How about the food-reinforced group? During trials 1–10 the food-reinforced rats learned where food wasn't (early part of maze) and where it was (end of maze). Both the latent learning group and the food-reinforced group of rats, then, had a sufficient number of foraging trials to map the maze. The addition of the food incentive determined their terminal level of performance.[4]

A traditional interpretation of Tolman and Honzik's (1930b) concept of

---

[4] On examining Figure 6.4, the reader should not assume that the terminal performance of the two food-rewarded groups differed significantly. The mean number of errors of one group was less than the mean number of errors of the other, but no statistical analysis was reported in this study. In addition, the terminal level of performance theoretically could be shifted by either increasing or decreasing the rat's hunger level, by increasing or decreasing the palatability of the food reinforcer, and so forth.

latent learning is that learning can occur in the absence of food reinforcement and that other sources of reinforcement cannot be ruled out. Why are there fewer errors across the first few trials for all groups in Figure 6.4? Making fewer errors means that the rat arrives at the goal box sooner, either to eat food (reinforced group) or to be taken out of the goal box and returned to the home cage more quickly (other two groups). Animals in the nonfood reward groups had a history of being fed in the home cage and a history of never being fed in the maze; therefore, the home cage would have more secondary reinforcing cues associated with it.

Latent Learning or Foraging?   An alternative interpretation of Tolman and Honzik's (1930b) experiment stresses the rats' innate behavioral predispositions: Making fewer errors in a maze makes a rat more efficient in that it expends less energy in locating the source(s) of food. Innate feeding tendencies are further played out in differentially reinforcing environments (i.e., food found in the goal box or food found in the home cage). In this view, hungry rats are disposed to systematic foraging, and these foraging experiences, whether successful or not in finding food in the maze, are remembered (Olton et al., 1977; Olton & Samuelson, 1976).

Purposive Behavior.   Ironically, Tolman would be in complete agreement with this alternative interpretation in that he was among the first learning psychologists to propose that behavior is *purposive* (Tolman, 1932). In Tolman's view, rats ran in order to secure food incentives rather than food acting to mechanically *stamp in* faster running speeds. For this and other reasons, as we see again in Chapter 9, Tolman is one of the first animal learning theorists who attributed *cognitive processes* to infrahumans.

(Recall that Skinner was aware of Tolman's experiments and agreed with him that rats brought innate tendencies into the laboratory. Skinner stopped using alleys and mazes and designed an arbitrary operant response, lever pressing, to study the effects of reinforcement. He reasoned that rats might have evolved foraging behaviors but not lever-pressing ones. Lever pressing, therefore, was a more arbitrary response. Free from innate behavioral tendencies, the effects of reinforcement could more easily be determined.)

Reinforcing Innate Feeding Tendencies in Humans.   Let us move from hungry rats seeking food in a maze to a human neonate seeking food from her immediate environment. Are there similarities? Human babies innately *root* when hungry. Environmental stimulation (tactile stimulation around her mouth) provides feedback as to her progress in finding a food source. (Not here. Not there. What's that smell? Here it is!) Sweet, warm milk from a nipple is a powerful primary reinforcer that both elicits and then reinforces the consummatory behaviors of sucking and swallowing. The sweet milk likely stimulates pleasure-producing neurons in the brain, as does the drive reduction of hunger being satisfied. That learning occurs and that memories of this learned behavior are formed are evidenced by the increased sucking proficiency of older, more experienced nursers.

Interim Summary

1. Reinforcers as either pleasing events or engaging in pleasing behaviors appear to have common brain bases; current candidates are the *medial forebrain bundle* and the *mesotelencephalic dopamine system*.

2. A contemporary theory of (brain) reinforcement is based on studies using electrical stimulation of the brain (ESB) in traditional learning situations and on observations regarding addictive drugs such as crack cocaine.

3. ESB reinforcers are so potent that animals choose them in preference to food, water, and other life-giving reinforcers. This seemingly maladaptive behavior can be understood as the artificial stimulation of selected neurons normally stimulated by life-giving reinforcers.

4. Premack's theory of reinforcement focuses on *behaving* rather than on reinforcers as pleasing stimuli. The *Premack principle* states that more probable behaviors reinforce less probable behaviors and that this reinforcement relationship is reversible.

5. Tolman studied the role that reinforcement plays in how rats learn to run mazes. He found evidence that food reinforcement was not necessary for learning, a phenomenon he called *latent learning*.

6. An alternative interpretation of the latent learning experiment is that rats engage in species-specific foraging behavior. Successful foraging involves reinforcement at any of a number of the various stages of foraging, including, but not restricted to, the attainment of food.

To now we have restricted discussion of theories of reinforcement to only the top left-hand cell of Figure 6.1. We have seen that learning occurs when our responses produce events that make us feel good. Let us now look at the many instances of behavior in which our responses make us feel good—by preventing bad things from happening.

NEGATIVE REINFORCEMENT

Students and researchers (Kimble, 1992) alike dislike Skinner's term *negative reinforcement,* probably for the same reason that no one enjoys reading a sentence in which *alike* and *dislike* appear side by side. *Negative reinforcement* seems to be an oxymoron. If reinforcement is a process that *increases* the rate of response, *negative* reinforcement should *decrease* it. But, by convention, procedures that decrease the rate of response are called *punishment* (see right-hand side of Figure 6.1).

For present purposes students should simply memorize the traditional distinction between the concepts of negative reinforcement and punishment: Reinforcement *of any kind,* including **negative reinforcement,** increases the rate of the preceding response. Punishment of any kind decreases the same. Let us take a closer look at a number of procedures that are used to study negative reinforcement.

Negative Reinforcement, Escape, and Avoidance

Imagine being trapped barefooted in a dimly illuminated Skinner box with a steel grid floor and a lever sticking out of one wall. Unable to escape, and just as you decide to relax and make the best of it, you feel electric shock on the soles of your feet. Aroused, you begin hopping around and accidentally bump up against the lever. The shock stops. About the time you start to relax, the scenario repeats itself. Again, by hitting the lever, you escape the shock. The third time the shock occurs, you make a beeline for the lever, hit it, and terminate the shock.

(By Jove, I think I've got it! This lever, my response, and electric shock seem to be associated together. Can I verbalize the contingencies after a few trials? It seems that my lever-pressing response allows me to escape or remove myself from the punishing stimulus called *electric shock*. Whether I can verbalize it or not, I think I'll hang around this lever.)

Escape and Avoidance Procedures. Murray Sidman (1953) accomplished this in an experiment with rats. Not only did his rats learn an **escape procedure**— that is, they learned to make a response that terminated an aversive stimulus— but also with additional training they learned another behavior. Sidman reprogrammed his apparatus so that a lever-pressing response would both terminate a shock and also delay the onset of the next shock. Not surprisingly, in this **avoidance procedure** the rats eventually learned to respond *before* the onset of the shock, thereby avoiding the shock altogether. After several sessions, rats' lever pressing on this unsignaled **Sidman avoidance** task soon begins to respond at relatively high rates. Sidman avoidance is also known as *free-operant avoidance* because to avoid shock, the operant responses must be repeated by the animal during a work session. In this procedure, Sidman's rats learned to make avoidance responses to aversive stimuli by the process of *negative reinforcement* (see Figure 6.1).

Determinants of Avoidance Response Rates

Sidman avoidance is unsignaled in that only the lever and other cues of the Skinner box set the occasion for the lever-pressing response. Because levers and electric shocks do not exist in the rat's world outside the Skinner box, in reality the box and the lever are highly distinctive signals. The rat has no way to know that a distinctive cue is important to the experimenter! The point is that we should not make too much of any alleged differences between unsignaled and the signaled avoidance tasks discussed in the next section.

Role of Shock Intensity.   What other stimuli control responding in a Sidman avoidance task? Certainly, the intensity of shock the animal experiences influences its rate of response. An occasional low-intensity shock is presumably tolerated better than one of higher intensity. Predictably, lever-pressing response rates vary as a direct function of shock intensity (see Theios, Lynch, & Lowe, 1966, for relevant experiments). But a shock level *too* high is likely to condition the passivity of *learned helplessness* rather than responses that are instrumental in avoiding pain.

Role of Time's Passage.   In the unsignaled Sidman avoidance task the animals must respond at least often enough to avoid shock. That they learn this schedule (and learn it well—see Box 6.2) attests to the ability of birds, rats, dogs, monkeys, and humans to effectively use the passage of time as a cue. Earlier we saw that Pavlov reliably conditioned salivary responses in dogs using only regularly spaced food USs and no CS (see *temporal conditioning*, p. 139). Monkeys also exhibit an exquisite sense of timing of their lever-pressing responses on a DRL schedule (p. 250). Regularly spaced responses on a Sidman avoidance schedule can be interpreted similarly as reflecting rats' very precise sense of time.

Discrete Trial Avoidance Schedules

When a *specific* discriminative stimulus is added to the experimental environment, even more precise stimulus control of avoidance responding can be achieved. For example, a *signaled* **discrete trial** avoidance procedure was reported by Solomon and Wynne (1953). They placed a dog in a **shuttle box** having two compartments separated by a low barrier wall. When a tone was sounded, escape/avoidance contingencies were put into effect. During each discrete trial, signaled by a tone, the dog was allowed first to *escape* and with further training to *avoid* electric shock. It did this by jumping across the barrier from the electrified compartment of the shuttle box to the shock-free side. When the researcher electrified this side, the dog could escape by reversing and jumping back across the barrier into the now safe compartment. Soon the dog learned to avoid electric shock entirely by jumping from one compartment to the other at the onset of the tone, a task known as **shuttle avoidance.**

The use of discriminative stimuli (S^ds) to control responding allows different types of avoidance schedules to be combined. Box 6.2 describes two types of concurrent avoidance behavior in monkeys trained to respond to each of three different S^ds.

Box 6.2 High Performance Motivated by Avoidance Schedules

(a)

(b)

Animal research supported the Apollo expeditions to the moon in the 1960s. In simulations of the performance requirements of astronauts in spacecraft, chimpanzees (*Pan troglodytes*) were trained on signaled Sidman avoidance and other discrete avoidance schedules (Koestler & Barker, 1965). A work session sequence involved both appetitive and aversive schedules of reinforcement. Why use aversive schedules? Because both appetite and appetitively based performance are hindered under conditions of high stress, including, for example, stressful drug effects (Dews, 1958) and suffocation following loss of breathable atmosphere (Koestler & Barker, 1965).

A red light above one lever was the discriminative stimulus (S^d) for the *Sidman avoidance* task. When the red light was on, lever pressing delayed (avoided) electric shock (a). Both the response-to-shock interval (*r-s interval*) and the shock-to-shock interval (*s-s interval*) were set at 5 seconds. That is, the chimp had to make one response every 5 seconds (*r-s interval* = 5 seconds) to avoid electric shock. If it did not respond, it received a 1-second shock every 5 seconds

(*s-s interval* = 5 seconds) throughout the work session.

Discriminative stimuli (S^ds) for the **discrete avoidance** tasks were backlit stimulus-response keys on the animal's performance panel. Each was illuminated in turn for 1 second. After 1 second the light terminated, and electric foot shock was applied to the chimp's foot. The shock could be avoided if the chimp pushed the key (depressing a microswitch) before 1 second elapsed. A tone served as the S^d for another unlit key, which, when depressed within 1 second, allowed the shock to be avoided (b).

Even with the low levels of electric shock used in these studies, chimpanzees rarely failed to respond to the negative reinforcement contingencies. Most performed flawlessly session after session, day after day, without receiving an electric shock.

As a historical note, this experiment could no longer be accomplished. For ethical reasons, chimpanzees cannot be subjected to restraints (such as being confined to sitting in a chair), electrical shock, or other insults. An exception is their use in AIDS research.

Analyzing Avoidance Learning by Humans.   In the previous chapter we analyzed ways in which traffic signals exercised control over our driving behavior. Think about collisions in intersections as events to be avoided. Can you verbalize parallels between pushing a key on a performance panel (as in Box 6.2) or jumping a barrier in a shuttle box and hitting the brakes as your automobile approaches an intersection? What are the discriminative stimuli (S^ds) controlling each of these responses? What motivates each response?

Assume that you could train someone to hit the brakes and that you could explain how such signaled, discrete trial avoidance behavior illustrates the concept of negative reinforcement. Are you ready for a more challenging task? Explain the following two examples of avoidance learning in humans: Small children learning to play soccer often turn their heads and bodies when an opposing player kicks the ball in their direction. What motivates this behavior? Both skiing and riding a bicycle require a person to make small behavioral adjustments collectively known as *maintaining balance.* After learning both skilled acts, (a) why do people seldom fall and (b) under what conditions do they fall? *Hint:* You might want to consider both skiing and riding a bicycle as *free operants.*

Where Is the Reinforcement in Negative Reinforcement?

Referring once again to Figure 6.1, note that in the lower left cell the process of negative reinforcement is accomplished in the *absence* of a reinforcing stimulus. The question learning theorists have raised for half a century is how the *absence* of a stimulus can reinforce behavior (Mowrer, 1960; Mowrer & Lamoreaux, 1942). It is interesting that when we consider specific examples of the phenomenon, negative reinforcement does not seem to be counterintuitive. For example, after sufficient avoidance training, people can ride bicycles for years on end without ever falling. We are initially motivated to keep our balance because it hurts to fall down. The predictable answer to the question "Why are you skiing so cautiously?" is "Because I don't want to fall." We can't ask rats, monkeys, and dogs why they keep responding even though they are no longer being shocked. But we can put ourselves in their place and their behavior seems reasonable enough.

What Persists Following Aversive Training?   We accept the preceding statements regarding our motivation underlying avoidance behavior because we suspect that at least some aspect of the reinforcer is never totally absent. The negative reinforcer is present in the form of a memory. For example, we remember the pain of falling off bikes and skis. When a skier says, "I ski slowly because I don't want to fall," is it possible that we are not hearing a dispassionate statement of fact but rather a disguised fear (or wariness) of falling? Perhaps the lessons learned during avoidance training remain with us in terms of memories of a painful experience translated into fear that it might occur again.

Two-Factor Theory of Avoidance

Such an analysis, known as **two-factor theory,** was first proposed by Mowrer (1947, 1960). According to this theory, the two factors underlying avoidance behavior are Pavlovian-conditioned emotional behavior and instrumentally conditioned motor (skeletal) responses. Two-factor theory posits that fear is conditioned first and separately from instrumentally reinforced avoidance responses. Fear is classically conditioned by the pairing of pain with stimuli in the avoidance training environment. The stimuli may be easily specified, such as the presence of a lever in a Skinner box or a tone or color signaling that shock-induced pain is imminent. Or the conditioned stimuli can be more subtle, such as the sensations of losing balance afforded by our vestibular apparatus. Vestibular sensations as well as skis and bikes have been associated with the pain of falling down.

According to two-factor theory, after the fear response is conditioned, the second step involves conditioning instrumental responses (such as lever pressing, jumping a barrier to avoid shock, or maintaining one's balance by turning a handlebar). Mowrer assumed that conditioned fear was present at all times during avoidance training. The (negative) reinforcement for such instrumental responses, he asserted, was the termination of the fear response. He reasoned that alleviation of fear is a positive experience and that this positive experience acts as the reinforcer for the preceding instrumental response.

Evaluation of the Two-Factor Theory of Avoidance

Are people who ride bikes, who ski, and who study their books to avoid failing classes really motivated by fear? Or is it more a feeling of *uneasiness* that is elicited when confronted with cues that have been associated with the training of the avoidance response? For example, on a Sidman avoidance schedule as well as in shuttle boxes, animal responses are distributed in time. Is the *fear* of electric shock ever present during a 1-hour session, day in and day out? Or is it more likely that rats, dogs, and humans are merely wary and uneasy when faced with cues that predict aversive consequences unless they do something? Is fear reduced with each response, or is it more likely that responding becomes automatic and that animals are less conscious of the response-shock contingency?

The Kamin, Brimer, and Black Experiment. An experiment by Kamin, Brimer, and Black (1963) provides some insight into these complicated issues. Rats were first trained to bar press for food. Then they were put into a shuttle box where a tone S^d set the occasion for shuttle-avoidance behavior. Four groups were trained to avoid electric shock on 1, 3, 9, or 27 consecutive trials. All rats were then returned to the Skinner box where they continued bar pressing for food. The tone was sounded while they bar pressed, and the effect this tone had on their response rate was measured. Kamin et al. (1963) found that following shuttle-avoidance training, the tone produced different levels of suppressed responses in each group. The groups that reached the shuttle-avoidance criterion of being successful on 3 and 9 consecutive shock avoidance trials apparently were more fearful of the tone to which they had been conditioned (i.e., the tone suppressed more responding than in the 1-trial group). Those rats with extensive experience on the shuttle-avoidance task that in the presence of the tone reached the criterion of 27 consecutive avoidance responses, however, showed a very different pattern. The somewhat surprising finding was that the tone did *not* suppress lever-pressing responses in this group.

Vigilance Replaces Fear.   One interpretation of this experiment is that fear first increases and then diminishes with increasing experience (and increasing success) in successfully making avoidance responses. We humans have no way to know whether these rats were fearful or merely uneasy as we would be. Because their avoidance behavior was maintained at a high level of proficiency, we know they were *motivated* to respond even though they were independently assessed as being less fearful (see Mineka, 1979, for a discussion of the independence of fear measures and avoidance responding). Humans monitoring radar screens in submarines and in air control terminals report high levels of *vigilance,* and autonomic nervous system measures tell us that they are physiologically aroused. But until and unless an emergency (a particularly configured pattern on the radar screen) occurs, fear is *not* present during these stressful avoidance tasks. As a final consideration, review the continuous and discrete avoidance tasks required of chimpanzees reported in Box 6.2. While maintaining a relatively high rate of lever pressing in the presence of the red S^d, 1-second duration discrete avoidance visual and auditory stimuli were presented. These stimuli elicited successful avoidance responses within a fraction of a second of their onset. Again, a state of vigilance rather than fear better characterizes the mental state of these monkeys (and of humans playing computer games).

Cognitive Analysis of Avoidance Behavior

Of the following two possibilities, which is more likely? Is the behavior of playing computer games maintained more by positive or by negative reinforcement contingencies? That is, is the attraction of playing games reinforcing because skilled responses produce positive consequences or because skilled responses prevent disaster? Another example: In playing a melody on the piano, depressing middle C on the keyboard is reinforced by the sound of middle C at the right time and in the right sequence in relation to other sounds. Pressing the middle C key when middle C is called for is positively reinforcing. Is it not also the case that the very same response is reinforcing because making the response *avoids* violating the expectation that the note should be there?

That is, appropriate responses to middle C avoid disharmony and prevent violation of the expected tempo.

Do animals develop *expectations* about the occurrence and nonoccurrence of events, and can they become more vigilant? Apparently so. Characterizing an animal's avoidance behavior in these terms provides a cognitive perspective to questions inherent in avoidance behavior (see Seligman & Johnston, 1973). For example, consider again Sidman's unsignaled avoidance task. Responding by rats to avoid shock has been demonstrated even when time cues predicting the shock-shock and response-shock intervals, were masked (Herrnstein, 1969; Herrnstein & Hineline, 1966). Instead of fear reduction, these researchers argued, rats merely learn that a contingency exists between their responses and shock reduction. Sometimes called a *one-factor theory of avoidance*, this theory stresses that rats are sensitive to rates of shock and that their lever-pressing patterns change in response to the shock schedule. Although the simplicity of this one-factor theory is appealing, it does not adequately address *why* the rat responds to avoid shock in the first place. Merely detecting a response-shock reduction contingency is not adequate *motivation* for a rat to bother to respond. Pain, fear, and vigilance are certainly the underlying motivation for animals trained with electric shock.

Persistence of Avoidance Responses

The preceding analysis helps us understand why avoidance responding is so slow to extinguish. Each avoidance response is at one and the same time *being reinforced* and *not being punished*. First, *a response is reinforced because it produces the desired outcome* (avoiding shock; avoiding falling on the ski slopes; avoiding an *F* on a test; avoiding hitting keyboard D when you wanted C; avoiding GAME OVER on the video screen, etc.). In addition, *the response prevents an undesirable, punishing outcome* (electric shock, falling, failing, fumbling, choking, etc.). Finally, a response is reinforced because *not responding* is punished. In learning avoidance responses, humans and animals are punished for not responding appropriately. Hitting keyboard D instead of C is punishing to an ear expecting C. Falling, failing, fumbling, and choking are punishing to an athlete.

Avoidance responses extinguish slowly, therefore, because the consequence of responding is reinforcement, and the consequence of not responding is punishment.

Interim Summary

1. *Negative reinforcement* is a process in which a response that is instrumental in either escaping or avoiding an aversive event is strengthened. A *negative reinforcer* is operationally defined as an event that when escaped from or avoided increases the rate of the preceding response.

2. In an *escape procedure,* a response is instrumental in removing or terminating an aversive stimulus; opening an umbrella in a torrential down pour is an example.

3. In an *avoidance procedure,* a response is instrumental in preventing or avoiding an aversive stimulus; opening an umbrella before walking out into a rain storm is an example.

4. Common laboratory investigations of negative reinforcement include *continuous,* or *free operant avoidance (Sidman avoidance)* or *discrete avoidance* tasks. These tasks may be either *signaled* or *unsignaled.*

5. On a Sidman avoidance task an animal must respond on a lever repeatedly to delay (avoid) an electric foot shock. If this free operant avoidance task is unsignaled, both the lever (and other stimuli within the Skinner box) and time cues act as discriminative stimuli that control the response rate.

6. Skilled human behavior is maintained by negative reinforcement. Examples include piano playing, operating word processors and automobiles, and following directions in filling out forms.

7. The two-factor theory of avoidance was first proposed by Mowrer (1947). Pavlovian-conditioned emotional behavior and instrumentally conditioned motor (skeletal) responses underlie two-factor theory.

8. Vigilance rather than fear seems to better characterize long-term avoidance behavior of both infrahumans and humans.

9. Avoidance responses are highly resistant to extinction because these responses have been reinforced in two different ways.

PUNISHMENT

Anyone who has received a speeding ticket can appreciate the complexity of emotional responses accompanying punishment: a sinking feeling when you notice the flashing blue lights in your rearview mirror. It is not quite fear, perhaps, unless there is an open container of alcohol in the car or your probationary period from the last ticket hasn't yet expired. Perhaps you feel confused and anxious as you anticipate the unknown. Yes. The fear may soon give way to denial and anger as you review the unjust contingencies to which you have been subjected. (No way could I have been going that fast! Why didn't you ticket the one that had just passed me? Cops should be out catching the *real* criminals. This is cruel and unusual punishment because it is going to cost me far more than it should. I drive fast but safely. Etc. Etc.)

Applying an Aversive Stimulus. The preceding scenario is an example of punishment because—as indicated in the top right-hand cell of Figure 6.1—a response (speeding) has produced an aversive consequence (a ticket and a fine). Response tendencies that diminish because they produce aversive consequences define the process of punishment. Does getting a speeding ticket result in less speeding? Not necessarily. We will consider the effectiveness of punishment below.

Withholding a Positive Stimulus.   Let us take another example. Your exam is returned and 67 is scrawled by your name. You vaguely remember that you had two other exams on that day and instead of studying all the material in the assigned chapters, you read only the chapter outlines. But the 67 still gives you the sinking feeling, followed perhaps by confusion, anger, resignation, and so forth. One way to analyze this complex behavioral sequence is to point out that you were punished for studying too little. The 67 is punishing only in reference to a 97 that you would have earned if you had read all of the assigned material. Your response (reading only the chapter outlines) was punished by *not* earning a good grade. Referring again to Figure 6.1, the bottom right cell describes the punishment contingency of a response not producing an expected reward. Another common example of this type of punishment is the time-out procedure used by parents and educators. Removing children from their social environment ("Go to your room!") prevents them from receiving reinforcers.

To summarize, the process of punishment can be effected by either applying a response-contingent aversive stimulus or by withholding an expected positive stimulus.[5]

What Is Punishing?

Innate or Primary Punishers.   What Thorndike labeled *annoyers* Skinner simply described as *aversive,* or *punishing, stimuli*. For humans and most other animals, common aversive stimuli include cold, heat, hunger and thirst, loud noises, and a host of environmental stimuli that can cause pain, nausea, and illness. A stimulus that is inherently aversive is called a **primary punisher.** The pain induced by spanking a child is an example of a physical or primary punisher.

Acquired or Secondary Punishers.   Neutral stimuli can also acquire secondary punishing properties through association with primary aversive stimuli. In one method described earlier, rats heard a neutral tone that was followed by a painful electric shock. In this *conditioned suppression* procedure, we hypothesized, the tone had two effects. It acted to suppress lever pressing and caused

---

[5] Punishment is a singular process described by two procedures. Some theorists use the term *positive punishment* to describe responses that produce an aversive consequence (i.e., speeding followed by a ticket) and *negative punishment* to describe responses that do not produce expected rewards (i.e., getting a grade of 67 rather than an *A* or *B*). The adjectives *positive* and *negative* are confusing in this context and will not be used here. (*Positive punishment* is another oxymoron, and *negative punishment* is redundant.)

emotional responses not unlike those you feel when you see lights flashing on a police car. Punishing properties of stimuli, then, can come from both innate predispositions and can be acquired through conditioning. The latter describes a **secondary punisher.** Spanking (physical pain) is a *primary* punisher, whereas scolding (psychological pain) is a *secondary* punisher. Another term for *psychological pain* is *learned pain*.

Combining Punishments.   Secondary punishers include social disapproval (nasty glances), ridicule, and other violated expectancies. Punishments are often combined. For example, having your phone service disconnected due to late payment combines two kinds of punishment. Disconnection violates your expectancies by depriving you of convenience (*removes* you from Thorndike's pleasing state of affairs). The cost in dollars (a penalty) to reconnect is the application of a punishing stimulus. *Penalty* is defined as "an imposed punishment for violating a rule." Penalties in our culture run the gamut from a yellow hanky thrown for being offside, to expulsion from school for low grades, and to fines, imprisonment, and capital punishment.

Separating Innate from Acquired Punishers.   Characterizing punishment as innate or acquired can be difficult. Consider, for example, the punishing effects of isolation. Solitary confinement in prison is considered to be one of the worst punishments a human can experience. Why is this so? One might argue that mammals are by nature gregarious or that they have a freedom reflex (Pavlov, 1927/1960). Or you might argue that a human acquires expectancies of social contact during a lifetime and that isolation violates these learned expectancies. Each is a reasonable explanation.

Another example of the difficulty of separating innate and acquired aspects of punishment can be found in how we use language. Consider the parent who uses abusive language to control a child's behavior. The abusive language may acquire some of its punishing properties by being paired with physical punishment. In addition, because loud noise by itself is punishing, innate aspects of abusive language cannot be ruled out. (Men are often accused of arguing unfairly because their voices are typically louder and arguably more innately punishing than women's voices.) Certainly, the secondary punishing properties of abusive language are confounded by a scolding or bullying delivery.

Reviewing the Nature and Procedures of Punishment.   Before considering whether punishment is effective in controlling behavior, let us briefly summarize and review what we have learned to this point by having you sort the following examples of punishment into four categories: (1) innate or (2) acquired and produced by either (3) applying a negative stimulus or (4) withholding an expected positive stimulus.[6]

---

[6] 1. acquired, withhold; 2. innate, withhold; 3. innate, apply; 4. acquired, withhold; 5. mixed, withhold; 6. mixed, withhold; 7. mixed, applied; 8. innate, applied; 9. acquired, applied.

1. Having one's driver's license revoked following a serious driving infraction.
2. Not feeding a hungry baby.
3. Spanking a crying baby.
4. Removing a hockey player to the penalty box for fighting.
5. Confining a child to her room for lying.
6. Reducing an employee's rank or salary because of incompetent behavior.
7. Making a child sit quietly in a classroom that is 90 degrees Fahrenheit.
8. Getting sick after eating a meal.
9. Quietly informing your lover you have found another.

How Effective Is Punishment?

On the basis of limited observations, both Thorndike (1932) and Skinner (1953) independently decided that punishment is relatively ineffective in controlling behavior. The general perception is that punishment can have long-lasting effects. It is especially ironic that Skinner concluded that relative to the way in which reinforcement permanently changed behavior, the effects of punishment are only temporary. During the past 40 years, new observations have led behavioral scientists to different conclusions, namely, that under the right conditions, punishment can have specific and permanent effects on behavior. Let us first look at factors we now know are important in punishment and then return to evaluate Skinner's position.

Rules of Punishment

In Chapter 3 we summarized many observations about the determinants of Pavlovian conditioning by specifying five rules that govern the acquisition of conditioned responses. Here we will also organize conclusions from many different experiments that have investigated the effect of punishment on behavior.

Punishment Is Associative.   A quick comparison of the rules governing the effectiveness of Pavlovian conditioning (including both acquisition and resistance to extinction measures) with those of punishment reveals a considerable degree of overlap. Both punishment training and Pavlovian conditioning are in part determined by (a) the intensity of the US or the punisher, (b) the number of conditioning trials, (c) the interval of time between the response and the punisher (or the CS and the US), and (d) the sequence (response→ punisher, or CS→US).

Other Common Associative Features.   In addition to these common processes during acquisition, both punishment procedures and Pavlovian conditioning procedures share the common effects of extinction, latent inhibition, generalization, and so on. From these observations we can tentatively conclude that punishment is an associative process. Under many circumstances punishment experiments yield outcomes similar to those of classically and reinforcement-based learning.

Punishment Intensity

The effect of punishment on responses is *directly related to the intensity of the pain-inducing stimulus*. Because it is easy both to quantify and to control, electric shock is used in many animal experiments. Severity of electric shock affects how rats run in the alley of a maze (Karsh, 1962) or bar press in a Skinner box (Storms, Boroczi, & Broen, 1962). Intensity of electric shock also affects how quickly humans learn *not* to open a cigarette case when they *are* punished for opening it (Powell & Azrin, 1968). Other commonly used punishing stimuli are aversive chemicals and toxins that, by their sickness-inducing properties, punish eating, drinking, and other consummatory responses. The familiar dose-response curves of nausea-inducing drugs accurately predict their punishing effects, for example, on suppressing the drinking of saccharin solution (Gamzu, 1977). Predictably, rats don't run as fast or lever press or lick as often, and humans become leery of opening a cigarette case when they have been shocked for doing so. Animals learn more or less rapidly, depending on shock intensity, level of poisoning, and intensity of other punishment treatments.

Skinner's Failed Punishment Experiment. Let us reexamine Skinner's (1953) mistaken conclusion about the effects of punishment. In one experiment, he used a low-intensity aversive stimulus—a spring-loaded lever that slapped the rat as it lever pressed for food (Skinner, 1938). After punishing lever-pressing responses with this slapping device, Skinner first demonstrated response suppression for a short period of time and then watched the response rate recover in extinction. Because responding recovered to baseline levels relatively quickly under these conditions, Skinner reasoned that punishment was ineffective in permanently altering behavior. As we saw in the preceding section, however, a punishment must be sufficiently intense to "work." From other experiments with other punishers, we now know that rats can be permanently trained not to lever press by consistently applying a relatively intense punishing stimulus. A simple conclusion is, then, that Skinner's slapping stimulus was too weak. His conclusion regarding punishment is suspect for an additional reason, namely, that extinction has the same effect on *reinforced* behavior as he observed for the slapped lever pressing. Responses diminish in extinction following both reinforcement and punishment procedures. A more parsimonious conclusion is that punished behavior is neither more nor less permanent than food-based behavioral change when the intensity of reinforcers and punishers is equated.

Does Low-Intensity Punishment Habituate?   Azrin, Holz, and Hake (1963) reported another interesting finding relating shock intensity and lever pressing. If the intensity of the punishing stimulus is low on the first few trials, the cumulative effect of numerous trials is less than it is in Pavlovian- or reinforcement-based conditioning. Initial trials with low-intensity punishment have the effect of *diminishing* the punishing properties of later trials using higher intensity aversive stimuli (Azrin et al., 1963). Again, the animals act as if they become habituated to the effects of electric shock in that higher shock intensity is ineffective in punishing behavior.

Performance Masks Punishment Effects.   An alternative explanation to shock habituation is that hunger-motivated lever pressing is sufficiently strong to mask the effects of punished responding. The question then becomes one of performance rather than learning. A human example illustrates this point quite well. Both children and adults can train themselves to self-administer insulin by painfully sticking a needle into their thigh muscle. Needle-sticking behavior should diminish because the response produces immediate pain. Out of necessity, however, some people stick themselves daily over many years.

Recently, following surgery, an elderly acquaintance of mine hired a home nurse. The nurse then afforded the opportunity to have someone else administer his daily insulin, and, not surprising, he was more than content to let the nurse do the honors. Why? The needle stick had been self-punishing over many years, and the response was clearly aversive. The needle-stick response, however, had been a necessity that prevented the aversive learning from showing. Recall, again, that hunger-motivated rats do not respond to low-intensity shock. If they had the alternative of *not* being hungry, the punishing properties of low-intensity shock would no doubt suppress a lever-pressing response. The point is that the *performance level* of a response is not always a reliable indicator that a response has (or has not) been learned.

Trials Effect

When an aversive stimulus is of sufficient intensity, punishment shows a *trials effect: The more frequently that responses are punished, the lower is the subsequent response rate*. A common way to measure the effects of punishment is to shock the lever-pressing responses of an animal working on a food-based schedule of reinforcement. Each response followed by shock is a trial. Using a moderately high-intensity shock, if every response in a work session is punished, rats stop bar pressing altogether. By contrast, rats shocked on every 100th or 500th response merely slow their rate of response. The rate of response is proportional to the number of punished responses (Azrin et al., 1963).

Results of Continued Punishment Training.   Once animals have learned the response-punishment contingency, their long-term behavior may change as they continue to be shocked. For high-intensity shocks, responses may remain suppressed indefinitely. For low-intensity aversive stimuli, the punishment may lose its effectiveness altogether. Under these conditions, the response rate has been demonstrated to recover even to its preshock level (Camp, Raymond, & Church, 1962). Low-intensity painful stimuli habituate, and, as a result, responses are not as effectively punished by the shock. Such habituation seems to act as if it immunizes the animal against experiencing higher levels of pain.

Response-to-Punishment Interval Rule

Earlier we argued that a 67 grade on a test paper punished the reading of chapter outlines in lieu of studying the text more thoroughly. It was also suggested that a 67 exam score might not change studying behavior in the same way that a traffic ticket often is ineffective in slowing drivers. One reason that a 67 might be ineffective in changing this student's behavior is that it was delivered 3 weeks after the response. In this example, many nonspecific responses are being punished by a secondary punisher delivered 3 weeks too late!

The preceding example not withstanding, punishment *is* an adaptive process that changes behavior. Punishment no less than reinforcement guides behavior by selecting from alternative responses those that produce the most pleasure and/or avoid the most pain. The CNS is designed to accomplish this task optimally under certain conditions. For example, some pain fibers are especially fast conducting. Both bee stings and touching a hot curling iron produce rapid reflexive responses and equally rapid association formation. A key to effective punishment is to mimic the reflexive S-R action of the nervous system by rapidly applying an aversive stimulus to the desired response. *The shorter the response-to-punishment interval, the more effective is the punishment treatment.* The adverse effects of delaying the punishing properties of electric shock following a lever-pressing response are detailed in Box 6.3.

Response-to-Punishment Contingency

A 67 on a test paper delivered 3 weeks after the examination is arguably noncontingent. Such treatment resembles the noncontingent punishment group described in Box 6.3. The noncontingent group violates the response-to-punishment *sequence* common to the other treatment groups (groups that in turn varied only by the response-to-punishment *interval*).

Why did we see a suppression of responses by this noncontingent punishment group? First, a few lever-pressing responses might have been paired with punishment in the same way that a *truly random control group* produces chance pairings. Second, we can speculate about nonassociative punishment effects. Third, punishment effects can be attributed to associations of aversive stimuli with the *context* in which they occurred rather than with specific responses. A general wariness about the testing environment might develop that

Box 6.3   Catch Him in the Act

THE FAR SIDE   By GARY LARSON

© 1984 FarWorks, Inc./Dist. by Universal Press Syndicate   9-26

"Harold! The dog's trying to blow up the house again! Catch him in the act or he'll never learn."

Gary Larson's cartoon captures the behavioral law relating to the ineffectiveness of delayed punishment. The effects of delaying the interval of time between a response and an electric shock is clearly seen in an experiment by Camp, Raymond, and Church (1962). The response-to-shock delays were 2.0, 7.5, and 30.0 seconds, and the results of these three groups were compared with a zero-second delay (i.e., immediate punishment), noncontin-gent punishment (group NC), and unshocked control group (control). Note that immediate shock is best, both in faster acquisition (asymptotic during the second training session) and in maintaining suppressed responding for the duration of the experiment. Note also that 2.0- and 7.5-second delays yield better suppression of responses than did 30-second delays.

The *noncontingent* punishment group was shocked during the session but not when it lever pressed. Note both the initial suppression and the long-term "dampening" effects on behavior of this group, relative to the control group. Apparently the NC group found the Skinner-box environment to be more aversive than did the control group. (Figure from Camp et al., 1962)

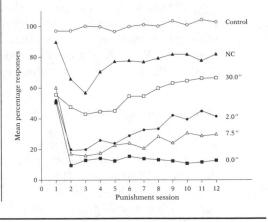

in turn affects the *performance* of the learned response. Is it possible that a general disdain for school in part reflects noncontingent punishment far removed from specific performances? Whether the response in question is lever pressing or writing the answer to a question, an immediate response-punishment contingency is the most effective way in which to change the desired response.

Another way to analyze the sequencing effects of aversive stimulation is to note that, by definition, punishment works only in one direction. If an aversive stimulus *precedes* a response and the response terminates that stimulus, the procedure is defined as *escape*. Responding *increases* following escape training procedures.

Latent Inhibition of Punishment

Recall that prior exposure to a CS or a US makes these stimuli familiar and that familiar stimuli do not condition as readily as novel stimuli. The phenomenon, known as *latent inhibition,* included the US preexposure effect (see p. 154). One explanation for the finding that a low-intensity punisher habituates and is no longer effective in controlling behavior is that punishers can also be latently inhibited. A number of laboratory demonstrations using a variety of stimuli have shown this to be the case. For example, shock is not as effective in punishing bar pressing when rats are familiar with it. In addition, a prior history with lithium makes it less effective in punishing saccharin drinking (Suarez & Barker, 1976). Punishers, then, can be latently inhibited in the same manner as CSs and USs.

Theories of Punishment

As was noted in Chapter 5, Thorndike's theory of punishment is a negative version of the law of effect—a recognition that animals have innate tendencies to seek pleasure and to avoid pain. Thorndike's theory of punishment, then, is an adaptive/evolutionary one. Skinner's atheoretical description of the effects of punishing stimuli on responding provides a contemporary *behavioral definition* rather than a theory of punishment.

In this section we look at one other theory of punishment, namely, the **two-factor theory of punishment** of Mowrer (1947, 1960) as elaborated by Dinsmoor (1954, 1977). As previously noted, Mowrer's theory of avoidance posited that learning proceeds in two stages. First, a fear response is conditioned classically and then an avoidance response is learned by reducing the fear response. Mowrer's punishment theory is similar. Cues in the environment, including the stimuli produced by the animals while responding, are classically (S-S) conditioned to the aversive punishing stimulus. In psychological terms, rats and humans *fear* or are wary of situations in which punishment has previously been meted out. Rats and humans can escape from their fear by engaging in some behavior other than the responses that have been punished (Dinsmoor, 1954). Humans, for example, often change those study habits that produced punishing consequences. Similarly, when faced with stimuli-predicting punishment, rats suppress lever pressing (measured) presumably by engaging in other behaviors (unmeasured).

Applying Punishment

> *"Beat me! Beat me!" said the masochist.*
> *"No!" said the sadist.*

We began this chapter by raising questions about *acquired motivation*. We now have several conceptual tools that may allow us to shed light on the intriguing bit of human behavior captured by the verbal interchange of these two maladjusted individuals. What reinforcement contingencies maintain the quite different roles that pain plays in the lives of the sadist and masochist?

Sadists.   We can dispose of the sadist quickly. Both sharp tongues and the playground bully's fists produce small victories in complex social interactions. Children reared in competitive environments are rewarded for being aggressively stronger, faster, and smarter and along other dimensions by which individual differences can vary.

Behavior learned in competition, however, does not always translate well in social interactions calling for cooperation. Winners deliver the punishment to losers. Sadists are reinforced for their behavior in part by not being punished for it. In social interactions, the sadist becomes a *discriminative stimulus* predicting punishment. Most humans are both wary of and suppress ongoing behavior in the sadist's presence.

Masochists.   The masochist's motivation is far more intriguing because the following simple question cannot be easily answered: How can pain become reinforcing? How do people apparently learn to use pain to give themselves pleasure?[7] Several psychologists have attempted to model this behavior using laboratory animals and have been surprisingly successful. Assuming that a low-intensity punisher can be used to signal as well as to punish, Holz and Azrin (1961) first trained pigeons to peck a key on a VI schedule for food. With the VI schedule still in effect, each pecking response was then punished with mild electric shock. The result was to halve the rate of key pecking. These food-reinforced sessions in which each peck was also punished alternated with non–punished, non–food-reinforced sessions. From the hungry pigeon's perspective, only electric shock predicted food availability. Therefore, the pigeon had to engage in masochistic behavior (self-induced pain) to find out whether food was available. Pain in this situation acts as an S^d that signals the presence of food. The pigeons eventually learned to continue pecking for food only if their key pecks were punished and to stop pecking if key pecking was *not* punished! Punished key pecking served as the S^d for food reinforcement.

Pain as an S^d for Pleasure.   Is it possible that masochists also learn to use pain as an S^d for pleasure? Another clever animal experiment suggests that this might be the case. First, rats were taught to run quickly down an electrified

---

[7] Recognize that theories of reinforcement and punishment *demand* that masochistic behavior be reinforcing. If masochism were punishing, our theory predicts that it would not exist because the masochistic responses would be consistently punished and thereby suppressed.

runway to a nonelectrified goal box. In this *escape* procedure, the rats were re-inforced by the termination of electric shock (cf. Figure 6.1, lower left cell). Af-ter learning this response, the rats were divided into two groups. For half the rats, the shock was turned off. For the other half, the section of the runway nearest the goal box remained electrified. You be the rat. What would you do under these circumstances? Let us first consider the extinction group—the group with the nonelectrified runway. For the first few trials you might run quickly even though you were not being shocked. (Recall that the experi-menter interprets your running speed to be a measure of *resistance to extinc-tion* of the learned escape response. The more slowly you run, the more your learned escape response has extinguished.) Eventually you might learn, as the rats in this group did, that you could take your time getting to the goal box, there to be removed and returned to your home cage.

What about the group encountering the electrified runway near the goal box? One might argue that the electric shock punishes entry into both the last part of the alley and the goal box. Since punished responses normally decrease in frequency, you might predict that rats would stay in the first part of the al-ley where they are not punished. The interesting finding in this situation is that punishment *increases* the speed of running relative to the nonshocked rats (Brown & Cunningham, 1981). By not entering the last part of the alley, the an-imal could escape shock altogether; apparently, however, the shock acts as a signal that the escape contingency is still in effect. Rather than freeze (for which there is no penalty—they would eventually be removed and returned to their home cage), they run in pain through the electrified portion into the goal box.

Abusive Relationships.   Perhaps like these rats, masochists seek punishment that when terminated is reinforcing. In other words, pain may become an S^d that is reinforced by its termination. For example, after being beaten by their abusive husbands, women leave them only to cyclically return. Such behavior appears to be maladaptive, and these women are often criticized for intention-ally putting themselves in harm's way. What is maintaining their behavior? A number of reinforcement and punishment contingencies can be identified. In addition to financial pressures of going it alone and learned social pressures to keep the family together, such women often have a learning history that in-cludes feelings of affection for the husband. In addition, beatings also have sig-nal value other than the pain induced. In abusive relationships, beatings are often followed by pleasurable sexual experiences with the same man who a few minutes earlier was inflicting pain. In these situations, then, pain signals are reinforced in two ways: first, by their cessation, and second, by pleasurable sensations of sex. It is no wonder that the cycle continues.

Interim Summary

1. Punishment is a process by which the application of an aversive stimulus decreases the frequency of response that precedes the aversive stimulus.

2. Punishment is associative and is affected by latent inhibition, extinction, generalization, and so forth.

3. The process of punishment is most effective when the punisher is intense, when the response-punishment interval is minimal, and when the response-punisher contingency is not degraded.

4. Noncontingent effects of punishment include a general response suppression. The response suppression may be due to the associative conditioning of aversive stimuli with environmental cues so that an adverse emotional state causes a performance decrement.

5. The effects of punishment are likely due to two processes: emotional conditioning of environmental cues and relief from aversive emotional states by making responses that minimize or remove these cues.

6. Masochistic behavior can be understood by recognizing that the cessation of pain is reinforcing, that the presence of pain becomes positive in that it signals that relief from pain is imminent, and that putting oneself into painful situations often reflects a past reinforcement history of pleasure derived from pain cessation.

INTEGRATION OF THEORIES: REINFORCEMENT AND PUNISHMENT WITH PAVLOVIAN AND INSTRUMENTAL CONDITIONING

We began this chapter by reviewing the role of reinforcement and punishment in learning theories. Each theorist suggested that a symmetry of sorts exists for the processes of reinforcement and punishment. For Skinner and Thorndike, punishment effects were construed not to be equivalent to reinforcement effects. Contemporary research has found that to the extent that a symmetry exists, it holds for a limited upper range of punishment intensities. In general, as summarized in Figure 6.1, punishment can be conceptualized as a mirror-image reversal of the associative process of reinforcement. Reinforcement increases and punishment decreases behavioral responses.

Similarities of Pavlovian and Instrumental Conditioning

This text has drawn parallels between reinforcement and punishment as well as between the processes and procedures of instrumental and Pavlovian conditioning. Is it possible to summarize the results of thousands of experiments in Pavlovian conditioning and instrumental learning? Risking oversimplification, Figure 6.5 is presented as an attempt to integrate these two systems of learning.

Note that the 2×2 matrix in Figure 6.5 incorporates some of the notation used in Figure 6.1. The matrix summarizes the associative effect of either (a)

	Pleasing Stimulus (S⁺)	Annoying Stimulus (S⁻)
The experimenter or a response **introduces**	(1) Name: *Positive reinforcement* (2) Effect: ↑ response rate (3) UR to S^+ → "pleasure" (4) CS^+ or S^d → "hope"	(1) Name: *Punishment* (2) Effect: ↓ response rate (3) UR to S^- → "pain" (4) CS^+ or S^d → "fear"
The experimenter or a response **removes**	(1) Name: *Punishment* (2) Effect: ↓ response rate (3) Absence of S^+ when expected → "confirmed disappointment" (4) CS^+ or S^d → "disappointment"	(1) Name: *Negative reinforcement* (2) Effect: ↑ response rate (3) Absence of S^- when expected → "relief" (4) S^d → "fear" or "vigilance"

FIGURE 6.5 Comparison of Classical and Instrumental Conditioning

Summary of sequence of events in both classical and instrumental conditioning, including (1) the name of the procedure, (2) the effect on ongoing behavior, (3) the psychological consequences of the procedures, and (4) expectancies in the presence of stimuli that signal the various procedures.

introducing or removing (b) pleasing or annoying stimuli (c) contingent upon either a response or another stimulus. The four possible outcomes are based on either increasing (positive and negative reinforcement) or decreasing the frequency of the preceding response (punishment).

Minimizing Differences in S-S and R-S Contingencies

The key to integrating Pavlov's system with the instrumental system is provided by notation to the immediate left of the matrix; namely, the experimenter, or a response *introduces* or *removes* (a pleasing stimulus, S⁺, or an annoying stimulus, S⁻). The experimenter introduces an *unconditioned stimulus*, and a response introduces a *reinforcer*. The terminology is different, but in both instances the animal is delivered a pleasing stimulus (S⁺). The present schema minimizes the traditional distinction between stimulus-stimulus (S-S) and response-stimulus (R-S) contingencies.

Moving inside the matrix, each of the four possible outcomes (1) has a name—*positive reinforcement* and *negative reinforcement*—and two different ways to *punish* behavior. Each process (2) either increases or decreases response rate, presumably because of (3) affective responses to the stimuli. The unconditioned psychological responses (as opposed to the measured be-havioral responses) to positive and negative USs are pleasure and pain. The conditioned psychological responses to the CSs that predict positive and aversive USs are (4) hope and fear, respectively. A similar analysis for pun-ishment and negative reinforcement can be found in the lower two panels of Figure 6.5.

As noted in earlier sections, learning occurs within stimulus contexts that set the occasions for responses to be either rewarded or punished. Examples from this chapter include red lights (S^ds) that come to control the behavior of both a monkey lever pressing to avoid shock and a human applying brakes to avoid a collision at an intersection. By way of comparison, in Pavlov's experi-ments dogs can be trained to salivate in the presence of a circle (CS^+) and not to respond to an ellipse (CS^-). The point is that in both systems responses come to be controlled by stimulus cues.

Unmeasured Emotional Responses.   These stimulus cues come to control affec-tive (emotional) responses in both systems. Presumably dogs are *disappointed* (bottom left cell) when an ellipse predicts no food, and rats are *disappointed* when their lever-pressing responses do not produce food as expected. Certainly humans would be. These emotional responses are seldom measured in learn-ing situations; rather, in the black box behaviorist tradition, emotional re-sponses are ignored. Recognizing that emotional responses likely accompany all learning situations, however, aids our understanding of an animal's learned behavior (Mowrer, 1960). Stimulus cues that have been associated with food or with shock set up expectations: *hope* that food is forthcoming and *fear* of im-pending shock. When expectations are not met, animals are *disappointed* and *relieved*, respectively.

Continuing our analysis of (4) in the lower left cell of Figure 6.5, we note that CS^- and S^D designate stimulus cues that set the occasion for the absence or removal of a reinforcing stimulus. After training, emotional responses elicited by CS^- and S^D cues have been labeled *disappointment*.

Interim Summary

1. A comparison of S-S and R-S conditioning paradigms in Figure 6.5 pre-sents the overwhelming impression that their similarities outweigh their differences.

2. From the animal's perspective, distinctive stimuli can be associated read-ily with good and bad outcomes. To the extent that animals respond in the presence of these stimuli, their responses—and those of humans—tend to be understandable within an adaptive/evolutionary framework.

3. R-S and S-S contingencies are important to theorists. From the animal's perspective, the experience of reinforcers and punishers may be more im-portant than whether a response was required to produce it.

4. Learned emotional responses are seldom measured in animal learning experiments.

5. Animals behave as if they have expectancies even though experimenters cannot effectively measure them.

6. Ignoring the cognitive/affective dimension of animal learning for the sole purpose of maintaining the integrity of a descriptive behaviorism is counterproductive at our present stage of theory development.

CHAPTER SUMMARY

1. Pavlov, Thorndike, Skinner, and Hull proposed traditional theoretical conceptions of reinforcement and punishment. Their terminology and methods of studying the two categories of reinforcing and punishing stimuli varied.

2. Pavlov identified appetitive and defensive reflexes and conditioned reflexes. Thorndikean satisfiers and annoyers stamped in and inhibited learned responses, respectively. Maintaining homeostatic balance was reinforcing in Hull's approach. All three recognized the adaptive/evolutionary significance of two classes of positive and negative stimuli having opposite effects on behavior.

3. By contrast, in Skinner's descriptive behaviorism, *reinforcement* is defined as the process of strengthening and *punishment* as the process of weakening responses, regardless of adaptive-evolutionary considerations.

4. Hull initially proposed a formal *drive-reduction theory* of behavior, later modified to a *drive-stimulus reduction theory*. Recognizing that physiological needs induce drives, he proposed to replace an S-R model of behavior with an S-O-R model. *Organismic* variables such as hunger determined the manner in which instrumental responses could be learned.

5. Reinforcers can be viewed as pleasing events or as the opportunity to engage in pleasing behaviors. Based on studies using electrical stimulation of the brain (ESB), many such operationally defined reinforcers have been found to have a common brain basis.

6. Tolman used the term *latent learning* to account for the fact that food reinforcement was not necessary for maze learning. Our current understanding of latent learning is that hungry rats in mazes engage in species-typical foraging behavior. Rats learn where food is not as well as where it is.

7. Escaping or avoiding aversive events is *negatively reinforcing*. Responses that either terminate aversive events or are instrumental in avoiding aversive events increase in frequency through the process of negative reinforcement. Accelerating to avoid an automobile collision is an example of a behavior maintained by negative reinforcement.

8. Mowrer (1947) proposed that avoidance responses were learned by two processes, classically conditioned emotional responses followed by instrumentally conditioned motor responses. Following conditioning, vigilance or fear responses to cues associated with the aversive stimulation are highly resistant to extinction.

9. Punishment is a process that results in lower rates of the response with which the punishing stimulus is associated. Punishment is affected by latent inhibition, extinction, generalization, intensity of punisher, short response-to-punishment intervals, and number of punishment trials.

10. A general decrement in overall performance following punishment is likely due to the conditioning of contextual cues with the punishing stimuli. The decrement is presumably due to a spread of negative affect, in the same way that food-reinforced contexts acquire secondary reinforcing properties.

11. Masochistic behavior is maintained by two sources of reinforcement: relief from pain and pain as a signal that its termination will follow shortly.

12. Parallels were drawn (Figure 6.5) between the use of pleasurable and aversive stimuli in two types of conditioning. Much evidence suggests that similar processes underlie S-S and R-S conditioning. It is most certainly the case that common affective responses are conditioned in all combinations of Pavlovian and instrumental reinforcement and punishment procedures.

DISCUSSION QUESTIONS

1. It has been commonly observed that only when sick do we become aware of how good we normally feel when healthy. That is, when healthy, most of us wouldn't describe our everyday lives as being *pleasurable* because a state of pleasure is subjectively better than *normal*. Tasty foods and jokes induce pleasure over and above our normal well-being. With this in mind, how would you answer the following question: Is pleasure the opposite of pain?

2. Is punishment the opposite of reinforcement?

3. Why is kissing not considered to be a *drive-reducing reinforcer?* Why is it reinforcing in some contexts but not in others?

4. Most parents attempt to use the secondary punishing properties of language to control their children's behavior. "No" (sometimes accompanied by spanking a hand) is understood by most English-speaking 18-month-olds. Under what conditions will the word "no" alone become a punishing stimulus? Why does "no" not work for some parents?

5. Gauging the appropriate intensity of secondary punishment is highly problematical. An interaction I had with a 4-year-old daughter made me acutely aware of my overreliance on (and the ineffectiveness of) parental scolding and bullying. My goal was to teach her to say "please" and "thank you." My method was to constantly scold her for omissions and to reinforce her (praise her) for correct language usage. Leaving a restaurant one evening (after having scolded her during the meal), we happened on a window display of sides of beef hanging in a butcher shop. Curious as to what a 4-year-old thought about the display, I asked her why she thought they were hanging there. "Because they didn't say 'please'? " she offered.

What have you learned about the nature of punishment that makes her response understandable? Why should parents use punishment more sparingly than most of us do? Assuming that you will want your children to say please and thank you, what reinforcement (and punishment) contingencies will *you* use?

6. High school coaches and aerobic instructors alike talk about "no pain, no gain." The long-distance runner is exhorted to push through the pain barrier. In what way is athletes' use of pain to perform better similar to the way a person in an abusive relationship uses pain to achieve pleasure? What are the differences?

7. Many skiers look for increasingly difficult downhill runs, perhaps to experi-

ence the pleasure of conquering fear as well as to experience the exhilaration of speed and control. Many skiers also think that falling down is a signal that they are sufficiently challenging themselves and that only through such challenges will they become better skiers. Why is "no pain, no gain" too simple to account for a skier's motivation?

8. What motivates you to study for your exams? Why do many people spend a great deal of time watching TV? Can you identify positive and/or negative reinforcement contingencies for each behavior?

DISCUSSION STARTERS

1. *Is pleasure the opposite of pain?* Pleasure, pain, and other subjective psychological experiences are the product of interactions of brain and neuroendocrine activity. The apparent dichotomy of pain and pleasure is belied by the complexity of human experiences. People can be tickled until they cry. Ballet dancers experience pleasure while their feet are bleeding. Presumably, these complex experiences result from other unique forms of brain activity.

2. *Is punishment the opposite of reinforcement?* The effect of reinforcement and punishment in laboratory experiments using lever pressing, alley-way entries, and other simple responses suggests the simple symmetry of a push-pull system. Punishment appears to be neither as addictive as certain reinforcers can become, however, nor as selective in its effects on a particular behavioral response.

3. *Why is kissing not considered to be a drive-reducing reinforcer? Why is it re-*

inforcing in some contexts but not in others? Kissing as foreplay to orgasm would not constitute *drive reduction*. On the other hand, assume that physical contact is a biological drive. It could then be argued that extending to a socially isolated individual, for example, a child or a lover, the opportunity to kiss could be drive reducing. Evidence that kissing is not reinforcing to all individuals? A 10-year-old boy overheard telling his sister to go kiss a fish.

4. *Why does "no" not work for some parents?* The word *no* could become a punishing stimulus by itself if it were consistently punished and/or never reinforced. For a variety of reasons many parents are not consistent in reinforcing and punishing behavior. See the next question.

5. *Why should parents use punishment more sparingly than most of us do?* Assuming that you will want your chil-

dren to say please and thank you, what reinforcement (and punishment) contingencies will you use? Being consistent and gauging the appropriate intensity of punishment are difficult tasks. In addition, punishment lacks the selectivity of response that reinforcement offers. Because parents are busy and because they provide only a portion of the environment that administers reinforcers and punishers, children's responses are not consistently reinforced or punished. Advice regarding table manners: Primarily use reinforcement and prepare to be patient for many, many years.

6. *In what way(s) do athletes use pain to improve performance?* Athletes use pain as one form of feedback to monitor their physical efforts. A common misperception, to take one example, is that athletes running marathons are in some way insensitive to pain or that they are able to push themselves through the pain barrier. On the contrary, exceptional marathoners are highly sensitive to any pain they might be experiencing. A cramp or blister one third of the way through a race is often interpreted as a nuisance by the occasional runner, but as a race-ending or race-limiting injury to the professional. Unlike other types of masochistic behavior, however, the pleasure for most athletes is in competing, and pain is not a sought-after end in itself. Having said this, my impressions are that this is one of those proverbial gray areas and that humans are fully capable of concurrently being both masochistic and hedonistic.

7. *Why is "no pain, no gain" too simple to account for a skier's motivation?* Skiers of different abilities ski for various reasons. Some abhor pain while others take competitive risks that incur pain. *Sensation-seeking* behavior is beyond the scope of this book. I assume that the roots of both *sensation-seeking* and of *competitive behavior* are psychobiological, that is, that both have biological origins tuned by the environment.

8. *What motivates you to study for your exams? Why do many people spend a great deal of time watching TV? Can you identify positive and/or negative reinforcement contingencies for each behavior?* The answer to the first question is a personal one because each reader has different goals and aspirations and reasons for being in school. It would be worth your while to stop and examine yours in terms of the concepts of reinforcement you learned in this chapter.

TV watching is more of a challenge to analyze. In your analysis, don't neglect both escape and avoidance contingencies.

KEY TERMS

Acquired Incentives Stimuli paired with innate incentives such as food and water in Hull's system (and *secondary reinforcers* in Skinner's system).

Acquired Motivation Behavior motivated by secondary reinforcers. (Primary reinforcers provide innate motivation.)

Avoidance Procedure Any procedure in which an animal's instrumental response prevents an aversive consequence. Example: a lever press prevents or avoids delivery of electric shock.

Behavioral Contrast A contrast procedure that demonstrates that reinforcement/punishment effects are determined in part by the immediate context in that these stimuli are delivered and the animal's prior history with other reinforcers/punishers. (Also known as *incentive contrast;* see *negative contrast.*)

Discrete Avoidance A procedure in which a stimulus sets the occasion for an avoidance response that, when emitted, delays or prevents an aversive stimulus.

Drive Reduction Theory (Hull) Behavior that fulfills specific *needs* (i.e., restores an organism to homeostatic balance) reduces drives. *Drive reduction* reinforces the instrumental behavior in Hull's theory.

Drive States (Hull) Motivated behavior translated from specific physiological needs resulting from food and water deprivation.

Drive-Stimulus Reduction The theory that stimulus properties of incentives, not the necessity of meeting physiological needs, are sufficient to reduce drive states.

Drive Theory See *drive reduction theory.*

Electrical Stimulation of the Brain (ESB) Passing minute amounts of electric current through an implanted electrode to specific areas of the brain to act as a reinforcer.

Escape Procedure A procedure in which an animal makes an instrumental response that has the effect of terminating an aversive stimulus.

Incentive Motivation Motivation to behave that can be attributed to the quality and amount of a reinforcer.

Latent Learning (Tolman) Learning that is alleged to occur in the absence of specific food rewards.

Needs Physiological requirements (such as food and water) necessary for maintaining life.

Negative Contrast The proposal that after experiencing both a small and a large reward, their comparison makes the perception of the smaller reward more negative than it would be in the absence of the contrast. See also *behavioral contrast.*

Negative Reinforcement The process by which responses that are instrumental in preventing or avoiding an aversive stimulus *increase* in frequency. (Cf. *Punishment.*)

Premack Principle David Premack's theory that the more probable of two responses always reinforces the less probable response.

Primary Punisher A stimulus that is inherently aversive.

Punisher Any stimulus whose application acts to decrease the rate of emission of the preceding response.

Punishment The process by which an aversive stimulus acts to decrease the rate of the response to which it is applied.

Secondary Punisher Stimuli that acquire punishing properties through a conditioning procedure. Example: The word *no*. (Cf. *Secondary Reinforcement.*)

Shuttle Box An apparatus in which animals can be conditioned to *escape* and/or *avoid* electric shock by jumping across a barrier dividing the two compartments of the shuttle box.

Shuttle-Avoidance Avoidance conditioning in which the terminal behavior is to jump over a barrier (cf. *shuttle*) separating two compartments of a shuttle box.

Sidman Avoidance A negative reinforcement procedure designed by Murray Sidman in which the lever in a Skinner box is the only signal that electric shock can be delayed/avoided by continuously lever pressing.

Social Reinforcement Theory (Bandura) A theory that human learning is accomplished primarily by innate imitation and modeling of observed behavior.

S-O-R Theory (Hull) A neobehaviorist S-R theory in which intervening variables, specifically *organismic* variables such as thirst and hunger, are considered in the functional relationship between stimulus and response variables.

Two-Factor Theory (Mowrer) A theory proposing that two factors underlying avoidance behavior are Pavlovian-conditioned emotional behavior and instrumentally conditioned motor (muscle) responses.

Two-Factor Theory of Punishment A theory that punishment learning is accomplished in two stages (i.e., a fear response that is first conditioned classically and then an avoidance response that reduces the fear response).

CHAPTER 7

INTEGRATION OF LEARNING, PHYSIOLOGY, AND BEHAVIOR

Among the many human feelings that, although culturally mediated, may be fundamentally preprogrammed, we might list sexual attraction, falling in love, jealousy, hunger and thirst, horror at the sight of blood, fear of snakes and heights and "monsters," shyness and suspicion of strangers, obedience to those in authority, hero worship, dominance of the weak, pain and weeping, laughter, the incest taboo, the infant's smiling delight at seeing members of its family, separation anxiety, and maternal love. There is a complex of emotions attached to each, and thinking has very little to do with any of them. Surely, we can imagine a being whose internal life is nearly wholly composed of such feelings, and nearly devoid of thought.
    Sagan and Druyan, *Shadows of Forgotten Ancestors* (1992, p. 169)

INTRODUCTION

Before this we have been concerned with laboratory animal-based studies of learning and behavior. Specifically, we have seen that reinforcement and punishment can modify both simple reflexes and simple responses in all animals, including, of course, humans. In this chapter we shift our focus to analyses of more complex behavior. How well does what we have learned about simple systems stand up?

The opening quotation from *Shadows of Forgotten Ancestors* raises questions about defining aspects of complex human behavior. Sagan and Druyan (1992) assert that such behaviors are as innately determined as are the patellar and eye-blink reflexes. The truth of their assertions await further research in the fields of behavioral genetics, primatology, sociobiology, and neuroethology. For now we can continue to ask questions about the role that learning plays in modifying such complex behaviors. Our task is formidable and the outcome of great importance. A learning theory that cannot address human arenas of sex and love, of relationships and family, of education and therapy, of popular culture and careers, of eating and drinking, of drug taking and health is a waste of our time.

ANALYSIS OF COMPLEX BEHAVIOR

We know that simple reflexes and simple motor responses are easily conditioned. We need to know the answers, however, to a number of questions. How does learning affect more complex physiological functioning? How can learning affect the immune system, for example? Humans behave in ways that seem to involve conscious choice; we select certain foods, drinks, and drugs. Does our human consciousness, our human language, and our so-called voluntary behavior change the rules regarding processes of behavioral change? Does our humanness make suspect a reliance on animal models of learning, thereby requiring more sophisticated learning theories than those based on simple association? Or, as suggested in the opening quotation, do we humans, not unlike other animals, live emotionally charged lives without much thought?

We begin by analyzing several of these questions: Given similarities in human and nonhuman physiology and behavior, what inferences can we make regarding differences in mind and consciousness? What is the relationship of mind to learning and behavior?

Comparative Analysis of Physiology, Behavior, and Mind

Geneticists posit the continuity of all life forms through evolutionary processes (Chapter 2), and within this framework, behavioral scientists have developed a conception that general processes of learning exist across vertebrates (Chapters 3–7). A common vertebrate physiology reflects our continuous genetic history. Most people in our culture readily accept the fact that a comparative mammalian physiology exists, that lungs are lungs, and that lymphatic systems, immune systems, and the physiology of digestion work in about the same way. We recognize that bacterial infections are the scourge of humans and animals alike.

Continuous Brains, Discontinuous Minds?

Moreover, our culture generally acknowledges that research in animal physiology directly underlies our knowledge of human physiology, of human disease states, and of medical practice. Most people would even agree that brain structures of humans and animals are related. Nonetheless, many think that brain *functioning* of nonhuman animals is somehow discontinuous with that of humans.[1]

Recall our discussion in Chapter 2 of the question of conditioning differences in humans and other animals. There we advocated that researchers should follow the law of parsimony (interpret findings using the simplest explanations possible) and should adopt a zoomorphic position (recognize that humans are animals). Here we raise a question that can be asked of all animals: Is a distinction between voluntary and involuntary behavior a meaningful one?

Voluntary and Involuntary Behavior

Two distinctions have traditionally been made regarding the concepts of **voluntary behavior** and **involuntary behavior.** One is that humans alone are capable of voluntary behavior. The second is that there are voluntary and involuntary aspects of human behavior. Walking and talking are examples of voluntary behavior, and digestion, breathing, and the regulation of fluids are examples of involuntary behavior.

CNS and ANS.   Historically, the central nervous system (CNS) has been said to cause voluntary behavior while the autonomic nervous system (ANS) controls involuntary behavior. This partitioning of behavior permeated learning theory into the 1960s. B.F. Skinner, among others, proposed that S-S conditioning was ANS mediated and R-S conditioning was CNS mediated (Skinner, 1938). That is, responses by skeletal muscles (such as those used in running a maze, or pressing a lever, or talking) controlled by the CNS could be conditioned by reinforcement and punishment. By contrast, salivation was ANS controlled, and Pavlovian conditioning (Skinner used the term *respondent conditioning*) was presumed to be controlled by the brain's involuntary functioning.

Experiments by Neil Miller and Associates.   Several researchers set out to test the preceding relegation of two types of conditioning to different nervous systems. They questioned whether it was possible to get *voluntary* control over autonomic nervous system functioning. They made skeletal muscles (controlled by

---

[1] See Ludvigson (1989) for a brief history of how psychologists have wrestled with human/animal issues of mind during this century. A more detailed treatment of comparisons of the human and animal minds can be found in Boaks (1984).

the CNS) nonfunctional to rule out their inadvertent effect on the ANS. Laboratory rats were totally paralyzed with curare (*d-tubocurarine*) and put on artificial respiration for the duration of the experimental procedure (Miller & Banuazizi, 1968). An ESB reinforcer was made contingent on slight changes in the rat's heart rate. As illustrated in Figure 7.1, they demonstrated that heart rate was effectively controlled by the ESB reinforcement. Miller and his colleagues

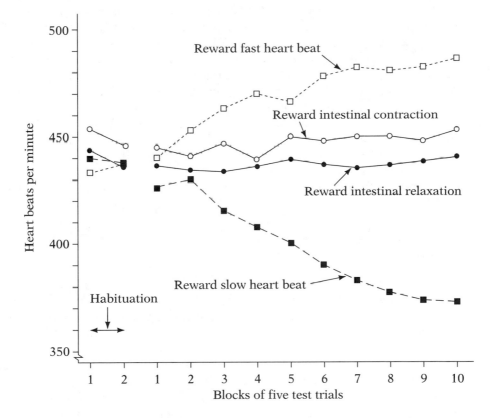

FIGURE 7.1   Conditioning Heart Rate

Using ESB to reinforce slightly increasing (top dashed line) or slightly decreasing (bottom dashed line) changes in heart rate elevates or lowers heart rate throughout a 50-trial period of time. A control group in which ESB reinforced intestinal contraction or relaxation had no effect on heart rate. The control group allows us to conclude that the pleasant sensation of ESB by itself does not systematically increase or decrease heart rate. (From Miller & Banuazizi, 1968) concluded that voluntary control over involuntary brain functioning was possible.[2]

Can we resolve the issue of whether voluntary behavior is the exclusive province of humans? Probably not to the reader's satisfaction. Consider the following irony. Voluntary behavior is behavior under stimulus control (Jonas, 1972). If asked to voluntarily raise your arm, you can, on cue. The words *raise your arm,* or your thoughts to raise your arm are discriminative stimuli (S^ds) that control your behavior. You can voluntarily play music on the piano. The music you play is tied to past instruction in which the notes you play cue the next notes and so on. Jonas (1972) argues that any demonstration of voluntary behavior is tied to past learning, making voluntary behavior no different from other learned responses. Shades of Skinner! Miller's experiments show that visceral responding (under the control of the ANS) can also be brought under stimulus control. Obviously, the voluntary responses of animals can also be brought under stimulus control, making unnecessary yet another artificial division of humans from other animals.

Thought question 1: What is the difference between demonstrations of one's heart racing because of revolving blue and white lights in the rearview mirror and heart-rate increases in rats reinforced for doing so?

Thought question 2: What are the implications of Miller's demonstration experiment for *behavioral medicine* (i.e., medicine based on behavioral manipulation rather than drugs or surgery)? We return to these questions later.

ARE CNS AND ANS SEPARATE?

The blurring of distinctions between S-S and R-S conditioning in the last chapter may allow you to answer the first thought question. Behavioral scientists are currently less interested in S-S and R-S distinctions than they once were. Similarities in the presumed processes underlying "both" kinds of learning have been detailed (e.g., Bindra, 1972), and there is now evidence of remarkable interactions among what were once thought to be relatively isolated physiological systems. So, Thought Question 2 is of more interest. Which physiological systems, in what ways, can be controlled by the environment? If, as alluded to earlier, the immune system can be affected by Pavlovian conditioning, distinctions between ANS and CNS and between S-S and R-S conditioning become less important. Keep in mind that resolution of this issue also has implications for questions of voluntary and involuntary behavior.

---

[2] The experiment is technically difficult to accomplish, and several attempts to replicate it have been unsuccessful. In light of other demonstrations and experiments in this chapter, however, the conclusion that voluntary control can be achieved over certain aspects of involuntary brain functioning seems irrefutable.

Studies of neuroendocrine, immune system, CNS, and ANS functioning in the past decade have led to a new integration and redefinition of these systems (Booth & Ashbridge, 1992). Evidence from a wide variety of studies (Husband, 1992) now attests to the fact that these systems are interconnected: One such holistic configuration is diagrammed in Figure 7.2. The conclusions are that (a) the central and autonomic nervous systems are more interconnected than they are conceptually separate, (b) distinctions between voluntary and involuntary behavior have become blurred, and (c) S-S and R-S differences, to the extent that they exist, likely have little basis in brain organization.

COMPLEX REFLEXES

Simple reflexes were listed in Table 3.1 (p.91). Compare them with those listed in Table 7.1. These added reflexes are more complicated, highly integrated response systems that involve the brain, immune, and neuroendocrine systems. Consider pain, eating and drinking, and sexual behavior. Are these merely reflexive behaviors, or is more mind involved? Are we reflexive machines, or is will involved in the experience of pain and pleasure, in what we eat and drink, and in how we select mates and make love? These are among the issues considered in this chapter.

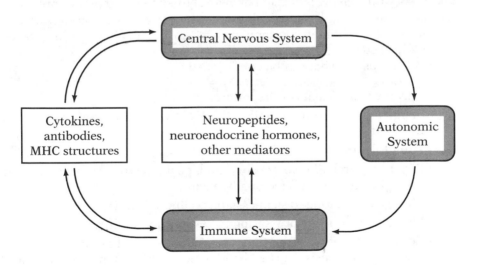

FIGURE 7.2

A schematic representation of the interactions of CNS, ANS, immune, and neuroendocrine systems. (From Booth & Ashbridge, 1992)

TABLE 7.1   Types of Complex Reflexive-Like Behavior

Eliciting Stimulus (Source: Environment, Darwin's "Nature")	*Reflex* (Source: DNA's programmed response)
Ingestion of toxin	Nausea, loss of appetite, vomiting
Salt loss	Aldosterone release, salt appetite
Morphine	Pupillary dilation, warming
Cedar pollen	Histamine release
Antigens	T-lymphocyte release
Stimulation of genitalia	Erection (M), vaginal lubrication (F)
Tissue damage	Pain, crying, clenching teeth
Localized heat	Tissue damage, pain, blister
Strange food	Wariness, caution (neophobia)
Strange human, animal	Wariness, caution (neophobia)
Death of a loved one	Weeping, wailing, sadness, depression

Conditioning Complex Physiological Systems

Mind and behavior are integral to the interconnected functioning of these physiological systems. In the remainder of this chapter we explore research and theory underlying issues in behavioral medicine and other applications of learning relative to physiological functioning. How do physiology and behavior interrelate? Is human consciousness a factor? Can all physiological systems be conditioned?

A brief list of what *can* be conditioned follows:

- Various components of the immune system.
- Temperature, reactivity, and pain (ANS) when drugs are used as unconditioned stimuli.
- Drug tolerance.
- Physiology relating to sensory and postingestive homeostatic mechanisms concerned with feeding behavior.
- Physiology relating to sickness and wellness behavior.
- Physiology of behavior relating to sexual functioning.
- Components of both the CNS and ANS relating to emotional responses (including neurosis, learned helplessness, phobias, post-traumatic stress disorder, etc.).

This list is impressive. We begin our analysis of conditioning complex physiological systems by examining psychosomatic interactions in the next section.

Interim Summary

1. Historically, the DNA, physiology, and reflexive behavior of humans has been viewed as continuous with that of other animals. Voluntary behavior, however, has been attributed only to humans.

2. Voluntary behavior has been attributed to the higher cortical functioning of humans. Other complicated animals have similar brain structures and brain functioning, however.

3. The distinction between voluntary and involuntary physiological systems—mediated by the CNS and ANS, respectively—has been blurred by evidence of their interdependence.

4. Miller and his associates accomplished heart-rate conditioning research that broke down the distinctions between CNS and ANS, voluntary and involuntary behavior, and Pavlovian and instrumental conditioning.

PSYCHOSOMATIC INTERACTIONS

With his simple demonstrations of psychic secretions at the turn of the century, Pavlov (1927/1960) began the experimental study of *psychosomatic interactions* (*psyche,* meaning *mind; soma,* meaning *body*). The perception of a ringing bell affected the body's saliva flow. He could not have foreseen that Pavlovian conditioning would become the primary research methodology for contemporary studies of behavioral medicine. When psychosomatic interactions produce deleterious effects in either the anatomy or physiology, they are called **psychosomatic disorders.**

Let us take as an example of a psychosomatic interaction the following bit of intriguing human behavior. By applying research findings and theories encountered in preceding chapters, try to hypothesize what is happening. A hypnotist and his subject, both males, performed this demonstration on "live" television:

> A hypnotic trance is induced and then deepened. After sufficient preparation, the hypnotist shows the audience a piece of chalk, tells the subject "I'm now going to burn you with a lighted cigarette," and then places the chalk on an exposed forearm. The subject's arm jerks away.
> "Did it hurt?" the hypnotist asks.
> "Yes, it did," the subject replies.
> The camera focuses on the arm. First there is a reddening of the skin where the chalk had been placed, and, within minutes, a blister appears.[3]

[3] I saw this demonstration on "The Paul Coates Show," truly "live" television without interuptions or gimmicks in the early 1950s in Los Angeles. It has since been replicated in the laboratory (Spanos & Chaves, 1989).

The Blister Reflex

Assume that the demonstration was not rigged. How might the blister be explained? We could focus on the hypnotic state or perhaps posit subconscious (or unconscious) mechanisms. Perhaps cognitive processes mediated the behavior. By contrast, a more parsimonious Pavlovian might begin by asking about reflexes and about how normal blisters are formed. Could the arm jerk be a conditioned withdrawal reflex initiated by chalk touching the skin? Note in Table 7.1 that blister formation can be thought of as a reflexive response to localized heat: In Pavlovian terms, the US = localized heat; the UR = blister (and tissue damage, pain, etc.). The physiology is somewhat more complicated.

Physiology of Blisters

Capillaries become increasingly permeable when skin is heated (the eliciting stimulus), and plasma loss produces the localized edema called a *blister* (the reflexive response). Might blister formation in the absence of heat be considered a *conditioned reflex?* If so, how was it conditioned? The student might want to stop and construct a possible conditioning scenario that might have preceded the televised demonstration.

Analysis of Blisters as CRs.   If the phenomenon in question is a conditioned response, what might the CS or CS-complex be? Three possible CSs are (a) the chalk, (b) the touch on the forearm, and (c) the hypnotist's words. The placement of the chalk on the forearm informed the brain where to place the blister. The operative CS, however, was the word *burn*. Had the hypnotist done everything the same except to use a different word for *burn* (such as, "I'm now going to *murph* you with a lighted cigarette"), it is unlikely that the blister would have formed.

Remembering Pavlov's Second Signal System.   Given the preceding analysis, what the TV camera did not show us were the conditioning trials preceding the demonstration. More than likely the subject had previously experienced burns (including cigarette burns) and consequent blister formation. Most humans have had such experiences. It is likely that the word *burn* functions as a CS in this and other situations. As we saw in an earlier section, Pavlov's (1927/1960) analysis of the *second signal system* detailed how our language can be considered the signal of signals, a representation of reality one level removed from incoming first-order sensory signals. To the extent that language is learned, many of our nouns and verbs have been associated with objects and actions in the environment. A lighted cigarette is an object that burns. Apparently, the word signaled the reflex, thereby eliciting blister formation.

Differences in Reflexive Conditioning?

Does the preceding conditioning analysis completely explain the phenomenon in question? No. Too many questions remain. Blisters and warts can apparently be readily conditioned in a hypnotic state (Spanos & Chaves, 1989), while other demonstrations of conditioning occur during normal consciousness.[4] Although normal conditioning can be accomplished with all conscious vertebrates, estimates are that probably only 10 to 30% of adult humans could make conditioned blisters (Hilgard, 1979). Another argument against a general process learning theory account of the blister phenomenon is that similar demonstrations involving nonhuman animals have not been reported. (Taking the argument in a different direction, blister formation is merely a reflex, and reflexes are readily conditioned in all animals.)

If one maintains that only humans can make conditioned blisters, however, because humans alone have higher cognitive processes, the law of parsimony would be violated. Indeed, if a blister were to appear on the skin of a human (in the absence of heat or known disease process), psychological dysfunctioning would be suspected. The fake blister would likely be seen as a psychosomatic disorder. It is more parsimonious to ask whether evidence exists that complex physiological responses can be conditioned in humans and animals. The answer to this question is a resounding yes. Does conditioning provide a good model for psychosomatic disorders in general? Again the answer is yes, as we will see throughout the chapter (see also Ader, Weiner, & Baum, 1988).

Interim Summary

1. Behavior affects physiology as readily as physiology affects behavior.
2. The distinction between voluntary and involuntary physiological systems, between voluntary and involuntary behavior, and between S-S and R-S conditioning becomes clouded when one considers their many interactions.
3. Heart rate and other aspects of the cardiovascular system regulated by both CNS and ANS can be conditioned.
4. As a result of their interactions, the CNS, ANS, immune system, and other physiological systems are now better conceptualized as an interdependent, integrative holistic system.
5. Behavior mediated by the CNS, ANS, and immune system provides the basis for psychosomatic interactions.
6. Blisters can be conditioned.

---

[4] While nonhypnotized subjects in theory could be conditioned to blister, I am not aware of controlled demonstrations to this effect. (See, however, the related example of hive formation in this chapter.)

7. Pavlovian conditioning provides a defensible account of psychosomatic disorders and is one of the primary research methodologies of contemporary behavioral medicine.

THE IMMUNE SYSTEM AND PSYCHONEUROIMMUNOLOGY

> *The biological sciences have become compartmentalized and bureaucratized—and that simply reflects our ignorance. I'm a psychologist, you're a biochemist, a pharmacologist, [or] an immunologist. We've divided the pie into manageable pieces. But this division has no bearing on the biology. The biology doesn't recognize these disciplines. There is only one organism, and the nature of the relationships among systems is every bit as important, functionally, as the relationships within a system.*
>
> *The mind and the body [are] the same thing. . . . they are inseparable components of the whole. . . . You see, we have a funny language. To talk about mind and body is to set up a dichotomy. . . . We have a one-dimensional language for a three-dimensional problem.*
>
> Robert Ader, in Bill Moyer, *Healing and the Mind* (1993, p. 245)

As suggested by Figure 7.2, the term **psychoneuroimmunology** is an area of research that studies the interconnectedness of the immune system, brain, mind, and behavior. As we will see, Ader has developed an animal model that demonstrates how the immune system can be conditioned. Let us start by trying to understand how the immune system is believed to function *without* the complications of psychology.

Immune System Functioning

The function of the immune system in mammals is to resist toxins and infectious organisms that might cause damage to tissues and organs. *Acquired immunity* describes the process whereby antibodies and sensitized lymphocytes (white blood cells) destroy invading organisms and toxins.

T-lymphocytes play an integral role in the immune system. Present at birth, they directly bind to the membranes of invading cells (such as a cancer cell or the cells of a transplanted heart). T-lymphocytes then release both *lysomal enzymes* (that directly attack the cell's integrity) and a *macrophage chemotaxic factor* (that attracts other killer cells to the site). From a Pavlovian reflex perspective, infectious organisms can be thought of as the US and T-lymphocyte production and functioning as the UR.

Conditioning the Immune System: T-lymphocytes

Ader and his associates demonstrated that the number of T-lymphocytes present in rats could be manipulated by a simple conditioning experiment (Ader, 1985). First, they injected rats with a drug called Cytoxan® (the US). The next day they recorded a reduced T-lymphocyte count (the UR). (Cytoxan® is a ra-diomimetic drug known generically as *cyclophosphamide*.[5] It is routinely used in chemotherapy to suppress immune system functioning, including the low-ering of T-lymphocyte production.)

Conditioned Immunosuppression.   Ader and associates then conditioned the rats by allowing them to drink a saccharin solution (the CS), followed by the Cy-toxan® injection (the US). A control group received saccharin and Cytoxan® noncontingently. After several trials, one per day, they recorded the number of T-lymphocytes when the rats drank saccharin. Drinking saccharin in the ab-sence of the drug is an extinction test. Ader found fewer T-lymphocytes relative to controls that drank saccharin but had not been conditioned.

The reduction of T-lymphocytes following this conditioning procedure is called **conditioned immunosuppression.** Presumably, the saccharin had become associated with the drugs, and components of the immune system re-sponded to the saccharin flavor in the same way that it had to the drug. It is likely that the mechanisms that allow conditioning of the immune system are recently discovered CNS nerve fibers serving immune system cells (Felten, 1993).

Conditioned Facilitation of Immune Response.   Ader's demonstration of condi-tioned immunosuppression was the first of many investigations in a research area now called *psychoneuroimmunology*. **Conditioned facilitation** of the im-mune response has since been reported, using exteroceptive stimuli as CSs (Bovbjerg, Cohen, & Ader, 1987; Gorczynski, Macrae, & Kennedy, 1982; Krank & MacQueen, 1988). In the research by Krank and MacQueen, for example, *in-creases* in antibody production were conditioned. They injected mice with cy-clophosphamide while the mice drank water in a distinctive environment (a novel room in which 80 dB music was played). Mice exposed to this distinctive room and music in extinction produced higher levels of antibodies compared to groups of mice in which there was no prior pairing of these stimuli with the drug. Possible reasons for the differences between this study and Ader's find-ing of suppression of antibodies are discussed later. (See *Conditioned Compen-satory Responses,* p. 361.)

Importance of Psychoneuroimmunology.   Why is psychoneuroimmunology im-portant? These experiments demonstrate that elements of the immune system can be "tricked" into functioning in the absence of stimuli that normally trig-ger them. We should not be surprised by these findings. In Chapter 3 we learned that a dog's salivary response could be brought under the control of an arbitrary stimulus, such as a bell. The present findings are more important, however. Salivation and changes in salivation via conditioning have implica-tions for the preliminary stages of digestion. By contrast, the integrity of the

---

[5] *Radiomimetic* means that it acts like (mimics) ionizing radiation.

immune system is vitally important for optimal functioning of all physiological systems and behavior. The immune system is critically important for health and longevity.

Thoughts Affect Immune Systems.   That the immune system can be conditioned using an arbitrary taste stimulus opens the door to other kinds of control. Is it possible that words, thoughts, beliefs, and other cognitive stimuli acting as CSs can become associated with immune system functioning? What do you think? Can thought processes, such as the perception of stressors, affect your health?

Several studies using both rats and humans provide supportive evidence. For example, the immune systems of rats given the opportunity to escape the stress of electric shock have been found to be normal in comparison with immunosuppressed rats unable to escape the same shocks (Laudenslager, Ryan, Drugan, Hyson, & Maier, 1983). The *perception* of the stressor, not the stressor alone, produced these changes in the immune system.

Other evidence suggests that human immune systems can be conditioned. Levels of IgA (immunoglobin A1, an antibody that protects the upper respiratory tract from infection) were compared in dental students before, during, and after final exams. The IgA levels were lower during the exams, reflecting a somewhat compromised immune system (Jemmott & Magloire, 1988). Personality variables have also been found to affect immune function. Both perceived stress and immunosuppression during test taking were found to differ as a function of students' personality profiles (Jemmott et al., 1990).

There is converging evidence, then, that the perception of stressors can affect one's immune system and, by extrapolation, one's health. Later in this chapter we look at evidence that psychological stress is also a conditioned response.

Conditioning Asthma

Nine million Americans suffer from a baffling condition called *asthma*. Although these people come from every walk of life and range in age from infants to the very old, they have one thing in common—difficulty in breathing, alternatively described as "hungry for air." Some asthma attacks can be fatal.

The sign in the allergist's office summarizes what the allergy sufferer already knows: Asthma attacks occur under a variety of conditions. (See Figure 7.3.) Another way to say this is that the same amount of external stimulus (cedar pollen, for example) doesn't always produce an identical asthmatic response, as would be the case if asthma were a simple reflex. Let us look more closely at this physiological condition.

Physiology of Asthma.   Asthma is a type of allergy involving yet another component of the immune system. In normal people, certain stimuli called *antigens* that invade the body activate immune responses. The presence of large

Environment	Provides antigen (allergen) and irritant (harsh, dry, cold)
Exertion	Causes irritation of mucous membranes
Emotion	Always heightens symptoms with any combination of the preceding or may induce asthma even in the absence of these factors

FIGURE 7.3   The Rule of E's

The rule of e's summarizes three of the most important variables that contribute to asthma attacks.

quantities of *reagins,* or sensitizing antibodies, causes some individuals to overreact to certain types of antigens known as *allergens*. When this occurs in allergic or asthmatic individuals, an allergic response called an *allergen-reagin reaction* takes place.

Serious health problems may ensue from such overly sensitive immune systems, and asthma can be thought of as a disorder involving overly sensitive airways. Allergen-reagin reactions involve attaching antibodies to cells and thereby damaging them throughout the body. If a sufficient number of cells are damaged in this *anaphylactoid* reaction, death can ensue.

The allergen-reagin reaction can therefore be understood as a US-UR reflex. Is it possible to condition an asthmatic reaction? That is, can asthmatic and allergic responses be brought under the control of neutral stimuli? A related question is the role emotion plays in the *rule of e's*. How can emotion be a facilitating factor in this reflex? We begin by looking at asthma in animals.

Asthma in Guinea Pigs

Guinea pigs have overly sensitive airways, making them good animal subjects on which to do asthma research. Guinea pigs can be made asthmatic by first injecting them with a foreign protein, such as egg albumin.[6] The albumin acts as a US. Their immune system responds by making sensitizing antibodies (reagins) to the invading protein (a UR). On subsequent encounters with the allergen, an allergen-reagin reaction occurs in the bronchioles of the lungs. There, mast cells release a slow-reacting substance of anaphylaxis causing the bronchial smooth muscle to spasm. Breathing difficulties ensue. The response of the guinea pig following one sensitizing treatment is so severe that unless a vasoconstrictor (such as Isuprel®) is immediately administered, the guinea pig will die. The breathing difficulties are another UR to the US.

---

[6] Any protein that is not "self" is foreign. The exception is the interchangeability of body parts of identical twins. Someone else's transplanted liver is a foreign protein.

Conditioning Asthma in Guinea Pigs.   Asthma in guinea pigs has been conditioned (Justesen, Braun, Garrison, & Pendleton, 1970). The sensitizing treatment just described makes the pig asthmatic. Breathing is measured by a pressure transducer in a sealed environment (see Figure 7.4). Recordings

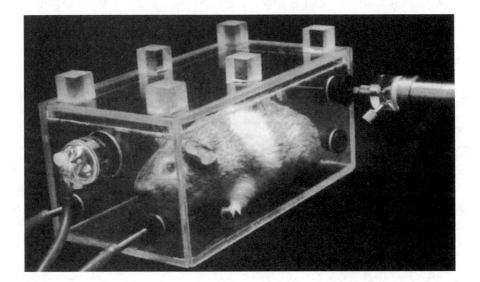

FIGURE 7.4   Conditioning Asthma in Guinea Pigs

Whole-body plethysomograms (breathing records) are recorded from fluctuations in air pressure within a sealed Plexiglas chamber. The guinea pig shown weighs about 850 grams (compared to laboratory rats that weigh about 350 to 400 grams). The nebulizer is attached at the back of the box. The record shows the breathing described in the text in which aerosol egg albumin causes the allergic attack. Isuprel® returns breathing to basal, or control, levels. The conditioned allergic response (conditional attack) shows disrupted breathing caused by sounding the nebulizer alone. (From Justesen, Braun, Garrison, & Pendelton, 1970) are made of slight changes in air pressure as the animal breathes normally. When aerosol egg albumin (the US) is administered into the air stream serving the chamber, breathing is disrupted (the UR) (see panel [b] of Figure 7.4).

A hissing nebulizer squirts the egg albumin (the US) into the air stream in an aerosol form. A conditioning trial consists of the hissing sound (the CS), the aerosol egg albumin (the US), and disrupted breathing (the UR). Finally, on administering aerosol Isuprel, breathing returns to baseline levels.

In the research by Justesen et al. (1970), *all* guinea pigs showed conditioned disruptions in breathing to the sound of the nebulizer alone after 6 to 12 trials. The hissing sound alone caused the asthma attack. Such demonstrations of conditioned asthma raise several important issues. Would it be possible, for example, to maximize conditioning (more trials, more salient CSs, etc.) and fatally disrupt breathing using only a CS? Note in the record that Isuprel was used to recover baseline breathing following a conditioned asthma attack. Another experiment: Could one train a discrimination between the aerosol egg albumin and aerosol Isuprel so that the CSs associated with the latter could be shown to relieve breathing disruptions to the former?

Conditioning Asthma in Humans.   The behavioral conditioning of asthma has also been reported in humans. For example, in a design similar to the guinea pig study just noted, two allergic individuals were first exposed to allergens when using a breathing apparatus. After several trials, they produced allergic symptoms when asked to use the breathing apparatus alone in the absence of allergens.[7]   Within the clinical literature on the treatment of asthma are numerous reports of psychosomatic (i.e., conditioned) asthma. Included is an allergic reaction to an artificial rose in a patient allergic to the smell of roses (reported by Gauci, Husband, & King, 1992). Apparently, the visual features of the rose acted as a CS, and the fragrance was the US.

Allergic rhinitis (hay fever) is related to asthma. It has also been conditioned in humans, using both mast-cell mediators and a subjective symptom score as dependent variables (Gauci et al., 1992). In this research, a number of asthma sufferers were recruited to participate in a study concerned with alternative treatments for hay fever and allergic rhinitis. Divided into three groups, they were given water, a medicine (actually an inert soft drink), or nothing. Each treatment was conceptualized as the conditioned stimulus. Immediately thereafter, each subject was challenged with an allergen (the US). Both subject symptom scores (a self-report measure) and mast-cell activity were measured. Two days later, the treatment was repeated. The CSs were given but not the allergen. These researchers reported that the medicine treatment diminished mast-cell activity—known as a **placebo effect**—relative to the other two

---

[7] After hearing a lecture on asthmatic conditioning, a student reported to me that he had replaced the Isuprel in his asthmatic roommate's nebulizer with water, and for one week watched symptomatic relief obtained from the water placebo. Ethics aside, the point is that drug administration is *always* accompanied by environmental CSs that may act as conditioned stimuli.

groups. A placebo (*placebo*, from the Greek, "I will please") effect is a conditioned response that mimics the effects of a drug treatment (the unconditioned stimulus). In humans, via the second signal system, a placebo effect may reflect the expectation of drug or other treatment effect. Interestingly, in the present study, Gauci et al. (1992) hypothesized that subjects' *expectations* regarding treatment were a confounding variable. These asthma sufferers apparently did not expect the medicine treatment to exert placebo properties. These researchers concluded that the entire experimental treatment had CS properties and that one-trial conditioning had been effected.

Asthma and Emotionality.   All asthma sufferers are likely to experience conditioned allergic reactions. For example, have you ever had your breathing forcibly disrupted for any length of time? Without special training, most people panic. That suffocation produces such extreme emotional responses is adaptive. Oxygen is our most critical homeostatic need, and its availability demands our immediate attention. The point is that the emotional components of allergic responses are also excellent USs, available for conditioning to a variety of environmental cues. It is no wonder that allergists have long recognized the inherent circularity of this medical condition; emotion causes the asthma causes the emotion, and so on. (See Figure 7.3.)

It is not unreasonable to suggest that guinea pigs also suffer emotional responses as they gasp for air. Concurrently with disruptions in breathing, the stimuli attendant with these emotional responses readily enter into association with the nebulizer sounds. After several pairings, the sound of the nebulizer alone produces a "panic" response, further disrupting normal breathing.

In any case, both the Justesen et al. (1970) and Gauci et al. (1992) experiments provide compelling demonstrations of the conditioning of human psychophysiological (cf. *psychosomatic*) disorders. Human food allergies are also subject to conditioning, as we will see in a later section.

Conditioning Hives

Urticaria is an immune system response commonly known as *hives*. Though not well understood, hives result when antigens enter specific skin areas and cause histamine release. Among other actions, histamine produces a local vascular dilation and capillary permeability. Within a few minutes of its release, it causes a red flare and swelling (a hive). Many individuals produce hives in situations in which the antigen either is not present or is present but is not causing a reaction. Consider the following example:

> *A woman in her mid-30s appears stressed by the presence of visiting in-laws. After several hours she is overheard telling her husband that she must get away from his family or she will "go crazy." A few minutes later the first hive appears on her arm. She retires to her bedroom, saying she will be okay. ". . . if left alone." Within the next*

15 minutes, several 6-inch diameter, half-inch raised welts appear on her arms, legs, and torso. An hour later all hives disappear without leaving a mark.[8]

It is tempting to speculate that the presence of in-laws acted as proximal conditioned stimuli, setting the occasion for the emotional/stress response. Given the time course of the appearance and disappearance of the response, it is likely that histamine was released locally as a conditioned rather than as an unconditioned response. Another example of an emotionally induced change in the skin is blushing. Blushing is caused by localized vasodilation of the face and neck, most noticeably the cheeks. Which particular conditioned stimuli control your blushing reflex? Certain people? Certain words?

Interim Summary

1. The *immune system*'s function in animals is to recognize and resist toxins and infectious organisms. For example, *T-lymphocytes* attack and ultimately destroy invading cells.

2. Psychoneuroimmunology is a research area that integrates physiology and behavior. Pavlovian conditioning is the primary methodology used in psychoneuroimmunology.

3. The immune system can be conditioned to respond to CSs. Rats drink flavored water followed by toxins that suppress immune functioning. Ultimately, *conditioned immunosuppression* results when these rats merely taste the flavors—a conditioned response. Conditioned *immunofacilitation* also has been demonstrated.

4. The perception or interpretation of stressors has been demonstrated to have immune system consequences in rats and humans.

5. Asthma has been classically conditioned in guinea pigs and humans. The emotional consequences of disrupted breathing are potential USs available for association with environmental cues.

6. Blushing and hives can be interpreted as conditioned responses.

DRUGS, DRUG EFFECTS, AND CONDITIONED DRUG EFFECTS

Drugs

Drugs act on humans and other animals alike. Using animal models of drug effects for several decades, pharmacologists identified both physical addiction and tolerance to certain drugs, but they cannot tell us why humans abuse

---

[8] Personal observation by the author.

drugs while other animals, for the most part, do not. By applying Pavlovian conditioning theory to the study of drug effects during the past two decades, behavioral scientists have provided insight into both drug-taking behavior and drug tolerance.

Drugs as Stimuli

Stimuli can be conceptually grouped into simple and complex categories. Pavlov's short duration tones and light panels that control a pigeon's pecking responses can be charcterized as "simple" CSs. Simple stimuli are experienced as such; they produce definable afferent neuronal responses of limited duration that project to primary sensory areas of the brain. By contrast, Pavlov's USs (biologically meaningful stimuli) are more complex. These USs evoke motivational and emotional responese from more diverse areas of the brain and neuroendocrine system.

Drugs as USs.   Drugs are complex stimuli. They have sensory properties, and each drug has one or more sites of action, including specific brain sites. The pharmacological effects of a drug constitute its unconditioned stimulus properties.

Drug Overdoses.   Given the complexity of drugs as stimuli, should we anticipate that conditioning using drugs as USs differs from conditioning salivation in dogs? Surprisingly, simple associative models work quite well. Consider the following case history of a drug overdose:

> An elderly man in the terminal stages of cancer, suffering acute, chronic pain, was being maintained on a high dosage of morphine. Bedridden, the patient was administered the morphine on a strict schedule by a relative. On one occasion the relative was late, and the patient crawled into the next room where he administered the drug to himself. Though the drug dosage was equivalent to what he had been taking, the patient died of an "overdose." (Siegel, Hinson, Krank, & McCully, 1982)

How can this be? How can the same dosage of a drug have two different effects? Fortunately, experimental work accomplished in this area provides a conceptual framework to help us understand how a normal drug dosage can sometimes be an overdose. The process is not unlike that of a drug dosage *losing* its effectiveness with repeated usage. Let us first look at various aspects of drugs and drug-taking behavior, and then we return to the issue of overdosing.

Drug-Taking Behavior

On the surface, taking drugs seems to be an example of a voluntary behavior. Addictive drugs, however, are often craved. Both food and drug cravings can be analyzed as resulting from physiological need states. After a thorough literature review, Tiffany (1990) concluded that drug-seeking behavior of habitual drug users may largely be determined by automatic (involuntary) processes rather than as the result of voluntary processes.

Drugs are powerful unconditioned stimuli, and addictive drugs are potent reinforcers. Each drug-taking episode can be considered a conditioning trial in which environmental stimuli (CSs) are paired with drug effects (USs). Each drug-taking episode is also one in which drug-taking behaviors may be reinforced or punished by the drug's effects.

As is the case with many other stimuli used in conditioning, both the effectiveness and the associability of drugs change with repeated trials. The reduced effectiveness of drugs repeatedly taken, called **drug tolerance,** is especially true of addictive drugs. An example of an addictive drug that loses its effectiveness over time is morphine.

Drugs as USs: Conditioning and Drug Tolerance

Morphine

Morphine is an alkaloid derivative of opium primarily used by humans at analgesic (pain-relieving) dosages. It has an effect on the central nervous system. Complex, endogenous opioid receptors (such as endorphins) are activated by morphine, producing a number of changes in CNS functioning and physiological systems. Among the easily measured unconditioned responses to morphine are respiratory depression (at high doses), analgesia, euphoria, and increased body temperature (at moderate doses).

Simple Conditioning with Morphine.   Pavlov (1927/1960) reported some of the first conditioning experiments using injections of morphine in dogs. The contextual cues attendant with morphine injection, including the appearance of the white-coated researcher who injected the animal, eventually became CSs that produced druglike responses in the absence of morphine administration (see Box 7.1).

Pavlov's observations of conditioning using morphine as a US and sights and sounds as CSs produced results similar to his other preparations. We now know, however, that drug effects are more complicated than his simple picture suggests.

Pharmacological Tolerance Is Not Behavioral Tolerance

Tolerance is defined as a reduction in the intensity of the effect of a dose of a drug over repeated trials. Tolerance has been likened to habituation (Baker & Tiffany, 1985). Another way to assess tolerance is to note the increasing requirement of a larger dose to achieve the same level of drug effect over trials.

Box 7.1   Conditioning Drug Responses in Dogs

Drugs are such powerful USs that we should not be surprised at their control over human behavior. Pavlov was among the first researchers to document the intensity of conditioned responses using morphine as a US:

> It is well known that the first effect of a hypodermic injection of morphine is to produce nausea with profuse secretion of saliva, followed by vomiting, and then profound sleep. . . .
>
> When the injections were repeated regularly . . . after five or six days the preliminaries of injection were in themselves sufficient to produce all these symptoms—nausea, secretion of saliva, vomiting and sleep. . . .
>
> In the most striking cases all the symptoms could be produced by the

dogs simply seeing the experimenter. Where such a stimulus was insufficient, it was necessary to open the box containing the syringe, to crop the fur over a small area of skin and wipe with alcohol, and perhaps even to inject some harmless fluid before the symptoms could be obtained. The greater the number of previous injections of morphine the less preparation had to be performed in order to evoke a reaction simulating that produced by the drug. (Pavlo, 1927/1960, pp. 35–36)

Is it obvious that what Pavlov referred to as a "harmless fluid" is what is now called a *placebo* and that the responses to the CSs that he observed were the placebo effect?

Mechanisms of tolerance vary from drug to drug. For example, *metabolic* tolerance to the daily ingestion of alcohol is characterized by compensatory changes in biochemicals (such as increased levels of alcohol dehydrogenase) that inactivate (metabolize) the drug. Because it is metabolized, less of the drug is available to reach receptor sites in the brain. *Physiological* tolerance to alcohol occurs when the presumed receptive sites on (as yet unspecified) neurons change so that the effects of the drug at these sites are reduced.[9] These and other biological mechanisms for other drugs characterize the many ways in which **pharmacological tolerance** for a drug develops.

It is also the case that in addition to the development of pharmacological tolerance over trials, animals experience a **behavioral tolerance.** Behavioral tolerance helps animals cope with the effects that drugs have on sensing and moving. For example, given enough trials in a drug state, rats under the influence of alcohol can learn to balance better while traversing a narrow ledge (Wenger, Tiffany, Bombardier, Nicholls, & Woods, 1981). This sensory-motor adjustment is a form of behavioral tolerance. Indeed, demonstrations of tolerance to stimuli other than drugs suggests a general mechanism. Homeostatic adjustments ensue to a number of repetitive stimuli. For example, tolerance

---

[9] Physiological tolerance is far more complicated than indicated here. In addition to changes in receptor number and receptor sensitivity, changes probably occur in intracellular second-messenger systems with which opiate receptors couple.

develops to a variety of physical circumstances such as heat, cold, delivery of electric shocks, exercise (cf. *training effect*), and even to the effects of brain lesions. In addition to studying drug tolerance processes, then, the question is how animals learn to tolerate or adjust to repetitive stimuli.

Conditioning Morphine Tolerance

How much tolerance can a person develop to morphine? A great deal. An initial dose of 100 to 200 mg produces sedation and respiratory depression to the point of death. After repeated administrations, tolerant subjects can take 20 to 40 times this dosage (as much as 4.0 gm) without adverse effect (Baker & Tiffany, 1985). The trick is determining how much tolerance is pharmacological and how much is behavioral.

We are now ready to consider an elegant demonstration of the way that Siegel (1975, 1977) partitioned morphine tolerance into *behavioral* and *pharmacological* components. He injected rats with 5.0 mg/kg morphine sulfate subcutaneously (under the skin) on a daily basis. This dosage of morphine produced several unconditioned responses: increased body temperature (hyperthermia), decreased heart rate (bradycardia), and decreased sensitivity to pain (analgesia).

How is the response to pain measured? Rats without morphine immediately withdraw and lick their paw when it is placed on a hot plate. Morphine's effects reduce their sensitivity to pain, and they may wait 20 to 30 seconds before removing their paw from the hot surface.

Drug administration took place in a room in which 60 dB white noise provided a constant background. (White noise is the sound parents make when "shushing" a child.) This distinctive environment, we will see, provided the contextual cues that eventually controlled some of the responses to the morphine.

Effects of Environment on Tolerance.   As tolerance to the morphine accrued (about 6 days), each injection produced less analgesia and less hyperthermia. The question Siegel wanted to answer was how much of the reduction in analgesia and hyperthermia was due to decreases in the drug's pharmacological action and how much was due to behavioral tolerance. To find out, he interrupted the schedule of drug administration by taking the rats to yet another room having different background cues. The morphine administered in this new environment again became effective. That is, the morphine once again produced analgesia (less pronounced pain) and again warmed the animals (see Figure 7.5).

Conditioned Compensatory Responses.   Siegel concluded that the context of the familiar room (in which the rats had been injected with morphine) had become conditioned. The rat's tolerance to the morphine was due in part to being administered the drug *in this environment*. The familiar environment,

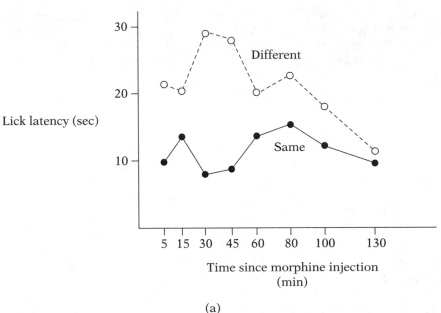

FIGURE 7.5a   Conditioning Pain and Temperature
Responses

After 6 trials, morphine loses its pain-killing effectiveness as is evidenced
by rats withdrawing their paws from a hot surface and licking them within
about 10 seconds. The same rats injected with the same dose of morphine,
when tested in a different environment, however, do not experience as
much pain: They leave their paws on the hot surface 2 to 3 times as long.
(After Siegel, 1977)

Siegel reasoned, contained CSs that had come to control **conditioned compensatory responses.** How so? The rats' normal physiology, he argues, allows
homeostatic mechanisms to counteract the effects of drugs. That is, the ANS
responds by cooling to counteract the warming effects of morphine, and by increasing heart rate (tachycardia) to counteract the bradycardia produced by
morphine. An increased sensitivity to pain counteracts the analgesia produced
by morphine.

Siegel concluded that the previously neutral stimuli present during drug
administration became conditioned stimuli. As such, these CSs were important
components in the development of drug tolerance. If this model were correct,
he further assumed, these CSs would act as CSs in other associative situations.
First, he showed that contextual cues without morphine administration (i.e.,
extinction trials) would extinguish the environmental component of acquired

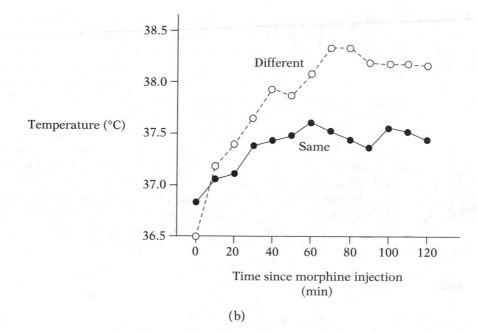

(b)

FIGURE 7.5b

Morphine normally increases body temperature until tolerance occurs. This effect, however, also depends on the environment in which the morphine is administered. In a *different* environment, morphine again warms the body. (After Siegel, 1977)

tolerance. Siegel called these *placebo sessions*. Second, he demonstrated that placebo sessions prior to conditioning acted to retard the acquisition of tolerance (cf. *latent inhibition*).

Let us return to the case study of apparent morphine overdose. Recall that the sickly individual was given daily morphine injections in his *familiar* bedroom. The fatal dose was self-administered in a *different* room. Taking the drug in a novel room bypassed the familiar environmental stimuli that would have elicited the conditioned compensatory responses. The effectiveness of the high dosage of morphine was thereby increased, unfortunately, to a fatal level (Siegel et al., 1982).

Conditioning Withdrawal Responses in Humans

Other drug-conditioning phenomena have been demonstrated in humans. One study used the drug naloxone. Naloxone mimics a host of heroin withdrawal effects, including subjective components (craving, nausea, and cramps), be-havioral components (blinking, yawning, restlessness), and ANS components (decreased skin temperature, increased heart rate, tears from the eyes). Ad-dicts volunteered to be studied during drug withdrawal in methadone mainte-nance programs (O'Brien, 1975). Naloxone was paired with a tone/odor condi-tioned stimulus complex. After 7 to 10 trials, the CS complex reliably produced conditioned responses similar to the naloxone treatment.

Street addicts coming into the treatment centers carry their drug condi-tioning history with them. When asked to perform a "cook-up" ritual under laboratory conditions, the detoxified addicts' pupils dilate and skin tempera-ture decreases prior to any drug action (O'Brien, Testa, Ternes, & Greenstein, 1978). The conditioned stimuli controlling the response is a complex including the sight of a bag of heroin, the odor of the cooker, and anticipation of shoot-ing up. Such naturalistic stimuli easily become conditioned stimuli (Ternes, O'Brien, Grabowski, Wellerstein, & Jordan-Hays, 1980).

Conditioning Alcohol Tolerance

Few readers of this text are either heroin addicts or morphine users. If it turns out that conditioned compensatory responses are specific only to conditioning with opiates, application to humans, while interesting, is limited. Research by Le, Poulos, and Cappell (1979) is important, then, in extending the generality of Siegel's framework to a commonly used drug, ethanol. Ethanol is found in beer, wine, and distilled spirits; its pharmacological action is quite different from the opiates. The research by Le et al. and of others in this area now pro-vides a conditioning model of alcohol tolerance that has important treatment implications (Melchior & Tabakoff, 1984).

Among its more interesting pharmacological actions, ethyl alcohol has a cooling effect on the body.[10] Le et al. (1979) injected rats intraperitoneally with 2.5 g/kg for 9 trials in a distinctive environment. When first administered, this dosage produces substantial motor impairment (rats appear drunk) and drops the body temperature from 98.6° to about 95° Fahrenheit. The change in the hypothermic unconditioned response over 9 alcohol treatments (one every other day) is noted in Figure 7.6.

When on the 10th day alcohol was administered in the rat's home cage rather than in the distinctive (familiar) environment, the cooling effect again reappeared. Le et al. (1979) interpreted this finding within Siegel's framework: Conditioned *hyper*thermic compensatory responses were interfering with the

[10] St. Bernards carrying brandy kegs provide a substance to stranded mountaineers that may burn the throat and stomache (and thereby arouse the RAS). Nevertheless, the result is to fur-ther cool the body—unless the person has an extensive history with ethanol consumption in cold climates. See the text.

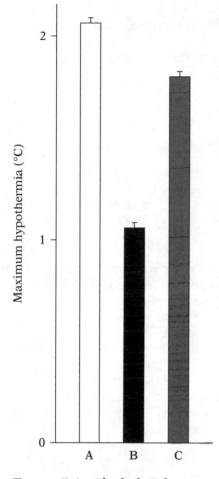

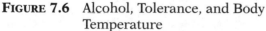

FIGURE 7.6   Alcohol, Tolerance, and Body
Temperature

Rats injected with alcohol experience a rather profound hypothermia.
Condition A shows a 2-degree Centigrade drop in body temperature
following a 2.5 gm/kg intraperitoneal injection of ethanol (dropping the
rat's body temperature to approximately 95–96 degrees Fahrenheit). After
nine such injections, the body temperature of alcohol-tolerant rats does
not decrease as much (condition B) unless the rat is injected in a novel
environment (condition C). See text for further details of this *conditioned
compensatory response*. (After Le, Poulos, & Cappell, 1979)

normal pharmacological action of ethanol. With respect to the development of alcohol tolerance, environmental cues were controlling at least a portion of the temperature UR to alcohol. Therefore, not all of the observed tolerance could be due to loss of pharmacological action at a receptor site.

Conditioning Changes in Body Temperature

Because body temperature itself is a factor in how well the immune system functions, there is increasing interest in demonstrating that body temperature changes can also be conditioned (Bull, Brown, King, Husband, & Pfister, 1992). Novel flavored fluids (CSs) are paired with either pyretics or antipyretics (USs).[11] Conditioned temperature changes to the CS are of the order of magnitude reported by Le et al. (1979) to ethanol (Bull, Brown, King, & Husband, 1991). Body temperature, therefore, can be conditioned by a variety of mechanisms.

Drug Craving.   Humans are creatures of habit, and for obvious reasons it is important to understand habitual alcohol-drinking behavior. When people are asked why they drink alcohol, many simply respond, "I crave it." Others drink alcohol but do not report consciously craving it (Kassel & Shiffman, 1992). Le et al. (1979) speculated that periodic drinking in familiar environments produces both time and place cues for the conditioned compensatory responses, including hyperthermia. They further reasoned that a slight warming effect could provide the somatic basis for the psychological craving for alcohol. Treatment of alcoholism should consider this learning component. Specifically, the treatment of alcoholics should include the extinction of conditioned compensatory responses as well as alcohol abstinence (Melchior & Tabakoff, 1984).

Similarities of Food Allergies to Drug Responses

The finding that both morphine and alcohol tolerance are determined in part by whether they are experienced in novel or familiar places raises questions about other environmentally sensitive conditioning phenomena. For example, food allergies occur in 8% of children. The role of environment in conditioning allergic responses to flavors of foods, however, has not been investigated. In a recent report of 13 children who had life-threatening food allergy incidents, five of the six fatal cases occurred outside the home (novel environment), whereas the remaining seven nonfatal reactions occurred at home (Sampson, Mendelson, & Rosen, 1992). Of the nonfatal reactions to foods, two of the children who came closest to dying were visiting in other people's homes. The report focused on somewhat longer delays in the administration of epinephrine in the fatal versus nonfatal incidents; however, the role of environment cannot be ruled out.

---

[11] A pyretic is any drug, toxin, or treatment that increases body temperature. Common antipyretics are aspirin and Tylenol®.

Reinforcing Properties of Drugs

In Chapter 6 we saw evidence of the tremendous reinforcing effects of electrical stimulation of the so-called pleasure centers in the brain. Among other dopamine-releasing sites, the medial forebrain bundle (MFB) was singled out. Given the limited availability of ESB and cognizant of Premack's conception that the value of a reinforcer changes as a function of opportunities to engage in behaviors that produce it, what is *your* most reinforcing stimulus?

For some individuals the most reinforcing stimulus is crack cocaine (Flynn, 1991). Money (secondary reinforcer) and crack (primary reinforcer) command and control the behaviors that produce the intense reinforcing effect reported by those who use the drug. Some human lives are totally rearranged to provide the opportunity for the next "hit," including bypassing food and sex. Seldom do reinforcers exert quite the total control that this drug does, presenting major difficulties for those wishing to apply some form of remedial therapy. Indeed, chemical dependency on a gamut of drugs of abuse, including alcohol, presents major challenges to health care. By one analysis, alcohol is addictive because it produces both positive reinforcement (a slight euphoria, presumably caused by the release of dopamine) and negative reinforcement (i.e., alcohol reduces the discomfort of anxiety). This one-two punch makes it difficult for many people to resist (Carlson, 1992).

Thought question: Can you apply *Premackian reinforcement* to identify a more powerful reinforcer than crack cocaine? If not, what is the prognosis for behavioral treatment of those chemically dependent on (and highly reinforced by) crack?

Addicts may also seek drugs because their brain chemistry has been sensitized by drugs (Berridge & Robinson, 1995). These researchers point to evidence suggesting that pleasure has been disconnected from the drug-taking process. Even when drugs no longer give pleasure, when no withdrawal exists, and when a craving would have just been satisfied following drug administration, addicts continue to crave drugs. Much is to be learned about human drug-taking behavior.

Interim Summary

1. A drug's pharmacological effects are its unconditioned stimulus properties.
2. Both the pharmacological properties of the drug and the conditioned responses to the environment in which the drug effects were experienced influence drug-taking behavior.
3. Early experiments with morphine demonstrated that conditioned stimuli could produce morphinelike effects in the animal.
4. Morphine tolerance is due both to the waning of the drug's effects (*pharmacological tolerance*, presumably adaptations in tissue) and to *behavioral tolerance*, the *conditioned compensatory responses* investigated by Siegel (1979).

5. Conditioned compensatory responses are understood as homeostatic adjustments elicited by drug-predictive environmental cues. When rats and humans experience the drug in a novel environment (that does *not* contain drug-predictive cues), tolerance disappears and the drug again becomes more effective.

6. Siegel's conditioning model of drug tolerance for morphine has been successfully extended to ethyl alcohol.

7. Drugs affect the immune system, and the drug tolerance conditioning models discussed here have had the heuristic effect of research in conditioning body temperature changes.

8. Alcohol has both positive and negative reinforcing properties. Cocaine and other drugs have reinforcing properties that can come to control behavior.

EATING, DRINKING, AND CONDITIONING

During the past century, hundreds of researchers have been drawn to the study of ingestive behaviors, that is, eating and drinking. Why? Because foods and fluids, more tangible than the air we breathe, sustain life. Ingestive behaviors are among the ethologists' *consummatory* behaviors—behaviors essential for survival. Researchers recognize that eating and drinking are among life's great pleasures. Throughout a lifetime, eating makes us feel good. Eating and drinking help define our social interactions.

Using animal models, nutritionists and dietitians have learned a great deal about the chemical makeup of foods and their ingestional consequences. These experts are not so much concerned with psychological and sociocultural factors—the when, what, and why of food and drink selection. Psychological factors are important. Why, for example, do some people overeat and others undereat to the detriment of their health? Do they learn this, or are the determinants of these disorders found in a combination of genes and physiology? A quick comparison of the cuisines of different cultures attests to the idiosyncratic food choices humans *learn* during their lifetimes. In this section we see how the application of learning theory using animal models aids our understanding of human eating and drinking behavior. The interested reader is directed to Logue (1991) and Capaldi and Powley (1990) for more extensive overviews of this enormous and increasing behavioral literature.

Sensitivity to Foods

Animals evolved membranes having properties that allowed them to be selectively sensitive to their interface with the environment. In meeting the challenge of efficiently securing palatable foods and avoiding toxins, our taste and smell receptors evolved in ways that took advantage of this sensitivity (Beidler, 1982; Young, 1966; Pfaffman, 1959). Among their behavioral predispositions, newborn humans display innate preferences for sweet and dislike of bitter substances.

Receptor-Driven Feeding of Simple Animals.   Unlike those receptors found on flies, human receptors do not determine appetite. Earlier in the text (p. 44) we looked at an example of a relatively simple behavioral system that is receptor driven. Specifically, we saw that a house fly reflexively lowers its proboscis to feed when taste receptors on its legs are stimulated (Dethier, 1978). Other animals—carnivores and herbivores to name but two well-known relatively restricted feeding niches—also occupy relatively more circumscribed feeding niches than do humans. As we discover shortly, it is with omnivores that eating and drinking becomes dicey.

Evolution of Eating Behaviors

In addition to taste and olfactory receptor tissue, specific food-related brain structures evolved in humans and other animals. An ability to monitor food value once it is past the peripheral sensing receptors is also part of our physiology. Homeostatic mechanisms are as much a product of evolution as are bitter and sweet receptors. A few examples of how human ingestive behaviors may have evolved reveal the complexities of what, how, and why we eat. These examples serve notice as to the limitations of a purely physiological approach.

Corn.   The quality of the digestible protein in corn is increased if, during food preparation, the corn is treated with an alkali solution. Katz (1982) wondered whether this was the reason that some American Indian cultures treated their corn with alkali and others did not. He found that those who *did* treat their corn with alkali grew and ate more corn than those not using the alkali treatment. He reasoned that the alkali food preparation method increased the nutritional value of the corn, which in turn influenced how corn was incorporated into the diet.

Two points are stressed: First, selecting to eat corn (or other foods) involves more than its taste and smell. Second, somehow, for unknown reasons, certain American Indians *learned* to treat corn with alkali. Did they recognize the value of this treatment in the course of a lifetime and transmit the acquired information to the next generation? It seems so.

Fava Beans, Bitter Manioc, and Soybeans.   Katz (1982) performed similar studies on African tribes eating fava beans, bitter manioc, and soybeans. He noted that cultural transformations of foods often enhanced adaptive fitness. For example, when bitter manioc is prepared in a certain way, the food offers increased protection against sickle cell anemia. Food preparation that enhances adaptive fitness often becomes part of the culture, a process that Katz (1975) called **biocultural evolution.**

Similar work on the relationship of African tribes that historically use cow's milk and the prevalence or absence of lactose insufficiency was reported by Simoons (1973). He theorizes that the consumption of particular types of food but not others over time may have led to divergence of human populations. Katz and Simoons view both the choice of food for consumption and methods of food preparation as an evolutionary interface. Those people who do this more successfully than others enjoy a reproductive advantage. A cultural trend develops as this behavior is successfully passed to the next generation.

Origin of Cuisines.   What humans learn about foods during their lifetimes is important. Learning complements the functioning of taste and smell receptors as well as innately organized homeostatic regulatory processes. Furthermore, the cross-generational transmission of food information is the basis for the origin of the world's various cuisines. Learning, therefore, is an important determinant of culture.

Thought question: What do you know about the origins of food choices within the ethnic cuisine of your subculture?

Specific Hungers

Evolution aside for the moment, individuals survive by eating foods selected from within their local environments several times each day. The task is not particularly easy even with a full complement of evolved food selection mechanisms and a supportive culture. Some insight into the complexity of this process can be gained by examining a case history. Box 7.2 reports the way that one particular child with faulty physiology learned to eat and drink. What is remarkable about this example is that it points out the redundant physiological systems we have for (a) recognizing salt and water in both the internal and external environment and (b) regulating their intake. We have **specific hungers** for salt and water. Salt and water are considered to be special cases for many reasons. Both are essential to survival in the short term. Animals can survive only a few days without fluid replenishment, and, as we see in the case of D.W., salt is also a critical need.

Special Nature of Salt and Water.   Another indication of the "special" nature of salt and water is that every language around the globe has words for these nutrients. By contrast, no language (other than the language of science) has a word for *thiamin, magnesium, selenium,* and other vitamins and minerals (or for the words *vitamins* and *minerals* themselves!). Salt joins sweet, bitter, and sour as one of the four basic tastes. Along with water, these tastes are presumably sensed by evolved receptors attuned to foods containing them.

Specific hungers are mediated by peripheral receptors (CNS), neuroendocrine systems, and homeostatic mechanisms of the ANS. These interrelated

Box 7.2   Salt Craving and Personality
            Development: A Mystery Story

A child known to us only by his initials, D.W., was born in the mid-1930s near Baltimore. What happened to him in his short lifetime contains the drama of a good mystery as well as an introduction to complexities of appetite.

Sickly from birth, D.W. would drink milk only when mixed with water. He regurgitated most "solid" foods. A watery, salted gruel barely kept him alive. At about 18 months of age, physically and mentally slowed by dietary deficiencies, he began to say a few words—among them were "Ma-ma," "Wa-wa," and "Salt!" His mother described D.W.'s behavior at this time:

> As soon as he knew what the word *water* meant, he would cry for it every time he heard the word mentioned. And when he saw the river or the ocean, he always thought he had to have some to drink. We were finally able to explain to him that it wasn't drinking water.

And then he discovered the salt shaker.

> He poured some out and ate it by dipping his finger in it. After this he wouldn't eat any food without having the salt, too. . . . He really cried for it and acted like he had to have it . . . practically everything he liked real well was salty, such as crackers, pretzels, potato chips, olives, pickles, fresh fish, salt mackerel, crisp bacon, and most fruits and vegetables if I added more salt. (Wilkins & Richter, 1940, p. 867)

Between 1 and 3 years old, D.W.'s obsession with salt and water found him searching magazines looking for pictures of lakes. During playtime he liberally "salted" imaginary meals.

His parents obviously knew that D.W.'s abnormal cravings were peculiar. But they must have been horrified when the tiny child became *virilized*.

(His voice deepened, and he began growing pubic hair and an adult-size penis.) Referred to Dr. Lawson Wilkins, the founder of pediatric endocrinology at Johns Hopkins School of Medicine, D.W. was admitted to a large children's ward. Placed on a standard hospital diet, he had restricted access to salt and water. He died 7 days after admission.

The child's death would be unnoted and unremarkable at the time were it not for Curt Richter, a somewhat reclusive scientist at Johns Hopkins University. Richter had spent the latter part of the 1930s investigating how and why laboratory rats ate and drank. He was particularly interested in why rats with adrenal glands removed died within a few days. If he gave them extra salt and unrestricted water, however, they lived quite normally (Richter, 1936).

Richter heard about the boy in the hospital who had craved salt. He contacted Wilkins and suggested that D.W.'s unusual salt craving might indicate problems with his adrenal glands. Richter and Wilkins performed an autopsy and found an adrenal tumor (Wilkins & Richter, 1940). The tumor had been responsible for two separate disorders. D. W.'s adrenal gland had secreted too much androgen (causing virilization) and too little aldosterone. Aldosterone regulates how much salt is excreted in the urine, and too little of it caused D.W. to excrete too much salt. He didn't get enough salt on the restricted hospital diet. The child's obsession with salt and water had helped him survive for more than three years—a remarkable example of the interplay of physiological regulation and the behavioral selection of essential nutrients in a preverbal child.

systems comprise the innate equipment that allows us to regulate calories, electrolytes, minerals, and other specific nutrients. We do not cover these systems here. Rather, we continue our focus on the role that learning plays in modifying and directing our innately organized eating and drinking behaviors.

Carnivores, Herbivores, and Omnivores

The Omnivore's Paradox.   As is the case with carnivores, herbivores, and all other living creatures, omnivores must secure from the environment those nutrients essential for survival. On the surface, the omnivores' strategy appears to be an ideal solution in meeting these needs. If plant sources dry up, eat meat (too bad, herbivores). If rabbits and small rodents disappear, eat plants (sorry, carnivores). Accompanying these benefits are costs, however. The paradox facing the omnivore is that this more open eating strategy increases the risk of making mistakes. If *everything* is fare [sic] game, recognize that *everything* includes toxic plants, *salmonella*, environmentally contaminated shellfish, and so on. Because it is less specialized, a wide open system contains fewer safeguards. That is the reason that the omnivores' strategy, beneficial during famine, can also be detrimental to health and well-being. The preceding cost-benefit analysis has been called the **omnivore's paradox** (Rozin & Kalat, 1971).

Nature and Nurture of Eating.   As we saw in a previous chapter, one innately organized behavior that helps us resolve the omnivore's paradox is food *neophobia,* a wariness concerning new foods. Are there other adaptive behavioral strategies that function to aid in food selection? In Box 7.3 we examine the eating behavior of another child, this one named Jane B. We assume that she has had less opportunity to *learn* to select foods than those humans who have eaten thousands of meals over several years. Her experiences allow us to see what innately predisposed behaviors she brings to this task. Some ques-

BOX 7.3   AND THIS IS NORMAL?

Unlike D.W.'s earliest eating experiences (Box 7.2), Jane B. was a perfectly normal infant. She nursed healthily at mama's breast for 1 year and maintained an optimal growth curve. Her physical and psychological development was textbook normal.

Omnivory begins with selecting choices from alternative foods as well as learning when, what, and where to eat. At about 10 months, Jane B. was offered apple juice from a nursing bottle, and she drank avidly. On her first birthday she abruptly refused breastmilk and all other animal milk offered her. (Mother was devastated.) Jane B. drank apple juice for the next 8 to 9 years of her life and then other sweetened drinks. At age 14 she continues to reject milk but still loves her mother.

Box 7.3

What did Jane B. learn from her first omnivorous (open) encounter? Did she learn that the sight of a baby bottle (CS) contained a very sweet fluid (US) that she could drink more rapidly than nursing from a breast? That is, was the sweeter, more rapidly attained apple juice a more potent reinforcer that shaped her preference over breast milk? In this particular instance, were the apple flavor and rapid glucose repletion more reinforcing than the over-

all more nutritious but less sweet, less rapidly digested milk? (These questions are not easily answered. See Weiffenbach, 1977).

During the second year of her life, Jane B. ate bread, fruit, ice cream, Jell-O®, some vegetables, and most anything sweet. No meat, poultry, or fish, and rarely cheese. She was avid about her likes and dislikes; she has always seemed to know exactly what and when she wanted to eat and ex-

actly what and when she did *not* want to eat. Familiar, not novel, foods were the rule. Two examples: From 16 months to about 2 years of age, she ate an egg and toast for every breakfast, 7 days a week. One day she abruptly stopped eating eggs and, to the present day, does not eat them (she prefers not to eat breakfast). At age 6 she could not get enough of McDonald's Chicken McNuggets, but then as abruptly rejected them. Any food item offered her that is either new or that she no longer likes is treated as poison, and the caretaker regarded as a probable assassin.

Jane B. has always had a wide variety of foods from which she was allowed to choose with few restrictions. In a busy household during her first 4 to 5 years, she ate pretty much on her own schedule, with only a nod to that of her family. While at grandmother's she was allowed to eat in the middle of the night if she woke up and was hungry. Grandmother's philosophy was to let her eat whatever she wanted, in whatever amount, around the clock (in a laboratory setting this is known as an *ad libitum* or *ad lib* feeding schedule— cf. *liberty*).

Bright, alert, and happy, at age 14, Jane B. is average in size and above average in intellectual achievement. (Apparently her brain *did* manage to get enough protein during development, a constant source of worry for her parents.) Other than normal childhood diseases and accidents, her health appears to be near optimal.

tions to keep in mind: What is the role of caretakers in Jane's culture? How well could she accomplish her food selection task without the help of adult caretakers?

Open Feeding Systems of Young Humans.   We can learn the following lessons from Jane B.'s case history of early omnivore behavior.

1. In large measure, the choices expressed by very young humans seem to be determined primarily by the *flavors* of food and drink. Preference for sweet may lead to the selection of (overall) less nutritious foods. A reinforcer is not choosy about the behavior it reinforces. (See discussion by Pliner, Herman, & Polivy, 1990.)

2. Food *neophobia* (translated as finickiness) describes the overall pattern of eating among young humans. Moreover, the highly conservative food selections that children make belie labeling them omnivorous.

3. Although the foods offered Jane B. were culturally determined, her selections were highly idiosyncratic. She seems to have learned from direct experience that "if it looks like A, then it tastes/smells like B." And how B tastes and smells, *not* the caretaker's admonitions, guided her ingestive behavior. Is this true throughout a lifetime?

4. Selecting one food and eating it nearly exclusively and then abruptly switching has been described as a "feeding jag" (Davis, 1939). We discuss feeding jags as an adaptive specialization of eating in the next section. In her classical *cafeteria feeding studies*, Davis (1928, 1939) also concluded that *ad libitum* selections of type and amount of food could be as readily accomplished by rug rats as by adult caretakers.

5. Advice for new parents: (a) Prepare to worry about your child's nutrition (worrying about your child's nutrition is adaptive and contributes to inclusive *fitness*), (b) provide many alternative foods (some of them nutritious) from which your child can choose, (c) put the poisons out of reach, (d) get real laid back, and (e) get out of the way.

Learning Appropriate Food Choices

Recall from Chapters 3 and 4 that *conditioning taste aversions* was a method used to illuminate general properties of association formation. Conditioned taste aversions decrease the preference for flavored foods and fluids, thereby influencing future food choices. In this section we shift our focus from general associative mechanisms to the specifics of how learning determines food choices.

The Role of Sickness in Learning to Recognize Nutrients.   The tragic history of D.W. underscored the innate regulation of salt and water. Rozin and his colleagues posed research questions about other specific hungers (Rodgers &

Rozin, 1966; Rozin, 1967). Identifying, ingesting, and regulating salt, they reasoned, must be performed differently from the way animals locate other nutrients, such as iron and thiamin. Why? Because animals have *not* evolved taste receptors sensitive to approximately 100 other vitamins, minerals, and essential nutrients. These trace elements are typically masked within food complexes and, as such, are not consciously recognized.

How Is Thiamin Recognized?   Rozin and colleagues set out to determine how a trace element such as thiamin is recognized in diets. The question they asked was how do animals know which foods contain thiamin if it cannot be detected by peripheral receptors? Recognize that this is not an academic question. On the contrary, the answer to this question would go a long way toward helping us understand how Jane B. managed to survive and thrive the first 14 years of life. She somehow selected the right foods, in the right amounts, and at the right time from a variety of food sources.

Rats eating a diet lacking thiamin become *thiamin deficient*.[12] They lose appetite and weight, their coat does not shine, and they die unless they replace the thiamin they lack. If given thiamin in a saccharin-flavored solution, they drink it avidly, ingest the thiamin, and recover from the deficiency state. They tend to like the saccharin better than control rats do, presumably because of the positive association of the flavor with recovery from sickness (Garcia, Ervin, Yorke, & Koelling, 1967). Other experiments have revealed that the analysis of increasing a flavor's preference by its association with recovery from deficiency is more complicated than suggested by Garcia et al. Zahorik (1977) analyzed the problem as follows, based on research with her colleagues (see Zahorik, Mair, & Pies, 1974):

1. Animals learn to dislike the flavor of the thiamin-deficient diet. Rats prefer a familiar-safe diet to a novel one, but they will choose a novel diet if the alternative is a familiar-deficient diet.

2. The familiar-deficient diet having become aversive, hungry rats overcome their innate neophobia and choose an alternative diet. If the alternative diet is familiar and safe—*not* associated with thiamin deficiency—it is selected over a novel diet. Rats select a novel diet in preference to a familiar-deficient diet.

3. Recovery from deficiency after eating a novel-flavored diet (that contains thiamin) increases the preference for that novel flavor. This *conditioned preference* is greater than for control rats that like the flavor merely because it has become familiar—*preference due to familiarity*.

From Zahorick's (1977) analysis we can conclude that salt detection differs from thiamin detection. Although we are conscious of salt on our tongue,

---

[12] The acute condition of thiamine deficiency in humans is called *beriberi,* a continuing problem in third world countries.

the taste of thiamin is not recognized in food. Thiamin is "recognized" over the long term by sickness (deficiency) and recovery states. Illness or well-being is attributed to flavored foods that alternatively lack and contain the needed substance, respectively.

Hedonic Conditioning.   What an interesting push-pull system! The possibility is raised that many dozens of nutrients are "unconsciously" regulated by an associative mechanism. Flavors of foods (of which we *are* presumably conscious) are associated with repletion of nutrients (of which we are unaware). Booth (1982) has called this regulation of nutrient selection by the association of flavored foods with their postingestional consequences **hedonic conditioning** (cf. *hedonism*). In his schema, following every meal flavors of foods consumed during that meal are hedonically adjusted according to their nutritional effects. If the consequences are positive (reinforcing), we increase our preference for the items most recently eaten. If the consequences are negative (i.e., punishing, such as when deficiency states are induced), we are less likely to continue eating those particular flavored foods.

Recall that rats prefer familiar-safe diets to novel diets. A child's feeding jags (Davis, 1939) are followed by abrupt switches to new foods. Such switches may reflect the formation of conditioned aversions to a familiar-deficient diet. In the case history described in Box 7.3, Jane B.'s abrupt rejection of eggs may have reflected a shift to meet other nutritional needs.

Conditioned Flavor Preferences.   Are changes in preference for flavored foods and beverages restricted to recovery from a thiamin deficiency state? No. The phenomenon is quite general. Increased preference for flavors has been associated with *protein replacement* (Baker, Booth, Duggan, & Gibson, 1987), *calories* (Bolles, Hayward, & Crandall, 1981; Capaldi, Campbell, Sheffer, & Bradford, 1987; Mehiel & Bolles, 1984), *recovery from gastrointestinal sickness* (Barker & Weaver, 1991; Green & Garcia, 1971), *ethanol (beer, spirits, etc.)* (Deems, Oetting, Sherman, & Garcia, 1986; Sherman, Hickis, Rice, Rusiniak, & Garcia, 1983), and a *physiological state accompanying low food deprivation* (Campbell, Capaldi, & Myers, 1987; Capaldi & Myers, 1982). Excellent evidence exists, then, to support Booth's notion of hedonic conditioning. The reader is referred to Capaldi and Powley (1990) for an overview.

Both genes and cultures determine our relationship with foods. What is missing in the preceding analysis is how food is interrelated with other aspects of our lives. Much of the world's political maneuvering, diplomacy, and business is conducted in the context of power breakfasts/lunches/formal dinners. In addition, the phrases "Let's do lunch sometime" or "Wanna get a cup of coffee?" often play a role in human courtship patterns. Let us turn our attention to sex.

Interim Summary

1. Eating and drinking behaviors are best understood as an interplay of genes and environment, of physiology and behavior.

2. In addition to taste and olfactory receptors that allow the location of foodstuffs in the environment, homeostatic mechanisms have evolved to regulate essential nutrients.

3. Food selection and food preparation processes have evolutionary consequences. This schema is called *biocultural evolution*. Feeding behaviors that are adaptive are selected because they enhance inclusive fitness. What humans learn about foods during their lifetime and transmit to their offspring complements (a) basic taste and smell receptors and (b) innate homeostatic regulatory processes.

4. Salt and water are examples of *specific hungers*. Both peripheral receptors and homeostatic mechanisms have evolved to recognize and regulate these critically essential nutrients.

5. Humans are omnivores. The *omnivore's paradox* is that their relatively more open feeding system allows them a diverse range of potential foods but increases the risks of ingesting toxins.

6. Children often display profound food preferences, food *neophobias*, and prolonged *feeding jags*. They also manage to self-select foods without adverse consequences.

7. General associative mechanisms complement innately organized eating and drinking behavior. Essential nutrients such as thiamin seem to be regulated by learning which flavors produce postingestional deficiency or recovery states.

8. The punishing and reinforcing properties of foods experienced postingestionally is called *hedonic conditioning*. Such conditioning appears to complement innate flavor preferences in determining food selections.

LEARNING ABOUT SEX AND LOVE

> . . . abortion, abstinence, adolescent sexuality, aging and sex, anatomy and physiology of sex, animal sexuality, aphrodisiacs, art and dance, attitudes towards sex, autoerotism. . . .
>
> (Ellis and Abarbanel, Eds., Table of Contents,
> *The Encyclopedia of Sexual Behavior*, 1961)

At the outset of this chapter, Sagan and Druyan (1992) challenged us to entertain the possibility that a great deal of complex human behavior is biologically predisposed. Emotions rule behavior, they have argued, and thinking has very little to do with various aspects of sex and love. These include sexual attraction, falling in love, jealousy, and maternal love.

Is there anything new in their assertions? We have already discussed issues of "biologically predisposed," or instinctive human behavior. Without exception, all such behaviors have been shown to be highly sensitive to environmental effects. Can we not also anticipate that expressions of human love and sexual behavior are also highly determined by the environment in which such behaviors are expressed?

Another assertion of Sagan and Druyan (1992) is that "emotional behavior" is a distinctively different category from "thinking." Certainly, different areas of brain and nervous system are involved in Watson's "fear, rage, and sex" relative to specific language areas on the surface of the left temporal lobe of the cerebral cortex. But the convenience of a dichotomous distinction between emotion and reason belies the integrity of adaptive behavior. Seldom are we dispassionate in our rationality, and seldom are our emotional behaviors devoid of plans and goals.

Issues of love and sexual behavior cover much ground. To select but a few topics in these realms runs the risk of trivializing themes of central importance in life. Indeed, the argument has repeatedly been made that an organism's behavior can best be understood in terms of *inclusive fitness:* How does the behavior contribute to survival, reproduction, and caretaking of offspring? For humans, issues of love and sex are essential in courting, mating, and caring for offspring. There are no more important issues.

Where to begin? The table of contents cited at the beginning of this section goes on to list more than 100 chapters in an encyclopedia of sexual behavior (Ellis & Abarbanel, 1961). The present strategy is to take two behaviors—sexual attraction and maternal love—that Sagan and Druyan (1992) asserted to be "biologically predisposed." Both are examples of behavior involving emotion, and both have been investigated in the laboratory. Let us begin by looking at the Harlows' interesting research on the development of maternal love in *Rhesus* monkeys.

Maternal Love

In a famous series of studies, the Harlows investigated the role of mother-infant feeding in pair bonding (Harlow & Harlow, 1962a, 1962b). In doing so they later found that they had inadvertently studied the effects of isolating infant *Rhesus* monkeys from their mothers. The infant monkeys in question were given surrogate mothers. One was a monkey-shaped wire frame to which a nursing bottle was attached. Next to it was a terry-cloth covered wire frame that didn't nurse. The Harlows measured which of the two surrogates the infants spent the most time with. Not surprising, the young monkeys nursed from the wire frame and then clung for hours to the terry cloth monkey mother. The Harlows speculated that primates had a biological need for contact comfort that was not met by the life-sustaining but uncomfortable wire monkey mother.

When these motherless monkeys became adults, the Harlows discovered that rather profound changes had occurred in their socialization. Neither the males nor females knew how to appropriately court the opposite sex or how to engage in copulation. Following artificial insemination, a number of the females successfully delivered infant monkeys, but they proved to be ineffective mothers. These surrogate-raised mothers were neither protective of their young nor effective in nursing them. Some were totally neglectful and physically abusive. Conclusion? Social isolation can have severe consequences. Primates, undoubtedly including humans, must have supportive environments in which various aspects of sexual and maternal behaviors are learned.

Effects of Isolation.   For convenience as well as for control over extraneous variables that might influence experimental outcomes, laboratory animals (mammals) are typically housed in single cages. Social isolation has identifiable effects. Raising young rats in isolation, for example, has been found to influence brain development: Group-housed rats have more cortical development (Bennett, Diamond, Krech, & Rosenzweig, 1964) and more synapses per neuron (Turner & Greenough, 1983). Concomitant changes occur in the behavior of isolated animals as well, as the Harlows and others have discovered. Harlow and colleagues also found a simple preventative to counteract the pronounced social effects of isolation.

Effects of Social Play.   We might suspect that the *Rhesus* monkeys that had surrogate mothers were ineffective because they had not modeled the appropriate behaviors from "real" mothers. For example, you might argue that to become an effective nurser, you must first have had the experience of being nursed. The answer is even simpler but raises even more questions. What Harlow and his collaborators eventually found was that the effects of being raised with a surrogate mother could be mitigated if the isolated infant monkey could play with same-age peers for as little as an hour a day (Harlow, 1969). This finding suggests that total isolation per se—and not the specific experience of being mothered—was critical to the development of maladaptive maternal behavior.

Perhaps the recuperative effects of this minimal social contact can be better understood by imagining what a roomful of infant monkeys at play looks, sounds, and smells like. Sensory and motor systems, limbic and affective systems, forebrain, midbrain, hindbrain, and spinal cord—all get a workout. As is the case with other primates, monkey play by both sexes involves wrestling, chasing, and aggressive play (Harlow, 1963). Early social interactions influence brain development and adult social behavior in adaptive ways. Likewise, early and profound social isolation is implicated in both maladaptively developed brains and behavior.

Learning Individual Differences in Sexual Behavior

> . . . beauty, chastity, nudism, coitus, contraception, courtship, divorce, extramarital sex, families, femininity, fertility, fetishism, homosexuality, impotence, love,

> sexual love, marriage, music and sex, orgasm, perversions, pornography, premarital sex, prostitution, transvestism. . . .
>
> (Ellis and Abarbanel, Eds., Table of Contents,
> *The Encyclopedia of Sexual Behavior,* 1961)

Most humans are preoccupied with love and sex. For example, Americans spend billions of dollars yearly—more than they spend on elementary education—on perfumes, deodorants, and other smell-enhancing attractants. Pick up a newspaper, a weekly newsmagazine, or novels; go to movies, or watch TV shows, and you will likely find a number of the topics in the preceding list of sexual behaviors.

That these areas of sexual behavior exist in all cultures speaks to their biological predisposition. The wide-ranging scope of sexual topics speaks to a plasticity of sexual behavior. Consider the following:

What is *beautiful;* attitudes toward *abortion, contraception,* and *premarital sex;* and what is and is not sexually *perverse* vary from individual to individual within a culture as well as among cultures. Learning has played a large role in the development of your particular outlook on these issues. There is no reason to expect that you have learned these attitudes and behaviors about sex and love any differently from how you learned other behaviors. Reinforcers and punishers control their very expression.

Within a lifetime, you may learn that too much of the wrong perfume is not sexually attractive (is not reinforced). Some hair styles are better for you (more reinforcing to other people) than others. You may learn that the same sexual practices that were reinforced during your unmarried teen years may be punished after 5 to 10 years of marriage.

Sexual Attraction

Even animals that we might suspect to lead simpler, more reflexive sex lives than humans exhibit unusual plasticity of behavior. Michael Domjan and his colleagues looked at the role conditioning plays in various aspects of the sexual behavior of the Japanese quail. Domjan's animal model is highly suggestive of the subtle ways in which sexual advances can be conditioned in other animals. For example, male quail make indiscriminate sexual approaches to quail of either sex. They apparently learn to prefer female quail after successful copulation (S⁺) and not to prefer males because of unsuccessful (S⁻) attempts at copulation (Nash & Domjan, 1991). Successful copulation with a female quail then becomes associated with their distinctively colored feathers; subsequently, males spend more time with a model (stuffed bird) with such feathers (Domjan, 1992).

Among the most interesting of Domjan's studies is his animal model of sexual fetishes. If, in the preceding study, artificially colored feathers are associated with successful copulation, male quail preferentially select models with artificially colored feathers over naturally colored female feathers (Domjan,

O'vary, & Green, 1988). Their analysis that nonsexual stimuli may become sexually attractive by their association with sexually reinforcing experiences may explain why black leather, for example, can become a turn on. In recognizing the complexities of quail sexuality, Domjan (1994) cautions against too simplistic Pavlovian conditioning accounts.

Interim Summary

1. Sexual behaviors are best understood as interplays of genes and environment and of physiology and behavior.

2. Love and sex are of utmost importance to humans because they bear directly on each individual's inclusive fitness.

3. The Harlows' research with *Rhesus* monkeys demonstrated that courting, mating, and maternal caretaking behaviors could be severely disrupted by isolation. Minimal social interactions with same-age peers during early development prevented the sexual deficiencies found in the Harlows' early surrogate mother studies.

4. The variability found within individuals during their lifetime, within a given culture, and cross-culturally attests to the plasticity of many aspects of human sexual behavior.

5. Domjan's animal model of sexual behavior using quail demonstrates that simple conditioning processes, including discrimination learning, account for gender preferences. In addition, visual stimulus characteristics become preferred as a result of sexual reinforcement.

ROLE OF CONDITIONING IN BEHAVIORAL DISORDERS AND BEHAVIORAL THERAPY

Health

In our culture physicians are entrusted with applying their knowledge of anatomy, physiology, and pharmacology in providing health care for people who become ill. The very existence of the concept of *mental health* and the field of **behavioral medicine** attest to the fact that health encompasses both physiology and behavior. Behavioral medicine is an interdisciplinary field concerned with the etiology of illness and wellness, preventative medicine, biofeedback, and other forms of psychophysiology, treatment, and rehabilitation strategies (Schwartz & Weiss, 1978). Learning theory also aids our understanding of health issues by spanning the behavioral gap between the physical and the mental realms. In the last part of this chapter, we analyze the role of learning in issues of behavioral medicine.

By the mid-1970s a growing number of health care professionals were advocating major revisions in the basic way that physicians and patients alike viewed issues of health (Knowles, 1977). A **biopsychosocial model** of health was proposed as the most meaningful alternative to an outmoded **biomedical model.** The coup was bloodless. Cultural practices, learned behavior, and genetically determined anatomy and physiology are now viewed as interlocking determinants of an individual's health. Figure 7.2 is one version of the contemporary understanding of the determinants of health.

Earlier in this chapter we reviewed strong evidence attesting to the power of the associative conditioning of immune system responses. We also saw that both the perception of pain and a drug's effectiveness could be markedly influenced by learning experiences. Finally, the open feeding systems of omnivores allow not only ingestional errors such as poisoning and nutritional deficiency but also the possibility of eating disorders in the form of clinical obesity, anorexia nervosa, and bulimia, which are three examples of disorders whose etiology and treatment fall within the purview of behavioral medicine. In this section we review several conditioning examples that have implications for health and then look ahead to the promising integration offered by behavioral medicine.

Neurosis and Conditioned Fear

Experimental Neurosis.   Remember Pavlov's experiment reported in Chapter 4 in which he conditioned a dog to discriminate between a circle and an ellipse (see Figure 4.9)? When the ellipse became too similar to the circle, the discrimination broke down. So did the dog. The biting and snarling behavior exhibited when the discrimination was further tested—when the dog continued to be challenged beyond its perceptual capacities—indicated to Pavlov a strong link between the dog's personal experience and its mental health. His dog's behavior changed for several weeks and extended beyond the immediate testing situation to other aspects of its life. Pavlov labeled the phenomenon **experimental neurosis.** He thought his model had direct parallels with some examples of human neurotic behavior.

What do you think? Can you relate Pavlov's findings to what you know about human responses to stressful situations? When faced with deciding how to split your study time the night before three tests, are there emotional consequences? Pavlov noted individual differences in how dogs responded to training. Do you know *your* limits?

Conditioning Emotional Responses in Humans.   *Conditioned suppression* was discussed in Chapter 4. Razran (1971) has noted that the most widely used method of investigating associative processes in the United States is, sadly, the conditioning of fear responses. Recall that when a tone or light (CS) is repeatedly paired with electric shock (US), the neutral stimulus takes on shocklike properties. Rats, dogs, and humans respond fearfully in the presence of the formerly neutral stimulus. Conditioned fear responses are presumed to be the basis of both phobias and anxiety.

What is the evidence that humans learn to be anxious and fearful? Alternatively, these conditions may be innately predisposed behavioral patterns. The reason is that both phobias and anxiety are highly idiosyncratic among individuals, and classical conditioning continues to be the best way to account for their origins (Davey, 1992). Let us look at a historical example of conditioned fear.

Watson and Little Albert.   John B. Watson asserted that human behavior could be controlled by reinforcing and punishing stimuli. His infamous experiments on Little Albert bear directly on questions of emotional health and well-being, the etiology of phobias, and related issues in behavioral medicine. Watson assumed that fear, rage, and love were three basic emotions innately shared by all humans. All other emotions (emotional behavior) are based on these. Watson and Rayner (1920) conditioned a fear response in Albert, an 11-month-old child. Watson's point was to demonstrate that innate fears could be arbitrarily attached to any neutral stimulus, the result being a maladaptive phobic response. On numerous occasions in his laboratory, Watson showed Albert a white rat (CS) and paired it with a very loud clanging noise (US). Albert soon responded in the presence of the white rat in the same way he responded to the loud noise; he startled, cried, and initiated escape responses.

Given the wealth of findings from general process learning, it should come as no surprise that Watson's "attachment" of fear responses through conditioning was found to *generalize* to other furry objects presented Albert. These included an inanimate fur coat and a Santa Claus mask. Indeed, the whole gamut of related associative phenomena might have been used to analyze the extent of Albert's emotional conditioning. Perhaps fortunately, Albert was removed from Watson's and Rayner's care before treatment of this phobia could be initiated. They were prepared to present the fear-inducing white rat and stimulate Albert's genitals at the same time to attach pleasurable feelings to the rat.

Anyone care to predict another likely outcome? We look at more reasonable treatment strategies in the last section of this chapter.

Post-Traumatic Stress Disorder

Ample evidence attests to the positive health outcomes of many of life's experiences. In a very real sense, the status of our health "when things go right" provides the control condition by which to gauge compromised health caused when bad things happen to people. For example, the health we enjoy due to the foods we normally eat may be appreciated only during times of malaise caused by famine or poisoning. Pain makes us appreciate its absence. Likewise, the role that catastrophe, trauma, and Thorndike's annoyers (i.e., loud clangs, mild electric shock, and gastrointestinal distress) play in our health gets our attention precisely because so often the behavioral consequences of these events are unusually unpleasant and long lasting.

Post-traumatic stress disorder (PTSD) sometimes results in individuals who experience intense aversive stimuli. The human response to overwhelming events that occur during war and as a result of rape, child abuse, and natural disasters (fires, hurricanes, etc.) is often severe and unique enough to be categorized as a disorder in the DSM-IV (*Diagnostic and Statistical Manual of Mental Disorders*, 4th ed., American Psychiatric Association).

The incidence of PTSD in the general population is estimated to be as high as 9.2% (Breslau, Davis, Andreski, & Peterson, 1991) compared to estimates of drug abuse (5.9%) and depression (8.3%) (Solomon, Gerrity, & Muff, 1992).

PTSD is not the inevitable result of trauma. Some humans suffer similar trauma and return to high levels of functioning within months. Why after the passage of many years do some otherwise talented, intelligent individuals continue to suffer debilitating nightmares, to continue to reexperience the trauma of war or rape via memories and flashbacks? Some forms of PTSD are considered to be associative; that is, a special type of conditioned emotional response (Kolb, 1984). The distinctive sounds of a helicopter, for example, may elicit intense conditioned fear responses in Vietnam vets. The conditioned response may be of such intensity that the person reports reliving, or reexperiencing, the original event. No other examples of conditioned responses having this characteristic come to mind.

Other features of the disorder (explosive outbursts, atypical dreams, hyperirritability, and startle reflex) seem to be better described in terms of *sensitization*. One prominent researcher (van der Kolk, 1987) invokes Pavlov's notion of an innate reflexive response, or defensive reaction, to environmental threat. Recognizing that flashbacks, nightmares, and intrusive recollections cannot be studied in animals, other researchers have pointed out that biological and behavioral processes have been successfully modeled. Both passive avoidance and dissociative symptoms (called *numbing* in humans) occur in all animals in response to intense stress (Foa et al., 1992). Reflexes typically are adaptive, however; they promote inclusive fitness. By contrast, the PTSD response pattern appears to be maladaptive. The interested reader is referred to van der Kolk (1987) for an in-depth analysis of this fascinating disorder.

Learned Helplessness

Initially described by Overmier and Seligman (1967) and Seligman and Maier (1967), *learned helplessness* is another apparently maladaptive behavior pattern. In research using dozens of dogs, they found that following administration of intense electric shocks, two of every three dogs failed to respond adaptively thereafter. In Chapter 3 it was argued that intense electric shocks should *sensitize* the dogs, making them tend to respond to future electric shocks even more vigorously. Following these researchers' treatment, however, the dogs were immobile. In the presence of shock, though unrestrained, they whined and defecated rather than attempting to escape the shock by moving away. This *reduction* in responsiveness is opposite to some PTSD behavior just described. PTSD patients are characterized by explosive outbursts, hyperirritability, and a hypersensitive startle reflex. Learned helplessness *is* characteristic of other PTSD victims whose response to rape, for example, is sometimes characterized by immobility, passivity, helplessness, and dissociative memory (Burgess & Holstrom, 1974). Why the responses to intense aversive stimuli are so unpredictable is unknown.

Learned Helplessness in Humans. The application of the learned helplessness research with dogs and rats has been applied to humans (Seligman, 1975). In his earliest formulation, Seligman identified three consequences of learned helpless training in humans; namely, *motivational, cognitive,* and *emotional* deficits. The motivational deficit is characterized by performance changes not unlike that seen in dogs. Whereas dogs do not bother to get off the grid floor to avoid electric shock, a human might not get out of bed for several days. Along with this reduction in a human's behavioral response is his or her *cognitive* interpretation that "responding is futile." Finally, *emotional* distress accompanies both the performance decrements and cognitive ideation. People who perceive themselves as helpless and depressed simply feel bad.

Critics of Seligman's (1975) theory pointed out that not all people who are subjected to uncontrollable events suffer these three deficits (Buchwald, Coyne, & Cole, 1978). For example, some individuals continue to live relatively normal lives even after having found out that they have a terminal illness with only months to live. Nevertheless, learned helplessness theory does fit the response patterns of many individuals and continues to receive serious attention in psychophysiological theories of stress and other psychosomatic disorders. For example, withdrawal and concomitant depression is a common response seen in college students who fail the first test, study hard for the second one, and then fail it. In this example, which response(s) are withdrawn in the face of what "uncontrollable events"?[13]

Eating Disorders: Anorexia Nervosa, Bulimia, and Obesity

Earlier in this chapter evidence was offered supporting two views of human ingestional behavior—that it is both innately organized and culturally determined (i.e., learned). The prevalence of eating disorders in our culture is hard

---

[13] Studying and class attendance because neither response seems to affect the grades earned on tests.

evidence for ingestional *plasticity*. Some individuals learn to override the multiple and redundant homeostatic mechanisms that are designed to preclude disorders such as anorexia nervosa and bulimia.

Failure of Primary Reinforcers and Punishers.   Because the topic is highly visible, most readers are aware of the prevalence of eating disorders in our culture. The etiology of *anorexia nervosa* and *bulimia* is unknown. Because of a paucity of animal models for these disorders, they will likely remain a mystery for some time. That these disorders are due to maladaptive learned behavior is assumed (Hsu, 1990). The sequence of conditioning experiences underlying this learning, however, has never been described. *Secondary reinforcers* seem to be maintaining both anorexia nervosa and bulimia. Primary reinforcers (i.e., alleviating hunger in anorexia nervosa) and normally punishing stimuli (vomiting in bulimia) no longer function to reinforce and punish behavior, respectively. Another way to say this is that the normal mechanisms that maintain homeostasis are out of whack. Why? The reasons are many. The maladaptively learned (mis)perception of thinness serves to act as a reinforcing stimulus maintaining the maladaptive eating behaviors.

Pain as Reinforcement.   Under the slogan "no pain, no gain," athletes use the response-produced stimuli of exertion and pain to motivate even greater pain-producing exertion. Such behavior is not considered maladaptive.[14] Rather, the more bench press repetitions or miles run, the greater the pleasure of attaining personal goals.

The intense motivation of the anorexic to stay thin appears to be achieved in a similar manner. *Not* responding to the hunger pains (normally unpleasant and simply alleviated) to achieve the goal of thinness becomes highly reinforcing. The trick of the masochist is to perceive normally painful stimuli—from a broad spectrum of life—as pleasurable. Then the law of effect continues to work as predicted. Though maladaptive, anorexia nervosa and bulimia should not be considered as exceptions to the law of effect. Rather, hunger and pain become discriminative stimuli *not* to eat. Furthermore, the ingestion of tasty food sets the occasion for vomiting in the bulimic and serves as highly effective punishment for the anorexic.

Obesity.   Merely overweight or obese? Obesity has been defined as being 40% or more above the ideal weight as determined by Metropolitan (standard) weight charts (Bray, 1976). Although classified as an eating disorder and typically included in the same discussions with anorexia nervosa and bulimia, obesity is both more familiar and better understood than the "thin" disorders. One difference is that being overweight isn't nearly as life-threatening as anorexia nervosa. At 20% above average weight, only very slight increases in morbidity

---

[14] This is so unless it so totally dominates all aspects of life that personal and social obligations are not met.

and mortality exist. At 40% above average, however, overweight men are two and a half times more likely to die from all causes (Van Itallie, 1979).

Food as Reinforcer.   Clearly, the role of learning in creating obesity is different from the other two eating disorders in that tasty foods *reinforce* the behavior of eating tasty foods. As predicted, reinforcement increases the frequency of the preceding behavior. A simple view of obesity, then, is one in which normal homeostatic control mechanisms are overridden by the reinforcing power of tasty foods. Animal models support this theory. Rats allowed a frequently changing diet of bananas, chocolate, chocolate-chip cookies, cheese, fat, marshmallows, peanut butter, sweetened condensed milk, and salami gained 269% more weight than controls eating lab chow (Sclafani & Springer, 1976). Not surprising, sugar and fat mixed together produced greater weight gains than diets of sugar, or fat, or lab chow alone (Lucas & Sclafani, 1990). Now, if you just add chocolate. . . .

The animal model described here does not begin to account for the individual differences observed among humans. There is some evidence (Jirik-Babb & Katz, 1988) that bulimics and anorexics are *less* sensitive to tastes (and, arguably, are less reinforced for eating tasty food) while flavors are *more* reinforcing for the obese (Schiffman, 1983). An implication of these opposing findings is that these disorders are presumably under more complex stimulus control than merely the taste of foods. Both self-perception and learned social roles are precipitating conditions, and the changing of maladaptive cognitive and emotional variables are common therapeutic goals in dealing with these disorders.

Let us turn to behavioral therapy.

Behavioral Therapies

Behavioral therapy and cognitive behavior therapy are among the most successful of the various psychotherapies used to effect changes in maladaptive cognitive and emotional behaviors. The fact that the various techniques now used in behavioral therapy were developed using Pavlovian conditioning models is reflected in their earliest descriptions, that is, *conditioned reflex therapy* (Salter, 1949) and the *conditioning therapies* (Wolpe, Salter, & Reyna, 1964). Likewise, one of the more important methodologies used in therapy, **behavior modification,** is a direct application of Skinner's operant conditioning. Extinction procedures and the systematic application of reinforcers and punishers are applied to change target behaviors.

Diverse Applications of Behavioral Therapy.   The treatment of phobias and other psychophysiological disorders involving the ANS using behavioral modification techniques is highly effective. Outcome studies generally indicate long-term remediation of symptoms with little recidivism. That behavioral therapies can be as effective as invasive biomedical therapies (such as drugs and surgery) has been demonstrated for such disorders as low back pain (Fordyce, Brockway, Bergman, & Spengler, 1986; Heinrich, Cohen, Naliboff, Collins, & Bonebakker, 1985); survival time in terminal cancer (Grossarth-Maticek & Eysenck, 1989); pain management (Turk, Meichenbaum, & Genest, 1983); and enuresis (Kimmel & Kimmel, 1970). Box 7.4 shows how behavioral therapy can be used as an alternative to biomedical therapy.

BOX 7.4   BLADDER CONTROL: SURGERY OR BEHAVIORAL MODIFICATION?

What was merely an embarrassment to the 5-year-old was perceived as a major problem by mom. Every day, a half-dozen or more of Kris's wet underpants accumulated in the laundry, testimony to a weak external spinctor connecting her bladder with her urethra. Her incontinence occurred while running and playing, when excited at her dance competitions, and if she waited too long between voidings.

Behavioral modification is now recognized as a treatment of choice for this condition (Philips, Fenster, & Samson, 1988), so Kris's parents initiated a home behavioral modification program.

Her behavioral treatment was both simple and noninvasive. Kris was asked to make a mark on her chart by the toilet each time she urinated. If, when she went to urinate, she discovered dry underpants, she was asked to place a gold stick-on star on her chart. If she discovered wet underpants, she merely changed herself and put an *X* on the chart instead of the star. The dependent variables, then, were *frequency of micturition* and *daily count of wet underpants*. At the end of each day, she received a dime for each star.

What are the relevant components of this behavior modification program? Her *baseline,* or *operant,* level of micturition was determined by the first day's count of stars and *X*s. Discovering wet pants (a) increased her awareness of the target behavior and (b) helped focus her attention on subtle previoiding sensations. The preceding intervention consisted of several forms of *reinforced* and *punished* behaviors:

BOX 7.4

Primary Reinforcers
- Parental attention and interest.
- The absence of parental concern and disappointment.
- The comfort of dry underpants.

Secondary Reinforcers
- Gold stars, dimes, and words of praise.

Punishers
- Discomfort of wet pants.
- Loss of expected gold stars and dimes.

What was the success of this program? The short-term and long-term outcome was mixed. The frequency of wet pants went down rapidly within the first few days. Among the behaviors that had been reinforced was spending more time on the toilet. In part the decreased frequency of wet pants can be attributed to the fact that she wore them less and sat on the toilet more. Increasing her frequency of attempted bladder voidings was a desirable outcome for two reasons: It helped Kris focus on the attendant sensations preceding micturition, and frequent bladder emptying is healthier than prolonged urine retention. In addition, the 5-year-old's successes gave her a sense of personal control. As time passed, she was encouraged to regard occasional incontinence as "accidents." Her parents communicated to her that her self-worth would not be measured by absolute continence, and that more girls than boys had this problem because of different plumbing.

Therapy from a Behavioral Viewpoint

Suppose that during his 30s, Little Albert had presented himself to a psychotherapist for treatment due to an inordinate fear of animals—especially dogs—that interfered with his job as a letter carrier. During an interview with his patient, the therapist attempts to determine the boundaries of Albert's phobia. All animals? Furry animals? Large or small animals? Neither knowing nor especially caring about the reasons underlying the phobia, the behavioral therapist tries to *target* the specific behavior in question and to get some idea of the extent of the *generalization gradient* around the target behavior.

Systematic Desensitization. Albert's therapist would probably have decided to employ a common behavioral technique called *systematic desensitization*. Systematic desensitization involves first extinguishing fear responses to stimuli far removed from the target. The sensitive target behavior is approached in small steps, allowing responses to extinguish at each step. For example, the therapist might ask Albert, while in a relaxed state, to visualize an elephant sleeping safely behind bars in a zoo. Assuming that Albert showed no fear responses (ANS activity—altered breathing, sweating, nausea) to this image, the therapist might direct Albert to visualize the animal awakening, beginning to move, getting to its feet, and so on. A next step might be to ask Albert to visualize the cage bars being removed or to have him visually walk to another cage containing a furry animal such as a lion.

The fear responses evoked by these images are allowed to extinguish in the safety of the therapist's office. Assuming that the target response to be alleviated is *fear in the presence of dogs,* the therapist is little by little incorporating more of the distinguishing characteristics of dogs in situations that have caused the patient's past fear responses.

Each of the following actions involves the patient to allow extinction of conditioned fear response (AECFR):

Say the word *dog* (allow extinction of conditioned fear response, AECFR).

Imagine the dog barking (AECFR).

See the stuffed toy dog (AECFR).

Approach the stuffed toy dog (AECFR).

Touch the stuffed toy dog (AECFR).

See the live dog from a distance (AECFR).

Approach the live dog (AECFR).

Touch the live dog (AECFR).

Walk the neighborhood (AECFR).

Biofeedback.   **Biofeedback** refers to a procedure in which a patient (or experimental subject) is provided *feedback* regarding unconscious physiological processes. For example, even though the human brain frequently produces *alpha waves* (8–13 Hz), we are not normally aware of this or any other pattern of brainwaves. Biofeedback equipment can be programmed to monitor a particular waveform and to signal the subject by beeping when the waveform occurs. When patients are then asked to make the equipment beep by outputting alpha, they can do so voluntarily. *Voluntarily* must be qualified because, when asked, they report, "I don't know how I'm doing it." In and of itself, this demonstration indicates that conscious control can be exerted over involuntary processes. From a training perspective, the target waveform can be considered an operant response and the beeper a secondary reinforcer via verbal instructions. (A therapist, for example, might say "good" when the patient is successfully producing alpha; the beeper is associated with "good.") That the reinforcement procedure is effective is evidenced by the increased frequency of outputting alpha.

In addition to changes in brain waves, other physiological responses that can be manipulated by biofeedback reinforcement procedures are muscle tension, skin temperature, blood pressure, heart rate, gastric motility, and skin conductance. That such physiological changes can be accomplished in the laboratory is not in question. The usefulness of biofeedback as behavioral therapy, however, is controversial. For example, comparison of biofeedback with relaxation training for headache pain (Blanchard, Andrasik, Ahles, Teders, & O'Keefe, 1980) and for control of blood pressure (Blanchard & Epstein, 1977) has led some researchers to question its practical clinical usefulness. Relaxation training appears to be equally effective and doesn't require the expensive instrumentation used in biofeedback.

Analysis of Biofeedback Efficiency.   Given that biofeedback training is a form of operant conditioning and that operant conditioning has proven to be a highly effective way to train instrumental responses, we might ask why biofeedback is not a more effective therapeutic procedure. In the first place, biofeedback uses a rather weak secondary reinforcer to effect permanent psychophysiological changes. Recall that in a biofeedback situation the reinforcement procedure of verbal praise ("good") follows the target psychophysiological response. Pavlov's *second signal system* describes how verbal praise (the word *good*) attains its reinforcing value due to second-order conditioning. The beeper sound is then paired with "good"; any reinforcing value of the beeper is attained by conditioning of the third order. Outside the biofeedback situation, it is unlikely that the beeper has any reinforcing value at all. That is, outside a 1-hour training session once or twice weekly, the conditioned change in the target psychophysiological response is "in extinction." Since these target responses are for the most part not consciously experienced, there is no awareness of the response-outcome contingency. The conditioned response can therefore extinguish without the person realizing it. To summarize, it is highly likely that the therapeutic goals of biofeedback are not being realized because of less than optimal operant conditioning methods during acquisition and due to simple extinction of the conditioned response.

Evaluating Behavioral Therapy.   How effective is behavioral therapy? We saw earlier that phobias are successfully treated. Some problem behaviors are more resistant to therapeutic intervention than others, however. For example, programs to change the drinking of alcohol, smoking tobacco, and weight control behaviors have follow-up success rates of only 20 to 30% (Kaplan, 1984). Extrapolation of laboratory results using short-term behavior change in laboratory animals to lifelong habits of humans is problematic. Adult humans in therapy must overcome literally years of reinforced trials, and neither therapists nor patients should expect 1-hour weekly sessions to reverse these lifetime habits. Such cautions, however, are tempered by the observation that both *behavior therapy* and *cognitive behavior therapy* are the most efficacious of the various types of psychotherapy. For example, for treating PTSD, better outcomes result from behavioral techniques than the use of drugs or other forms of therapy (Solomon et al., 1992).

Interim Summary

1. A *biopsychosocial* model of health has replaced a strictly *biomedical* model.

2. Pavlov and others have investigated animal models of neurosis in laboratory settings.

3. Conditioning emotional responses such as fear and anxiety is easily accomplished in humans and other animals.

4. Post-traumatic stress disorder (PTSD) and learned helplessness occasionally result from intense aversive stimulation. These disorders can be analyzed from both associative and nonassociative perspectives using animal models.

5. Eating disorders such as anorexia nervosa, bulimia, and obesity are maladaptive but are explainable by applying the law of effect. In obesity, the reinforcing effects of palatable foods override homeostatic regulatory mechanisms. In the "thin" disorders, secondary reinforcing effects of perceived image override the primary reinforcers of palatable foods.

6. *Behavioral therapies* (or conditioning therapies) are effective as well as noninvasive methods used in *behavioral medicine*. In *behavior modification*, problem behaviors are identified and modified by the systematic application of reinforcers and punishers, by systematic desensitization, and by biofeedback.

CHAPTER SUMMARY

1. Learning theory can be applied to analyze the interaction of physiology and behavior. Animal models of drug-taking behavior, ingestional behavior, and immune system functioning provide insight into complex human behavior in these realms.

2. Historical distinctions tying instrumental conditioning to CNS functioning and Pavlovian conditioning to the ANS have broken down for several reasons. There is general agreement that common processes underlay S-S and R-S conditioning. CNS, ANS, endocrine, and immune systems are interactive in functioning.

3. Laboratory studies of the behavior and physiology of humans and animals

have had the cumulative effect of blurring the distinctions between so-called voluntary and involuntary behavior.

4. Due to their interactions, the CNS, ANS, neuroendocrine system, immune system, and other physiological systems are now best conceptualized as an interdependent, integrative holistic system.

5. Psychosomatic (cf. *psychophysiological*) disorders have their origin in Pavlovian conditioning. Apparently any physiological reflex can be conditioned, including blisters. Words/beliefs often function as conditioned stimuli that control responses.

6. Psychoneuroimmunology defines a research area in which immune system functioning can come under the control of previously neutral stimuli. Asthma and hives can be conditioned to respond to neutral stimuli. The emotional consequences of disrupted breathing are potential USs available for association with environmental cues. Both immunosuppression and immunofacilitation of T-lymphocytes can be conditioned. Psychoneuroimmunology provides the mechanism by which words/ thoughts/ emotions can effect immune system functioning.

7. Drugs such as morphine and ethyl alcohol can function as unconditioned stimuli. By entering into association with environmental cues, the pharmacological effects of drugs can be enhanced or reduced by environmental cues.

8. Drug tolerance can be understood as a conditioned response rather than merely being a pharmacological phenomenon. Drugs can also function as reinforcers that increase drug-taking behavior.

9. Ingestional behavior reflects evolutionary predispositions in the form of innate flavor receptors, systems of feeding such as carnivore and omnivore, and homeostatic regulatory mechanisms. The latter include innate recognition of certain foodstuffs such as salt and water, called *specific hungers*, and specialized eating behaviors such as feeding jags and neophobia.

10. Ingestional behavior also has plastic components, including the conditioning of flavor aversions and flavor preferences. Thiamin and other essential nutrients can be identified in flavored foods by a conditioning process. Conditioning based on application of the law of effect, called *hedonic conditioning*, is a mechanism that regulates and readjusts food preferences based on each meal's postingestive consequences.

11. Environment plays a crucial role in the development of various aspects of sexual behavior. Visual stimuli associated with sexual reinforcement have been conditioned in laboratory animals.

12. Behavioral disorders including phobias and other conditioned fear responses are understood in terms of laboratory models initially developed by Pavlov (*experimental neurosis*) and Watson (who conditioned Little Albert).

13. Learned helplessness and PTSD are serious disorders resulting from intense aversive experiences. Laboratory models of these disorders indicate that they are caused by both associative and nonassociative components.

14. Disorders of eating behavior (anorexia nervosa, bulimia, and obesity) are also learned. They can be successfully analyzed by the application of principles of reinforcement and punishment.

15. Behavioral therapies, including behavioral modification, attempt to change behaviors using reinforcement, punishment, and extinction procedures. Behavioral medicine employs a variety of animal-based methodologies as therapeutic alternatives to invasive procedures such as drugs and surgery.

DISCUSSION QUESTIONS

1. Charged with buying illegal amounts of valium, Jennifer Whitt spent almost 10 months in a prison in Reynosa, Mexico. A 24-year-old college student from Austin, Texas, she survived this time period without her asthma medication. Two hours after her release in September 1992, Jennifer suffered an asthma attack while her parents drove her across the border into southern Texas. A lifelong asthma sufferer, she died a few hours later in a U.S. hospital. Can you think of some reasons that her attack might have been so severe the day she reentered the United States?

2. Ted drinks five beers at a party while his twin brother Ned consumes the same amount of alcohol bar hopping. Given equal histories with alcohol (and, hence, equivalent amounts of alcohol tolerance), which twin would you predict would be the most wasted after five drinks? Why? Under what conditions might they be similarly affected?

3. *Dorland's Illustrated Medical Dictionary* (1974) defines *pica* as "a craving for unnatural articles of food; a depraved appetite, as seen in hysteria, pregnancy, and in malnourished children." What reasons can you come up with for changes in appetite in these three categories of abnormality?

4. Is conscious awareness necessary for a person to exhibit voluntary behavior? Must a person be aware of the response being made for that response to be reinforced? Must a rat be aware of its lymphocytes for them to decrease or increase in number, depending on whether the rat tastes saccharin following a conditioning episode? Must a preverbal human be aware of the relationship of his or her responses to the reinforcing or punishing stimulus that changes those responses?

5. Referring to Table 7.1 on p. 346, we see that stimulation of genitalia causes erections in males and vaginal lubrication in females. Could you describe a conditioning scenario in which CSs could come to control these responses?

6. As mentioned earlier, many years ago a student related to me that after hearing my lecture on the placebo effect, he emptied his roommate's asthma medicine bottle (that attached to a nebulizer) and filled it with water. For one week he watched his roommate get breathing relief from inhaling the water vapor. Understandably, his roommate became angry when he was told what had happened. He resumed his prescribed treatment. Can you explain why inhaling water vapor seemed to work? Any ideas on how long it would have continued to work?

7. Let CS_1 be a high-frequency nebulizer sound that accompanies the introduction of aerosol egg albumin into a chamber, causing a disruption in guinea pigs' breathing. Let CS_2 be a *low*-frequency nebulizer sound that accompanies the introduction of Isuprel into the chamber, allowing the guinea pigs to again breath without distress. Could these two distinctive CSs first induce and then relieve breathing disruptions? What would you call the effect of CS_2?

8. Premack's reinforcement theory can be applied to selecting therapy options for chemical dependency. To get someone to quit using crack cocaine, Premack would argue that the therapist needs to find a more powerful reinforcer than crack for the client. Assuming that Premack's analysis is correct, what is the prognosis if a therapist can't find a more powerful reinforcer?

9. Can you develop a conditioning scenario for a woman who becomes sex-

ually aroused only by males with mustaches? And while we're at it, why does that particular cologne smell so good?

10. *Pseudocyesis* is a psychosomatic condition more commonly known as *pseudopregnancy* or *false pregnancy.* In addition to cessation of the menstrual cycle, some females experience breast swelling, morning sickness, pica, and, as the ninth month approaches, the appearance of *colostrum* (a clear, sweet fluid that precedes breast milk), the onset of labor, and dilation of the cervix in preparation for delivery. In pseudocyesis there is no fetus. Women who experience the most symptoms have previously had a child or have read about the sequences of symptoms. Most such women want to be pregnant and grieve when they find that they have merely experienced some of the signs of pregnancy. Can you make the case that pregnancy is an elaborate 9-month "reflex" and that pseudopregnancy is a conditioned reflex?

11. After training Little Albert to fear a white rat, Watson and Rayner wanted to experiment further to remove the conditioned fear. They were prepared to stimulate Albert's genitals at the same time they aroused his fear by placing the rat near him. The idea was for Albert to attach pleasurable feelings to the rat. Anyone care to predict a more likely outcome? Can you think of an alternative therapy?

DISCUSSION STARTERS

1. *Can you think of some reasons that Jennifer Whitt suffered a fatal asthma attack the day she reentered the United States?* Given the similarity of environment, it is not likely that allergens differed in South Texas and Reynosa, Mexico. They may have been present but triggered the attack only when she entered a new environment. Among the possibilities that might have exacerbated her condition were heightened emotion at being released from prison and being reunited with parents. Another possibility is that being reunited with parents provided precipitating CSs associated with previous asthma attacks.

2. *Why would identical twins be differently affected by the same amount of alcohol?* Going from club to club, it can be argued, provides novel environments. Other considerations are the prior histories of Ted and Ned. Bar hopping itself may have become a familiar activity. Certainly the familiar (or novel) people you include in social situations would be among the most significant stimuli controlling your drug responses. You could also make the case that one of alcohol's effects is to alter perception, making the same environment continually renewing and novel. The latter analysis predicts less an effect for bar hopping and relatively more for a pharmacological effect.

3. *Why does pica occur?* Recall Rozin's category of a familiar-deficient diet. A familiar-deficient diet becomes aversive because the flavor of it produces a conditioned taste aversion to it. A marginally adequate familiar diet

could become a deficient diet because of increased nutritional demands of pregnancy. Familiar-deficient diets would initiate (trigger) a reduction (reversal?) in neophobia and a concomitant increase in "searching for new nutrients." Sounds like pica.

4. *Is conscious awareness necessary for a person to exhibit voluntary behavior?* No.

5. *Could you describe a conditioning scenario in which CSs could come to control these responses?* Design an experiment in which erections and vaginal lubrication are conditioned responses to formerly neutral CSs.

6. *Why might an asthma sufferer get breathing relief from inhaling water vapor?* This example defines the conditioned response properties of placebos. A question about how long the placebo will be effective becomes a question about the determinants of resistance-to-extinction (Chapters 3 and 4). Anger at being informed of a placebo effect reflects violated expectations: Our culture has prepared this individual to expect that only drugs have pharmacological ("real") properties.

7. *Could two distinctive CSs first induce, and then relieve, breathing disruptions? What would you call the effect of* CS_2? In preceding examples we have seen that $S^d – S^\Delta$, and $CS^+ – CS^-$ discriminations can be conditioned with ease. This leads us to expect that indeed, Justeson and his colleagues could have paired a distinctive sound, CS_2, with Isuprel and then demonstrated a placebo effect. (I wish someone would do this research. Imagine conditioning a near death response with one sound and recovering the animal with a different sound!)

8. *Premackian reinforcement and crack cocaine.* Assume that Premack's analysis of reinforcement relationships is correct and that the opportunity to engage in a higher probability behavior will reinforce engaging in a lower probability behavior. Securing and taking cocaine is the highest probability behavior in many an addict's behavioral repertoire. What, then, is a therapist to use to reinforce cocaine abstinence? Stating the problem doesn't solve it. Chemical dependency treatment programs are notoriously ineffective, especially for individuals who have few lifestyle alternatives. I have no solutions.

9. *Mustaches and sexual arousal.* This should not be much of a challenge after reviewing Domjan's animal model of sexual fetishism in quail. The idea is that visual (and other) stimuli can become associated with sexual encounters. Perfumes and colognes are designed to be sexual attractants in themselves and then become CSs that are reinforced by sexual arousal—a double whammy.

10. *Is pregnancy a nine-month "reflex"? Is pseudopregnancy a conditioned reflex?* Given that pseudopregnancies are common in dogs and cats (for equally unknown reasons), we need not invoke a uniquely conscious, uniquely thinking human to accomplish this interesting psychological/ physiological feat. Pregnancy can be broken down into a large number of physiological, reflexive, S-R chains. Assume that the female body "knows" how to accomplish each stage of a successful pregnancy via preexisting DNA programs. A false pregnancy can be attributed to initiating the sequence of S-R

chains and then suppressing disconfirming signals that fetal implantation in the uterine wall has failed. Suppressing disconfirming signals probably involves both conscious and unconscious mechanisms in humans. For example, the finding that those women who display the most symptoms of pregnancy have either had a child *or have read the most about having a child* suggests conscious influences. If words and *hope, despair,* and other *emotions* can influence immune system functioning, why not the myriad of interrelated physiological systems underlying reproduction?

11. *Predicting the outcome of mixing rats, fear, and sex.* Several problems with Watson's reasoning come to mind.

Earlier we looked at bidirectional conditioning. In bidirectional conditioning, two powerful stimuli—essentially two USs—enter into association in both a forward and a backward manner. In the present situation, it is more likely that fear (and the rat) would become associated with stimulation of the genitals than that the fear of the rat would be counterconditioned by genital pleasure. (As a matter of fact, if a mad scientist were interested in conditioning some weird sexual preferences, he or she might want to consider Watson and Rayner's scenario.) A better therapy would be simply to use systematic desensitization to extinguish the phobic response to rats.

KEY TERMS

Behavior Modification The systematic application of reinforcers, punishers, extinction, and other classical and operant conditioning procedures to change target behaviors.

Behavioral Medicine An interdisciplinary field concerned with the etiology of illness and wellness, preventative medicine, biofeedback, and other forms of psychophysiology, behavioral treatment, and rehabilitation strategies.

Behavioral Therapy Any psychotherapeutic procedure involving the systematic application of reinforcers or punishers or the implementation of extinction or other classical or operant procedure known to be effective in bringing about behavioral change.

Behavioral Tolerance That portion of total drug tolerance that can be attributed to learned or environmental variables as opposed to pharmacological variables.

Biocultural Evolution (S. Katz) The process by which the selection, preparation, and consumption of particular types of food by some individuals gives them a reproductive advantage that, over time, has probably led to the divergence of human populations.

Biofeedback A procedure used in both research and therapy in which a human subject through differential reinforcement can be made aware of and can gain voluntary control over his or her involuntary processes (such as brain waves, heart rate, skin conductance, etc.).

Biomedical Model The traditional approach to health care that, in emphasizing anatomy and physiology, assumes that almost all illness can be attributed to a specific pathogen or specific biochemical malfunction.

Biopsychosocial Model An approach to health care that attempts to integrate cultural, social, psychological, and behavioral factors with the traditional biomedical model.

Compensatory Responses See *conditioned compensatory responses.*

Conditioned Compensatory Responses In conditioning experiments using drugs as USs, a conditioned response opposite in direction to the preconditioning UR to the drug. Example: morphine produces hyperthermia, and the CR following conditioning is hypothermia (Siegel).

Conditioned Facilitation Conditioning the immune system as demonstrated by an increase in antibody production in the presence of a conditioned stimulus.

Conditioned Immunosuppression Conditioning the immune system as demonstrated by a decrease in antibody production in the presence of a conditioned stimulus.

Drug Tolerance Reduction in the effectiveness of a drug resulting from repeated exposure to the drug.

Experimental Neurosis (Pavlov) The outcome of a conditioning experiment in which an animal becomes emotionally distraught for an extended period of time.

Hedonic Conditioning A theory proposed to account for meal-to-meal changes in particular foods selected based on the positive or negative postingestional consequences of previous selections. Tastes and textures are CSs that become associated with postingestional consequences (USs).

Involuntary Behavior Physiology and behavior under the control of the autonomic nervous system; unintentional, unwillful behavior. (Cf. *Voluntary Behavior.*)

Omnivore's Paradox An eating pattern that *enhances* fitness during famine but *diminishes* fitness by increasing the risk of poisoning (Rozin).

Pharmacological Tolerance That portion of total drug tolerance that can be attributed to pharmacologic properties of drugs.

Placebo Effect A conditioned response that mimics the effects of a drug treatment (the unconditioned stimulus); in humans, via the second signal system, the expectation of drug or other treatment effects.

Post-Traumatic Stress Disorder (PTSD) A disorder characterized by one or more of the symptoms of intense fear, feelings of helplessness, and recurrent intrusive memories/dreams and whose etiology is thought to be caused by an unusual, markedly distressing event such as rape or battle fatigue.

Psychoneuroimmunology The field of research attempting to describe and integrate the interconnectedness of the immune system, central and autonomic nervous systems, neuroendocrine system, and behavior.

Psychosomatic Disorders Disorders of anatomy and/or physiology that can be attributed in part to psychological or behavioral variables.

Specific Hungers The translation of physiological needs into cravings and hungers for specific, identifiable nutrients. Examples: salt and water.

Voluntary Behavior Physiology and behavior under the control of the central nervous system; intentional, willful behavior. (Cf. *Involuntary Behavior.*)

CHAPTER 8

CHOICE BEHAVIOR

Science has probably never demanded a more sweeping change in a traditional way of thinking about . . . (what it means to be an individual). In the traditional picture a person perceives the world around him, selects features to be perceived, discriminates among them, judges them good or bad, changes them to make them better (or, if he is careless, worse), and may be held responsible for his action and justly rewarded or punished for its consequences. In the scientific picture, a person is a member of a species shaped by evolutionary contingencies of survival, displaying behavioral processes which bring him under the control of the environment in which he lives, and largely under the control of a social environment which he and millions of others like him have constructed and maintained during the evolution of a culture. The direction of the controlling relation is reversed: a person does not act upon the world, the world acts upon him.

Skinner, Beyond Freedom and Dignity (1971, p. 211)

INTRODUCTION

Decisions, decisions. Two tests tomorrow—do I study psychology or Spanish? Gaining weight—should I eat dessert or not? Call Margaret or mom first? Watch the soaps or listen to my newest CD? Study now, or sleep and get up early tomorrow? Sleep in, or make my 9:00 class? Blue jeans or slacks? Is this person I've been seeing significant or not?

Daily, hourly, and by the minute, people engage in decision making. Making choices of one kind or another is characteristic of all animal life. As an animal you make the basic decision to move, to engage in voluntary behavior, or not. The simplest voluntary responses of animals involve choice.

What is known about this process? Are many processes involved? How do we make choices? How do we choose from among alternatives? Are there rules or laws governing our behavior? For example, are we born knowing how to make the best decisions, or do we simply make decisions based on the moment?

Freedom and Determinism.   As we saw in Chapters 5 and 6, one way to approach the question of choice is to raise the issue of free choice. Are we truly autonomous individuals—free agents, so to speak—who are the masters of our destiny? Or are our decisions the product of past reinforcement history; that is, do we choose on the basis of maximizing reinforcement? In the opening quotation, Skinner says that we are controlled by our personal reinforcement histories as well as by a wisdom of our species. If animals who consistently make bad choices became extinct, then those of us who remain alive are off-spring of animals who consistently have made good choices over millions of years.

Can we even agree on how to use the term *choice*? Let us put a recently fed and watered hamster in its cage and attach a water bottle to it. Can we say that the hamster is free to choose to drink from the bottle—or not? Let us now repeat the experiment but not let the same hamster drink water for 48 hours before allowing it water access. Is the hamster free to choose to drink from the bottle? Less free?

Consider another incident. You choose to go to Momma Rollo's and select pepperoni pizza from the menu. Later you get sick. You attribute your sickness to Momma Rollo's pepperoni pizza. Are you as free to choose this restaurant and this food item after getting sick? Can you see that the first example is what Skinner alludes to when he talks about how our evolutionary history constrains choice and that the second example shows how the environment acting on us constrains what we choose?

Choice Behavior and Economics

How people make choices is of as much interest to the marketing divisions of businesses around the world as it is to philosophers and psychologists. When more people choose to buy widgets than whatnots or imported rather than domestic automobiles, investors will line up behind the preferred choice. The tasks of the marketing divisions of companies making whatnots and domestic cars is to influence the decisions of purchasers to buy *their* products. Notice in this example that neither the purchaser nor the marketer much cares whether humans are *free to choose* from among alternatives. Philosophical positions of determinism versus free will do not allow us to predict *how* individuals make choices. Here we are interested in choice behavior, not the philosophy of choice. The question of widgets or whatnots focuses our observations: (a) selecting one object rather than another is a common human behavior and (b) choices are influenced (even if not determined) by environment.

Evaluating Decision Making

Assume that widgets are better made than whatnots. Will everyone choose widgets? Highly unlikely. This question goes to the heart of individual differences in choice behavior; there are no simple answers to why people make the choices they do. Choices are multivariably determined.

All humans make questionable decisions at one time or another. A questionable decision is one with which someone else disagrees. Indeed, some of us are more notorious than others for the consistency of our bad judgment. For example, what are some circumstances in which whatnots rather than widgets might be purchased? Whatnots are available nearby, and widgets are across town; whatnots are $1 cheaper; whatnots are a more pleasing color of purple. You prefer widgets, however, but they are sold out, and a whatnot will do. No one in your family would be caught dead buying a widget; your ex-boyfriend flaunts his widget, and you can't wait to buy a whatnot out of spite.

Value.   One word can be used to summarize the reasons people choose between widgets or whatnots, namely the object's **value.** The value of whatnots in this example was determined by how it looked (*esthetics*—the color purple), how useful it was (*utility*), what its price was (*cost*), how near it was (*availability*), and, all factors considered, your perception of its worth (*perceived utility*). Note that most all of these variables can be subsumed under the rubric of *perceived utility:* esthetics, cost, and availability.

To give you a flavor of the complexity of this situation, let us note just a few of the choice determinants in this example: A $1 difference in purchase price is *everything* to a person with only a few dollars to his or her name, is *nothing* to a millionaire, and is *something* to the rest of us, depending on how near it is to payday. Likewise, taking a half-hour drive across town to buy a widget rather than a whatnot is nothing to a person with plenty of free time and an automobile at his or her disposal, but is everything to someone with no time to spare. (Let's not even consider the cost of gasoline to make that drive relative to what he or she "saves.") The color purple? Wonderful, or unimportant, unless you have a conditioned emotional response to that particular shade because your ex was partial to it.[1]

Limitations of Theory.   Now the astute reader should have antennae out. If we can't predict something as unimportant as whether a person will buy a widget or a whatnot, we're not going to be able to do a very good job either predicting or helping advise on the choice of a career, a marriage partner, or the advantages of renting versus buying your own home. This being the case, perhaps we should fold our tent and cut to Chapter 9 because in reality the analysis of choice behavior is even more complex than choosing between two items that are matched on most dimensions, such as whatnots and widgets. As is the case with all such human enigmas, we have more than one model, more than one law, and many observations about choice behavior for which we have neither models nor laws.

Retrospective and Chapter Preview

However deficient our state of knowledge is, the issue of choice behavior is too important to ignore. From health decisions at the personal level, to political

---

[1] That perceived utility is learned is illustrated by a recent experience I had helping a friend with a garage sale. We were setting the price of items for sale. I noticed that some items that he valued for sentimental reasons were overpriced relative to those to which he had less emotional attachment. For example, his memories of a certain dish his mother had used caused him to place an inflated dollar value on it.

decisions at the social level, and to environmental decisions at the world level, good and bad choices are made daily. Indeed, a prominent learning theorist (Tolman, 1938) proposed that all behavior can be analyzed as choice behavior, and that a science of behavior would be greatly advanced if we could understand and predict the behavior of a rat at a choice point in a maze!

In this chapter we begin our inquiry into the origins of choice behavior with an overview of utility theory. Can we mathematically model the factors leading to choice decisions? From utility theory we turn to an in-depth examination of a model of choice based on adaptive-evolutionary considerations. Is there a genetic basis for making decisions? We then turn to a variety of animal models of choice behavior and examine several interesting laws that have come from laboratory experimentation. Can we design meaningful animal models to help us predict the choices that humans make? In the last section, we attempt to apply what we have learned to your situation. Can we use our theories to help train people to make better decisions in their personal lives, in educational settings, and in behavioral therapy? We begin with utility theory.

Interim Summary

1. Humans and other animals make choices throughout their lifetimes regardless of whether their behavior is determined or whether they have "free will."

2. A theory of choice behavior must take into account both adaptive-evolutionary considerations and personal reinforcement history.

3. People decide between two or more alternatives based on their perceived value.

UTILITY THEORY

Assume that an eccentric uncle has died. His will is being read, and you are to be a beneficiary. Among the conditions of his will are that you have to make a choice between these two alternatives: (a) You can choose to receive $3,000 outright or (b) you can gamble to win $4,000 by spinning a wheel-of-inherited-fortune. You can land on one of 10 slots on the wheel. Eight of 10 slots will earn you $4,000, but two of the slots read $0. You are assured that the game is not fixed and that the two probabilities are correct: $3,000 with the probability of 1.0; $4,000 with a probability of 0.8. What do you choose to do? When a study outlining this proposition was conducted in the late 1970s, more than 80% of the people responded that they would take the $3,000; only 20% were willing to gamble at even these high (80% chance of winning) odds (Kahneman & Tversky, 1979). I would be very surprised if the findings would be any different today; the old axiom to the effect that a bird in the hand is worth two in the bush is a timeless, accurate prediction concerning human behavior. But why do people make this choice?

Expected Utility

A model that came to be known as **expected utility** was proposed in the 18th century by Bernoulli, a mathematician, who described, among other mathematical functions, the probabilities associated with gambling. In this century his work was incorporated into both economic gaming theory (von Neuman & Morganstern, 1944) and *decision theory* (French, 1986). Bernoulli's analysis of humans making decisions that didn't match the odds of winning bets was that people preferred to focus on the risk of losing and of the *perceived value* of the money involved rather than on winning and the absolute value of the money involved.

In some ways the concept of *expected utility* is similar to the findings of traditional *psychophysics* formulated by the 19th-century German mathematician (and early psychologist) Gustav Fechner. Recall that the study of psychophysics described the mathematical relationship of the responses of the senses to the physical stimulus energy in the environment. *Brightness* and *loudness*, for example, are psychological terms referring to (and mapping) the intensity of visual and auditory stimuli, respectively. Likewise, the expected utility or expected gain from a decision made about money is a psychological function related to the real-world value of money. Assume that such decisions must be made repeatedly about a given wager (X). Equation (8.1) describes this relationship mathematically. Note that the perceived or expected utility (EU) of an amount of money (X) is a function of expected gain (G), the mean value of X (μ_x), and the standard deviation of x (s_x^2).

$$EU\ (X) = G(\mu_x,\ s_x^2) \tag{8.1}$$

The important thing to remember about this equation is that human and animal judgments about gains (G) in money, food, or anything of value depend in part on how much money we're talking about (i.e., μ_x) and how variable it is (i.e., s_x^2). In a wager, the risk of losing is worth taking only under certain conditions.

Economics of Choice in Animals

Equation (8.1) has been used to analyze decisions that people and animals make relating to their perception of the real world. As stated earlier, because most humans are risk averse, their *expected utility* does not match the actual values of their transactions. That is, because humans are risk averse, they do not maximize the gains available to them. What their expected utility *does* reflect are the multitudinous psychological variables that govern their decisions:

Buying a whatnot because an ex-boyfriend has a widget is one example. For this reason, a number of researchers have decided to investigate choice behavior in nonhuman animals. Presumably, the learned psychological complexity that motivates animals is less than that found in humans. In the next section we begin with a simple model of the choice behavior of honeybees. The question raised by Real's (1991) investigation seems simple enough: What is the biological and evolutionary basis of expected utility?

Interim Summary

1. Value is determined by the *expected utility* of an item.
2. Factors affecting *expected utility* are esthetics, utility, cost, availability, and perceived utility.

ADAPTIVE-EVOLUTIONARY CONSIDERATIONS IN CHOICE BEHAVIOR

Yes, honeybees. Your presumed question as to the ecological validity of studying the behavior of honeybees as a model for human choice behavior is a legitimate one. Having raised questions regarding the extrapolation of research results from animals to humans throughout the text, I would be remiss to not comment here about the use of honeybees as a model of choice behavior. First, Real's (1991) investigation of choice behavior in honeybees succeeds at several levels; he does not conceptualize his research regarding how bees make decisions to be an exact model of how humans make choices. Second, the abilities of bees are quite remarkable (see Box 8.1), and their decision making is orderly with respect to the expected utility model described earlier. Finally, some remarkable consistencies of choice behavior exist whether bees, rats, pigeons, or humans are studied. Let us take an in-depth look, then, at the decisions of which bees are capable. (The superskeptical among you might want to take an extended look at Box 8.1 before proceeding. Call it consciousness raising or whatever. I think you will find that these insect brains are not what you thought they were.)

Foraging in Honeybees

What kinds of decisions do foraging honeybees make? Simply put, bees must determine which nearby flowers contain the most nectar. Energy is expended in foraging, and the return (gain in nectar) must always be balanced against this energy loss. Real (1991) studied how bees adjust their behavior (make their next decision about which flowers to visit) as a function of the reinforcement value of previously visited flowers. His method is to allow wild bumble-

BOX 8.1   ARE BEE BRAINS SMART ENOUGH TO MAKE DECISIONS?

Sejnowski and Churchland (1992a, 1992b) are intrigued by the parallels of both organization and performance of computers and living brains. They start by comparing what a small honeybee can do that powerful computers can't. A honeybee brain has only 1 million neurons compared to a human's 100 billion. The honeybee brain operates at about 10 TFLOPS (10,000 GFLOPS), while powerful computers approach speeds of only 10 GFLOPS (i.e., 1 billion operations per second).

Honeybees share a number of sensory and motor abilities with vertebrates: They can see, sense vibration, smell, fly, walk, and maintain their balance. They are able to navigate long distances, recognize high-energy nectar sites, and remember those flowers they have already visited. Returning to the hive, they can communicate the location of nectar sources to other bees.

In the hive they recognize and attack intruders. Their housekeeping abilities include the removal of garbage and dead bees from the hive. When the hive becomes crowded, responding to cues not yet understood, some bees will swarm and establish a new hive.

Whereas supercomputers need the constant care of humans, honeybees manage their activities independently of humans.

---

bees to search a large, netted enclosure in which they can sample artificial cardboard flowers of different colors. Let us look at the details.

Colored Flowers Predict Reinforcement.   In the middle of each cardboard flower is a well containing a specified amount and concentration of diluted honey ("nectar"). That bees rapidly associate the color of the flower with the nectar has long been known. That is, bees learn to return to the color of flowers that have the most nectar. In one experiment Real allowed single bees to visit a patch containing 100 blue and 100 yellow flowers randomly spaced. All of the blue flowers contained 2 µl (microliter) and one-third of the yellow flowers contained 6 µl nectar. A foraging bee, by Real's analysis, could therefore sample each color equally often and receive an average 2 µl nectar per trip (6 µl divided across visits to three yellow flowers equals an average of 2 µl per visit). Remember, however, the bird-in-hand concept. Even though bees choosing blue flowers will never experience the 6 µl nectar jackpot of some yellow flowers, the blue flowers always have some nectar. What is your prediction of what bees would do in Real's (1991) experiment?

Bees Avoid Risk, Favor Consistency.   Figure 8.1 shows the results of this experiment (using the average performance of five bees) after allowing these bees a 40-visit foraging bout. We presume that the bees learned what the reinforce-

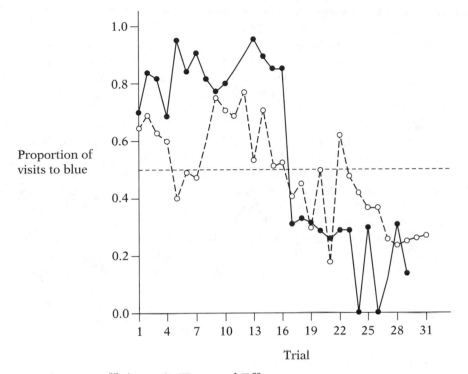

FIGURE 8.1   Efficiency in Time and Effort

Two separate experiments are plotted in the figure. The solid line shows that bees prefer blue to yellow flowers when blue flowers are consistently paired with 2 μl reinforcing nectar and when only one-third of the yellow flowers are reinforced (with 6 μl nectar; the remaining two-thirds with no nectar). After 16 trials, the reinforcement contingencies of the blue and yellow colors are switched, and bees continue to prefer the consistently reinforced color.

The dashed lines are the result of a second experiment in which blue flowers continued to be reinforced with 2 μl nectar, one-third of the yellow flowers with 5 μl nectar, and two-thirds of the yellow flowers with 0.5 μl. The consistently reinforced blue flowers on trials 1–16 (dashed lines) were visited 62% of the time on average. Following a color switch (trials 17–31), visits to blue flowers dropped to 27%.

---

ment contingencies were during these first 40 visits. Over the first 16 trials (see Figure 8.1), bees chose to visit the 2 μl-rewarded blue flowers approximately 84% of the time. On trials 17–31, the colors of the flowers were reversed: Yellow flowers always contained 2 μl, one-third of the blue flowers had 6 μl, and two-thirds contained nothing. Again, the solid line after trial 17 shows a major reversal of preference mirroring the switch in reinforcement contingencies; now only about 23% of the visits were made to blue flowers.

Computing Risky Choices

How good are bees at adjusting their behavior as a function of even more sub-tle changes in reinforcement contingencies? That is, what if the problem were not quite so simple as having bees decide between consistent reinforcement and low probability reinforcement? In another experiment Real (1991) contin-ued to reinforce blue with 2 μl nectar, one-third of the yellow flowers with 5 μl nectar, and the remaining two-thirds of the yellow flowers with 0.5 μl. In this case, choosing half yellow and half blue flowers over the long run will continue to provide equivalent amounts of nectar (i.e., the reinforcement contingencies of blue and yellow flowers are equal). *All* choices will be reinforced. Again, for bees, the *expected utility* of these two conditions are *not* equivalent: Apparently, bees (and probably humans in a similar situation) prefer the less risky propo-sition of consistent reward. The dashed lines in Figure 8.1 indicate that the consistently reinforced blue flowers on trials 1–16 were visited 62% of the time, on average, and following a color switch, the now consistently reinforced yellow flowers were visited approximately 63% of the time. Real (1991) specu-lates that because the variance in expected reward was narrower in the second experiment (5% vs. 0.5% compared to 6% vs. 0.0% in the first experiment) the bees' preference for consistently rewarded colors was commensurably less in the second experiment (62% vs. 84% in the first experiment).

Raising the Stakes. Let us return to our initial gamble to better compare what bees do relative to humans. Few of us would turn down $3,000 cash for an 80% chance at $4,000. Let us up the ante. Would you take $3,000 cash or an 80% chance at $10,000? Or $100,000? Or $1,000,000? An 80% probability means that four out of five times you are going to win the bet: Try getting those odds out of Las Vegas for any athletic contest! The point is that the expected utility function Equation (8.1) predicts that risk taking will increase—that uncer-tainty can be compensated for—by increasing expectation. The prediction is that bees (and humans) will take more risks for higher than average expected rewards. In a second experiment, Real (1991) covaried the probability of find-ing a reward with the size of the reward and found just that: greater risk tak-ing. As predicted in our human example, he reported a linear relationship con-necting risk taking and reward size; specifically, he concluded from his studies that uncertainty can be compensated for by increasing the amount of the ex-pected reward.

Maximizing Energy Gain

At several places in the text (typically within an adaptive-evolutionary context), reference has been made to the concept of *maximizing reinforcement opportu-nities*. Never well specified, the general idea being proposed was that behavior is neither trivial nor random. To behave entails costs. To *behave* means to *ex-pend energy*. The Brelands' pigs and raccoons (Chapter 5) that engaged in behaviors that delayed reinforcement (i.e., washing or rooting tokens rather than trading them for food) were viewed as being maladaptive. Choosing larger rewards over smaller ones is viewed as adaptive. Why? Because of an implicit awareness that energy well expended is more adaptive than energy wasted. Engaging in behavior incurs an (energy) cost, and the benefit should at a minimum equal that cost.

Biomechanics of Utility

As you might expect from reading about bees in Box 8.1, expected utility theory can be profitably applied to the problems faced by bees in meeting energy needs (Harder & Real, 1987). Bees, indeed, maximize their net energy gain by the decisions they make about which flowers to visit during foraging. Equation (8.2) is introduced with the following cautions: The student is not expected to either memorize or solve it (unless your prof. wants you to, in which case I sincerely apologize). Rather, the equation is introduced for two reasons: First, to draw parallels with Hull's formidable equation—Equation (6.1), p. 293—which attempted to predict the likelihood of occurrence of a learned response based on both physiology and learned performance and second, to address risk aversion (a psychological construct) by examining niche behaviors.

Equation (8.2) (from Real, 1991) predicts that the rate of net energy uptake (E) for each flower visited by a bee equals

$$E = \frac{epSV - W(K_p(T_a + V/I) + K_fT_f)}{T_f + T_a + (V/I)} \tag{8.2}$$

in which e = the energy content of the nectar (15.48 Joules/per mg sucrose); p = the nectar density (mg/μl); S = nectar concentration; V = nectar volume; W = the bee's mass in grams; K_p and K_f = the energy costs of probing and flying, respectively; T = the total time duration of the visit to the flower; T_f = flight time between flowers; T_a = total time at a flower; and I = ingestion time, in seconds.

Equation (8.2) predicts that the costs associated with foraging are real and that because of these costs, the rate of energy intake is a deceleration, rather than a linear function, of nectar volume (Harder & Real, 1987). Such a function predicts that smaller, consistent rewards are more energy efficient than foraging for larger but more variable rewards. (Going to a yellow flower that has little or no nectar is a high energy cost.) At least in this simple animal, a cognitive function called *choosing* can be modeled and predicted merely by measuring simple biomechanical factors of energy expenditure and energy intake! *Choosing* is italicized here because the term implies a level of consciousness that bees and other nonhuman animals likely do not share with humans. Bees and birds in the following example presumably respond to the results of a concluded foraging experience and adjust their foraging behavior involuntarily, that is, without being aware of what they are doing. A model incorporating neurobiological and behavior data for how bees make their choices has been proposed (Montague, Dayan, & Sejnowski, 1993).

Take one last look at Equation (8.2). Would you say that the science of behavioral analysis has been successful in delving into the *black box?* Certainly, the analytical model proposed by Hull, which was maligned in his lifetime, was on the right track.

The question of animal awareness aside for the moment, effectively choosing from among foraging alternatives has Darwinian, life-and-death implications. When foraging involves feeding hungry offspring, the importance of making good decisions is paramount. Here we look at two examples. In the first, laboratory rats were offered two different water patches from which to choose. The effort involved to secure the water was manipulated by requiring the rats to bar press on schedules that produced different amounts of water. The rats solved the problem in a way that reduced their overall energy costs relative to the costs associated with random sampling (Collier, Johnson, Borin, & Mathis, 1994). We return to another example of Collier's research later in this chapter.

So Much for Rats and Bees. How Do Birds Do It?   To take another example, the manner in which mountain chickadees (*Parus gambeli*) located in the mountains of northern California go about poking insects into voracious mouths in their nests has recently been reported by Grundel (1992). His results can be summarized in the form of decision trees regarding whether to return to a previous foraging location and what type of prey to take from there. In essence, his findings parallel what we now know about the decisions that bees make in foraging.

Beginning with a successful foraging expedition and having fed their offspring, chickadees typically adopt a *win-stay* strategy. (If prey is found, that is, if they *win*, then they *stay* with that location.) But not always. Grundel (1992) found that the proximity of the foraging location to the nest was important. If it took too long to get there on the previous flight, the chickadee would shift to another location. The operative rule was that if the time to get there was approximately 30% longer than the shortest successful foraging distance, even though prey was found at the more distant site, the chickadee was unlikely to return—a *win-shift* strategy.

Once at a site, which prey do they take? Grundel reported three rules that account for most of the variance in his observations of chickadee foraging patterns. The best predictor was *number* of prey; chickadees appear to take *whatever* size insect that was available in the largest numbers. In other words, number of insects was a better predictor of prey selection than *size* of prey, the second best predictor. Confounding both of these observations, Grundel (1992) noticed a trend that if the foraging time was sufficiently short (i.e., if the location was a very short distance from the nest), chickadees would be even less selective of prey and would be more likely to select the same as last time.

These strategies, presumably inborn response tendencies honed by experience, serve both bees and birds and do not seem to be unreasonable for humans.

Interim Summary

1. Bees and other animals are risk averse; the axiom "a bird in the hand is worth two in the bush" is descriptive of the behavior of many animals.

2. Given a choice of alternatives in which work expended is covaried with energy attained, bees, rats, and birds maximize their net energy gain by making adaptive choices.

THE MATCHING LAW

You are a hungry pigeon trapped in a Skinner box in Richard Herrnstein's laboratory. Two keys in front of you seem to have something to do with food because you have learned to peck at the red key on the left-hand side and the white key on the right-hand side and the grain hopper has sometimes magically appeared. Now, however, you find that you must peck more often yet receive less food. If you were able to understand English, you might have heard a lab assistant mumble something about putting you on a *partial schedule of reinforcement*. And, if you could read, you might notice that one piece of apparatus used to schedule your reinforcement on the left-hand key is labeled VI-135, and the schedule of reinforcement on the right-hand key is a VI-270 seconds. These are lean schedules; you are reinforced for pecking on these keys on the average of only every 2 minutes (plus) and every 4.5 minutes. The reinforcement schedules run simultaneously, and each is independent of the other. They are called **concurrent schedules** of reinforcement.

Thought question: How would you distribute your responses? As a hungry bee would in a way that *minimizes* risk? Recall that bees distributed more than 80% of their responses to the color of flower that was consistently reinforced (and less than 20% of their responses to a color that was not consistently reinforced). Or would you distribute your responses in a way that *maximizes reinforcement?*

The Matching Law in Pigeons

Herrnstein (1961) found that pigeons made twice as many responses to the VI-135 as they did to the VI-270. That is, they matched their responses to the available reinforcement. In a 1-hour work session, for example, pigeons working on the VI-135 averaged approximately 3,100 responses to earn 27 reinforcements and concurrently responded approximately 1,600 times, earning 13 reinforcements on the VI-270. Herrnstein then continued working his pigeons on different combinations of concurrent VI schedules to see whether the percentage of key-pecking responses would consistently match the percentage of available reinforcement on each schedule. As can be seen in Figure 8.2, pigeons match their responses to available reinforcement almost flawlessly—a behavioral regularity called the **matching law.**

Equation (8.3) mathematically describes the relationship of responses made and reinforcement earned (Baum, 1974).

$$\frac{R_A}{R_B} = b \left(\frac{r_A}{r_B} \right)^a \tag{8.3}$$

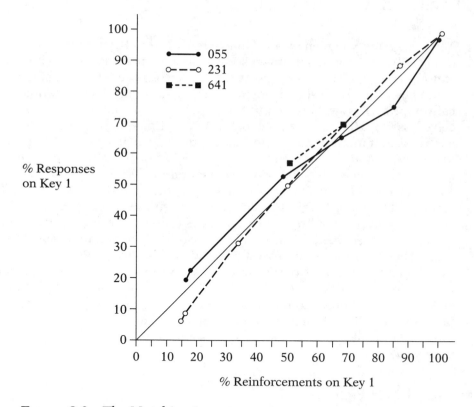

FIGURE 8.2   The Matching Law

A perfect match between percentage of responses and percentage of reinforcements is indicated by the diagonal line. Depicted are the performances of three birds on several different concurrent schedules (see text). These behavioral data lie on top of the predicted line, the basis for what Herrnstein (1961) has called the *matching law*.

R_A and R_B refer to the *rates* of responding on keys A and B (i.e., left and right), and r_A and r_B refer to the rates of reinforcement on those keys. When the value of the exponent a is equal to 1.0, the matching law entails; responses perfectly match available reinforcement. (Variable b can be used to weight nonmatched response topographies or nonmatched reinforcers.)

Although the derivation of the matching law from the expected utility function expressed in Equation (8.1) is beyond the scope of this text, these two functions are related. The regularity (low variability) of Herrnstein's data is reminiscent of Real's bee-foraging data (Figure 8.1). Prediction of behavior is high for both the bees and pigeons under the circumstances of these experiments. How do we know this? Because the observed functions lie very close to their predicted values. There are circumstances in which pigeons do *not* match responses to reinforcements. By way of illustrating these exceptions, consider the following scenario.

Undermatching

You talk on the phone with your two best friends several times daily. Assume that they both work odd hours, make other phone calls, and the longer you delay your respective calls to them, the higher is the probability that they will be home to take them. Friend A is home more than Friend B, and so the probability of Friend A answering when you call is twice that of Friend B. Not surprising, you match these reinforcement contingencies by calling Friend A twice as often as Friend B. Your phone calling/hit rate would fall along the diagonal in Figure 8.2.

Undermatching Phone Calls.   Further assume that over a period of time, you consistently call Friend A first, thereby introducing a delay in calling Friend B. Your strategy thereby *increases* the likelihood of being reinforced when you call Friend B. Under these conditions your phone-calling responses no longer match the reinforcement contingencies of getting through; by delaying, you increase your hit rate for Friend B. Reinforcement theory predicts that you would increase the rate of phone calling to Friend B relative to Friend A. If in fact you respond by calling Friend B more than predicted by the matching law, you are **undermatching** the predicted 2:1 ratio of phone calls. This is, by calling Friend B more, your ratio might come closer to a 50–50 match (i.e., 1:1), undermatching the predicted 2:1 ratio. Such undermatching has been observed under a variety of conditions, and several alternative explanations for undermatching have been proposed (Baum, 1974, 1979; Myers & Myers, 1977).

Changeover Delays.   The hit rates for phone calls to Friend A and Friend B are similar to pigeons pecking on key A and key B for food reinforcement in Herrnstein's (1961) experiment. Recall that key A was reinforced twice as often as key B (VI-135 vs. VI-270). In fact, Herrnstein's pigeons initially *undermatched* by getting more reinforcements/pecks on the VI-270 than predicted by the matching law. Why? First, they learned that key A delivered the most reinforcement. Then, primarily by responding to key A (VI-135) for a long period of time, key B (VI-270) was more likely to deliver reinforcement on the pigeon's first peck on key B. These changeover responses would have the highest probability of being reinforced than any other responses in the session. To keep this from happening, Herrnstein introduced a **changeover delay (COD)** to separate the two components of the concurrent schedules. Whenever a pigeon switched from the left to right or from the right to left key, no reinforcement was available for 1.5 seconds. Herrnstein viewed this 1.5-second changeover delay as a punishment contingency for switching (see also Davison, 1991). Another view is that the COD differentially punished switching from key A to key B and made the animal respond with a few more pecks on key B than it normally would have. Without the COD, a pigeon could even better maximize reinforcement on the VI-270 by virtually ignoring it and only minimally responding on it.

The Matching Law and Human Behavior: An Example

When you are among a group of friends, do you find yourself talking to one or two individuals more than the others? Do you tend to talk more with people who agree with you than with those who don't? A clever experiment reported by Conger and Killeen (1976) examined the effect that concurrent schedules of reinforcement had on how individuals distributed their responses (talking to one or another person). The test subject was introduced into a videotaped four-way discussion under false pretenses. The other three individuals involved were trained as confederates by the experimenter. One discussed an agreed upon topic with the test subject while the other two reinforced statements made by the test subject on a concurrent schedule. Reinforcement consisted of comments such as "I agree" or "Good point" or a simple head nod with a yes. In the first phase of the experiment, one person reinforced about 80% of the subject's comments (the other reinforced far fewer comments). During a final 15-minute period the other confederate reinforced about 40% of the test subject's statements. The dependent variable was how much time the test subject spent talking to the confederates. After studying five individuals in this situation, Conger and Killeen (1976) reported good matches between talking and being reinforced: About 80% of responses were directed to the individual delivering reinforcement 80% of the time. When the source of reinforcement shifted from one to the other confederate, the responses followed reliably (the match was ~30% responses for a 40% reinforcement schedule).

Melioration

A more recent interpretation of matching and undermatching has been proposed by Herrnstein and Vaughan (1980) and by Vaughan (1981, 1985). Their analysis of pigeons responding on concurrent schedules is that the pigeons' response strategy is continually changing within a session. After gaining experience with the two VI schedules, within each session a pigeon shifts from one key to the other, always attempting to meliorate, or maximize, local (moment-to-moment) changes in available reinforcement. The difference in the **melioration** position from that of *matching* is that the latter term better describes an overall (daily) maximizing strategy, whereas melioration places more emphasis on a pigeon's short-term memory and key-to-key shifts depending on the most recently obtained reinforcement. The issue of molar versus molecular strategies is far from settled (see Williams, 1991). Bees, it is argued, are short-term energy maximizers, perhaps due to constraints on their memory systems that do not allow them to keep daily running totals of the results of their choices (Real, 1991). By contrast, humans have both excellent short-term and long-term memories. You are as likely to remember that Friend B answered the phone each of the last three times you called and at the same time know that in the long run of events, Friend A is usually easier to contact.

Overmatching

Recall the rats that had electrodes implanted in their brains and had learned to bar press for ESB. Anderson et al. (1992) reported that when these hungry rats were allowed sequential access to either food or ESB reinforcement, after experience with both schedules they quit responding for food entirely. He called the phenomenon absolute *negative contrast*, a special case of *incentive contrast*. In general, when rewards of different value are repeatedly experienced, the better one becomes even better, and by comparison the lesser one sinks even further in value (see Flaherty, 1991). Similar behavior observed on concurrent schedules of reinforcement has been called **overmatching.** In overmatching, a rat or pigeon spends too much time responding on the better of the two VI schedules; it does not distribute enough responses to the less reinforced lever to match the available reinforcement. In one study, for example, switching between levers was punished by electric shock, and pigeons restricted a higher proportion of their responses (than predicted by matching theory) to the richer schedule—hence, *overmatching* (Todorov, 1971). (Recall that the COD also acted as a punisher, yet it improved the match between responses and available reinforcement on two VI schedules.) The increment of food available on the lesser VI schedule apparently did *not* offset the painful cost of switching. Another way to interpret the phenomenon is that the introduction of shock magnified the contrast between the two schedules.

Overmatching in Play.   Have you ever watched two young children playing with toys? During a play session, both children play with a variety of toys. Each toy has a particular value, as reflected by the amount of time a child plays with it. It is often the case that in the midst of plenty both zero in on one particular toy, Toy X. If Child A then asserts ownership of Toy X, a wary game of who plays with what ensues. The cost of choosing Toy X by Child B now includes the penalty of being harassed for attempting to play with it. One outcome is that when Toy X becomes available (when Child A shifts interest to other toys), Child B is less likely to choose it. The reinforcement is now available, but Child B does not respond commensurate with his or her availability—behavior similar to pigeons that overmatch on concurrent schedules.

Labor, Leisure, Wages, and the Matching Law

Regularities of behavior are indicative of adaptive-evolutionary mechanisms, that is, of responses that fit (match) the environment. Perhaps this is the reason that pigeons' behavior on concurrent schedules is not especially surprising; indeed, the *matching law* has an intuitive ring to it. Two common colloquialisms are "dogs [or people] respond to the way they are treated" and "hard work will be rewarded." Both sayings suggest that behavioral responses match (agree with) the reinforcement and punishment contingencies that have shaped and that maintain behavior. We are puzzled by misbehaving pigs and raccoons precisely because for the most part our personal behavioral experiences conform closely to the matching law. In this section we continue with more examples demonstrating that work ouput typically matches the reinforcement contingencies. Most animal research on choice uses the concurrent schedules of reinforcement methodology (see Williams, 1988, for a review), making the studies that follow exceptional.

Matching Law in an Ecological Niche

Searching and Working for Food. Collier (1983) expanded on the empirical evidence demonstrating that behavior often matches available reinforcement. He built a controlled ecological system for rats in which he could more precisely measure the relationship of energy expended in work (pumping iron) and energy attained through such work (i.e., food). Rats were trained to press one lever (called the *search bar*) and were reinforced by the onset of S^ds that signaled additional work requirements. Energy expended in work was varied on each lever by adjusting both the weight and the number of repetitions of the lever press. If an S^d associated with an additional low-work requirement was illuminated (an FR-10 with little added weight, for example), the rat could complete the work requirement and then eat. Other S^ds, however, required more repetitions at higher weights. The experimenter chose the various work schedules that the rats had to complete for their food reinforcement. Rats could choose *not* to work on a particular schedule with a high-energy requirement by returning to the search bar. There the rat could complete an additional work assignment and search for other S^ds that required less work.

(Note that like Real's, 1991, foraging bees, the energy that these rats expended shopping around for an easier schedule on the search bar [cf. *procure-*

ment costs] is "real" energy that must be made up. That is, searching for an easier job takes time and energy, and these costs must at some point be recovered.)

What did Collier (1983) find? Rats entered into a trade-off between minimizing search time by working on high-energy-expending schedules and increasing search time if the costs were *too* high. That is, if the energy costs associated with pumping iron were too high, rats would spend more time searching for a low-energy-expending schedule leading to food. As has been found with other species, then, given a variety of options, rats are able to adjust their work schedules to maximize calories from food relative to calories expended in earning it.

Matching Law in the Workplace

How much is one's labor worth? The answer lies somewhere between what the worker thinks is fair and what the boss thinks is adequate. Unfortunately, the workplace constitutes a large part of the ecological niche for many humans. Is there any evidence that the matching law applies to the work output of laborers and the money expended by owners? That is, do people work harder if they are paid more? Economists have analyzed this problem and have modeled this relationship as a **labor supply curve,** one version of which is depicted in Figure 8.3. Let us analyze this function and then see whether human economics conforms to the matching law studied in animals.

Working for Wages. Note in Figure 8.3 that a person making $500 per hour works less (fewer hours) to earn a relatively high wage. By contrast, a person making $50 per hour must work more hours to earn less money. This relationship holds for the intermediate wage levels: An individual's effort (hours worked) can be conceptualized as an attempt to maximize total wages earned. Such are the workings of a free enterprise economy, and most readers are familiar with this reality.

As the wage rate drops even more precipitously, however, to $2 per hour, less than the minimum wage, an interesting thing happens; most individuals no longer work longer hours to make more money. The flat slope of the $2 per hour wage rate in Figure 8.3 indicates that very little is gained in wages even when many more hours are worked. In the vernacular, "The juice isn't worth the squeeze" (i.e., the extra money isn't worth the effort).

Labor Supply Curves and the Matching Law. Is this backward-bending curve in Figure 8.3 indicative of a breakdown in the matching law? Probably not. Among the differences between our animal models and the human experience is that (at least in some experiments) animals are very hungry and their work efforts result directly in eating and alleviating hunger. Humans earn wages that are traded for other amenities of life as well as for food.

The Labor-Leisure Trade-Off. Look again at the idealized performance in Figure 8.3. It shows the behavior of individuals working during a typical work-

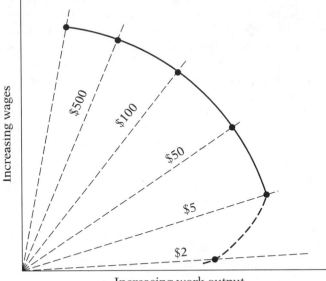

FIGURE 8.3 A Labor Supply Curve

Wages earned are plotted as a function of work output for wage rates between $2 and $500 per hour. For the medium and high wage rates, people work to maximize total wages earned; however, at the lowest wage rate, individuals appear to give up and no longer work as hard. At this lowest wage rate of $2 per hour, the tiny increment in wages attainable by additional work is apparently not worth the expended energy. The reversal in the function at this lowest wage level gives the standard labor supply curve its backward-bending character—presumably reflecting a work-leisure trade-off.

week. Even working 40 hours per week, humans have much discretionary time in which to spend the wages they have accrued. Leisure time is valuable; much of the wage not spent on meeting energy needs (food) and in meeting other consummatory response needs (clothing, shelter, family needs, etc.) is spent on leisure. Not working costs and is considered worth the cost by many humans. One interpretation of the $2 per hour wage earner who limits total work is that this individual's leisure time has become more valuable relative to the benefits of working. Once basic energy needs are met, humans have earned the choice of not working.

We have no animal model for the work/leisure trade-off other than to note that when work requirements become too high for the payoff (i.e., when it appears that the juice isn't worth the squeeze), having met their energy needs, animals also quit responding for discretionary pleasure. For example, rats love sucrose solutions and will work (press a lever) for the sweet taste. (Assume in this study that the rat's energy needs have been met independently of this sucrose option.) What happens if you continue to increase the number of lever presses a rat must make just for the taste of sucrose? Given the option of not doing anything or working for a brief pleasure, rats eventually chose to do nothing (Kelsey & Allison, 1976), and, likewise, pigeons quit rather than work hard for nominal rewards (Green, Kagel, & Battalio, 1987). Not unlike the $2 wage earner, these animals chose to work less with two consequent results: (a) They did without the few extra reinforcements they might have earned, and (b) they were reinforced for doing nothing (leisure) as opposed to expending energy on work.

Interim Summary

1. Choice is conveniently studied in laboratory animals using *concurrent schedules of reinforcement*.

2. Using concurrent schedules of reinforcement, Herrnstein (1961) found that the rate of key pecking in pigeons matched the reinforcement that was available on the two schedules, a phenomenon he called the *matching law*.

3. *A changeover delay (COD)* discourages animals on concurrent schedules from switching to the alternate schedule to pick up an easy reinforcer. Without a COD, animals tend to *undermatch*.

4. *Melioration* describes short-term shifts from one key to the other (while on a current schedule), presumably due to the most recently obtained reinforcement. By contrast, *matching* describes a session-long strategy the end result of which is to maximize reinforcement.

5. *Overmatching* describes an animal that responds too much on the better of the two VI schedules, thereby not maximizing reinforcement available on both schedules.

6. Collier (1983) found that rats adjusted their work in a way that maximized the intake of calories relative to calories expended.

7. A backward-bending *labor supply curve* can be understood as another example of matching (work to wages) and is influenced by the reinforcement value of leisure.

SELF-CONTROL

Put yourself in the following two situations.

Scenario A. You have stopped in the middle of a hectic day to have a bite of lunch and are reviewing your schedule. You have a psychology exam tomorrow for which you *must* study. At that moment your best friend calls and begs you to go to the movies that night. The show you have been dying to see is playing, and you are now torn between two alternatives: go to the show or study for your exam. You tell your friend that you have to study. Your friend counters that you can study before and after the show, but you are skeptical; you have been down that road before. After another 15 minutes of agonizing indecision, you say no. You reluctantly choose to study.

Scenario B.   You have a psychology exam tomorrow for which you *must* study. You finish a bite to eat, and at 7 P.M. you open your book. At that moment your best friend calls and begs you to go to the show. It starts at 7:20. You have been dying to see this movie, and you are now torn between two alternatives: go to the show or study for your exam. You tell your friend that you have to study. Your friend counters that you can study after the show. You have a moment of self-doubt. Your friend says, "Let's get going or we'll be late." You look at your watch, at your psychology textbook, and hear yourself say "okay." You can always study after the show.

Immediate and Delayed Gratification.   Which scenario is more likely? If you answer that both choices are likely, what are the circumstances that account for these two different courses of action? Assume that studying for the exam was a better decision: Is it the case that we make better decisions earlier in the day (i.e., noon as opposed to supper time)? Likely the person was more tired when the decision was made to go to the show. Do people consistently make bad decisions when they are tired? Not too likely. What we can agree on is that the decision to go to the show was made more impulsively. Deciding on a moment's notice allows less time for reflecting on the consequences of one's actions. We can also make a value judgment. Deciding to go to the show rather than study showed a lack of self-control. Let us begin with this issue.

Immediate Gratification and Self-Control

One very useful application of animal research on choice behavior is in the area of self-control. **Self-control** is defined as the ability to delay immediate gratification, usually with the goal of attaining a larger reinforcer at a later time. Achieving self-control is viewed as a defining feature of civilized behavior. Certainly self-control is conceptualized as being learned; the selfish behavior of infants and small children is accepted as normal. Should a student fail to graduate from school due to bad decisions about when and how much to study, a counselor would likely label the person (and the behavior) as immature.

The Sins of Immediate Pleasure.   Other decisions we make daily reflect a conflict between achieving an immediate (proximal) pleasure at the expense of a delayed (distal) reinforcer. (Should I go to class or not?) Many decisions that affect a person's health fall into these categories. Choosing to drink alcohol may lead to immediate pleasure at the expense of incurring less favorable, more distal outcomes (such as automobile injuries and hangovers). Choosing not to drink produces the greater pleasure of not being hurt and not having a hangover. The same can be said for impulsive sexual encounters that may lead to unwanted pregnancies and diseases. Likewise, choosing not to smoke (proximal) increases longevity (distal). Choosing not to eat the double banana fudge sundae (proximal) allows for the reinforcement of reduced obesity/increased longevity (distal). In this section we explore what is known about how self-control is trained in both animals and humans.

Training Self-Control in Pigeons

Hungry again, you find yourself in a Skinner box. One peck at key A raises the grain hopper immediately, allowing you to feed a short while. One peck at key B raises the grain hopper for a longer period of time, allowing you to eat more food—but a 4-second delay has been imposed between your pecking response and food availability. Your choices are, then, a small immediate reward versus a large delayed reward. You more often than not choose the key producing the immediate small reward. (Why should I delay gratification? I'm only a bird!)

Time Delays and Self-Control. Rachlin and Green (1972) then tried to train self-control in these pigeons by increasing the time interval between making the choice and receiving the reinforcement (see Figure 8.4). Using a *concurrent chain* procedure, a single response to key A put the pigeon into a second schedule, an FR-10 on key A. Likewise, a response to key B put the pigeon in a FR-10 on key B. Completing the 10 pecks on key A produced the small immediate reward; completing the 10 pecks on key B produced a 4-second delay and then the large (delayed) reward. Under these circumstances, pigeons began to peck key B, leading to the large delayed reward. They delayed immediate gratification, overcame their impulsive behavior, and (to the extent a pigeon can be a "self"), they exhibited self-control. Why? Rachlin (1974) developed a theory of self-control expanded on by Logue (1988). These researchers argue that the results of many other experiments using both humans and animals can be interpreted as shifts in reward value over time. Let us analyze their reasoning.

Self-Control, Immediate Gratification, and Expected Utility

Figure 8.5 shows the relationship of the value of a reward (i.e., its expected utility) as a function of time prior to experiencing the reward. Note that if a choice between a large and small reward is made just prior to the small reward becoming available (i.e., point T_1 on the time line), the reward value of the small reward is greater than the reward value of the large reward. As we saw in Equations (8.1) and (8.2), expected utility theory describes the relative value of

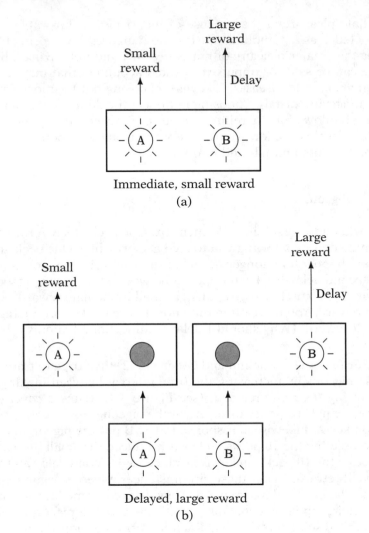

FIGURE 8.4 Teaching Patience to Pigeons

In (a), pigeons are first taught that their choice of the left or right key produces either a small reward immediately or a larger reward after a delay. After this training (b), responding to key A leads to an FR-10 requirement (on key A), followed by a small reinforcement delivered immediately. Responding to key B (b) leads to an FR-10 requirement, followed by a 4-second delay, followed by a larger reinforcer. Pigeons choose the small reward in (a) and the larger reward in (b).

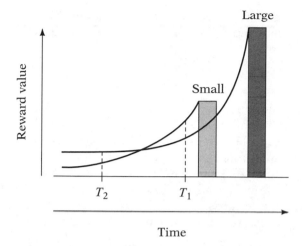

FIGURE 8.5   Expected Value of Large and Small
Rewards

A reward's expected utility changes as a function of time. The value of a
reward increases as the experience of the reward approaches. At time T_2,
the expected values of two rewards are more in synchrony with their
actual values. At time T_1, the expected value of the small reward exceeds
the expected value of the large reward because the small reward is
imminent. Choices for small rewards made at time T_1 reflect the fulfilling
of immediate gratification; those made for large rewards at time T_2 reflect
self-control.

rewards. The value of an item or action is in part determined by its ready availability; for example, your inheritance is of limited value if you can't get to it for
30 years. "A bird in the hand is worth two in the bush" is as much a statement
about *time* (*now* versus the *future*) as it is about certainty and uncertainty.

Do you want to go to the show, or do you want to study? The relative
value of studying versus going to the show varies as a function of when the
question is asked and when the decision is made. If, for example, the question
is posed and the decision is made at time T_2 (hours, weeks, days before the
event), the relative values of activity A (two hours of pleasure enjoying a
movie) versus activity B (studying to pass a class; earn a degree, etc.) can be
more fairly weighed.[2] If the question is posed at time T_1, however, the immediate anticipation of activity A may outweigh that of activity B. The moral of the

---

[2] Note in the time prior to T_2 in Figure 8.5 that the expected reward values are in agreement
with the "real" values of small and large rewards. This may not always be the case in real life, when
often there exists disagreements about the relative values of events and activities.

story is to decide with your children in early December, not on Christmas Eve, that their presents will be opened on the morning of December 25.

Training Self-Control in Children

Earlier it was asserted that learning self-control is culturally based. Several studies have demonstrated that children learn to tolerate delays and thereby to make better choices. For example, 6-year-old children and older ones select large delayed rewards from two alternatives, while the 4-year-olds typically choose smaller, immediate rewards (Sonuga-Barke, Lea, & Webley, 1989). In another study, impulsive children were first allowed direct, immediate experience with both small and large rewards. A delay interval was gradually lengthened for access to the larger reward while the smaller reward continued to be immediately available. Several hyperactive children learned to choose the larger, delayed reward with this training, thereby demonstrating increased self-control (Schwitzer & Sulzer-Azaroff, 1988). Finally, children have been found to model on adults who verbalize the benefits of delayed rewards as being "worth the wait" (Mischel, 1966). It is as likely that other children model on impulsive parents with less desirable results.

This chapter began with a quote from Skinner pondering whether an individual should "be held responsible for his [or her] action and justly rewarded or punished for its consequences." Skinner argues that your decisions and choices have been determined by your genes and by your unique reinforcement history. Because you are not a free agent, the environment is responsible for your actions.

In this chapter we have seen that there is some truth in Skinner's analysis: Certainly, for simple organisms such as bees and even some small-brained vertebrates—birds and rats—choices are constrained by innate strategies that minimize energy expenditure and maximize energy consumption. Likewise, our responses seem to be keenly tuned to the available reinforcement contingencies. Only with training can we learn the patience of self-control—delaying immediate gratification for the goal of a larger anticipated award.

CHAPTER SUMMARY

1. Humans and animals engage in decision making throughout their lifetimes. Choices are influenced by feedback from the environment.

2. People and animals decide between two or more alternatives based on the perceived value of alternatives. Value is determined by esthetics, utility, cost, availability, and perception of worth. Together these factors compose the *expected utility* of an item.

3. Choice behavior can be understood within an adaptive-evolutionary context. Choices among food alternatives are seen as adaptive when they maximize energy attained (food) for energy expended (foraging, work).

4. Bees choose among alternatives in a way that avoids risk and favors consistency. Humans and other animals do likewise.

5. Initially measured in pigeons working on VI-VI concurrent schedules of reinforcement, the *matching law* describes a form of choice behavior in which responses match the available reinforcement. If one component of the concurrent schedule makes available three times the reinforcement compared to the other, pigeons make three times as many responses, matching the schedule.

6. *Undermatching* is likely to occur when the passage of time obscures or distorts the reinforcement contingencies of the leanest of the concurrent VI schedules. In undermatching, proportionately more responses are made to the lean schedule. The insertion of *changeover delays* in the concurrent schedules corrects for undermatching.

7. *Melioration* describes attempts by experienced animals to maximize reinforcement on two keys by paying attention to the most recently obtained patterns of reinforcement. *Overmatching* refers to pigeons on current schedules that by spending a disproportionate amount of time on the rich VI component underrespond on the lean VI component. Theoretical accounts of both melioration and overmatching disagree on whether molecular (short-term effects) or molar (long-term maximization) better accounts for the phenomena.

8. When *labor supply curves* are compared to the matching law, breakdowns in matching occur for the lowest-level wage earner. Leisure has value, and expending energy to work is balanced against the costs of lost leisure. Matching laws predict the behavior of hungry birds better than they predict the behavior of humans motivated by nonhunger variables.

9. Animals have been trained to choose between receiving either immediate or delayed reinforcement. Choosing delayed reinforcement demonstrates self-control.

10. The preference of both humans and animals for immediate gratification obtained by choosing small rewards (relative to selecting larger rewards that are delayed) can be accounted for by *expected utility theory*. Expected utility theory takes into account the relative value of immediate and delayed reinforcers. Expected utility theory predicts that choices between two alternatives will vary as a function of time preceding the experience of the reinforcers.

DISCUSSION QUESTIONS

1. Carley Brock, from Silverton, Oregon, is the 61-year-old father of three children. He was recently ticketed by local police and eventually fined $100 for "improperly supervising" his 16-year-old son Michael. Michael was caught smoking at school—his latest run-in with school officials and juvenile authorities. The elder Brock was one of 13 parents cited following the enactment of a new "parental responsibility" law. A number of states have enacted similar laws.[3] What do you suspect that Skinner would have thought about such laws?

2. A friend of mine is about to buy an off-road vehicle. Living in a small town with a single dealership, he compares vehicles and prices available there with those in a large town 100 miles away. He has one decision to make from three choices: (a) He can buy outright a locally available vehicle he likes—except for an automatic transmission (he prefers a manual transmission); (b) he can buy the model he wants with a manual transmission from a town 100 miles away; or (c) he can order his choice of model and features from the factory, deliverable after 30 days. He is leaning toward buying the car locally. Why?

3. What is the meaning of the following sayings?

   a. "Beggars can't be choosers."
   b. "I've saved the best for last."
   c. "Let me sleep on it, and I'll give you my decision tomorrow."

   d. "Never go grocery shopping when you are hungry."

   Are these sayings descriptive of human behavior? What theories help account for their truth?

4. What different food choices might you make from a menu as compared to a cafeteria line? Why?

5. A couple is in love. Compare and contrast their choices either to elope or to have a long engagement.

6. The NCAA has ruled that an athlete transferring to a new school is typically ineligible to play the first year at the new school. What is this rule attempting to influence/control?

7. Note that the labor supply curve in Figure 8.3 is for *wages* earned. What is the difference between a salary and a wage? How do employers' expectations differ for those employees paid wages and those paid salaries? From the employees' perspective, are there different expectations regarding leisure while on the job?

8. Why is impulse control training an important aspect of child rearing in most (all?) of the world's cultures?

DISCUSSION STARTERS

1. *Skinner's likely response to "parental responsibility" laws?* Skinner's consistent theme was that there was no such thing as free choice. Behavior, including deviant behavior, was controlled by reinforcement and punishment contingencies. To the extent that a child's inappropriate behavior was being maintained by parents, Skinner might agree with a law that shifted some responsibility to the parents. Recall, however, that Skinner saw all of society as sources of environmental control, not just caregivers. And he was not an advocate of punishment (the fine) to control behavior. Interestingly enough, in this case, the son was reported to be embarrassed by the incident, and his behavior changed so as to not cause his father any more trou-

---

[3] Cox News Service release, January 8, 1996.

ble. You may want to review how negative reinforcement controls behavior (p. 312ff.).

2. *Why does my friend decide to buy locally a new car that has fewer desirable features than those available elsewhere?* You can begin to explain his decision by reference to Figure 8.5. The relevant factors are all present—time, instant versus delayed gratification, bird in hand—even for an automobile. Should we be surprised that most humans have difficulty setting and maintaining lifelong goals?

3. *What is the meaning of the saying "Beggars can't be choosers"?* Two ideas come to mind: First, energy needs must be met before entertaining the option (and the luxury) of becoming less risk averse. Second (at the risk of being mean spirited!) in observing others, we compare the amount of energy expended for what is gained and expect something resembling a match. For many of us, the salaries of some administrators and entertainers and sports stars and radiologists do not seem to match the effort expended. The saying "I've saved the best for last" relates to the expectation of a larger reward making the passage of time more tolerable. The sayings "Let me sleep on it, and I'll give you my decision tomorrow" and "Never go grocery shopping when you are hungry" suggest that decisions change as a function of time. Immediate gratification is more primal, more emotional. The passage of time allows ANS activity to subside and the possibility of more rational thought to commence. The saying probably reflects a learning history of having made more poor decisions "on the spur of the moment" and therefore a distrust of immediate gratifica-

tion. Personally, I now let 24 hours pass and reread my letter to the editor rather than send it immediately after writing it.

4. *Different food choices ordering from a menu compared to those made in a cafeteria line?* The passage of time plays different roles in each scenario. Referring to Figure 8.5, by resisting the immediate gratification of appetite—a task made more difficult by the sights and smells of the cafeteria line—you can make the case that from the standpoint of health and nutrition, better overall choices will be made from the menu.

5. *Elope or have a long engagement?* Merely a different kind of appetite—see previous question.

6. *Why does the NCAA make athletes who change schools ineligible to play for one year?* This rule was implemented to discourage the reinforcement of immediately playing at another school. The inducements another coach or school might make to entice the athlete to switch are offset by the time delay. This penalty has the same effect as the *changeover delay* that prevents pigeons from undermatching by switching for high probability, immediate food on the alternate schedule.

7. *Differences between work and wages and work and salary?* One observation is that a salaried worker's job is less well defined than that of a wage earner. Also, compare FI and FFI schedules. Not all salaried workers are on FFI schedules (free fixed intervals, with no response contingency), but the traditional distinction is that wage earners are expected to produce each hour, while salaried workers are expected to get the job done with less reference to the passage of time.

8. *Why is impulse control training important?* The existence of civilization depends on the impulse control—delay of immediate gratification—of its citizens. Aldous Huxley's *Brave New World* and B.F. Skinner's *Walden Two* are utopian novels that specifically address the necessity of a technology to train impulse control in children. Toilet training is an example. Most group activities require discipline to accomplish group goals, be it a minimally functioning household, a preschool classroom, or, later, a workplace, athletic team, or military unit. Individual differences are evident in classroom discussions of impulse control. Most readers who have yet to reproduce espouse an ideal of less parental control and more freedom for children. Most parents see the world differently. Your position on impulse control can easily extend into both religious and political realms.

Key Terms

Changeover Delay (COD)   In a *concurrent schedule* procedure, a brief period of time during which reinforcement is not available immediately following a switch, or changeover, from one reinforcement schedule to the other.

Concurrent Schedules   A training procedure in which two or more reinforcement schedules run simultaneously and independently of each other and a subject can respond on either, used in the measurement of choice behavior.

Expected Utility   The expected gain from a decision made about a wager or transaction involving money or other tangible valuable.

Labor Supply Curve   A backward-bending curve that deviates from the matching law, reflecting a breakdown in the general rule that effort will increase indefinitely to match available reinforcement.

Matching Law   A monotonic functional relationship typically found between the rate of responding and available reinforcement. Response rates typically match available reinforcement (Herrnstein).

Melioration   Maximization of local (moment-to-moment) changes in available reinforcement.

Overmatching   Responding *more* than predicted for available reinforcement. (Cf. *Matching Law.*)

Self-Control   The ability to delay immediate gratification, usually with the goal of attaining a larger reinforcer at a later time.

Undermatching   Responding *less* than predicted for available reinforcement. (Cf. *Matching Law.*)

Value   The relative worth, merit, or importance of an object or activity, based on *esthetics, cost, availability, perceived utility,* and other properties.

CHAPTER 9

CONCEPTUAL LEARNING AND THINKING

Inquiring human beings of our day have been taught that among the distinctions between humankind and animal life are, first, the ability to use language; second, the ability to make and use tools; third, a sense of consciousness about oneself; and fourth, the ability to transmit culture. Each of these distinctions, as is true of all icons scientific and scriptural, has crumpled and fallen to make dust and detritus. As human beings have come to invest in the study of animal life, they come to understand also that whatever may be thought to be unique and defining about human beings is also characteristic of other animals. The remaining candidates for distinction are metaphysical and spiritual, such as the idea that only human beings are conscious of death or that humankind, alone among animal life, desires to know. These icons may not be as solid as we think.
                        Candland, *Feral Children and Clever Animals* (1993, p. 3*)*

INTRODUCTION

We have come full circle. To this point we have studied common processes of learning in animals and through the use of animal models have been successful in achieving a better understanding of human behavior. In this chapter we return to themes and issues set forth in Chapters 1 and 2.

In preceding chapters the strategy has been to apply relatively simple models of association formation—both Pavlovian and instrumental conditioning—to account for acquired behaviors in both humans and animals. There is little disagreement, for example, that nonhuman animals and human infants and adults can be conditioned. Insights attained through the application of conditioning enhance our understanding of health issues, eating behaviors, emotional behavior, behavioral control, skilled performance, and so forth.

Nevertheless, this general process view was likely to have frustrated the reader when it was applied to human behavior. The reason is that most humans believe that there are *qualitative* differences between human behavior and the human mind, on the one hand, and animal behavior and animal minds on the other. Unless you are familiar with the evidence of language, tool making, the transmission of culture, and other alleged behaviors of animals alluded to in the opening statement by Candland, scepticism remains in order. Indeed, many behavioral scientists who have studied animal behavior share your scepticism.

In this and in the following chapter, we turn to the study of conceptual learning, thinking, and language. Can we continue to extrapolate findings from animals to humans as we conduct research into conceptual and other forms of complex learning? Animals and human infants can't talk. Are they *conscious?* Can they *think?* Or, because only older humans think and talk, are thinking and talking *prerequisites* for complex learning? If so, then animal models become irrelevant, and our study of thinking, language, and complex learning should be reconceptualized as species-specific behaviors of the adult form of *Homo sapiens*. Let us first look at an example of concept formation in a nonhuman primate as studied in the laboratory.

Concept Formation in Nonhuman Primates: An Example

Earlier we learned that monkeys and chimpanzees make key-pressing responses for food reinforcement. In one experiment (Koestler & Barker, 1965), a display of visual stimuli such as those seen in Figure 9.1 were presented to a chimpanzee. (A picture of the chimpanzee working on the stimulus display panel can be seen in Box 6.2 on p. 314. The three backlit keys were located in the middle of the panel immediately below two other backlit keys.) A response to the odd stimulus—the triangle, for example (Problem 1, Figure 9.1)—was reinforced with food. A response to either of the same shapes (i.e., either of the circles) displayed in Problem 1 was not reinforced.

All responses, reinforced or not, terminated the visual display for 10 seconds. If correct, on the second training trial, a new stimulus array was presented. Note that the formerly correct triangle is incorrect in the same position. The *position* of the odd stimulus has been altered (i.e., placed on the far right). On the third training trial, a new stimulus (square) is correct, and so on for a sequence of 18 problems. One way to think about this task is that the *odd* stimulus is a discriminative stimulus (S^d) and the two identical stimuli are S^Δs.

With extensive training, eight chimpanzees were able to pick the odd stimulus from these 18 arrays with an average efficiency of 60 to 70% (33% = chance performance). The researchers concluded that the chimpanzees learned the **oddity concept** using these two-dimensional representational stimuli. This conclusion may or may not be warranted. Nevertheless, the example is instructive in showing that animals can be asked far more interesting questions than those asked in a standard Skinner box. Certainly you will agree

Problem no.	Symbol on display		
	1	**2**	**3**
1	○	△	○
2	△	△	○
3	○	○	□
4	△	○	○
5	△	○	△
6	□	□	△
7	○	□	□
8	△	□	□
9	△	△	□
10	□	○	□
11	□	△	△
12	○	□	○
13	○	○	△
14	○	△	△
15	△	□	△
16	□	○	○
17	□	△	□
18	□	□	○

FIGURE 9.1   Oddity Problems

The sequence of oddity problems used by Koestler and Barker (1965).
Symbols were projected on backlit keys. Each display would terminate if the
chimp hit any key or would timeout if the chimp failed to respond within 10
seconds. Responding to the correct key was reinforced with a banana-
flavored pellet. Correct responses advanced the display to the next problem;
incorrect responses re-presented the display until the chimp got it right.

that the task *might* require more complex properties of mind than the task of hitting a lever. Anthropomorphic speculation is always risky; however, in the example given, following extensive training, chimpanzees (and other animals in other experiments noted later) seem to "get the idea" of a pattern of responding rather than performing a conditioned reflex to a particular stimulus element. Given that *concept formation* is arguably a form of *thinking*, nonhuman animals may not be doomed to be the machinelike automatons envisioned by Descartes, forever restricted to behavior generated by the lowest level of conditioned reflex.

In a later section we return to the question of the concept of oddity and look at an alternative explanation for these animals' performance. These complex properties of mind generate behaviors that raise yet other questions— about the nature of *consciousness* and of *intelligence*. Our cultural knowledge leads us to assume that language, intelligence, thinking, and consciousness *go together*, for example, that you can't be intelligent if you are not conscious and that conceptual thinking is impossible without language. Given that these terms are typically defined in reference to and are characteristic of adult humans, what does it mean to question whether nonhuman animals have **cognitive processes**? What concepts, if any, can they learn? What is the nature of animal *thinking*, animal *language*, and animal *intelligence?* A brief history of why we use different language to address cognitive issues in humans and nonhuman animals can be found in Box 9.1.

Comparative Cognition

What is the evidence that animals think? That they are *conscious*? That they *communicate*? Unlike most of the subject matter of animal learning, the American public is interested in the animal mind, as attested to by an issue of *Time* magazine (March 22, 1993) featuring a six-page cover story, "Can Animals Think?"

In Chapter 10 we ask how different humans are from other primates in these regards. Does *Homo sapiens'* use of language and other highly developed cognitive abilities require extension and further revision of the simple associative frameworks we have studied, or should they be scrapped if found inadequate? For example, Chomsky (1975) and others think that language is so uniquely human that it determines the nature of human thought and behavior; learning and simple associative frameworks are irrelevant. Chomsky's analysis, however, begs the question of whether humans alone can form concepts, think, and be conscious.

The Question of Animal Consciousness

The preceding are not easy questions, and not everyone agrees on what constitutes evidence bearing on their answers. Some answers may surprise you. For example, it was suggested earlier that only humans can think conceptually,

Box 9.1   A Brief History of Cognitive Science

Introducing cognitive terms into a textbook on animal learning forces us to acknowledge the historical gap between animal *learning* and human *cognition* and *memory*. Recall that in formulating behaviorism, both John B. Watson and B.F. Skinner were reacting against "soft" conceptions of mind. Confident that the human *mind* could not be investigated scientifically, they opted for experimental analyses of *behavior*. Rejecting *mind* properties that could not be operationally defined, they implicitly accepted the Darwinian notion of continuity among animals and adopted instead animal models of behavior. To this behavioral framework, both adaptive/ evolutionary theory and the findings of contemporary neuroscience have been incorporated. This textbook is written from within such a perspective.

In the 1950s and 1960s, a different epistemology developed outside the behaviorist framework. *Cognitive psychologists* focused their study exclusively on humans and developed their own language and methodologies (see Gardner, 1985, for an excellent history and review). During the past 40 years, a very interesting pattern has developed. Cognitive psychologists have conducted research and written books and published articles in journals that dealt with properties of mind *exclusively human* including learning, intelligence, memory, attention, cognition, language, problem solving, and thinking. During the same time period, *comparative psychologists* and other behavioral scientists conducted research, wrote books and published articles in journals that dealt with properties of mind almost as *exclusively nonhuman*. For the most part their focus has been on animal learning and behavior.

Many textbooks written in the 1970s, for example, reflected this strange dichotomy. Several had titles like *Learning and Memory* and were written in a fairly standardized format: The first part of these books dealt with animal learning, the last half with human memory and cognition (e.g., J. Hall, 1982; Tarpy & Mayer, 1978; see also Schwartz & Reisberg, 1991). With exceptions (Dennett, 1983; Griffin, 1985; Weiskrantz, 1988, provide examples) few contemporary theorists attempt to bridge the conceptual gaps created by these different philosophical approaches, different research methods, and different terminology.

This issue has not been resolved, nor, it seems, will it be in the near future. But the conduct of science is a slow, very human endeavor, and scientists, their thinking constrained by empirical observations, are conservative. Some researchers *are* bridging the gap by using animals to study parallel problems in human memory (for example, Kesner, 1990). At the same time, however, behaviorists continue to decry the cognitive psychologists' plethora of "mind" terms and hypothetical constructs devoid of empirical reference (Malone, 1982; Schlinger, 1993; Wright & Watkins, 1987). Lewontin (1981), for example, argues for "replacing the clockwork mind with something less silly. Updating the metaphor by changing clocks into computers has got us nowhere." Ironically, rapid advances in the study of the central nervous system by behavioral neuroscientists may shape both disciplines, forcing them to *pay more attention* to each other.

presumably because we have language that allows us the conscious ability to talk about concepts as well as to each other. As shown in Focus on Research 9.1, however, Weiskrantz and other respected neuroscientists are of the opinion that even in the absence of language, some higher animals are every bit as conscious as humans.

Weiskrantz's position on the question of human and animal consciousness is controversial (see also Weiskrantz, 1988). Most of the issues dealt with in this chapter are controversial. Why? Because the issues in this chapter help us to define human nature and our place in the universe.[1] Each of us has a conception of who and what we are and of our place in the universe, and most of us become uncomfortable when our closeness to nonhuman animals is so baldly made apparent. In this chapter the intent is not to make monkeys of us all but to inquire into the rudiments of our human nature. It is a reasonable strategy to study other animals as well as humans to find out, and researchers in the field of *comparative animal cognition* do just that.

Searching for Human Capabilities in Animals.   One path to understanding what it is that discriminates the human mind from the minds of other animals is to see what we *can* and what other animals *cannot* accomplish. Even if some animals are capable of forming simple concepts, the fact remains that we are qualitatively better than all other animals in the realm of language and thinking. As we see later, even after extensive, painstaking training, to take another example, chimpanzees may exhibit some language capabilities, but nothing resembling the ability of a 3-year-old human with little formal training.

We study animals because we have so little insight into human complexity. It is human nature to talk, and yet the process of acquiring speech and generating language remains an enigma. Possessing analytical skills that far exceed those of other animals, we are puzzled over how we do it and why they can't. Recognizing at the outset that no other animal has even the rudiments of what we humans call *culture*, nevertheless we shall seek clues to human uniqueness in the behavior of our smaller-brained animal cousins. Before further addressing the complexities of thinking and language, let us begin at the beginning by asking how nonhuman animals learn about simple patterns in time and space.

Interim Summary

1. Both human and nonhuman animals engage in complex behaviors. Some of these complex behaviors are learned.

---

[1] A biased sampling of recent contributions to these "big issue" questions include Barkow, Cosmides, and Tooby's (1992) *The Adapted Mind: Evolutionary Psychology and the Generation of Culture;* Candland's (1992) *Feral Children and Clever Animals;* Corballis's (1991) *The Lopsided Ape;* Degler's (1991) *In Search of Human Nature;* Dennett's (1995) *Darwin's Dangerous Idea;* Diamond's (1992) *The Third Chimpanzee;* and Griffin's (1992) *Animal Minds.*

FOCUS ON RESEARCH 9.1

Do Animals Think?

Dr. Larry Weiskrantz, Department of Experimental Behavior, University of Oxford, Oxford, England

"All multi-cellular animals show changes in behavior as a result of experience—from habituation in the simpler organisms to complex forms of learning and memory in mammals. It cannot be this capacity to learn, per se, that distinguishes animals from humans. The challenging difference concerns the issue of animal *thought*. Undoubtedly thought is immensely enriched by language, but the question is whether it absolutely *requires* language. Many philosophers, from Locke in 1690 to Wittgenstein in 1922, have been resolutely unwilling to make concessions to nonverbal animals in this regard, largely on *a priori* grounds. That language is not essential for complex cognitive skills is clear even at the human level: severely aphasic patients can score highly on IQ tests like Raven's Matrices (Kertesz, 1988; Newcombe, 1987), and preverbal infants can segment and categorize their causal world (Leslie, 1988; Spelke, 1988). Therefore, there is no logical necessity to deprive animals of advanced mental skills because they lack language. Many impressive demonstrations have been reported, such as the ability of the chimpanzee to perform arithmetical addition or ratios (Premack, 1988), of rats to show 'intentional' behavior (Dickinson, 1985, 1988), and the spatial cognitive abilities of a number of animals (Thinus-Blanc, 1988). (For examples and a review of 'thought without language' in both animals and humans, cf. Weiskrantz, 1988.)

"But complex cognition, it might be argued, is not the same as having mental imagery. What about animals' images and imaginings? There are a number of approaches to this question. Detailed analysis of S-S classical conditioning suggests a control of behavior by representations of absent events, which have been interpreted as being 'imagined' (cf. review by Holland, 1990). Second, evidence of deception by primates leads to the suggestion that they have 'theories of other minds,' that is, imagine what the consequence of their behavior will be, based on their beliefs about other's belief (Woodruff & Premack, 1979). Finally, human neuropsychology has revealed a large number of residual cognitive capacities caused by brain damage of which the patient is 'unconscious' or 'unaware,' capacities sometimes called *implicit processes*. One can consider comparable cognitive dissociations in animals based on homologous brain systems. It may be possible to study the difference between 'conscious' (explicit) and 'thoughtless' (implicit) performance in animals (cf. Milner & Rugg, 1992; Weiskrantz, 1986)."

2. Training chimpanzees to perform an oddity task is an example of concept formation.

3. Little agreement exists among scientists concerning comparisons of consciousness, cognition, and language in humans and nonhuman animals although related questions are among the most interesting to ask.

4. The cognitive abilities of animals are often studied within two separate domains (i.e., nonhuman animal learning and human cognitive psychology).

5. *Animal learning* uses a *descriptive behaviorism* terminology that has two effects: It tends to (over)explain complex processes using a simple associative framework and in doing so probably oversimplifies the cognitive abilities of humans.

6. *Cognitive psychologists* use a plethora of cognitive terms that are not always operationally defined; many of which are a priori restricted to humans. This practice probably underestimates cognitive processes in animals.

LEARNING ABOUT PATTERNS IN TIME AND SPACE

Learning about concepts and rules involves learning about relationships. Given the large numbers of trials it takes to train above-chance performances, *odd* and *even* appear to be difficult concepts even for chimpanzees. Let us begin, then, by analyzing how humans and animals learn about even simpler relationships. Among the simplest of relationships that animals can learn are that events are distributed in *time* and that events can occur in *patterns*.

Timing Behavior in Animals

In previous chapters we have marveled at the ability of animals to keep track of time. Beyond speculating that their time perception likely differs from that of humans, we know very little about other animals' psychological appreciation of time. There is no disagreement that the rats, monkeys, and pigeons we have studied have the ability to use the passage of time as a discriminative stimulus to control the patterning of their responses. For example, monkeys on DRL schedules of reinforcement can *withhold* lever-press responding for specified durations of time within margins measured in *hundredths* of a second. Their behavior is evidence that monkeys have an excellent sense of *timing*. Rats and pigeons as well as monkeys and chimpanzees can be trained to make panel-push or lever-press responses within seconds of the onset of a stimulus to avoid an electric shock or to secure food (see Box 6.2, p. 314).

Indeed, the very basis of conditioning is predicated on the animal's ability to discriminate the time relationships of stimuli and of responses. Only a fraction of a second differentiates *forward* from *trace* or *backward* conditioning; yet as we have seen, such differences are critical in determining both the amount and nature of the resulting association.

A number of models of timing behavior in animals have been proposed (see Gibbon & Church, 1984; Roberts, 1981). At present, however, the existence of a central nervous system mechanism (a biological "clock") that would mediate precise timing behaviors is only speculative. All we can say is that an animal's sensitivity to time attests to the precision of sensory and motor nerve conduction velocities measured in fractions of a second and to the overall adaptive functioning of a nervous system whose very survival depends on such exquisite time-keeping functions.

Counting Behavior in Animals

When information provided the animal by the environment concerns the *number* of events rather than the *duration* of events in a given period of time, *counting* rather than *timing* behavior is described (Meck & Church, 1983).

Counting behavior can be considered to be another example of preconceptual pattern learning. Children learn to count, initially from 1 to 10, and then, with conceptual training, to identify odd and even numbers, to learn the multiplication tables, prime numbers, imaginary numbers, and so on. Counting is therefore a precursor to each human's mathematical abilities. While recognizing that the word *mathematics* is seldom used in reference to infrahuman capabilities, is it not unreasonable to inquire into the abilities of animals to quantify; that is, is the ability to *count* restricted to humans?

Counting and Rhythmic Timing.   That counting and timing behavior are related is evidenced by the musical abilities of humans; the timed beats of varying duration can be considered a form of rhythmic counting. An example of similar behavior in *Rhesus* monkeys has been previously described (see p. 250). Recall that these monkeys were reinforced with a sugar pellet for *withholding* responses for 15 seconds before striking a lever. One animal's incredible timing accuracy (responses were repeatedly within hundredths of a second) was apparently achieved by a sequenced pattern resembling rhythmic counting. After making a reinforced response, this seated monkey would (a) rhythmically chew the pellet for a few seconds; (b) then begin to sway from side to side, metronome-like, for the next few seconds; (c) then still swaying, with her left hand begin to rhythmically tap the upper center section of the performance panel positioned in front of her; (d) then, as the end of the 15-second interval approached, with exaggerated intensity her sway switched from side to side to front to back, and her tapping speeded up to about two taps per second; and (e) finally, with her right hand she deftly slapped the appropriate lever located on the lower left-hand portion of the performance panel. She would then pick up her sucrose pellet and begin the sequenced pattern again, her interresponse latencies not varying by more than a fraction of a second (Barker, 1968).

Was this monkey *counting?* I think the answer is yes, unless counting is restricted to the realm of human verbal behavior. If a human were instructed to repeatedly make a chalk mark on a chalkboard every 15 seconds, a rhythmic motion that resembled the monkey's behavior (probably accompanied by rhythmic subvocalization) would likely occur. Counting appears to be one of the simplest possible timed patterns.

Counting, Timing, Attention, and Memory

Counting and timing behaviors require the animal to *pay attention* to what it is doing. The monkey's rhythmic counting and precisely timed lever-pressing response are reflections of the animal's *memory* for what it has previously learned. In a sense, each timed response matches the monkey's memory for how much time had passed from the previous response. Using the words *attention* and *memory* is a departure from the descriptive language used to this point to account for animal learning and animal behavior. As discussed earlier, the law of parsimony is applied whenever possible. Working within the rigorous methodologies afforded by Skinner's descriptive behaviorism, a great deal of learned human and animal behavior has been accounted for without formally acknowledging the cognitive processes of *paying attention*, of *remembering*, and of *memory*. To the extent that these cognitive terms and constructs help us both to explain patterned and other complex animal behavior and to bridge the gap with behaviors that humans engage in, these terms are used with caution in discussions of complex behavior throughout this chapter.

Serial Pattern Learning in Animals

In addition to counting and timing, quite a good deal of research has been directed toward understanding how sensitive animals are to serial patterns. Again, this research is best understood within the frameworks of both *animal memory* for patterns and simple *rule learning*. Given a series of items to remember, which patterns presented them can rats and pigeons recognize (i.e., *remember*) and use to solve problems?

Serial Pattern Methodology.   The methodology used by Hulse and his graduate students illustrates how rats can learn serial patterns. Given that hungry rats run faster or slower in a runway depending on whether they receive food, Hulse (1978) measured the running speed of rats rewarded with a *monotonic series* of reinforcer amounts. Over five successive trial runs, one group of rats found consistently decreasing amounts of pellets of food in the goal box (i.e., 14, 7, 3, 1, and, finally, 0 pellets. This same sequence was repeated (five runs × five sequences of reinforcements each day). Eventually, these rats were found to run more slowly on those trials that ended in an empty goal box. Note that the only way the rats could *know* that there would be no food in the goal box (as evidenced by their slow rate of running) was that they had learned the sequence of the serial pattern of reinforcement. For this reason, the phenomenon is called **serial pattern learning.**

Cued Counting.   What was the pattern learned in this task? Several analyses are possible. The most parsimonious argument is that these rats may be doing something akin to rhythmic counting. That is, they may have learned the simple rule that they will be reinforced only on every fifth run down the runway. Count to 4, pause, count to 4, pause, *cha-cha-cha*. If this were the case, then *any* sequence of four reinforced trials preceding a nonreinforced trial would suffice. Or are *some* serial patterns more easily learned than others? Hulse (1978) compared the performance of rats on the monotonic series as described earlier with another group of rats that successively found 14, 1, 3, 7, and 0 pellets in the goal box. The same training conditions were used; however, notice that the sequence of pellets was *not* monotonic (amounts did not consistently decrease). After training, however, these rats *also* learned to slow down on the fifth run, although (a) they took more trials to learn the pattern and (b) they didn't ever slow as much on the fifth, nonreinforced trial as did the group with the monotonic pattern. We can conclude that rats learned the *pattern* of reinforcement and that the decreasing monotonic series was the more effective cue than the nonmonotonic sequence of 14, 1, 3, 7, and 0 pellets.

Phasing Cues Improve Performance.   What else do we know about serial pattern learning? Other researchers have reported that eliminating the delay between the end of one series (i.e., 0 pellets) and the beginning of the next series (i.e., 14 pellets) makes the pattern unlearnable. Apparently, without the pause in the series, the individual elements of the "pattern" become one long sequence with no discernible elements (to the rat). The time delay between each repeating series is conceptualized as a *phasing cue* that serves to demarcate each series (Fountain, Henne, & Hulse, 1984). These investigators also found that a series longer than five elements can be effectively learned by rats if *phasing cues* that effectively break the long series into a sequence of shorter elements are introduced. Their finding parallels our understanding of how humans reduce long serial patterns into shorter ones, such as telephone numbers (817/829-1979), social security numbers (569-xx-2280), and the like.[2]

Summary of Serial Pattern Learning in Rats.   Rats are apparently capable of learning to respond to patterns of stimuli grouped together in time. The task is probably best conceptualized as one in which various cues allow the rat to memorize short repeating patterns, separated by discrete periods of time. For reasons that are at present not understood, monotonic series cues (which are orderly for humans) produce better serial learning performance than do non-

---

[2] The phenomenon of grouping elements into smaller units is called *chunking*. The phone number is for the post office in Elm Mott, Texas.

monotonic cues for rats. Rats are apparently able to detect the pattern of monotonicity and to use it in addition to a serial pattern of reinforcement.

Maze Learning in Animals

The learning of serial patterns as demonstrated by Hulse and his colleagues is in some ways similar to the way a rat learns to find its way through a maze. For example, the running speed of rats changes as they learn the pattern of the maze in which they are placed. Note the two different patterns of mazes in Figure 9.2. One, the eight-arm radial maze (often called the *Olton Maze*), has a central start box: Any of the eight arms can be baited with food and used as a goal box. A famous maze (used in experiments by Edward Tolman) has a start box and paths containing a number of *choice points* leading to either *cul-de-sacs* or the shortest path to the *goal box*. After many trials in the traditional maze, appropriately patterned responses occur; the rat eliminates blind alleys and wrong turns, allowing rapid entry into the goal box. Let us analyze experiments conducted in these two types of maze and then compare maze learning with the serial pattern learning described by Hulse.

How Rats Learn Mazes

A traditional type maze (see Figure 9.2) was used by Tolman and Honzik (1930). On successive trials, rats typically run faster and make fewer errors at the choice points on their way to food reinforcement in the goal box. For this reason, much early attention was directed to the rat's performance at these choice points. Among the questions raised were, for example, whether rats make more errors in the first or last part of the maze; whether they learned a *sequence* of left and right turns in an associative manner; and/or whether they *memorized* the maze or learned to map it. It is beyond the scope of this book to summarize 90 years of research devoted to how rats learn mazes.[3] But for present purposes, let us briefly look at the three questions raised.

In Early Trials, Do Rats Learn the First or Last Part of the Maze?   Rats eliminate errors nearest the goal box, and only after many trials do they successfully make appropriate left and right turns in the early part of the maze (Hull, 1932). Hull described this in terms of the principle of *delay of reinforcement;* responses at the end of a series of responses are closest to the reinforcing stimu-

---

[3] Small (1901) built a rat-size replica of the high-hedged human maze located in the gardens of Henry VIII's Hampton Court palace and was the first psychologist to study the rat's maze-learning abilities. Having been hopelessly lost in the Hampton Court maze on several occasions (trials), I find it incredible that Small's rats ever found their way out. The reader interested in the historical use of mazes in animal experiments is directed to Woodworth and Schlosberg (1954).

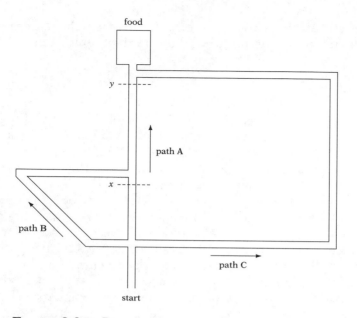

food

y

path A

x

path B

path C

start

FIGURE 9.2a   Rats in Mazes

(a) The plan of Tolman and Honzik's (1930) "insight" maze. Note that path A is the shortest one unless blocked at point *x* or point *y*. With both blocks in place, path C, the longest route, is the only way to get to the food in the goal box.

lus. Furthermore, Hull (1943) hypothesized that rats learn the maze from back to front by a conditioning process. By his analysis, stimuli encountered on entry into the goal box are paired with food reinforcement. Fractional traces of even earlier stimuli in the maze are also conditioned; these stimuli in turn become secondary reinforcers for the earliest responses in the maze. In Hull's system of terminology and notation, these stimuli are called **fractional anticipatory goal responses (r_Gs).** So, to the second question of whether rats learn a *sequence* of left and right turns in an associative fashion, Hull's answer would be a resounding yes. Stimuli composing each choice point (the shape, color, smell, vestibular and somesthetic cues, orientation of the maze in the room, etc.) are reinforced by secondary reinforcement and eventually by primary reinforcement in the goal box.

Role of r_Gs's in Serial Pattern Learning.   Recall that Hulse's rats learned a serial pattern of reinforcement. After four straight reinforced trials, they learned to run more slowly on a fifth trial that was never food reinforced. One hypothesis is that rats *connect* the individual elements of this sequence into a *pattern*. The

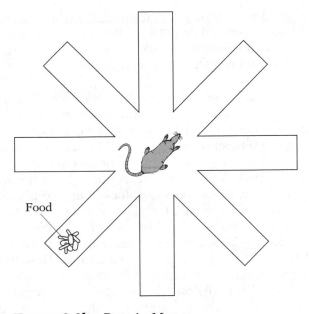

Food

FIGURE 9.2b   Rats in Mazes

(b) Olton's eight-arm radial maze (Olton & Samuelson, 1976). Rats are placed in the center and are free to enter any of the eight arms at any time. Several of the eight arms may contain food; hungry rats will systematically forage all eight arms, seldom repeating those previously visited.

---

rat uses each reinforced trial as a discriminative stimulus for the next trial. That is, each trial is part of a pattern of trials; each trial has distinctive stimulus properties that signal the rat where it is in the pattern. The patterned sequence of four reinforced trials signals a fifth, nonreinforced trial, in a manner similar to the patterned sequence of left and right turns that signal reinforcement in a goal box.[4] The interested reader is directed to Capaldi and Molina (1979), and Capaldi, Verry, Nawrocki, and Miller (1984) for further analysis and discussion of this hypothesis.

Cognitive Maps of Mazes.   Tolman (1932) provided another hypothesis concerning the way rats learn the pattern of mazes; rats make a **cognitive map** of the maze. Tolman was well aware that the term *cognitive map* represented a departure from the connectionist model of association formation. That is,

---

[4] Note that this analysis can likewise be applied to the learning of a long musical piece in which one sequence of finger placements and sounds signals the next sequence of finger placements and sounds, and so on.

rather than learning a maze dumb-dumb fashion through a trial and error sequence of reinforced and nonreinforced responses, Tolman assumed that a rat "got the idea" of where, in two dimensional space, *I am located,* of where *food is located,* and of the *shortest path connecting me to the food.*

Tolman and Honzik's (1930) Experiment.   What is the evidence for *cognitive maps?* Look again at the maze in Figure 9.2, and notice that points *x* and *y* represent blocked passages in the maze. Using an analysis of *learning by association,* rats encountering these blocked passages could not make the appropriate instrumental responses leading to reinforcement and, therefore, could learn nothing directly about path A (i.e., the straight path from the *starting place* to the *food box*). Indeed, with the passage blocked at two places, Tolman's rats had no alternative but to learn to take the long route (path C) through the maze. When the blockades were then removed, however, the rats quickly took the shortcut, path A. They had never before been food reinforced for taking path A, and they had no direct experience with it. How did they know about the shorter path? Tolman argued that the rats could do this only if they had a *mental representation* of the maze's configuration. The rat's *memory* for the overall pattern of the maze, apparently attained even in the absence of direct experience, allowed the rat, given the opportunity, to efficiently solve the maze.

Exploration, Investigation, and Spatial Memory

Whether or not we buy into Tolman's "mentalistic" terminology, his analysis of this problem in terms of the acquisition of *spatial memory* is probably correct. Bowe (1984) argues that psychologists have long ignored the ability of animals to learn about *spatial relationships,* focusing instead on *time relationships*. Rats bring to new environments inborn tendencies to spontaneously *explore* and to *investigate* (Renner, 1988; Renner & Seltzer, 1991). In a series of experiments, Renner and his colleagues demonstrated that nonhungry rats systematically explore an experimental space and investigate both new and familiar objects within it. Days following these experiences, they return to previous locations looking for objects that were removed in their absence (Renner & Seltzer, 1991).

Renner's work can be thought of as the study of species-specific exploration and investigation patterns. In addition, research with both traditional mazes and the eight-arm maze (Olton et al., 1977; see Figure 9.2) now leads us to believe that rats are expert in the domain of spatial relationships (see Figure 9.3). Rats actively explore and investigate their environment even when not hungry. When hungry, their search for food in a spatial domain uses innately determined **foraging patterns** (Haig, Rawlings, Olton, Mead, & Taylor, 1983). For example, rats first become familiar with the eight-arm pattern of this type of maze by finding food placed in one or more of its "arms." After training,

FIGURE 9.3   Liberal Arts Rats in Maze

Frank and Ernest by Bob Thaves. Reprinted by permission of Newspaper Enterprise Association, Inc.

when placed in the start box, rats conduct systematic searches of the maze's eight arms. Defining an error as reentry of an arm previously searched for food, *rats seldom make errors* under these conditions. On a given series of trials, they enter each arm in turn, even if a previously visited arm is rebaited or if shaving lotion is used to mask *trail cues* (Olton & Samuelson, 1976). Note that rebaiting the arm with food should provide usable odor cues; because rats don't reenter these arms, odor cues apparently do not play a role in their search pattern. If not food odor, what *does* determine their search pattern? If rats are allowed to visit a few arms and then are removed while the entire maze is rotated 45° (so that the previously visited arms are now in new locations), rats will go to the new locations. That is, they seem to be responding almost exclusively in terms of spatial cues, not to characteristics of individual arms of the maze.

Foraging Behavior of Other Animals.   Rats are not the only animals that bring innately determined patterns of behavior to their task of securing food from the environment. Pigeons (Olson & Maki, 1983), marsh tits (Shettleworth & Krebs, 1982), and chimpanzees (Menzel, 1978) join humans in their ability to conduct patterned searches, the result of which is to rapidly locate and remember where food is located in three-dimensional space. Menzel's (1978) chimpanzee experiment is reminiscent of Tolman and Honzik's (1930) blockaded maze experiment. Chimps were carried around an acre of rough outdoor terrain and were allowed to watch as fruits and vegetables were hidden at 18 different locations. A short time later, they were turned loose from a central location. Not surprising, without hesitation, the chimps went by the shortest paths to their most preferred foods (sweet fruits) and then systematically collected the remaining vegetables from all 18 sites. In making few errors, each acted as if it had memorized the area through which it conducted a patterned search.

Interim Summary

1. Among the simplest of complex behaviors are timing and rhythmic counting. Many animals are highly sensitive to the passage of time.

2. One form of counting is evidenced by the fact that rats can learn *serial patterns* of events distributed in time and can break down long serial patterns into shorter ones by the use of *phasing cues*.

3. Many animals have been demonstrated to have excellent memories for spatial events. Rats behave in ways that suggest they have predispositions to explore and investigate their environments.

4. Rats learn not only to negotiate mazes without errors but also to form *cognitive maps* of the areas they are traversing. Some response tendencies at choice points in mazes can be accounted for by Hull's principle of *fractional anticipatory goal responses*.

5. The readiness by which different species of animals learn complex spatial patterns is highly suggestive of an innately *prepared* form of learning. By this analysis, species-specific innate foraging behaviors locate food via patterned searches rather than a random trial-and-error approach. Locating food both stops the search and reinforces the pattern; searching continues on nonreinforced trials.

LEARNING ABOUT RULES AND CONCEPTS

This chapter opened by describing the behavior of chimpanzees that apparently had learned a *general rule* governing the oddity task they were confronted with (i.e., they appeared to learn to select the *odd* stimulus of three stimuli presented on a display panel, see Figure 9.1). In some ways this oddity configuration is similar to the mazes and patterned reinforcement sequences described in the preceding section. Each oddity problem has a pattern, and the animal's task is to learn the pattern.

The oddity task and the animal's behavior differ, however, in that the "pattern" these primates had to learn changed from trial to trial. In the other examples, both the maze pattern and Hulse's reinforcement pattern remained fixed from trial to trial over many sessions. And, unlike maze learning, chimpanzees and other animals do not bring innately predisposed foraging strategies to the solution of an oddity problem. Rather, the food hopper is in a fixed position, and animals must learn to solve symbolic problems unrelated to the location of food in space. Symbolic conceptual learning, then, is a different task, presumably a more complex form of learning. Let us take a closer look at the oddity task.

Associative Conditioning, Memorization, or Conceptual Learning?

Note in Figure 9.1 the various positions that triangles, circles, and squares can assume in the oddity problem. Recall that responding to a square in the center position, for example, was sometimes reinforced and sometimes punished. The same was true for a triangle, circle, or square in any position. Throughout the 18 presentations of stimuli in every session, responding to the triangle (S^d) when it appeared with either two squares or two circles was reinforced on each of six occasions and in each of three positions. During the same session, responding to any of the 12 triangles when they were S^Δs did *not* produce reinforcement. The animals learned to respond to a particular stimulus only when it was positioned in a particular array with other stimuli.

How did chimpanzees accomplish this task? Is it a case of "simple" differential conditioning of a relatively large number of S^ds and S^Δs? Given the limited number of stimulus arrays (18 in total; see Figure 9.1), following extensive conditioning, perhaps they *memorized* which response went with each array. (A human analogy would be the rote memorization of the multiplication tables.) Or did the animals truly learn to respond to the *odd* stimulus in each array? (A human analogy would be using rules to memorize the multiplication tables, such as any odd number multiplied by 5 ends in 5; any number multiplied by an even number ends in an even number; etc.) Recognize that the latter alternative is typically what is meant by *conceptual learning;* the former can be considered a repertoire of conditioned responses. Note also that when humans memorize the multiplication tables, presumably both kinds of learning are involved.

Memory Capacity Versus General Rule Learning?   How can we decide whether the chimpanzees who were able to solve this oddity task *memorized particular stimulus configurations* or *learned a general rule*? Unfortunately, for reasons that soon should become apparent, in these experiments we *cannot* decide between these two alternatives. We require at least two kinds of information to help us decide: First, we need information regarding the abilities of nonhuman primates and other animals to memorize (to learn to recognize) a large number of stimulus arrays. Can chimpanzees memorize the correct response to the 18 stimulus arrays depicted in Figure 9.1? If so, they could solve the problem without having developed a *concept* of oddity. Second, we need a methodology that allows us to bypass specific memories for previously learned items. We need a task that requires the animal to select novel (untrained) stimuli using a general rule rather than relying on conditioned responses to particular stimuli that had been reinforced. Let us first look at evidence that chimpanzees can memorize a large number of complex stimulus arrays.

Match to Sample

Figure 9.4a depicts Minnie, a chimpanzee making a conditioned response on a **match-to-sample** task. In this experiment, Farrar (1967) trained Minnie and two other chimpanzees to perform with better than 90% accuracy. A work session consisted of presenting the chimp a sequence of the 24 different problems, each involving a different stimulus array; see sequence of visual stimuli in Figure 9.4b. Each problem began with the appearance of a single visual stimulus displayed on a backlit key located above four similar side-by-side

FIGURE 9.4a Minnie and the Story of Picture Memory

Chimpanzee 46 (Minnie) is seen performing on the *match-to-sample* task described in the text. Note the large size of the equipment used to measure responses and to control timing and stimulus configurations in the precomputer era of the early 1960s. Minnie continues to live in New Mexico. Now in her mid-30s, she has successfully born and raised 15 chimpanzees in captivity. A good mother, she remains a joy to all humans who have had the pleasure of working with her.

Problem no.	Pictures				Correct position
	Lever no. 1	Lever no. 2	Lever no. 3	Lever no. 4	
1	+	Ⓖ	|	×	4
2	⧌	—	▣	◎	2
3	Ⓖ	Ⓦ	+	×	3
4	Ⓑ	—	Ⓡ	▣	1
5	Ⓖ	⧌	—	×	2
6	+	×	Ⓡ	Ⓑ	4
7	|	Ⓖ	Ⓦ	⧌	3
8	|	Ⓖ	—	◎	1
9	+	◎	ⓄⓇ	×	3
10	△	▣	|	×	2
11	Ⓦ	◎	Ⓑ	|	4
12	◎	ⓄⓇ	▣	—	1
13	ⓄⓇ	Ⓦ	—	Ⓖ	1
14	×	▣	ⓄⓇ	Ⓡ	2
15	Ⓡ	—	+	▣	3
16	⧌	Ⓖ	|	Ⓡ	4
17	×	▣	◎	Ⓑ	3
18	Ⓑ	|	×	—	4
19	Ⓑ	+	▣	—	1
20	+	Ⓖ	|	Ⓑ	2
21	×	Ⓦ	—	Ⓑ	2
22	⧌	×	Ⓖ	Ⓡ	1
23	▣	Ⓑ	×	|	3
24	⧌	—	▣	Ⓡ	4

FIGURE 9.4b

Table of the 24 problems in Farrar's (1967) study of *picture memory*. Note that Problem 2 (*triangle, horizontal line, square,* and *circle*) is displayed on the performance panel in Minnie's cage; see (c).

Figure 9.4c

Match-to-sample problem 2 from Minnie's view. See text.

keys. This stimulus, called the *sample*, was displayed for 3 seconds. The sample was varied in shape and/or color (i.e., a *blue circle*). After the 3-second display of the sample, four backlit keys located below the sample were also illuminated, displaying stimuli varying in color and shape. The chimpanzee's task was to survey the four keys and to locate and push the one key on which the symbol matched the sample above—hence, match to sample. After learning this task (which required hundreds of trials; see following discussion), the procedure was slightly changed. The sample was illuminated for 3 seconds and *terminated* at the onset of the four-stimulus array. Technically, this procedure is called a **delayed match to sample** (with a 0-second delay). Using *delayed match to sample* (especially with longer delays), the animal must remember what the stimulus was and select its match from memory.

For example, the sample stimulus displayed for 3 seconds in Problem 2 was a horizontal line; when it terminated, a *triangle, horizontal line, square,* and *circle* lit up for 10 seconds (see Fig 9.4c) . The chimp was reinforced by delivery of a banana pellet for pressing the key displaying the *horizontal line* in the second position. If the wrong stimulus was selected, the display would terminate without food, and the same problem (beginning with the sample) would be presented until a correct response was made.

The three chimpanzees in Farrar's study learned this task and performed at high levels of proficiency. Minnie, for example, achieved perfect scores (144 correct/144 problems per day) on 5 of 10 test days; the occasional "misses" appeared to be due to lack of attention and to problems timing out before responses were made. Minnie and two other chimpanzees' 10-day average accuracy percentage rates were 99.3, 95.4, and 93.7, respectively. Farrar had noted that Minnie's lack of attention to the display panel did not seem to impede her performance. On several occasions she did not look at the 3-second sample stimulus, but when the four-stimulus display was illuminated, she nevertheless made the correct response.[5] One day a technician noticed that the light bulb used to illuminate the sample stimulus was burned out. He checked each of the three animal's records for that day and found that none of the three had suffered any performance decrement.

Picture Memory. Farrar (1967) concluded that each stimulus arrangement composed a *picture* and that the chimps had memorized each of the 24 different pictures in Figure 9.4b, a phenomenon he called **picture memory**. But note that each picture, while distinctive, has common elements. For example, a green circle appears on 9 of the 24 pictures but is reinforced only on Problem 20. On the seven occasions in which a red circle is part of the picture, it is reinforced twice in position 4 but is *not* reinforced on five other occasions (including twice in position 4, twice in position 3, and once in the first position). What aspect of each picture, then, is controlling the animal's response?

Randomizing the Serial Position Pattern. Intrigued, Farrar (1967) ran a series of experiments to attempt to determine how these chimpanzees were solving the problem in the absence of a sample. He first randomized the order of the sequence of presentation of the 24 pictures and left the sample light off. The chimps' performance did not change. Farrar concluded that the chimps had not solved the problem by responding based on the serial presentation of the 18 pictures. That is, the chimps had apparently *not* learned the sequence: on trial 1, *far right key;* on trial 2, *second from the left,* and so forth.

Removing Elements of Each Picture. In subsequent daily tests (again with the sample light off), Farrar (1967) systematically eliminated one or two of the symbols in each of the 24 pictures. The deleted stimulus elements appeared as blank (unlighted) response keys. Only one of the three chimps suffered *any* change in performance (i.e., 85% rather than 95% accuracy) even when *half the picture* (i.e., *two of the four distracter stimuli, or $S^\Delta s$) was eliminated.* For example, in Problem 2 (see Figure 9.4c), the triangle and the square were re-

[5] D. Farrar, November 1992, personal communication.

moved. Only the circle and the horizontal line appeared. Having never seen this picture before and in the absence of a sample, the chimps nevertheless picked the horizontal line, the S^d previously associated with reinforcement. Apparently, Farrar concluded, merely the presence of the S^d in a particular position and at least one other stimulus element were enough of the composite picture for the animal to solve the problem.

What Is the S^d in "Degraded" Pictures?   Farrar then gambled ingeniously. What if the consistently rewarded stimulus in each picture does *not* by itself constitute the S^d? What would happen if instead of removing two of the three S^Δs from each picture, he removed the S^d and one S^Δ? How would the animals respond in the absence of the correct stimulus element? On each of the next two days, all three chimpanzees were presented with pictures that contained only 50% of the elements with which they originally had been trained. On the first day, one each of 12 S^ds and S^Δs were deleted from half the pictures; two S^Δs were deleted from each of the other 12 pictures. The second day was like the first except Farrar deleted different S^ds and S^Δs. Recall that these deleted stimulus elements appeared as blank (unlighted) response keys, and if the blank key was in the position that an S^d usually occupied, responding to the blank key would be reinforced.

The performance of the three chimps deteriorated but, again, far less than one might assume. Assuming that the animals would continue to respond to blank keys (which they did), their chance performance, or guessing, on this problem can be computed as an efficiency of 25%. (Given four keys, the chimps had a one in four chance of being reinforced on each trial.) The three chimps' performance on the first test day with S^ds missing was 49.3, 57.6, and 50.0%, and on the second day, with totally new S^ds missing, was 68.1, 72.9, and 62.5%. Farrar speculated that the improvement on the second day represented relearning a *new* picture, a picture in which the blank keys effectively served as stimulus elements. Unfortunately, training was disrupted at this point, and terminal performance on such highly degraded pictures was not realized.

Learning About Pictures or Learning Concepts?

What have we learned? Or better, what have these animals learned? This rather long section on *picture memory* was introduced to answer a specific question about the memory capabilities of chimpanzees for this type of problem. Specifically, we wanted to know whether chimpanzees were capable of *memorizing* which response went with each of the 18 oddity problems displayed in Figure 9.1, or whether they learned a *general rule* (i.e., did they learn to respond to the *odd* stimulus in each array?). From Farrar's (1967) experiment we know that chimpanzees are capable of memorizing at least 24 pictures, each of which has more pictorial elements than the three-symbol oddity problem. So it is possible that in the previously discussed oddity research, chimpanzees did *not* learn the concept of oddity; rather, they learned to make specific conditioned responses to 18 different pictures. Although supporting records do not exist, the chimpanzees' performance in Koestler and Barker's (1965) study was low (60–70% efficiency) because they consistently missed *particular* problems: Errors were not randomly distributed throughout the set of 18 problems. Their pattern of performance suggests *picture memory* rather than a *concept of oddity*.

Indeed, Farrar's (1967) study of picture memory raises problems for all concept formation methodologies that use a relatively small number of items. Memorization precedes and perhaps precludes rule learning in these tasks. Given the apparently excellent memory of chimpanzees for pictures, we are faced with devising a task that requires an animal to select a novel stimulus using a general rule rather than relying on conditioned responses to particular stimuli. Harlow (1949) showed us how to do just that.

Learning a Win-Stay, Lose-Shift Strategy

Harlow's (1949) task was simpler than the oddity task described earlier. His monkey-training apparatus is depicted in Figure 9.5a. The experimenter lowers a screen so the *Rhesus* monkey cannot watch where food is hidden in either of two food cups located beneath two objects arranged on a tray. (The stimulus objects were small toys and other novelty items purchased from the local variety store.) One of the items is designated as the correct choice for six consecutive trials (i.e., the reward is hidden beneath it), and the position of the correct item is determined by a randomization scheme. The monkey has a 50% chance of being right on each trial. It can maximize reinforcement by a **win-stay, lose-shift strategy,** as follows.

Let a red block be the correct stimulus and a thimble be incorrect. If the monkey selects the red block on the first trial, it will be rewarded (i.e., "win") and on the next trial with the same pair of stimuli, continue to be reinforced by continuing to select the red block (i.e., "stay" with the red block). Selecting the thimble is never reinforced. After six trials, the monkey is confronted with two new objects, one of which is reinforced, the other not. Note that the sooner this rule is learned (i.e., "if reinforced, stay with that choice; if not reinforced, shift to the other choice"), the more reinforcements will be attained. Harlow (1949) found that after having six trials with each of eight pairs of objects, monkeys averaged about 75% correct responses on their sixth trial with the eighth pair; see panel (b) of Figure 9.5. He concluded that monkeys were capable of learning a *win-stay, lose-shift* rule.

Learning Sets or Learning to Learn

As Harlow's (1949) monkeys continued their training with new objects (i.e., trained beyond the first eight paired objects), another phenomenon emerged.

They got better at the task. To perform at only 75% efficiency on the sixth trial of a two-choice task means that during these first eight successive pairs of objects, the monkeys required several trials to learn to *stay* (if reinforced) and several trials to learn to *shift* (if punished). These monkeys apparently were learning anew the solution to each novel problem within the six training trials. Once each monkey had mastered this concept, however, and had learned a *strategy*, it no longer needed six trials to learn the correct response. Rather than having to be differentially conditioned to each new S^d and S^Δ, these monkeys applied a *general rule* to each new set of paired objects. Harlow described this as **learning to learn.**

Our attention, therefore, shifts to the animal's behavior on the *second* trial. Figure 9.5b shows how these monkeys continued to improve their performance so that after a hundred or so sets of six trials (with two new objects in each set), they began to *stay* or *shift* on trial two of the six-trial set. That is, with each new pair, they did not have to learn the strategy anew but had only to implement a strategy (apply a rule) already learned. Harlow called this task a **learning set**. The monkey, he reasoned, had *learned how to learn* novel learning sets. After 250-plus trials, the monkeys were about 98% accurate on the second through sixth trials with each newly introduced pair of stimuli.

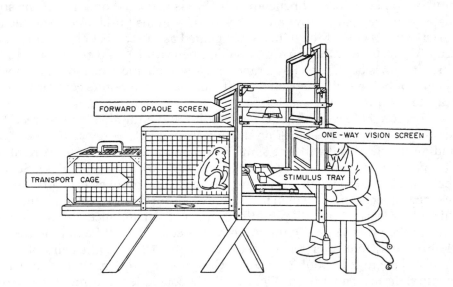

FIGURE 9.5a   Learning to Learn

An apparatus called the *Wisconsin General Test Apparatus* (*WGTA*) placed an experimenter across from a monkey. A series of screens could be raised and lowered, allowing the experimenter, out of view of the monkey, to "bait" the correct food cup over which a stimulus object was placed. Once in place, the monkey's screen could be raised, allowing it to respond to the testing situation (see text for further details).

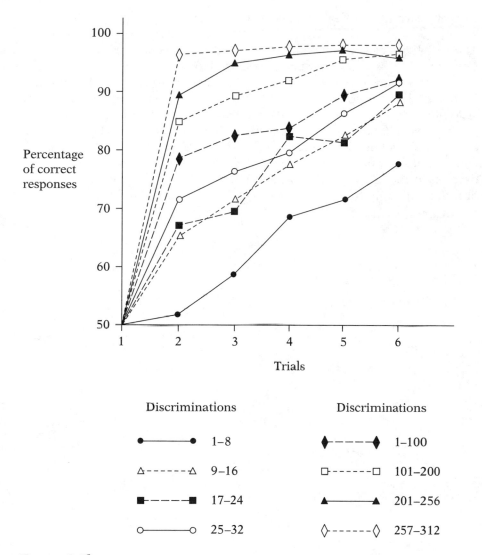

FIGURE 9.5b

Harlow's (1949) *learning set* data that show the acquisition of a *win-stay, lose-shift* strategy over several hundred trials. Each learning set consists of six consecutive trials in which two objects were presented to a monkey, one of which is arbitrarily and consistently rewarded if the monkey chooses it rather than the other. Mean percentage correct responses are plotted for the first eight problems the monkeys encountered, then the next eight (i.e., 9–16), the next eight (17–24), and so on. The data are then regrouped and plotted in blocks of 100 problems. Note the performance for problems 257–312; after this number of trials, the *win-stay, lose-shift* strategy has been almost perfectly learned as evidenced by 97% correct performance on the second trial.

Comparison of Learning Set Performance Across Species

The simplicity of Harlow's method allowed for the comparison of *learning set formation* across different species. Figure 9.6 is a composite of studies conducted by different researchers and plotted by Warren (1965). Data on children aged 2 to 5 years reported by Harlow (1949) have been added to Warren's (1965) figure. As can be seen, rats and squirrels seem to be pretty much incapable of learning a win-stay, lose-shift strategy; squirrel monkeys, marmosets, and cats are somewhat better after 1,000 problems (six trials per problem); Harlow's *Rhesus* monkeys do well after several hundred trials; and human children learn the most rapidly of all animals tested. Although some of the children (presumably the older ones) were 85% accurate in fewer than 20 trials,

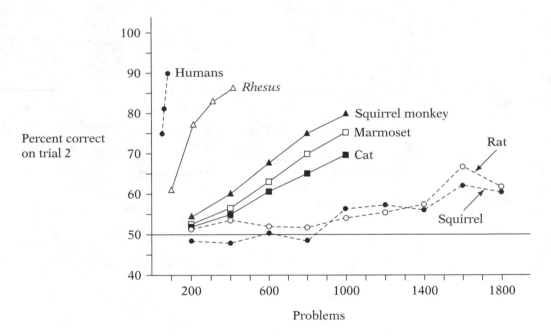

Figure 9.6 Learning a Win-Stay, Lose-Shift Strategy:
A Between-Species Comparison

The percentage of correct responses on trial 2 is plotted as a function of the number of problems encountered in *learning set* training. Note that after a thousand trials rats and squirrels finally begin to perform slightly better than chance. *Rhesus* monkeys clearly outperform cats and squirrel monkeys (from Warren, 1965). The data from children aged 2 to 5 years (Harlow, 1949) have been added to Warren's (1965) comparative data.

their group means nevertheless showed a typical negatively accelerated learning curve. In this study, then, young humans also had to learn a rule before they could apply it with a high degree of accuracy. The process by which they learned this rule is presumably similar to the process by which *Rhesus* monkeys and other animals learned. Only humans are smarter; they learned much more quickly.

New Stimulus Test in Both Match-to-Sample and Oddity Problems

The importance of Harlow's learning-to-learn demonstration is that it clearly shows that animals can learn to apply a rule to solve a novel problem. By contrast, the ability of monkeys and chimpanzees to solve novel problems was not tested using the discrete number of both *oddity* and *match-to-sample* problems described earlier. Is there other evidence that monkeys can learn concepts of match-to-sample and oddity by applying a general rule to novel items? The short answer is yes. After extensive training, Capuchin and squirrel monkeys (both New World monkeys) can solve oddity problems with novel items on the first trial (Thomas & Boyd, 1973). Capuchin monkeys are also capable of learning to apply a rule to solve a simplified version of the match-to-sample task. In this task, a sample stimulus such as a square is illuminated, and next to it an identical square and a "different" stimulus are presented. The monkey is reinforced for matching two identical stimuli. After approximately 1,000 to 1,500 trials, monkeys are able to correctly match a novel sample with a high level of efficiency (D'Amato, Salmon, & Colombo, 1985). Had the chimpanzees who had learned the 18 array oddity task (Figure 9.1) and the 24 array match-to-sample task (Figure 9.4b) been given *new stimulus* tests, based on these results with monkeys, it is likely they could have performed as well as monkeys.

Transitive Inference Reasoning by Chimpanzees

If *a* is greater than *b*, and *b* is greater than *c*, is *a* greater than *c*? Most (but not all) schoolchildren can answer this riddle. We call the ability of those who can solve this problem **transitive inferential reasoning.** Can chimpanzees *reason* in this way? If, after having learned that $a > b$ and that $b > c$, a chimp can answer, "Yes, *a* is greater than *c*" without ever having been reinforced for choosing $a > c$, we have evidence of reasoning and have also satisfied the requirement of a *new stimulus* test.

Sadie, Luvie, and Jessie.   Some evidence exists that with difficulty some (but not all) chimpanzees can be trained to solve this problem (Gillan, 1981, 1983). The method was simple. On a given trial two of five different containers were presented to the animal; choosing the "correct" one was reinforced with a preferred food. The five containers each had a distinctively colored lid by which the chimp could tell one from the other. The rules governing reinforcement were that for every pair, one color was consistently "greater than" the other color. For example, in a green versus blue pairing, green was reinforced; in a red versus green pairing, red was reinforced. After extensive training, a novel question could then be asked of the animal: Which do you choose from a red versus blue pairing? Those chimps consistently choosing red over blue provided evidence for *transitive inferential reasoning*. Gillan reports that after extensive training, Sadie performed at 89% accuracy and Luvie and Jessie were 72% and 69% accurate, respectively (50% = chance performance). Chimpanzees, then, are marginally capable of learning a series of specific relationships taken two at a time and, by extrapolation, of applying these learned rules to construct a larger pattern of relationships. This ability of chimps, albeit halting and puny, resembles the transitive inferential reasoning abilities of most children.

Pigeons Can Learn the Concept of Sameness

Note in Figure 9.6 the marginal performance of rats and squirrels on a learning set problem. Are the above conceptual abilities of rule learning (such as win-stay, lose-shift, oddity, and match to sample) restricted to primates? The answer is a qualified "no." Pigeons, for example, cannot perform oddity tasks, but how they learn concepts has been extensively studied, with surprising results. In a **sameness** task, for example, pictures of objects are sequentially presented to pigeons. Following this series, a final picture is presented that either was or was not in the series (i.e., *same* or *different*). Pigeons are apparently able to remember a series of pictures seen on only one previous occasion because they can solve this problem for food reinforcement by responding to one key if this final picture is the same and to another key if this picture is different from those in the preceding series (Wright, Santiago, Sands, & Urcuioli, 1984).

Natural Concepts in Pigeons

The ability of pigeons to extract information from complex pictures of natural environments is truly remarkable. In a series of experiments by Hernstein and his colleagues (reviewed by Herrnstein, 1984), pigeons were trained to respond to photographs in a way that indicated that they recognized such **natural concepts** as trees, people, and other "open-ended" categories. For example, pigeons who pecked at slides of pictures (projected onto keys in the Skinner box) containing trees (S^ds) were reinforced, but pecking at slides *not* containing trees (S^Δs) was not reinforced (Herrnstein, Loveland, & Cable, 1976). The pigeons learned this discrimination to a discrete set of stimuli, and the concept generalized to new pictures. Herrnstein et al. (1976) also were successful in training pigeons to discriminate photos of a particular person (S^d) from photos of other people (S^Δs). This discrimination was learned even when similar clothing was worn by the target and the distracters. This is surprising. Shouldn't clothing be as discriminative a stimulus as facial features, hair, and whatever other human attributes controlled the response?

Abstracting Taxonomic Classifications. How are pigeons able to learn this difficult discrimination? Even though pigeons are unable to learn to solve oddity problems, and physical dissimilarity of the pictures alone cannot account for what is learned about them, Roitblat (1987, p. 307) argues that pigeons are apparently capable of learning "relatively abstract *taxonomic classifications*" of objects. Another mystery surrounding the pigeon's ability to abstract a rule from highly ambiguous information is that fewer trials are needed relative to the number of trials chimpanzees and monkeys require to learn oddity and match-to-sample tasks. Let us examine this issue more closely.

Number of Trials in Learning Abstract Concepts

Fifteen hundred trials? Why does it take monkeys and chimpanzees so many trials to learn seemingly simple rules? Learning strategies such as *win-stay, lose-shift* and abstract concepts such as *oddity, match to sample,* and *inferential reasoning* tasks are difficult for chimpanzees, where *difficulty* is operationally defined as the number of trials to criterion. In the absence of language, it is apparent that animals learn strategies and rules via basic associative processes. After many hundreds of consistently reinforced responses to stimuli with specifiable characteristics, they begrudgingly acquire a response strategy that allows them to solve new problems. No *Eureka!* experience. No *A-ha* phenomenon. Nothing that resembles what humans typically mean when they use the term *insight*. Rather, the cognitive processes that these animals display after extensive training appear to have been learned by differentially reinforced responding. "Rules" governing the selection of specific reinforced choices are learned slowly and appear to be applied to untrained stimulus objects without keen insight. Indeed, it was argued earlier that chimpanzees working *oddity* and *match-to-sample* problems seem to prefer to memorize pictures rather than to learn rules.

Pigeons Prepared to Learn Natural Concepts? In this regard, as noted earlier, pigeons remain a mystery. Granted that they also learn the S^d–S^Δ discrimination in an associative manner, they seem, however, to be prepared (in an adaptive/evolutionary sense) to learn some discriminations more easily than others. What is the evidence for *prepared* learning by pigeons? Learning *natural concepts* requires fewer trials than learning a complex visual discrimination without such taxonomic features. For example, Herrnstein and de Villiers (1980) reported that fish slides are more easily discriminated from nonfish slides than a control condition in which one set of slides is arbitrarily grouped as S^ds and another set as S^Δs. More rapid acquisition of natural concepts (i.e., fish, people, trees) is taken as evidence for *prepared learning* as discussed in

Chapters 4 and 5. For unknown reasons, pigeons have preferences for some pictures over others and seem to use a taxonomic grouping rule without extensive training.

In addition, after learning a set of fish pictures, a *new* fish picture also tends to be treated as an S^d on the pigeon's first encounter with that picture. Reinforcement of a particular picture is not necessary for it to be included in a category. Pigeons learn faster than monkeys that, after learning either *win-stay, lose-switch* strategies (Harlow, 1949) or an *oddity* concept (Thomas & Boyd, 1973), are able to respond meaningfully to novel stimuli. The pigeon's task may be easier, however; recall that pigeons are *unable* to learn to solve oddity problems (Roitblat, 1987). Perhaps we have underestimated just how difficult the oddity task is to learn.

Primates Contraprepared to Learn Concepts?

Given that small-brain pigeons can learn *natural concepts,* what can be said of the pitiful efforts of larger-brain primates who require trials numbering in the thousands? Normally, monkeys and chimpanzees never encounter match-to-sample or oddity problems and other conceptual tasks as presented them in human laboratories. So, from an adaptive-evolutionary perspective, we are asking them to do something other than what their brains were designed to do. Having trained many chimpanzees to solve such conceptual problems, I have observed that their task-solving behavior often brought to mind that of children—and of mentally retarded and otherwise brain-impaired human adults and of college professors and students—who are confronted with a very difficult problem to solve. Chimpanzees often vocalized their frustration, anger, and sadness when they failed and exhibited happiness when they succeeded. And, like many bright school children I know, on many occasions chimpanzees also expressed disdain and disinterest for the task at hand.

Do All Humans Form Concepts?　The latter point is not unimportant. Conceptual learning does not come easily to all children or, for that matter, to all adults. College-educated students find some concepts easy to understand but others to be impossible. How many trials? After how many *years* of formal instruction in school do we continue to find "bright, mature adults" who, in the words of Diamond (1988, p. 337), continue to "show the same dumb behaviours seen in infants—e.g., failure to show transfer of training, absence of systematic hypothesis testing or planning, rigidity, and perseveration."

An alternative view of the relatively poor performance of primates compared to pigeons on concept-learning tasks is that primates bring to these tasks more hypotheses or strategies that must be discarded. Their poor performance might be viewed as resulting from their relatively greater cognitive resources. Though possible, I find this alternative unlikely. Humans are considered intelligent in no small measure because they rapidly learn response-reinforcement relationships. Why primates do so poorly is a mystery.

Some forms of conceptual learning, then, seem to be acquired by trial and error rather than by insight. Our association models *are* relevant to accounts of conceptual learning, but, you may argue, we have yet to consider language. What is the role of language in abstract thinking processes? Let us now turn to language, something that humans in fact do better than animals.

Interim Summary

1. Primates (humans, monkeys, and chimpanzees) are able to learn simple concepts and form general rules to solve such problems as delayed match-to-sample and oddity. Rats and pigeons are incapable of forming such concepts as *oddity*.

2. Chimpanzees can be trained to reason.

3. After many hundreds of training trials, chimpanzees are able to form memories for pictures. They can respond in meaningful ways when the pictures are highly degraded, even to the point of continuing to respond in the absence of the discriminative stimulus element.

4. Given a two-choice task, a variety of animals (including children, pigeons, and rats) can learn a win-stay, lose-shift rule that can then be applied to successfully solve novel problems.

5. Pigeons are capable of extracting a surprising amount of information from pictures presented to them in the laboratory. Pigeons can remember whether they have (or have not) seen a particular picture from a series of pictures presented earlier. They are also capable of learning so-called natural concepts: taxonomically grouping trees, fish, humans, and so on, and responding to new examples by including them in the correct categories.

6. The large number of trials required to learn even the simplest of concepts suggests that primates, including humans, are *not* evolutionarily prepared to think conceptually. The fact remains that humans can outperform all other animals on every conceptual task devised.

COMMUNICATION AND ANIMAL "LANGUAGE"

Thinking Without Language

In Focus on Research 9.1 Larry Weiskrantz presented convincing arguments that language is *not* essential for complex cognitive skills in animals or in humans. The fact that severely aphasic (nonlanguage-using) patients often score highly on nonverbal IQ tests is among the evidence for this assertion. In addition, preverbal infants "can sometimes apprehend the unity, the boundaries, the persistence, and the identity of objects," thereby presumably displaying conceptual knowledge of the world (Spelke, 1988, p. 180). Humans think in language, but humans also "think" musically, mathematically, visually, gastro-nomically, athletically, and so forth. Finally, as we learned in the preceding sec-tion, nonverbal animals are capable of learning simple rules, strategies, and concepts that arguably constitute evidence for simple *thinking*.

Nevertheless, language usage is considered by many scientists and philosophers to be *the* distinctive, defining characteristic of *Homo sapiens*. What species-specific capability is universally recognized as quintessentially human? Language. What do humans use language to do and to do better than any other animal? To think abstractly. So one of the questions entertained in this section is not whether animals can *think without language* (cf. Weiskrantz, 1988) but what, if anything, might language *add* to thinking processes.

Framing the Arguments.   The strategy for tackling these difficult issues proceeds along several venues. First, we consider evidence as to whether animals other than humans (a) display rudimentary communication skills/language; (b) can be trained to manipulate *words* in the form of symbols that stand for agents, ac-tions, and objects; and (c) having learned symbolic communication skills can appropriately and spontaneously use this artificial language as humans use their language. We look at animal communication/language in this section, an-ticipating that in the next chapter we explore the role that associative learning plays in both the acquisition and usage of human language. Do simple laws of association help us understand human language, or can language be under-stood only by reference to higher—specifically human—cognitive functioning? In the exploration of human language, inevitably we return to questions of thinking and of human consciousness. Let us begin with animal communica-tion and animal language.

What Is Animal "Language"?

Are humans the only animals capable of learning language? Before examining the evidence for language capabilities among animals, the semantic problem of what constitutes language seemingly must be addressed, but this is so thorny that for present purposes we merely look at what some investigators *think* is evidence for language capabilities in animals. As the argument devel-ops, I hope that you will begin to have a better understanding of just how mar-velous your language behavior is.

Communication

A traditional approach to these complex questions is to distinguish between animal *communication* and animal *language*. Many animals communicate with each other (i.e., with conspecifics—members of the same species). Among the ways by which animals communicate are pheromones, visual displays, and vocalizations. Recognize that these types of communication involve both the production and reception of signals, typically meaningful only to conspecifics.

Such communications seem to have similar functions to those of human language.

Are these signals language? Although modifiable by experience, these animal communications are considered to be reflexively tied to specific eliciting conditions in the environment. By contrast, human language is considered to be less reflexive and more *intentional*. Humans, the argument goes, *know* what they are talking about, but animals don't.

Vervet Monkeys.   Perhaps the most intriguing example of animal communication is some clever research on vervet monkeys first reported by Seyfarth, Cheney, and Marler (1980). Vervet monkeys make what are called *alarm calls* in the presence of predators. Seyfarth et al. recorded the alarm calls and systematically observed the various reactions of the monkeys when (in the absence of predators) particular calls were replayed from carefully hidden speakers. These researchers found evidence of a primitive form of language; one of the alarm calls caused the monkeys to look up (for predatory eagles), another to look around on the ground (for pythons), and yet another to take to the trees (to escape leopards). Infant vervet monkeys vocalized these alarm calls imperfectly but improved with age and experience.

Intentionality.   What are we to make of vervet monkey alarm calls? Are they *words?* Does a monkey making an alarm call *intend* to warn others, or is the sight of a predator merely acting as a *sign-releasing stimulus* that triggers a *fixed action pattern* (FAP) consisting of both a particular vocalization and attendant movement response? Dennett (1983) argues in favor of *intentionality* in vervet monkey calls and in other forms of animal communication. He cites Seyfarth et al.'s (1980) observation that when alone (out of hearing range of other monkeys), on seeing a leopard a vervet monkey will silently climb to safety rather than vocalize an alarm call. By this analysis, the vocalization response to seeing a leopard is not reflexive (involuntary); rather, alarm calls are *intended* (voluntary) to warn other nearby members of predators.

Origins of Animal Communication.   Not all behavioral scientists who study comparative animal cognition agree with Dennett's (1983) analysis. Monkeys may or may not be that smart. Others would like to see evidence of intentionality independent of the monkey's innate vocalization, for example, shaking a branch, throwing something, and so forth. What is unarguably clear from this example of vervet monkey behavior, however, is that primates other than humans use vocalized signals to communicate with each other. Our special interest in asking these questions about *primate* communication is an acknowledgment of both our genetic relatedness and our curiosity regarding the *origins* of human language. In the movie *Quest for Fire*, primitive hominids are characterized as having limited language capabilities—simple words and phrases directly related to meeting survival needs. It is assumed that human language evolved, presumably from simple to complex, but no evidence of such transformation exists. Because language does not fossilize, we have no record of the origins of language. When we ask questions about early hominid capabilities, we are restricted to studies of extant primates.

Bridging the Language Gap.   No matter how close the brain organization of other primates resembles that of humans, we are left with the fact that humans speak but animals do not. If animals could only talk, we might know more about their *intentions* as well as other aspects of their psychological experience. The Seyfarth et al. (1980) research strategy was to eavesdrop on what vervet monkeys were saying in their ecological niche and then by analyzing their behavioral responses to interpret what the vocalizations meant. We leave this area of research in animal communication to look at the results of a different research strategy. What happens if researchers try to teach animals an artificial, symbolic language? Because untrained animals do not understand human language and we likewise struggle with theirs, why not try to develop a common, simplified, symbolic language? In doing this we remove the animal from its ecological niche and ask it to do the "unnatural" task of communicating on human terms. We first look at research with porpoises and dolphins and then return to primates.

Porpoises and Dolphins

As was alluded to in the previous section, many animals, porpoises and dolphins included, vocalize among themselves in their natural habitats. Presumably because of these abilities and their apparent eagerness to both interact and communicate with humans (Lilly, 1961), a number of dolphins have been subjected to intensive symbolic language training regimens. Here we concentrate on research by Louis Herman and his associates and another research program headed by Ronald Schusterman. Although both use similar training methods and get similar results, their various interpretations of the language capabilities of dolphins differ markedly, along the behavioral-cognitive split alluded to in Box 9.1. The issues raised by these two interpretations reemerge in a later discussion of what both chimpanzees and humans "mean" when they use "language."

What Can Dolphins Learn About Symbols?   If you have ever had the good fortune to watch a trained dolphin perform, you probably wondered how it was able to respond to a series of verbal and hand-signal commands. Did the porpoise really *understand* the signaled instructions to fetch the *red* ball and shoot the ball at the basket on the *right-hand side* of the pool? Herman, Richards, and Wolz (1984) consider that Ake, a bottlenose dolphin, after learning such a task, has a "tacit knowledge of syntactic rules," allowing the animal to comprehend three- to five-word "sentences." Each "sentence" learned by the dolphin had three essential components, hand-signaled in sequence: the (direct) *object* (the "basket on the right-hand side of the pool"), the *action* ("fetch"), and the *agent* ("red ball"). Both the color of the objects and the positions (right, left) were modifiers that required Ake to select from alternatives. Herman et al. (1984) consider the sentence components to be "words" and that "dolphins are sensitive to the semantic and syntactic features of the sentences we construct in those languages, because their responses covary with variations in those features" (Herman, 1989, p. 46).

Language or Rule Learning?   While acknowledging the complexity of the tasks that Ake was able to learn, other researchers challenge Herman's (1989) linguistic analysis. For example, Schusterman and Gisner (1988, 1989) have trained both dolphins and sea lions using the same techniques and with the same results reported by Herman. Invoking the law of parsimony, however, they argue that animals are performing conditioned responses, not understanding language. They see the animal's task as a *conditional sequential discrimination* problem, involving three categories of signs and using two rules:

1. **If** an OBJECT is designated by one, two, or three signs (an OBJECT sign and up to two modifiers), **then** perform the designated ACTION to that object.
2. **If** two OBJECTS are designated (again, by one to three signs each) and the ACTION is *FETCH*, **then** take the second designated object to the first. (Schusterman & Gisner, 1988, p. 346)

Analysis of "Language-Trained" Dolphins.   Which analysis is correct? In this text we have consistently taken the position that given two accounts, the more parsimonious explanation is better. In doing so we run the risk of underattributing complexity of thought that may in fact accompany the dolphin's performance. Let us here, then, simply emphasize what can be agreed upon. There is no disagreement that these dolphins' trained behaviors required many hundreds of trials using both Pavlovian and Skinnerian techniques. Nothing emerged from the system that was not put into it. Following this elaborate training, we have no window into the dolphin's mind. We do not know (to paraphrase Dennett, 1983, p. 344) what dolphins *know*, what they *want*, what they *understand*, and what they *mean*. Other aspects of human language, including such possibilities as irony, metaphor, storytelling, and confabulation (Dennett, p. 347) did not emerge, nor could it, given the primitive language components provided the dolphin. In this regard, the more parsimonious behavioral account is probably closer to the truth of the matter. Rather than language comprehension, their behavior is better construed as an additional example of the ability of animals to learn complex rules. For example, their "If *x*, then *y*" rule is similar to the *win-stay, lose-shift* response strategy described earlier. Indeed, previously considered examples of how S^ds can come to control behavior of rats and pigeons in *multiple* and *chained* schedules of reinforcement approach the complexity of these dolphins' behavior.

Language Studies with the Common Chimpanzee
(*Pan troglodytes*)

Donald, Gua, and Viki.   Kellogg's interest in both porpoise and chimpanzee behavior resulted in two classic publications, *Porpoises and Sonar* (1961) and *The Ape and the Child* (Kellogg & Kellogg, 1933). In both books he addressed questions of comparative cognition: Can these animals communicate with humans, and can we use their vocalizations as a window into animal consciousness?[6] Kellogg was among the first of many researchers in this century who systematically attempted to break the communication barrier with chimpanzees (Benjamin & Bruce, 1982). *The Ape and the Child* chronicled Luella and Winthrop Kellogg's 9-month experiment of raising an infant chimp named Gua along with their 10-month-old child, Donald, in their home environment (see Figure 9.7). Among their research objectives, simply stated, was whether humanlike behavior would emerge if a chimp was raised in a human environment. One finding, simply stated, is that not only did Gua remain mute, he seemed to have a retarding effect on Donald's acquisition of language (Benjamin & Bruce, 1982). Other efforts (Hayes, 1951) over several years to teach a chimpanzee named Viki to talk proved equally ineffective. Conclusion? The common chimpanzee, *Pan troglodytes*, is unable to talk to us.

Washoe, Nim, and Koko.   Though unquestionably fascinating, the Kelloggs' and Hayes's failure to communicate with their chimps speaks more to these investigators' methodological deficiencies than to the chimpanzees' lack of capacity for language. Both attempted to use the chimpanzees' innate vocalizations, but chimps rarely make humanlike sounds. Allen and Beatrice Gardner provided a solution to this problem by training a chimpanzee named Washoe to sign, using American Sign Language (ASL) (Gardner & Gardner, 1969). Using both food and praise as reinforcers, they reported that Washoe learned well over 100 signed words. Terrace (1979) also trained Nim Chimpsky (cf. Noam Chomsky) in ASL; but, contrary to the Gardners' conclusions about Washoe's language capabilities, Terrace was struck more by the differences between humans and chimps. He cites (a) the intensity of training effort required of even the simplest of words with his chimp, relative to the little effort expended on humans; (b) the number of signs Nim learned increased at a painstakingly slow pace; (c) the lack of either spontaneity or creativity in language use when not prompted by the experimenter; and (d) evidence that the chimp echoed back the same "multiword" sentences *as trained* rather than as novel combinations of signs (Terrace, 1979). Although not all primate researchers agree with Terrace, similar criticism has been made of the language skills of a lowland gorilla named Koko following ASL training (Patterson & Linden, 1981). Terrace's (1979) assessment, you might note, is similar to that of Schusterman and Gis-

---

[6] A staunch behaviorist, Kellogg would not have used terminology referring to consciousness.

FIGURE 9.7   Gua and Donald Kellogg

Walking together serves at different times as evidence of a common
"understanding" of the command, "Take Gua's hand." This remark,
addressed to Donald, is at first responded to more successfully by the ape
than by the child. In a number of other instances Donald likewise
demonstrates that he comprehends commands originally reserved for
Gua, by suddenly responding to them before she is able to do so. (Photo
and text from Kellogg & Kellogg, 1933, p. 274)

ner (1989) who concluded that after extensive training, dolphins exhibited
conditioned responses rather than "language." This question can be alternatively framed as one of whether animal language is ever proactive (i.e., gener-
ative) or merely reactive (elicited after training). Humans definitely exhibit
both proactive as well as reactive language.

Sara and Lana.   Two other methodological attempts to talk to chimpanzees
were independently implemented in the 1970s by Premack and Rumbaugh
and their respective collaborators. In both methods chimps were trained to associate artificial symbols with actions and objects using food reinforcement.
For example, Premack and Premack (1972) trained a chimp named Sara to as-

sociate uniquely marked *lexigrams* with particular *agents, actions,* and *objects* (cf. Aka's dolphin "language"). The language was called *Yerkish* because the work was done at the Yerkes Primate Center in Atlanta. Sara was taught to first "read" and then to physically arrange a three-token sequence standing, for example, for "give"—"Sara"—"M&M." After several years of training, the Premacks reported that Sara eventually learned to use the *agent-action-object* format to create unique "sentences" never before reinforced with a functional vocabulary of about 130 words.

It is interesting that the initial association of a symbolic "word" with the meaning of "agent" (or action or object) took Sara thousands of trials.[7] This finding constitutes further evidence that chimpanzees seem to be contraprepared to learn to use the same symbols in a variety of settings (cf. the previous findings on difficulty in training an oddity problem).

Chimpanzee-Computer Interactions.   The method designed by Rumbaugh and colleagues to train Lana (Rumbaugh, 1977; Rumbaugh & Gill, 1976), although not conceptually different from the training of Sara, involved building a chimp-computer-human interface. Lana (and her trainers) interacted with a control panel that contained keys with illuminated geometric symbols (lexigrams). Each lexigram symbolized an object, agent, action, or other grammatical elements. The lexigrams could be activated by the experimenter, either requesting or instructing Lana to respond. Lana in turn could communicate by pressing a sequence of keys. For example, she could ask for food. If the sequence of lexigrams was correct, she received food reinforcement. A four-lexigram sequence standing for "please"—"machine"—"give"—"M&M" is shown in Figure 9.8.

Sherman and Austin.   A more sophisticated computer-controlled interface continues to be used in modified form at the *Language Research Center* in Georgia (e.g., Savage-Rumbaugh, McDonald, Sevcik, Hopkins, & Rubert, 1986). Savage-Rumbaugh and her colleagues trained the chimps Sherman and Austin during the 1970s using a combination of lexigrams, ASL, and real-world objects and reported results that exceeded previous efforts with other chimps. Specifically, Sherman and Austin could (a) sort and categorize both objects and lexigrams on the first trial of a blind test; (b) carry out commands in the absence of seeing the object (i.e., go into a different room and bring back a designated object); (c) make statements (arrange lexigrams) about future actions; and (d) engage in cooperative behavior (sharing reinforcement) after using their language to solve a problem (Savage-Rumbaugh, 1987).

Is There a Message in the Medium?   A concern of all animal language researchers has been that the various means of communication afforded chimpanzees—ASL, plastic tokens, and computer interfaces—are artificial and

---

[7] As it did for Lana, Sherman, and Austin—chimps trained by Rumbaugh and his colleagues. See further discussion.

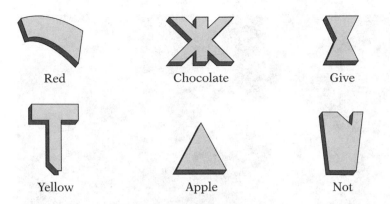

FIGURE 9.8 Yerkish Language

A sample of the artificial symbol used to associate with agents, objects, and actions in the Yerkish language.

highly limiting. An analogy would be to take a young child into a laboratory, give her a saxophone, and measure how well she "uses language" by which notes she plays on certain occasions, whether she plays it spontaneously, whether she tries to get other children to play it, and so on. Her language abilities under these conditions would likely be found wanting. Both vocalization and signing are the preferred patterns of language in humans. Is there a preferred pattern of communication in chimpanzees? Let us look at another species of chimpanzee.

Language Studies with the Pygmy Chimpanzee (*Pan paniscus*)

Just when many comparative psychologists thought that the animal language story had become pretty uninteresting, fortuitous observations of the behavior of a young pygmy chimpanzee named Kanzi breathed in new life (Savage-Rumbaugh et al., 1986; see Figure 9.9). Pygmy chimpanzees are known as *bonobos;* their scientific name is *Pan paniscus*. A half century of intensive effort had produced rather meager language results in the common chimpanzee, *Pan troglodytes*. The training gains were hard to attain and easy to lose. Two possibilities suggested themselves: Either these chimps were not especially interested in talking with humans or they were incapable of entering the conversation. Scientists have argued over whether signing ASL or manipulating artificial symbols are merely conditioned responses or are true attempts at

FIGURE 9.9

Dr. Sue Savage-Rumbaugh with Kanzi, an adult bonobo chimpanzee (*Pan paniscus*) at the Language Research Center, Georgia State University. Notice the portable Yerkish keyboard.

symbolic communication. For many psychologists the chimpanzees' performance was so minimal that it really didn't matter who won the argument.

Kanzi.   Kanzi's behavior was a different matter. Without formal training—from merely watching other chimps and humans interact—Kanzi learned more language than any other chimpanzee. And, though his accent is still thick, he also seems to have learned a bit of English. Let's look at the details.

From 6 months of age Kanzi found himself in the artificial language environment of his mother, Matata, who was a subject learning lexigrams on a keyboard. One year later Kanzi began to show interest in the symbols; without prodding or training he quickly learned to respond to lexigrams on the keyboard. At no time, according to Savage-Rumbaugh et al. (1986), was Kanzi food rewarded for the appropriate use of a symbol. Part of his training took place on a 55-acre forest. At 3 years of age, Kanzi had learned the location of food stashes throughout the forest and was able to "select each location by pointing to either a photograph or a lexigram . . . [and then proceed] to guide the experimenter to the location of the food he had selected." This behavior both confirms previous reports of chimpanzee foraging abilities (i.e., Menzel, 1978) and signals *intentionality* of a planned behavior (some of the locations were 30 minutes distant from where Kanzi initially signaled).

Kanzi's comprehension of English has continued to increase for several years. Recently, Kanzi's language skills were compared with those of a 2-year-old human child (Savage-Rumbaugh et al., 1993). In a test of 660 human-chimp interactions and in comparison with an equal number of human-child interactions conducted in a manner as similar as possible, Kanzi was found to *understand* more English than the child did. Language production was a different matter; the child's spoken language was decidedly better than the chimp's attempts.

Having said this, perhaps the most interesting finding of Savage-Rumbaugh's research with Kanzi is his apparent attempt to vocalize/talk to humans. Although both species of chimpanzees are said to lack the ability to form consonants, Savage-Rumbaugh and her colleagues are nevertheless convinced that Kanzi, a bonobo chimp, engages in intentional vocal efforts, "answering, disagreeing, or expressing emotion" (Savage-Rumbaugh et al., 1986). This behavior is totally lacking in the common chimpanzee, *Pan troglodytes*. Kanzi has spoken and used appropriately the English words *bunny, good, groom, sweet potato,* and *tomato* and has used appropriately words that "sound like" *lettuce, orange drink, raisins, carrot* (all foods) as well as *yes, there, knife, snake, hot, oil, paint, get it,* and others (Savage-Rumbaugh et al., 1993). Apparently, *pan promiscus* doesn't suffer to the same extent the vocalization disabilities of *Pan troglodytes*.

Analysis of Kanzi's Language Abilities.   What can be concluded from this study of Kanzi? I believe that Savage-Rumbaugh and her colleagues are correct in their analysis that *Pan paniscus,* the pygmy chimp, qualitatively differs in language ability from *Pan troglodytes,* the common chimp. One has more of a propensity for language than the other (probably species specific), the same argument, we see in the next chapter, that is proposed to account for the qualitative differences between human and nonhuman forms of communication. The crucial difference appears to be that "someone's home" in the pygmy chimp's head. When Savage-Rumbaugh talks about differences in these chimpanzees' receptive language, she is positing that pygmy chimps "listen" and that common chimps, for the most part, do not. She also suggests that language *receptivity* precedes language *productivity* and that "when an ape can, simply by virtue of human rearing, begin to comprehend human speech, the power of culture learning looms very large indeed" (Savage-Rumbaugh et al., 1986, p. 231). I would add the coda that a *talking* chimpanzee far exceeds the language capabilities of any other species. Savage-Rumbaugh's interactions with Kanzi may be considered the most successful attempt yet in establishing contact with another species.

What Can Be Concluded About Animal "Language"?

We began this section by asking whether animals other than humans (a) can communicate, (b) can be trained to engage in languagelike behaviors, and (c) can use an acquired artificial "language" as a human might. The evidence from porpoises and chimpanzees allows us to say yes to propositions (a) and (b) but only with grave reservations to (c). With the exception of Kanzi, animals other than humans seem to have very little to say to humans, and are little interested in talking to each other as humans do.

Interim Summary

1. Animal communication can be meaningfully distinguished from animal "language." Many animals innately vocalize and otherwise signal conspecifics in meaningful ways.
2. Among the issues raised by the question of animal language is the difficult question of *intentionality*. Vervet monkeys make predator-alerting vocalizations that can be alternately conceived of as involuntary (reflexive, species specific) behavior or as an intentional (voluntary) act.
3. Some animals have been taught to associate artificial symbols with objects and behaviors; they occasionally engage in languagelike behavior.
4. Porpoises and dolphins learn to use artificial signals to perform relatively complex acts. Although some theorists talk about their accomplishments in terms of their having learned a simple *grammar*, others view their behavior as conditioned responses and the application of learned rules.
5. The common chimpanzee (*Pan troglodyte*) has been the subject of numerous language investigations during this century. Although these chimpanzees for the most part do not vocalize "words," they do learn to use American Sign Language (e.g., Washoe), plastic tokens (e.g., Sara and Nim), and other artificial symbols (e.g., Lana, Sherman, and Austin) to engage in meaningful languagelike behaviors with their human caretakers.
6. The most promising nonhuman candidate to exhibit language abilities is *Homo sapiens'* most genetically similar relative, the pygmy chimpanzee (*Pan paniscus*). According to Savage-Rumbaugh, Kanzi's speech comprehension and vocalizations are qualitatively different from the common chimpanzee. Nevertheless, compared to humans, pygmy chimpanzees have meager language abilities.

Chapter Summary

1. Conceptual learning, thinking, and language can be studied from within a comparative perspective. Insight can be attained into the human mind by (a) comparing what we can do but other animals can't do and (b) examining the respective roles of genetics and environment as determinants of conceptual learning, thinking, and language.

2. Evidence from a variety of experiments leads to the conclusion that the categories of conceptual learning, reasoning, thinking, and language (a) can be differentiated from one another and (b) are not exclusive properties of the human mind.

3. Evidence from many sources leads us to the conclusion that animals can think: Rats and other animals can (a) count, (b) keep track of time, (c) solve serial pattern problems, (d) explore and investigate their environments, and (e) memorize complex maze patterns (cf. *cognitive maps*).

4. A variety of animals have been trained to apply rules and concepts to solve *learning-set* problems (win-stay, lose-shift strategy) *match to sample* and *delayed match to sample, oddity, sameness,* and so on. Even though they require many hundreds of trials, monkeys and chimpanzees learn these problems better than other nonhumans do. Pigeons learn *sameness* and *natural concepts* tasks in surprisingly few trials but cannot solve oddity problems.

5. Although a number of animals show communication patterns in the real world (some even resembling primitive language), the results of having animals learn symbolic language in laboratories have been discouraging. Among the issues related to animal "language" are questions of intentionality, spontaneity (proactive rather than reactive language), and cost benefit (few demonstrations of even minimal animal language following intensive training efforts by different experimenters).

6. Despite numerous efforts to engage porpoises and chimpanzees in symbolic conversation throughout this century, in the realm of language humans remain in a class by themselves. The most encouraging findings have come from work with Kanzi, a pygmy chimpanzee (*Pan paniscus*) who differs from other chimpanzees in (a) voluntarily entering the conversation as opposed to being trained into it, (b) being seemingly interested in learning about humans and their language, and (c) attempting to vocalize language as humans do.

Discussion Questions

1. Some animals have a keen sense of time. Recall the *Rhesus* monkeys that were conditioned to time their lever-pressing responses on a DRL schedule of reinforcement. Their reinforcement for correct responses was a tiny sugar pellet—candy as opposed to food. After training for hundreds of sessions, one monkey became so accurate that her interresponse interval never varied by more than a few hundredths of a second. Why do you think these monkeys were able to make such accurately timed responses? Could primates do equally well? Vertebrates?

2. Humans have a great sense of timing, as attested to by such skilled performances as hitting a curve ball or playing the piano. However, could you ever train *yourself* to do as well as this monkey on her task (i.e., hit a lever every 15 seconds for 5 minutes and never vary the response interval by more than a few *hundredths* of a second)? Under what conditions could you do this? Would you concentrate or try to "get in a zone"? Would it help or hurt your performance if $100 rode on every response or if you received a rather severe electric shock if your responses varied too much? Is it possible that monkeys are able to do this task so well because they *don't* think as much, or as well, as you do?

3. I've often wondered what animals think when you give them a problem that can be solved only by application of a *rule*. Their bewilderment reminds me of my own at a recent party in which a woman played a game involving *mime:* She modeled a series of different movements (simple dance steps, pulling her ears, patting her arms, etc.) and asked her audience to find the one thing in common she did on each different occasion. As person after person was able to solve the puzzle by applying the discovered rule, those of us who couldn't figure out the pattern became increasingly uncomfortable. It turned out that the only thing that was common to the series of different movements she made was that she cleared her throat before each one. So easy when you know what the rule is. . . . In your own experience, is rule learning difficult? Can you verbalize *rules* you memorized in algebra or trigonometry? Were your "a-ha" experiences better characterized as having been attained by trial and error or by *insight?* (After reading this chapter, do you suspect that these terms are not mutually exclusive?)

4. Related to the preceding question, are you of the opinion that human language so changes the nature of human thought and behavior that simple associative frameworks become irrelevant? Alternatively, can you use the concepts of reinforcement and punishment to help account for your rule learning in Spanish 101, math, computer science, spelling, and so forth?

5. Given the tens of thousands of species of life on earth, why do you think that only humans talk to and listen to each other?

DISCUSSION STARTERS

1. *Why do monkeys make such accurately timed responses? Primates? Vertebrates?* The question is *why* rather than *how* monkeys make such accurately timed responses. Because we know that synaptic transmission is timed on the order of milliseconds, we can argue that the nervous system is full of potential timing devices. I'm intrigued by the motivation of monkeys to do this because each sugar pellet—while desirable—does not seem to this human to

be worth the effort to be so accurate. Other primates certainly have the nervous system and response capabilities to perform as well as these monkeys. Frankly, I have a hard time seeing all mammals doing this well: cows no, birds yes, amphibians and fish, likely not. Perhaps monkeys and birds need accurately timed responses to fly from limb to limb in trees?

2. *Could you make accurately timed responses as well as these monkeys?* Undoubtedly, you could because skilled performers do this well with time intervals that vary enormously (as opposed to the same 15-second interval over and over). Think of the timing involved in music, where a trained ear can hear a few thousandths of a second differences in a performance. Given the contingencies of $100 for each correct response or avoiding electric shock for each incorrect response, one could learn to perform this task with great efficiency.

3. *In your own experience, is rule learning difficult? How do you learn rules?* The inability to solve problems via a rule leads to frustration in chimpanzees, monkeys, and humans (as evidenced by vocalization; listen to young humans sigh, grunt, and groan during a test or while working on a math problem). Some rules can be verbalized while others—including rules for playing musical instruments—seem to be conditioned responses stored in nonverbal memory. Language makes some rule learning easier. In the example given, if I had been given the verbal instruction that "clearing the throat" would be an S^d for what followed, I would have had "insight" and made no errors. Other verbalized rules are more difficult to follow: The speed limit is 65 mph; the AIDS virus can be transmitted during unprotected sex.

4. *Are simple associative frameworks irrelevant given human language? Do reinforcement and punishment underlie rule learning in language usage?* This topic is addressed more completely in the next chapter. Here it is noted that both primary and secondary reinforcement and punishment can be clearly identified in many classroom and on-the-job performance situations. Terminal reinforcement and punishment take the form of good grades/payday and failure/bad performance reports, respectively. Secondary reinforcement consists of the incentives and motivation of humans to learn verbal rules of language, math, science, and so on. Experientially, a sense of satisfaction is an emotional experience, suggesting basic associative rather than cognitive processes. Would you agree that the emotion of self-satisfaction is acquired, the result of experience with caregivers?

5. *Given the tens of thousands of species of life on earth, why do you think that only humans talk to and listen to each other?* As we see in the next chapter, language and all other species-specific behaviors are the outcome of natural selection processes. Receptivity to language/words and sounds/words production promoted inclusive fitness in ways about which we can only speculate. Why humans? One idea is that human ancestors left (were driven from?) a tropical niche presently occupied by gorillas and chimpanzees and had to face survival in harsher environments. Language/intelligence was another tool to enhance survival in these more challenging environments. Let us turn to the final chapter.

KEY TERMS

Cognitive Map (Tolman) The hypothesis that some animals (including rats) can form memories of where they are located relative to a food source and, even without direct experience of the route, "know" the shortest path connecting them with the food.

Cognitive Processes Psychological processes of perceiving, thinking, knowing, remembering, and so on.

Delayed Match to Sample A task measuring learning and memory processes that involves briefly presenting a target stimulus (i.e., the stimulus to be remembered) and, after a delay, again presenting the target with a number of distractor stimuli. The animal is reinforced for selecting the target from the distractors, thereby *matching the sample*.

Foraging Patterns Innately disposed behavior that results in the conduct of patterned searches and the remembering of where food is located in three-dimensional space.

Fractional Anticipatory Goal Responses (r$_G$s) (Hull) The theory that stimuli encountered in the pathway prior to entry into the goal box are reinforced and in turn become secondary reinforcers for even earlier responses in the maze. This theory allows a single reinforcer to connect complex sequences of behavior.

Learning Set (Harlow) A learning procedure in which two stimuli are presented to an animal for a *set* of six consecutive trials. Selecting one, arbitrarily designated as the "correct" choice, is reinforced. After completing many sets of such problems, animals learn a win-stay, lose-shift strat-

egy and are able to consistently respond correctly on the first opportunity. (See *Win-Stay, Lose-Shift Strategy; Learning to Learn.*)

Learning to Learn (Harlow) The term that describes the ability of animals to slowly learn a *general rule* that they could then apply to rapidly solve new problem sets. (See *Win-Stay, Lose-Shift Strategy; Learning Sets.*)

Match-to-Sample Task The difference between the two procedures is that in match to sample the target stimulus does not terminate prior to presentation of the target plus distractors. (See *Delayed Match to Sample.*)

Natural Concepts A term used to describe the ability of pigeons to extract information from complex pictures of natural environments and to respond in a way that indicates that they recognize trees, people, and other "openended" categories.

Oddity Concept Learning to select the odd stimulus from a three-stimulus display containing two that are identical and one that is different.

Pan Paniscus The *bonobo* chimpanzee, sometimes referred to as the *pygmy chimp*. (Cf. the common chimpanzee, *Pan troglodytes*.)

Pan Troglodytes The common chimpanzee. (Cf. the pygmy chimpanzee, *Pan paniscus*.)

Picture Memory (Farrar) The term used to describe the performance of the chimpanzee, Minnie, in which she memorized 24 pictures with common elements.

Sameness Task A learning task in which pictures of objects are sequentially presented to pigeons. A final picture is presented that either was or was not in the series (i.e., *same* or *different*). Pigeons solve this problem for food reinforcement by responding to one key if the same and to another key if different.

Serial Pattern Learning A learning task in which rats are exposed to and learn a sequence of patterns of reinforcement (or nonreinforcement) in the goal box over a succession of trials.

Transitive Inferential Reasoning A problem of the following type: If *a* is greater than *b*, and *b* is greater than *c*, is *a* greater than *c*? Its solution indicates reasoning ability and a knowledge of relationships that extend beyond immediate experience.

Win-Stay, Lose-Shift (Harlow) A strategy that animals are capable of learning. When presented with repeated opportunities to solve a two-choice discrimination problem in which one of the choices is consistently rewarded, reinforcement can be maximized by adopting the two-part rule: (a) to continue selecting the reinforced choice (i.e., win-stay) and (b) to shift to the alternative choice when not reinforced (i.e., lose-shift). (See *Learning Set; Learning to Learn*.)

CHAPTER 10

LANGUAGE, INTELLIGENCE, AND CULTURE

There is a difference between our minds and the minds of other species, a gulf wide enough to make a moral difference. It is—it must be—due to two inter-meshed factors, each of which requires a Darwinian explanation: (1) the brains we are born with have features lacking in other brains, features that have evolved under selection pressure over the last six million years or so, and (2) these features make possible an enormous elaboration of powers that accrue from the sharing of Design wealth through cultural transmission. The pivotal phenomenon that unites these two factors is language. We human beings may not be the most admirable species on the planet, or the most likely to survive for another millennium, but we are without a doubt at all the most intelligent. We are the only species with language.

Dennett, *Darwin's Dangerous Idea* (1995, p. 371)

INTRODUCTION

Humans are the only species with language. This observation alone has such great import that most humans in most cultures believe we have little to learn about ourselves by studying other animals. Our brief look at nonhuman language in Chapter 9 served to reinforce the view that humans "do language" in a qualitatively different way than other animals do. Dennett (1955) attributes our species' intelligence to our unique brains and the language afforded us by these brains. Language makes us special.

Language by itself, however, does not guarantee either civilization or even cultural development much beyond that of other primates. The Tasmanians, a race destroyed by European settlers several hundred years ago, had been isolated from other humans for so long that they had not shared the accumulated "Design wealth" alluded to by Dennett in the opening quotation. The last Tasmanian died in 1876 (see Box 10.1).

In this final chapter we seek an understanding of our human language behavior. Is it the most important species-specific behavior exhibited by hu-

BOX 10.1   THE LAST OF THE TASMANIANS

Diamond (1992) recounts a story of cultural clash that began in the 1600s when Europeans began to settle in Tasmania. Tasmania is a large island 200 miles south of the Australian continent, populated with people that had been separated from their aboriginal ancestors for an estimated 10,000 years.

About 5,000 Tasmanians lived in hunter-gatherer societies when discovered. Their lifestyles were primitive by most standards:

> Like the mainland Aborigines, they lacked metal tools, agriculture, livestock, pottery, and bows and arrows. Unlike the mainlanders, they also lacked boomerangs, dogs, nets, knowledge of sewing, and the ability to start a fire. (Diamond, p. 278)

Their European discoverers enslaved, imprisoned, and slaughtered these indigents over the next few hundred years until the last Tasmanian, named Truganini, died over a century ago. The Tasmanians had language (Chomsky's universal grammar) but lacked written language.

Language is common to all *Homo sapiens*. Language alone, however, does not guarantee the sophisticated culture that modern humans associate with civilization. You may argue that there was nothing "civilized" about a European culture that committed genocide on the Tasmanians. Unfortunately, neither language nor written language can completely insulate humans from those parts of their genetically determined brain that will always be capable of generating uncivilized behavior. Conclusion: Human language is a necessary but not sufficient condition for civilization.

---

mans? In the study of human language behavior, what role does environment play? Do we learn to speak? Will we discover that we need unique learning concepts to account for how we speak, read, and write? What role does language play in allowing humans to become civilized? We turn to the study of human language behavior.

"Pup-pee" was the sound my daughter Jane made at 17 months of age when together we turned the pages of her picture book of animals. A "pup-pee" was any picture of a cow, horse, or dog, and, for a while, even an elephant. As she rapidly acquired words during the next year of her life, each incorrect label of "puppy" was replaced by the appropriate word (i.e., *cow, horse,* and *dog*).[1] During this time she learned to discriminate a rhinoceros from an elephant, and, with apparent ease, correctly applied the verbal label *dog* to both

---

[1] This process is called *schema extraction* by Hintzman (1986). Simple generalization and discrimination processes account equally well for an initial broad umbrella of brown furry animals ultimately becoming discriminable.

real dogs and pictures of dogs. *Puppy* ultimately was a word restricted to small, young dogs with puppylike characteristics.

How did Jane do this? Did she "learn" to say these words? Or, as America's foremost linguist Noam Chomsky (1980) argues, did she use an innate, species-specific, language-acquisition mechanism? The latter process, Chomsky asserts, does not at all resemble learning. Indeed, for Chomsky, the associative processes of learning discussed in this text are meaningless and irrelevant to *all* questions of human language.

Throughout the first nine chapters of this text the case has been made that humans share associative processes with other animals. Without a doubt these shared processes can result in meaningful behavioral change. And so many learning theorists find themselves in vigorous disagreement with many—but not all—of Chomsky's analyses concerning human language behavior. We see later that one way to begin to frame the initial argument concerning human language is to tie down both ends of a nature-nurture continuum.

Revisiting the Nature-Nurture Argument

By the late 1950s, in the process of defining a new discipline of language studies called *psycholinguistics*, Chomsky had adopted a radical nativist position. By contrast, in this and other arguments, Skinner occupied the ground of an extreme environmentalist. For Chomsky, humans talk the talk, walk the walk, and do both because that is what humans are born capable of doing without much help from the environment. For Skinner, language acquisition and usage only superficially resembled walking: Different environments around the world resulted in the same walk but talk in different languages and in other ways that seemed to reflect both their culture and their unique reinforcement and punishment history. How could language *not* be learned, Skinner argued?

Naming Objects.   Learning to name objects, for example, is an instance of associative conditioning not unlike those you have studied throughout this text. Recall Pavlov's *second signal system*. Pavlov presented a parsimonious description of how humans are conditioned to apply arbitrary names to objects in the environment; how the sounds of words become CSs for objects; how conditioned responses (such as saying "pup-pee") can *generalize* along any of a number of stimulus dimensions to similar objects in the environment; and how, with further training, *discriminations* between words can be learned. Then, following *discrimination training*, specific responses can become consistently associated with specific stimuli. Adding to Pavlov's account, Skinner pointed out that children who are reinforced for speaking speak more and that those punished for speaking speak less. Mispronunciations of words and misnamed objects are corrected by caregivers. Finally, through conditioning, words acquire the power to both signal and control emotions in different environments.

The problem with a learning analysis, Chomsky countered, is that regardless of environmental differences around the world, humans acquire grammar in a remarkably similar way—inevitably—without consistent intervention by their caregivers. Human language is far more complicated than learning what is, and is not, a puppy. Nor is human language restricted to naming objects; indeed, *naming* is considered a relatively unimportant component of language by some psycholinguists.

And so the issue is joined. Let us continue examining evidence on both sides of this argument.

Interim Summary

1. Cross-culturally children learn how to talk without formal instruction.
2. Chomsky's radical nativist position asserts that humans talk and walk because innate programs unfold due to maturation with minimal help from the environment.
3. Skinner's behaviorist position stresses the role of environment in shaping language acquisition and usage through processes of reinforcement and punishment.
4. For Chomsky, language has more to do with the structure of grammar and less with signaling and naming.

FIRST SOUNDS, FIRST WORDS

For every instance of behavior described in this text, we have been able to identify both inherited and learned components. There is no reason to expect that human thought and language behavior should be analyzed otherwise. Here we first examine the amazing development of language abilities of children and then reiterate the positions of the main players on both sides of the argument: Language due to nature is a *species-specific behavior*, but the nurture camp notes that language is shaped and molded by experience.

The intensity with which these respective positions on language acquisition are guarded affords us the rare opportunity to declare both sides wrong at the outset. That is, neither of the protagonists, nativist Chomsky, or environmentalist Skinner, nor their adherents can alone account for the known facts of human language. That this argument has gone on for more than 30 years with both sides asserting the supremacy of their philosophical positions is due as much to the tenaciousness of both ego and theory in science as it is to the complexity of the phenomenon. Let us first look at what can be agreed on, and then inquire further into what the argument is about.

First Sounds

Crying as an FAP.   Human infants vocalize distress cries at birth. As is the case with other animals, such crying is adaptive. Vocalizations alert and sensitize caregivers to action, typically to alleviate hunger, pain, temperature changes, and other discomforts. Such crying can be characterized as a *species-specific behavior* with each species having a particular pattern of both sound production and sound reception. More specifically, crying can be analyzed as a fixed action pattern (FAP).[2]

Crying as an Instrumental Behavior. Crying behavior can be reinforced or punished; that is, infants (especially older, more experienced ones) are afforded the opportunity of crying *instrumentally*. Caregivers adopt various strategies to deal with instrumental crying behavior. For example, if, after a feeding and a diaper change, the infant continues to cry, a parent might decide to let it "cry itself out."[3] In this behavioral contingency, the child is not picked up when it cries.

From Skinner's perspective, crying is an emitted behavior. As is the case with all learned behaviors, instrumental crying extinguishes in the absence of reinforcement. Alternatively, at grandma's the child might be reinforced for instrumental crying by being held and rocked through the night. The frequency of an infant's vocalizations, then, can be manipulated by reinforcement and punishment contingencies in different contexts. To summarize, infants cry innately; the environment acts to modify even the earliest of such vocalizations.

Cooing and Babbling

The first noncrying sounds made by infants appear within a few months of being born. Because deaf children make these *cooing* and *babbling* sounds, there is no argument that these vocalizations are innately determined. By about 1 year of age, hearing babies begin to produce "intonal patterns" that resemble the sound characteristics of the caregiver's language—English, Spanish, or Vietnamese (Weir, 1966). Once again, this innate behavior is modified by the child's immediate environment.

Parents in different cultures do not act the same way toward their babies. Most caregivers interact with infants, however, by talking back to them as they make their endearing sounds. It is likely, then, that this caregiver behavior also has genetic basis.

"Language-impoverished" environments are those that provide both less modeling of the target language and less reinforcement (paying attention, smiling, cuddling, etc.) for the *babbling* behavior. Language *will* develop in children from language-impoverished environments. But the enormous individual differences seen in adult human language behavior likely have their origins at least in part as a result of these earliest interactions (see following discussion).

---

[2] You may want to review the criteria that Moltz (1963) proposed for a behavioral sequence to be considered an FAP (see p. 61).

[3] The author is describing, not prescribing, this approach to parenting.

First Words

Although infants are highly variable in their time to first word, at about 1 year of age the average child begins to speak the language he or she has been hearing. The first words are usually names for objects encountered in the environment (such as *mama* and *milk*) and for actions such as *get* and *go*. This is known variously as the **one-word utterance stage** or as *holophrastic speech.* Adults judge the meaning of these single words by the context in which they are delivered. For example, sitting in a high chair and reaching for her cup, a child might say "wa-wa," short for "I'm thirsty, I want some water." Later, "wa-wa" might be playfully splashed (and drunk) during an evening bath. Parents typically have no problems either understanding or meeting the needs expressed by such utterances. Again, the child learns to use these first words instrumentally. How such words are reinforced (or extinguished or punished) thereafter influences their frequency of usage.

Where do these first words come from? How and why are they produced? Theories abound. Let us join the argument by reviewing both cognitive and behavioral theories.

Biological Theory.   For Chomsky (1965, 1975) a child's first words reflect the operation of an innate **language acquisition device (LAD).** For the same reason that children begin to babble, they are evolutionarily prepared to speak their first word.[4] From this perspective, the infant's task is to "map" each new word onto a previously acquired concept (Levine & Carey, 1982). For example, according to this biological/cognitive view, an infant must have entertained a preverbal concept of *mama* before being able to *map* the word *mama* onto her. From this perspective, language acquisition is preceded by and predicated on these innate cognitive categories. (*Note:* Some cognitive psychologists assume that these preverbal cognitive categories are innate. What would John Locke have thought about this assumption?)

The Behaviorist's View.   It goes without saying that postulating the existence of innate cognitive structures prior to language acquisition was anathema to early behaviorists. For Skinner (1957), first words, like babbling sounds, were described as *emitted operants.* Skinner was less concerned about where the words come from than in how they could be manipulated—reinforced and punished—once they were spoken.

An offshoot of Skinner's behavioral position that *does* address the origin of first words is that they appear as a result of "generalized imitation" and subsequently are maintained by conditioned reinforcement (Baer & Sherman,

---

[4] Chomsky conceptualizes LAD as an innate, biological capacity but one that is not necessarily the outcome of a natural selection process. See Pinker (1994) for his analysis of Chomsky's position. Most theorists, including Pinker, have adopted the stronger position that the innate propensity humans have for language production and reception *is* the end product of a natural selection process.

1964; Kymissis & Poulson, 1990). In this analysis, imitation is itself viewed as an innate behavior that, when combined with reinforcement, produces the first French or Japanese word. Contemporary behaviorists referring to an *innate* mechanism of imitation? What an interesting development!

Two Words and the Beginning of a Grammar.　**Telegraphic speech** is the term used to define the next stage of language output, during which, at around a year and a half, children universally begin to string together two words (Bloom, 1970). That the two words are not randomly spoken together is indicated by the fact that some of the grammatical conventions of the parent language are observed. For example, a child will say in English, "get cookie," not "cookie get."

As every parent knows, preverbal children understand more than they can say. In other words, the child's *receptive language* is better at the one- and two-word utterance stage than is the child's *productive language*. Even though some parents on some occasions simplify their language for the child, "normal" language will develop without this help. From the child's perspective, parental language usage extends beyond the child's productive language capability. Recall Savage-Rumbaugh et al.'s (1986) observation that the pygmy chimpanzee named Kanzi had far more receptive than productive language.

Interim Summary

1. Crying is the first vocalized, prelanguage communication patterns in humans. Crying can be thought of both as an innate FAP and as one of the first emitted instrumental behaviors that can be reinforced and punished.
2. Cooing and babbling next occur during a time when infants begin to hear/discriminate the phonemic sounds of the culture in which they live.
3. A child's first words (holophrastic speech) occur cross-culturally at about 1 year of age. The process by which this occurs is unknown.
4. First words that *are* reinforced continue to be expressed in the vocabulary.
5. Chomsky proposed an innate mechanism—a *language acquisition device* (*LAD*)—to account for how the child generates first words. An imitation theory has also been proposed.
6. During these first few years, receptive language capacity far exceeds productive language.

FIRST GRAMMAR

As remarkable as the language acquisition process is up to 18 months of age (by which time the average child has about 25 words), a virtual word explosion occurs during the next few years. By age 6, an average child's lexicon contains more than 15,000 words (Medin & Ross, 1990).[5] Long before that, by about age 3 and one-half, a child has acquired the grammar and speech patterns (if not the working vocabulary) of the parents' language.

How can this happen? Parents spend less, not more, time eliciting and shaping language behavior after age 3. Can the rapid growth of words and the grammar adopted by the child be considered innate or rather be accounted for by environmental processes of imitated, reinforced, and punished verbal exchanges?

Chomsky's Universal Grammar

In his earliest writings Chomsky was struck by the appearance of the two-word utterance stage in cultures around the world. He postulated the existence of an innate **universal grammar** to account for these observations. In no meaningful way, he reasoned, could *learning* account for this time-locked appearance of patterned communication by 18-month-olds. As revealed in the following quote taken from a recent interview, Chomsky's theoretical position resembles a *doctrine of innate ideas:*

> I'm not . . . convinced that there ever is going to be such a thing as a theory of learning. . . . I see what we call learning as one kind of growth. You know we don't learn to grow arms. We also don't learn to have language in any very interesting sense. What happens is that systems that are sort of pre-formed in a certain fashion, or pre-adapted to certain consequences will interact with the environment in such a way as to sharpen them by filling in blanks, and you develop a system. . . . We can hardly fail to be struck by the fact that so-called "learning theory" has been pursued for seventy or eighty years, and is so limited in its results—very little has come out of it. (Noam Chomsky, in Beckwith & Rispoli, 1986, p. 195)

We can join with Chomsky and proud parents cross-culturally in marveling at the amazing abilities of children who so rapidly acquire language. But let us reserve judgment on his *ad hominem* attack of all learning theories. What evidence, gathered rather early in the argument, suggested to Chomsky that shaping, reinforcement, and punishment do little to affect the acquisition of grammar?

Home Studies.   Behaviorally oriented researchers (Brown & Hanlon, 1970) went into homes and recorded parent-child verbal interactions. They concluded that middle-class parents do *not* consistently reinforce proper grammatical conventions. For example, a toddler whose mother was brushing her hair said, "Her curl my hair" and was immediately reinforced by mom saying,

---

[5] This lexicon refers to receptive, not productive language capabilities. The reading and writing vocabulary at age 6 would be far less. What is interesting about this number is that it is identical to the 15,000 distinct words found in all of Shakespeare's written works (according to Pinker, 1994) and the estimated number of words in an average reading vocabulary of a Chinese adult (Holender, 1987, cited in Adams, 1990).

"That's right, darling." By contrast, a grammatically correct comment by this child ("Walt Disney comes on Tuesday") was punished with a parental response, "No it doesn't, it comes on Thursday." Brown and his colleagues concluded that "truth value" of the utterance (i.e., the semantic meaning rather than grammar) was being reinforced. Note also in this example that the parents' "words" (having presumably acquired secondary reinforcing and punishing properties) by themselves shape the child's language behavior.

Brown and Hanlon (1970) rediscovered that children apparently grow up in less than optimal language environments. Nevertheless, most children acquire the major grammatical features of their parents' language. Does that mean that Chomsky's theory of *universal grammar* is correct? Further, is his assertion that learning plays no role in language acquisition a reasonable one?

Associative Learning of the Lexicon

Not everyone agrees with all aspects of Chomsky's theory. Pinker (1991, 1994), for example, divides the language instinct into two parts: naming, or attaching arbitrary sounds to their meanings, and grammar, putting words together in meaningful ways. He agrees with Chomsky's position on grammar but disagrees regarding naming. The latter is accomplished by an associative process, that is, by learning.

Other researchers agree with Pinker that empiricist theories provide a better account for certain parts of the language acquisition process than do biological/cognitive theories. Stemmer (1989) in particular rejects cognitivists' claims that a child innately *maps* language onto objects in the environment. Mapping, he reasons, is nothing more than what Pavlov described as the *pairing of two stimuli*. Stemmer reasons that children, not unlike Pavlov's dogs, have an *inductive capacity*. After pairing neutral stimuli (the sounds of words) with known objects, the child can then meaningfully respond to (i.e., induce) "new" objects as long as they are within the *generalization gradient*. The (mis)application of the word *ma-ma* in reference to daddy, for example, can be interpreted as an example of the Pavlovian phenomenon of generalization. With further conditioned discrimination trials, the appropriate response can be consistently paired with the appropriate stimulus (i.e., the word *mama* becomes associated with mama; *papa* with papa).

Stemmer's (1989) analysis of language acquisition is a logical extension of Pavlov's *second signal system*. The role of generalization and the learning of discriminations enable an individual (human or animal) to learn *perceptual concepts*. An elaboration of this theory can be found in Hall (1991).

Associative Learning of Language Behavior

Parents Simplify Language.   In what other way does the environment affect the acquisition and use of language? We have already noted that parents simplify and structure language at the one- and two-word utterance stages. Young children, after all, more often than not do *not* know what adults are talking about. The fact of the matter is that many children enjoy several years of a structured, hand-tailored interactive language environment before being gradually incorporated into the realm of adult language. Children also speak when no one is around.[6]

Attaching Emotion to Words and Vice Versa.   The most telling deficiency of Chomsky's biological/cognitive theory of language acquisition is his lack of consideration for the psychological and behavioral world of the hearing and speaking child. For the infant, toddler, and child, emotions, objects, and words are embedded in the experience of life. The language structure provided by parents includes the attachment of emotion, through conditioning, to words and phrases. To say that the word *mama*, for example, is associated (or mapped) with the object mama is a gross oversimplification. Mama is a composite of pleasure. Mama is the *feel good* of our earliest experiences: of food in the stomach, warmth, familiar smells and tastes, and physical contact. Mama is the emotional contract against fear, the dark, the unknown, and Binky's nightmare closet. Mama is symbolic of the lifelong quest for self-understanding that begins with coping when she is not there. Throughout a lifetime, each experience with mama continues the growth of the associative framework of the word, person, and emotional attachment. And then there is papa and other moving animals, including siblings, spouses, pets, and . . .

Language is only a small part of the experience of living. "Experiencing" other living beings includes feeling unique sensations and emotions as well as the attachment of a language that refers to them. Chomsky's LAD totally ignores the reality of humans, especially of children, who learn to use language in their complex cognitive, emotional, and experiential environments.

Unique Emotional Attachments to Words.   Remember D.W., the 3-year-old who survived as long as his mother allowed him to eat salt and drink water around the clock (Box 7.2, p. 371)? Do you suspect that satisfying physiological needs produced emotional attachments to salt and to water and that the words *salt* and *water* became conditioned stimuli that gave D.W. pleasure? That the meeting of unusual needs attaches special meaning to some words is not the point. Rather, each of us lives in a unique flux; we share a common language, but the meanings of our *own* words reflect idiosyncratic learning histories.

Consider another example. A newly married couple find themselves arguing about each other's families. One says, "I don't want anything to do with *family*." The other says, "*Family* is very important to me." They are both using the same word, but their experience with the meaning of that word and the

---

[6] A conservative estimate is that during the first 5 years of life, 10,000 hours of time are spent "practicing speaking" (Anderson, 1990). (I wonder if they listen to themselves talk?)

emotions attached to it are very different. To one, negative emotions—possibly from bad experiences with family—are attached to the word. The same word, even the same sentences, can mean different things to both speakers and listeners.

The Role of Context in Language Meaning

Do all of us learn the same meaning of even simple words such as *yes* and *no?* Or do we learn *conditional yes's* and *no's?* Arguments for a *universal grammar* ignore the subtleties and idiosyncrasies of language learning and language usage experienced by everyone who learns to speak.

Many demonstrations of classical and operant conditioning of language meaning have been reported (see Cicero & Tryon, 1989). For example, strict parents attach strong emotions to *yes* and *no*, to *right* and *wrong.* Less strict parents use *yes* and *no* in a looser fashion. Recall the verbal interchanges of Joey and his mother in the grocery store (summarized in Table 5.1, p. 263). *No* never meant more than *maybe.* Joey had learned that with enough verbal persistence (a behavior that had been consistently reinforced), the "No, you can't" would soon become "Oh, all right, but this is the last time."

Few linguists question that the *meaning* of words is associatively conditioned, and for clinical psychologists, reconditioning the meaning of words is one goal of psychotherapy (Staats & Staats, 1957). In summary, postulating a universal grammar doesn't tell us much at all about *what* will be verbalized *when,* what such verbalizations *mean,* or why the same words mean different things to different people. Language is embedded in behavior and culture as much as in biology.

Language "Growth" or Language "Learning"?

Chomsky (1980) conceptualizes the environment as a *triggering* and *shaping* instrument that determines the manner in which language grows. An analogy is that acorns do not *learn* to be oaks but *grow* into oaks; likewise, language growth is viewed as a genetic unfolding shaped by environment (Pateman, 1985). Perhaps, then, in seeking to determine language behavior, we are merely arguing over the relative roles of environment and genetics, as we have encountered so often in analyses of other areas of animal learning.

But surely Chomsky underestimates the role of environment. In the first place, as Skinner (1957) pointed out, language *behavior* is not synonymous with linguistic *structure.* Postulating a universal grammar and noting similarities across the world's different languages accounts more for the form than the function of language. Where do we see the influence of environment? Examples abound. Chinese isn't French, and the differences between these and hundreds of other languages are *environmentally* determined. In addition, language *fails to develop* in language-deficient environments (Candland, 1993; Curtiss, 1977).[7]

Environment and Individual Differences in Language

Listen to speaking humans in your particular subculture. Do some have more to say than others? Is it likely that Chomsky's *universal grammar* affords us all a "lowest common denominator" of verbal expression? Isn't it just as likely that unique environments produce the vast range of expressed human language, from perfunctory utterances to finely crafted storytelling? The tremendous variation in language acquisition and usage both within and across cultures can be tied directly to unique environmental experiences.

Postulating a *universal grammar* doesn't address the enormous individual differences we find in spoken vocabulary, estimates of which range from a few thousand words in some individuals to tens of thousands of words in others. Nor does postulating a *universal grammar* address other than spoken language; reading and writing are two examples. Not surprising, those environments that support reading and writing are responsible for the profound individual differences in thought and consciousness that accompany differences in word usage. In the next section we look at the behaviors that humans engage in to get from highly prepared spoken language to the beginnings of reading and writing.

Interim Summary

1. One-word utterances merge into a *two-word utterance* stage during the second year. Cross-culturally, rules of syntax appear to govern how words are used. Chomsky proposed an innate *universal grammar* mechanism.

2. Observation of parent-child interactions in homes does not support the proposition that parents are instrumental in shaping a child's grammar by reward and punishment.

3. The role of environment *can* be seen in the specifics of phoneme production and receptivity, in the associative learning of the lexicon, in the role parents play in simplifying language, and in the unique ways in which words acquire emotional meanings.

4. The meaning of words is conditioned as the child interacts with his or her verbal environment. Likewise, the context, or environment, in which words are used helps to determine their meaning.

---

[7] In addition to Genie, the language-deficient child who was raised in a closet in Los Angeles (Curtiss, 1977), other well-documented cases of nonspeaking "wild children" raised without language givers include Peter (found in Germany in 1724); Victor (found in France in 1799); and Kamala and Amala (found in India in 1920). Their stories are recounted in a highly readable book by Candland (1993).

5. The range of spoken language and language comprehension is enormous. Individual differences are better accounted for by reference to environment rather than an innate language mechanism.

6. For these reasons language acquisition is best conceptualized as being determined by the interaction of biology, behavior, and culture.

SPEAKING AND LEARNING BUT NOT YET READING

> Since [John] was six weeks old, we have spent 30–45 minutes reading to him each day. By the time he reaches first grade at age six and a quarter, that will amount to 1000 to 1700 hours of storybook reading—one on one, with his face in the books. He will also have spent at least as many hours fooling around with magnetic letters on the refrigerator, writing, participating in reading/writing/language activities in preschool, playing word and "spelling" games in the car, on the computer, with us, with his sister, with his friends, and by himself, and so on. [Furthermore] to account for such variation [within households], we may therefore add or subtract a thousand hours from John's total.
>
> Adams, *Beginning to Read: Thinking and Learning About Print* (1990, p. 85)

We have seen that the nativist position focuses on the ease of language acquisition. Chomsky's analysis is that, like walking, speaking grammatically requires no training. By contrast, hundreds of hours are required for a toddler to make "basic" letter-sound correspondences (Adams, 1990). The child spends these hours in more structured environments than one in which speech is merely heard. A "reading environment" minimally requires printed text and, at least part of the time, a literate caregiver to direct the child's interaction with the text.

Parents who read with their toddlers do more than "teach letters" to them. As a secondary gain the child benefits from the transmission of values, lifestyle, and the positive affect that accompanies reading and learning (Wigfield & Asher, 1984). From the child's perspective, these moments are among the most intense and most personally directed of all their interactions with caregivers. Children identified by Teale (1986) who had limited interactions with reading parents—an estimated 4 hours *per year* (compared to the thousands of hours per year in middle-class homes) not only are poor readers, but also miss out on these other benefits.

By contrast with learning to talk, learning to read is so painfully slow and difficult that after 12 years of formal schooling, some high school illiteracy estimates remain as high as 25% (Weaver, 1994). Children who will become the *best* readers have, prior to formal schooling, several thousand hours or more of exposure to print. Such effort is reminiscent of our primate relatives who also require thousands of trials to learn to use artificial symbols both to communicate and to solve problems.

Whereas it is impossible for adults to recapture the feeling of being overwhelmed with the task of "learning letters," the observations of preschool, kindergarten, and primary school teachers (especially those teaching first grade) and parents who are sensitive to the task are instructive. Neither my wife nor I have ever "taught" reading, but we helped get our four daughters ready for formal schooling. By first grade, these children had already learned their "letters." In addition, they could sound out some syllables, and recognize (read?) a few simple words. Successful performance of these tasks took hundreds of hours to accomplish.

Associative Theory and Reading.   Both Pavlovian and instrumental versions of associative theory account very well for how a child (or an adult) learns to read. From a Pavlovian perspective, both letters and their sounds are CSs. The visual letters signal the associated sound: The symbolic visual letter *D* is pronounced (and heard as) *dee*. The child's learning task is to make discriminated sight-sound associations—a process obviously more complex than this simple associative analysis suggests. (The *kinesthetic cues* of vocal cords, tongues, and air passage also become associated with the *sight* and *sound* of the letter.) Caregiver(s) correctly vocalizes (models) each letter. Correct vocalizations by the child are imitated and/or shaped by successive approximation.

Conditioning Performance Factors.   In reading to the child, parents direct attention to visual features of letters (and colors and pictures) in special children's books. (In doing this, parents are presenting the CSs in the form of discrete trials.) With reinforced practice, the mechanics of holding the book and of turning pages become automatic.

Attention spans are systematically lengthened (shaped) in children as longer reading periods are demanded. The child develops expectations about the amount of information per unit time that can be processed. By contrast, television programmers condition shorter attention spans by changing images in fractions of seconds.

Also, while reading (but not while watching television), the child controls the pace of behavioral engagement and, hence, the flow of information. The value of books and of reading is further conditioned by parental attention, physical contact, pleasing sights, sounds, odors, and so on.[8] Such early conditioning might account for lifelong emotional attachment to books by some people, such as librarians and others who *love* both libraries and the smell of books and who consider books to be best friends. Note that these positive preverbal, prereading conditioning factors occur prior to the additional reinforcing properties of being entertained by stories and the reinforcement that occurs when concepts and ideas contained in the print are understood.

---

[8] A Jewish custom is to give candy to children during their first encounters with books. In an even older custom, infants were allowed to taste a drop of honey from a book cover, thereby conditioning a love of books by their pleasurable association with a sweet taste.

Preparing to Read: Cognitive or S-R Mechanism?

We have seen how easy it is for children to begin to speak. How do children learn to read? Can performance of this task be explained by the associative methods discussed in the preceding chapters, or do we need to invoke a specially human "cognitive" mechanism? There is now enough research to come to some tentative answers regarding this issue (Adams, 1990), but let us first take a closer look at the demands of reading.

Letter Recognition. English-speaking readers have forgotten how foreign (and how similar) the letters *H* and *F* once looked. Lowercase *p, b,* and *d* not only look alike but also sound similar. Learning letters in English requires 52 sight-sound associations. These must be memorized before any reading takes place. The "empiricist principles—contiguity, recency, frequency, and similarity" provide the best account of how this procedure occurs (Adams, 1990, p. 202).

Compared to the evolutionarily prepared "no training" acquisition of speaking, the fact is that learning to make sight-sound associations requires hundreds (thousands?) of trials over many hundreds of hours. This large number of training trials suggests that learning these rudimentary prereading tasks is as contraprepared as are chimps learning a symbolic oddity task. It is safe to conclude that no special cognitive mechanism facilitates the learning of the elements of printed language.

Phoneme Recognition. What other prereading experiences prepare a 6-year-old child to read? Although letter knowledge has been found to be the strongest predictor of those who will be reading at the end of the first year of school, the ability to discriminate phonemes (syllable and letter sounds) was the second most important variable (Bond & Dykstra, 1967). These are not mutually exclusive skills. If the letters *b* and *p* are to be learned, the child has to hear the difference between these two sounds as well as recognize the differences in their letter shapes.

Interim Summary

1. Middle-class parents spend a few thousand hours teaching children their letters and helping them sound out simple words before, at about age 6, the child encounters formal reading instruction.

2. The child's prereading preparation in English involves many hundreds of hours memorizing the sound-sight associations of 52 (upper- and lowercase) letters. The process is best described as simple associative conditioning involving contiguity of the stimulus elements and frequency of presentation.

3. Individual differences in a child's prereading preparation are enormous, ranging from a few hours to thousands of hours per year. Parent-child

reading interactions also provide optimal settings for learning other tasks and for the transmission of cultural values.

4. Before becoming a reader, the child must learn to discriminate the phonemic sounds of the language being learned (probably preceding and during the time they learn their letters).

5. Letters and their sounds are CSs that are paired in an associative manner.

6. Among the performance factors conditioned during early training are attention spans, holding books, and turning pages.

LANGUAGE, LITERACY, AND INTELLIGENCE

Humans have been compared to other animals throughout this text. We have seen that nonhuman animals can think but cannot talk. Nonhuman animals are conscious but arguably *not* in the same way as humans. Monkeys and chimpanzees can learn relatively complex rules and concepts more easily than other mammals, and humans require fewer trials to learn even higher-order concepts. No surprises here.

What makes us so different from other animals? Certainly, language defines us, but the activities of yet other areas of our brain also make us different. No other animal composes music, records it symbolically, builds the instruments on which to play it, or invests the time and effort necessary to accomplish a virtuoso performance. (Nor would any animal—except humans—attend the performance if it *were* to be given.)

No other animal behavior comes anywhere near the accomplishments of humans in the arts, home construction, mathematics, cooking, literature, fashion design, athletics, editorial cartoons, science, or technology. So it is easy to agree with Dennett's comparisons of humans with other animals (p. 479): Humans are the only ones that use language, and we are smarter than all other animals. Given this observation, it is not unreasonable to inquire into the relationship of language to intelligence.

Finally, humans with written language are the only animals to have developed culture and, among some groups of humans, civilization. Here we entertain some of the complex relationships that exist among language, literacy, and intelligence.

Literacy and Cognitive Processes

Slow reading acquisition has cognitive, behavioral, and motivational consequences that slow the development of other cognitive skills and inhibit performance on many academic tasks. In short, as reading develops, other cognitive processes linked to it track the level of reading skill. Knowledge bases that are in reciprocal relationships with reading are also inhibited from further development. The longer this developmental sequence is allowed to continue, the more generalized the deficits will become, seeping into more areas of cognition and behavior. Or to put it more simply—and sadly—in the words of a tearful nine-year-old, already falling frustratingly behind his peers in reading progress, "reading affects everything you do." (Stanovich, 1986, p. 390)

In this quotation Stanovich alludes to **cognitive processes** that will not develop if reading skills are developmentally delayed. The implication is that literacy is a building stone on which some aspects of thought and intelligence are based. Let us look at some data relevant to these issues.

Vocabulary Growth and Print Exposure

Consider the following facts: An excellent reader in the fifth grade is encountering six million printed words each year in *out-of-school* reading while the average student sees only 650,00 words (Anderson, Wilson, & Fielding, 1988; Fielding, Wilson, & Anderson, 1987).[9] Furthermore, the amount of print exposure for fifth graders reading at the 90th percentile is *200 times greater* than for those reading at the 10th percentile. First conclusion: Profound individual differences exist in time spent reading.

Next, consider vocabulary growth. An average school-age child is acquiring an English vocabulary at a rate of about 8 words per day, or about 3,000 words per year (Miller & Gildea, 1987; Nagy & Anderson, 1984). Vocabulary growth appears to be determined largely by the frequency with which words are encountered in print. Second conclusion: Those children who are exposed to more print (who read more) ultimately acquire a larger vocabulary.

The most important point to be gleaned from these data concerns the *size* of the differences in both print exposure and vocabulary at age 11. Not only does reading affect everything you do, as the 9-year-old says in the quote from Stanovich (1986), the effects of these differences on the development of intellectual life are profound.

Another important finding in the print exposure study cited is that the *quality* of reading material is a less important factor than is the *quantity* of reading. In college-age students, the single best predictor of IQ is the amount of print exposure. Conclusion? We should encourage our children to read whatever interests them. The evidence indicates that their overall cognitive abilities will be enhanced. One outcome of thousands of hours of exposure to the printed word is that it allows them to use language better than those who don't read as much. But does it make them smarter? Let us look next at the relationship of language and intelligence.

[9] I doubted this statistic the first time I encountered it. Since my daughter Jane was then an avid reader in the fifth grade, she and I used two different methods to compute her print exposure for the year. Our estimates from both methods were 5 and 9 million words per year.

Literacy and Intelligence

The development of written language during the past several thousand years has allowed some human cultures to develop new ways of thinking—about what it means to be human and about the universe. Western culture is the product of cumulatively written as well as orally transmitted knowledge. Now, since all living humans have ancestors that could not read or write, literacy is neither a necessary nor sufficient condition to survive and reproduce the next generation.[10] Intelligence as a collection of behaviors that enhance inclusive fitness can be defined without reference to either oral or written language. But intelligence at a higher level *is* tied to language, especially to written language.

Language Acquisition and Intelligence.   Among the questions that can be asked about language and intelligence is whether more intelligent children read sooner and better than less intelligent children. The answer is a mixed one, depending on one's definition of intelligence (Adams, 1990). Some studies show no relationship of early reading ability and tests of nonverbal intelligence. What does seem to be the case, however, is that the better readers (those who have more print exposure) soon begin to score higher on IQ tests (also, see pp 494–495, the quote from Stanovich, 1986). Even after controlling for differences in nonverbal cognitive ability (differences that are considerable), a recent study reports that mere exposure to large numbers of words enhances the verbal intelligence of college students (Stanovich & Cunningham, 1992).

Literacy and the Brain

The Tasmanian culture described in the opening section led a primitive lifestyle.[11] By contrast, those cultures in which reading and writing developed (7 to 10 thousand years ago) produced sophisticated civilizations. Why is it that literate humans seem to make a *qualitative* leap over other animals, including nonliterate humans?

This question has occupied scholars for centuries and will not be adequately answered here. Chomsky has pointed to a unique human brain organization that supports language. Reading and writing add to the language areas of the human brain by incorporating the visual cortex into the loop (see Figure 10.1). Hundreds of millions of neurons in the striate cortex and other portions of the occipital lobe become available for symbolic manipulation when a person reads language. The increased computational

[10] All other animals do just fine without language.
[11] Anthropologists and some other learned people do not like to use the word *primitive* to describe an extant human culture. I use the term because I think it is a highly descriptive term understood by most people who speak English. I apologize for causing discomfort to those who do not like it.

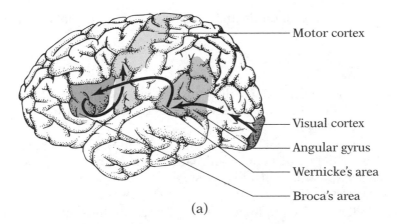

(a)

Written Word

Early visual processing:
Striate cortex

↓

Visual word recognition:
Extrastriate cortex

Spoken Word

Early auditory processing:
Primary auditory cortex

↓

Auditory word recognition:
Angular gyrus

Semantic association:
Inferior frontal cortex

↓

Premotor coding:
Supplementary motor area
Other areas near sylvian fissure

↓

Motor control of speech:
Primary motor cortex

↓

Speech

(b)

FIGURE 10.1 Brain Areas Involved in Literacy

(a) When a person repeats a written word, according to the Wernicke-Geschwind model, visual areas of the brain are involved before the "language areas" (i.e., the angular gyrus, Wernicke's area, and Broca's area) are activated (Geschwind, 1970). (b) A comparison of the flow in information in the brain when a word is read (left column) or heard (right column).

power of the brain may underlie the intellectual achievements that define civilization.

Interim Summary

1. The development of reading skills leads to the development of other cognitive skills. Developmentally delayed readers fall behind in other areas of school performance.
2. Print exposure differences measured in thousands of hours separate good from poor readers and people with large vocabularies from those with small ones. Exposure to print is the single best predictor of *verbal intelligence* measures of IQ.
3. Literate individuals score higher on nonverbal intelligence tests than do the illiterate.
4. Reading uses areas of the occipital cortex that would not otherwise be activated.

LANGUAGE, LITERACY, AND CULTURE

People in all cultures acquire spoken language in the same way (i.e., as described by Chomsky), but not all cultures enjoy literacy. In an earlier chapter, for example, a young Cherokee Indian named Little Tree learned survival skills from his grandfather, who told him and showed him how to walk on a hillside, how to catch fish with his hands, and so forth. But neither the Cherokees nor any other native American Indian developed written language. It is likely that the oral transmission of cultural knowledge preceded writing by tens of thousands of years.

Human culture differentiates us from other animals because of our unique brains and behavior, including language behavior, and, through literacy, by the transmission of one generation's accomplishments to the next. A working assumption is that *written* history has allowed the tremendous explosion in knowledge and culture humans have entertained during the past few thousand years. Finally, among humans with written language, civilization emerged.[12]

Written Language and Human Culture

From a comparative perspective, then, it is reasonable to assume that human language preceded and allowed the development of important aspects of human thought. Language as a species-specific behavior that enhances inclusive fitness remains the most important difference separating humans from other animals. Moreover, with the development of written language we see opening an

---

[12] The Incas of Peru are an exception: They developed a relatively sophisticated civilization without the benefit of a written language.

enormous cavern among members of the human species—those who *learn* to read and write and do so, and those who do not. Consider, for example, the following devastating effects of illiteracy on success in our culture:

> Illiterate adults account for 75% of the unemployed, one-third of the mothers receiving Aid to Families with Dependent Children, 85% of the juveniles who appear in court, 60% of prison inmates, and nearly 40% of minority youth; of people in the work force, 15% are functionally illiterate, including 11% of professional and managerial workers, and 30% of semiskilled and unskilled workers. *Fortune* magazine reports that "of the 3.8 million 18-year-old Americans in 1988, fully 700,000 had dropped out of school, and another 700,000 could not read their high school diplomas." (Adams, 1990, p. 27)

With few exceptions, someone who cannot read or write is a beneficiary of, but not a major contributor to, civilization.

Human Learning and Culture

We began this chapter seeking an understanding of our most unique behavior, human language. We have found that all humans speak and that this is best understood as the most important species-specific behavior in our repertoire. We have also found that learning plays an enormous role in how we use language and whether or not we become literate. We have determined that it is learning to read and write, and not language per se, that best accounts for the role a person will play in our culture. It is for these reasons that Chomsky's assertion to the effect that learning plays no meaningful role in human behavior is so baffling.

What is the counterpoint? First, language behavior affords humans the opportunity to occupy a unique place among other animals on this planet. Second, reading and writing allow some fortunate humans (and cultures) to achieve a qualitatively higher level of discourse—of conceptual thinking, of realized consciousness, and of intelligence—than that enjoyed by speaking but illiterate humans.

Human culture is *not* synonymous with human civilization. The Tasmanians were uncivilized, and had they survived without being influenced by other cultures, would probably still not be able to start a fire. Unfortunately, the culture of the civilized Europeans they encountered allowed for their destruction. But a variety of that same European culture allowed humans to land on the moon several hundred years later.

Contrary to Chomsky's message, literacy is *learned* and learned only by tremendous effort within a supportive environment. Literacy is much like the other things you have learned as a human, be it dancing or ice skating, or playing soccer, the guitar, or the piano. The role of learning and environment is of *critical* importance. We are not the only animals who learn, but because of our unique genetic makeup, we certainly learn and behave in more interesting ways.

Interim Summary

1. Illiterate individuals do not do well in our culture. Illiteracy is associated with unemployment, crime, and other societal problems.
2. Humans are the only animals that enjoy language and the only animals to have developed culture. Civilization depends on literacy.
3. Literacy is learned in an associative manner.

CHAPTER SUMMARY

1. Children learn how to talk without formal instruction, a phenomenon that is best accounted for by a nativist position.

2. Language is readily modifiable by environment. Individual differences in language, best accounted for by traditional theories of learning, include *which* language is spoken, the unique meanings and emotions conditioned to words, and the role of environmental context.

3. Crying is an FAP and can be modified by reinforcement and punishment.

4. At 6 to 12 months human infants begin to discriminate the phonemic sounds of the language they hear.

5. First words (holophrastic speech) occur at about 1 year of age, via a *language acquisition device* (Chomsky).

6. Chomsky's innate *universal grammar* mechanism mediates a *two-word utterance* stage during the second year. Syntax is similar cross-culturally. The child's spoken grammar is little affected by traditional learning processes.

7. The meaning of some words is conditioned by association of word sound with objects and actions.

8. Environments vary with respect to how much language a child hears. Children do not learn to speak in language-absent environments.

9. Reading skills are acquired even more slowly than speaking. Reading is best understood from within a framework of learning by association (i.e., of sight of printed text with the sound of the spoken language).

10. Other behaviors are conditioned while a middle-class child learns to "read" during the several thousands of hours of preschool instruction. These include attachment of positive emotions to caregivers, books, and the reading process itself.

11. The child's prereading preparation involves memorizing (by simple associative conditioning) the sound-sight associations of 52 (upper- and lowercase) letters and by learning to discriminate their phonemic differences.

12. Reading skill development allows for further cognitive development. Poor readers fall behind in other areas of school performance.

13. Print exposure differences among readers are enormous. Amount of print exposure is a predictor of verbal intelligence scores.

14. Readers score higher than nonreaders on nonverbal tests of intelligence.

15. Language skills, including literacy, differentiate humans from other animals and make civilization possible.

16. Language behavior, not unlike other behavior, is best understood as the interaction of biology, behavior, and culture.

DISCUSSION QUESTIONS

1. Given the restricted range of behaviors of human neonates and the necessity of a caregiver (by far the majority of these being mothers), how surprising is it that cross-culturally, children begin to say the same things at the same time?

2. Chapter 4 (p. 149) was introduced with a passage from *The Education of Little Tree*. A sampling of the cultural knowledge of Cherokee Indians in this century illustrates how much can be learned merely from noting the associations between stimuli. Is language necessary to acquire this knowledge? Is language necessary to transmit this knowledge to the next generation?

3. Brown and his colleagues studied how parents reinforced and punished their children's language behavior. Their conclusion was that correct grammar was less important to parents than how well the child's language accurately reflected what was going on around them. These researchers pointed out the irony of all children being consistently reinforced for telling the truth but who then lie so much as adults. Can you identify the contingencies of reinforcement and punishment that maintain confabulation, lying, and other deceptive language practices? That is, under what conditions is lying reinforced and when is it punished? What are "white lies"? Does a universal grammar predict white lies?

4. Tamil says, "I love to read!" Roberto says, "I hate to read!" Does their language reflect unique conditioning histories?

5. Recall that "no" meant "maybe" for Joey (p. 262ff). Now accused of rape, Joey's defense attorney has argued that his 18-year conditioning history absolves him of his behavior. You are the prosecuting attorney . . .

6. Given the finding that children who have their noses in books most of the time do better in school, score higher on intelligence tests, and are generally smarter and have more successful careers than their less scholarly contemporaries throughout a lifetime, how are *you* going to raise your own children?

DISCUSSION STARTERS

1. *How surprising is it that children everywhere in the world begin to say the same things at the same time?* We are not surprised that children sit up unassisted, take their first steps, and begin to eat solid food, according to an unfolding biological timetable. It makes equally good sense that children would begin to coo, babble, and generate their first words at about the same time. Other features of language are also somewhat predictable. No one would a priori expect an infant to use five words before speaking a first word, and two-word utterances predictably follow one-word utterances. The first and most important entity in the environment is mom, and mom was probably called *mom* because it is one of the first sounds infants begin to make.

Other first words are nouns, including, not surprisingly, an indispensable nutrient, *water*. What am I missing here?

2. *Is language necessary to acquire a knowledge of nature and to transmit this knowledge to the next generation?* Little Tree recounts that "dandelions . . . are good when you mix them with . . . nettles. Nettles . . . have little tiny hairs that sting you when you're picking. . . . Fireweed has a long stalk which you can peel and eat raw, or you can cook it . . . like asparagus." All omnivores have favorite foods that they have learned about through associative experiences. Nothing in this passage makes language necessary. Language allows this cultural knowledge to be transmitted more efficiently probably by allowing rehearsal of this information in the absence of direct experience of it—one of the primary functions of Pavlov's second signal system.

3. *What is the origin of lying and other deceptive language practices? Under what conditions is lying reinforced, and when is it punished? Does a universal grammar predict white lies?* We can speculate about the origin of deceptive language practices. One tack is to ask whether verbal behavior that allows the speaker to escape punishment is reinforced. You can think of any of a number of situations in which it is. A "universal grammar" predicts nothing about the function of language.

4. *Do loving to read and hating to read reflect unique conditioning histories?* When adults read to children, the books involved and the activities of reading (page turning, looking at pictures, thinking) are being paired with a variety of reinforcers: physical closeness (cf. Harlow's *contact comfort*, p.

378), familiar smells, and two acutely interactive voices—soft, melodic, rhythmic, and rhyming. It's magic time. By contrast, Roberto encountered the alphabet and books for the first time at age 6 when he started first grade. The instruction may be the same but not the context in which the instruction is received. And it may be that the loving context is the most important component of a child's development.

5. *How should the prosecuting attorney counter? Is Joey's crime voluntary or involuntary?* You might start by pointing out the implications for a society that can't agree on the meaning of words or that allows idiosyncratic interpretations of words. Laws would be difficult to write and impossible to enforce. Regarding Joey's crime being "involuntary," recall the recent law that allows for the prosecution of parents for the misbehavior of their children (Discussion Question 1, p. 425). The law in question presumes that children are not free agents; rather, that their behavior is (should be?) controlled by their parents. Ask a lawyer what she or he thinks about this issue.

6. *How are you going to raise your own children?* Do you suppose that the world's best artists, musicians, and athletes spent disproportionate amounts of time doing something *other* than reading as a child? What are *your* values? What do you want for your child? Are you up to the task of helping your child "choose" his or her ultimate direction in life by providing the appropriate early environment? Or are you content to hand them the remote control and let them choose their own channel? Decisions, decisions! Have a good life.

GLOSSARY

Cognitive Processes   Psychological processes of perceiving, thinking, knowing, remembering, and so on.

Language Acquisition Device (LAD) (Chomsky) A proposed species-specific brain mechanism (or series of mechanisms) that allows a human child to rapidly acquire language once triggered by a minimal language environment.

One-Word Utterance Stage   The first words spoken in any language, typically referring to names for objects encountered in their environment, such as *mama* and *milk* and for actions such as *get* and *go*. (Also known as *holophrastic speech.*)

Telegraphic Speech   The term used to define a stage of language when, at the age of about 1½ years, children begin to string together two words in a grammatically meaningful fashion.

Universal Grammar (Chomsky)   A theoretical position that postulates the existence of innate structures underlying the rapid acquisition and output of grammatically correct language and that denies any role for Pavlovian and instrumental conditioning processes.

GLOSSARY

Acquired Incentives (Hull) Secondary reinforcers.

Acquired Motivation Behavior motivated by secondary reinforcers. (Primary reinforcers provide innate motivation.)

Adaptation Any characteristic that improves an organism's chances of transmitting its genes to the next generation.

Adaptive Describing a characteristic or behavior that enhances survival.

Animal Model The use of animals in research that bears on the human condition. Example: An animal model of alcohol addiction.

Annoyer (Thorndike) Aversive stimuli. When an unpleasant stimulus (an *annoyer*) follows a response, the response is less likely to be repeated. (Cf. *Punisher; Law of Effect*.)

Antecedent Condition In a causal relationship, the event that precedes, and causes an event to occur.

Anthropomorphism The attribution of human characteristics to animals, deities, and others.

Appetitive Conditioning (Pavlov) Food-based Pavlovian conditioning. (Cf. *Appetite*.)

Appetitive Salivary Conditioning (Pavlov) Pavlovian conditioning in which a conditioned salivary response to a food stimulus is measured.

Association Theory The relationship (connection, union) that results when two or more stimuli are paired together in time.

Associationism Basic learning defined as the association of two or more sensory experiences. (Cf. *Association Theory*.)

Automaintenance Maintenance of key-pecking behavior due to the contiguity between response and reinforcement. Pigeons that have a history of being fed in the presence of a lighted key will unnecessarily peck at the light even though their pecking response has no effect on when food is made available.

Autoshaping Occurrence of key-pecking responses in the absence of a reinforcement contingency. An untrained pigeon is placed in a Skinner box, and food is presented in the presence of a lighted key.

Without specific training, the bird will begin to peck at the lighted key. See *Sign-Tracking*.

Aversive Conditioning   Conditioning experiments using aversive unconditioned stimuli (as opposed to appetitive food stimuli). Three contemporary *aversive* conditioning procedures are eye-blink conditioning, conditioned suppression, and taste aversion conditioning, employing aversive air puffs to the eye, electric shock, and toxins, respectively.

Avoidance Procedure   Any procedure in which an animal's instrumental response prevents an aversive consequence. Example: a lever press prevents or avoids delivery of electric shock.

Backward Conditioning   (Pavlov) A conditioning procedure in which the onset of the unconditioned stimulus precedes the onset of the conditioned stimulus. (Cf. *Negative Contingency*.)

Baseline   The preexperimental, or normal, level of a measured response. The baseline often constitutes the control condition to which the effects of an experimental treatment are compared.

Behavior   The way in which an animal acts or responds within the environment.

Behavioral Contrast   Incentive contrast. A procedure that demonstrates that reinforcement/punishment effects are determined in part by the immediate context in that these stimuli are delivered and the animal's prior history with other reinforcers/punishers. (See *Negative Contrast*.)

Behavioral Control   The past and present reinforcement and punishment contingencies that determine the expression of a behavior.

Behavioral Ecology   The study of interrelationships among organisms and their environments focusing on the development of survival behaviors—feeding, reproduction, social organization, and so on.

Behavioral Genetics   The study of the interaction of environment and patterns of inheritance in expressed behavior.

Behavioral Medicine   An interdisciplinary field concerned with the etiology of illness and wellness, preventative medicine, biofeedback, and other forms of psychophysiology, behavioral treatment, and rehabilitation strategies.

Behavioral Therapy   Any psychotherapeutic procedure involving the systematic application of reinforcers or punishers, or the implementation of extinction or another classical or operant procedure known to be effective in bringing about behavioral change.

Behavioral Tolerance   That portion of total drug tolerance that can be attributed to learned or environmental variables as opposed to pharmacological variables.

Behaviorism   A philosophical position espousing an extreme environmental determinism; the assertion that human and animal behavior is directly and inevitably determined and controlled by the reinforcing and punishing contingencies of the local environment. (John B. Watson and B. F. Skinner are two famous proponents of behaviorism.)

Behavior Modification   The systematic application of reinforcers, punishers, extinction, and other classical and operant conditioning procedures to change target behaviors.

Behavior Theory   An analysis of the way in which animals act or respond with environments as encompassing the interplay of genes and environment.

Between-Groups Design   The design of an experiment in which the effect of manipulating an independent variable (i.e., the treatment group) is compared to a control group not having the independent variable. (Cf. *Within-Groups Design*.)

Biocultural Evolution   (S. Katz) The process by which the selection, preparation, and consumption of particular types of food by some individuals gives them a reproductive advantage that, over time, has probably led to the divergence of human populations.

Biofeedback   A procedure used in both research and therapy in which a human subject through differential reinforcement can be made aware of and can gain voluntary control over his or her involuntary processes (such as brain waves, heart rate, skin conductance, etc.).

Biological Determinism The philosophical position that behavior is caused by the immutable action of genes. (Cf. *Environmental Determinism*.)

Biomedical Model The traditional approach to health care that, in emphasizing anatomy and physiology, assumes that almost all illness can be attributed to a specific pathogen or specific biochemical malfunction.

Biopsychosocial Model An approach to health care that attempts to integrate cultural, social, psychological, and behavioral factors with the traditional biomedical model.

Blocking Following excitatory conditioning of CS_1, the failure to condition CS_2 in a CS_1-CS_2 compound. One hypothesis is that CS_2 is blocked because it is a *redundant* stimulus.

Causality The relationship of cause and effect. A goal of science is to investigate why events occur on the assumption that nothing can happen without a cause.

Chained Operants A behavioral sequence analyzed in terms of a succession of discriminative stimuli that set the occasions for operant responses, eventually leading to reinforcement. (Cf. *Stimulus-Response Chains*.)

Changeover Delay (COD) In a *concurrent schedule* procedure, a brief period of time during which reinforcement is not available immediately following a switch, or changeover, from one reinforcement schedule to the other.

Classical Conditioning See *Pavlovian Conditioning*.

COD See *Changeover Delay*.

Cognition The acts of perceiving, thinking, knowing, and remembering.

Cognitive Map (Tolman) The hypothesis that some animals (including rats) can form memories of where they are located relative to a food source and even without direct experience of the route, "know" the shortest path connecting them with the food.

Cognitive Processes Psychological processes of perceiving, thinking, knowing, remembering, and so on.

Comparative Psychology The study of animal behavior, stressing both similarities and species-specific differences.

Compensatory Responses See *Conditioned Compensatory Responses*.

Concept of Oddity A learning task in which an animal must pick the odd stimulus from a three-stimulus array in which two stimuli are identical.

Concurrent Schedules A training procedure in which two or more reinforcement schedules run simultaneously and independently of each other, and a subject can respond on either; used in the measurement of choice behavior.

Conditioned Compensatory Responses In conditioning experiments, using drugs as USs, a conditioned response opposite in direction to the preconditioning UR to the drug. Example: Morphine produces hyperthermia, and the CR following conditioning is hypothermia (Siegel).

Conditioned Discrimination A procedure used to train an animal to discriminate and respond differently to two different stimuli. One stimulus (CS^+) is reliably paired with an unconditioned stimulus, and, on alternating trials, another stimulus (CS^-) is *not* paired with the US. The animal learns to respond to CS^+ and not to respond to CS^-, thereby demonstrating that it can *discriminate* one from the other. (Cf. *generalization*, in which an animal responds in a *similar* manner to different stimuli.)

Conditioned Emotional Response (CER) The outcome of an experimental treatment in which emotional responses are conditioned to neutral (non-emotion-inducing) stimuli. (Cf. *Conditioned Suppression*.)

Conditioned Excitor A descriptive term for the CS after it has been conditioned in a forward, or excitatory, manner. The CS acquires excitatory properties; for example, the excitor can be used "as a US" in higher-order conditioning.

Conditioned Facilitation Conditioning the immune system as demonstrated by an increase in antibody production in the presence of a conditioned stimulus.

Conditioned Immunosuppression Conditioning the immune system as demonstrated by a decrease in antibody production in the presence of a conditioned stimulus.

Conditioned Inhibition The opposite of conditioned excitation, usually resulting from induction procedures or negative contingencies. Example: If *fear* is the conditioned (excitatory) response, *safety* or *elation* is the conditioned inhibitory response. (Cf. *Induction Method; Negative Contingencies.*)

Conditioned Inhibitor A descriptive term for the CS after it has been conditioned in a backwards, or inhibitory, manner. The CS acquires inhibitory properties; for example, the inhibitor can retard the conditioning of another stimulus.

Conditioned Response (CR) (Pavlov) A new response, learned to the CS, following pairings of a neutral stimulus (i.e., the CS) with an unconditioned stimulus. Salivation to the sound of a bell is an example.

Conditioned Stimulus (CS) (Pavlov) A stimulus that comes to control a reflexive response following pairings with an unconditioned stimulus. Example: A bell controls salivation after pairings with food.

Conditioned Suppression A laboratory technique used to measure aversive (fear) conditioning. A neutral stimulus is paired with electric shock while an animal is lever pressing for food. Following tone-shock conditioning, the tone disrupts (suppresses) lever pressing, allowing the experimenter to easily quantify the amount of fear conditioning the animal has experienced.

Conditioning See *Pavlovian Conditioning.*

Confounded Variables Variables that con-tribute to changes in behavior, and that can be mistaken for learning effects. These variables include light-dark cycles, changes in diet and sleep, age and sex of organism, and so on.

Consummatory Behaviors (Ethology) Innate, genetically determined "survival" behaviors, including fixed action patterns, which determine species-specific patterns of feeding, courting, reproduction, social interactions, and so on.

Contiguity Theory of Association The theory that stimulus-stimulus associations occur when two stimuli are perceived close together in time.

Contingency Theory of Association The theory that stimulus-stimulus associations occur when one stimulus is perceived to precede and signal the occurrence of a second stimulus.

Continuity of Species (Darwin) The theory that all living organisms are evolutionary adaptations of earlier life forms and, therefore, are all genetically related.

Continuous Reinforcement (CRF) A procedure in which each emitted response is rewarded.

Contraprepared The opposite of a prepared, or easily conditioned, response. When associations between two stimuli, or a stimulus and a response, require many trials to learn, an animal is said to be contraprepared for association.

Control Group A comparison group for a treatment group. In an experiment, a group of subjects exposed to all conditions that the treatment group experiences but *not* to the independent variable.

CRF See *Continuous Reinforcement.*

Critical Period (Ethology) A specific time period (usually early in an animal's development) when an animal is particularly sensitive to certain features in the environment. Exposure to such sign stimuli "releases" genetically determined behavioral responses. (Cf. *Imprinting; Sign Stimulus.*)

CS Preexposure Effect The reduced associability of familiar stimuli. Preexposed, or familiar, conditioned stimuli require more trials to become associated with a given US than do novel conditioned stimuli. (Cf. *Latent Inhibition*.)

CS⁺ and CS⁻ Trials A method used to condition a discrimination between two different CSs. One is paired with food (called *CS⁺ trials*) and the other without food (called *CS⁻ trials*). Following training, the animal responds in extinction to CS⁺ but not to CS⁻.

CS See *Conditioned Stimulus*.

CS-US Interval A time interval measured from the onset of the conditioned stimulus to the onset of the unconditioned stimulus.

Culture The arts, beliefs, customs, inventions, language, technology, and traditions of a group of people.

Cumulative Record A visual record of responses and reinforcement patterns in time generated by an ink-writing instrument called a *cumulative recorder*.

Defense Conditioning Pavlov's term for experiments that used aversive unconditioned stimuli—now referred to as *aversive conditioning*.

Delayed Match to Sample A training procedure used to measure short-term memory. An animal is briefly presented a target stimulus and later is required to remember the target and select it from a stimulus array that includes distractor stimuli. (Cf. *Match to Sample*.)

Dependent Variable In an experiment, the treatment effect of an independent variable assessed by measuring changes in the dependent variable. In the behavioral sciences, most dependent variables are changes in behavior. Example: A drug (independent variable) causes increased activity (dependent variable).

Determinism The philosophical position that behavior is caused by the joint actions of genes (i.e., biological determinism) and environmental influences (i.e., environmental determinism).

Differential Reinforcement of High Rates (DRH) A schedule of reinforcement designed to reinforce bursts of lever pressing. (Example: The 10th response within a 5-second time period would be reinforced.)

Differential Reinforcement of Low Rates (DRL) A schedule of reinforcement designed to reinforce timed pauses between operant responses. (Example: The first response after 5 seconds of nonresponding would be reinforced.)

Discrete Avoidance A procedure in which a stimulus sets the occasion for an avoidance response, that, when emitted, delays or prevents an aversive stimulus.

Discrete Trial Testing an animal's response on a single trial, such as presenting a stimulus requiring a single response. (Cf. *Free Operant*.)

Discriminated Operant A particular operant response under stimulus control. (Example: removing the wrapper [S^d] from a stick of gum [reinforcer].)

Discriminative Stimulus (S^d) A stimulus (S^d) that signals that a particular response-reinforcement contingency is in effect, therefore setting occasions during which operant responses become highly probable.

Disinhibition (Pavlov) An extraneous stimulus that disrupts the ongoing effects of an inhibitory stimulus. Example: the effect of a loud noise on a drowsy state.

Distal Causes See *Ultimate Causes*.

DRH See *Differential Reinforcement of High Rates*.

DNA (deoxyribonucleic acid) A double-stranded, helix-shaped structure containing genetic material.

Drive Reduction Theory (Hull) When behavior is instrumental in fulfilling specific *needs* (i.e., that restores an organism to homeostatic balance) the drive is said to be *reduced*. *Drive reduction* reinforces the instrumental behavior in Hull's theory.

Drive States (Hull) Physiological states such as hunger and thirst that underlie motivated behavior.

Drive-Stimulus Reduction The theory that stimulus properties of incentives, not the necessity of meeting physiological needs, are sufficient to reduce drive states.

Drive Theory   See *Drive Reduction Theory*.

DRL   See *Differential Reinforcement of Low Rates*.

Drug Tolerance   Reduction in the effectiveness of a drug resulting from repeated exposure to the drug.

Dyzygotic   Developed from two zygotes; fraternal, or two-egg, twins. Dyzygotic twins have different genotypes.

Ecological Niche   The place of an animal or plant in nature; the interrelatedness of plants and animals with their local environments.

Ecological Validity   In animal experiments, requiring an animal to learn a task that is likely to be encountered in the real world, for example, learning about foods. Learning to maintain balance on a hind paw while inebriated is of questionable ecological validity.

Electrical Stimulation of the Brain (ESB)   Passing minute amounts of electric current through an implanted electrode to specific areas of the brain to act as a reinforcer.

Elicited Behavior   (Skinner) Reflexive or otherwise innately organized behavior, sometimes characterized as *involuntary behavior*. (Cf. *Emitted Behavior*.)

Embedded Conditioning   A variation of simultaneous conditioning in which the onset and offset of either the CS or US occurs during the other element. Embedded conditioning situations often involve the pairing of long-duration stimuli, such as flavors experienced during meals and sensory events during drug effects.

Emitted Behavior   (Skinner) Instrumental responses, sometimes characterized as *voluntary* behavior, that are not readily tied to specific eliciting stimuli. (Cf. *Elicited Behavior*.)

Empiricism   The primary method (and philosophy) of observation and experimentation that distinguishes science from other ways humans obtain knowledge about the world. (Cf. *Intuitionism*, which has no real-world referents.)

Environment   The sum of conditions and influences affecting the growth and development of living things, including air, water, soil, other plants and animals, and so on.

Environmental Determinism   The philosophical position that behavior is caused (determined) by environmental influences (Cf. *Behaviorism; Biological Determinism*.)

ESB   See *Electrical Stimulation of the Brain*.

Escape Procedure   A procedure in which an animal makes an instrumental response that has the effect of terminating an aversive stimulus.

Evolution   Changes taking place in the genetic makeup of populations. Darwinian, or neo-Darwinian, evolution is a complex theory (comprising many subtheories) proposed to account for the history of life on earth.

Excitatory Conditioning   (Pavlov) "Normal" forward conditioning in which a CS is paired with a US and the conditioned response resembles the unconditioned response.

Expected Utility   The expected gain from a decision made about a wager or transaction involving money or other tangible valuable.

Experimental Extinction   See *Extinction*.

Experimental Neurosis   (Pavlov) The outcome of a conditioning experiment in which an animal becomes emotionally distraught for an extended period of time.

External Inhibition   (Pavlov) Temporarily disrupting the ongoing process of conditioned excitation by introducing an extraneous stimulus. The extraneous stimulus acts as a distractor, a temporary inhibitory stimulus.

Extinction   (Pavlov) A reduction of responding in the presence of the CS in the absence of the US (or reinforcer). The conditioned response is said to *extinguish*.

Extinction Curve   A plot of responses during nonreinforced trials. In a typical extinction curve, response magnitude diminishes to preconditioning levels.

Extinction Gradient   See *Extinction Curve*.

Extrapolation   The real-world application of experimental results found in field and laboratory experimentation with animals to the human condition.

FAP See *Fixed Action Pattern*.

FI See *Fixed Interval Schedule*.

Fixed Action Pattern (FAP) (Ethology) A fixed series of movements ordered in time and space and triggered by an environmental stimulus. FAPs are species typical and, once initiated, proceed through sequence to completion.

Fixed Interval Schedule (FI) A schedule of reinforcement in which an animal is reinforced for its first response following a specified *time interval* from the preceding reinforcer.

Fixed Ratio Schedule (FR) A schedule of reinforcement in which reinforcement is contingent on the completion of a fixed number of operant responses.

Foraging Patterns Innately disposed behavior that results in the conduct of patterned searches and remembering where food is located in three-dimensional space.

Forward Conditioning (Pavlov) Occurs when CS onset precedes US onset; the most common form of excitatory conditioning. Example: A bell CS is followed immediately by a food US.

FR See *Fixed Ratio Schedule*.

Fractional Anticipatory Goal Responses (r_Gs) (Hull) The theory that stimuli encountered in the pathway prior to entry into the goal box are reinforced and in turn become secondary reinforcers for even earlier responses in the maze. This theory allows a single reinforcer to connect complex sequences of behavior.

Free Operant An easy, repeatable operant response, such as a lever press. (Cf. tasks requiring *discrete trials*.)

Frequency (Association theory) The number of times two stimuli occur together.

Frustration Theory (Amsel) Following a history of continuous reinforcement, an extinction procedure that produces a state of negative emotions.

Functional Relationship An orderly relationship existing between stimulus and response. Example: Higher drug doses cause higher levels of activity.

Gene Composed of deoxyribonucleic acid (Cf. *DNA*); a part of a chromosome that, during the reproductive process, influences the inheritance and development of characteristics in the offspring.

General Process Learning Theory Basic associative theory. Animals have common brain areas that mediate common learning processes. General processes are contrasted with species-specific processes of learning and behavior. (Cf. *Vertebrate Plan; Species-Specific Behaviors*.)

Generalization The tendency of animals to both perceive (*stimulus generalization*) and to respond (*response generalization*) in a similar manner to stimuli that share common properties.

Genetics The study of patterns of heredity and variations in plants and animals.

Genotype The total of an organism's genetic information.

Habituation Reduced responsiveness of an organism to repeated stimulation.

Habituation Control Group A nonassociative control group that receives the CS but not the US during conditioning.

Hedonic Conditioning A theory proposed to account for meal-to-meal changes in particular foods selected based on the positive or negative post-ingestional consequences of previous selections. Tastes and textures are CSs that become associated with postingestional consequences (USs).

Hedonism The philosophical position that the sole motivation of humans and other animals is to seek pleasure and to avoid pain.

Heredity The genetic transmission of characteristics from one generation to the next.

Heritability The fraction of the total phenotypic variance that is accounted for by genetic variation.

Higher-Order Conditioning (Pavlov) The process by which an arbitrary (conditioned) stimulus (CS_1) acquires unconditioned stimulus properties. CS_1 is first paired with a US. Following conditioning, CS_1 is then paired with yet another arbitrary stimulus (CS_2). CS_2 acquires US properties through the higher-order conditioning process.

Hypothesis A hunch, idea, or theory that is formally tested in an experiment.

Hypothetical Construct Psychological terms used to label alleged processes of the mind, such as personality, learning, memory, motivation, perception, and intelligence. (Cf. *Intervening Variable*.)

Imprinting (Ethology) Genetically programmed aspects of behavior change involving the rapid development of a response to a specific stimulus at a particular stage of development. (Cf. *Critical Period; Innate Releasing Mechanism*.)

Incentive Motivation Motivation to behave that can be attributed to the quality and amount of a reinforcer.

Independent Variable In an experiment, the variable that is manipulated to see how it affects the dependent variable. The *independent variable* is seen as the cause, and the dependent variable is the effect. Example: A drug (independent variable) causes increased activity (dependent variable).

Induction Method A method that produces inhibition. An excitatory stimulus (such as a tone) is paired with shock. When another stimulus (such as a light) is paired with the tone, and the pair is not shocked, the tone "induces" the light to become an inhibitory, or "safe," stimulus.

Inhibition of Delay (Pavlov) A psychological state produced by the passage of time during conditioning. Responding is suppressed, or inhibited, during the first part of regularly spaced long intervals. An extraneous stimulus can disinhibit this inhibition of delay.

Innate Releasing Mechanism (IRM) (Ethology) A postulated neural mechanism that, when stimulated by a sign-releasing stimulus, triggers an innately organized motor program. (Cf. *Critical Period; Sign Stimulus*.)

Instinct Innately organized behavior.

Instinctive Drift (Breland) The theory that arbitrarily established responses erode (drift) in the face of more innately organized (instinctive) behavior.

Instrumental Conditioning See *Instrumental Learning*.

Instrumental Learning (Thorndike) The modification of voluntary (nonreflexive) behavior by the application of reinforcers or punishers. (Cf. *General Process Learning Theory; Operant Conditioning*.)

Instrumental Response Voluntary, nonreflexive responses that act on the environment in a meaningful, or instrumental, fashion.

Intensity (Association theory) The strength of a stimulus. More intense stimuli are more associable. (Cf. *Law of Strength*.)

Intermittent Reinforcement See *Partial Reinforcement*.

Internal Inhibition A process proposed by Pavlov as a counterpart to external inhibition, and by Hull as a counterpart of an excitatory process.

Intertrial Interval The elapsed time between conditioning trials in a conditioning experiment.

Intervening Variable Processes of the mind, such as learning, memory, and motivation that are inferred from observations of behavior. When "learning," for example, is operationally defined and investigated, it is conceptualized as an *intervening variable* that bridges the gap between measurable *stimulus* and *response variables*. (Cf. *Hypothetical Constructs*.)

Involuntary Behavior Physiology and behavior under the control of the autonomic nervous system; unintentional, unwillful behavior. (Cf. *Reflexive Behavior, Voluntary Behavior*.)

IRM See *Innate Releasing Mechanism*.

Labor Supply Curve A backward-bending curve that deviates from the matching law, reflecting a breakdown in the general rule that effort will increase indefinitely to match available reinforcement.

LAD See *Language Acquisition Device.*

Lamarckian Evolution The theory that genetic changes in populations (i.e., evolution) can occur through the inheritance of characters acquired during a lifetime.

Language Acquisition Device (LAD) (Chomsky) A proposed species-specific brain mechanism (or series of mechanisms) that allows a human child to rapidly acquire language once triggered by a minimal language environment.

Latent Inhibition Reduced associability of familiar stimuli. (Cf. *CS Preexposure Effect.*)

Latent Learning (Tolman) Learning that is alleged to occur in the absence of specific food rewards.

Law of Effect (Thorndike) The effect of reinforcement and punishment on behavior. A response that is followed by a pleasant consequence will tend to be repeated and a response followed by an unpleasant consequence will tend to decrease in frequency.

Law of Parsimony Explaining phenomena in the simplest possible terms.

Law of Strength (Pavlov) Three interrelated factors that account for the *strength* (or magnitude) of a conditioned response. The three factors are the intensity of the CS, the intensity of the US, and the interstimulus interval between the CS and US.

Learned Helplessness The outcome of an experimental treatment in which an animal is initially prevented from escaping intensely painful stimuli. Thereafter, when allowed the opportunity, the animal fails to respond in an adaptive fashion and does not attempt to escape pain.

Learning A relatively permanent change in observable behavior that results from experience within the environment.

Learning-Performance Distinction The difference between what is measured (performance) and what is inferred from the measurement (learning). Example: Changes in lever pressing are measured; learning is inferred.

Learning Set (Harlow) A procedure demonstrating that animals learn strategies to solve problems. Sets of unique problems are presented the animal for 6 trials, and animals eventually learn a win-stay, lose-shift strategy.

Learning Theory The proposition that a limited number of general principles of learning can account for much of the observed variability in animal behavior.

Learning to Learn (Harlow) The term used to describe the ability of animals to slowly learn a *general rule* that could then be applied to rapidly solve new problem sets. (See *Win-Stay, Lose-Shift Strategy; Learning Sets.*)

Long-Term Depression (LTD) Decreased responsiveness of certain neurons stimulated rapidly and repeatedly that may last for days and even weeks. LTD may mediate associative effects between neurons.

Long-Term Potentiation (LTP) Increased responsiveness of certain neurons stimulated rapidly and repeatedly that may last for days and even weeks. LTP may mediate associative effects between neurons.

LTD See *Long-Term Depression.*

LTP See *Long-Term Potentiation.*

Magazine Training An initial stage of operant conditioning in which the sound of the food delivery mechanism becomes associated with food delivery.

Match to Sample A procedure in which an animal is presented a target stimulus and then required to select it from a stimulus array that includes distractor stimuli. (Cf. *Delayed Match to Sample.*)

Matching Law (Herrnstein) A monotonic functional relationship typically found between the rate of responding and available reinforcement. Response rates typically match available reinforcement.

Melioration Maximization of local (moment-to-moment) changes in available reinforcement.

Molar Level In research, investigations of the behavior of whole, intact organisms. (Cf. *Molecular Level.*)

Molecular Level In research, investigations of behavior by determining which parts of the brain (anatomy) or which biochemicals are involved concomitant with the behavior. (Cf. *Molar Level*.)

Monozygotic Developed from a single zygote; identical, or one-egg, twins. Monozygotic twins have identical genotypes.

Morgan's Canon Complex psychological processes should not be attributable to animals if their behavior can be understood in simpler terms.

Natural Concepts A term used to describe the ability of pigeons to extract information from complex pictures of natural environments and to respond in a way that indicates that they recognize trees, people, and other open-ended categories.

Natural Selection (Darwin) An aspect of the theory of evolution that stresses the reproductive advantage of certain offspring suited to their environment over others not suited. Darwin argued that environment (i.e., nature) selects those individuals who will reproduce the next generation depending on their relative fitness. Animals not able to overcome these selection pressures drop out of the gene pool. (Cf. *Selective Pressure*.)

Needs Physiological requirements (such as food and water) necessary for maintaining life.

Negative Contingency A US-CS pairing. By contrast, a CS-US pairing sets up a positive contingency. Negative contingencies often result in the formation of conditioned inhibition.

Negative Contrast After experiencing both a small and a large reward, their comparison makes the perception of the smaller reward more negative than it would be in the absence of the contrast. See also *Behavioral Contrast*.

Negative Discriminative Stimulus (S^Δ) A stimulus that signals that response-food contingencies are *not* in effect. Responding in the presence of this stimulus is not reinforced.

Negative Reinforcement The process by which responses that are instrumental in preventing or avoiding an aversive stimulus *increase* in frequency. (Cf. *Punishment*.)

Neophobia A behavioral tendency to approach new objects cautiously (literally, *fear of the new*). When applied to rats and humans responding to unfamiliar foods, their innate feeding tendencies are to cautiously approach and sniff before tasting, to be generally finicky, and (for a few human children) to suspect that someone is trying to poison them.

Neuroethology The study of the relationship between the nervous system and consummatory behaviors.

Nonassociative Learning Relatively permanent changes in behavior that result from an animal experiencing a particular stimulus. Sensitization and habituation are two examples. (Cf. *AssociationTheory*.)

Null Hypothesis The research hypothesis that *no* differences exist between a *treatment* group and a *control* group. Rejecting the null hypothesis (using a statistical analysis) leads to the conclusion that the two groups in fact differ and that the treatment effect caused this difference.

Occasion Setting A procedure in which a stimulus or context signals that a following stimulus will be either a discriminative or a negative-discriminative stimulus.

Omnivore's Paradox (Rozin) An eating pattern that *enhances* fitness during famine but also *diminishes* fitness by increasing the risk of poisoning.

One-Word Utterance Stage The first words spoken in any language, typically referring to names for objects encountered in their environment, such as *mama* and *milk* and for actions such as *get* and *go*. (Also known as *holophrastic speech*.)

Ontogenetic History A history of an animal's entire development from fertilization through death.

Operant (Skinner) A designated response, such as a lever press, that effectively *operates* on the environment. (Cf. *Instrumental Response*.)

Operant Conditioning (Skinner) A variant

of instrumental conditioning. (See *Instrumental Conditioning*.)

Operant Level (Skinner) An existing baseline rate of a response as measured prior to the administration of reinforcement and punishment contingencies. (Cf. *Baseline*, or *Free-Operant, Level*.)

Operant Response See *Operant*.

Operational Definition A definition of a term or concept that refers to the operations that measure the presumptive process. Example: Intelligence is that which IQ tests measure.

Orienting Reflex (Pavlov) The response that occurs when a CS such as a tone is first sounded. A dog will prick up its ears and turn its head, locating the source of the sound.

Overmatching Responding *more* than predicted for available reinforcement. (Cf. *Matching Law*.)

Overshadowing The acquisition of more associative strength by one stimulus when conditioned in compound with another. One CS is said to overshadow the other CS.

Pan paniscus The *bonobo* chimpanzee, sometimes referred to as the *pygmy chimp*. (Cf. *Pan troglodytes*.)

Pan troglodytes The common chimpanzee. (Cf. *Pan paniscus*.)

Parameters The various levels that an independent variable can assume. Example: Low, medium, and high dosages are the *parameters* of a drug treatment.

Partial Reinforcement Any reinforcement situation other than continuous reinforcement. Also called *intermittent reinforcement*.

Partial Reinforcement Effect The tendency for animals maintained on partial reinforcement schedules to be highly resistant to extinction.

Pavlovian Conditioning An experimental procedure in which a basic *reflex*, consisting of an *unconditioned stimulus* (US) and an *unconditioned response* (UR) is paired in time with a neutral stimulus (the *conditioned stimulus, CS*). After several pairings, the CS by itself can elicit components of the original reflex, called the *conditioned response* (CR). (Also called *classical conditioning*.)

Peak Shift Following S^+/S^- discrimination training of two wavelengths, the shift of the peak response of the generalization gradient to the target S^+ opposite to (away from) the S^- wavelength.

Pharmacological Tolerance That portion of total drug tolerance that can be attributed to pharmacologic properties of drugs.

Phenotype A genotype expressed in an environment. Defining an organism by its appearance, and not by its genetic constitution or hereditary potential.

Phylogenetic History The entire evolutionary history of a specific taxonomic group of organisms. Collectively, the natural history of life on earth.

Picture Memory (Farrar) The term used to describe the performance of the chimpanzee, Minnie, in which 24 pictures with common elements were memorized.

Placebo Effect A conditioned response that mimics the effects of a drug treatment (the unconditioned stimulus); in humans, via the second signal system, the expectation of drug or other treatment effects.

Positive Reinforcement The process by which the application of a reinforcer contingent on a desired response increases the frequency of that response.

Positive Reinforcer Any stimulus (such as food) delivered to an animal immediately following a designated response that leads to an increase in the frequency of that response. (Cf. *Satisfiers*.)

Postreinforcement Pause A break in responding following delivery of a reinforcer. Longer pauses are seen for higher FR schedules than for lower FR schedules (i.e., for FR-100 vs. FR-10), and very *short* postreinforcement pauses are typically found using VI and VR schedules of reinforcement.

Post-Traumatic Stress Disorder (PTSD) A

disorder characterized by one or more of the following symptoms of intense fear, feelings of helplessness, and recurrent intrusive memories/dreams and whose etiology is thought to be caused by an unusual, markedly distressing event such as rape or battle fatigue.

Potentiation   Enhanced conditioning of a stimulus due to the presence of a flavor stimulus. The flavor stimulus is said to *potentiate* the conditioning of the CS.

Premack Principle   David Premack's theory that the more probable of two responses always reinforces the less probable response.

Preparedness   A genetically determined rapid form of learning. Associations between certain stimuli, and between some stimuli and certain responses, are more easily learned presumably because they enhance fitness. (Cf. *Stimulus Specificity in Conditioning*.)

Primary Punisher   A stimulus that is inherently aversive.

Procedural Memory   Memory for skills; hypothesized memory store for conditioned responses.

Proximate Causes   (of behavior) Causes of behavior that focus on immediate, local (psychological and sociological) determinants as opposed to ultimate causes (genetic).

Psychic Secretion   (Pavlov) Pavlov's term for salivation attributable to psychological factors.

Psychobiology   An interdisciplinary approach to questions of physiology, learning, and behavior that draws on and attempts to integrate observations and experiments in, among other sciences, psychology, ethology, physiology, and genetics.

Psychoneuroimmunology   The field of research attempting to describe and integrate the interconnectedness of the immune system, central and autonomic nervous systems, neuroendocrine system, and behavior.

Psychosomatic Disorders   Disorders of anatomy and/or physiology that can be attributed in part to psychological or behavioral variables.

PTSD   See *Post-Traumatic Stress Disorder*.

Punisher   Any stimulus whose application acts to decrease the rate of emission of the preceding response.

Punishment   The process by which an aversive stimulus acts to decrease the rate of the response to which it is applied.

R-S Conditioning   In instrumental conditioning, the requirement of a response prior to presentation of a food stimulus. Hence, instrumental conditioning is sometimes referred to as *response-stimulus*, or *R-S, conditioning*. (Cf. *Instrumental Conditioning*.)

Random Control Group   A nonassociative control group in which the CS and US are presented separately, never together, in time.

Reductionism   Explaining a phenomenon by reference to a more molecular analysis (i.e., a biochemical level). Reductionism is the primary means of scientific explanation.

Reflexes   Innate, involuntary responses an animal makes to specific stimuli in the environment. Example: Iris closure in response to sudden bright light.

Reification   Asserting the existence of a presumptive process independent of evidence for that process. Example: Intelligence is *there*, awaiting its measurement.

Reinforcement   See *Positive Reinforcement* and *Negative Reinforcement*.

Reproduction   The behavioral and physiological means by which animals produce offspring.

Rescorla-Wagner Model   A theory of association. Rescorla-Wagner modeled the growth of association during conditioning by (a) quantifying the effects of using stimuli of different novelty and salience; (b) predicting and quantifying the greater growth of associative potential in early training trials; and (c) predicting and quantifying the effects of extinction and blocking procedures.

Resistance-to-Extinction   A measure of conditioning. Greater resistance-to-extinction is found following many conditioning trials compared to a few conditioning trials.

Response Contingency In instrumental conditioning, making a reinforcer or punisher contingent on a specified response. No such requirement exists for Pavlovian conditioning.

Response Variable The measured response in a behavioral experiment. (In chemistry, the response variable is typically called a *reaction*.) In the behavioral sciences, the response variable is a measure of behavioral change.

Retardation Test A procedure that allows indirect measurement of conditioned inhibition. A stimulus is first made a conditioned inhibitor and is then conditioned as an excitor. The acquisition of conditioned excitation is retarded when a conditioned inhibitor is used, relative to a neutral stimulus.

r_Gs See *Fractional Anticipatory Goal Responses*.

Salience The relative associability of stimuli. More salient stimuli are more easily conditioned.

Salivary Reflex An innate response (salivation) to food placed on a dog's tongue.

Sameness Task A learning task in which pictures of objects are sequentially presented to pigeons and a final picture is presented that either was or was not in the series (i.e., *same* or *different*). Pigeons solve this problem for food reinforcement by responding to one key if the same, and to another key if different.

Satisfiers Positive stimuli. Thorndike's law of effect proposed that when pleasant stimuli, which he called *satisfiers*, followed a response, the response would more likely be made thereafter. (Cf. *Reinforcer*.)

Schedules of Reinforcement Rules specified by the experimenter that govern the relationship of reinforcing events to an animal's responses. Example: In *continuous reinforcement*, the rule is that each response is reinforced. Other schedules include fixed ratios, variable intervals, and so forth.

SΔ See *Negative Discriminative Stimulus*.

S^d See *Discriminative Stimulus*.

Second-Order Conditioning (Pavlov) The lowest, most common level of higher-order conditioning. After CS_1 has been paired with a US, CS_1 is then paired with CS_2—called *conditioning of the second-order*. CS_2 acquires US properties through the process called *higher-order conditioning*.

Second Signal System Pavlov's theory that words act as CSs. Words are the signal of signals, hence, the second signal system.

Secondary Punisher Stimuli that acquire punishing properties through a conditioning procedure. Example: The word *no*. (Cf. *Secondary Reinforcers*.)

Secondary Reinforcers Properties of stimuli acquired by the process of higher-order conditioning. (Cf. *Conditioned Reinforcers*.)

Selective Pressure Any feature of an environment that allows one phenotype to have reproductive advantage over another.

Self-Control The ability to delay immediate gratification, usually with the goal of attaining a larger reinforcer at a later time.

Sensitization Increased responsiveness following presentation of a stimulus. Sensitization is an example of nonassociative learning.

Sensitization Control Group A nonassociative control group (also referred to as a *pseudoconditioning* control) that is exposed only to the US during conditioning.

Sensory Preconditioning A method used to measure CS-CS associations. In the first step, two conditioned stimuli (CS_1 and CS_2) are repeatedly paired. CS_1 is then conditioned to a US, after which CS_2 is tested as if it had been conditioned. In sensory preconditioning, CS_2 shows (indirect) evidence of conditioning through its prior association with CS_1.

Serial Pattern Learning A learning task in which rats are exposed to and learn a sequence of patterns of reinforcement (or nonreinforcement) in the goal box over a succession of trials.

Shaping by Successive Approximation A training system that involves the selective reinforcement of responses that approximate the target behavior. Increasingly stringent response requirements are placed on the animal, until only the successful completion of the target response (i.e., a lever press) is reinforced.

Sherringtonian Reflexes Reflexes characterized by identifiable *sensory neurons* synapsing on identifiable *interneurons* and *motor neurons*.

Shuttle-Avoidance Avoidance conditioning in which the terminal behavior is to jump over a barrier (Cf. *shuttle*) separating two compartments of a shuttle box.

Shuttle Box An apparatus in which animals can be conditioned to *escape* and/or *avoid* electric shock by jumping across a barrier dividing the two compartments of the shuttle box.

Sidman Avoidance A negative reinforcement procedure designed by Murray Sidman in which the lever in a Skinner box is the only signal that electric shock can be delayed/avoided by continuously lever pressing.

Sign Stimulus (Ethology) A specific environmental stimulus that triggers innately organized behaviors. (Cf. *Fixed Action Pattern; Innate Releasing Mechanism*.)

Sign Tracking See *Autoshaping*.

Similarity (Association theory) Two stimuli that are perceived as being similar to each other are more associable. (Cf. *Preparedness*.)

Simultaneous Conditioning (Pavlov) Conditioning trials in which the CS and US have identical onsets, durations, and offsets. Very little conditioning results from these trials.

Single-Stimulus Effect (Association theory) Behavioral change due to the action of a single stimulus, as opposed to the association of two or more stimuli. (See *Habituation; Nonassociative Learning; Sensitization*.)

Skinner Box An experimental environment consisting of a small box containing one or more (a) levers or response keys, (b) lights/speakers, and (c) feeding/watering devices used in animal learning experiments (named for B. F. Skinner).

Social Reinforcement Theory (Bandura) A theory that human learning is accomplished primarily by innate imitation and modeling of observed behavior.

Sociobiology The study of the genetic determinants of social behavior.

Species-Specific Behaviors Innate perceptual and response patterns typical of a species.

Species-Specific Defense Reaction (SSDR) An innately organized hierarchy of defense behaviors elicited by signals indicating potential danger.

Specific Hungers The translation of physiological needs into cravings and hungers for specific, identifiable nutrients. Examples: salt and water.

Spontaneous Recovery (Pavlov) The reappearance of a higher level of conditioned response following a delay in the extinction process.

S-S Conditioning One stimulus is paired with another. Pavlovian conditioning is sometimes referred to as stimulus-stimulus, or *S-S, conditioning*. (Cf. *Instrumental Conditioning*.)

SSDR See *Species-Specific Defense Reaction*.

Stimulus Control Specified operant responses in the presence of an S^d. The response is not made in the presence of an S^Δ.

Stimulus Generalization Gradient Following training to a target stimulus, a predictable pattern of responses to similar stimuli. More responses are made to the most similar, and the fewest responses are made to stimuli most different from the target.

Stimulus-Response Chains The theory that in learning to perform a sequence of responses (such as left and right turns in a maze) responses acquire stimulus properties that cue the next response. (Cf. *Chained Operants*.)

Stimulus Specificity in Conditioning Genetically determined (prepared) brain structures allow rapid learning of certain (specific) stimuli. Other associations are more difficult. Examples: Garcia's telereceptor-cutaneous and gustatory-visceral conditioning systems. (Cf. *Preparedness*.)

Stimulus Substitution (Pavlov) A theory of conditioning. Animals come to consider the conditioned stimulus to be a "substitute" for the unconditioned stimulus. (Example: chimpanzees that hoard tokens associated with prior food reinforcement.)

Stimulus Variable The experimental manipulation imposed on a subject in an experiment. (Cf. *Independent Variable*.) Stimulus variables impinge on animals, causing responses.

Successive Approximation See *Shaping by Successive Approximation*.

Summation Test A procedure that allows indirect measurement of conditioned inhibition. Following conditioning of CS_2 (a conditioned inhibitor) and CS_1 (a conditioned excitor) and when presented together in extinction, CS_1 and CS_2 will algebraically combine, or summate, to lessen both the excitatory and inhibitory response.

Target Response The instrumental or operant response that, when executed, is reinforced.

Taste Aversion Conditioning A method of studying aversive Pavlovian conditioning. Rats drink a flavored solution (the CS) and then are given an illness-inducing toxin (the US). Conditioned taste aversions to the target flavor result from one or a few pairings.

Telegraphic Speech The term used to define a stage of language, when, at the age of about 1½ years, children begin to string together two words in a grammatically meaningful fashion.

Temporal Conditioning (Pavlov) A variation of conditioning in which dogs are presented food at regular intervals. After many such trials, salivation occurs just prior to food administration. The inter-food time interval acquires conditioned stimulus properties.

Temporal Contiguity Two events perceived as being closely related in time.

Thorndikean Conditioning See *Instrumental Learning*.

Tolerance Changes in the effectiveness of drugs taken repeatedly as measured by the necessity to increase a drug dosage to get the same effect or the decreased effectiveness of a given drug dosage taken repeatedly.

Trace Conditioning (Pavlov) An example of forward conditioning in which both the CS onset *and offset* precede the US onset.

Transitive Inferential Reasoning A problem of the following type: If *a* is greater than *b* and *b* is greater than *c*, is *a* greater than *c*? Its solution is indicative of reasoning ability and a knowledge of relationships that extends beyond immediate experience.

Treatment Group In an experiment, the group of subjects that receives the *independent variable*.

Trial A CS–US pairing.

Tropism A differential growth movement in a plant away from or toward a directional stimulus.

Two-Factor Theory (Mowrer) A theory proposing that two factors underlying avoidance behavior are Pavlovian-conditioned emotional behavior and instrumentally conditioned motor (muscle) responses.

Two-Factor Theory of Punishment A theory that punishment learning is accomplished in two stages (i.e., a fear response that is first conditioned classically and then an avoidance response that reduces the fear response).

Two-Stage Theory of Association Stage 1: Two stimuli perceived as being temporally contiguous and correlated. Stage 2: S_2 perceived as being contingent upon, and caused by, S_1.

Ultimate Causes (of behavior) Causes of behavior that focus on evolutionary and genetic determinants rather than psychological and sociological explanations.

Unconditioned Response (UR) (Pavlov) The reflexive response to an unconditioned stimulus (the US). Salivation is the unconditioned response to food.

Unconditioned Stimulus (US) (Pavlov) A stimulus that innately and involuntarily elicits a reflexive response (i.e., the UR). Example: Food is an unconditioned stimulus that elicits reflexive salivation.

Undermatching Responding *less* than predicted for available reinforcement. (Cf. *Matching Law*.)

Universal Grammar (Chomsky) A theoretical position that postulates the existence of innate structures underlying the rapid acquisition and output of grammatically correct language and that denies any role for Pavlovian and instrumental conditioning processes.

Unprepared A form of learning that takes an intermediate number of trials to accomplish. (Cf. *Preparedness; Contraprepared*.)

UR See *Unconditioned Response*.

US See *Unconditioned Stimulus*.

US Preexposure Effect Preexposed, or familiar, unconditioned stimuli requiring more trials to become associated with a given CS than do novel unconditioned stimuli. (Cf. *CS Preexposure Effect*.) Example: Exposing an animal to an electric shock before conditioning makes the electric shock a less effective unconditioned stimulus.

Value The relative worth, merit, or importance of an object or activity, based on *esthetics, cost, availability, perceived utility*, and other properties.

Variability (Darwin) An aspect of the theory of evolution that describes the role played by the wide range of genetic variation (i.e., variability) within a species. Genetic variance is the raw material on which natural selection works. (Cf. *Natural Selection; Selective Pressure*.)

Variable Interval Schedule (VI) A partial schedule of reinforcement. An animal is reinforced for its first response following a *variable interval* of time from the preceding reinforcer. Example: An animal on a VI-60 is reinforced at varying time periods averaging 60 seconds from the preceding reinforcement.

Variable Ratio Schedule (VR) A partial schedule of reinforcement. Delivery of a reinforcer is contingent on the completion of a variable number of operant responses from the preceding reinforcement. Example: An animal responding on a VR-10 is reinforced for different numbers of responses, their average being ten.

Vertebrate Plan The observed similarities in brain structure among all vertebrates, characterized by their common bilaterality, cranial nerves, thalamus, medulla, and other structures.

VI See *Variable Interval Schedule*.

Voluntary Behavior Physiology and behavior under the control of the central nervous system; intentional, willful behavior. (Cf. *Involuntary Behavior*.)

VR See *Variable Ratio Schedule*.

Win-Stay, Lose-Shift (Harlow) A strategy animals learn. Presented with repeated opportunities to solve a two-choice discrimination problem, animals stay with reinforced choices and shift away from nonreinforced choices.

Within-Groups Design An experimental design in which a pretreatment measure of the dependent variable is compared with a post-treatment measure *in the same subjects*. (Cf. *Between-Groups Design*.)

Working Hypothesis A simple statement of what is expected to happen in an experiment. Example: A low dose of drug X will have less effect on activity than a high dose of drug X.

Written History The transmission of cultural knowledge; a cumulative record of the ontogenetic histories of many individuals that provides the basis for civilization, which is an invention unique to *Homo sapiens*.

Zoomorphism The attribution of animal qualities and properties to humans.

References

Abramson, C. I. (1994). *A primer of invertebrate learning*. Washington, DC: American Psychological Association.

Adams, M. J. (1990). *Beginning to read: Thinking and learning about print*. Cambridge, MA: MIT Press.

Ader, R. (1985). Conditioned taste aversions and immunopharmacology. *Annals of the New York Academy of Sciences, 443,* 293–307.

Ader, R. (1993). Conditioned responses. In B. Moyers, (Ed.), *Healing and the mind.* New York: Doubleday.

Ader, R., & Cohen, N. (1982). Behaviorally conditioned immunosuppression and murine systemic lupus erythematosus. *Science, 215,* 1534–1536.

Ader, R., Cohen, N., & Bovbjerg, D. (1982). Conditioned suppression of humoral immunity in the rat. *Journal of Comparative and Physiological Psychology, 96,* 517–521.

Ader, R., Weiner, H., & Baum, A. (Eds.). (1988). *Experimental foundations of behavioral medicine: Conditioning approaches.* Hillsdale, NJ: Erlbaum.

Amsel, A. (1958). The role of frustrative nonreward in partial reinforcement and discrimination learning. *Psychological Review, 69,* 306–328.

Anastasia, D., & LoLordo, V. M. (1994). Evidence for simultaneous excitatory and inhibitory associations in the explicitly unpaired procedure. *Learning and Motivation, 25,* 1–25.

Anderson, C. D., Ferland, R. J., & Williams, M. D. (1992). Negative contrast associated with reinforcing stimulation of the brain. *Society for Neuroscience Abstracts, 18,* 874.

Anderson, J. R. (1990). *Cognitive psychology and its implications*. New York: W. H. Freeman.

Anderson, R. C., Wilson, P. T., & Fielding, L. G. (1988). Growth in reading and how children spend their time outside of school. *Reading Research Quarterly, 23,* 285–303.

Annau, Z., & Kamin, L. J. (1961). The conditioned emotional response as a function of intensity of the US. *Journal of Comparative and Physiological Psychology, 54,* 428–432.

Archer, T., & Sjoden, P. O. (1982). Higher-order conditioning and sensory preconditioning of a taste aversion with an exteroceptive CS1. *Quarterly Journal of Experimental Psychology, 34B,* 1–17.

Ayllon, T., & Azrin, N. (1968). *The token-economy: A motivational system for therapy and rehabilitation*. New York: Appleton-Century-Crofts.

Ayres, J. J., Philbin, D., Cassidy, S., & Bellino, L. (1992). Some parameters of latent inhibition. *Learning & Motivation, 23,* 269–287.

Azrin, N. H., & Holz, W. C. (1966). Punishment. In W. K. Honig (Ed.), *Operant behavior: Areas of research and application.* New York: Appleton-Century-Crofts.

Azrin, N. H., Holz, W. C., & Hake, D. F. (1963). Fixed-ratio punishment. *Journal of the Experimental Analysis of Behavior, 6,* 141–148.

Azrin, N. H., Hutchinson, R. R., & Hake, D. F. (1966). Extinction-induced aggression. *Journal of the Experimental Analysis of Behavior, 9,* 191–204.

Baer, D. M., & Sherman, J. A. (1964). Reinforcement control of generalized imitation in young children. *Journal of Experimental Child Psychology, 1,* 37–49.

Baker, A. G., & Baker, P. A. (1985). Does inhibition differ from excitation: Proactive interference, contextual conditioning, and extinction. In R. R. Miller & N. E. Spear (Eds.), *Information processing in animals: Conditioned inhibition.* Hillsdale, NJ: Erlbaum.

Baker, A. G., & Mackintosh, N. J. (1977). Excitatory and inhibitory conditioning following uncorrelated presentations of CS and UCS. *Animal Learning & Behavior, 5,* 315–319.

Baker, A. G., & Mercier, P. (1982). Extinction of the context and latent inhibition. *Learning and Motivation, 13,* 391–416.

Baker, A. G., Mercier, P., Gabel, J., & Baker, P. A. (1981). Contextual conditioning and the US preexposure effect in conditioned fear. *Journal of Experimental Psychology: Animal Behavior Processes, 7,* 109–128.

Baker, A. G., Singh, M., & Bindra, D. (1985). Some effects of contextual conditioning and US predictability on Pavlovian conditioning. In P. Balsam & A. Tomie (Eds.), *Context and learning.* Hillsdale, NJ: Erlbaum.

Baker, B. J., Booth, D. A., Duggan, J. P., & Gibson, E. L. (1987). Protein appetite demonstrated: Learned specificity of protein-cue preference to protein need in adult rats. *Nutrition Research, 7,* 481–487.

Baker, T. B., & Tiffany, S. T. (1985). Morphine tolerance as habituation. *Psychological Review, 92,* 78–108.

Balsom, P. D., & Tomie, A. (Eds.). (1985). *Context and learning.* Hillsdale, NJ: Erlbaum.

Bandura, A. (1962). Social learning through imitation. In M. R. Jones (Ed.), *Nebraska symposium on motivation.* Lincoln: University of Nebraska Press.

Bandura, A. (1971). *Social learning theory.* Englewood Cliffs, NJ: Prentice Hall.

Bandura, A., & Walters, R. H. (1963). *Social learning and personality development.* New York: Holt, Rinehart, & Winston.

Barash, D. (1979). *The whisperings within: Evolution and the origin of human nature.* New York: Harper & Row.

Barash, D. (1982). *Sociobiology and behavior* (2nd ed.). New York: Elsevier.

Barker, L. M. (1968). *Effects of (classified drug) on aversive and appetitively motivated behavior of Rhesus monkeys in aeronautical simulation studies.* Unpublished USAF Technical Report.

Barker, L. M., Best, M. R., & Domjan, M. (Eds.). (1977). *Learning mechanisms in food selection.* Waco, TX: Baylor University Press.

Barker, L. M., & Smith, J. C. (1974). A comparison of taste aversions induced by radiation and lithium chloride in CS-US and US-CS paradigms. *Journal of Comparative and Physiological Psychology, 87,* 644–654.

Barker, L. M., Suarez, E. R., & Grey, D. (1974). Backward conditioning of taste aversions in rats using cyclophosphamide as the US. *Physiological Psychology, 2,* 117–119.

Barker, L. M., & Weaver, C. A. (1991). Conditioning flavor preferences in rats: Dissecting the "medicine effect." *Learning and Motivation, 22,* 311–328.

Barkow, J. H., Cosmides, L., & Tooby, J. (1992). *The adapted mind: Evolutionary psychology and the generation of culture.* New York: Oxford University Press.

Barnett, S. A. (1981). *Modern ethology.* New York: Oxford University Press.

Batson, J. D., Hoban, J. S., & Bitterman, M. E. (1992). Simultaneous conditioning in honeybees (*Apis mellifera*). *Journal of Comparative Psychology, 106,* 114–119.

Baum, W. M. (1974). On two types of deviation from the matching law: Bias and undermatching. *Journal of the Experimental Analysis of Behavior, 22,* 231–242.

Baum, W. M. (1979). Matching, undermatching, and overmatching in studies of choice. *Journal of the Experimental Analysis of Behavior, 32,* 269–281.

Baum, W. M. (1981). Optimization and the matching law as accounts of instrumental behavior. *Journal of the Experimental Analysis of Behavior, 36,* 387–403.

Beach, F. (1950). The snark was a boojum. *American Psychologist, 5,* 115–124.

Beckwith, R., & Rispoli, M. (1986). Aspects of a theory of mind: An interview with Noam Chomsky. *New Ideas in Psychology, 4,* 187–202.

Beidler, L. M. (1982). Biological basis of food selection. In L. M. Barker (Ed.), *The psychobiology of human food selection.* Westport, CT: AVI Publishing.

Benedict, J. O., & Ayres, J. J. B. (1972). Factors affecting conditioning in the truly random control procedure in the rat. *Journal of Comparative and Physiological Psychology, 78,* 323–330.

Benjamin, L. T., & Bruce, D. (1982). From bottle-fed chimp to bottlenose dolphin: A contemporary appraisal of Winthrop Kellogg. *The Psychological Record, 32,* 461–482.

Bennett, E. L., Diamond, M., Krech, D., & Rosenzweig, M. R. (1964). Chemical and anatomical plasticity of the brain. *Science, 146,* 610–619.

Bernstein, A. M., Philips, H. C., Linden, W., & Fenster, H. A. (1992). Psychophysiological evaluation of female urethral syndrome: Evidence for a muscular abnormality. *Journal of Behavioral Medicine, 15,* 299–312.

Bernstein, I. L. (1978). Learned taste aversions in children receiving chemotherapy. *Science, 200,* 1302–1303.

Bernstein, I. L., & Borson, S. (1986). Learned food aversion: A component of anorexia syndromes. *Psychological Review, 93,* 462–472.

Bernstein, I. L., & Webster, M. M. (1980). Learned taste aversions in humans. *Physiology and Behavior, 25,* 363–366.

Berridge, K. C., & Robinson, T. E. (1995). The mind of an addicted brain: Neural sensitization of wanting versus liking. *Current Directions in Psychological Science, 4,* 71–76.

Best, M. R. (1975). Conditioned and latent inhibition in taste-aversion learning: Clarifying the role of learned safety. *Journal of Experimental Psychology: Animal Behavior Processes, 1,* 97–113.

Best, M. R., & Barker, L. (1977). The nature of "learned safety" and its role in the delay of reinforcement gradient. In L. M. Barker, M. R. Best, & M. Domjan (Eds.), *Learning mechanisms in food selection.* Waco, TX: Baylor University Press.

Best, P. J., Best, M. R., & Henggeler, S. (1977). The contribution of environmental noningestive cues in conditioning with aversive internal consequences. In L. M. Barker, M. R. Best, & M. Domjan (Eds.), *Learning mechanisms in food selection.* Waco, TX: Baylor University Press.

Best, P. J., Best, M. R., & Mickley, G. A. (1973). Conditioned aversion to distinct environmental stimuli resulting from gastrointestinal distress. *Journal of Comparative and Physiological Psychology, 85,* 250–257.

Best, M. R., Brown, E. R., & Sowell, M. K. (1984). Taste mediated potentiation of non-ingestional stimuli in rats. *Learning & Motivation, 15,* 244–258.

Best, M. R., & Gemberling, G. A. (1977). The role of short-term processes in the CS preexposure effect and the delay of reinforcement gradient in long-delay taste-aversion learning. *Journal of Experimental Psychology: Animal Behavior Processes, 3,* 253–263.

Best, M. R., & Meacham, C. L. (1986). The effects of stimulus preexposure on taste mediated environmental conditioning: Potentiation and overshadowing. *Animal Learning & Behavior, 14,* 1–5.

Bindra, D. (1972). A unified account of classical conditioning and operant training. In A. H. & W. F. Prokasy (Eds.), *Classical conditioning II: Current research and theory.* New York: Appleton-Century-Crofts.

Bitterman, M. E. (1975). The comparative analysis of learning. *Science, 188,* 699–709.

Bitterman, M. E., Menzel, R., Fietz, A., & Schäfer, S. (1983). Classical conditioning of proboscis extension in honeybees (*Apis mellifera*). *Journal of Comparative Psychology, 97,* 107–119.

Black, A. H. (1971). Autonomic aversive conditioning in infrahuman subjects. In F. R. Brush (Ed.), *Aversive conditioning and learning.* New York: Academic Press.

Blanchard, E. B., Andrasik, F., Ahles, T. A., Teders, S. J., & O'Keefe, D. (1980). Migraine and tension headache: A meta-analytic review. *Behavior Therapy, 11,* 613–631.

Blanchard, E. B., & Epstein, L. H. (1977). The clinical usefulness of biofeedback. In M. Hersen, R. M. Eisler, & P. M. Miller (Eds.), *Progress in behavior modification* (Vol. 4). New York: Academic Press.

Bliss, T. V. P., & Lomo, T. (1973). Long-lasting potentiation of synaptic transmission in the dentate area of the anaesthetized rabbit following stimulation of the perforant path. *Journal of Physiology* (London), *232*, 331–356.

Bloom, L. (1970). *Language development: Form and function in emerging grammars.* Cambridge, MA: MIT Press.

Boakes, R. A. (1984). *From Darwin to behaviourism.* Cambridge, UK: Cambridge University Press.

Boakes, R. A., & Halliday, M. S. (Eds.). (1972). *Inhibition and learning.* London: Academic Press.

Boice, R. (1973). Domestication. *Psychological Bulletin, 80,* 215–230.

Boice, R. (1977). Burrows of wild and albino rats: Effects of domestication, outdoor raising, age, experience, and maternal state. *Journal of Comparative and Physiological Psychology, 91,* 649–661.

Boice, R. (1981). Behavioral comparability of wild and domesticated rats. *Behavior Genetics, 11,* 545–553.

Boland, F. J., Mellor, C. S., & Revusky, S. (1978). Chemical aversion treatment of alcoholism: Lithium as the aversive agent. *Behaviour Research and Therapy, 16,* 401–409.

Bolles, R. C. (1970). Species-specific defense reactions and avoidance learning. *Psychological Review, 71,* 32–48.

Bolles, R. C. (1971). Species-specific defense reactions. In F. R. Brush (Ed.), *Aversive conditioning and learning.* New York: Academic Press.

Bolles, R. C. (1972). The avoidance learning problem. In G. H. Bower (Ed.), *The psychology of learning and motivation* (Vol. 6). New York: Academic Press.

Bolles, R. C., Hayward, L., & Crandall, C. (1981). Conditioned taste preferences based on caloric density. *Journal of Experimental Psychology: Animal Behavior Processes, 7,* 59–69.

Bond, G. L., & Dykstra, R. (1967). The cooperative research program in first grade reading instruction. *Reading Research Quarterly, 2,* 5–142.

Booth, D. A. (1982). How nutritional effects of foods can influence people's dietary choices. In L. M. Barker (Ed.), *The psychobiology of human food selection.* Westport, CT: AVI Publishing.

Booth, R. J., and Ashbridge, K. R. (1992). Implications of psychoimmunology for models of the immune system. In A. J. Husband (Ed.), *Behavior and Immunity.* London: CRC Press.

Bouchard, T. J. (1994). Genes, environment, and personality. *Science, 264,* 1700–1701.

Bouchard, T. J., Lykken, D. R., McGue, M., Segal, N. L., & Tellegen, A. (1990). Sources of human psychological differences: The Minnesota study of twins reared apart. *Science, 250,* 223–228.

Bousfield, W. A. (1955). Lope de Vega on early conditioning. *American Psychologist, 10,* 828.

Bouton, M. E. (1984). Differential control by context in the inflation and reinstatement paradigms. *Journal of Experimental Psychology: Animal Behavior Processes, 10,* 56–74.

Bouton, M. E. (1991). Context and retrieval in extinction and in other examples of interference in simple associative learning. In L. Dachowski & C. F. Flaherty (Eds.), *Current topics in animal learning.* Hillsdale, NJ: Erlbaum.

Bouton, M. E. (1993) Context, time, and memory retrieval in the interference paradigms of Pavlovian learning. *Psychological Bulletin, 114,* 80–99.

Bouton, M. E., & Bolles, R. C. (1979a). Contextual control of the extinction of conditioned fear. *Learning and Motivation, 10,* 455–466.

Bouton, M. E., & Bolles, R. C. (1979b). Role of conditioned contextual stimuli in reinstatement of extinguished fear. *Journal of Experimental Psychology: Animal Behavior Processes, 5,* 368–378.

Bouton, M. E., Dunlap, C. M., & Swartzentruber, D. (1987). Potentiation of taste by another taste during compound aversion learning. *Animal Learning & Behavior, 15,* 433–438.

Bouton, M. E., & Swartzentruber, D. (1986). Analysis of the associative and occasion-setting properties of contexts participating in a Pavlovian discrimination. *Journal of Experimental Psychology: Animal Behavior Processes, 12,* 333–350.

Bovbjerg, D., Cohen, N., & Ader, R. (1987). Behaviorally conditioned enhancement of delayed-type hypersensitivity in the mouse. *Brain Behavior Immunology, 1,* 64.

Bowe, C. A. (1984). Spatial relations in animal learning and behavior. *The Psychological Record, 34,* 181–209.

Bower, G. H., & Hilgard, E. R. (1981). *Theories of learning* (5th ed). Englewood Cliffs, NJ: Prentice Hall.

Bray, G. A. (1976). *The obese patient.* Philadelphia: Saunders.

Breland, K., & Breland, M. (1961). The misbehavior of organisms. *American Psychologist, 16,* 681–684.

Breslau, N., Davis, G. C., Andreski, P., & Peterson, E. (1991). Traumatic events and post-traumatic stress disorder in an urban population of young adults. *Archives of General Psychiatry, 40,* 216–222.

Brett, L. P., Hankins, W. G., & Garcia, J. (1976). Prey-lithium aversions III: Buteo hawks. *Behavioral Biology, 17,* 87–98.

Brown, J. S., & Cunningham, C. L. (1981). The paradox of persisting self-punitive behavior. *Neuroscience & Biobehavioral Reviews, 5,* 343–354.

Brown, P. L., & Jenkins, H. M. (1968). Autoshaping the pigeon's key peck. *Journal of the Experimental Analysis of Behavior, 11,* 1–8.

Brown, R., & Hanlon, C. (1970). Derivational complexity and the order of acquisition of speech. In R. Brown (Ed.), *Psycholinguistics.* New York: Free Press.

Buchwald, A. M., Coyne, J. C., & Cole, C. S. (1978). A critical evaluation of the learned helplessness model of depression. *Journal of Abnormal Psychology, 87,* 180–193.

Buckabee, C. I., & Abramson, D. A. (1996). Methodological considerations in classical conditioning of the proboscis extension reflex in honeybees (*Apis mellifera*): Support for the single US method.

Buckley, K. W. (1989). *Mechanical man: John Broadus Watson and the beginnings of behaviorism.* New York: Guilford Press.

Bull, D. F., Brown, R., King, M. G., & Husband, A. J. (1991). Modulation of body temperature through taste aversion conditioning. *Physiology and Behavior, 49,* 1229–1233.

Bull, D. F., Brown, R., King, M. G., Husband, A. J., & Pfister, H. P. (1992). Thermoregulation: Modulation of body temperature through behavioral conditioning. In A. J. Husband (Ed.), *Behavior and immunity.* London: CRC Press.

Bull, J. A. III, & Overmier, J. B. (1968). Additive and subtractive properties of excitation and inhibition. *Journal of Comparative and Physiological Psychology, 66,* 511–514.

Burgess, A. W., & Holstrom, E. (1979). Adaptive strategies in recovery from rape. *American Journal of Psychiatry, 136,* 1278–1282.

Bush, R. R., & Mosteller, F. (1951). A model for stimulus generalization and discrimination. *Psychological Review, 58,* 413–423.

Caggiula, A. R., & Hoebel, B. G. (1966). "Copulation-reward" site in the posterior hypothalamus. *Science, 153,* 1284–1285.

Camp, D. S., Raymond, G. A., & Church, R. M. (1962). Response suppression as a function of the schedule of punishment. *Psychonomic Science, 5,* 23–24.

Campbell, D. H., Capaldi, E. D., & Myers, D. E. (1987). Conditioned flavor preferences as a function of deprivation level: Preferences or aversions? *Animal Learning and Behavior, 15,* 193–200.

Candland, D. K. (1993). *Feral children and clever animals.* Oxford: Oxford University Press.

Capaldi, E. D., Campbell, D. H., Sheffer, J. D., & Bradford, J. P. (1987). Conditioned flavor preferences based on delayed caloric consequences. *Journal of Experimental Psychology: Animal Behavior Processes, 13,* 150–155.

Capaldi, E. D., & Myers, D. E. (1982). Taste preferences as a function of food deprivation during original taste exposure. *Animal Learning and Behavior, 10,* 211–219.

Capaldi, E. D., & Powley, T. L. (Eds.). (1990). *Taste, experience, and feeding.* Washington, DC: American Psychological Society.

Capaldi, E. J., & Miller, D. J. (1988). Counting in rats: Its functional significance and the independent cognitive processes that constitute it. *Journal of Experimental Psychology: Animal Behavior Processes, 14,* 3–17.

Capaldi, E. J., & Molina, P. (1979). Element

discriminability as a determinant of serial pattern learning. *Animal Learning & Behavior, 7,* 318–322.

Capaldi, E. J., Verry, D. R., Nawrocki, T. M., & Miller, D. J. (1984). Serial learning, interim association, phrasing cues, interference, overshadowing, chunking, memory, and extinction. *Animal Learning & Behavior, 12,* 7–20.

Carew, T. J., Hawkins, R. D., & Kandel, E. (1983). Differential classical conditioning of a defensive withdrawal reflex in *Aplysia californica. Science, 219,* 397–400.

Carlson, N. R. (1992). *Foundations of physiological psychology* (2nd ed.). Boston: Allyn & Bacon.

Carter, Forrest. (1976). *The education of Little Tree.* Albuquerque: University of New Mexico Press.

Chambers, K. C. (1990). A neural model for conditioned taste aversions. *Annual Review of Neuroscience, 13,* 373–385.

Chomsky, N. (1965). *Aspects of the theory of syntax.* Cambridge, MA: MIT Press.

Chomsky, N. (1972). *Language and mind.* New York: Harcourt Brace Jovanovich.

Chomsky, N. (1975). *Reflections on language.* New York: Pantheon.

Chomsky, N. (1980). *Rules and representations.* New York: Columbia University Press.

Church, R. M., Wooten, C. L., & Matthews, T. J. (1970). Discriminative punishment and the conditioned emotional response. *Learning and Motivation, 1,* 1–17.

Cicero, S. D., & Tryon, W. W. (1989). Classical conditioning of meaning—II. A replication of triplet associative extension. *Journal of Behavioral Therapy and Experimental Psychiatry, 20,* 197–202.

Coleman, S. R., & Gormezano, I. (1979). Classical conditioning and the "law of effect": Historical and empirical assessment. *Behaviorism, 7,* 1–33.

Collier, G. (1983). Life in a closed economy: The ecology of learning and motivation. In M. D. Zeiler & P. Harzem (Eds.), *Advances in analysis of behavior: Vol. 3: Biological factors in learning.* Chichester, England: Wiley.

Collier, G., Hirsch, E., & Hamlin, P. H. (1972). The ecological determinants of reinforcement in the rat. *Physiology & Behavior, 9,* 705–716.

Collier, G., Johnson, D. F., Borin, G., & Mathis,

C. E. (1994). Drinking in a patchy environment: The effect of the price of water. *Journal of the Experimental Analysis of Behavior, 62,* 169–184.

Conger, R., & Killeen, P. (1976). Use of concurrent operants in small group research. *Pacific Sociological Review, 17,* 399–416.

Corballis, M. C. (1989). Laterality and human evolution. *Psychological Review, 96,* 494–505.

Corballis, M. C. (1991). The lopsided ape. Oxford: Oxford University Press.

Curtiss, S. (1977). *Genie: A psycholinguistic study of a modern day wild child.* New York: Academic Press.

D'Amato, M. R., Salmon, D. P., & Colombo, M. (1985). Extent and limits of the matching concept in monkeys (*Cebus apella*). *Journal of Experimental Psychology: Animal Behavior Processes, 11,* 35–51.

D'Amato, M. R., & Schiff, E. (1964). Further studies of overlearning and position reversal learning. *Psychological Reports, 14,* 380–382.

Dantzer, R., Arnone, M., & Mormede, P. (1980). Effect of frustration on behavior and plasma corticosteroid levels in pigs. *Physiology & Behavior, 24,* 1–4.

Dantzer, R., & Kelley, K. W. (1989). Stress and immunity: An integrated view of relationships between the brain and the immune system. *Life Sciences, 44,* 1995–2008.

Darwin, C. (1859/1962). *The origin of species.* New York: Collier Books.

Darwin, C. (1871). *The descent of man and selection in relation to sex.* London: John Murray.

Darwin, C. (1872/1965). *The expression of emotions in man and animals.* Chicago: University of Chicago Press.

Davey, G. C. L. (1992). Classical conditioning and the acquisition of human fears and phobias: A review and synthesis of the literature. *Advances in Behavior Research & Therapy, 14,* 29–66.

Davis, C. M. (1928). Self-selection of diet by newly weaned infants. *American Journal of Diseases of Children, 36,* 651–659.

Davis, C. M. (1939). The results of self-selection of diets by young children. *The Canadian Medical Association Journal, 41,* 257–261.

Davis, M. (1974). Sensitization of the rat startle response by noise. *Journal of Comparative and Physiological Psychology, 87,* 571–581.

Davis, M., & File, S. E. (1984). Intrinsic and extrinsic mechanisms of habituation and sensitization: Implications for the design and analysis of experiments. In H. V. S. Peeke & L. Petrinovich (Eds.), *Habituation, sensitization, and behavior.* New York: Academic Press.

Davison, M. (1991). Choice, changeover, and travel: A quantitative model. *Journal of the Experimental Analysis of Behavior, 55,* 47–61.

Dawkins, R. (1976). *The selfish gene.* London: Oxford University Press.

Dawkins, R. (1995). The evolved imagination. *Natural History, 104,* 12–24.

Deems, D. A., Oetting, R. L., Sherman, J. E., & Garcia, J. (1986). Hungry, but not thirsty, rats prefer flavors paired with ethanol. *Physiology and Behavior, 36,* 141–144.

Degler, C. N. (1991). *In search of human nature.* New York: Oxford University Press.

Dennett, D. C. (1975). Why the law of effect will not go away. *Journal of the Theory of Social Behavior, 5,* 169–187.

Dennett, D. C. (1983). Intentional systems in cognitive ethology: The "Panglossian paradigm" defended. *The Behavioral and Brain Sciences, 6,* 343–355.

Dennett, D. C. (1995). *Darwin's dangerous idea.* New York: Simon & Schuster.

Dess, N. K. (1991). Ingestion and emotional health. *Human Nature, 2,* 235–269.

Dess, N. K., & Minor, T. R. (1996). Taste and emotionality in rats selectively bred for high versus low saccharin intake. *Animal Learning & Behavior, 24,* 105–115.

Dethier, V. G. (1978). Other tastes, other worlds. *Science, 201,* 224–228.

Deutsch, R. (1974). Conditioned hypoglycemia: A mechanism for saccharin-induced sensitivity to insulin in the rat. *Journal of Comparative and Physiological Psychology,* 86, 350–358.

Dews, P. B. (1958). Studies on behavior. IV: Stimulant actions of methamphetamine. *Journal of Pharmacology and Experimental Therapeutics, 122,* 137–147.

Diamond, A. (1988). Differences between adult and infant cognition: Is the crucial variable presence or absence of language? In L. Weiskrantz (Ed.), *Thought without language.* Oxford, UK: Clarendon Press.

Diamond, J. (1992). *The third chimpanzee: The evolution and future of the human animal.* New York: HarperCollins.

Dickinson, A. (1985). Actions and habits: The development of behavioural autonomy. *Philosophical Transactions of the Royal Society (London), B308,* 67–78.

Dickinson, A. (1988). Intentionality in animal conditioning. In L. Weiskrantz (Ed.), *Thought without language.* Oxford, UK: Clarendon Press.

Dinsmore, J. A. (1954). Punishment I. The avoidance hypothesis. *Psychological Review, 61,* 34–46.

Dinsmore, J. A. (1977). Escape, avoidance, punishment: Where do we stand? *Journal of the Experimental Analysis of Behavior, 28,* 83–95.

Domjan, M. (1977). Attenuation and enhancement of neophobia for edible substances. In L. M. Barker, M. R. Best, & M. Domjan (Eds.), *Learning mechanisms in food selection.* Waco, TX: Baylor University Press.

Domjan, M. (1983). Biological constraints on instrumental and classical conditioning: Implications for general process theory. In G. H. Bower (Ed.), *The pyschology of learning and motivation* (Vol. 17). New York: Academic Press.

Domjan, M. (1987a). Animal learning comes of age. *American Psychologist, 42,* 556–564.

Domjan, M. (1987b). Comparative psychology and the study of animal learning. *Journal of comparative psychology, 101,* 237–241.

Domjan, M. (1992). Adult learning and mate choice: Possibilities and experimental evidence. *American Zoologist, 32,* 48–61.

Domjan, M. (1994). Formulation of a behavior system for sexual conditioning. *Psychonomic Bulletin & Review, 1,* 421–428.

Domjan, M., & Burkhard, B. (1988). *The principles of learning and behavior.* Belmont, CA: Brooks/Cole.

Domjan, M., O'vary, D., & Greene, P. (1988). Conditioning of appetitive and consummatory behavior in male Japanese quail (*Coturnix coturnix japonica*). *Journal of Comparative Psychology, 105,* 157–164.

Domjan, M., & Wilson, N. E. (1972). Specificity of cue to consequence in aversion learning in the rat. *Psychonomic Science, 26,* 143–145.

Dorland's Illustrated Medical Dictionary, 25th

Edition (1974). Philadelphia: W. B. Saunders Press.

Durlach, P. J., & Rescorla, R. A. (1980). Potentiation rather than overshadowing in flavor-aversion learning: An analysis in terms of within-compound associations. *Journal of Experimental Psychology: Animal Behavior Processes, 6,* 175–187.

Eibl-Eibesfeldt, I. (1970). *Ethology: The biology of behavior.* New York: Holt, Rinehart and Winston.

Eikelboom, R., & Stewart, J. (1982). Conditioning of drug-induced physiological responses. *Psychological Review, 89,* 507–528.

Elkins, R. L. (1973). Attenuation of drug-induced baitshyness to a palatable solution as an increasing function of its availability prior to conditioning. *Behavioral Biology, 9,* 221–226.

Ellis, A., & Abarbanel, A. (Eds.). (1961). *The encyclopedia of sexual behavior.* New York: Hawthorn Books.

Emmelkamp, P. M. G. (1982). *Phobic and obsessive-compulsive disorders: Theory, research, and practice.* New York: Plenum.

Estes, W. K., & Skinner, B. F. (1941). Some quantitative properties of anxiety. *Journal of Experimental Psychology, 29,* 390–400.

Falk, J. L. (1961). Production of polydipsia in normal rats by an intermittent food schedule. *Science, 133,* 195–196.

Farrar, D. (1967). Picture memory in the chimpanzee. *Perceptual and Motor Skills, 25,* 305–315.

Felten, D. (1993). *The brain and the immune system.* In B. Moyers (Ed.), *Healing and the mind.* New York: Doubleday.

Fielding, L., Wilson, P., & Anderson, R. (1987). A new focus on free reading: The role of trade books in reading. In T. E. Raphael & R. Reynolds (Eds.), *Contexts of literacy.* New York: Longman.

Fiori, L., Barnet, R., & Miller, R. (1994). Renewal of Pavlovian conditioned inhibition. *Animal Learning and Behavior, 22,* 47–52.

Fisher, J., & Hinde, R. A. (1949). The opening of milk bottles by birds. *British Birds, 42,* 347–358.

Flaherty, C. F. (1982). Incentive contrast: A review of behavioral changes following shifts in reward. *Animal Learning and Behavior, 10,* 409–440.

Flaherty, C. F. (1991). Incentive contrast and selected models of anxiety. In L. Dachowski & C. F. Flaherty (Eds.), *Current topics in animal learning.* Hillsdale, NJ: Erlbaum.

Flynn, J. C. (1991). *Cocaine.* New York: Birch Lane Press.

Foa, E. B., Zinbarg, R., & Rothbaum, B. O. (1992). Uncontrollability and unpredictability in post-traumatic stress disorder: An animal model. *Psychological Bulletin, 112,* 218–238.

Fordyce, W. E., Brockway, J. A., Bergman, J. A., & Spengler, D. (1986). Acute back pain: A control group comparison of behavioral vs. traditional management methods. *Journal of Behavioral Medicine, 9,* 127–140.

Fountain, S. B., Henne, D. R., & Hulse, S. H. (1984). Phasing cues and hierarchical organization in serial pattern learning by rats. *Journal of Experimental Psychology: Animal Behavior Processes, 10,* 30–45.

French, S. (1986). *Decision theory.* New York: Halstead Press.

Freud, S. (1930/1961). *Civilization and its discontents.* New York: Norton.

Furumoto, L., & Scarborough, E. S. (1987). Placing women in the history of comparative psychology: Margaret Floy Washburn and Margaret Morse Nice. In E. Tobach, (Ed.), *Historical perspectives and the international status of comparative psychology.* Hillsdale, NJ: Erlbaum.

Galef, B. G. (1984). Reciprocal heuristics: A discussion of the relationship of the study of learned behavior in laboratory and field. *Learning and Motivation, 15,* 479–493.

Gamzu, E. (1977). The multifaceted nature of taste-aversion-inducing agents: Is there a single common factor? In L. M. Barker, M. R. Best, & M. Domjan (Eds.), *Learning mechanisms in food selection.* Waco, TX: Baylor University Press.

Gamzu, E. R. (1985). A pharmacological perspective on drugs used in establishing conditioned food aversions. *Annals of the New York Academy of Sciences.*

Gamzu, E., & Schwartz, B. (1973). The maintenance of key pecking by stimulus-contingent and response-independent food presentation. *Journal of the Experimental Analysis of Behavior, 19,* 65–72.

Gamzu, E., & Williams, D. R. (1971). Classical conditioning of a complex skeletal act. *Science, 171,* 923–925.

Gamzu, E., & Williams, D. R. (1973). Associative factors underlying the pigeon's key pecking in autoshaping procedures. *Journal of the Experimental Analysis of Behavior, 19,* 225–232.

Gamzu, E., Vincent, G., & Boff, E. (1985). A pharmacological perspective on drugs used in establishing conditioned food aversions. *Annals of the New York Academy of Sciences, 443,* 231–249.

Gantt, W. H. (1964). Schizokinis. In J. Wolpe, A. Salter, & L. J. Reyna (Eds.), *The conditioning therapies.* New York: Holt, Rinehart, & Winston.

Gantt, W. H. (1966). Conditional or conditioned, reflex or response? *Conditioned Reflex, 1,* 69–74.

Garb, J. J., & Stunkard, A. J. (1974). Taste aversions in man. *American Journal of Psychiatry, 131,* 1204–1207.

Garcia, J., Ervin, F. R., & Koelling, R. A. (1966). Learning with prolonged delay of reinforcement. *Psychonomic Science, 5,* 121–122.

Garcia, J., Ervin, F. R., Yorke, C. H., & Koelling, R. A. (1967). Conditioning with delayed vitamin injections. *Science, 155,* 716–718.

Garcia, J., Hankins, W. G., & Rusiniak, K. W. (1974). Behavioral regulation of the milieu interne in man and rat. *Science, 185,* 824–831.

Garcia, J., Kimeldorf, D. J., & Koelling, R. A. (1955). Conditioned aversion to saccharin resulting from exposure to gamma radiation. *Science, 122,* 157–158.

Garcia, J., & Koelling, R. A. (1966). Relation of cue to consequence in avoidance learning. *Psychonomic Science, 4,* 123–124.

Gardner, B. R., & Gardner, R. A. (1971). Two-way communication with an infant chimpanzee. In A. M. Schrier & F. Stollnitz (Eds.), *Behavior of nonhuman primates* (Vol. 4). New York: Academic Press.

Gardner, H. (1985). *The minds new science: A history of the cognitive revolution.* New York: Basic Books.

Gardner, R. A., & Gardner, B. T. (1969). Teaching sign language to a chimpanzee. *Science, 165,* 664–672.

Gauci, M., Husband, A. J., & King, M. G. (1992). Conditioned allergic rhinitis: A model for central nervous system and immune system interaction in IgE-mediated allergic reactions. In A. J. Husband (Ed.), *Behavior and immunity.* London: CRC Press.

Geshwind, N. (1970). The organization of language and the brain. *Science, 170,* 940–944.

Gibbon, J., & Church, R. M. (1984). Sources of variance in information processing theory of timing. In H. L. Roitblat, T. G. Bever, & H. S. Terrace (Eds.), *Animal cognition.* Hillsdale, NJ: Erlbaum.

Gibbons, A. (1993). Evolutionists take the long view of sex and violence. *Science, 261,* 987–988.

Gillan, D. J. (1981). Reasoning in the chimpanzee: II. Transitive inference. *Journal of Experimental Psychology: Animal Behavior Processes, 7,* 150–164.

Gillan, D. J. (1983). Inferences and the acquisition of knowledge by chimpanzees. In M. L. Commons, R. J. Herrnstein, & A. R. Wagner (Eds.), *Quantitative analyses of behavior: Vol. 4; Discrimination processes.* Cambridge, MA: Ballinger.

Gillan, D. J., Premack, D., & Woodruff, G. (1981). Reasoning in the chimpanzee: I. Analogical reasoning. *Journal of Experimental Psychology: Animal Behavior Processes, 7,* 1–17.

Goddard, M. E., & Beilharz, R. G. (1983). Genetics of traits which determine the suitability of dogs as guide-dogs for the blind. *Applied Animal Ethology, 9,* 299–315.

Gorczynski, R. M., Macrae, S., & Kennedy, M. (1982). Conditioned immune response associated with allogeneic skin grafts in mice. *Journal of Immunology, 129,* 704.

Gormezano, I., Kehoe, E. J., & Marshall, B. S. (1983). Twenty years of classical conditioning research with the rabbit. In J. M. Prague & A. N. Epstein (Eds.), *Progress in psychobiology and physiological psychology* (Vol. 10). New York: Academic Press.

Gormezano, I., & Tait, R. W. (1976). The Pavlovian analysis of instrumental conditioning. *The Pavlovian Journal of Biological Science, 11,* 37–55.

Gottlieb, G. (1984). Evolutionary trends and evolutionary origins: Relevance to theory in comparative psychology. *Psychological Review, 91,* 448–456.

Gould, J. L., & Marler, P. (1987). Learning by instinct. *Scientific American, 256,* 74–85.

Gould, S. J. (1989). *Wonderful life: The burgess shale and the nature of history.* New York: W. W. Norton.

Gould, S. J., & Lewontin, R. C. (1979). Spandrals of San Marco and the Panglossian paradigm: A critique of the adaptionist program. *Proceedings of the Royal Society of Britain, 205,* 581–598.

Grahame, N. J., Barnet, R. C., Gunther, L. M., & Miller, R. R. (1994). Latent inhibition as a performance deficit resulting from CS-context associations. *Animal Learning & Behavior, 22,* 395–408.

Gratton, A. P., & Wise, R. A. (1988). Comparisons of connectivity and conduction velocities for medial forebrain bundle fibers subserving stimulation-induced feeding and brain stimulation reward. *Brain Research, 438,* 264–270.

Gray, J. A. B. (1964). *Pavlov's typology.* New York: Pergammon Press.

Green, K. F., & Garcia, J. (1971). Recuperation from illness: Flavor enhancement for rats. *Science, 173,* 749–751.

Green, L., Kagel, J. H., & Battalio, R. C. (1987). Consumption-leisure tradeoffs in pigeons: Effects of changing marginal wage rates by varying amount of reinforcement. *Journal of the Experimental Analysis of Behavior, 47,* 17–28.

Greenberg, G. (1987). Historical review of the use of captive animals in comparative psychology. In E. Tobach (Ed.), *Historical perspectives and the international status of comparative psychology.* Hillsdale, NJ: Erlbaum.

Griffin, D. R. (1978). Prospects for a cognitive ethology. *Behavioral and Brain Sciences, 4,* 527–538.

Griffin, D. R. (1985). Animal consciousness. *Neuroscience and Biobehavioral Reviews, 9,* 615–622.

Griffin, D. R. (1992) *Animal minds.* Chicago: University of Chicago Press.

Grossarth-Maticek, R., & Eysenck, H. J. (1989). Length of survival and lymphocyte percentage in women with mammary cancer as a function of psychotherapy. *Psychological Reports, 65,* 315–321.

Grundel, R. (1992). How the mountain chickadee procures more food in less time for its nestlings. *Behavioral Ecology and Sociobiology, 31,* 291–300.

Guttman, N., & Kalish, H. I. (1956). Discriminability and stimulus generalization. *Journal of Experimental Psychology, 51,* 79–88.

Haig, K. A., Rawlins, J. N. P., Olton, D. S., Mead, A., & Taylor, B. (1983). Food searching strategies of rats: Variables affecting the relative strength of stay and shift strategies. *Journal of Experimental Psychology: Animal Behavior Processes, 9,* 337–348.

Hake, D. F., & Azrin, N. H. (1965). Conditioned punishment. *Journal of the Experimental Analysis of Behavior, 8,* 279–293.

Hall, G. (1991). *Perceptual and associative learning.* Oxford, UK: Clarendon Press.

Hall, J. F. (1982). *An invitation to learning & memory.* Boston: Allyn & Bacon.

Hallam, S. C., Matzel, L. D., Sloat, J. S., & Miller, R. R. (1990). Excitation and inhibition as a function of posttraining extinction of the excitatory cue used in Pavlovian inhibition training. *Learning and Motivation, 21,* 59–84.

Halliday, T. R., & Slater, P. J. B. (Eds.). (1983). *Animal behavior: Vol. 3. Genes, development, and learning.* New York: W. H. Freeman.

Hanson, H. M. (1959). Effects of discrimination training on stimulus generalization. *Journal of Experimental Psychology, 58,* 321–333.

Harder, L. D., & Real, L. A. (1987). Why are bumble bees risk averse? *Ecology, 68(4),* 1104–1108.

Harlow, H. F. (1949). The formation of learning sets. *Psychological Review, 56,* 51–65.

Harlow, H. F. (1963). Basic social capacity of primates. In C. H. Southwick (Ed.), *Primate social behavior.* Princeton, NJ: Van Nostrand.

Harlow, H. F. (1969). Age-mate or peer affectional system. In D. S. Lehrman, R. H. Hinde, & E. Shaw (Eds.), *Advances in the study of behavior* (Vol. 2). New York: Academic Press.

Harlow, H. F., & Harlow, M. K. (1962a). The effect of rearing conditions on behavior. *Bulletin of the Menninger Clinic, 26,* 213–224.

Harlow, H. F., & Harlow, M. K. (1962b). Social deprivation in monkeys. *Scientific American, 207,* 137–146.

Harriman, A. E. (1955). The effect of a preoperative preference for sugar over salt upon compensatory salt selection by adrenalectomized rats. *Journal of Nutrition, 57,* 271–276.

Hartman, T. F., & Grant, D. A. (1960). Effect of intermittent reinforcement on acquisition, extinction, and spontaneous recovery of the conditioned eyelid response. *Journal of Experimental Psychology, 60,* 89–96.

Hayes, C. (1951). *The ape in our house.* New York: Harper & Row.

Hearst, E. (1972). Some persistent problems in the analysis of conditioned inhibition. In R. A. Boakes & M. S. Halliday (Eds.), *Inhibition and learning.* London: Academic Press.

Hearst, E., & Jenkins, H. M. (1974). Sign-tracking: The stimulus-reinforcer relation and directed action. Austin, TX: Psychonomic Society.

Heath, R. G. (1963). Electrical self-stimulation of the brain in man. *American Journal of Psychiatry, 120,* 571–577.

Hedges, S. B., Kuman, S., Tamura, K., & Stoneking, M. (1991). Human origins and analysis of mitochondrial DNA sequences. *Science, 255,* 737–739.

Heinrich, R. L., Cohen, M. J., Naliboff, B. C., Collins, G. A., & Bonebakker, A. D. (1985). Comparing physical and behavioral therapy for chronic low back pain on physical abilities, psychological distress, and patients' perceptions. *Journal of Behavioral Medicine, 8,* 61–78.

Herman, L. M. (1989). In which procrustean bed does the sea lion sleep tonight? *Psychological Record, 39,* 19–50.

Herman, L. M., Richards, D. G., & Wolz, J. P. (1984). Comprehension of sentences by bottlenosed dolphins. *Cognition, 16,* 129–219.

Herrick, C. J. (1948). *The brain of the tiger salamander.* Chicago: University of Chicago Press.

Herrnstein, R. J. (1961). Relative and absolute strength of response as a function of frequency of reinforcement. *Journal of the Experimental Analysis of Behavior, 4,* 267–272.

Herrnstein, R. J. (1969). Method and theory in the study of avoidance. *Psychological Review, 76,* 49–69.

Herrnstein, R. J. (1970). On the law of effect. *Journal of the Experimental Analysis of Behavior, 13,* 243–266.

Herrnstein, R. J. (1984). Objects, categories, and discriminative stimuli. In H. L. Roit-

blat, T. G. Bever, & H. S. Terrace (Eds.), *Animal cognition.* Hillsdale, NJ: Erlbaum.

Herrnstein, R. J., & deVilliers, P. A. (1980). Fish as a natural category for people and pigeons. In G. H. Bower (Ed.), *The psychology of learning and motivation* (Vol. 14, pp. 60–97). New York: Academic Press.

Herrnstein, R. J., & Hineline, P. N. (1966). Negative reinforcement as shock frequency reduction. *Journal of the Experimental Analysis of Behavior, 9,* 421–430.

Herrnstein, R. J., Loveland, D. H., & Cable, C. (1976). Natural concepts in pigeons. *Journal of Experimental Psychology: Animal Behavior Processes, 2,* 285–301.

Herrnstein, R. J., & Vaughan, W., Jr. (1980). Melioration and behavioral allocation. In J. E. R. Staddon (Ed.), *Limits to action.* New York: Academic Press.

Heth, C. D. (1976). Simultaneous and backward fear conditioning as a function of number of CS-UCS pairings. *Journal of Experimental Psychology: Animal Behavior Processes, 2,* 117–129.

Hilgard, J. R. (1979). *Personality and hypnosis: A study of imaginative involvement* (2nd ed.). Chicago: University of Chicago Press.

Hinde, R. A. (1981). Biological approaches to the study of learning: Does Johnston provide a new alternative? *Behavior and Brain, 4,* 146–147.

Hintzman, D. L. (1986). Schema extraction in a multiple trace memory model. *Psychological Review, 93,* 411–428.

Hodos, W., & Campbell, C. B. G. (1969). *Scala Naturae:* Why there is no theory in comparative psychology. *Psychological Review, 76,* 337–350.

Hogan, J. (1973). How young chicks learn to recognize food. In R. A. Hinde & J. Stevenson-Hinde (Eds.), *Constraints on learning.* London: Academic Press.

Hogan, J. (1977). The ontogeny of food preferences in chicks and other animals. In L. M. Barker, M. R. Best, & M. Domjan (Eds.), *Learning mechanisms in food selection.* Waco, TX: Baylor University Press.

Holender, D. (1987). Synchronic description of present-day writing systems: Some implications for reading research. In J. K. O'Regan & A. Levy-Schoen (Eds.), *Eye movements: From physiology to cognition.* Amsterdam: Elsevier North Holland.

Holland, P. C. (1986). Temporal determinants of occasion setting in feature-positive discriminations. *Animal Learning and Behavior, 14,* 111–120.

Holland, P. C. (1990). Event representation in Pavlovian conditioning: Image and action. *Cognition, 37,* 105–131.

Holz, W. C., & Azrin, N. H. (1961). Discriminative properties of punishment. *Journal of the Experimental Analysis of Behavior, 4,* 225–232.

Honig, W. K., Boneau, C. A., Burstein, K. R., & Pennypacker, H. S. (1963). Positive and negative generalization gradients obtained under equivalent training conditions. *Journal of Comparative and Physiological Psychology, 56,* 111–115.

Honig, W. K., & James, P. H. R. (Eds.). (1971). *Animal memory.* New York: Academic Press.

Hsu, L. K. G. (1990). *Eating disorders.* New York: Guilford Press.

Hull, C. L. (1932). The goal gradient hypothesis and maze learning. *Psychological Review, 39,* 25–43.

Hull, C. L. (1943). *Principles of behavior.* New York: Appleton.

Hull, C. L. (1952). *A behavior system.* New Haven: Yale University Press.

Hulse, S. H. (1978). Cognitive structure and serial pattern learning by animals. In S. H. Hulse, H. F. Fowler, & W. K. Honig (Eds.), *Cognitive processes in animal behavior.* Hillsdale, NJ: Erlbaum.

Hursh, S. R., Navarick, D. J., & Fantino, E. (1974). "Automaintenance": The role of reinforcement. *Journal of the Experimental Analysis of Behavior, 21,* 117–124.

Husband, A. J. (Ed.). (1992). *Behavior and immunity.* London: CRC Press.

Jaynes, J. (1969). The historical origins of "ethology" and "comparative psychology." *Animal Behavior, 17,* 601–606.

Jemmott, J. B. III, Hellman, C., McClelland, D. C., Locke, S. E., Kraus, L., Williams, R. M., & Valeri, C. R. (1990). Motivational syndromes associated with natural killer cell activity. *Journal of Behavioral Medicine, 13,* 53–73.

Jemmott, J. B. III, & Magloire, K. (1988). Academic stress, social support, and secretory immunoglobulin A. *Journal of Personality and Social Psychology, 55,* 803–810.

Jenkins, H. M., & Moore, B. R. (1973). The form of the autoshaped response with food or water reinforcers. *Journal of the Experimental Analysis of Behavior, 20,* 163–181.

Jirik-Babb, P., & Katz, J. L. (1988). Impairment of taste perception in anorexia nervosa and bulimia. *International Journal of Eating Disorders, 7,* 353–360.

Johnson, M. H. (1992). Imprinting and the development of face recognition: From chick to man. *Current Directions in Psychological Science, 1,* 52–54.

Jonas, G. (1972). *Visceral learning.* New York: Viking Press.

Justesen, D. R., Braun, E. W., Garrison, R. G., & Pendleton, R. B. (1970). Pharmacological differentiation of allergic and classically conditioned asthma in the guinea pig. *Science, 170,* 864–866.

Kagel, J. H., Rachlin, H., Green, L., Battalio, R. C., Basmann, R. L., & Klemm, W. R. (1975). Experimental studies of consumer demand behavior using laboratory animals. *Economic Inquiry, 13,* 22–38.

Kahneman, D., & Tversky, A. (1979). Prospect theory: An analysis of decision under risk. *Econometrica, 47,* 263–291.

Kalat, J. (1977). Status of "learned-safety" or "learned noncorrelation" as a mechanism in taste aversion learning. In L. M. Barker, M. R. Best, & M. Domjan (Eds.), *Learning mechanisms in food selection.* Waco, TX: Baylor University Press.

Kalat, J. (1984, 1994). *Biological psychology.* Belmont, CA: Wadsworth.

Kalat, J., & Rozin, P. (1973). "Learned safety" as a mechanism in long-delay taste-aversion learning in rats. *Journal of Comparative and Physiological Psychology, 83,* 198–207.

Kamin, L. J. (1965). Temporal and intensity characteristics of the conditioned stimulus. In W. F. Prodasy (Ed.), *Classical conditioning.* New York: Appleton-Century-Crofts.

Kamin, L. J. (1968). "Attention-like" processes in classical conditioning. In M. R. Jones (Ed.), *Miami symposium on the prediction of behavior: Aversive stimulation.* Miami: University of Miami Press.

Kamin, L. J. (1969). Predictability, surprise, attention, and conditioning. In B. A. Campbell & R. M. Church (Eds.), *Punishment and aversive behavior.* New York: Appleton-Century-Crofts.

Kamin, L. J., & Brimer, C. J. (1963). The effects of intensity of conditioned and unconditioned stimuli on a conditioned emotional response. *Canadian Journal of Psychology, 17,* 194–200.

Kamin, L. J., Brimer, C. J., & Black, A. H. (1963). Conditioned suppression as a monitor of fear of the CS in the course of avoidance training. *Journal of Comparative and Physiological Psychology, 56,* 497–501.

Kandel, E. R., & Schwartz, J. H. (1982). Molecular biology of learning: Modulation of transmitter release. *Science, 218,* 433–443.

Kaplan, R. M. (1984). The connection between clinical health promotion and health status. *American Psychologist, 39,* 755–765.

Karsh, E. B. (1962). Effects of number of rewarded trials and intensity of punishment on running speed. *Journal of Comparative and Physiological Psychology, 55,* 44–51.

Kassel, J. D., & Shiffman, S. (1992). What can hunger teach us about drug craving? A comparative analysis of the two constructs. *Advances in Behavioral Research and Therapy, 14,* 141–167.

Katz, S. (Ed.). (1975). *Biological anthropology: Selected readings from Scientific American.* San Francisco: W. H. Freeman.

Katz, S. (1982). Food, behavior, and biocultural evolution. In L. M. Barker (Ed.), *The psychobiology of human food selection.* Westport, CT: AVI Publishing.

Kellogg, W. N. (1961). *Porpoises and sonar.* Chicago: University of Chicago Press.

Kellogg, W. N., & Kellogg, L. A. (1933). *The ape and the child.* New York: Whittlesey House.

Kelsey, J. E., & Allison, J. (1976). Fixed-ratio lever pressing by VMH rats: Work vs. accessibility of sucrose reward. *Physiology and Behavior, 17,* 749–754.

Kelso, S. R., Ganong, A. H., & Brown, T. H. (1986). Hebbian synapses in hippocampus. *Proceedings of the National Academy of Sciences USA, 83,* 5326–5330.

Kertesz, A. (1988). Cognitive function in severe aphasia. In L. Weiskrantz (Ed.), *Thought without language.* Oxford, UK: Clarendon Press.

Kesner, R. P. (1990). New approaches to the study of comparative cognition. In *Research monograph by the National Institute on Drug Abuse: Alcohol, drug abuse, and mental health administration.* (pps. 22–36).

Washington, DC: United States Department of Health and Human Services.

Kimble, G. A. (1992). *A modest proposal for a minor revolution in the language of psychology.* Paper presented at the 4th Annual Meeting of the American Psychological Society, San Diego, CA.

Kimmel, H. D., & Kimmel, E. (1970). An instrumental conditioning method for the treatment of enuresis. *Journal of Behavior Therapy and Experimental Psychiatry, 1,* 121–123.

Klopf, A. H. (1988). A neuronal model of classical conditioning. *Psychobiology, 16,* 85–125.

Knowles, J. H. (1977). The responsibility of the individual. In J. H. Knowles (Ed.), *Doing better and feeling worse: Health in the United States.* New York: W. W. Norton.

Koestler, F. G., & Barker, L. M. (1965). *The effect on the chimpanzee of rapid decompression to a near vacuum* (Contractor Report No. NASA CR-329). Washington, DC: NASA.

Kolb, L. (1984). The posttraumatic stress disorders of combat: A subgroup with a conditional emotional response. *Military Medicine, 149,* 237–243. (As cited in van der Kolk, B. S. [1987]. *Psychological trauma.* Washington, DC: American Psychiatric Press.)

Kombian, S. B., & Malenka, R. C. (1994). Simultaneous LTP of non-NMDA- and LTD of NMDA-receptor-mediated responses in the nucleus accumbens. *Nature, 368,* 242–246.

Konorski, J. (1948). *Conditioned reflexes and neuron organisation.* Cambridge, UK: Cambridge University Press.

Krane, R. V., & Wagner, A. R. (1975). Taste aversion learning with a delayed shock US: Implications for the "generality of the laws of learning." *Journal of Comparative and Physiological Psychology, 88,* 882–889.

Krank, M. D., & MacQueen, G. M. (1988). Conditioned compensatory responses elicited by environmental signals for cyclophosphamide-induced suppression of antibody production in mice. *Psychobiology, 16,* 229–235.

Kymissis, E. & Poulson, C. L. (1990). The history of imitation in learning theory: The language acquisition process. *Journal of the Experimental Analysis of Behavior, 54,* 113–127.

Lalonde, R. (1994). Cerebellar contributions to instrumental conditioning. *Neuroscience and Biobehavioral Reviews, 18,* 161–170.

Lalonde, R., & Botez, M. I. (1990). The cerebellum and learning processes in animals. *Brain Research Reviews, 15,* 325–332.

Laudenslager, M. L., Ryan, S. M., Drugan, R. C., Hyson, R. L., & Maier, S. E. (1983). Coping and immunosuppression: Inescapable but not escapable shock suppresses lymphocyte proliferation. *Science, 221,* 568–570.

Lavond, D. G., Kim, J. J., & Thompson, R. F. (1993). Mammalian brain substrates of aversive classical conditioning. *Annual Review of Psychology, 44,* 317–342.

Le, A. D., Poulos, C. X., & Cappell, H. (1979). Conditioned tolerance to the hypothermic effect of ethyl alcohol. *Science, 206,* 1109–1110.

Lehner, G. F. J. (1941). A study of the extinction of unconditioned reflexes. *Journal of Experimental Psychology, 29,* 435–456.

Lennartz, R. C., & Weinberger, N. M. (1992). Analysis of response systems in Pavlovian conditioning reveals rapidly versus slowly acquired conditioned responses: Support for two factors, implications for behavior and neurobiology. *Psychobiology, 20,* 93–119.

Leslie, A. L. (1988). The necessity of illusion: Perception and thought in infancy. In L. Weiskrantz (Ed.), *Thought without language.* Oxford, UK: Clarendon Press.

Lett, B. T. (1980). Taste potentiates color-sickness associations in pigeons and quail. *Animal Learning & Behavior, 8,* 193–198.

Levine, S. C., & Carey, S. (1982). Up front: The acquisition of a concept and a word. *Journal of Child Language, 9,* 645–657.

Levis, D. J. (1976). Learned helplessness: A reply and alternative S-R interpretation. *Journal of Experimental Psychology: General, 104,* 47–65.

Lewontin, R. (1981). [Review of Gould's The mismeasure of man]. *New York Times* pp. 12–16. (As quoted in D. C. Dennett [1983]. Intentional systems in cognitive ethology: The "Panglossian paradigm" defended [p. 355]. *The Behavioral and Brain Sciences, 6,* 343–390.)

Lewontin, R. C. (1977). The selfish gene. *Nature, 267,* 202.

Lewontin, R. C. (1983). Gene, organism, and environment. In D. S. Bendell (Ed.), *Evolution from molecules to men.* Cambridge, UK: Cambridge University Press.

Lilly, J. C. (1961). *Man and dolphin.* New York: Doubleday.

Lockard, R. B. (1969). The albino rat—a defensible choice or a bad habit? *American Psychologist, 23,* 734–742.

Locke, J. (1690). An essay concerning human understanding. Reprinted in E. Sprague & P. W. Taylor (Eds.) (1959). *Knowledge and value.* New York: Harcourt, Brace.

Loehlin, J. C., Willerman, L., & Horn, J. M. (1988). Human behavioral genetics. *Annual Review of psychology, 39,* 101–133.

Logue, A. W. (1979). Taste aversion and the generality of the laws of learning. *Psychological Bulletin, 86,* 276–296.

Logue, A. W. (1985). Conditioned food aversion learning in humans. *Annals of the New York Academy of Sciences, 443,* 316–329.

Logue, A. W. (1988). Research on self-control: An integrating framework. *Behavioral and Brain Sciences, 11,* 665–709.

Logue, A. W. (1991). *The psychology of eating and drinking* (2nd ed.). New York: W. H. Freeman.

LoLordo, V. M. (1979). Selective associations. In A. Dickinson & R. A. Boakes (Eds.), *Mechanisms of learning and motivation.* Hillsdale, NJ: Erlbaum.

Long, M. E. (1991). Secrets of animal navigation. *National Geographic, 179,* 70–99.

Lorenz, K. (1935). Der Kumpan in der Umwelt des Vogels; die Artgenosse als auslosende Moment sozialer Verhaltungswiesen. *Journal fur Ornithologie, 83,* 137–213. (As cited in Hess, E. H. [1973]. *Imprinting.* New York: Van Nostrand.)

Lorenz, K., & Tinbergen, N. (1938). Taxis und instinkthandlung in der eirollbewegung der graugans. *Zeitschrift fur Tierpsychology, 2,* 1–29. (As cited in Eibl-Eibesfeldt, I. [1975]. *Ethology, the biology of behavior* [2nd ed.]. New York: Holt, Rinehart, & Winston.)

Lubow, R. E. (1989). *Latent inhibition and conditioned attention theory.* Cambridge, UK: Cambridge University Press.

Lubow, R. E., & Moore, A. U. (1959). Latent inhibition: The effect of nonreinforced preexposure to the conditioned stimulus.

Journal of Comparative and Physiological Psychology, 52, 415–419.

Lucas, F., & Sclafani, A. (1990). Hyperphagia in rats produced by a mixture of fats and sugar. *Physiology and Behavior, 47,* 51–55.

Ludvigson, H. W. (1989). *Commentary: The dilemma of mind and the quest for understanding in comparative psychology.* Paper presented at the 35th Annual Meeting of the Southwestern Comparative Psychological Association, San Antonio, TX.

McCarthy, Cormac. (1992). *All the pretty horses.* New York: Vintage International.

MacCorquodale, K., & Meehl, P. E. (1948). On a distinction between hypothetical constructs and intervening variables. *Psychological Review, 55,* 95–107.

Mackenzie, S. A., Oltenacu, E. A. B., & Houpt, K. A. (1986). Canine behavioral genetics— A review. *Applied Animal Behavior Science, 15,* 365–393.

Mackintosh, N. J. (1983). *Conditioning and associative learning.* New York: Oxford University Press.

McCormick, D. A., & Thompson, R. F. (1984). Cerebellum: Essential involvement in the classically conditioned eyelid response. *Science, 223,* 296–299.

MacLean, P. D. (1970). The limbic brain in relation to the psychoses. In P. Black (Ed.), *Physiological correlates of emotion.* New York: Academic Press.

MacLean, P. D. (1977). The triune brain in conflict. *Psychotherapy & Psychosomatics, 18,* 207–220.

MacNeilage, P. F. (1991). The postural origins theory of neurobiological asymmetries in primates. In N. Krasnegor, D. Rumbaugh, M. Studdert-Kennedy, & R. Schiefelbusch (Eds.), *The biological foundations of language development.* Hillsdale, NJ: Erlbaum.

Maier, S. F., & Jackson, R. L. (1979). Learned helplessness: All of us were right (and wrong): Inescapable shock has multiple effects. In G. H. Bower (Ed.), *The psychology of learning and motivation* (Vol. 13). New York: Academic Press.

Malone, J. C. (1982). The second offspring of general process learning theory: Overt behavior as the ambassador of the mind. *Journal of the Experimental Analysis of Behavior, 38,* 205–209.

Marler, P., & Peters, S. (1988). Sensitive periods for song acquisition from tape recordings and live tutors in the swamp sparrow, *Melospiza georgiana. Ethology, 77,* 76–84.

Maslow, A. (1954). *Motivation and personality.* New York: Harper.

Mason, F. B. (Ed.). (1928). *Creation by evolution.* New York: Macmillan.

Mayr, E. (1991). *One long argument: Charles Darwin and the genesis of modern evolutionary theory.* Cambridge, MA: Harvard University Press.

Meachum, C. L., & Bernstein, I. L. (1990). Conditioned responses to a taste CS paired with LiCl administration. *Behavioral Neuroscience, 104,* 711–715.

Meck, W. H., & Church, R. M. (1983). A mode control model of counting and timing processes. *Journal of Experimental Psychology: Animal Behavior Processes, 9,* 320–334.

Medin, D. L., & Ross, B. H. (1990). *Cognitive psychology.* Fort Worth, TX: Harcourt Brace Jovanovich.

Mehiel, R., & Bolles, R. C. (1984). Learned flavor preferences based on caloric outcome. *Animal Learning and Behavior, 12,* 421–427.

Melchior, C. L., & Tabakoff, B. (1984). A conditioning model of alcohol tolerance. In M. Galanter (Ed.), *Recent developments in alcoholism* (Vol. 2). New York: Plenum Press.

Meltzoff, A. N., & Moore, M. K. (1983). Newborn infants imitate adult facial gestures. *Child Development, 54,* 702–709.

Melzac, R. (1990, February). The tragedy of needless pain. *Scientific American, 262,* 27–33.

Menzel, E. W. (1978). Cognitive mapping in chimpanzees. In S. H. Hulse, H. F. Fowler, & W. K. Honig (Eds.), *Cognitive processes in animal behavior.* Hillsdale, NJ: Erlbaum.

Miller, A. D., & Rugg, M. D. (Eds.). (1992). *The neuro-psychology of consciousness.* London: Academic Press.

Miller, G. A., & Gildea, P. M. (1987). How children learn words. *Scientific American, 257,* 94–99.

Miller, N. E. (1969). Learning of visceral and glandular responses. *Science, 163,* 434–445.

Miller, N. E., & Banuazizi, A. (1968). Instrumental learning by curarized rats of a specific visceral response, intestinal or cardiac. *Journal of Comparative and Physiological Psychology, 65,* 1–7.

Miller, R. R., & Matzel, L. D. (1988). The comparator hypothesis: A response rule for the expression of associations. In G. H. Bower (Ed.), *The psychology of learning and motivation.* Orlando, FL: Academic Press.

Miller, R. R., & Matzel, L. D. (1989). Contingency and relative associative strength. In S. B. Klein & R. R. Mowrer (Eds.), *Contemporary learning theories: Pavlovian conditioning and the status of learning theory.* Hillsdale, NJ: Erlbaum.

Miller, R. R., & Schactman, T. R. (1985a). The several roles of context at the time of retrieval. In P. D. Balsam & A. Tomie (Eds.), *Context and learning.* Hillsdale, NJ: Erlbaum.

Miller, R. R., & Schactman, T. R. (1985b). Conditioning context as an associative baseline: Implications for response generation and the nature of conditioned inhibition. In R. R. Miller & N. E. Spear (Eds.), *Information processing in animals: Conditioned inhibition.* Hillsdale, NJ: Erlbaum.

Milner, P. M. (1976). Theories of reinforcement, drive, and motivation. In L. L. Iverson & S. H. Snyder (Eds.), *Handbook of psychopharmacology* (Vol. 7). New York: Plenum Press.

Mineka, S. (1979). The role of fear in theories of avoidance learning, flooding, and extinction. *Psychological Bulletin, 86,* 985–1010.

Mineka, S. (1985). Animal models of anxiety based disorders. In R. Tuma & J. Maser (Eds.), *Anxiety and anxiety disorders.* Hillsdale, NJ: Erlbaum.

Minor, T. R., Dess, N. K., Ben-David, E., & Chang, W. C. (1994). Individual differences in vulnerability to inescapable shock in rats. *Journal of Experimental Psychology: Animal Behavior Processes, 20,* 402–412.

Mischel, W. (1966). Theory and research on the antecedents of self-imposed delay of reward. *Progress in Experimental Personality Research, 3,* 85–132.

Mitchell, D. (1976). Experiments on neophobia in wild and laboratory rats: A reevaluation. *Journal of comparative and physiological psychology, 90,* 190–197.

Moltz, H. (1963). Imprinting: An epigenetic approach. *Psychological Review, 70,* 123–138.

Monroe, B., & Barker, L. M. (1979). A contingency analysis of taste aversion conditioning. *Animal Learning and Behavior, 7,* 141–143.

Montague, P. R., Dayan, P., & Sejnowski, P. J. (1993). Foraging in an uncertain world using predictive Hebbian learning. *Society for Neuroscience, 19,* 1609.

Moore, T. (1994). *Soul mates.* New York: HarperCollins.

Morgan, C. L. (1903). *An introduction to comparative psychology.* New York: Scribner.

Mowrer, O. H. (1947). On the dual nature of learning: A reinterpretation of "conditioning" and "problem solving." *Harvard Educational Review, 17,* 102–148.

Mowrer, O. H. (1960). *Learning theory and behavior.* New York: Wiley.

Mowrer, O. H., & Lamoreaux, R. R. (1942). Avoidance behavior and signal duration: A study of secondary motivation and reward. *Psychological Monographs, 54* (Whole No. 247).

Moyers, B. *Healing and the mind.* New York: Doubleday.

Myers, D. L., & Myers, L. E. (1977). Undermatching: A reappraisal of performance on concurrent variable-interval schedules of reinforcement. *Journal of the Experimental Analysis of Behavior, 25,* 203–214.

Nagy, W. E., & Anderson, R. C. (1984). How many words are there in printed school English? *Reading Research Quarterly, 19,* 304–330.

Nash, S., & Domjan, M. (1991). Learning to discriminate the sex of conspecifics in male Japanese quail (*Coturnix coturnix japonica*): Tests of "biological constraints." *Journal of Experimental Psychology: Animal Behavior Processes, 17,* 342–353.

Newcombe, F. (1987). Psychometric and behavioral evidence: Scope, limitations, and ecological validity. In H. S. Levin, J. Grafman, & H. M. Eisenberg (Eds.), *Neurobehavioral recovery from head injury.* Oxford, UK: Oxford University Press.

Nottebohm, F. (1980). Testosterone triggers growth of brain vocal control nuclei in adult female canaries. *Brain Research, 189,* 429–436.

Nottebohm, F. (1991). Reassessing the mechanisms and origins of vocal learning in birds. *Trends in Neurosciences, 14,* 206–211.

O'Brien, C. P. (1975). Experimental analysis of conditioning factors in human narcotic addiction. *Pharmacological Reviews, 27,* 533–543.

O'Brien, C. P., Testa, T., Ternes, J. W., & Greenstein, R. (1978). Conditioning effects of narcotics in humans. In *Behavioral Tolerance* (NIDA Research Monograph no. 18, pp. 67–71). Washington, DC: NIDA.

Olds, J. (1962). Hypothalamic substrates of reward. *Psychological Review, 42,* 554–604.

Olds, J., & Milner, P. (1954). Positive reinforcement produced by electrical stimulation of septal area and other regions of the rat brain. *Journal of Comparative and Physiological Psychology, 47,* 419–427.

Olson, D. J., & Maki, W. S. (1983). Characteristics of spatial memory in pigeons. *Journal of Experimental Psychology: Animal Behavior Processes, 9,* 266–280.

Olton, D. S. (1979). Mazes, maps, and memory. *American Psychologist, 34,* 583–596.

Olton, D. S., Collision, C., & Werz, M. A. (1977). Spatial memory and radial arm maze performance of rats. *Learning and Motivation, 8,* 289–314.

Olton, D. S., & Samuelson, R. J. (1976). Remembrance of places passed: Spatial memory in rats. *Journal of Experimental Psychology: Animal Behavior Processes, 2,* 97–116.

Ornstein, R. (1974). *The psychology of consciousness.* New York: W. H. Freeman.

Overmier, B., & Seligman, M. (1967). Effects of inescapable shock upon subsequent escape and avoidance responding. *Journal of Comparative and Physiological Psychology, 63,* 28–33.

Palya, W. L. (1993). Bipolar control in fixed interfood intervals. *Journal of the Experimental Analysis of Behavior, 60,* 345–359.

Papini, M. R., & Bitterman, M. E. (1990). The role of contingency in classical conditioning. *Psychological Review, 97,* 396–403.

Pateman, T. (1985). From nativism to sociolinguistics: Integrating a theory of language growth with a theory of speech practices. *Journal of the Theory of Social Behavior, 15,* 38–58.

Patterson, F., & Linden, E. (1981). *The educa-tion of Koko.* New York: Holt, Rinehart and Winston.

Pavlov, I. (1927/1960). *Conditioned reflexes.* New York: Dover. (First published 1927, Oxford University Press.)

Peeke, H. V. S., & Petrinovich, L. (Eds.). (1984). *Habituation, sensitization, and behavior.* New York: Academic Press.

Pfaffman, C. (1959). The sense of taste. In J. Field (Ed.), *Handbook of physiology. Neurophysiology* (Vol. 1). Washington, DC: American Physiological Society.

Pfaffman, C. (1960). The pleasures of sensation. *Psychological Review, 67,* 253–268.

Philips, H. C., Fenster, H., & Samson, D. (1988). An effective treatment for voiding dysfunction: A control treatment trial. *Journal of Behavioral Modification, 15,* 45–63.

Phillips, A. G., & Fibiger, H. C. (1989). Neuroanatomical bases of intracranial self-stimulation: Untangling the Gordian knot. In J. M. Liebman & S. J. Cooper (Eds.), *The neuropharmacological basis of reward* (pp. 66–105). Oxford, UK: Clarendon Press.

Pinel, J. P. J. (1993). *Biopsychology.* Boston: Allyn & Bacon.

Pinker, S. (1991). Rules of language. *Science, 253,* 530–535.

Pinker, S. (1994). *The learning instinct.* London: Penguin Press.

Pliner, P., Herman, P. C., & Polivy, J. (1990). Palatability as a determinant of eating: Finickiness as a function of taste, hunger, and the prospect of good food. In E. D. Capaldi & T. L. Powley (Eds.), *Taste, experience, and feeding.* Washington, DC: American Psychological Society.

Plomin, R. (1990). The role of inheritance in behavior. *Science, 248,* 223–228.

Powell, J., & Azrin, N. (1968). The effects of shock as a punisher for cigarette smoking. *Journal of Applied Behavior Analysis, 1,* 63–71.

Premack, A. J., & Premack, D. (1972). Teaching language to an ape. *Scientific American, 227,* 92–99.

Premack, D. (1962). Reversibility of the reinforcement relation. *Science, 136,* 255–257.

Premack, D. (1971). Language in chimpanzee? *Science, 142,* 808–822.

Premack, D. (1976). *Intelligence in ape and man.* Hillsdale, NJ: Erlbaum.

Premack, D. (1988). Minds with and without

language. In L. Weiskrantz (Ed.), *Thought without language*. Oxford, UK: Clarendon Press.

Rachlin, H. C. (1974). Self-control. *Behaviorism, 2,* 94–107.

Rachlin, H. C., & Green, L. (1972). Commitment, choice, and self-control. *Journal of the Experimental Analysis of Behavior, 17,* 15–22.

Randich, A., & LoLordo, V. M. (1979). Preconditioning exposure to the unconditioned stimulus affects the acquisition of the conditioned emotional response. *Learning and Motivation, 10,* 245–275.

Razran, G. (1957). The dominance-contiguity theory of the acquisition of classical conditioning. *Psychological Bulletin, 54,* 1–46.

Razran, G. (1971) *Mind in evolution*. Boston: Houghton Mifflin.

Real, L. A. (1991). Animal choice behavior and the evolution of cognitive architecture. *Science, 253,* 980–986.

Renner, M. J. (1988). Learning during exploration: The role of behavioral topography during exploration in determining subsequent adaptive behavior. *The International Journal of Comparative Psychology, 2,* 43–56.

Renner, M. J., & Seltzer, C. P. (1991). Molar characteristics of exploratory and investigative behavior in the rat (*Rattas morregicus*). *Journal of Comparative Psychology, 105,* 326–339.

Rescorla, R. A. (1967). Pavlovian conditioning and its proper control procedures. *Psychological Review, 74,* 71–80.

Rescorla, R. A. (1968). Probability of shock in the presence and absence of CS in fear conditioning. *Journal of Comparative and Physiological Psychology, 66,* 1–5.

Rescorla, R. A. (1969). Pavlovian conditioned inhibition. *Psychological Bulletin, 72,* 77–94.

Rescorla, R. A. (1971). Summation and retardation tests of latent inhibition. *Journal of Comparative and Physiological Psychology, 75,* 77–81.

Rescorla, R. A. (1985). Conditioned inhibition and facilitation. In R. R. Miller & N. E. Spear (Eds.), *Information processing in animals: Conditioned inhibition*. Hillsdale, NJ: Erlbaum.

Rescorla, R. A. (1990a). The role of information about the response-outcome relation in instrumental discrimination learning. *Journal of Experimental Psychology: Animal Behavior Processes, 16,* 262–270.

Rescorla, R. A. (1990b). Evidence for an association between the discriminative stimulus and the response outcome association in instrumental learning. *Journal of Experimental Psychology: Animal Behavior Processes, 16,* 326–334.

Rescorla, R. A., & Cunningham, C. L. (1978). Within compound flavor associations. *Journal of Experimental Psychology: Animal Behavior Processes, 4,* 267–275.

Rescorla, R. A., & Wagner, A. R. (1972). A theory of Pavlovian conditioning: Variations in the effectiveness of reinforcement and nonreinforcement. In A. H. Black & W. F. Prokasy (Eds.), *Classical conditioning II: Current research and theory*. New York: Appleton-Century-Crofts.

Reynolds, G. S. (1968). *A primer of operant conditioning*. Glenview, IL: Scott, Foresman.

Richter, C. P. (1936). Increased salt appetite in adrenalectomized rats. *American Journal of Physiology, 115,* 155–161.

Richter, C. P. (1942). Total self-regulatory functions in animals and human beings. *Harvey Lectures, 38,* 63–103.

Richter, C. P. (1958). Rats, man, and the welfare state. *American Psychologist, 13,* 1–17.

Riley, A., & Tuck, D. L. (1985). Conditioned taste aversions: A behavioral index of toxicity. *Annals of the New York Academy of Sciences, 443,* 272–292.

Roberts, S. (1981). Isolation of an internal clock. *Journal of Experimental Psychology: Animal Behavior Processes, 7,* 242–268.

Rodgers, W., & Rozin, P. (1966). Novel food preferences in thiamine deficient rats. *Journal of Comparative and Physiological Psychology, 61,* 1–4.

Roitblat, H. L. (1987). *Introduction to comparative cognition*. New York: W. H. Freeman.

Rolls, B, J., Rolls, E. T., and Rowe, E. A. (1982). The influence of variety on human food selection and intake. In L. M. Barker (Ed.), *The psychobiology of human food selection*. Westport, CT: AVI Publishing.

Romanes, G. (1884). *Animal intelligence*. New York: Appleton.

Ross, R. T., & Holland, P. C. (1981). Conditioning of simultaneous and serial feature-positive discriminations. *Animal Learning and Behavior, 9,* 293–303.

Routtenberg A., & Lindy, J. (1965). Effects of

the availability of rewarding septal and hypothalamic stimulation on bar pressing for food under conditions of deprivation. *Journal of Comparative and Physiological Psychology, 60,* 158–161.

Rozin, P. (1967). Thiamine specific hunger. In C. F. Code (Ed.), *Handbook of physiology (Section 6): Alimentary canal (Vol. 1): Control of food and water intake.* Washington, DC: American Physiological Society.

Rozin, P., & Kalat, J. W. (1971). Specific hungers and poison avoidance as adaptive specializations of learning. *Psychological Review, 78,* 459–486.

Rudy, J. W. (1994). Ontogeny of context-specific latent inhibition of conditioned fear: Implications for configural associations theory and hippocampal formation development. *Developmental Psychobiology, 27,* 367–379.

Rumbaugh, D. M. (Ed.). (1977). *Language learning by a chimpanzee: The LANA project.* New York: Academic Press.

Rumbaugh, D. M., & Gill, R. V. (1976). The mastery of language-type skills by the chimpanzee (*Pan*). *Annals of the New York Academy of Sciences, 280,* 562–578.

Rzoska, J. (1953). Bait-shyness: A study in rat behavior. *The British Journal of Animal Behavior, 1,* 128–135.

Sagan, C. (1977). *The dragons of Eden: Speculations on the evolution of human intelligence.* New York: Random House.

Sagan, C., & Druyan, A. (1992) *Shadows of forgotten ancestors.* New York: Ballantine Books.

Salter, A. (1949). *Conditioned reflex therapy.* New York: Farrar, Straus.

Sampson, H. A., Mendelson, L., & Rosen, J. P. (1992). Fatal and near fatal anaphylaxis reactions to food in children and adolescents. *Journal of the American Medical Association, 327,* 380–384.

Savage-Rumbaugh, S. (1987). Communication, symbolic communication, and language: Reply to Seidenberg and Petitto. *Journal of Experimental Psychology: General, 116,* 288–292.

Savage-Rumbaugh, S., McDonald, K., Sevcik, R. A., Hopkins, W. D., & Rubert, E. (1986). Spontaneous symbol acquisition and communicative use by pygmy chimpanzees (*Pan paniscus*). *Journal of Exper-*

imental Psychology: General, 115, 211–235.

Savage-Rumbaugh, S., Murphy, J., Sevcik, R. A., Brakke, K. E., Williams, S. L., & Rumbaugh, D. M. (1993). Language comprehension in ape and child. *Monographs of the Society for Research in Child Development,* Serial No. 233, Vol. 58 (3–4), pp. 30–170. Chicago: Society for Research in Child Development.

Schiffman, S. S. (1983). Taste and smell in disease. *New England Journal of Medicine, 308,* 1337–1342.

Schlinger, H. D. (1993). Learned expectancies are not adequate scientific explanations. *American Psychologist, 48,* 1155–1156.

Schmajuk, N. A., & Christiansen, B. A. (1990). Eyeblink conditioning in rats. *Physiology and Behavior, 48,* 755–758.

Schneiderman, N., Fuentes, I., & Gormezano, I. (1962). Acquisition and extinction of the classically conditioned eyelid response in the albino rabbit. *Science, 136,* 650–652.

Schusterman, R. J., & Gisner, R. (1988). Artificial language comprehension in dolphins and sea lions: The essential cognitive skills. *Psychological Record, 38,* 311–348.

Schusterman, R. J., & Gisner, R. (1989). Please parse the sentence: Animal cognition in the procrustean bed of linguistics. *Psychological Record, 39,* 3–18.

Schwartz, B., & Reisberg, D. (1991). *Learning and memory.* New York: W. W. Norton.

Schwartz, B., & Williams, D. R. (1972). The role of the response-reinforcer contingency in negative automaintenance. *Journal of the Experimental Analysis of Behavior, 17,* 351–357.

Schwartz, G. E., & Weiss, S. M. (1978). Behavioral medicine revisited: An amended definition. *Journal of Behavioral Medicine, 1,* 249–251.

Schwitzer, J. B., & Sulzer-Azaroff, B. (1988). Self-control: Teaching tolerance for delay in impulsive children. *Journal of the Experimental Analysis of Behavior, 50,* 173–186.

Sclafani, A., & Springer, D. (1976). Dietary obesity in adult rats: Similarities to hypothalamic and human obesity. *Physiology and Behavior, 17,* 461–471.

Sears, L. L., & Steinmetz, J. E. (1991). Dorsal accessory inferior olive activity diminishes during acquisition of the rabbit classically conditioned eyelid response. *Brain Research, 545,* 114–122.

Sejnowski, T. J., & Churchland, P. S. (1992a). *The computational brain.* Cambridge, MA: MIT Press.

Sejnowski, T. J., & Churchland, P. S. (1992b). Silicon brains. *BYTE, 17* (10), 137–146.

Seligman, M. E. P. (1970). On the generality of the laws of learning. *Psychological Review, 77,* 406–418.

Seligman, M. E. P. (1975). *Helplessness: On depression, development, and death.* San Francisco: W. H. Freeman.

Seligman, M. E. P., and Johnston, J. C. (1973). A cognitive theory of avoidance learning. In F. J. McGuigan & D. B. Lumsden (Eds.), *Contemporary approaches to conditioning and learning.* Washington, DC: Winston-Wiley.

Seligman, M. E. P., & Maier, S. F. (1967). Failure to escape traumatic shock. *Journal of Experimental Psychology, 74,* 1–9.

Seligman, M. E. P., & Weiss, J. (1980). Coping behavior: Learned helplessness, physiological activity, and learned inactivity. *Behavior Research and Therapy, 18,* 459–512.

Seyfarth, R. M., Cheney, D. L., & Marler, P. (1980). Vervet monkey responses to three different alarm calls. Evidence of predator classification and semantic communication. *Science, 210,* 801–803.

Sheffield, F. D., & Roby, T. B. (1950). Reward value of a non-nutritive sweet taste. *Journal of Comparative and Physiological Psychology, 43,* 471–481.

Sheffield, F. D., Roby, T. B., Campbell, B. A. (1954). Drive reduction versus consummatory behavior as determinants of reinforcement. *Journal of Comparative and Physiological Psychology, 47,* 349–354.

Sheffield, F. D., Wulff, J. J., & Backer, R. (1951). Reward value of copulation without sex-drive reduction. *Journal of Comparative and Physiological Psychology, 44,* 3–8.

Sherman, J. E., Hickis, C. F., Rice, A. G., Rusiniak, K. W., & Garcia, J. (1983). Preferences and aversions for stimuli paired with ethanol in hungry rats. *Animal Learning and Behavior, 11,* 101–106.

Sherrington, C. S. (1906). *Integrative action of the nervous system.* New York: Scribner.

Shettleworth, S. J. (1975). Reinforcement and the organization of behavior in golden hamsters: Hunger, environment, and food reinforcement. *Journal of Experimental Psychology: Animal Behavior Processes, 1,* 56–87.

Shettleworth, S. J., & Krebs, J. R. (1982). How marsh tits find their hoards: The roles of site preference and spatial memory. *Journal of Experimental Psychology: Animal Behavior Processes, 8,* 342–353.

Shumake, S. A., Thompson, R. D., & Caudill, C. J. (1971). Taste preference behavior of laboratory versus wild Norway rats. *Journal of Comparative and Physiological Psychology, 77,* 480–494.

Sibley, C. G., Comstock, J. A., & Ahlquist, J. E. (1990). DNA hybridization evidence of hominoid phylogeny: A reanalysis of the data. *Journal of Molecular Evolution, 30,* 202–206.

Sidman, M. (1953). Avoidance conditioning with brief shock and no exteroceptive warning signal. *Science, 118,* 157–158.

Siegel, S. (1975). Evidence from rats that morphine tolerance is a learned response. *Journal of Comparative and Physiological Psychology, 89,* 498–506.

Siegel, S. (1977). Morphine tolerance acquisition as an associative process. *Journal of Experimental Psychology: Animal Behavior Processes, 3,* 1–13.

Siegel, S. (1983). Classical conditioning, drug tolerance, and drug dependence. In Y. Israel, F. B. Glaser, H. Kalant, R. E. Popham, W. Schmidt, & R. G. Smart (Eds.), *Research advances in alcohol and drug problems* (Vol. 7). New York: Plenum.

Siegel, S., Hinson, R. E., Krank, M. D., & McCully, J. (1982). Heroin "overdose" death: Contribution of drug-associated environment cues. *Science, 216,* 436–437.

Simoons, F. J. (1973). New light on ethnic differences in adult lactose intolerance. *American Journal of Digestive Disorders, 18,* 595–611.

Skinner, B. F. (1938). *The behavior of organisms.* Englewood Cliffs, NJ: Prentice Hall.

Skinner, B. F. (1948). *Walden two.* New York: Macmillan.

Skinner, B. F. (1950). Are theories of learning necessary? *Psychological Review, 57,* 193–216.

Skinner, B. F. (1953). *Science and human behavior.* New York: Macmillan.

Skinner, B. F. (1957). *Verbal behavior*. New York: Appleton.

Skinner, B. F. (1959). A case history in scientific method. In S. Koch (Ed.), *Psychology: A study of a science*. New York: McGraw Hill.

Skinner, B. F. (1960, January). Pigeons in a pelican. *American Psychologist, 14*, 5–23.

Skinner, B. F. (1963). Behaviorism at fifty. *Science, 140*, 951–958.

Skinner, B. F. (1966). The phylogeny and ontogeny of behavior. *Science, 153*, 1204–1213.

Skinner, B. F. (1971). *Beyond freedom and dignity*. New York: Knopf.

Skinner, B. F. (1989). The origins of cognitive thought. *American Psychologist, 44*, 13–18.

Small, W. S. (1901). An experimental study of the mental processes of the rat. *American Journal of Psychology, 12*, 206–239.

Smith, J. C., & Roll, D. L. (1967). Trace conditioning with x-rays as the unconditioned stimulus. *Psychonomic Science, 9*, 11–12.

Soler, J. (1979, June 14). The dietary prohibitions of the Hebrews. *The New York Review of Books*, p. 24.

Solomon, P. R., Brennan, G., & Moore, J. W. (1974). Latent inhibition of rabbits' nictitating membrane response as a function of CS intensity. *Bulletin of the Psychonomic Society, 4*, 445.

Solomon, R. L. (1977). An opponent-process theory of motivation: V. Affective dynamics of eating. In L. M. Barker, M. R. Best, & M. Domjan (Eds.), *Learning mechanisms in food selection*. Waco, TX: Baylor University Press.

Solomon, R. L. (1980). The opponent-process theory of acquired motivation: The costs of pleasure and the benefits of pain. *American Psychologist, 35*, 691–712.

Solomon, R. L., & Corbit, J. D. (1974). An opponent-process theory of motivation: I. The temporal dynamics of affect. *Psychological Review, 81*, 19–145.

Solomon, R. L., & Wynne, L. C. (1953). Traumatic avoidance learning: Acquisition in normal dogs. *Psychological Monographs, 67* (Whole No. 354).

Solomon, S. D., Gerrity, E. T., & Muff, A. M. (1992). Efficacy of treatments for posttraumatic stress disorder: An empirical review. *Journal of the American Medical Association, 268*, 633–638.

Sonuga-Barke, E. J. S., Lea, S. E. G., & Webley, P. (1989). The development of adaptive choice in a self-control paradigm. *Journal of the Experimental Analysis of Behavior, 51*, 77–85.

Spanos, N. P., & Chaves, J. F. (Eds.). (1989). *Hypnosis: The cognitive-behavioral perspective*. Buffalo, NY: Prometheus Books.

Spelke, E. S. (1988). The origins of physical knowledge. In L. Weiskrantz (Ed.), *Thought without language*. Oxford, UK: Clarendon Press.

Spetch, M. L., Wilkie, D. M., & Pinel, J. P. (1981). Backward conditioning: A reevaluation of the empirical evidence. *Psychological Bulletin, 89*, 163–175.

Staats, C. K., & Staats, A. W. (1957). Meaning established by classical conditioning. *Journal of Experimental Psychology, 54*, 74–80.

Staddon, J. E. R. (1971). The "superstition" experiment: A reexamination of its implications for the principles of adaptive behavior. *Psychology Review, 78*, 3–43.

Stanovich, K. E. (1986). Mathew effects in reading: Some consequences of individual differences in the acquisition of literacy. *Reading Research Quarterly, 21*, 360–406.

Stanovich, K. E., & Cunningham, A. E. (1992). Studying the consequences of literacy within a literate society: The cognitive correlates of print exposure. *Memory & Cognition, 20*, 51–68.

Stein, L. (1969). Chemistry of purposive behavior. In J. T. Tapp (Ed.), *Reinforcement and behavior*. New York: Academic Press.

Stellar, E. (1982). Preface. In L. M. Barker, (Ed.), *The psychobiology of human food selection*. Westport, CT: AVI Publishing.

Stemmer, N. (1989). The acquisition of the ostensive lexicon: The superiority of empiricist over cognitive theories. *Behaviorism, 17*, 41–61.

Stoddart, D. M. (1990). *The scented ape: The biology and culture of human odour*. Cambridge, UK: Cambridge University Press.

Storms, L. H., Boroczi, G., & Broen, W. E. (1962). Punishment inhibits an instrumental response in hooded rats. *Science, 135*, 1133–1134.

Stringer, C. B., & Andrews, P. (1988). Genetic and fossil evidence for the origin of modern humans. *Science, 239*, 1263–1268.

Suarez, E. M., & Barker, L. M. (1976). Effects

of water deprivation and prior lithium chloride exposure in conditioning taste aversions. *Physiology & Behavior, 17,* 555–559.

Tarpy, R. M., & Mayer, R. E. (1978). *Foundations of learning and memory.* Glenview, IL: Scott, Foresman.

Teale, W. H. (1986). Home background and young children's literacy development. In W. H. Teale & E. Sulzby (Eds.), *Emergent literacy.* Norwood, NJ: Ablex Publishing.

Ternes, J. W., O'Brien, C. P., Grabowski, J., Wellerstein, J., & Jordan-Hays, J. (1980). Conditioning drug responses to naturalistic stimuli. In *Problems of drug dependence, 1979.* (Research Monograph no. 27, pp. 67–71. Washington, DC: NIDA.

Terrace, H. S. (1979). *Nim.* New York: Alfred A. Knopf.

Terrace, H. S. (1984). Animal cognition. In H. L. Roitblat, T. G. Bever, & H. S. Terrace (Eds.), *Animal cognition.* Hillsdale, NJ: Erlbaum.

Terry, W. S., & Wagner, A. R. (1975). Short-term memory for "surprising" versus "expected" unconditioned stimuli in Pavlovian conditioning. *Journal of Experimental Psychology: Animal Behavior Processes, 1,* 122–133.

Theios, J., Lynch, A. D., & Lowe, W. F. (1966). Differential effects of shock intensity on one-way and shuttle-avoidance conditioning. *Journal of Experimental Psychology, 72,* 294–299.

Thinus-Blanc, C. (1988). Animal spatial cognition. In L. Weiskrantz (Ed.), *Thought without language.* Oxford, UK: Clarendon Press.

Thomas, R. K., & Boyd, M. G. (1973). A comparison of *Cebus albifrons* and *Saimiri sciureus* on oddity performance. *Animal Learning and Behavior, 5,* 151–153.

Thompson, R. F. (1986). The neurobiology of learning and memory. *Science, 233,* 941–947.

Thompson, R. F., & Spencer, W. A. (1966). Habituation: A model phenomenon for the study of neuronal substrates of behavior. *Psychological Review, 73,* 16–43.

Thorndike, E. L. (1898). Animal intelligence: An experimental study of the associative processes in animals. *Psychological Review Monograph Supplement, 2,* 1–109.

Thorndike, E. L. (1911). *Animal intelligence: Ex-*

perimental studies. New York: Macmillan.

Thorndike, E. L. (1932). *Fundamentals of learning.* New York: Teachers College, Columbia University.

Tiffany, S. T. (1990). A cognitive model of drug urges and drug use behavior: The role of automatic and non-automatic processes. *Psychological Review, 97,* 147–168.

Timberlake, W. (1984). Behavior regulation and learned performance: Some misapprehensions and disagreements. *Journal of the Experimental Analysis of Behavior, 41,* 355–375.

Timberlake, W. (1993). Animal behavior: A continuing synthesis. *Annual Review of Psychology, 44,* 675–708.

Timberlake, W. (1994). Behavior systems, associationism, and Pavlovian conditioning. *Psychonomic Bulletin and Review, 1,* 405–420.

Timberlake, W., & Grant, D. S. (1975). Autoshaping in rats to the presentation of another rat predicting food. *Science, 190,* 690–692.

Timberlake, W., Wahl, G., & King, D. (1982). Stimulus and response contingencies in the misbehavior of rats. *Journal of Experimental Psychology: Animal Behavior Processes, 8,* 62–85.

Tinbergen, N. (1951). *The study of instinct.* Oxford, UK: Clarendon Press.

Todorov, J. C. (1971). Concurrent performances: Effect of punishment contingent on the switching response. *Journal of the Experimental Analysis of Behavior, 16,* 51–62.

Tolman, E. C. (1932). *Purposive behavior in animals and men.* New York: Appleton-Century-Crofts.

Tolman, E. C. (1938). The determiners of behavior at a choice point. *Psychological Review, 45,* 1–41.

Tolman, E. C., & Honzik, C. H. (1930a). Degrees of hunger; reward and non-reward; and maze learning in rats. *University of California Publications in Psychology, 4,* 241–256.

Tolman, E. C. & Honzik, C. H. (1930b). "Insight" in rats. *University of California Publications in Psychology, 4,* 215–232.

Turk, D. C., Meichenbaum, D., & Genest, M. (1983). *Pain and behavioral medicine: A cognitive behavioral perspective.* New York: Guilford Press.

Turner, A. M., & Greenough, W. T. (1983). Synapses per neuron and synaptic dimensions in occipital cortex in rats reared in complex, social, or isolation housing. *Acta Stereologica, 2,* 239–244.

Twitmyer, E. B. (1974). A study of the knee jerk. *Journal of Experimental Psychology, 103,* 1047–1066.

Vaccarino, F. J., Schiff, B. B., & Glickman, S. E. (1989). Biological view of reinforcement. In S. B. Klein & R. R. Mowrer (Eds.), *Contemporary learning theories: Instrumental conditioning and the impact of biological constraints on learning.* Hillsdale, NJ: Erlbaum.

Valenstein, E. S., Cox, V. C., & Kakolewski, J. W. (1967). Polydipsia elicited by the synergistic action of a saccharin and glucose solution. *Science, 157,* 552–554.

van der Kolk, B. S. (1987). *Psychological trauma.* Washington, DC: American Psychiatric Press.

Van Itallie, T. B. (1979). Adverse effects on health and longevity. *American Journal of Clinical Nutrition, 32,* 2723–2733.

Vaughan, W., Jr. (1981). Melioration, matching, and maximizing. *Journal of the Experimental Analysis of Behavior, 36,* 141–149.

Vaughan, W., Jr. (1985). Choice: A local analysis. *Journal of the Experimental Analysis of Behavior, 43,* 383–405.

Vega, L. de. (1615). El Capellan de la Vergen [*The Chaplain of the Virgin*]. In W. A. Bousfield. *American Psychologist, 10,* 828.

Vigilant, L., Stoneking, M., Harpending, H., Hawkes, K., & Wilson, A. C. (1991). African populations and the evolution of human mitochondrial DNA. *Science, 253,* 1503–1507.

von Neuman, J., & Morganstern, O. (1944). *Theory of games and economic behavior.* Princeton, NJ: Princeton University Press.

Wagner, A. R. (1976). Priming in STM: An information processing mechanism for self-generated and retrieval-generated depression in performance. In T. J. Tighe & R. N. Leaton (Eds.), *Habituation: Perspectives from child development, animal behavior, and neurophysiology.* Hillsdale, NJ: Erlbaum.

Wagner, A. R., & Rescorla, R. A. (1972). Inhibition in Pavlovian conditioning: Application of a theory. In R. A. Boakes & M. S. Halliday (Eds.), *Inhibition and learning.* London: Academic Press.

Warren, J. M. (1965). Primate learning in comparative perspective. In A. M. Schrier, H. F. Harlow, & F. Stollnitz (Eds.), *Behavior of non-human primates* (Vol. 1). New York: Academic Press.

Washburn, M. F. (1908). *The animal mind: A textbook of comparative psychology.* New York: Macmillan.

Washburn, S. L., & Moore, R. (1974). *Ape into man.* Boston: Little, Brown.

Watson, J. B. (1913). Psychology as the behaviorist views it. *Psychological Review, 20,* 158–177.

Watson, J. B. (1919). *Psychology from the standpoint of a behaviorist.* Philadelphia: Lippincott.

Watson, J. B. (1924). *Behaviorism.* New York: Norton.

Watson, J. B., & Rayner, R. (1920). Conditioned emotional reactions. *Journal of Experimental Psychology, 3,* 1–14.

Weaver, C. A. (1994). The psychology of reading. In *The encyclopedia of human behavior.* San Diego: Academic Press.

Weiffenbach, J. M. (Ed.). (1977). *Taste and development: The genesis of sweet preference.* (Publication No. (NIH) 77–1068). Bethesda, MD: DHEW.

Weingarten, H. P. (1990). Learning, homeostasis, and the control of feeding behavior. In E. D. Capaldi & T. L. Powley (Eds.), *Taste, experience, and feeding.* Washington, DC: American Psychological Society.

Weir, R. H. (1966). Some questions on the child's learning of phonology. In F. Smith & G. A. Miller (Eds.), *The genesis of language.* Cambridge, MA: MIT Press.

Weiskrantz, L. (1986). *Blindsight: A case study and implications.* Oxford, UK: Oxford University Press.

Weiskrantz, L. (Ed.). (1988). *Thought without language.* Oxford, UK: Clarendon Press.

Wenger, J. R., Tiffany, T. M., Bombardier, C., Nicholls, K., & Woods, S. C. (1981). Ethanol tolerance in the rat is learned. *Science, 213,* 575–577.

West, M. S., & King, A. P. (1980). Enriching cowbird song by social deprivation. *Journal of Comparative Psychology, 94,* 263–270.

Whorf, B. (1956). *Language, thought, and reality.* Cambridge, MA: MIT Press.

Wickler, W. (1973). Ethological analysis of

convergent adaptation. *Annals of the New York Academy of Science, 223,* 65–82.

Wigfield, A., & Asher, S. R. (1984). Social and motivational influences on reading. In P. D. Pearson, R. Barr, M. L. Kamill, & P. Mosenthal (Eds.), *Handbook of research and reading.* New York: Longman.

Wilcoxson, H. C., Dragoin, W. B., & Kral, P. A. (1971). Illness-induced aversions in rats and quail: Relative salience of visual and gustatory cues. *Science, 171,* 826–828.

Wilkins, L. & Richter, C. P. (1940). A great craving for salt by a child with a cortico-adrenal insufficiency. *Journal of the American Medical Association, 114,* 866–868.

Williams, B. A. (1988). Reinforcement, choice, and response strength. In R. C. Atkinson, R. J. Herrnstein, G. Lindzey, & R. D. Luce (Eds.), *Stevens' handbook of experimental psychology* (2nd ed.). New York: Wiley.

Williams, B. A. (1991). Choice as a function of local versus molar reinforcement contingencies. *Journal of the Experimental Analysis of Behavior, 56,* 455–473.

Williams, D. A., Overmier, J. B., & LoLordo, V. M. (1992). A reevaluation of Rescorla's early dictums about Pavlovian conditioned inhibition. *Psychological Bulletin, 111,* 275–290.

Williams, D. R., & Williams, H. (1969). Automaintenance in the pigeon: Sustained pecking despite contingent non-reinforcement. *Journal of the Experimental Analysis of Behavior, 12,* 511–520.

Wilson, E. O. (1975). *Sociobiology: The new synthesis.* Cambridge, MA: Harvard University Press.

Wolfe, J. B. (1934). Effectiveness of token rewards for chimpanzees. *Comparative Psychology Monographs, 12,* (5) (Serial No. 60).

Wolpe, J., Salter, A., & Reyna, L. J. (1964). *The conditioning therapies.* New York: Holt, Rinehart and Winston.

Woodruff, G., & Premack, D. (1979). Intentional communication in the chimpanzee: The development of deception. *Cognition, 7,* 333–362.

Woodworth, R. S., & Schlosberg, H. (1954). *Experimental psychology.* New York: Holt, Rinehart and Winston.

World Book Encyclopedia. (1991). Chicago: World Book.

Wright, A. A., Santiago, H. C., Sands, S. F., & Urcuioli, P. J. (1984). Pigeon and monkey serial probe recognition: Acquisition, strategies, and serial position effects. In H. L. Roitblat, T. G. Bever, & H. S. Terrace (Eds.), *Animal cognition.* Hillsdale, NJ: Erlbaum.

Wright, A. A., & Watkins, M. J. (1987). Animal learning and memory and their relation to human learning and memory. *Learning and Motivation, 18,* 131–146.

Xie, X., Berger, T. W., & Barrionuevo, G. (1992). Isolated NMDA receptor-mediated synaptic responses express both LTP and LTD. *Journal of Neurophysiology, 67,* 1009–1013.

Yin, H., Barnet, R., & Miller, R. (1994). Second-order conditioning and Pavlovian conditioned inhibition: Operational similarities and differences. *Journal of Experimental Psychology: Animal Behavior Processes, 20,* 419–428.

Young, P. T. (1966). Hedonic organization and regulation of behavior. *Psychological Review, 73,* 59–86.

Zahorik, D. (1977). Associative and non-associative factors in learned food preferences. In L. M. Barker, M. R. Best, & M. Domjan (Eds.), *Learning Mechanisms in Food Selection.* Waco, TX: Baylor University Press.

Zahorik, D., & Bean, C. A. (1975). Resistance of "recovery" flavors to later association with illness. *Bulletin of the Psychonomic Society, 6,* 309–312.

Zahorik, D., Mair, S. F., & Pies, R. W. (1974). Preferences for tastes paired with recovery from thiamine deficiency in rats. *Journal of Comparative and Physiological Psychology, 87,* 1083–1091.

ACKNOWLEDGMENTS

P. 52, Fig. 2.3a from Robert A. Wallace, *Animal Behavior: Its Development, Ecology, and Evolution.* Santa Monica, CA: Goodyear Publishing Company.

P. 53, Fig. 2.3(b) from Strickberger, M. W. (1990). *Evolution,* second edition. Fig. 19.2 Copyright © 1995 by Jones and Bartlett Publishers, Boston. Reprinted by permission. Adapted from Schultz, A. H., 1933. Die körperproportionen der erwachsenen catarrhinen Primaten, mit spezieller Berücksichtigung der Menschenaffen. *Anthropol. Anz., 10,* 154–185.

P. 62, Box 2.5 from Eibl-Eibesfeld, I., *Ethology: The Biology of Behavior,* Fig. 3.1. Copyright © 1967 by R. Piper & Co. Verlag, Munich. Reprinted by permission from the English translation of Eibl-Eibesfeld, I. *Grundrib der vergleichenden Verhaltensforschung: Etho logie* by permission of R. Piper & Co. Verlag.

P. 72, Table 2.2 from Goddard, M. E. & Beilharz, R. G. (1993). Genetics of traits which determine the suitability of dogs as guide-dogs for the blind, Table 1. *Applied Animal Ethology, 9,* 299–315. Reprinted by permission of Elsevier Science Publishers BV.

P. 183, Fig. 3.7(a) from Kamin, L. J. & Brimer, C. J. (1963). The effects of intensity of conditioned and unconditioned stimuli on a conditioned emotional response, Figure 1. *Canadian Journal of Psychology, 17,* 194–200. Reprinted by permission.

Figure 3.7(b) from Kamin, L. J. (1965). Temporal and intensity characteristics of the conditioned stimulus. In Prokasy, W. F., editor. (1965). *Classical conditioning.* New York: Appleton-Century-Crofts, 1965. Reprinted by permission.

P. 185, Fig. 3.8(a) from Schneiderman, N., Fuentes, I., & Gormezano, I. (1962). Acquisition and extinction of the classically conditioned eyelid response in the albino rabbit. *Science, 136,* 650–652. Copyright 1962 by the A.A.A.S. Reprinted by permission of the American Association for the Advancement of Science.

P. 301 Fig. 6.3 reprinted courtesy of Dr. Clint D. Anderson.

P. 308, Fig. 6.4 from Tolman, E. C. & Honzik, C. H. (1930). Degrees of hunger; reward and non-reward; and maze learning in rats, Figure 1. *University of California Publications in Psychology, 4,* 241–256. Reprinted by permission of the University of California Press.

P. 326, Box 6.3, from Camp, D. S., Raymond, G. A., & Church, R. M. (1962). Response suppression as a function of the schedule of punishment. *Psychonomic Science, 5,* 23–24. Reprinted by permission of the Psychonomic Society, Inc.

P. 343, Fig. 7.1 from Miller, N. & Banuazizi, A. (1968). Instrumental learning by curarized rats of a specific visceral response, intestinal or cardiac, Figure 1. *Journal of Comparative and Physiological Psychology, 65,* 1–7. Copyright 1968 by the American Psychological Association. Reprinted by permission.

P. 345, Fig. 7.2 from Booth, R. J. & Ashbridge, K. R. (1992). Implications of psychoimmunology for models of the immune system, Figure 1. In Husband, A. J., editor, *Behavior and immunity.* London: CRC Press. Reprinted by permission of CRC Press, Boca Raton, Florida.

P. 354, Fig 7.4 from Justesen et al. (1970). Pharmacological differentiation of allergic and classically conditioned asthma in the guinea pig, Figure 1. *Science, 170,* 864-866. Copyright 1970 American Association for the Advancement of Science. Reprinted by permission.

P. 407, Fig. 8.1 from Real, L. A. (1991). Animal choice behavior and the evolution of cognitive architecture. *Science, 253,* 980–986. Copyright 1991 American Association for the Advancement of Science. Reprinted by permission.

P. 412, Fig. 8.2 from Herrnstein, R. J. (1961). Relative and absolute strength of response as a function of frequency of reinforcement. *Journal of the Experimental Analysis of Behavior, 4,* 267–272. Copyright 1961 by the Society for the Experimental Analysis of Behavior, Inc. Reprinted with permission.

P. 442, Fig. 9.2(a) from Tolman, E. C. & Honzik, C. H. (1930). "Insight" in rats. *University of California Publications in Psychology, 4,* 215–232. Copyright 1930 by the University of California Press. Reprinted by permission of the University of California Press.

P. 443, Fig. 9.2(b) from Olton, D. S. & Samuelson, R. J. (1976). Remembrance of places past: spatial memory in rats. *Journal of Experimental Psychology: Animal Behavior Processes, 2,* 97–116. Copyright ©1976 by the American Psychological Association. Reprinted by premission.

Pp. 448–550, Fig. 9.4 from Farrar, D. N. (1967). Picture memory in the chimpanzee. *Perceptual and Motor Skills, 25,* 303–315. ©Southern Universities Press. Reproduced with permission of author and publisher.

P. 456, Fig. 9.6 from Warren, J. M. (1965). Primate learning in comparative perspective, Figure 4. In Schrier, A. M., Harlow, H. F., & Stollnitz, F., editors. *Behavior of nonhuman primates.* New York: Academic Press. Reprinted by permission of Academic Press, Orlando, FL.

Photo Credits

Pp. 41, 125, 314, 448, and 450 courtesy of United States Air Force; p. 41 used by permission of Don Van Piper and USAF; p. 46, courtesy of National Portrait Gallery, London, England; p. 56, courtesy of Dr. Stephen Jay Gould and Harvard University; p. 60, Thomas McAvoy/Life Magazine, © Time Warner; p. 70, courtesy of Dr. Nancy K. Dess; pp. 110 and 226, Bettmann Archive; p. 122, courtesy of Dolores Buckbee; p. 132, courtesy of Prof. Ilene Bernstein; p. 167, courtesy of Dr. Michael Best; p. 192, courtesy of Dr. John Garcia; p. 209, courtesy of Prof. Robert A. Rescorla; p. 367, Fig. 5.9, photos of pigeons from H. M. Jenkins and B. R. Moore (1973), The form of the autoshaped response with food or water reinforcers. *Journal of the Experimental Analysis of Behavior, 20,* 163–181. Copyright 1973 by the Society for the Experimental Analysis of Behavior, Inc., and reprinted by permission of Dr. Herbert Jenkins; p. 231, courtesy of Dr. Charles Brewer and Furman University; p. 235, Nina Leen/Life Magazine, © Time Warner; pp. 163, 224, 297, 354, and 388, courtesy of the author; p. 467, © McGraw-Hill; p. 436, courtesy of Dr. Larry Weiskrantz; and p. 470, courtesy of Dr. Sue Savage-Rumbaugh.

Cartoons

p. 108, Zamorano; p. 169, The Far Side ©1992 Farworks Inc. Reprinted by permission of Universal Press Syndicate. All rights reserved; p. 326, The Far Side ©1992 Farworks Inc. Reprinted by permission of Universal Press Syndicate. All rights reserved; p. 445, Frank and Ernest by Bob Thaves. Reprinted by permission of Newspaper Enterprise Association, Inc.

AUTHOR INDEX

Subject Index

552